INDIANA HISTORICAL COLLECTIONS
Volume XIX

INDIANA BOUNDARIES

INDIANA LIBRARY AND HISTORICAL BOARD

Lyman S. Ayres, *President*
John P. Goodwin, *Vice-President*
Mrs. Benjamin Saks, *Secretary*
Mrs. A. T. Carpenter		John E. Horner

HISTORICAL BUREAU
Hubert H. Hawkins, *Director*
Dorothy Riker, *Editor*

In view of the continued interest in this volume, a second printing, by offset process, has been authorized.
April, 1967

INDIANA BOUNDARIES
TERRITORY, STATE, AND COUNTY

By
GEORGE PENCE
and
NELLIE C. ARMSTRONG

Reprinted by the
INDIANA HISTORICAL BUREAU
Indianapolis, 1967

COPYRIGHT, 1933
BY THE
INDIANA HISTORICAL BUREAU
STATE DEPARTMENT OF EDUCATION

INDIANAPOLIS:
WM. B. BURFORD PRINTING CO., CONTRACTOR FOR STATE PRINTING AND BINDING
1 9 3 3

PREFACE

THE object of this volume is to show as exactly as may be the boundaries of the State of Indiana, the territories preceding it, and the counties which have been organized within it. The knowledge of the limits of political units at different times is essential to the use of public records, election returns, land records, or genealogical data. It has not been practicable to extend this work to cover congressional, judicial, and legislative districts nor civil townships; it is to be hoped that these less permanent political units may be covered later.

The boundaries described in this volume were determined primarily by executive and legislative acts. In cases in which the action of local authorities, such as county commissioners, was required, it has been taken into account. There have been cases, doubtless rather numerous in the earlier history of the state, in which local usage and jurisdiction of courts did not follow with precision boundaries fixed by law. Some county lines were not surveyed. These and other instances of deviation from the statutes cannot be given recognition here.

The maps represent the boundaries of a given unit as in existence upon the date when the statute governing formation or change became effective. Organization of a government within a county, when provided for in the same act as the formation, usually took place at some later time, under specific provisions of the law. When organization was carried out under a separate law, it should be noted that the "effective" date given is the date on which the law was put in force, not the date on which organization was completed.

The publication of the volume has been delayed by the death of the original author, George Pence, on September 13, 1929, not long after he had finished the preliminary work upon this volume. His lifelong interest in the history of Indiana and its counties made possible its compilation. As civil engineer, county surveyor, and field examiner of the State Board of Accounts, he had accumulated during a long and useful life detailed information of records and practices, the recording of which was one of the reasons for this publication. No tribute can be too great to the industry and the patience which, under severe physical handicap, he gave to its development.

Mrs. Ruth Williams Spilver, formerly of the Historical Bureau staff, aided in the repeated and arduous checking of text and maps necessary in the compilation of these records. Her carefulness and persistence not only resulted in the elimination of many errors, but brought to settlement numerous baffling points. Mrs. Spilver and Miss Dorothy Riker, of the present staff, assisted in the examination of House and Senate *Journals* for records of legislation regarding the boundaries of counties and their attachments, and Miss Riker has shared the task of seeing the volume through the press. The completion of the volume by Miss Nellie C. Armstrong involved not only the difficulty of picking up the work of another person, but protracted research and most exacting work both in the text and on the maps.

The Bureau is indebted to the Indiana State Library for permission to use its collection of early maps and the rare volumes of the early laws; to the library of the Indiana Supreme Court, which made available the early laws from neighboring states; and to the department of land records in the office of the Auditor of State, for the use of survey field notes and maps. County officials have been most generous in supplying information from the commissioners' records, particularly concerning changes made in boundaries after the General Assembly delegated to the counties authority to make transfers of territory; in many cases they have also provided survey maps of disputed areas.

CHRISTOPHER B. COLEMAN,
Director of the Historical Bureau

CONTENTS

OUTLINE OF BOUNDARY LEGISLATION

Territorial and State Boundaries.......................... 1
Territorial Counties....................................... 20
Counties of the New State................................. 28
The Northern Counties..................................... 57
Later Counties.. 83
Changes under the Second Constitution....................103

TERRITORIAL AND STATE MAPS

Northwest Territory, 1787................................136

Indiana Territory..138
   I. 1800; II. 1802; III. 1805; IV. 1809

State of Indiana...146
   I. 1816; II. 1816-17; III. 1817-18; IV. 1818-19; V. 1819-20; VI. 1820-21; VII. 1821-22; VIII. 1822-23; IX. 1823-24; X. 1825; XI. 1825-26; XII. 1826-27; XIII. 1827-28; XIV. 1828-29; XV. 1829-30; XVI. 1830-31; XVII. 1831-33; XVIII. 1833-34; XIX. 1834-35; XX. 1835-36; XXI. 1836-38; XXII. 1838-39; XXIII. 1839-40; XXIV. 1840-42; XXV. 1842-44; XXVI. 1844-52; XXVII. 1859-73; XXVIII. 1923-33

RELATED COUNTIES

Randolph County, Northwest and Indiana Territories.........202
   I. 1795; II. 1801; III. 1803

St. Clair County, Northwest and Indiana Territories..........208
   I. 1790; II. 1795; III. 1801; IV. 1803

Wayne County, Northwest and Indiana Territories............216
   I. 1796; II. 1803

TEMPORARY COUNTIES

Wabash County, New Purchase, 1820.......................220

Delaware County, New Purchase, 1820.....................222

(ix)

x INDIANA HISTORICAL COLLECTIONS

COUNTIES OF INDIANA

Adams County, 1835....................................224

Allen County, 1823....................................226

Bartholomew County....................228
    I. 1821; II. 1828; III. 1836; IV. 1838

Benton County, 1840...................236

Blackford County, 1838.................238

Boone County, 1830....................240

Brown County, 1836....................242

KEY TO SECTION NUMBERS

Carroll County........................244
    I. 1828; II. 1839

Cass County..248
    I. 1828; II. 1832; III. 1834; IV. 1838

Clark County...256
    I. 1801; II. 1802, Jan. 1803; III. Mar. 1803; IV. 1808; V. 1810;
    VI. 1813; VII. 1815; VIII. 1819; IX. 1820; X. 1824; XI. 1836;
    XII. 1837; XIII. 1839; XIV. 1843; XV. 1844, 1846; XVI. 1873

Clay County, 1825.....................................288

Clinton County...290
    I. 1830; II. 1859

Crawford County.......................................294
    I. 1818; II. 1827

Daviess County...298
    I. 1816; II. 1818; III. 1820; IV. 1821; V. 1828

Dearborn County.......................................308
    I. 1803; II. 1810; III. 1814; IV. 1816; V. 1844; VI. 1845

Decatur County, 1821..................................320

De Kalb County, 1835..................................322

Delaware County, 1827.................................324

Dubois County..326
    I. 1817; II. 1818; III. 1820

Elkhart County...332
    I. 1830; II. 1832; III. 1836

Fayette County...338
    I. 1818; II. 1821; III. 1826

Floyd County...344
    I. 1819; II. 1823; III. 1828; IV. 1844

CONTENTS

Fountain County, 1825.....................................352
Franklin County...354
   I. 1810; II. 1818; III. 1820; IV. 1821; V. 1826
Fulton County...364
   I. 1835; II. 1838; III. 1840; IV. 1843; V. 1844; VI. 1846
Gibson County...376
   I. 1813; II. 1814; III. 1815; IV. 1816, 1817; V. 1818; VI. 1821; VII. 1823; VIII. 1824; IX. 1825; X. 1843; XI. 1844; XII. 1847; XIII. 1852
Grant County..402
   I. 1831; II. 1838
Greene County, 1821.......................................406
Hamilton County, 1823.....................................408
Hancock County, 1827......................................410
Harrison County...412
   I. 1808; II. 1810; III. 1813; IV. Jan. 10, 1818; V. Jan. 29, 1818; VI. 1819; VII. 1823; VIII. 1824, 1852
Hendricks County..428
   I. 1823; II. 1831; III. 1868
Henry County..434
   I. 1821; II. 1823; III. 1824; IV. 1827
Howard County (Richardville)..............................442
   I. 1844; II. 1845; III. 1859
Huntington County, 1832...................................448
Jackson County..450
   I. 1815; II. 1816; III. 1818; IV. 1820; V. 1821; VI. 1822; VII. 1824; VIII. 1828; IX. 1836; X. 1843; XI. 1859
Jasper County...472
   I. 1835; II. 1839; III. 1840; IV. 1841; V. 1859; VI. 1923
Jay County..484
   I. 1835; II. 1838
Jefferson County..488
   I. 1810; II. 1813; III. 1814; IV. 1815; V. 1816; VI. 1820; VII. 1830; VIII. 1835, 1836; IX. 1837
Jennings County...506
   I. 1816; II. 1820; III. 1830
Johnson County, 1822......................................512

xii   INDIANA HISTORICAL COLLECTIONS

Knox County..514
   I. 1790; II. 1796; III. 1798; IV. 1801; V. 1802, 1803; VI. 1808;
   VII. 1809; VIII. 1810, 1813; IX. 1814; X. 1815; XI. 1816; XII.
   1816; XIII. 1843

Kosciusko County..540
   I. 1835; II. 1840; III. 1843; IV. 1846

La Grange County, 1832..................................548

Lake County...550
   I. 1836; II. 1923

La Porte County...554
   I. 1832; II. 1842; III. 1850; IV. 1925; V. 1931

Lawrence County...564
   I. 1818; II. 1822; III. 1859

Madison County..570
   I. 1823; II. 1824; III. 1827; IV. 1831; V. 1838

Marion County...580
   I. 1821; II. 1831

Marshall County...584
   I. 1835; II. 1836

Martin County...588
   I. 1820; II. 1828

Miami County..592
   I. 1832; II. 1834; III. 1838; IV. 1844

Monroe County...600
   I. 1818; II. 1821; III. 1828, 1831; IV. 1836

Montgomery County.......................................608
   I. 1822; II. 1824; III. 1825

Morgan County...614
   I. 1821; II. 1861; III. 1868

Newton County...620
   I. 1835; II. 1836; III. 1859; IV. 1923

Noble County..628
   I. 1835; II. 1859

Ohio County...632
   I. 1844; II. 1845

Orange County...636
   I. 1815; II. 1818; III. 1818

Owen County...642
   I. 1818; II. 1821; III. 1822; IV. 1825

CONTENTS xiii

Parke County..650
   I. 1821; II. 1824

Perry County..654
   I. 1814; II. 1816; III. Jan. 10, 1818; IV. Jan. 29, 1818; V. 1827

Pike County...664
   I. 1816; II. 1817; III. 1824; IV. 1825; V. 1826

Porter County...674
   I. 1835; II. 1836; III. 1923

Posey County..680
   I. 1814; II. 1815; III. 1817; IV. 1818; V. 1821; VI. 1823

Pulaski County, 1835......................................692

Putnam County...694
   I. 1821; II. 1822; III. 1824; IV. 1825; V. 1861

Randolph County...704
   I. 1818; II. Jan. 1820; III. Dec. 1820; IV. 1824

Ripley County...712
   I. 1816; II. 1821

Rush County, 1821...716

St. Joseph County...718
   I. 1830; II. 1832; III. 1835; IV. 1836; V. 1850; VI. 1931

Scott County..730
   I. Jan. 1820; II. Dec. 1820; III. 1830; IV. 1839; V. 1843

Shelby County, 1821.......................................740

Spencer County..742
   I. 1818; II. 1825

Starke County...746
   I. 1835; II. 1842; III. 1925

Steuben County, 1835......................................752

Sullivan County...754
   I. 1816; II. Jan. 1818; III. Dec. 1818, 1819; IV. 1821; V. 1825; VI. 1843

Switzerland County..766
   I. 1814; II. 1821

Tippecanoe County, 1826...................................770

Tipton County, 1844.......................................772

Union County..774
   I. 1821; II. 1826

Vanderburgh County, 1818................................778

xiv INDIANA HISTORICAL COLLECTIONS

Vermillion County, 1824....................................780
Vigo County...782
    I. 1818; II. 1819; III. Jan. 1821; IV. Dec. 1821; V. 1822; VI. 1825
Wabash County..794
    I. 1832; II. 1838
Warren County, 1827....................................798
Warrick County...800
    I. 1813; II. 1814; III. 1818; IV. 1824; V. 1825; VI. 1826; VII. 1843; VIII. 1844; IX. 1847; X. 1852
Washington County......................................820
    I. 1813; II. 1814; III. 1815; IV. Jan. 1820; V. Dec. 1820; VI. 1839; VII. 1843; VIII. 1846; IX. 1873
Wayne County...838
    I. 1810; II. Jan. 1818; III. Dec. 1818; IV. 1821; V. 1823; VI. 1824; VII. 1827
Wells County, 1835.....................................852
White County...854
    I. 1834; II. 1838; III. 1839; IV. 1841
Whitley County...862
    I. 1835; II. 1859

OUTLINE OF BOUNDARY LEGISLATION

By

NELLIE C. ARMSTRONG

TERRITORIAL AND STATE BOUNDARIES

INDIANA'S present boundaries were first foreshadowed by provisions of the Ordinance of July 13, 1787, which established a government in the Territory of the United States Northwest of the River Ohio. The Ordinance did not specifically describe the boundaries of the territory to be governed, but it did outline the boundaries of three states to be formed within the territory at a later time, with a provision for two more, should Congress find their erection "expedient." The boundaries laid out for the future "middle state" were prophetic of those of the present state of Indiana.

Division of the northwestern country had been considered prior to this date, but the plan of partition suggested first by the Virginia delegates to the Continental Congress on September 6, 1780, embodied in a congressional resolution of October 10, 1780, and subsequently in Virginia's act of cession of December 20, 1783, proposed the erection of small states from one hundred to one hundred fifty miles square. In 1778 Virginia had set up a vaguely defined and incompletely organized county, embracing the territory on the western side of the Ohio River, but the act forming Illinois County, after one renewal in 1780, was allowed to lapse in January, 1782. On March 1, 1784, Virginia's deed of cession was signed by the Virginia delegates; on the same day a congressional committee headed by Thomas Jefferson presented a plan for the future erection of ten western states, to be bounded by designated lines of latitude and longitude. With some changes, the plan was adopted on April 23, 1784, and remained in force, so far as possible state boundaries were concerned, until 1787. By that year the country northwest of the Ohio was freed from the territorial claims of all the states, and the question of its government came before Congress. While a new ordinance embodying the existing provisions for western states was under discussion, western influence brought about a revision of the plan to allow for larger states. Virginia was asked to alter her deed of cession to allow its enactment, and it was adopted on July 13, 1787. It provided for the erection of three or five states.

The "middle state" was to be bounded on the west by "a direct line drawn from the Wabash and Post Vincent's due north to the territorial line between the United States and Canada," by "the Wabash from Post Vincent's to the Ohio; by the Ohio, by a direct line drawn due north from the mouth of the Great-Miami, to the said territorial line, and by the said territorial line." Should the two additional states be formed, they were to lie "north of an east and west line drawn through the southerly bend or extreme of lake Michigan."[1]

Indiana did not at any time conform exactly to these boundaries, but they served as guide lines for three of the four territorial changes which preceded the Indiana Enabling Act of April 19, 1816.

1800. The civil and judicial system set up for the Northwest Territory proved inadequate to the problems presented by great distance and scattered population. In December, 1799, William Henry Harrison, territorial delegate to Congress, secured the appointment of a House committee to investigate the "judicial establishment" of the territory. The resultant bill to reform the superior courts of the territory was recommitted on January 30, 1800, to a select committee, with instructions to report "on the expediency of dividing the said Territory into two distinct governments: *Provided,* That the line of division shall commence at the mouth of the Great Miami

[1] *Journals of the American Congress: From 1774 to 1788,* 4:754 (Washington, 1823). Kettleborough, Charles, *Constitution Making in Indiana* . . ., vol. 1 (*Indiana Historical Collections,* Indianapolis, 1916) reprints this and following documents preliminary to Indiana statehood.

BOUNDARY LEGISLATION 3

river, and run due north until it strikes the dividing line between the United States and Canada."[2]

On March 3 the committee reported in favor of a division, repeating in their report the line of separation drawn from the mouth of the Great Miami.[3] A bill for division was introduced on March 20 and passed the House on March 31.[4] After drastic amendment in the Senate, followed by a conference between the houses, an amended bill was agreed upon, although there was an attempt to postpone further action until the next session.[5]

In the bill as finally approved on May 7, 1800, effective on July 4, the boundary line between the eastern division, which continued to be called the Territory Northwest of the River Ohio, and the new Indiana Territory, which extended westward to the Mississippi River, had been altered to follow the Greenville Treaty line from a point on the Ohio River opposite the mouth of the Kentucky River, to Fort Recovery. From that point it ran due north to the territorial boundary in Lake Superior. This was a change greatly disappointing to the western

[2] *Annals of Congress*, 6 Congress, 1 session, 193, 197-98, 245, 507, 645 (Washington, 1851).

[3] This division was objectionable to persons interested in the development of Cincinnati. Arthur St. Clair, governor of the Northwest Territory, proposed to Harrison a division into three, instead of two districts, suggesting as the "most eligible" division "that the Scioto and a line drawn north from the forks of it, should form the western boundary of the eastern district—a line drawn north from that part of the Indian boundary opposite the mouth of the Kentucky the western boundary of the middle division and the western division to comprehend all the country between that line and the Mississippi." Such a subdivision would leave Cincinnati the capital of the middle district. Letter of February 17, 1800, in Esarey, Logan (ed.), *Governors Messages and Letters. Messages and Letters of William Henry Harrison*, 1:11-12 (*Indiana Historical Collections*, vol. 7, Indianapolis, 1922).

[4] *Annals*, 6 Congress, 1 session, 583, 635, 649. The committee report appears in *ibid.*, 1320-21, and is reprinted in Kettleborough, *op. cit.*, 39-41.

[5] *Annals*, 6 Congress, 1 session, 676, 684, 691, 698-99. For the wording of the act, see text with map, Indiana Territory I.

district, which had expected to include the comparatively well-settled triangular area, later known as the "Gore," between the Greenville Treaty line and the proposed boundary running north from the mouth of the Great Miami. Section 5 of the act provided, however, that whenever a state should be erected to the east of Indiana Territory, its western boundary should follow the line established by the Ordinance of 1787 and embodied in the original bill for the division of the Northwest Territory.[6]

1803. Three years later, when Ohio was carved out of the Northwest Territory and established as a state, the provisions of the Ordinance were observed. Ohio's northern boundary followed the due east line through the southerly extreme of Lake Michigan, and her western boundary, the due north line from the mouth of the Great Miami. Indiana Territory absorbed two large districts—that part of the Northwest Territory north of Ohio, and the coveted Gore. She lost only a narrow strip of land north of Fort Recovery between the old territorial boundary and the new state line.[7]

There is some question as to the date of effect of this change. On April 30, 1802, the Enabling Act for Ohio was passed by Congress. A state government had not yet been set up, and according to provisions of the constitution framed in November of that year, the territorial government was to continue until the new state government was formed. On March 1, 1803, the newly elected

[6] See Goebel, Dorothy B., *William Henry Harrison*, 47-51 (*Indiana Historical Collections*, vol. 14, Indianapolis, 1926) for a discussion of the move for separation. See also Dunn, Jacob P., *Indiana: a Redemption from Slavery*, 274 ff. (*American Commonwealths*, Riverside Press, Cambridge, 1888, revised edition, 1905).

[7] See map of Indiana Territory II. Washington, in 1783, had suggested the formation of one or possibly two states from the eastern part of the western territory, drafting roughly the present states of Ohio and Michigan. Ford, Worthington C. (ed.), *The Writings of George Washington*, 10:310-11 (G. P. Putnam's Sons, 1891); Dunn, *op cit.*, 187.

BOUNDARY LEGISLATION   5

legislature met, but the senators and representatives to Congress were not seated until October 17, 1803. Since there was no formal act admitting Ohio to the Union, controversy arose as to what date marked the establishment of the new state. On February 21, 1806, Congress passed an act allowing the salaries of territorial officers paid until March 1, 1803, and this date has been generally accepted.[8]

The actual running of the boundary line was a slow process.[9] Part of the meridian forming the Indiana-Ohio boundary line had been surveyed in 1798 as a base line for a congressional survey of the land east of the Greenville Treaty line and north of the Ohio River. This survey covered a distance of eighty-nine miles between the Ohio River and the intersection of the meridian with the Greenville Treaty line. After tentative moves in 1809, 1811, and 1812 toward tracing the entire Indiana-Ohio boundary, the matter dropped until 1816, when William Harris, of Indiana, was appointed by the surveyor-general of the United States to complete the survey northward. During the following year the work was carried out. Harris remarked that the line then interfered with no settlement. It was doubtless the increase of population in the neighborhood of the line which again brought into question its exact location. In 1837 the governors of Indiana and Ohio appointed John A. Watson and M. T. Williams commissioners to locate the exact spot on the

[8] King, Rufus, *Ohio. First Fruits of the Ordinance of 1787*, 292-95 (*American Commonwealths*, Riverside Press, Cambridge, 1888). This long-drawn-out procedure resulted in some uncertainties as to jurisdiction, particularly in the Gore. See text with maps, Clark County II and III. Certain landholders of the Gore in 1805 petitioned for attachment to the state of Ohio. *Annals*, 9 Congress, 1 session, 294, 467.

[9] For a detailed study of the establishment of the Indiana-Ohio boundary line, see the special reports of T. C. Mendenhall and A. A. Graham in *Ohio Archaeological and Historical Publications*, 4:127-51. See also Wilson, George R., *Early Indiana Trails and Surveys*, 428-29 (*Indiana Historical Society Publications*, 6: no. 3, Indianapolis, 1919).

Ohio River where the boundary line began. The commissioners met in November, and with a surveyor, Nathaniel L. Squibb, proceeded to establish the line "as nearly as possible and as could be ascertained with the field notes of the . . . survey of Israel Ludlow, made in 1798."[10] Two freestone monuments were erected to mark the line, one on the bank of the Ohio River, and the other where the line intersects the road from Elizabethtown, Ohio, to Lawrenceburg, Indiana.

In 1891, at the request of the governor of Ohio, an examination of the line was made by the United States Coast and Geodetic Survey to see whether or not it was seriously in error. By this time the monument which had been placed at the junction of the Miami and the Ohio rivers had disappeared, but the remaining marker a few miles north was used as a starting point. Considerable variation in the line was shown; the report states: "It is evident that the line is an irregular one, sometimes bending east, then curving west, as would probably be the case with any of the meridians traced out by the needle many years ago.

. . . . . .

"The examination proves that while the line is not a true meridian, it is not in error ten or twelve miles as is supposed by many.

"Should the line be traced out as a true meridian from the south end, it would probably cut from Indiana a strip of territory amounting to nearly 100 square miles in area."[11]

The line has never been officially marked along its entire extent. In 1929 the inscription on the marker near Lawrenceburg was renewed, and a commemorative

[10] Report of the commissioners, November, 1837, quoted in Mendenhall and Graham, *op. cit.*, 143. For authorization of the appointment of a commissioner from Indiana, see *Laws of Indiana*, 1836-37 (local), p. 430.

[11] Report of C. A. Sinclair, of the United States Coast and Geodetic Survey, to T. C. Mendenhall, November 5, 1891, quoted in Mendenhall and Graham, *op. cit.*, 149.

BOUNDARY LEGISLATION 7

bronze tablet was attached by the Colonel Archibald Lochry Chapter, Daughters of the American Revolution.

1805. As early as 1803 the inhabitants of the large northeastern district which had been added to Indiana Territory upon the admission of Ohio began to plead their great distance from the seat of government at Vincennes, and the vast intervening Indian holdings, as good and sufficient reasons for separate territorial organization.

Their memorial, presented on October 21 to the Senate, was favorably received, and a committee report of October 31 recommended the erection into a territory of all that part of Indiana Territory north of an east and west line run from the Mississippi River on the west, through the southern extreme of Lake Michigan to Lake Erie on the east. A bill forming the territory passed the Senate on December 6 in amended form.[12]

The House committee to which it was referred reported unfavorably, on the ground that similar arguments for organization could be advanced by various isolated settlements in the Mississippi and Louisiana territories. The adverse report was rejected, but the bill failed on February 21, 1804, by a vote of 58-59.[13]

In December, 1804, a second bill for the organization of Michigan Territory was introduced in the Senate. After amendment in the Senate and in the House, it was approved on January 11, 1805. This measure cut to less than half the territory which Michigan had been allotted by the unsuccessful proposal of 1803, running the western boundary of the new territory north from "the southerly bend, or extreme" of Lake Michigan "to its northern extremity, and thence due north to the northern boundary of the United States." Both southern and western boundaries were thus dependent upon an unestablished point on the southern shore of Lake Michigan.[14] The boundary was not surveyed.

[12] *Annals*, 8 Congress, 1 session, 16, 29-30, 212.
[13] *Ibid.*, 1040-41, 1041-42.
[14] *Ibid.*, 8 Congress, 2 session, 20, 21, 23, 26, 31, 32, 871, 872.

1809. Citizens of the eastern part of Indiana Territory were not anxious to see further subdivision take place.[15] A western separatist faction already existed, and had asked, in 1803, to be joined to Louisiana Territory.[16] In December, 1805, the Indiana House of Representatives and Legislative Council, in a petition to Congress, included a request that no division of the territory be permitted, and that formation of a state government be allowed as soon as the population should reach the required standard. The House of Representatives also sent a resolution stating its objections to division. But the western part of the territory was anxious for a separate organization, and in January, and again in March, 1806, the western counties, St. Clair and Randolph, asked that the territory be divided into two governments.[17]

At the next session of Congress, petitions both for and against the division were presented in the House. On February 26, 1807, a report was made to the effect that division was expedient, but no further action was taken in the matter. When similar petitions appeared in April of the next session, 1808, the lateness of the session, the "unpromising aspect of . . . fiscal concerns, and particularly the impolicy of increasing the number of Territorial Governments without its being manifestly necessary" were made the grounds for an unfavorable report.[18]

New resolutions and petitions requesting division of the territory were promptly put before the next session of Congress,[19] and the territorial delegate, Jesse B. Thomas, elected under pledge to exert his influence in

[15] For a discussion of the movement for the organization of Illinois Territory, see Philbrick, Francis S. (ed.), *The Laws of Indiana Territory, 1801-1809*, pp. xx ff. (*Illinois Historical Collections*, vol. 21, Springfield, 1930); see also Dunn, *Indiana*, 337 ff., 378-79; Esarey, Logan, *A History of Indiana*, 1:179 (Fort Wayne, 1924); Goebel, *William Henry Harrison*, 82-85.

[16] *Annals*, 8 Congress, 1 session, 489, 555, 623; 2 session, 1659-60.

[17] *Ibid.*, 9 Congress, 1 session, 293-94, 297, 342, 848-49.

[18] *Ibid.*, 9 Congress, 2 session, 590, 624; 10 Congress, 1 session, 1976, 2067.

[19] *Ibid.*, 10 Congress, 2 session, 18, 633, 862, 901.

BOUNDARY LEGISLATION

favor of separation, reported a bill for division on December 31, 1808. It was passed without amendment and was approved on February 3, 1809, to become effective the first of March following.[20]

There seems to have been no debate on the line of division. The Wabash formed a natural boundary within the settled area, and the line "from the Wabash and Post Vincent's" due north to the territorial boundary between the United States and Canada was provided in the Ordinance of 1787.

The next year the Assembly adopted a resolution "for settling the division line between the two territories," for the reason that "doubts have arisen as to the point or place from whence the line dividing the Indiana Territory . . . is to start from Post Vincennes; *And whereas* doubts also arise as to what part of the settlement formed above Vincennes on the north-west side of the river Wabash, will form a part of the Illinois Territory." The governor was empowered to enter into correspondence with the governor of Illinois Territory "for the purpose of settleing the point of the town of Vincennes, from which the line dividing the Illinois from this territory shall run . . . and to make arrangements with the governor of the Illinois, for running and marking the same for the distance of thirty miles, on the north west side of the Wabash." In case such negotiation failed, the governor of Indiana Territory was authorized to have thirty miles of boundary "run and marked, commencing at the lower end of Vincennes."[21]

[20] *Annals*, 10 Congress, 2 session (House), 815, 862, 971-73, 1093-94; (Senate), 326, 327, 338, 339. See Alvord, Clarence W., *The Illinois Country, 1673-1818*, 425 (Springfield, 1920).

[21] *Acts of Indiana Territory*, 1810, pp. 78-80. See map, Indiana Territory IV, and maps, Knox County VII ff. It will be noted that a direct line drawn "from the Wabash and Post Vincent's due North" puts into Indiana Territory a tract of land west of the river just above Vincennes, and into Illinois Territory a tract farther north, east of the river. Contemporary maps showing the Wabash River above Vincennes flowing much more directly from

1816. Indiana Territory began formal action to acquire statehood shortly after Illinois Territory had been formed. On December 11, 1811, a memorial from the House of Representatives was presented in the United

the northeast than it actually does, and crossing the Vincennes line only at Vincennes, lead to the inference that it was the intention of Congress both in 1787 and in 1809 to put all the land east of the Wabash into the "middle state." See "A Map of the Northern Parts of the United States," in Jedidiah Morse's *American Gazetteer*, Boston, 1797, reprinted without change in 1804; "Map of the Back Settlements," in Morse's *American Geography*, London, 1794; "N. W. Territory," in Carey's *American Pocket Atlas*, Philadelphia, 1801; "A Map of the United States," in the *United States Gazetteer*, by Joseph Scott, Philadelphia, 1795. An undated sketch map from the Indian Office, which does show the westward bend of the river above Vincennes, draws the territorial line north from the mouth of the Wabash, west of Vincennes, twice crossing the river above that point. Practically the same line appears on a map of the "Upper Territories of the United States," in Carey's *Atlas*, Philadelphia, 1814. There is evidence that the Wabash was commonly spoken of as the boundary above Vincennes in the period from 1809 to 1816 ("Field notes North of the Base Line, and West of the second Principal Meridian, Indiana," 11:617, 626, office of the Auditor of State); on the other hand, the resolution of 1810 quoted above, by any ordinary interpretation indicates that the Territorial Assembly took for granted that the territorial line left the river at Vincennes. As late as 1812, Jonathan Jennings said before the United States House of Representatives that "the acts of Congress establishing the Territories of Indiana . . . and Illinois, have bounded the territorial limits of the former . . . by the river Wabash, from its confluence with the Ohio to Vincennes; and from thence by a line to be drawn due north. . . ." (*Annals*, 12 Congress, 1 session, 1247). See also the description of the boundaries of Indiana in the Enabling Act as introduced (*post*, 11). John Tipton, in his Journal of the survey of the Indiana-Illinois line in 1821, after describing the running of the line north from Vincennes to the point at which it last touched the Wabash River, wrote: "Run our north line to the Bank of wabash in S 33 To 11 N of R 10 west beeing 45 miles 38 chain & 50 Links north from vincennes the River here 11 chain 4 Links wide the River is by an act of congress passed 1816 to be the line between Ia & Illinois to this place," from which one may infer that he regarded the Enabling Act of 1816 as changing the boundary below this point.

BOUNDARY LEGISLATION 11

States Senate, asking admission to the Union. The petition was presented in the House on January 1, 1812, and referred to a committee of which Jonathan Jennings, territorial delegate, was chairman. A protest signed by two members of the territorial legislature followed shortly. After three months of consideration the committee reported in favor of admitting Indiana as a state whenever "the population of its Federal numbers" should amount to thirty-five thousand.[22] Not until August, 1814, was the taking of a census provided for, the work to be carried out in 1815.[23]

The Territorial Assembly of December 4 to 28, 1815, directed immediate attention to measures preparatory to going into state government. A committee was appointed on December 6, and the next day reported a memorial to Congress praying that a time and place be appointed for the meeting of a convention to form a constitution. The amended memorial passed the House on December 11, was further amended by the Legislative Council, and on December 12, copies were ordered to be made for the speaker of the House, the president of the Senate, and the territorial delegate to Congress.[24]

On December 28, 1815, Jennings presented the petition in the House of Representatives. According to the report of the House committee to which the petition was referred, the state was to be bounded "on the East by the State of Ohio; on the South by the State of Kentucky; on the west by the river Wabash, from its mouth to a point opposite the town of Vincennes, and from thence by a due north line until it intersects a due east and west line which shall touch the southern extreme of Lake Michigan; and on the north by the line last described." By the time the bill had passed the House, on March 30, 1816, the north boundary had been placed, by amendment, at the 42° of latitude. A Senate amendment changed the

[22] *Annals*, 12 Congress, 1 session, 1:91; *ibid.*, 1:607, 749; 2:1247.
[23] Kettleborough, *Constitution Making*, 1:68-69.
[24] Territorial House Journal, 1815, *passim*.

line once more, moving it southward from the 42° to its present location ten miles north of the east and west line through the southern extreme of Lake Michigan.

The changes from the original bill, and from the provisions of the Ordinance of 1787, were certainly not made with a clear understanding of their effect, for the territory in question was known but vaguely, and inaccurate maps then in use represented the southern extremity of Lake Michigan as considerably farther north than it actually is, and the 42° of latitude as south of the lake. In view of this fact, it is possible that the actual effect of the changes was, in each case, exactly opposite to the intended result. One reason for the final wording of the bill may have been to assure Indiana of a frontage on Lake Michigan. Although Michigan Territory objected to this reduction of her territory, the fact that her jurisdiction had not been extended over this little known area, and that the change was formally acquiesced in by Congress, prevented the outbreak of any such boundary struggle with Indiana as occurred with Ohio.

The description of the Illinois-Indiana boundary was also reworded—continuing the boundary in the Wabash "to a point where a due north line drawn from the town of Vincennes, would last touch the northwestern shore of the said river." The bill was thus passed by the Senate and accepted by the House. The convention for drawing up a state government next approved the boundaries, and Congress passed a resolution admitting Indiana to statehood. It was approved on December 11, 1816.[25]

The survey of the Indiana-Illinois boundary was made in 1821. In compliance with provisions of an Indiana

[25] *Annals of Congress*, 13 Congress, 1 session, 1116; 14 Congress, 1 session, 388, 408, 459-60, 1293, 1300, 1367, 1373; 23 Congress, 1 session, *Senate Documents*, 4:no.354:31. For a full discussion of the Indiana-Michigan boundary line, see Sheehan, Mrs. Frank J., *The Northern Boundary of Indiana* (*Indiana Historical Society Publications*, vol. 8, no. 6, Indianapolis, 1928); see also Soule, Annah May, "The Michigan-Indiana Boundary," in *Michigan Historical Collections*, 27:341-45.

statute of January 8, 1821, and an Illinois statute of February 6, 1821, John Tipton, of Indiana, and Samuel McClintoc, of Illinois, were commissioned "to adjust, run and mark" the line.[26] John McDonald was employed as surveyor, and the work was completed in the summer of 1821. McDonald's plat and field notes, dated July 22, 1821, and approved by Tipton and McClintoc on July 26, were presented to the two state legislatures at their next term. The Illinois committee to which the survey was referred objected to the report on the ground that it did not fix any point of beginning at the town of Vincennes. Their commissioner "informed them that he was fully aware of the difficulty; that they commenced the line at the Court House in Vincennes; but as the Commissioner on the part of Indiana conceived he had thus given this state [Illinois] an advantage; and fearful he might injure his political standing, by stating the fact in the Report and the Field Book, refused to make any other return."[27]

The Indiana Assembly approved the line in a joint resolution of December 14, 1821, and the Illinois Assembly gave its confirmation by an act of February 17, 1823. This act provided for placing "where the line dividing the states of Illinois and Indiana last leaves the river Wabash, a hewn stone, of at least five feet in length and fifteen inches in diameter," to be inscribed "on west 'Illinois,' on the east, 'Indiana,' and on the north, '159 miles and 46 chains to lake Michigan.'" In September, 1928, this old stone marker, which had sunk from view, was recovered

[26] See directions for the marking of the line in *Laws of Indiana*, 1820-21, pp. 37-40.

[27] The Indiana State Library has the original of the report made by Tipton to the Indiana Assembly, and one of the two copies of the field notes and plat books. It has photostatic copies of the report made by McClintoc and the plat book submitted by him. Tipton's Journal, covering the boundary survey, has also been preserved. He says about the place of beginning the survey: "we commensed the line opisit the vincennes Hotell on the N W **Bank of** Wabash."

and reset in a permanent foundation.[28] The northern part of the Indiana-Illinois line was resurveyed in 1834, under directions from Micajah T. Williams, surveyor-general northwest of the Ohio. Beginning at the one hundred eighteenth mile post, the line was retraced north to Lake Michigan and many of the boundary mounds were rebuilt.[29]

That part of the Indiana-Illinois boundary formed by the Wabash River has been construed to be the middle of the river as it was in 1816. Changes in the meandering course of the river have effected the transfer of some Illinois lands to the east side of the present river bed, and some Indiana lands to the west, or Illinois, side, so that the jurisdiction of each state reaches in some instances across the river.[30] In this volume no attempt has been made to show such changes.

The northern boundary of Indiana was surveyed by E. P. Kendricks in 1827. That the matter was regarded as a source of possible trouble is evident from the letter in which Surveyor-General Edward Tiffin transmitted the completed plat to Governor Ray, of Indiana:[31]

"In order to avoid any colour of ground for complaint or jealousy on either side of the state line, I thought it

[28] *Laws of Indiana*, 1821-22, p. 173; *Laws of Illinois*, 1822-23, pp. 159-60; Scott, George A., "The Recovery of the Indiana-Illinois Boundary Stone," in *Indiana History Bulletin*, 6:extra no.2:32-39.

[29] See a statement concerning the resurvey in Wilson, *Early Indiana Trails and Surveys*, 429-30.

[30] For example, parts of sections 3, 4, 9, 10, 20, and 21, township 8 north, range 11 west, when surveyed by Arthur Henrie in 1815 lay on the west side of the river in two of its loops or meanders. The river has since cut a more direct course across the necks of these loops, and the two small tracts of land are left on the Indiana side, in the region of Truman Township, Sullivan County. Cut-offs in the river have transferred land in the other direction from Black and Harmony townships, Posey County, taking a considerable acreage to the Illinois side.

[31] Letter of November 28, 1827, printed in Indiana *House Journal*, 1827-28, pp. 75-76. The plat of the survey is reproduced in 20 Congress, 1 session, *House Executive Documents*, 5:no.187.

BOUNDARY LEGISLATION

best to select for this service a skilful deputy Surveyor, not a citizen of either Indiana or Michigan—a gentleman of this place [Chillicothe], with whose . . . abilities . . . I have the utmost confidence. And that in the manner in which he has executed the survey, will be satisfactory to the state of Indiana. I was apprehensive that it would have been unnecessary delay, to suspend the survey until legislative provision could be made by the state of Indiana, for sending out an agent to accompany the surveyor. And . . . it would have been but justice that an agent . . . of the territory of Michigan . . . should accompany the Surveyor likewise."

The boundary line run by Kendricks was approved by a joint resolution of the Indiana Assembly on January 17, 1828.[32]

In the seventies, eighties, and nineties a part of the Indiana-Kentucky boundary was in controversy between the two states. The boundary was agreed to be the northwestern shore of the Ohio River along a line representing low watermark at the time when Kentucky became a state in 1792. The controversy centered around Green River Island, an island about six miles in length and containing some two thousand acres, lying south and east of Evansville, and separated from the Indiana shore only by a slough. Kentucky claimed that the course of the river had changed since 1792, and that at that time low watermark lay north of the island. Indiana disputed the claim.

In 1873 bills were introduced in the legislatures of both states for the appointment of commissioners to determine the line. The Indiana bill was crowded out at the end of the session, but the Kentucky measure became law on April 21, 1873.[33] This was the beginning of negotiations and litigation which lasted until 1896.

[32] *Laws of Indiana*, 1827-28, p. 138. See a short account of the survey in Wilson, *Early Indiana Trails and Surveys*, 431-32.

[33] *Senate Journal*, 1873, pp. 719, 931-32, 949-50; *House Journal*, 1873, p. 846; *Acts of Kentucky*, 1873, pp. 51-52.

In 1875 Indiana passed a companion act providing for the appointment of a commissioner to aid in surveying the state boundary line through the disputed area. The commissioners were instructed to "be governed by the surveys originally made by the Government of the United States," to make a written report within ten days after establishing the line, and to record it in the counties of Henderson, Kentucky, and Vanderburgh and Warrick, Indiana, and in the office of the governor of Kentucky and the secretary of state of Indiana. Section 3 of the Indiana act concluded: "Such writing, or the record thereof, shall be conclusive evidence of the boundary line between the State of Indiana and Kentucky, between the points on said Green River Island heretofore indicated."[34]

Commissioners were duly appointed by the two states —August Pfafflin, of Evansville, for Indiana, and D. N. Walden, of Henderson County, for Kentucky. By July 17, 1875, they had completed a survey, and ten days later their written report was ready for record. Unfortunately for the claims of Indiana, the surveyors, following literally their instructions to be guided by government surveys, established the boundary along a meander line laid out by a government survey of 1806. This gave to Kentucky not only the territory she claimed, but additional land on the Indiana side, between low watermark and the meander line.

Unwilling to give such a report the authority it would automatically acquire if recorded, Governor Thomas A. Hendricks suspended Pfafflin's appointment on July 28, and after further investigation, ordered him by a letter of November 12, 1875, not to file for record any description of the survey. The report was put on file, however, in Henderson County, Kentucky.[35]

[34] *Laws of Indiana*, 1875 (general), pp. 8-9.
[35] The commissions to Pfafflin and Walden, and their report, are printed in the *Transcript of Record . . . the State of Indiana, complainant, vs. the State of Kentucky*, 168-71 (Washington, 1889). Governor Hendricks' later instructions to Pfafflin appear on pages 189-92.

Early in the session of 1877 a move was made to abrogate the law of February 27, 1875. Two laws were enacted, one repealing the 1875 measure, and declaring void the survey and other acts of commissioners under the act,[36] and the second authorizing the governor of Indiana to negotiate with the governor of Kentucky for the cession, by Kentucky, of all her rights to Green River Island and territory on the Indiana shore near the island, or to fix a boundary by agreement; the bill required ratification by the state legislature to make the negotiations binding, and depended upon the passage of a similar act by Kentucky and upon the consent of Congress to proceedings between the states. If neither cession nor an agreement could be effected, the attorney general, under direction of the governor, was to institute proceedings against the State of Kentucky.[37]

Instead of enacting a corresponding law for an amicable settlement, Kentucky passed an act in 1878 ratifying the report made by the commissioners under the law of 1875. This left Indiana no recourse but litigation. In 1881 an appropriation of $1500 was made for costs of suit.[38]

Contention between land owners made the situation a vexing and possibly dangerous one, but proceedings regarding the Indiana-Kentucky line were not instituted under the act of 1881 because the appropriation of $1500 was considered insufficient to pay costs of a suit in chancery. Governor Isaac P. Gray, in January, 1887, put the situation before the Senate,[39] and on February 16 Senate Bill No. 292 was introduced enlarging the appropriation and directing the governor to institute suit

[36] *Laws of Indiana*, 1877 (general), p. 23; *House Journal*, 1877, pp. 110, 880; *Senate Journal*, 1877, pp. 839-40.

[37] *Laws of Indiana*, 1877 (general), pp. 23-24; 1881, pp. 525-26; *State of Indiana vs. State of Kentucky, Brief in Behalf of Complainant*, pp. 128-29.

[38] *Acts of Kentucky*, 1877-78, pp. 56-58; *Laws of Indiana*, 1877 (general), pp. 525-26.

[39] *Senate Journal*, 1887, p. 354.

against the State of Kentucky. Under suspension of the rules, the measure was hurried through Senate and House, and on February 25, was approved.[40] McDonald and Butler, attorneys for the State of Indiana, filed a bill of complaint before the United States Supreme Court on October 12, 1887, and at the January term of court, 1888, Kentucky filed a cross bill. The case was argued on April 9 and 10, 1890, and decided on May 19, the Supreme Court confirming Kentucky's claim to Green River Island. The actual line of boundary was to be established by a commission to be appointed by the court.[41]

Indiana had by this time exhausted her appropriation for prosecution of the claim, and a bill to appropriate $5000 more for the conclusion of litigation and fees was introduced on February 9, 1891.[42] No further action on this bill is reported, and not until 1895 was definite action begun again for establishment of the Indiana-Kentucky line. On October 21 of that year the Supreme Court appointed three commissioners agreed upon by the two states—Gustave V. Menzies, of Mount Vernon, Indiana, Gaston M. Alves, of Henderson, Kentucky, and Colonel Amos Stickney, of the United States Army, with instructions to "ascertain and run the boundary line between the States of Indiana and Kentucky."[43]

The commissioners met on December 7, 1895, and by February 3, 1896, had completed the mapping of a boundary line. The chief problem in establishing the line centered around accretions near the head and foot of the

[40] *Senate Journal*, 1887, pp. 578-79, 679, 781.

[41] Indiana v. Kentucky, 136 *United States*, 479-519. The court attached great importance to the fact that Indiana had not prosecuted a claim against Kentucky at any earlier period during the seventy years since becoming a state, although Kentucky had by more than one act asserted jurisdiction over the contested area. The fact that the government survey of 1806 had not included any of the territory of Green River Island was also regarded as an indication that Indiana Territory did not make any claim to the area.

[42] Original House Bill No. 549; *House Journal*, 1891, p. 603.

[43] 159 *United States*, 275-78.

BOUNDARY LEGISLATION 19

island. These accretions were allotted to Indiana in the report of the commissioners which came before the Supreme Court in April, 1896. Kentucky filed exceptions, but the Court, on May 18, 1896, confirmed the commissioners' report.[44]

Although the boundary line itself was at last fixed and agreed upon, the question of jurisdiction on the Ohio River was still in controversy. Indiana claimed concurrent jurisdiction on the river. Kentucky denied her right to it. In 1904 the question was settled by a decree of the United States Supreme Court, upholding Indiana's right to "as much power—legislative, judiciary, and executive, as that possessed by Kentucky, over so much of the Ohio River as flows between them."[45]

[44] The description of this line appears in the report to the Supreme Court, 163 *United States*, 525-26. See also the *Biennial Report of the Attorney-General*, 1895-96, p. 25.

[45] See the case of Wedding v. Meyler, 192 *United States*, 573 ff. Justice Holmes pointed out that this jurisdiction must be "on" the river, and that it "does not extend to permanent structures attached to the river bed and within the boundary of one or the other State."

TERRITORIAL COUNTIES

THE first counties formed in the territory which later became the state of Indiana were established by proclamation of the governors of the Northwest and Indiana territories. Upon the advance of Indiana Territory to the second grade in 1805 the power of setting up new counties passed to the legislature. This procedure was provided for in the Ordinance of 1787.[1] The territory of the first organized counties was vast; their boundaries, where not established by waterways, were described by unmapped, sometimes impossible, lines; their organization was limited and vague. Under such conditions it was inevitable that the more remote tracts of country should be assigned now to one county, and now to another; boundaries of established counties were distorted by the formation of new ones, and large districts were sometimes separated entirely from the parent county.

At the beginning of the territorial period surveyed areas were small, disconnected, and usually limited to private grants. By 1808 and 1810, when county organization became more rapid, government surveys usually preceded the laying out of county boundaries, but accurate maps were not always at the disposal of the legislators, and errors and ambiguities of description obscured the intent of many early boundary acts. The survey of lines not defined by watercourses or government survey

---

[1] "For the prevention of crimes and injuries, the laws to be adopted or made shall have force in all parts of the district, and for the execution of process, criminal and civil, the governor shall make proper divisions thereof; and he shall proceed, from time to time, as circumstances may require, to lay out the parts of the district in which the Indian titles shall have been extinguished, into counties and townships, subject, however, to such alterations as may thereafter be made by the legislature." *Journals of Congress*, 4:752.

BOUNDARY LEGISLATION

lines was often considerably delayed, for it was not regularly provided for as part of the process of forming or changing counties.

Three main factors determined the establishment of new counties. First, there was the difficulty of providing adequate local jurisdiction in large counties where part of the citizens lived at great distance from their seat of government, or were separated from it by natural obstacles of rivers, forests, and hills. Second, there was the spread of population, particularly following the close of the War of 1812, into territory lately ceded by the Indians. Third, with the growth of towns, there sprang up a rivalry among the more populous for the prestige and commercial advantages enjoyed by county seats. Speculators in land values gambled on the probable location of new county boundaries to lay out towns which might logically become county seats, and county boundaries were juggled to favor towns already established.

1790-99. Knox County was formed by proclamation of Governor Arthur St. Clair on June 20, 1790. Of the four counties laid out in the Northwest Territory and later a part of Indiana Territory, Knox is the only one on the present list of Indiana counties. It included, at the time of its formation, all of the present state of Indiana, western Ohio, western Michigan, a strip of Wisconsin along Lake Michigan, and eastern Illinois.[2] St. Clair County had been formed along the Mississippi River about two months earlier in the year, and Randolph County was cut off the southern end of St. Clair in 1795. Both were included with a large western expanse of Knox County in the formation of Illinois Territory in 1809. The first Wayne County, created as a part of the Northwest Territory in 1796, and redefined as part of Indiana Territory in 1803, was taken over by Michigan

[2] Maps of Knox County I, II, and III, show the formation of the county and changes made in it before 1800. See also *History of Knox and Daviess Counties, Indiana* . . ., 168 ff. (The Goodspeed Publishing Co., Chicago, 1886); Dunn, *Indiana*, 271-74.

Territory upon its formation in 1805.[3] No additional county formations occurred before Indiana Territory was organized in 1800.

1800-1804. Clark County was created out of the southeastern part of Knox County in 1801, embracing all the expanse of country to the eastern territorial line, which ran from Fort Recovery to the mouth of the Kentucky River.[4] When the territorial line was pushed eastward at the time of Ohio's advance to statehood, the Gore between the old and new lines was temporarily attached to Clark County for jurisdiction. In March, 1803, in compliance with a petition from that district, Governor Harrison erected the Gore into the county of Dearborn.[5]

Up to this time there seems to have been no recognition of Indian titles in the laying out of county boundaries, although the provision in the Ordinance of 1787 authorizing the formation of counties limited them to ceded territory.[6] The Treaty of Greenville, signed in 1795, did, it is true, include all the territory which formed Dearborn County, but the vast territory included in Clark and Knox counties, excepting the Illinois Grant, the Vincennes Tract, and several small grants in the northeast, was still claimed by the Indians. Land purchases secured at Vincennes and at Grouseland in 1804 and 1805 completed a wide band of ceded territory between the Wabash River and the Gore.[7] From that time new counties were

[3] See maps, St. Clair County, and Randolph County, Northwest Territory, and Wayne County, Northwest Territory and Indiana Territory.

[4] See text with map, Clark County I; Baird, Lewis C., *History of Clark County, Indiana*, 46 ff. (Indianapolis, 1909); "Clarke and Floyd Counties, Indiana," in *History of the Ohio Falls Cities and their Counties*, 2:91 ff. (Cleveland, 1882).

[5] See text with map, Dearborn County I; *History of Dearborn and Ohio Counties, Indiana* . . ., 111 ff. (F. E. Weakley & Co., publishers, Chicago, 1885); Shaw, Archibald (ed.), *History of Dearborn County, Indiana* . . ., 132 ff. (Indianapolis, 1915).

[6] See note 1, above.

[7] Kappler, Charles J. (ed.), *Indian Affairs. Laws and Treaties*, 2:39-45, 70-72, 80-82 (Washington, 1904).

BOUNDARY LEGISLATION 23

usually limited by the Indian boundaries, and portions of the old counties which projected beyond the treaty lines gradually lost contact with their county organizations.[8]

1805-12. Harrison County, created out of Knox and Clark in 1808, was the first county to be established by legislative act. Early in the session begun on September 26, 1808, the Territorial House of Representatives received petitions both praying for and opposing the erection of the new county. A bill to form the county was introduced on October 5 and after amendment by the House and again by the Legislative Council was passed on October 11.[9] Requests of 148 petitioners for a second new county, out of Clark and Dearborn, were rejected on the grounds that the proposed county would be too thinly settled and that the formation would be expensive and to no purpose.[10] The northern part of Dearborn County also asked to be separately organized, presenting petitions with a total of 561 signers on October 7, 13, 14, 17, and 18. A difference of opinion among the petitioners as to whether the line of division should fall between townships 7 and 8 or 8 and 9 north resulted in a recommendation that the petition be renewed at the next session.[11]

The next year two large districts were purchased from the Indians at Fort Wayne, one of them, the "Twelve Mile Purchase," paralleling the 1795 treaty line north of the Grouseland cession.[12] During the meeting of the General Assembly in 1810, this purchase, with the north-

[8] See, for example, maps, Clark County IV and V, and accompanying text. See also map, Indiana I.

[9] Journal of Territorial House of Representatives, in the *Western Sun*, November 12, 19, 26, December 3, and 10, 1808; Journal of the Legislative Council, in *ibid.*, January 28, 1809; *Biographical and Historical Souvenir for the Counties of Clark, Crawford, Harrison* . . ., 123 ff. (Chicago, 1889).

[10] Territorial House Journal, *op. cit.*, November 12, 19, and 26.

[11] Territorial House Journal, *op. cit.*, November 26, December 10, and 17.

[12] Kappler (ed.), *Laws and Treaties*, 2:101-2.

ern part of Dearborn County, was laid out into Wayne[13] and Franklin counties.[14] Dearborn's northern boundary was put at the line dividing townships 7 and 8 north. Jefferson County came into existence the same year.[15] This formation, together with an enlargement of Harrison, reduced Clark County to a fraction of its former size, and cut off from it a large district north of the Indian boundary.

1813-14. The northern boundary of Knox County had not yet been legally redrawn, although the establishment of the "Ten o'Clock Line," in 1809, as the outer boundary of the Indian purchase adjoining the Vincennes tract, provided a boundary of much greater actual significance.[16] In the southern part of the county, as settlements increased, there was a move for new county organizations. Harrison had made the initial curtailment of Knox territory, and in March, 1813, the large area south of the Wabash River and a line through the center of township one north was divided into two new counties, Gibson and Warrick.[17] In December of the same year Washington County was formed, taking a portion of Knox County, and also the northern part of Harrison and Clark counties and a corner of Jefferson.[18] The Silver

[13] See map, Wayne County I; Young, Andrew W., *History of Wayne County, Indiana* . . ., 80 ff. (Cincinnati, 1872); *History of Wayne County, Indiana* . . ., 1:402 ff. (Inter-State Publishing Co., Chicago, 1884).

[14] See map, Franklin County I; Reifel, August J., *History of Franklin County Indiana* . . ., 77 ff., and maps preceding (Indianapolis, 1915).

[15] See map, Jefferson County I; *Biographical and Historical Souvenir for the Counties of Clark . . . Jefferson* . . ., 147 ff.

[16] See Kappler (ed.), *op cit.*

[17] See maps, Gibson County I and Warrick County I; Stormont, Gil R., *History of Gibson County Indiana* . . ., 64 ff. (Indianapolis, 1914); *History of Warrick, Spencer and Perry Counties, Indiana* . . ., 35 ff. (Goodspeed Bros. & Co., publishers, 1885).

[18] See map, Washington County I; *History of Lawrence, Orange and Washington Counties Indiana* . . ., 706 ff. (Goodspeed Bros. & Co., publishers, 1884); *Biographical and Historical Souvenir for the Counties of Clark . . . and Washington*, 252 ff.

BOUNDARY LEGISLATION   25

Creek Knobs formed a natural southeastern boundary, but the precise defining of the line along their height was the subject of legislative controversies and compromises until 1873.

1814. Three counties were laid out by the legislative session which met in August and September, 1814. A petition for the formation of Switzerland County from Jefferson and Dearborn was laid before the House on August 20, and was followed the next day by a protest against the division. An amended measure which created the new county and made a transfer from Jefferson County to Dearborn was approved on September 7.[19] The same day a Council bill was signed, dividing the elongated extent of Warrick County upon the Ohio River into three counties, Posey on the west, Warrick, and Perry on the east. Ten townships from Gibson County were allotted to Perry County.[20]

The Territorial Assembly of 1814 also extended the boundaries of Washington County northwest from the Grouseland Treaty line of 1805 to the Ten o'Clock Line of 1809.[21] This was the first incorporation into an organized county of any part of that Indian purchase,

---

[19] Territorial House Journal, 1814, August 19 (20), 21 (22), 22 (23), 28 (29), September 5, 7. The dates in the Journal are incorrect for the month of August; the correct date is given in parentheses. The manuscript Journal is in the office of the Secretary of State. See map, Switzerland County I; see also Dufour, Perret, *The Swiss Settlement of Switzerland County Indiana*, 6-7, 35 (*Indiana Historical Collections*, vol. 13, Indianapolis, 1925); *History of Dearborn, Ohio and Switzerland Counties, Indiana* . . ., 1009 ff. (Weakley, Harraman & Co., 1885).

[20] Territorial House Journal, 1814, September 3, 5; *History of Posey County Indiana* . . ., 327 ff. (Goodspeed Publishing Co., 1886); Leffel, John C. (ed.), *History of Posey County Indiana*, 64 ff. (Chicago, 1913); *History of Warrick, Spencer and Perry Counties*, 597 ff. See also maps, Posey County I, Perry County I, Warrick County II.

[21] Territorial House Journal, August 24 (25), 28 (29), 30 (31), September 1; *History of Lawrence, Orange and Washington Counties*, 709.

although, technically, the boundaries of old Knox County covered the entire area.

Another county organization, presumably to adjoin the Ohio River, was proposed by citizens of Harrison and Clark in a petition presented in the House on September 3. A protest from other citizens, and a second petition, from Washington County, favoring the change, were referred with the original request to a committee of three, which reported adversely on September 6.[22]

Franklin County citizens also presented a petition dealing with the division of counties. From the Journal record it is impossible to discover whether the petition dealt with the boundary between Franklin and Wayne, the formation of a new county, or with some more general matter. A bill was reported and passed the House on August 17, but was rejected by the Legislative Council.[23]

1815. The last Territorial Assembly created two counties: Jackson was formed from the northern part of Washington, with a small area from Clark and several townships from Jefferson;[24] Orange was erected as a long, narrow county beginning at the Perry County line and running northward past Harrison, Washington, and Jackson counties to the Ten o'Clock Line.[25] Most of Orange County came from the old Knox County, but several townships were taken from Gibson's eastern extremity.

Gibson also lost to Posey County a small triangular tract upon the Wabash River, forming the southeast corner of township 4 south, range 13 west. It was evidently the intention of the bill to include the Rappite

[22] Territorial House Journal, September 3, 5, 6.

[23] *Ibid.*, August 16, August 16 (17), 19 (20), 24 (25).

[24] *Ibid.*, 1815, December 5, 11, 12, 13, 14, 15, 16; see also *History of Jackson County, Indiana* . . ., 324 ff. (Brant & Fuller, Chicago, 1886); *History of Lawrence, Orange and Washington Counties*, 709. See map, Jackson County I.

[25] Territorial House Journal, 1815, December 14, 15, 16, 22; *History of Lawrence, Orange and Washington Counties*, 410 ff. See map, Orange County I.

settlement "Harmonie" in Posey County. The Rappite holdings extended beyond the line drawn in the enacted law, but the bill, before amendment, may have included the full extent of their lands. At any rate, Posey received adjoining territory at the following legislative session.[26]

The Legislative Council passed two bills which failed of final enactment. One contemplated the erection of a county out of Knox, apparently at the forks of White River. The other bill, proposing the attachment of part of Knox to Washington, was set aside as conflicting with the House act creating Orange County.[27]

There were, then, fifteen counties when Indiana became a state, one of which, Knox, had been created as part of the Northwest Territory. Knox, Clark, and Dearborn were formed by governors' proclamations; Harrison, Jefferson, Franklin and Wayne, Gibson and Warrick, Washington, Perry, Posey, Switzerland, Jackson, and Orange were created by the territorial general assemblies. In all these cases, the organization of the county was provided for in the act forming the county. No one of the fifteen had reached its present form.

[26] Territorial House Journal, 1815, December 8, 11, 12, 15; *History of Posey County*, 328. See map, Posey County II.

[27] Territorial House Journal, December 9, 11, 12, 15, 20, 21, 22. Daviess County was created in this territory the next year.

Conference committees appointed by House and Legislative Council to confer on certain petitions from Wayne and Franklin counties decided against legislative action. Although the content of the petitions is not given, the fact that the matter of county divisions was raised by citizens of the two counties at the preceding and succeeding sessions leads to the inference that the Assembly of 1815 was petitioned on the same subject. It is probable that Connersville hoped to become the seat of a new county. *Ibid.*, December 18, 19.

COUNTIES OF THE NEW STATE

UNLIKE some commonwealths, Indiana did not, upon admission to statehood, lay out a framework for the future county organization of her entire territory.[1] Nor did county organization in Indiana follow any other carefully prepared plan. Although there were occasional tentative moves during the early years of statehood toward laying out all unorganized territory into counties, their organization actually followed irregularly behind the lines of Indian cessions and pioneer settlements. More than half the area of the state was still Indian territory in 1816. The "New Purchase" of 1818, covering the central area of the state, was immediately divided into two unorganized "counties," but later purchases were not closely followed by such an experimental distribution. In 1835 all the territory which had not been incorporated in existing counties, with the exception of the interior of the Miami Reserve, was laid out into "paper" counties to await later organization as population increased.

The method employed to provide criminal and civil jurisdiction for districts not within county boundaries, consisted of attaching prescribed areas to organized counties. The attachments when first made were ordinarily explicitly defined, but as new counties appeared, new attachments were frequently made in such a way as to disrupt the boundaries of earlier attachments. There

---

[1] The first legislative assembly of California passed an act laying out twenty-seven counties, covering the entire area of the state. Coy, Owen D., *California County Boundaries* . . ., 1 ff. (Berkeley, 1823). Another example of the same system is Colorado. At the first assembly after reaching territorial standing, the entire area was divided into seventeen counties. Paxson, Frederic L., "The County Boundaries of Colorado," in *University of Colorado Studies*, 3:no. 4:197-215. In both cases the first arrangement was subsequently changed.

was seldom any attempt to clarify the status of attachments so invalidated.

Considerable controversy over county boundaries arose from the difficulty of interpreting general terms of description such as "north" and "south" to fit the irregularities of government surveys. Particularly where correctional survey lines left a range five sections wide, instead of the regulation six, or caused a break in the continuity of a range or township line, a description which did not specify the township, range, and section precisely was likely to bring on a boundary dispute. Another fertile source for contention was the custom of laying out boundaries along unsurveyed lines to follow natural divisions such as that along the Knobs between Clark and Washington counties.[2]

The proper size of counties was much discussed in the convention which formed the state constitution. It was first proposed that "No new county shall be established by the general assembly, which shall reduce the county or counties, or either of them from which it shall be taken, to less contents than four hundred square miles; nor shall any county be laid off of less contents."[3] Upon an attempt to amend the section to "except counties bordering on the Ohio and Wabash rivers, and in such other parts of the state as may be naturally circumscribed, so as to render such small county or counties necessary," the entire section was stricken out. It was reintroduced, however, minus the limitation upon the size of new counties, and passed by a vote of 23 to 16 in the following form: "The general assembly, when they lay off any new county, shall not reduce the old county or counties, from which the same shall be taken, to a less content than

[2] See, for example, text with map, Henry County I. The Clark-Washington boundary was explicitly defined during the revision of the laws in 1842-43.

[3] *Journal of the Convention of the Indiana Territory: begun and held at . . . Corydon . . . on the second Monday in June . . . in the Year of Our Lord, one thousand eight hundred and sixteen . . .*, 53 (Louisville, 1816).

four hundred square miles." There was an unsuccessful attempt to amend this to except counties on the Ohio River.[4]

1816-17. The establishment of a state government was followed by a period of great activity in the organization of counties. The two large counties of Sullivan and Daviess were cut out of that part of Knox County which had been opened to settlement along the Ten o'Clock Line following the Fort Wayne Treaty of 1809.[5] By this reduction the legal boundaries of Knox County were at last made to fit its organized extent. Pike County, created at this session, absorbed more than half of Gibson and a corner from Perry.[6] This formation, and a further loss of several townships to Posey County, left Gibson with an awkward appendage of four townships separating Pike and Warrick. On the east, Dearborn, Jefferson, and Jackson counties were reduced by the formation of Jennings and Ripley.[7]

[4] *Journal of the Convention, Indiana Territory*, 60, 61-62, 64.

[5] Wolfe, Thomas J. (ed.), *A History of Sullivan County Indiana* . . ., 1:22 ff. (New York, Chicago, 1909); *House Journal*, 1816-17, pp. 81, 84, 95, 98, 107; Fulkerson, A. O. (ed.), *History of Daviess County Indiana* . . ., 81 ff., 272 ff. (Indianapolis, 1915); *History of Knox and Daviess Counties*, 606 ff.; *House Journal*, 1816-17, pp. 19, 21, 30, 39, 65, 93. See maps, Sullivan County I, Daviess County I.

[6] *History of Pike and Dubois Counties Indiana* . . ., 273 ff. (Goodspeed Bros. & Co., publishers, 1885). See maps, Pike County I, and Gibson County IV. *House Journal*, 1816-17, pp. 19, 21, 29, 31, 32, 53, 59, 63, 69, 75. The probability of an almost immediate division of the new county was recognized by the commissioners who selected the county seat. They "were unanimously of the opinion that it would admit of a future division, and in all probability from the great emigration to the country" would "justify a division in a few years by the line dividing Sections two and three, in Range six." *History of Pike and Dubois Counties*, 335-36. The division was made by the succeeding legislature, with the boundary one mile west of the division line suggested. See map, Dubois County I.

[7] *House Journal*, 1816-17, pp. 52, 59, 70, 72, 78, 81, 88, 91; *Illustrated Historical Atlas of the State of Indiana*, 301-2, 321-22 (Baskin, Forster & Co., Chicago, 1876). See maps, Jennings County I, Ripley County I.

BOUNDARY LEGISLATION 31

The five counties erected in 1816-17 were all created in response to petitions asking the division of older counties, where long distances from the county seats worked hardship to the citizens in remote areas. Unsuccessful attempts were made at the same session to secure the establishment of four other new counties: one from Franklin and Wayne;[8] one from Clark, Harrison, and Washington;[9] one from Jefferson, Clark, and Jackson;[10] and one from Dearborn, or from Dearborn and Switzerland.[11]

A bill was passed at this session for the running of a boundary line between Clark and Jefferson counties.[12]

Ripley, created by an act of December 27, 1816, was the first county to have its boundaries laid out without an accompanying provision for its immediate organization. Such provision was not made until 1818, under a separate law; in the meantime, jurisdiction over the territory was divided between Jennings and Dearborn.

1817-18. During the next session, 1817-18, the number of counties increased by eight, although no new territory was brought under organization. Dubois County was formed out of Pike County,[13] and along the Ohio River, Vanderburgh and Spencer pushed their way in on

[8] *House Journal*, 1816-17, pp. 25, 29, 62, 71.

[9] *Ibid.*, 98. The petition asking this formation was introduced late in the session and was tabled immediately.

[10] *Ibid.*, 21, 41, 48, 64, 69.

[11] *Ibid.*, 32, 37, 38. The committee which reported on the petition for a new county from Dearborn pointed out that the formation would reduce Dearborn below "the constitutional quantity" of square miles, but suggested that a county about eight miles in width and twenty in length could be safely taken from the southern end of Dearborn. This report was made before the formation of Ripley reduced Dearborn's area. In 1818, when Ripley was organized, an attempt was made to exclude from it the territory taken from Dearborn. *Ibid.*, 1817-18, pp. 142, 147.

[12] *Senate Journal*, 1816-17, pp. 64-84 *passim*.

[13] *History of Pike and Dubois Counties*, 483 ff.; Wilson, George R., *History of Dubois County* . . ., 30 ff. (Jasper, Ind., 1910); *House Journal*, 1817-18, pp. 33, 37, 41, 53, 57, 65. See map, **Pike County I.**

either side of Warrick.¹⁴ No changes have been made in Vanderburgh's boundaries. At the same session Crawford made itself a place between Perry and Harrison.¹⁵ In response to a series of petitions, enough territory was taken from Sullivan, along the 1809 Indian boundary, to form the county of Vigo.¹⁶ Monroe and Lawrence were formed by lopping off the northern part of Orange County, thus reducing it to its present size.¹⁷ By the

¹⁴ The creation of Vanderburgh and Spencer counties illustrates the importance of county-seat rivalries in changing county boundaries. Evansville was the first county seat of Warrick County. When Perry and Posey counties were erected in 1814, a more central site became necessary and Evansville was forsaken for Darlington. But Hugh McGary, with interests in the town of Evansville, determined to preserve its importance, and evolved a plan for a new county for which Evansville should be the logical county seat. This involved negotiations with Ratliff Boon, who would oppose any measure calculated to subtract from his political scope in Warrick County, or to interfere with his interests in Darlington. Finally, there was Daniel Grass to be considered, also politically powerful in Warrick County, and with extensive holdings in its eastern part. A scheme was eventually adapted to everyone's uses. The formation of Vanderburgh County with Evansville as county seat pleased McGary; Boon abandoned Darlington, but saw the new county seat of Warrick called Boonville; the Grass interests were recognized in the creation of Spencer County with its county seat at Rockport. *History of Vanderburgh County Indiana* . . ., 42 ff. (Brant & Fuller, 1885); *History of Warrick, Spencer and Perry Counties*, 277 ff.; Vanderburgh, *House Journal*, 1817-18, pp. 40, 66, 73-74, 81, 91, 120, 121; Spencer, *ibid.*, 61, 66, 73-74, 91, 119.

¹⁵ Pleasant, Hazen H., *History of Crawford County, Indiana*, 1 ff. (Greenfield, Ind., 1926); *House Journal*, 1817-18, pp. 145, 156, 182, 183-84, 193, 194, 203, 215, 221-22. See map, Crawford County I.

¹⁶ The bill was amended by both houses. *House Journal*, 1817-18, pp. 59, 62, 75, 81, 89, 107, 121, 124-25, 127, 159-60; Bradsby, H. C., *History of Vigo County, Indiana* . . ., 285 ff. (Chicago, 1891).

¹⁷ Monroe was created by a Senate bill, and Lawrence by a House bill; both were amended in each house. The north boundary of Lawrence County was at one time placed at the Driftwood Fork of White River, and the name Hendricks was first suggested. *Senate Journal*, 1817-18, pp. 17, 25, 27, 32, 34-35, 66, 69, 95, 109; *House Journal*, 1817-18, pp. 11, 31-32, 36, 39-40, 56-57, 106. See also *History of Lawrence and Monroe Counties Indiana* . . ., 64 ff.,

same process, Randolph was erected out of northern Wayne County.[18]

Measures proposing the formation of two counties from Sullivan and Daviess, to be attached to Daviess and Monroe counties respectively, passed the House, but failed in the Senate.[19] Petitions for new counties from Clark and Harrison, and from Clark, Harrison, Washington, and Orange, failed of approval in committee.[20] In each house a bill was introduced for the formation of a new county from Franklin and Wayne, both of which failed in the House of Representatives.[21] The House also defeated an attempt to revive the movement for a new county from Dearborn.[22]

1818-19. The movement of settlers into the territory along the Ten o'Clock Line justified the formation of another county there in 1818-19, and Owen County was created from Sullivan and Daviess counties to complete a tier of new counties extending from the Illinois boundary to the Grouseland Treaty line of 1805.[23] Towards the end of the session a House bill was introduced for the formation of a second new county out of Daviess and Sullivan; the measure failed in the Senate.[24] Sullivan did, however, lose a strip of territory to Vigo.[25]

224 ff. (B. F. Bowen & Co., 1914); *History of Lawrence, Orange and Washington Counties*, 64 ff.

[18] *House Journal*, 1817-18, pp. 15, 66, 89, 107, 112, 129; Smith, John L., and Driver, Lee L., *Past and Present of Randolph County Indiana* . . ., 117 ff. (Indianapolis, 1914).

[19] *House Journal*, 1817-18, pp. 62, 201, 211, 217, and 208, 216; *Senate Journal*, 1817-18, pp. 156, and 158, 195.

[20] *House Journal*, 1817-18, pp. 12, 14, 20, and 138, 171.

[21] *Ibid.*, 66, 105, 108, 163; *Senate Journal*, 1817-18, pp. 50, 53-54, 68, 69.

[22] *House Journal*, 1817-18, p. 128.

[23] *Ibid.*, 1818-19, pp. 11, 14, 40, 51, 52, 61, 75. See Blanchard, Charles (ed.), *Counties of Clay and Owen, Indiana* . . ., 561-62 (Chicago, 1884), for an account of the eagerness of the inhabitants for organization. See also map, Owen County I.

[24] *House Journal*, 1818-19, pp. 127-28, 148; *Senate Journal*, 1818-19, pp. 83, 86. Greene County was formed from the two counties in 1821.

[25] *House Journal*, 1818-19, pp. 160-61, 164. See map, Vigo County II.

The district between Clark and Harrison, which had been agitating for separate county organization since 1814, made another vigorous effort in 1818-19, and in spite of remonstrances from opposing factions in the counties, unfavorable committee reports, and extensive amendments to the bill which was finally introduced, was at last erected as Floyd County.[26]

Like Clark and Harrison, Franklin and Wayne lost a tract of territory the inhabitants of which had determined on separation several years before. Persistent opposition to the bill forming Fayette County could not stop its passage, although it was amended in both houses.[27] Besides taking a part of Franklin and of Wayne, the new county reached out beyond the Twelve Mile Purchase boundary of 1809 into the New Purchase acquired at the Treaty of St. Mary's in October, 1818.

1819-20. The New Purchase gave the United States title to most of the central section of the state south of the Wabash River and a line northwest of and parallel to the Wabash west of the Tippecanoe River, with the stipulation that the Delaware Indians might have three years for their withdrawal from the ceded territory, should that time be needed.[28]

In 1820 the legislature disposed of the entire tract purchased at St. Mary's by enlarging Randolph, Franklin, and Jennings counties and by dividing the remainder into two counties—Delaware, east of the second principal

[26] *House Journal*, 1818-19, pp. 29-30, 37, 93, 121-22, 129, 152, 168, 170; *Senate Journal*, 1818-19, pp. 88, 96, 101, 103, 106. See map, Floyd County I.

[27] *House Journal*, 1818-19, pp. 30, 53, 60, 68-69, 80, 104; Barrows, Frederic Irving, *History of Fayette County, Indiana . . .*, 155 ff. (Indianapolis, 1917); *History of Fayette County Indiana . . .*, 57 ff. (Warner, Beers & Co., Chicago, 1885). See map, Fayette County I.

[28] The text of the treaties of October 2-6, 1818, between the United States and the Potawatomi, Wea, Delawares, and Miami appears in Kappler (ed.), *Indian Affairs. Laws and Treaties*, 2:168-74.

BOUNDARY LEGISLATION   35

meridian, and Wabash, west of it.[29] These so-called counties did not have the usual county organization. They were put under the jurisdiction of adjoining counties, and new counties were formed within their boundaries much as had happened in the old Knox County. Scott and Martin counties were also formed in 1820, but well within the settled area south of the 1805 and 1809 Indian boundaries.[30] Martin County took a small part of Dubois County south of Lick Creek or Lost River, but most of her territory came from Daviess County. Daviess was still further reduced in size by a curious act establishing a "permanent" northern boundary twenty miles south of the existing one, and making an attachment of the district thus removed. The act did not prevent later changes in the line.[31] Another measure provided for a survey of Clark County's boundaries.[32]

Several boundary proposals failed to pass. Unfavorable committee action disposed of petitions asking the erection of new counties out of Clark and Jefferson, and out of Daviess, Owen, and Sullivan. Later in the session, a bill was reported for the creation of a new county out of Daviess and Sullivan, but after second reading, further discussion was indefinitely postponed.[33] The effort to extend Fayette County eastward progressed as far as bill form, but was killed in Committee of the

[29] *House Journal*, 1819-20, pp. 38, 130-31, 211, 319; *Laws of Indiana*, 1819-20, pp. 95-96. See maps, Delaware and Wabash counties, New Purchase.

[30] The formation of Scott followed various petitions for the erection of a county, all embracing at least a part of the same area from Washington, Clark, Jefferson, Jennings, and Jackson. *House Journal*, 1819-20, pp. 25, 88, 157, 216-17, 224, 238. For the formation of Martin County, see *ibid.*, 75, 131, 178, 192, 220. This formation made the last change in Dubois' boundaries.

[31] *House Journal*, 1819-20, pp. 310-11, 337, 378; *Senate Journal*, 1819-20, pp. 234-35. See maps, Daviess County II and III.

[32] *Laws of Indiana*, 1819-20, pp. 121-23.

[33] Clark-Jefferson, *House Journal*, 1819-20, pp. 27, 73, 129; Daviess-Owen-Sullivan, *ibid.*, 86, 110, 220-21, 251.

Whole.[34] Similar action defeated a proposed transfer from Posey to Gibson; a bill to attach part of Spencer to Perry, after passing the Senate by a close vote, failed in the House.[35]

Other petitions for change, from Jackson, Jefferson, and Switzerland, show how general was the uneasiness on the subject of county boundaries.[36]

1820-21. Four counties were formed by the legislature of 1820-21. Two of these, Union and Greene—which still retains its original boundaries—were created out of old counties. Wayne, Fayette, and Franklin all contributed to the small new county of Union,[37] while Greene was erected in response to continued petitions for a new county from Daviess and Sullivan.[38] The new Parke County took the northern part of Vigo County, and extended well beyond the Indian boundary into Wabash County.[39] The fourth new county, Bartholomew, lay for the most part in Delaware, although a small strip of Jackson County was allotted to it in spite of some objection from the transferred section.[40] A controversy over

[34] *House Journal*, 1819-20, pp. 284-85. Union County was formed in this area in 1820-21.

[35] Posey-Gibson, *ibid.*, pp. 280, 317; Spencer-Perry, *Senate Journal*, 1819-20, pp. 156, 166, 172-73; *House Journal*, 1819-20, pp. 265, 297.

[36] *Ibid.*, 88, 110, 116.

[37] *Senate Journal*, 1820-21, pp. 86, 94, 97, 100, 101-2.

[38] *House Journal*, 1820-21, pp. 20, 60, 124, 146, 154-55, 157-58, 176. An amendment proposed in the House would have cut off the western tier of townships. *Ibid.*, 157. *History of Greene and Sullivan Counties* . . ., 34 ff. (Goodspeed Bros. & Co., Chicago, 1884).

[39] *House Journal*, 1820-21, pp. 191, 221, 285-86, 292, 317-18; *History of Parke and Vermillion Counties Indiana* . . ., 60 ff. (B. F. Bowen & Company, Indianapolis, 1913).

[40] *House Journal*, 1820-21, p. 78; *History of Bartholomew County, Indiana* . . ., 313 ff. (Brant & Fuller, Chicago, 1888). Accusations were made that John Tipton had influenced the laying out of the boundaries of Bartholomew County to further his own interests. He made a hot defense in a letter of August 3, 1821, to the *Indiana Gazette* of Corydon. "Extracts from Corydon Newspapers, 1820-1838," in the Irdiana State Library.

BOUNDARY LEGISLATION 37

Bartholomew's western boundary was settled by making a temporary attachment to the county, running westward to Monroe County.[41]

The most extensive boundary change made in 1820-21, aside from the formation of the four counties mentioned, was the elongation of Randolph to the northern boundary of the state.[42] An alteration was made in the Scott-Washington boundary,[43] and a bill was passed attaching to Floyd County all that part of Clark "south and west of the lines dividing Harrison and Floyd counties." What was intended by this last-mentioned act it is impossible to say. The fact that it is sometimes spoken of in the House as a bill "attaching part of Clark county to the county of Harrison," and sometimes as a bill "attaching part of the county of Clark to the county of Floyd" indicates that the problem was not altogether clear to the legislators.[44]

Two Senate bills which were crowded out in the House concerned an addition from the New Purchase to Monroe, and the formation of a new county from Wabash and Delaware.[45]

1821-22. The movement northward was only beginning. The expediency of laying off the counties of Delaware and Wabash into new counties of approximately four hundred square miles area had already had some consideration, and in the session of 1821-22 seven counties were created, all in, or extending into, the New Purchase. They were Decatur, Rush, and Shelby, which

[41] *House Journal*, 1820-21, pp. 204-5, 211-12, 215-16, 236; *Senate Journal*, 1820-21, pp. 156-57, 159-60, 174, 177.
[42] See map, Randolph County III.
[43] See maps, Scott County II, Washington County V.
[44] *Laws of Indiana*, 1820-21, p. 111; *House Journal*, 1820-21, pp. 157, 207, 222-23, 237, 251, 317.
[45] Monroe, *Senate Journal*, 1820-21, pp. 98, 103, 121; *House Journal*, 1820-21, pp. 164, 243; Wabash and Delaware, *Senate Journal*, 1820-21, pp. 97, 100, 102-3, 106; *House Journal*, 1820-21, pp. 144-45, 232, 263.

have had no boundary changes,[46] Morgan, Marion, Henry, and Putnam.[47] Putnam absorbed a part of Vigo and Owen; in partial compensation Owen received an addition from Wabash County; Monroe was given that part of the New Purchase which lay between Morgan and Monroe's former boundary. Extensive areas not included in the county boundaries proper were attached for jurisdiction to Parke, Putnam, Bartholomew, and Marion.

Minor changes affected Gibson and Posey, and brought Ripley and Switzerland to their final form.[48] A bill to attach part of Jackson County to Lawrence passed the House, but was blocked in the Senate, and leave to introduce a bill on the same subject later in the session was refused.[49] Another House bill, attaching part of Clark

[46] Harding, Lewis A. (ed.), *History of Decatur County Indiana* . . ., 69 ff. (Indianapolis, 1915); *History of Rush County, Indiana* . . ., 284 ff. (Brant & Fuller, Chicago, 1888); *History of Shelby County, Indiana* . . ., 273 ff. (Brant & Fuller, Chicago, 1887). Shelby County was called Marion in the House bill for its organization; the name was changed by a Senate amendment. *Senate Journal*, 1821-22, pp. 201-2, 213-14. See also formation maps of the counties.

[47] Sulgrove, B. R., *History of Indianapolis and Marion County, Indiana*, 33 ff. (Philadelphia, 1884); Dunn, Jacob Piatt, *Greater Indianapolis* . . ., 1:47 ff. (Chicago, 1910); Marion County was first called Centre County; the name was changed by a Senate amendment. *House Journal*, 1821-22, pp. 255, 262; *Senate Journal*, 1821-22, pp. 213, 218. Blanchard, Charles (ed.), *Counties of Morgan, Monroe and Brown, Indiana* . . ., 14 ff. (Chicago, 1884); *History of Henry County, Indiana* . . ., 295 ff. (Inter-State Publishing Co., Chicago, 1884); Hazzard, George, *Hazzard's History of Henry County Indiana* . . ., 2:868 ff. (New Castle, Ind., 1906; military ed.); *Biographical and Historical Record of Putnam County, Indiana* . . ., 208 ff. (Lewis Publishing Company, Chicago, 1887); Weik, Jesse W., *Weik's History of Putnam County Indiana*, 19 ff. (Indianapolis, 1910). See formation maps of the counties.

[48] See maps, Gibson County VI, Posey County V, Ripley County II, and Switzerland County II. There was an unsuccessful attempt at the next session to transfer part of Ripley to Switzerland. *House Journal*, 1822-23, pp. 136, 148, 285.

[49] *House Journal*, 1821-22, pp. 252, 256, 351-52; *Senate Journal*, 1821-22, pp. 248-49, 250, 264.

BOUNDARY LEGISLATION

to Washington, reached the Senate the day before adjournment and action was postponed until the first Monday of the following December.[50] A third unsuccessful House bill proposed the attachment of part of Floyd to Harrison.[51]

1822-23. The fitting in of three counties around Marion was accomplished in 1822-23. Hamilton and Johnson were laid out in their present boundaries to the north and south of Marion, respectively,[52] and Madison to the east and northeast.[53] Another change of considerable extent was the transformation of Putnam County. As the result of assignments of territory to Owen and Vigo, and the addition of territory from the New Purchase, Putnam was moved north and east into an entirely new set of boundaries.[54] North of this reconstructed county,

[50] *House Journal*, 1821-22, pp. 230, 245, 254, 402; *Senate Journal*, 1821-22, p. 281. At the session of 1825-26, the Speaker of the House decided that bills postponed by the last legislature to any day after its adjournment were not a part of unfinished business. *House Journal*, 1825-26, p. 87.

[51] *Ibid.*, 1821-22, pp. 284, 296-97, 386.

[52] Haines, John F., *History of Hamilton County Indiana* . . ., 119 ff. (Indianapolis, 1915); *History of Hamilton County, Indiana* . . ., 36 ff. (Kingman Brothers, Chicago, 1880). The bill forming Hamilton County was passed only upon a reconsidered vote. *Senate Journal*, 1822-23, pp. 93, 107, 110, 122, 125, 131, 136, 137, 146; *House Journal*, 1822-23, pp. 184-85, 206, 218, 229.

Concerning the authenticity of the petition for Johnson County, see *History of Johnson County, Indiana* . . ., 680 ff. (Brant & Fuller, Chicago, 1888); Branigin, Elba L., *History of Johnson County Indiana*, 34, 44 ff. (Indianapolis, 1913). The name Delaware was proposed for the county. *House Journal*, 1822-23, pp. 101-2.

[53] Forkner, John L., and Dyson, Byron H., *Historical Sketches and Reminiscences of Madison County, Indiana* . . ., 22 ff. (Anderson, Ind., 1897); Forkner, John L., *History of Madison County Indiana* . . ., 1:45 ff. (Lewis Publishing Company, 1914); Netterville, J. J. (ed.), *Centennial History of Madison County Indiana* . . ., 1:90 ff. (Anderson, Ind., 1925).

[54] See map, Putnam County II.

Montgomery was erected, within territory which had been under the jurisdiction of Putnam and Parke.[55]

Citizens of Parke and Vigo counties, living west of the Wabash River, and inconvenienced by the necessity of crossing the river to reach their county seats, made a strong effort to secure a new county west of the river. A bill creating such a county—to be called Clinton—passed the Senate in spite of opposition from the remaining Parke County voters, but its final passage in the House was blocked.[56] There were also two ineffectual attempts to dispose of the open territory north of Morgan County, one by creating a new county, the other by attaching the area in question to Morgan.[57]

All this activity in relation to new counties proved burdensome to the legislators, and the Senate sought relief in a resolution providing that a committee be appointed "to arrange all the new purchase, or so much thereof as they may deem expedient into counties, in such size and form as they may think best to prevent future legislatures being troubled therewith."[58]

Less important measures passed at the session included transfers of territory from Jackson to Lawrence, from Harrison to Floyd, and a transfer from Gibson to Posey which put Posey in its present form. A Wayne-Henry boundary adjustment was effected.[59] Bills proposing the cession of part of Perry County to Crawford and Spencer, respectively, failed.[60] Attempts to add to Scott from Jef-

[55] *History of Montgomery County Indiana* . . ., 1:49 ff. (A. W. Bowen & Company, Indianapolis, n. d.). See map, Montgomery County I.

[56] *Senate Journal*, 1822-23, pp. 171, 207, 222-23, 227, 233, 249-50; *House Journal*, 1822-23, pp. 278, 284, 302, 305-7.

[57] *Senate Journal*, 1822-23, pp. 47, 56-57, and 187, 249, 253-54.

[58] *Ibid.*, 57.

[59] See maps, Jackson County VI, Lawrence County II, Harrison County VII, Floyd County II, Gibson County VII, Posey County VI, Wayne County V, Henry County II.

[60] *House Journal*, 1822-23, pp. 106, 171, 181, 209-10, and 276, 284; *Senate Journal*, 1822-23, pp. 161, 181, and 166-67, 170, 231.

ferson and Clark were also unsuccessful,[61] as were proposals affecting Dubois, Martin, and Daviess.[62]

1823-24. The revision of the laws in 1823-24 provided an opportunity for a checking of county boundaries. The boundaries of all old counties were restated and three new ones were created. In response to the continued demand for a county west of the Wabash River, a long narrow strip of territory along the Illinois line was organized as Vermillion County and an attachment to Vermillion.[63] Hendricks County was formed out of that part of Delaware and Wabash north of Morgan, to bridge the gap between Putnam and Marion counties;[64] Allen cut in two the northern extension of Randolph.[65] Between Allen and Randolph and westward toward the Great Miami Reserve lay a wide stretch of territory which was at this time attached to the two last-named counties for jurisdiction.

The Gibson-Pike-Warrick boundaries were rearranged, the law defining county boundaries assigning to Warrick the southeastern projection of Gibson County which dated from Pike's formation in 1816-17, and Pike and Gibson

[61] *House Journal*, 1822-23, pp. 33, 283, and 94, 121, 131, 210.

[62] *Senate Journal*, 1822-23, pp. 107, 113, 172, 247, 259.

[63] *Biographical and Historical Record of Vermillion County, Indiana* . . ., 200 ff. (Lewis Publishing Company, Chicago, 1888); *History of Parke and Vermillion Counties Indiana* . . ., 249 ff. (B. F. Bowen & Company, Indianapolis, 1913); *House Journal*, 1823-24, pp. 32, 51, 58-59, 68, 69, 94, 97, 129. See map, Vermillion County. See also discussion of the north boundary of Vermillion County, *post* 59 ff.

[64] *History of Hendricks County, Indiana* . . ., 276 ff. (Inter-State Publishing Co., Chicago, 1885); Hadley, John V. (ed.), *History of Hendricks County Indiana* . . ., 44 ff. (Indianapolis, 1914); *Senate Journal*, 1823-24, pp. 40, 46, 51, 54-55, 60, 68, 75. See map, Hendricks County I.

[65] Slocum, Charles E., *History of the Maumee River Basin* . . ., 1:550 (Indianapolis, 1905); Griswold, Bert J., *The Pictorial History of Fort Wayne Indiana* . . ., 264 (Chicago, 1917); *House Journal*, 1823-24, pp. 11, 21, 43, 49, 62, 79. See map, Allen County.

making an exchange of small areas under a special law. The description of the line between Gibson and Warrick left open to question the intention of the legislature regarding twenty-four sections in the north half of township 4 south, range 9 west, and the northwest corner of township 4 south, range 8 west. Gibson and Warrick disputed the jurisdiction of this area for years, and attempts of subsequent legislatures to define the line invariably roused objections in one county or the other.[66]

There was an apparent readjustment between Clark and Harrison counties; although unfortunately their respective boundaries are described in general terms in the Act relative to County Boundaries, that area north and west of Floyd, which had never been explicitly detached from Harrison, was in this law treated as a part of Clark County. The two sections of land which had heretofore joined it to Harrison were overlooked entirely in the definition of county boundaries, and so remained for some years. Doubtless the difficulty of establishing a definite line along the Knobs was responsible for the vagueness of descriptions.[67]

The Wayne-Henry boundary underwent one of its frequent changes, Madison County was restricted on the north, and Jackson's northern boundary was altered.[68]

Attempts at change which failed of adoption included proposals to attach part of Greene to Sullivan; to enlarge Switzerland County; to enlarge Dubois from Martin or Daviess; to attach part of Perry to Spencer and a part to Crawford; to attach part of Warrick County to Spencer; to alter the boundary between Jennings and

[66] See accounts of the following sessions: 1837-38, 1838-39, 1839-40, 1842-43, 1843-44, 1846-47, 1851-52, 1853, 1855, and maps, Gibson County VIII, X, XI, XII, XIII, Warrick County IV, VII, VIII, IX, X.

[67] See sections 14, 15, and 16 of the act, *Revised Laws of Indiana*, 1823-24, pp. 95-96.

[68] See maps, Wayne County VI, Henry County III, Madison County II, Jackson County VII.

BOUNDARY LEGISLATION 43

Jefferson; and to form a new county from Owen, Putnam, and Vigo.[69]

Indiana had by this time fifty-one counties, more than half its present number, but in thirty-five of these, boundary changes were yet to be made. Part of the remaining ceded territory was placed under the jurisdiction of organized counties, in the form of enormous attachments; part was accounted for only under the general designation of Wabash and Delaware counties. Allen County trespassed on Indian lands, but its nearest neighbor, Randolph, lay forty miles to the south, and none of the other counties extended as far north as the south boundary of the Great Miami Reserve. Allen, Decatur, Dubois, Greene, Hamilton, Johnson, Orange, Parke, Posey, Randolph, Ripley, Rush, Shelby, Switzerland, Vanderburgh, and Vermillion had reached their present size and shape.

1825. The renewed demand for a county out of Putnam, Owen, and Vigo resulted in the formation of Clay in February, 1825.[70] Clay County, which retains its original boundaries, by its formation reduced Owen and Vigo to their present limits; Sullivan was also affected by its creation. Spencer was a fourth county to make its last boundary change in 1825, in a transfer with Warrick. A Gibson-Pike exchange completed the boundary alterations made at the session.[71] Marion was given jurisdiction over

[69] Greene-Sullivan, *House Journal*, 1823-24, pp. 77, 83, 101, 173, 206; *Senate Journal*, 1823-24, p. 242. This transfer was attempted at several later sessions, but was never actually made. Switzerland, *House Journal*, 1823-24, pp. 32, 51, 57, 65, and 328; Dubois-Daviess-Martin, *ibid.*, 35, 64, and 35, 40, 47, 67-68; Perry-Spencer-Crawford, *ibid.*, 20, 40, 67, and 239-40, 254; Warrick-Spencer, *ibid.*, 227, 260; Jennings-Jefferson, *ibid.*, 85, 152-53, 257; Owen-Putnam-Vigo, *ibid.*, 95.

[70] Blanchard (ed.), *Counties of Clay and Owen*, 11-12; Travis, William, *A History of Clay County Indiana* . . ., 1:1-4 (Chicago, 1909). Citizens of Putnam County presented a remonstrance against the formation, and an attempt was made in the Senate to postpone action until the next session. See *House Journal*, 1825, p. 102; *Senate Journal*, 1825, p. 152.

[71] See maps, Spencer County II, Warrick County V, Gibson County IX, Pike County IV.

a small part of Delaware, but its actual boundaries remained as before.[72]

A dozen proposed changes came to nothing or were obliged to wait until the next session for successful hearing. Among these were bills to define the Washington-Clark boundary; to attach part of Jefferson County to Scott, introduced over the protest that it would reduce the area of Jefferson below four hundred square miles; to attach part of Jennings and Ripley counties to Decatur; to transfer part of Daviess to Lawrence; and to alter the boundaries of Johnson County.[73]

Several petitions were directed toward the formation of a county north of Parke. A bill creating such a county passed the House, but was postponed to the following December, on second reading in the Senate.[74] Movements which did not reach bill form concerned transfers from Morgan to Hendricks and from Hendricks to Marion; from Perry to Crawford; from Vermillion to Parke; and from Greene to Sullivan.[75]

1825-26. Fountain County was erected in December, 1825, in response to a new series of petitions for a county north of Parke. Montgomery objected to the loss of a

[72] Description of the attachment is given with map of Marion County I. See also state map, 1825.

[73] Washington-Clark, *Senate Journal*, 1825, pp. 19, 57, 70-71, 95-96, 99; *House Journal*, 1825, pp. 145, 155, 246. The select committee in the House to which the Senate bill was referred reported that it did not definitely settle the boundary, and that they had "not been able to procure such a map of the county" as would "enable them by amending said bill, definitely to settle said boundary" during the session.

Jefferson-Scott, *ibid.*, 115, 160, 178; Jennings-Ripley-Decatur, *ibid.*, 53, 215, 222; Daviess-Lawrence, *Senate Journal*, 1825, pp. 74, 121, 134; Johnson, *ibid.*, 35, 42, 50, 59, 68.

[74] *House Journal*, 1825, pp. 26, 27, 62, 75, 112-13, 125; *Senate Journal*, 1825, pp. 84, 87, 93; see also *ibid.*, 77-78, 122, 157, and *House Journal*, 1825, p. 23. The name Fairfield was suggested by one group of petitioners.

[75] Morgan-Hendricks, *Senate Journal*, 1825, pp. 62, 85, 102; Hendricks-Marion, *ibid.*, 102; Perry-Crawford, *ibid.*, 52; Vermillion-Parke, *House Journal*, 1825, pp. 122, 152; Greene-Sullivan, *ibid.*, 81, 153.

BOUNDARY LEGISLATION

township and a half to Fountain, and Parke attempted to retain jurisdiction over the new county and territory north and west of it. Fountain, however, was not only allotted the territory from Montgomery but was granted independent jurisdiction within its own boundaries and, temporarily, over the territory north and west as far as the 1818 Indian boundary.[76]

Tippecanoe County was also formed at this session, lying north of Montgomery, and adjoining Fountain and its attachment.[77] Both these counties retain their original boundaries. The only other change in the northern part of the state was the attachment to Hamilton County, for jurisdiction, of the unassigned part of Delaware County.[78]

Three old counties, Franklin, Union, and Pike, made their last boundary changes at this session. Franklin County lost territory to both Fayette and Union, in spite of numerous spirited protests against reduction below the constitutional area of four hundred square miles.[79] A transfer from Pike to Warrick was made apparently without controversy.[80]

Unfavorable committee action disposed of petitions to attach part of Rush to Madison; part of Bartholomew to Johnson; part of Lawrence to Orange; and part of Hendricks to Marion.[81] A Senate bill to establish the

[76] *Senate Journal*, 1825-26, pp. 77, 86-87, 89-90, 91; Clifton, Thomas A. (ed.), *Past and Present of Fountain and Warren Counties Indiana*, 57 ff. (Indianapolis, 1913). See map, Fountain County.

[77] De Hart, R. P. (ed.), *Past and Present of Tippecanoe County Indiana*, 1:151 ff. (Indianapolis, 1909). Amendments made by the House to the bill caused considerable dissatisfaction in the Senate, and were finally dropped. *Senate Journal*, 1825-26, pp. 88, 91, 107, 192.

[78] See state map, 1825-26.

[79] *House Journal*, 1825-26, pp. 74-75, 114, 130, 166; *Senate Journal*, 1825-26, pp. 133, 169, 201-3.

[80] *House Journal*, 1825-26, pp. 61-62, 280, 301, 336, 352.

[81] Rush-Madison, *ibid.*, 83, 114; Bartholomew-Johnson, *ibid.*, 254, 280; Lawrence-Orange, *ibid.*, 108, 125; Hendricks-Marion, *ibid.*, 269, 331.

east boundary of Henry County went no further than second reading. Action on a second Senate bill, transferring part of Daviess to Dubois, was postponed until the following December.[82] Unsuccessful also was a House bill for the formation of a new county out of Delaware.[83]

1826-27. The building up of the New Purchase was continued in 1826-27 by the erection of Warren County northwest of the Wabash River, from territory under the jurisdiction of Fountain.[84] Another new county, north and east of Tippecanoe, was outlined in a House bill which did not survive third reading.[85] Delaware County was laid out west of Randolph,[86] and Madison County was almost completely transformed by the formation of Hancock from its southern end, and a compensatory extension northward around the corner of the Miami Reserve.[87] Madison retained civil and judicial jurisdiction over Hancock County. No boundary changes have been made in the three counties formed by that legislature.

[82] Henry County, *Senate Journal*, 1825-26, pp. 133, 139-40, 216; Daviess-Dubois, *ibid.*, 96, 138, 219.

[83] *House Journal*, 1825-26, pp. 166, 193, 216, 309-10.

[84] Clifton (ed.), *Past and Present of Fountain and Warren Counties*, 217 ff.; *Counties of Warren, Benton, Jasper and Newton, Indiana* . . ., 53 ff. (F. A. Battey & Co., Chicago, 1883); *Senate Journal*, 1826-27, pp. 78, 106, 153, 158, 168, 169. See map, Warren County.

[85] *House Journal*, 1826-27, pp. 69, 152, 164, 314-15, 323.

[86] Haimbaugh, Frank D. (ed.), *History of Delaware County Indiana*, 1:154 ff. (Indianapolis, 1924); Kemper, G. W. H. (ed.), *A Twentieth Century History of Delaware County Indiana*, 55 ff. (Chicago, 1908); *House Journal*, 1826-27, pp. 77, 161, 339-40, 355, 443. See map, Delaware County.

[87] Binford, J. H., *History of Hancock County, Indiana* . . ., 25 ff. (Greenfield, Ind., 1882); Richman, George J., *History of Hancock County Indiana* . . ., 56-59 (Greenfield, Ind., 1916). The *Journal* records of the passage of this bill are somewhat confused, but it is clear that there was strong opposition both in the House and in the Senate. An attempt was made in the House to change the name from Hancock to Tecumseh. *House Journal*, 1826-27, pp. 246-47, 252, 444, 450-51, 497-98, 511-12; *Senate Journal*, 1826-27, pp. 219-20, 228, 253, 258, 262-63. See maps, Hancock County, Madison County III.

BOUNDARY LEGISLATION 47

Early in the session the Senate adopted a resolution that the Committee on the Judiciary be "instructed to enquire into our constitutional jurisdiction over persons and property, upon lands occupied by Indians, within our territorial limits; and into the expediency of . . . designating county boundaries upon said lands . . . and whether in the opinion of said committee such enactments would, or would not be an unauthorized interference with any constitutional enactments of the United States, or in perfect conformity to our sovereignty as a state." No report appears to show what decision was reached by the committee.[88]

The transfer of part of a township to Crawford brought that county and Perry to their present form, and a Senate bill, redrawing for the fourth time the Wayne-Henry boundary, weathered a difficult passage in the House, and completed the changes in those two counties.[89] The troublesome question of county areas arising in connection with this latter bill, prompted the suggestion that Franklin, Union, Fayette, and Wayne be consolidated, but nothing came of this movement.[90] The House rejected a bill to attach part of Wayne to Fayette,[91] but passed a bill to reattach part of Union to Franklin; the bill did not pass the Senate, however.[92] Another House bill defeated in the Senate proposed the attachment of a strip of Greene County to Sullivan.[93]

Dissatisfaction with the existing county divisions is reflected in petitions for a rearrangement of the boundaries of Parke, Vermillion, and Fountain, and for a new county

[88] *Senate Journal*, 1826-27, pp. 7-8, 10.
[89] Perry-Crawford, *House Journal*, 1826-27, pp. 78, 112, 123, 181, 221; *Senate Journal*, 1826-27, pp. 359, 366, 381; Wayne-Henry, *House Journal*, 1826-27, pp. 184, 197, 294, 310, 410, 416, 432-33, 449.
[90] *Ibid.*, 221, 286.
[91] *Ibid.*, 124, 162.
[92] *Ibid.*, 98, 106, 152, 164, 253-54, 269, 286-88; *Senate Journal*, 1826-27, pp. 150-51, 157, 201, 202-3.
[93] *House Journal*, 1826-27, pp. 127, 139, 156, 401, 409; *Senate Journal*, 1826-27, pp. 220, 228. This transfer was attempted at several following sessions.

from Parke, Putnam, and Montgomery.[94] An attempted exchange of territory between Johnson and Morgan met remonstrances from both counties and the measure was dropped, while county-seat disturbances prevented the introduction of a bill to attach part of Daviess to Lawrence.[95] The Clark-Washington boundary as usual came in for a share of legislative attention, but a House bill to define the respective county boundaries failed.[96]

1827-28. The considerable amount of legislative action devoted to county boundaries during the session of 1827-28 resulted in the formation of but one new county. Early in January, Carroll was laid out in an area extending northeast of Tippecanoe County as far as the Miami Reserve, and was organized by the same act, although an attempt was made to attach it to Tippecanoe for jurisdiction.[97] Hancock County, formed by the preceding legislature, was also granted separate jurisdiction.[98]

In December, 1827, the House appointed a committee to inquire into the expediency of laying out unorganized territory into counties. The report made some six weeks later offered three principal reasons for prompt county organization: the laying out of counties would induce early settlement; it would lead to a more judicious and impartial choice of county-seat sites; and it would prevent the discontent likely to arise in relation to county boundaries fixed after partial settlement of the territory involved.[99] Instead of working out a plan for new counties

[94] *House Journal*, 1826-27, pp. 230, 245, 295.

[95] Johnson-Morgan, *ibid.*, 181-82, 194-95, 216, 238, 295, 420; Daviess-Lawrence, *ibid.*, 18, 33, 162.

[96] *Ibid.*, 73, 76-77, 139, 156, 375.

[97] *History of Carroll County, Indiana* . . ., 119 ff. (Kingman Brothers, Chicago, 1882); Stewart, James H., *Recollections of the Early Settlement of Carroll County, Indiana*, 16 ff. (Cincinnati, 1872); Odell, John C., *History of Carroll County Indiana* . . ., 73 ff. (Indianapolis, 1916); *House Journal*, 1827-28, pp. 56, 66, 103, 121, 168, 177, 220, 221, 236-37; *Senate Journal*, 1827-28, p. 106.

[98] *Ibid.*, 39-40, 43, 56, 75, 95; *House Journal*, 1827-28, pp. 102-3, 122, 131, 473.

[99] *Ibid.*, 68, 392-93.

BOUNDARY LEGISLATION 49

in accordance with these conclusions, a series of attachments was made, assigning to existing counties all the unorganized part of the state except the central part of the Miami Reserve and a strip of territory running north from Warren County. Allen, Delaware, Hendricks, and Tippecanoe had their jurisdiction thus enlarged. The Indian boundary established at Mississinewa in 1826 was ignored, and the Miami Reserve was invaded by these attachments.[100]

Actual additions were made to Bartholomew, Monroe, and Jackson counties by dividing among them territory which had been attached to Bartholomew since 1821.[101] Two sections between Floyd and Washington, unassigned since 1824, were given to Floyd County,[102] and the boundary changes of Daviess and Martin were completed by transferring from Daviess to Martin two townships lying north of Martin.[103]

Several county-boundary measures which had failed in the preceding session were unsuccessfully revived. The House defeated a Senate bill for a transfer of territory from Johnson to Morgan, and a House bill attaching part of Greene to Sullivan was lost in the Senate. The perennial problem of defining the Washington-Clark line, and the attachment of part of Wayne to Fayette were also under discussion.[104]

Among other proposed changes was the attachment of part of the town of Paris, lying in Jefferson County, to

[100] *Laws of Indiana*, 1827-28, pp. 13-14. See state map, 1827-28.
[101] *Laws of Indiana*, 1827-28, p. 15.
[102] *Ibid.*, 12, 17-18. See map, Floyd County III.
[103] Early in the session a petition to attach part of Daviess to Lawrence was unfavorably reported on because of probable county-seat difficulties. *House Journal*, 1827-28, pp. 88, 193. This had been proposed before. See map, Martin County II.
[104] Johnson-Morgan, *Senate Journal*, 1827-28, pp. 105, 129, 134, 140; *House Journal*, 1827-28, pp. 42, 59, 275, 299; Greene-Sullivan, *ibid.*, 172, 207, 302, 313, 327, 340; *Senate Journal*, 1827-28, pp. 183, 184, 206-7; Washington-Clark, *House Journal*, 1827-28, pp. 10, 137, 148, 197; Wayne-Fayette, *ibid.*, 172, 178-79, 234, 349-50, 470.

5—48526

Jennings.[105] This measure was carried out at a later session. The attachment of part of Rush to Hancock was declared inexpedient because it would reduce the area of Rush to less than four hundred square miles. A bill to attach part of Clay to Owen, and another attaching part of Greene to Monroe failed in the House.[106]

1828-29. On the fourth day of the session of 1828-29, a petition was introduced into the Senate for a new county at and contiguous to the mouth of Eel River. Cass County was duly formed around that center, and by an amendatory act passed in January, 1829, given jurisdiction over a great area extending north of the county to the Michigan boundary. These two acts reduced the jurisdiction of Carroll and Allen counties considerably.[107]

Petitions for two other counties, one from Montgomery, Parke, and Putnam, and one from Perry and Spencer, were withdrawn after unfavorable committee action.[108]

A bill for surveying and marking the Clark-Washington boundary came up for the third time at this session, and secured a passing vote. A similar bill, passed in January, provided for the marking and surveying of the Clark-Scott line.[109] A House bill to alter the Jefferson-Scott boundary was tabled, and the House also tabled bills for attaching part of Clark to Floyd County, and part of Henry to Wayne.[110]

[105] *House Journal*, 1827-28, pp. 191, 224, 238.

[106] Rush-Hancock, *ibid.*, pp. 220, 225, 360-61; Clay-Owen, *ibid.*, 46, 55, 83-84, 102, 125-26; Greene-Monroe, *ibid.*, 71, 180, 196, 366-67.

[107] Helm, Thomas B., *History of Cass County, Indiana* . . ., 265 ff. (Chicago, 1886); Powell, Jehu Z. (ed.), *History of Cass County Indiana* . . ., 1:57 ff. (Chicago, 1913); *Senate Journal*, 1828-29, pp. 27, 31, 46, 50, 58-59, 71, 75-76; *ibid.*, 220, 231, 247-48, 258, 290.

[108] Montgomery-Parke-Putnam, *ibid.*, 102, 127; Perry-Spencer, *ibid.*, 206, 327.

[109] *Laws of Indiana*, 1828-29, pp. 16, 17.

[110] Jefferson-Scott, *House Journal*, 1828-29, pp. 278, 361-62; Clark-Floyd, *ibid.*, 28, 132, 348; Henry-Wayne, *ibid.*, 128, 288-89, 376.

BOUNDARY LEGISLATION 51

Select committees in the House reported against movements to change the Warren-Tippecanoe boundary, and to attach part of Shelby County to Decatur. Like action disposed of petitions to the Senate for transfers from Greene to Sullivan County, and Tippecanoe to Carroll. A petition from Clay, asking the enlargement of the county, received an unfavorable report on the ground that such an enlargement would infringe on the boundaries of counties already reduced below four hundred square miles in area.[111]

The propriety of laying off that part of the state not already included in organized counties into a number of counties not less than twenty miles square was the subject of a House resolution adopted January 1, 1829. The question was referred for inquiry to the Committee on Education, but no report appears in the House record.[112]

1829-30. Indian holdings in the state had been gradually reduced by the treaties of Chicago, 1821, Mississinewa, 1826, and Carey Mission, 1828, until the inevitability of their complete extinguishment was no longer to be questioned.[113] During the session of 1829-30, the expediency of erecting into counties the unorganized part of the state was again suggested as a proper subject for committee investigation in the House. A select committee was appointed on January 6, 1830, to make an inquiry, but there is no report of their activities.[114] At the time of the committee appointment there was already in process a House bill for the erection of Clinton County. The next day, January 7, a bill was reported for the formation of a county north of Marion and Hendricks which

[111] Warren-Tippecanoe, *House Journal*, 1828-29, pp. 106, 329; Shelby-Decatur, *ibid.*, 201-2, 365; Greene-Sullivan, *Senate Journal*, 1828-29, pp. 31, 54-55, 66, 72; Tippecanoe-Carroll, *ibid.*, 314, 322; Clay, *ibid.*, 120-21, 172.
[112] *House Journal*, 1828-29, p. 301.
[113] Kappler (ed.), *Indian Affairs. Laws and Treaties*, prints the treaties mentioned: Chicago, 2:198-99; Mississinewa, 2:273-75; Carey Mission, 2:294. See also *ibid.*, 286.
[114] *House Journal*, 1829-30, p. 290.

was called Boone, after the names Ray and Mercer had been rejected in turn, and on January 15 a third House bill was introduced to establish "Elk Hart" and St. Joseph counties. During the passage of this bill through the Senate, an attempt was made to substitute the name Ross for St. Joseph, but the change was not adopted.

The three bills received the governor's signature on the same day. Clinton and Boone filled in the territory between Carroll and Hendricks, cutting down the jurisdictional attachments of several contiguous counties. Boone has had no boundary changes.[115] Elkhart and St. Joseph were laid out along the middle section of the state's northern boundary, with attachments running to east and west state lines respectively. By the erection of these two counties the jurisdiction of Tippecanoe and Carroll, Cass, and Allen counties was reduced somewhat.[116] Carroll's attachment was redefined and Warren County's jurisdiction slightly extended under a separate law.[117]

During this legislative session petitioners asked the formation of two counties from territory already organized. The House dismissed a petition for a county from Montgomery, Parke, and Putnam.[118] A bill for the formation of a county out of Lawrence, Jackson, and Monroe, to be called Highland, was introduced in the

[115] *History of Clinton County, Indiana* . . ., 337 ff. (Inter-State Publishing Co., Chicago, 1886); Claybaugh, Joseph, *History of Clinton County Indiana* . . ., 28 ff., 94 ff. (Indianapolis, 1913); *House Journal*, 1829-30, pp. 189, 219-20, 229, 291-92, 448; Crist, L. M., *History of Boone County Indiana* . . ., 1:79, 83 ff. (Indianapolis, 1914 [?]); *Early Life and Times in Boone County Indiana* . . ., 75-76 (Harden & Spahr, Lebanon, Ind., 1887); *House Journal*, 1829-30, pp. 255, 296, 300-1, 304-6, 355, 355-56, 495; *Senate Journal*, 1829-30, p. 275. See maps, Clinton County I, Boone County.

[116] *History of Elkhart County Indiana* . . ., 369 ff. (Chas. C. Chapman & Co., Chicago, 1881); Weaver, Abraham E. (ed.), *A Standard History of Elkhart County Indiana* . . ., 1:27 ff. (Chicago, 1916); Howard, Timothy E., *A History of St. Joseph County Indiana* . . ., 1:157 ff. (Chicago, 1907); *House Journal*, 1829-30, pp. 309, 359, 393, 449; *Senate Journal*, 1829-30, pp. 310, 316. See maps, Elkhart County I, St. Joseph County I.

[117] *Laws of Indiana*, 1829-30, pp. 26-27.

[118] *House Journal*, 1829-30, pp. 308, 386-87.

BOUNDARY LEGISLATION 53

House in spite of an adverse report, but further action was indefinitely postponed when the bill came up for third reading.[119]

Jefferson County was concerned in the only two actual territorial transfers of the session. It gave to Jennings that part of the town of Paris lying south of their common boundary, a cession which had been proposed before. The second change—with Scott—consisted in substituting a boundary run by section lines, for the former straight diagonal line across township three north, range eight east. A small amount of territory was added to Scott by this arrangement.[120]

Among county-boundary measures before the 1829-30 Assembly, were two which had failed the preceding year. One proposed attaching a part of Clark to Floyd; the other provided for reattaching to Wayne a strip of territory which had been transferred to Henry. Neither bill was allowed to become an act.[121] Remonstrances followed three petitions for boundary changes—to attach part of Ripley and Jennings to Decatur, to alter the Warren-Fountain boundaries, and to extend Madison's territory one mile further east; in each case the plea received an unfavorable committee report.[122]

1830-31. The laws of Indiana underwent a new revision during the legislative session of 1830-31. One of the bills reported by the Joint Committee on Revision and adopted by the Assembly defined the boundaries of all existing counties.[123] Two minor changes were incor-

[119] *Ibid.*, 289, 303-4, 329, 339, 346, 456.

[120] *Senate Journal*, 1829-30, pp. 172, 184, 296, 309; *House Journal*, 1829-30, pp. 90, 145, 187, 212, 354, 372. See map, Jefferson County VII.

[121] Clark-Floyd, *House Journal*, 1829-30, pp. 90-91, 220, 497-98; Wayne-Henry, *Senate Journal*, 1829-30, pp. 160, 248, 267-68, 355, 356-57, 366.

[122] Ripley-Jennings-Decatur, *House Journal*, 1829-30, pp. 308, 309, 500, 501; Warren-Fountain, *ibid.*, 211, 212, 260-61; Madison, *ibid.*, 334, 442-43, 482.

[123] Inaccuracies occur in the descriptions of several counties. Some were apparently due to carelessness in transcription; others resulted from a failure to take note of recent boundary changes.

porated in this law: one made the Hendricks-Marion boundary a due north and south line; the other assigned to Monroe a small unoccupied area at its northwest corner.[124]

A new county, Grant, was formed by a special act approved the same day as the general county-boundary law. It included a strip off the north end of Madison County, a portion of the Great Miami Reserve not before encroached upon by county organization, and a part of the territory which had been attached to Delaware for jurisdiction.[125]

The law forming Grant County also provided for a redistribution of jurisdiction in the territory attached to the northern counties, and all the open territory of the state except the central section of the Great Miami Reserve was apportioned to neighboring counties. Marion was the only county to reach its present form that year.

The number of petitions for boundary changes was noticeably less than usual during this session, but some persisted. Undeterred by former failures, proponents of a county to be formed from the surplus territory of Parke, Putnam, and Montgomery, early in the session made another plea for such a division. Remonstrances against the change were also filed, however, and the committee reported adversely, calling attention to the fact that the new county, if formed, could not have an area of more than two hundred square miles, and that the boundaries of Putnam and Montgomery would be left undesirably irregular.[126] A select committee appointed on December 11, 1830, to inquire into the expediency of laying off new counties between Logansport and Fort Wayne reported unfavorably on January 17.[127] In the meantime

[124] See maps, Hendricks County II, Monroe County III.

[125] *History of Grant County, Indiana* . . ., 270 ff. (Brant & Fuller, Chicago, 1886); *House Journal*, 1830-31, pp. 67, 130, 192, 244, 253, 260, 267, 294, 335, 367, 407, 415, 439, 485; *Senate Journal*, 1830-31, p. 450. The names Logan and Fulton were suggested for the new county.

[126] *House Journal*, 1830-31, pp. 179, 191, 271, 278, 313.

[127] *Ibid.*, 81, 315.

BOUNDARY LEGISLATION

leave had been given on January 7 to introduce a bill for the formation of a new county east of Cass. This bill was withdrawn shortly after the publication of the committee report just mentioned.[128]

Among the proposed transfers of territory, only one reached bill form—a third attempt to attach a part of Clark to Floyd. The attachment of part of Franklin to Fayette, and the extension of Elkhart County southward were disapproved in committee and the petitions were dropped.[129]

Sixty-four counties had now been formed, an increase of thirteen since 1824, when the boundaries of all the counties had been last defined. The Wabash County of 1820 was entirely built up into new counties. Organization in Delaware County had advanced less rapidly, because of the Indian holdings in that area, but jurisdictional divisions had been made beyond the lines of cession, covering all the northern part of the state except the central area of the Great Miami Reserve. Two counties jutting southward from the Michigan boundary were like the tightening of a vise upon the Indians, and emphasized the inevitability of their removal westward.

The number of counties which had completed their boundary development had more than doubled in the same seven years. In 1824 there were but sixteen; by the end of the session of 1830-31, Boone, Clay, Crawford, Daviess, Delaware, Fayette, Fountain, Franklin, Hancock, Henry, Marion, Martin, Montgomery, Owen, Perry, Pike, Spencer, Tippecanoe, Union, Vigo, Warren, and Wayne belonged within this group, and brought the total number to thirty-eight.

Not all the counties named were satisfied with the existing status, and further changes would undoubtedly have been made but for the constitutional provision against reducing counties below four hundred square miles in area, and the unwillingness of general assem-

[128] *Ibid.*, 262, 365.
[129] Clark-Floyd, *ibid.*, 85-86, 106, 151, 163, 444; Franklin-Fayette, *ibid.*, 76, 192, 202-3, 226; Elkhart, *ibid.*, 423, 444.

blies to make changes which might stimulate or complicate the already plentiful struggles over county-seat locations. Focal points of discontent included the contiguous districts of Putnam, Parke, and Montgomery, of Greene and Sullivan, and of Wayne and Henry counties. Topographical irregularities in the region of the Knobs made the establishment of well-defined boundaries there extremely difficult, and county-seat disturbances resulted in repeated petitions for change between Dearborn and Switzerland counties.

THE NORTHERN COUNTIES

UP TO this time, 1831, new counties had been formed as increasing population and the settlement of new areas made such erections feasible. There had resulted a gradual building up of the state from south to north, with outlying districts gradually drawn into county organization, or with established counties broken into smaller units as the number of inhabitants increased. With the establishment of Allen County, far north of the general line of settlement, and St. Joseph and Elkhart on the Michigan line, this solidarity of development was temporarily lost.

1831-32. In the legislative session of 1831-32 two new counties were created along the Michigan boundary. La Porte, for which the name Michigan was first suggested, included a part of St. Joseph County and territory under its jurisdiction to the westward.[1] By provision of two subsequent acts, St. Joseph received a strip of territory from Elkhart, and Elkhart an addition on the south.[2] La Grange, the second county formed, still occupies the boundaries in which it was laid out to the east of Elkhart. The jurisdiction of the county, however, at the time of formation extended beyond these limits eastward and southward into territory which had formerly been attached to Elkhart and Allen.[3]

The Wabash and Erie Canal project, with its promise

[1] *History of La Porte County, Indiana* . . ., 437 ff. (Chas. C. Chapman & Co., Chicago, 1880); Daniels, E. D., *A Twentieth Century History and Biographical Record of La Porte County Indiana* . . ., 33 ff. (Chicago, 1904); *Senate Journal*, 1831-32, pp. 32, 51, 94, 149, 205. See map, La Porte County I.

[2] *House Journal*, 1831-32, pp. 227, 238, 313, 343; *ibid.*, 214, 228, 297, 403. See maps, Elkhart County II, St. Joseph County II.

[3] *Counties of La Grange and Noble, Indiana* . . ., 32 ff.; *House Journal*, 1831-32, pp. 84, 121, 354, 406. See map, La Grange County. Warsaw, De Kalb, Ray, and Tecumseh were all suggested as names for the county.

of a rapid increase in population through the northern part of the state, stimulated other county formations. On January 20 leave was given to introduce a House bill for a new county, probably east of Cass. The bill was tabled on second reading, but on January 23 was taken up and referred to a select committee with instructions to lay off into counties all the territory between Cass and Allen. An act establishing Huntington, Wabash, and Miami counties and reshaping Cass was accordingly passed.[4] Due probably to the haste necessary to enact the bill during that session, ambiguities invalidated the descriptions of Wabash and Miami, a mischance of minor importance since separate jurisdiction was not granted to any of the counties created by the 1831-32 law.[5]

From three other sections of the state came pleas for new counties. No action seems to have been taken on petitions for the formation of a county out of Dearborn, with the seat of government at Rising Sun. House and Senate reported adversely upon new petitions asking for the establishment of a county in the contiguous areas of Putnam, Montgomery, and Parke, the petitions in favor of a bill being outweighed by protests as before. The inexpediency of erecting a county out of Tippecanoe, Carroll, and attached territory, under the name Brown, was also agreed upon.[6]

[4] *House Journal*, 1831-32, pp. 294, 314, 339, 406; *Senate Journal*, 1831-32, pp. 315, 316, 347, 349-50, 356; *History of Huntington County, Indiana* . . ., 321 ff. (Brant & Fuller, Chicago, 1887); Weesner, Clarkson W. (ed.), *History of Wabash County Indiana* . . ., 152 ff. (Chicago, 1914); *History of Miami County Indiana* . . ., 272 ff. (Brant & Fuller, Chicago, 1887); Bodurtha, Arthur L. (ed.), *History of Miami County Indiana* . . ., 1:96 ff. (Chicago, 1914). See maps, Huntington County, Wabash County I, Miami County I, Cass County II.

[5] *Senate Journal*, 1832-33, pp. 241, 280, 344, 346; *House Journal*, 1832-33, pp. 404-5, 474.

[6] Dearborn, *Senate Journal*, 1831-32, pp. 53, 105; Putnam-Parke-Montgomery, *House Journal*, 1831-32, pp. 169, 170, 186, 295; *Senate Journal*, 1831-32, pp. 261, 273, 283-84; Tippecanoe-Carroll, *House Journal*, 1831-32, pp. 170, 196, 216; *Senate Journal*, 1831-32, pp. 233 (misnumbered 231), 242.

BOUNDARY LEGISLATION 59

No less than nine transfers of territory were proposed. A bill was introduced in the House to alter and establish the lines of Wayne, Union, Fayette, and Henry counties, but met objections at every step and was finally withdrawn.[7] Petitions to attach part of Wayne to Fayette, and part of Wayne to Union were both tabled. There was an attempt to enlarge Floyd County, but it failed, although a bill attaching part of Harrison County to Floyd was introduced in the House. Earlier in the session a committee had been appointed to inquire into the expediency of a law for surveying the line of Clark, Floyd, and Washington. If the committee took any action it is not recorded. House bills to attach part of Putnam to Clay and part of Shelby to Decatur did not reach the Senate, and committees reported unfavorably on a petition to attach a quarter section of Jefferson to Jennings County, and on another to alter the Lawrence-Jackson boundary.[8]

The boundaries of Johnson County were corrected in an act amending the county-boundary law adopted at the previous session.[9] Another measure provided for the survey of the boundary between Vermillion and Warren counties. When Vermillion was created in January, 1824, its northern boundary was described as beginning on the state line at its intersection with the line dividing townships numbered 19 and 20 north, and running thence east to the Wabash River. No mention was made of the offset in the township line—a matter of more than a mile—at the range line dividing ranges 9 and 10 west. In March, 1824, however, when the commissioners of Vermillion County divided the county into townships, they did take into account this offset, and described the

[7] *House Journal*, 1831-32, pp. 131, 135, 152, 163, 214, 218-19.

[8] Wayne-Fayette-Union, *House Journal*, 1831-32, pp. 214-15, 235; Floyd, *ibid.*, 183, 204-5, 242, 414-15; Clark-Floyd-Washington, *ibid.*, 114; Putnam-Clay, *ibid.*, 131, 142, 164, 171, 204, 396-97; Shelby-Decatur, *ibid.*, 140, 161, 219; Jefferson-Jennings, *ibid.*, 54, 73; Lawrence-Jackson, *ibid.*, 109, 184, 416-17.

[9] *Laws of Indiana*, 1831-32, p. 267.

northern boundary of Highland Township as beginning on the state line where it is intersected by the township line dividing townships 19 and 20 north, and running "thence east with said line to the Wabash River."

Warren County came into existence in 1827, with a southern boundary running from "the north east corner of Vermillion county, on the Wabash river, thence west to the state line." In view of the fact that Vermillion's northernmost civil township was bounded by the government township line, and not by a due east and west line, it seems probable that citizens of both Warren and Vermillion counties at this time believed the inter-county boundary to follow the township line.

Some time before the legislative session of 1831-32, divergence of opinion arose. Early in December, 1831, the representative of Warren County presented a petition from his constituents asking for the enactment of a law "establishing the line between Vermillion and Warren counties." After a committee report advising against legislation on the subject, he introduced a bill, on leave, "for the more permanent establishment of the line." In its original form it defined the boundary as "beginning on the Wabash river, at the line dividing townships No. 19 and 20, in range 9, thence on said line, west to the state line." It was amended in the House to provide for the survey of the boundary, with instructions for a report of the proceedings to be laid before the speaker of the House at the next Assembly.[10]

1832-33. The required reports on the survey of the Vermillion-Warren line came before the House early in the session of 1832-33, accompanied by plats of survey. On December 20, 1832, a bill "to more permanently establish" the line was presented. On second reading it was amended on motion of the representative from Vermillion County by striking out from the enacting clause and in-

[10] *Laws of Indiana*, 1831-32, p. 106; *House Journal*, 1831-32, pp. 54, 160, 162, 401-2, 405; *Biographical and Historical Record of Vermillion County*, 203.

serting the following description: "Beginning on the west bank of the Wabash river, where the township line dividing Townships No. nineteen and twenty intersects the same, thence west with said Township line to the Range line dividing Ranges nine and ten west; thence north with said Range line to the Township line, dividing Townships nineteen and twenty north, in Range ten west; thence west with said township line to the line dividing the states of Indiana and Illinois." A provision for the repeal of that part of the 1831 boundary law describing the two counties was included in the amendment. The representative from Warren County attempted to secure an amendment which would run the line "west from the Wabash river, to the State line, on the line dividing townships 19 and 20 N., as said township line is defined in the survey, in range 9 west." This failed. After passage of the bill on third reading, the House reconsidered its vote, and the measure was recommitted to a select committee, with instructions to amend "so as to fix the line between Vermillion and Warren counties, where it has heretofore been acknowledged to be by the common consent of both parties." The bill was reported without change and passed House and Senate without further amendment. It is noticeable that nowhere in the titles of acts proposed or passed in either 1831-32 or 1832-33 is this action spoken of as an alteration of the boundary, but always as the establishment of the boundary. The implication is strong that the intention of the legislature was merely to define, precisely, an existing line.[11]

The Madison-Hancock-Henry line, also left open to question by discrepancies in the county-boundary law of 1831, was the subject of another clarifying act.[12] A third corrective law redrew the boundaries of Wabash and Miami. Forty-three Miami County residents petitioned for county organization, but an unfavorable report on

[11] *House Journal*, 1832-33, pp. 124, 126, 163, 264, 315, 316-17, 323, 360, 401.
[12] *Senate Journal*, 1832-33, pp. 167, 184, 194, 250, 286.

their petition pointed out that half the territory proposed for the new county still belonged to the Miami Indians, and that organization was plainly inexpedient.[13]

Desire for a new county in the neighborhood of Tippecanoe and Carroll declared itself in two sets of petitions. One group asked for the formation of a county out of Tippecanoe and territory attached to Carroll. In this case the number of remonstrances exceeded the number of petitions, and as the proposed boundary lay within four miles of the seat of justice of Tippecanoe, the committee returned an adverse report. The other proposal was to lay out the new county north of Tippecanoe and west of Carroll. A bill for the formation of Drayton County was introduced on January 18, but did not survive second reading.[14]

The House killed a bill to attach part of Putnam to Owen, and a counter movement to attach part of Owen to Putnam. An attempt to attach part of Shelby to Decatur failed on second reading. All other suggested transfers were disposed of while still in petition form, the House concurring in adverse committee reports on changes involving Franklin and Rush, Morgan and Hendricks, and Harrison and Floyd. Petitions for the last-named alteration were recognized as reasonable, in view of Floyd's limited size and Harrison's slight surplus of territory, but action was left to a later Assembly. A committee appointed early in the session to inquire into the expediency of altering the boundary between Jefferson and Clark failed to make a report.[15]

1833-34. The first county-boundary measure to come

[13] *Senate Journal*, 1832-33, pp. 165, 227.

[14] *House Journal*, 1832-33, pp. 64, 334, 341; *ibid.*, 335, 422, 474-75, 475-77, 500-1. The name White supplanted Drayton before the measure was dropped for the session.

[15] Putnam-Owen, *House Journal*, 1832-33, pp. 38, 133, 164, 210, 311; *ibid.*, 210, 317, 323; Shelby-Decatur, *ibid.*, 161, 380, 470; Franklin-Rush, *ibid.*, 303-4, 316, 329; Morgan-Hendricks, *ibid.*, 348, 422-23; Harrison-Floyd, *ibid.*, 90, 161, 177, 617; Jefferson-Clark, *ibid.*, 124.

BOUNDARY LEGISLATION 63

before the new Assembly provided for the organization of Miami County and attached to Miami a two-mile strip from eastern Cass County. Petitioners had requested the extension of Miami northward as well, but this change was not included in the organization law.[16]

Residents of the territory attached to Carroll had ready for the Assembly of 1833-34 a new plea for county organization. In spite of some remonstrances, a bill for the erection of Tecumseh County was introduced and passed, with the name changed to White. By this act all the territory straight west of White and north of Warren was attached to White for jurisdiction.[17] A petition to transfer part of Warren to Tippecanoe, under consideration during the passage of this bill, received an unfavorable report.[18]

La Porte County about the same time began a movement to acquire jurisdiction over certain unorganized territory, but a bill making the necessary attachment was crowded out at the end of the session.[19]

From the northeast section of the state came petitions accompanied by two sets of descriptions for a county to be laid out in the general area of the present Noble County. Finding that the petitions for such a county were outbalanced by the remonstrances and that the petitioners were charged with fraud, the select committee on the subject asked to be discharged.[20]

Like action disposed of a petition to transfer a strip of territory one mile in width from Madison to Hancock

[16] *Senate Journal*, 1833-34, pp. 71-72, 77, 84, 88, 170, 190. See map, Miami County II.

[17] *House Journal*, 1833-34, pp. 228, 319-20, 346 (misnumbered 246), 391, 447, 510-11; *Counties of White and Pulaski, Indiana* . . ., 15 ff. (F. A. Battey & Co., Chicago, 1883); Hamelle, W. H. (ed.), *A Standard History of White County Indiana* . . ., 1:61 ff. (Chicago, 1915).

[18] *House Journal*, 1833-34, pp. 107, 302.

[19] *Ibid.*, 195, 253, 382-83, 428; *Senate Journal*, 1833-34, pp. 321, 323. The Senate did not receive the bill until January 29.

[20] *House Journal*, 1833-34, pp. 107, 433-34.

County.[21] Only two other changes of boundary were proposed at this session, both with the idea of enlarging Floyd County. A select committee reported against the attachment of part of Clark to Floyd, "not being able to ascertain that Clark county had any territory over and above four hundred square miles," and on the question of attaching part of Harrison to Floyd, reported an equal division and asked to be discharged. A bill introduced on leave, to make the latter transfer, was tabled on second reading.[22]

1834-35. During the sessions of 1827-28, 1828-29, and 1829-30, the legislature had considered the propriety of laying out into counties all the unorganized territory of the state. The wisdom of connecting the northern, central, and southern portions of the state became apparent with the formation of counties along the northern boundary line, and with the acquisition, in 1832, of the remaining Indian holdings in the northwestern part of the state. In the session of 1834-35 the situation was examined by a House committee consisting of one member from each judicial circuit. There were objections to the measure on the ground that it was legislating in the dark, and that it was aiding speculation, but such attacks were insufficient to balance the advantages expected from a union of the various districts of the state, the advancement of settlements and furthering of roads and highways, and, particularly, the good effect such a measure would have upon the lands near the Wabash and Erie Canal. A bill laying out fourteen new counties was approved on February 7, 1835,[23] and a separate measure forming Noble County was signed the same day.[24]

The only areas left outside county boundaries by this

[21] *Senate Journal*, 1833-34, pp. 255, 354.
[22] *House Journal*, 1833-34, pp. 217, 228, 270, 310, 358, 367, 502.
[23] *Ibid.*, 1834-35, pp. 56, 188, 190, 197-98, 275-76, 311-12, 339-40, 451-52, 540, 627-28.
[24] *Ibid.*, 84-85, 139, 150, 177, 192, 223, 311, 564, 627-29; *Counties of La Grange and Noble*, 26-27; *History of Northeast Indiana* . . ., 1:325 ff. (Lewis Publishing Company, Chicago, 1920).

BOUNDARY LEGISLATION

act were the central section of the Miami Reserve, a small attachment to Hamilton just south of the Reserve, a narrow strip of territory north of Cass and White, attached to those counties, and a still smaller area between Kosciusko and the northern boundaries of Miami and Wabash counties which had apparently been overlooked in the general apportionment of lands.

Five of the new counties remain within their original boundaries. They are Adams, De Kalb, Pulaski, Steuben, and Wells.[25] The other counties laid out were Fulton, Jasper, Jay, Kosciusko, Marshall, Newton, Porter, Starke, and Whitley.[26] Organization of these "paper" counties

[25] Snow, J. F., *Snow's History of Adams County Indiana* . . ., 80 ff. (Indianapolis, 1907); Tyndall, John W., and Lesh, O. E. (eds.), *Standard History of Adams and Wells Counties Indiana* . . ., 1:29, 50 ff. (Adams); 1:304 ff. (Wells) [Chicago, 1918]; *Biographical and Historical Record of Adams and Wells Counties Indiana* . . ., 195 ff. (Adams); 570 ff. (Wells) [Lewis Publishing Company, Chicago, 1887]; *History of Northeast Indiana*, 1:179-80 (Steuben); 1:474 ff. (De Kalb); *History of Steuben County Indiana* . . ., 273 ff. (Inter-State Publishing Co., Chicago, 1885). Adams and Pulaski were organized in 1836; De Kalb, Steuben, and Wells, in 1837.

[26] "Fulton County," in Peattie, Ella W., *Pictorial History of America* . . ., pt. 3:4 ff. (Chicago, 1896); Esarey, Logan (ed.), *History of Indiana* . . . *also An Account of Fulton County* . . ., 3:33 ff. (Dayton, Ohio, 1923); *Counties of Warren, Benton, Jasper and Newton*, 409-11 (Jasper); 591 ff. (Newton); Hamilton, Louis H., and Darroch, William (eds.), *Standard History of Jasper and Newton Counties Indiana* . . ., 1:44 ff. (Chicago, 1916); an unsuccessful motion was made to change the name Newton to Watts. *Senate Journal*, 1834-35, pp. 365-66; Montgomery, M. W., *History of Jay County, Indiana*, 119 ff. (Chicago, 1864 [?]); *Biographical and Historical Record of Jay and Blackford Counties, Indiana* . . ., 198 ff. (Lewis Publishing Company, Chicago, 1887); *Biographical and Historical Record of Kosciusko County, Indiana* . . ., 641-42 (Lewis Publishing Company, Chicago, 1887); Royse, L. W. (ed.), *Standard History of Kosciusko County Indiana* . . ., 1:81-83 (Chicago, 1919); McDonald, Daniel, *Twentieth Century History of Marshall County Indiana*, 1:79 ff. (Chicago, 1908); Goodspeed, Weston A., and Blanchard, Charles (eds.), *Counties of Porter and Lake Indiana* . . ., 31 ff. (Chicago, 1882); *History of Porter County Indiana* . . ., 1:36-38, 42 ff. (Lewis Publishing Com-

was not provided for in the formation law, jurisdiction remaining temporarily as it had been under the attachments which preceded the creation of the new counties.

While this omnibus county organization bill was in progress, petitions came before the House for the erection of a new county out of Monroe, Bartholomew, Morgan, and Johnson. The organization of a county out of Bartholomew and Monroe was recommended, and a bill for that purpose was introduced and passed the House. It died, however, in committee in the Senate.[27]

In addition to creating fifteen counties, the Assembly passed bills organizing Wabash County, redefining the attachments to Cass, White, and Warren counties, and transferring a bit of territory from Jefferson to Jennings County at the town of Paris.[28] Bills affecting Carroll and White, and Carroll and Cass did not emerge from the originating house, and a bill to alter the south boundary of La Grange and change the county seat also failed to pass.[29]

There was the customary influx of prayers for boundary changes. Petitions and remonstrances in quantity had to do with the possible attachment of part of Harrison to Crawford County. A petition to transfer to Scott that part of Jackson County lying east of the north fork of the Muscatatuck River was followed by another asking

pany, Chicago, 1912); Goodspeed, Weston A., and Blanchard, Charles (eds.), *County of Whitley, Indiana* . . ., 54 ff. (Chicago, 1882); Kaler, S. P., and Maring, R. H. (eds.), *History of Whitley County Indiana* . . ., 46 ff. (B. F. Bowen & Co., 1907). Fulton, Jay, Kosciusko, Marshall, and Porter were organized in 1836, Jasper and Whitley in 1838, and Starke in 1850. The Newton County here laid out never had a separate county organization.

[27] *House Journal*, 1834-35, pp. 329, 403, 424-25; *Senate Journal*, 1834-35, p. 405.

[28] Wabash, *Senate Journal*, 1834-35, pp. 21, 37, 79, 124, 129-30, 380, 381, 422; Cass-White, *House Journal*, 1834-35, pp. 61, 142, 177, 199-200, 218; Warren, *ibid.*, 165, 177, 407, 451, 550; Jefferson-Jennings, *ibid.*, 219, 291, 363, 483, 597.

[29] Carroll-White-Cass, *ibid.*, 220, 228, 283, 511; *ibid.*, 318, 548; La Grange, *ibid.*, 149, 173, 192, 221-22, 273, 278, 311.

BOUNDARY LEGISLATION 67

a change in the Jackson-Lawrence line, and a transfer from Decatur to Jennings was again suggested. All failed to reach bill form.[30]

1835-36. Two of the seven counties formed since 1835 were erected in 1836. Brown County, succeeding in its second attempt to secure organization, absorbed the contiguous territory of Monroe and Bartholomew, and a small strip of Jackson County.[31] This formation made the last boundary change for Monroe County, while Brown itself has had no territorial readjustments. Brown County was organized under the formation law.

Following petitions asking the attachment to Porter County of that part of Newton north of the Kankakee River, a bill was passed which redistributed the territory in the northwest corner of the state. The northern boundary of Newton County was pushed southward to the Kankakee River, as suggested, and the territory north of it divided to provide for a new county, Lake, and a reduced Porter.[32] This law also granted Porter separate jurisdiction.

Adams, Jay, Noble, Kosciusko, Fulton, and Marshall counties applied for and received independent jurisdiction. A petition from Kosciusko County asking the detachment of six miles from the southern end of the county was not approved, and Fulton County failed in an attempt to extend her boundaries northward.[33] Marshall County

[30] Harrison-Crawford, *ibid.*, 94-95, 173, 293-94, 327, 470, 584, 605; Jackson-Scott, *ibid.*, 228, 297; Jackson-Lawrence, *ibid.*, 424; Decatur-Jennings, *ibid.*, 33, 43, 547.

[31] *Ibid.*, 1835-36, pp. 87, 96, 138, 169, 271, 366, 437. An error in description was corrected by an act of December 20, 1836. *Laws of Indiana*, 1836-37, pp. 100-1; *Counties of Morgan, Monroe and Brown*, 679 ff. See map, Brown County.

[32] *House Journal*, 1835-36, pp. 162, 178, 313, 335, 343, 368; Howat, William F. (ed.), *A Standard History of Lake County, Indiana* . . ., 1:100 ff. (Chicago, 1915); Ball, T. H., *Encyclopedia of Genealogy and Biography of Lake County, Indiana* . . ., 6 ff. (Chicago, 1904).

[33] Kosciusko, *House Journal*, 1835-36, pp. 260, 327; Fulton, *Senate Journal*, 1835-36, pp. 453, 541.

was permitted to add a strip of territory three miles wide along her northern boundary, taking small areas from St. Joseph and Elkhart counties for this enlargement. Marshall and Elkhart thus reached their present boundaries.[34] Warren County hoped for extension northward into unorganized Jasper County, but did not secure it.[35]

After remaining quiescent for three sessions, promoters of a county to be erected from Putnam, Montgomery, and Parke hopefully presented a petition for such a county, but failed again.[36] A petition for a change in the Jackson-Lawrence line was not reported on.[37]

In the southeastern section of the state, attempts at boundary alterations were not particularly successful. Clark County gained a small block of territory from Jefferson County. Transfers from Harrison to Floyd, and from Harrison to Crawford, both of which had been proposed before, again failed of enactment. Once more the feasibility of erecting a new county out of Dearborn was argued in petitions and remonstrances, and once more unfavorably reported upon. Another petition from citizens of Dearborn County asked that the town of Lawrenceburg be transferred from Indiana to Kentucky.[38]

1836-37. The importance of county-boundary legislation in the session of 1836-37 is not fully revealed by the laws passed. No new county came into existence, and the only transfer of territory—between Clark and Jefferson—was small, and part of a long and confusing series.[39] Another transfer law, attaching part of Carroll County to White, was vitiated by the misnumbering

[34] *Laws of Indiana*, 1835-36 (general), p. 50.
[35] *House Journal*, 1835-36, pp. 319, 328.
[36] *Ibid.*, 224, 290.
[37] *Ibid.*, 56.
[38] Clark-Jefferson, *House Journal*, 1835-36, pp. 369, 453, 482-84. See map, Clark County XI. Harrison-Floyd-Crawford, *House Journal*, 1835-36, pp. 114, 248, 259, 316; *Senate Journal*, 1835-36, pp. 398, 410, 541, 556; Dearborn, *House Journal*, 1835-36, pp. 263, 327, 387.
[39] See map, Clark County XII.

BOUNDARY LEGISLATION

of a township.[40] The granting of independent jurisdiction to Steuben, De Kalb, and Wells, laid out in 1835, and to Lake, formed in 1836, completes the list of acts passed.[41]

Practically every section of the state, however, proposed changes that were not carried out. On the third day of the session the Senate provided for the appointment of a select committee to see what amendments might be necessary to an act relative to county boundaries; a second resolution specified particular inquiry with regard to the boundaries of Delaware and Randolph; Madison and Grant; Scott, Clark, and Washington; and Wabash, Delaware, and Jay; and a third resolution suggested a bill designating the boundaries of all counties in the state.[42] The boundaries of Grant, La Porte, Marshall, Starke, and St. Joseph were also brought into question.[43]

In the House, petitions asking the attachment of part of Clark to Floyd and part of Greene to Monroe received little support.[44] Of five bills introduced to alter county boundaries, one, relating to Delaware and Madison, was rejected on first reading; two, relating to Jay County, and to the Daviess-Martin line, respectively, were tabled; and two, relating to an attachment to Warren from Jasper, and the creation of a new county out of Dearborn, passed the House, but failed in the Senate.[45]

Behind the demand for the division of Dearborn County lay the rivalry of Lawrenceburg, Wilmington, and Rising

[40] The transfer was made by an act of February 14, 1839. See text with map, White County III.
[41] *Laws of Indiana*, 1836-37 (general), pp. 55-60.
[42] *Senate Journal*, 1836-37, pp. 31, 71, 77. Such a bill was passed at the succeeding session.
[43] *Ibid.*, 223, 275.
[44] Clark-Floyd, *House Journal*, 1836-37, p. 67; Greene-Monroe, *ibid.*, 247, 329.
[45] Delaware-Madison, *ibid.*, 409; Jay, *ibid.*, 142, 231, 398; Daviess-Martin, *ibid.*, 216, 294, 309; Jasper-Warren, *ibid.*, 100, 122, 129; *Senate Journal*, 1836-37, pp. 237, 542.

Sun, all covetous of advantages accruing to county-seat towns. Discussion reached a heated pitch in the session of 1836-37, with a single petition for division bearing 962 names. A bill creating Ohio County struggled through the House in spite of strenuous opposition. In the Senate it was referred to the Judiciary Committee. That committee recommended an amendment which would nullify the act should a survey made at the expense of the petitioners show that Dearborn County would be left less than four hundred square miles by the creation of Ohio County. The committee also put before the Senate part of the testimony of the Dearborn County representatives in the House on the local problems involved. An amendment of the nature suggested was agreed to by the Senate, but action on the bill was then indefinitely postponed. Toward the close of the session the bill was again taken under consideration, only to fail on the question of engrossment for third reading.[46]

1837-38. Legislation enacted by the General Assembly of 1837-38 included a general law restating the boundaries of all counties and embodying certain changes.[47]

Cass and White counties were extended north to include attachments over which they already held jurisdiction, and the open territory north of Wabash and Miami was divided between those two counties and Fulton. These changes completed the evolution of Cass and Wabash counties to the present time, and a transfer between Grant and Madison brought them to their present form.

[46] Shockley, "County Seat Wars," in *Indiana Magazine of History*, 10:no.1:40-41; *House Journal*, 1836-37, pp. 75, 88, 97, 129, 132, 144; *Senate Journal*, 1836-37, pp. 252, 253, 260, 273, 297-300, 545-46.

[47] *Laws of Indiana*, 1837-38 (local), pp. 241 ff. This act should have been included in the *Revised Statutes*, and a committee was appointed at the following session to inquire why it had been omitted. A number of inaccuracies appeared in the descriptions as restated. See maps, Cass County IV, White County II, Wabash County II, Miami County III, Fulton County II, Grant County II, Madison County V.

BOUNDARY LEGISLATION 71

Bartholomew also made its most recent change, in the process of which three sections of land which had belonged to the county were overlooked entirely. They were eventually attached to Jackson County.[48]

Separate acts provided for the erection of Blackford County out of the western part of Jay County,[49] and for the organization of Whitley and Jasper counties.[50] The law organizing Jasper included a section which attached Newton County to White for judicial and representative purposes. Greene County was empowered to put to a vote at the August general election, the question of transferring to Monroe County a strip of territory three miles wide and twelve long, adjacent to the Monroe line, but the change was not made.[51]

The passage of these measures did not satisfy all demands in relation to county boundaries. Citizens of Bartholomew, Decatur, Rush, and Shelby petitioned for the erection of a county to be called St. Omer.[52] Groups of citizens from Fountain, Tippecanoe, and Warren, from Carroll, Clinton, and Indian territory east of Carroll, and from Tippecanoe, Carroll, Clinton, and White, also petitioned for county formations.[53] All were denied, adverse reports showing clearly the legislative fear of attendant disturbances in organized counties, such as the necessity of relocating county seats and providing new public buildings.

[48] See maps, Bartholomew County IV, Jackson County X.

[49] The new county was called Windsor in the original bill. The formation law set up machinery for Blackford County's organization the same year, but a second organization law was enacted in 1839. It is likely that the commissioners appointed by the first law failed to act. *House Journal*, 1837-38, pp. 172, 213, 257, 346, 375, 676; *Laws of Indiana*, 1838-39 (general), pp. 64-65. See also a short account of Blackford County in *Historical Atlas of Indiana*, 1876, p. 288.

[50] Whitley, *Laws of Indiana*, 1837-38 (local), p. 408; Jasper, *ibid.*, 268.

[51] *Ibid.*, 432.

[52] *House Journal*, 1837-38, pp. 194, 257.

[53] *Ibid.*, 527-28, 557.

Wayne and Fayette counties asked in vain for a change in their common boundary, and Clay County was unsuccessful in requests for territorial addition.[54] The question of the line between Gibson and Warrick, in dispute since 1824, was brought to the attention of the House by various communications asking a definite interpretation of the boundary. The bill reported was allowed to die in committee, and the question arose to annoy succeeding assemblies as late as 1855.[55]

1838-39. Publication of the general county-boundary law of February 17, 1838, brought upon the General Assembly of 1838-39 a flood of petitions for correction of errors and for specific alterations. Four purely corrective laws were passed,[56] and a fifth bill passed one house but failed in the second.[57] Several other acts, inspired by inadequacies in the law, aimed at specific definition of controversial lines. For example, commissioners were appointed by an act of February 15, 1839, to establish a part of the Clark-Floyd line; an act of February 16 "more particularly" defined the Scott-Clark-Washington boundary; an act of February 18 empowered the county boards of Warrick and Spencer to determine their common boundary; and the Carroll-White transfer contemplated by an act of February 4, 1837, was made actual, a change which brought Carroll County to its present form.[58] In connection with the establishment of the Scott-Clark-Washington boundary, it is interesting to note that an attempt was made to secure the forma-

[54] *House Journal*, 1837-38, pp. 241, 241-42, 330.

[55] *Ibid.*, 124, 172, 259, 264.

[56] Newton, *Laws of Indiana*, 1838-39 (general), p. 68; St. Joseph, Marshall, La Porte, Starke, Porter, Lake, *ibid.*, 70; Tippecanoe, *ibid.*, 79; Rush-Fayette, *ibid.*, 85-86. These laws were intended to eliminate discrepancies in the descriptions of contiguous counties, and errors of a typographical nature.

[57] *House Journal*, 1838-39, pp. 141, 250, 471-72; *Senate Journal*, 1838-39, pp. 604, 605.

[58] Clark-Floyd, *Laws of Indiana*, 1838-39 (general), p. 89; Scott-Clark-Washington, *ibid.* (local), 323-24; Warrick-Spencer, *ibid.*, 254; Carroll-White, *ibid.* (general), 93; map, Carroll County II.

BOUNDARY LEGISLATION 73

tion of a new county in the area.[59] There was also considerable legislation regarding possible transfers.[60]

Noteworthy in comparison with the group of amendatory measures was an act assigning the untouched central area of the Miami Reserve for judicial purposes to the surrounding counties, to be so held until increased population and the extinction of all Indian titles should warrant the establishment of the new county of Richardville within this area.[61] Carroll, Cass, Hamilton, and Miami were the counties affected.

Another change, unique in the development of Indiana counties, concerned Newton and Jasper. Newton County, formed in 1835, had never been organized. Under an act of January 29, 1839, commissioners appointed to establish the county seat of Jasper were authorized to inquire into the propriety of consolidating Newton and Jasper, and to make such a consolidation should it appear advisable. The county name Jasper was to be retained, and the county seat was to be called Newton. A later measure provided for Newton's attachment to White County for representative and judicial purposes, in case no consolidation should occur. The counties were united, however, some time during the year 1839.[62]

Two counties, Pulaski and Blackford, attained separate jurisdiction under organization laws passed at this session.[63] There was also some agitation for a new county

[59] *House Journal*, 1838-39, pp. 323, 431, 487-88; *ibid.*, 526-27, 622; *Senate Journal*, 1838-39, pp. 481, 689.

[60] Washington-Scott, *House Journal*, 1838-39, pp. 220, 266, 590; Clark-Jefferson, *ibid.*, 271, 412; Jefferson-Scott, *ibid.*, 248, 304, 306, 388, 606.

[61] *Laws of Indiana*, 1838-39 (general), pp. 75-76. Richardville County was never organized to include all the territory thus assigned.

[62] *Ibid.* (general), 83; (local), 261. Exact information concerning the change is difficult to find, due to the destruction of Jasper County records by fire. See map, Jasper County II.

[63] *Laws of Indiana*, 1838-39 (general), pp. 34-35, and 64-65. The Blackford organizing act also corrected a misprint in the formation law of February 15, 1838.

in the neighborhood of Blackford County, but it apparently received little consideration.[64] Another new county, to be called Chester, was proposed by citizens of Kosciusko and nearby counties, but remonstrances outweighed the petitions and postponement of legislation for at least twelve months was recommended.[65]

Committee reports were unfavorable to transfers from Franklin to Decatur, and from Owen to Clay.[66] The problem of the Gibson-Warrick line again demanded consideration. From the text of a committee report it appears that the Assembly was requested to transfer a part of township 4 south, range 9 west to Gibson County. Legislation was denied on the ground that nine sections of the area—which included the petitioners—were within the boundaries of Gibson County.[67]

1839-40. The new General Assembly had scarcely met before agitation was begun for the erection of a new county out of southern Kosciusko and the three-mile strip lately attached to Miami and Wabash counties. On December 21 a bill to form a county was introduced in the House. Amended on second reading, it was referred to the Committee on the Judiciary for investigation of the status of the three-mile strip. The committee reported that the attachment of that territory to Wabash had been for judicial purposes only, that Fulton County had wanted its permanent attachment, and that Kosciusko had protested. The intention had been to include the strip in Kosciusko when that county was formed, but it had been overlooked. The committee was satisfied that the majority of voters in the territory concerned favored a new county. In spite of this report, the bill to form Van Buren County passed the House only after a reconsidered vote, and subsequently failed in the Senate. The Senate

[64] *House Journal*, 1838-39, p. 509.
[65] *Senate Journal*, 1838-39, pp. 402-3, 457-58.
[66] Franklin-Decatur, *Senate Journal*, 1838-39, pp. 196-97, 612; Owen-Clay, *House Journal*, 1838-39, pp. 248, 405, 430.
[67] *Ibid.*, 46, 154. Later committee reports indicate that jurisdiction in the disputed area was divided.

BOUNDARY LEGISLATION

committee based their rejection on the assumption that to remove the three-mile strip from Miami and Wabash was illegal, since it would reduce them to less than four hundred square miles in area. A minority of the committee pointed out that this territory had been added to the original counties, and that the constitutional provision was not concerned with territory added after the formation of a county, and for temporary purposes, but the majority report was adopted by a vote of 25-18.[68] The addition to Fulton of the northeast quarter of township 30 north, range 4 east, was made permanent by an act of February 24, 1840, and the boundaries of Jay County were redefined in an act of February 20.[69] A petition for a new county from Noble and La Grange was laid on the table.[70]

While the bill for the county of Van Buren was moving slowly toward defeat, a measure forming Benton County from the southern end of Jasper County progressed rapidly through House and Senate, and was approved on February 18.[71]

Fountain, Montgomery, and Parke revived the question of the formation of a county from their contiguous territory, but were refused again.[72]

A petition to attach part of Tippecanoe to Carroll was

[68] *House Journal*, 1839-40, pp. 66-67, 165, 192, 195, 228, 313-15, 346, 365-66; *Senate Journal*, 1839-40, pp. 217, 246-47, 265-67, 284-85. The names Van Buren and Tipton were suggested for this county.

[69] Fulton-Kosciusko, *Laws of Indiana*, 1839-40 (local), p. 229. See map, Fulton County III. Jay, *Laws of Indiana*, 1839-40 (general), p. 79.

[70] *House Journal*, 1839-40, p. 340.

[71] *Ibid.*, 335, 628-29, 768, 913; *Senate Journal*, 1839-40, p. 344; *Counties of Warren, Benton, Jasper and Newton*, 226-27; Birch, Jesse S., "Benton County and Historic Oxford," 1:45 ff. This is an unpublished manuscript in the Indiana State Library. The name Tipton having already failed of adoption for one county was proposed again for Benton but was not adopted.

[72] *House Journal*, 1839-40, pp. 218, 358. The formation had been proposed in 1835-36.

tabled, and a bill attaching part of Carroll to Cass failed on second reading.[73] A bill to amend the act of the preceding session which assigned jurisdiction over the Miami Reserve to surrounding counties, was blocked by disagreement of the houses on an amendment.[74]

Owen and Clay, Gibson and Warrick, and Clark and Floyd prayed for exchanges of territory, but the three House bills providing for the alterations all failed of passage.[75]

1840-41. Sentiment favoring the erection of a county from southern Kosciusko and northern Wabash survived the defeat of 1839-40 and showed considerable strength in a renewed appeal before the Twenty-first General Assembly. After a second consideration of the petitions, the committee in charge, finding that 421 citizens of Kosciusko and 170 citizens of Wabash approved the division, as against 326 citizens of Kosciusko who opposed it, reported a bill for the formation of a county to be called Tipton. Remonstrances continued to come in, however; the form of the measure was not satisfactory, and the bill was tabled after second reading.[76] Kosciusko County was concerned also in an unsuccessful petition to attach part of Kosciusko to Fulton.[77]

In the meantime, the consolidation of La Grange and Noble counties had been petitioned for. Following a flurry of remonstrances from both counties, the House committee made an adverse report.[78] The Senate made the same disposition of petitions for a new county out of

[73] Tippecanoe-Carroll, *House Journal*, 1839-40, p. 888; Carroll-Cass, *ibid.*, 297, 639, 646, 664, 714.

[74] *Ibid.*, 683, 700, 814; *Senate Journal*, 1839-40, pp. 327-28, 358, 496.

[75] Owen-Clay, *House Journal*, 1839-40, pp. 486, 720, 877-78; Gibson-Warrick, *ibid.*, 151, 158, 228, 783, 960; Clark-Floyd, *ibid.*, 803, 878, 985; *Senate Journal*, 1839-40, pp. 477, 478, 481.

[76] *Ibid.*, 1840-41, pp. 319-20, 358-59, 446, 447, 450, 545-46.

[77] *House Journal*, 1840-41, pp. 359, 736.

[78] *Ibid.*, 412, 634; see also remonstrances to the Senate, in *Senate Journal*, 1840-41, pp. 241, 256-57, 346.

BOUNDARY LEGISLATION 77

Carroll and Clinton, and for transfers of territory from Carroll to Cass, and from Tippecanoe to Carroll.[79]

Bartholomew, Johnson, and Shelby counties sent to the House a petition signed by nine hundred citizens asking for the formation of a county from contiguous territory of the three counties. This was followed by a second petition with ninety-three signers. A bill for the formation of Macomb County was reported, but was tabled on second reading, and was not revived after the appearance of remonstrances from Johnson and Bartholomew counties.[80]

Less ambitious boundary measures fared little better than bills for new counties. One law was enacted, attaching a part of White to Jasper County, but an attempt to add to White that part of Carroll County west of the Tippecanoe River was unsuccessful.[81] White County has made no more boundary changes.

Marshall County citizens from a tract of some eleven sections of land southeast of the Tippecanoe River asked unsuccessfully for attachment to Fulton County. A transfer from Daviess to Martin was also proposed. The committee report on the petition was unfavorable, but a bill was introduced and after amendment passed to engrossment. A select committee appointed to examine its constitutionality brought out a divided report, the majority holding the measure inexpedient and unconstitutional because it not only reduced Daviess very slightly below the required area of four hundred square miles, but because it was not based on the petitions.[82]

Blackford County made an attempt to enlarge her small territory at the expense of Grant, Wells, and Jay. A bill for enlargement passed the House and progressed through

[79] *Ibid.*, 241, 309, 499, 502, 640.
[80] *House Journal*, 1840-41, pp. 445, 508, 517, 546, 554, 570.
[81] White-Jasper, *Laws of Indiana*, 1840-41 (general), p. 135. See map, Jasper County IV. White-Carroll, *House Journal*, 1840-41, pp. 64, 327.
[82] Marshall-Fulton, *House Journal*, 1840-41, pp. 95, 264, 299; Daviess-Martin, *ibid.*, 343, 415, 487, 527-28, 782-83.

second reading in the Senate. In the meantime, citizens of Jay County were asking for the repeal of the act forming Blackford County, and the restoration of all that territory. Bill and petition were referred to a select committee, the majority of which recommended passage, although the minority objected on constitutional grounds. After several attempts to block further action the bill failed for want of a constitutional majority.[83]

One of the few boundary measures enacted at the session of 1840-41 provided for the marking of part of the Clark-Floyd boundary. Commissioners appointed under the act were instructed to establish the boundary by sectional lines if that could be done without altering the area of the counties. Should this prove impossible, the line was to be surveyed along the summit of the Knobs.[84]

Another act, aimed at abuses in the petition system of demanding boundary changes, required public notice to be given thirty days before the circulation of any petition asking changes.[85] It was approved on February 4, 1841.

1841-42. Failure to comply with provisions of the act of February 4, 1841, destroyed the chances of at least five petitions filed with the General Assembly of 1841-42. Three of these had to do with proposed new counties out of Perry and Spencer, Kosciusko and Wabash, and Carroll, Clinton, and part of the Miami Reserve.[86] The two other boundary proposals which received unfavorable action on the same grounds both concerned Carroll, one suggesting an addition to Carroll from Tippecanoe

[83] *House Journal*, 1840-41, pp. 343, 367, 385; *Senate Journal*, 1840-41, **pp.** 307, 440, 441-42, 456, 487; *ibid.*, 351, 440.

[84] *Laws of Indiana*, 1840-41 (general), pp. 147-48.

[85] *Ibid.*, 149. This act applied also to petitions for changes of county seat.

[86] Perry-Spencer, *House Journal*, 1841-42, pp. 583-84; Kosciusko-Wabash, *Senate Journal*, 1841-42, pp. 250, 262, 320; Carroll-Clinton-Miami Reserve, *House Journal*, 1841-42, pp. 339, 409, 465, and 481.

BOUNDARY LEGISLATION

County, and the second requesting the transfer of Washington Township from Carroll to Cass.[87]

Citizens of Clay, Parke, Putnam, and Vigo counties had not given up hope of securing the county formation for which they had petitioned so obstinately, but a renewed plea for organization was refused.[88] Subsequently, a bill was put through the House attaching part of Vigo County to Clay, but the session was too far advanced to permit the Senate to act upon it.[89]

In the meantime, a bill organizing the central part of the Miami Reserve had passed one branch of the Assembly. The first petition on the subject asked for the formation of Richardville County, but the measure was reported out of the House committee on January 7 as a bill defining the southern boundary of Miami County and organizing Tipton County. The Senate made two amendments, in one of which the House concurred, but disagreement over the second was prolonged until January 29, when the conference committee from the two houses asked to be discharged.[90]

The future development of Benton County was brought before this Assembly by two opposed factions. On January 11, 1842, a bill was introduced in the House to provide for the location of a county seat in Benton County. On January 19, petitions came before the Senate asking for the disorganization of the county. The committee to which these latter petitions and some remonstrances were referred reported on January 21 that there were but eighty voters in the county, and that the majority had petitioned for disorganizing the county. In view of the prohibitive expense of erecting county buildings, they reported a bill in accordance with the petitioners' request.

[87] Carroll-Tippecanoe, *ibid.*, 121, 197; Carroll-Cass, *ibid.*, 287, 656.

[88] *Ibid.*, 351, 421, 484-85; *Senate Journal*, 1841-42, p. 510. Agitation for a county in this area began in 1826-27.

[89] *House Journal*, 1841-42, pp. 606, 634.

[90] *Ibid.*, 306, 319, 340, 419, 493-94, 519; *Senate Journal*, 1841-42, pp. 410-11, 467, 490, 506, 605.

Both bills, a House bill for organization, and a Senate bill for disorganization, passed their originating houses; each was tabled in the other chamber.[91]

One county-boundary measure mustered enough strength for enactment, after a temporary halt caused by failure to observe the new requirements as to circulation of petitions. A petition asking that Starke County transfer to La Porte all her territory north of the Kankakee River was filed on December 8. The next day the Senate committee reported that they did not feel authorized to legislate because the petitioners had not complied with the law of the preceding February 4. On January 25, thirty days' notice having presumably been given and the petition once more circulated, a bill was introduced making the transfer. It passed both houses without amendment, and was approved on January 29.[92]

Petitions asking for the attachment of part of Jackson to Scott, and of part of Decatur to Jennings, both presented late in the session, did not reach bill form.[93]

1842-43. Such boundary changes as occurred in 1842-43 were incorporated in an act of the *Revised Statutes* passed at that session, which defined all county boundaries. There were five such readjustments: the Scott-Clark, Clark-Washington line along the summit of the Knobs was explicitly defined; three unassigned sections of land bounded by Brown, Bartholomew, and Jackson counties were definitely included in Jackson County; the Gibson-Warrick boundaries were so defined as to give to Gibson County a disputed area of some twenty-four sections; the line between Knox and Sullivan was straightened, giving Sullivan a small strip of Knox; and nine sections were transferred from Fulton to Kosciusko County. Neither *House* nor *Senate Journal* records any

[91] *House Journal*, 1841-42, pp. 358, 424, 514, 534; *Senate Journal*, 1841-42, pp. 447, 480, 545.

[92] *Ibid.*, 35, 55. *Laws of Indiana*, 1841-42 (general), p. 152. See maps, La Porte County II, Starke County II.

[93] Jackson-Scott, *House Journal*, 1841-42, pp. 447, 615; Decatur-Jennings, *Senate Journal*, 1841-42, p. 504.

discussion on these changes, although all of them, excepting the one affecting Jackson County, were to be the subject of controversy in later assemblies.

Section 90 of the county-boundary law made a general provision intended to remove one source of frequent boundary disputes: "when any boundary line of any county is described as running east, west, north, or south, from any point in a range, township, or section line, such boundary shall be deemed to run with and along such range, township, or section line, unless the contrary is obviously intended."[94]

The most important of the unsuccessful county-boundary projects related to the organization of part of the Miami Reserve. A Senate bill forming Tipton County was introduced on January 27, 1843. The next day a House bill organizing Tipton County had its first reading and on January 31 it passed the House and was transmitted to the Senate; after second reading on February 2, it was referred to a select committee. On February 3 the Senate bill also passed second reading and was referred to the same committee. Failing to agree on either measure, the committee apparently suggested a substitute form for the House bill, but their report and the Senate bill were both tabled.[95]

The House, on January 28, 1843, rejected a bill to attach part of Tippecanoe to Carroll, introduced after a petition for that change had been tabled and then withdrawn. A second petition, bringing the request of citizens of Carroll for a new county, died in committee.[96] Still another request before this Assembly came from citizens of Daviess, Greene, Knox, and Sullivan counties and asked for the laying out of a new county from their surplus territory. The necessary bill was reported, but was tabled on January 8.[97]

[94] *Revised Statutes of Indiana*, 1842-43, p. 90.
[95] *Senate Journal*, 1842-43, pp. 397-98, 469, 470, 483, 605; *House Journal*, 1842-43, pp. 567, 610.
[96] *Ibid.*, pp. 91-92, 109, 576-77.
[97] *Ibid.*, 271, 310, 402.

7—48526

Of the two remaining proposals of 1842-43 relating to county boundaries, one was a resolution inquiring into the expediency of establishing the east line of Madison County on the line dividing ranges 8 and 9 east. The second was a bill for the appointment of a committee to determine the line between Clark and Floyd counties. Its course in the House was long and involved, and came to an ineffectual end in a vote on an amendment.[98]

[98] Madison, *House Journal*, 1842-43, p. 703; Clark-Floyd, *ibid.*, 151, 243, 355, 356-57, 679-81.

LATER COUNTIES

A S IN 1824 and in 1838, publication of a general county-boundary act roused general interest in the question of counties and their limits and gave a final stimulus to the organization of counties.

1843-44. The legislature of 1843-44 created three new counties, Ohio, Tipton, and Richardville, which later became Howard, bringing the number of Indiana counties to its present total of ninety-two. The formation of Ohio County was actually a compromise measure to quiet the long-standing rivalry between Rising Sun, which wanted to become a county seat, and Lawrenceburg, which had held that distinction in Dearborn County until 1836, and was determined to secure it again. A difficulty in the way of the establishment of the county was the small size of Dearborn County and the constitutional provision that no old county should be reduced by the formation of a new one to "a less content than four hundred square miles." To overcome this obstacle the area of Dearborn County was extended to its utmost by taking the measurement at low waterline, and the new county was laid out with strict attention to the necessity of preserving a safe four hundred square miles in Dearborn County. An attempt was made to amend the bill, providing that Ohio should "forever remain the same size," and should at no future time "have any portion of the territory from the adjacent counties," but the amendment failed.[1]

The erection of Tipton and Richardville counties within the unorganized remainder of the Miami Reserve gave

[1] See minority report of committee to which the bill was assigned, *House Journal*, 1843-44, pp. 178-79; communication of George P. Buell, senator from Dearborn County, favoring the bill, *Senate Journal*, 1843-44, pp. 245-46; *History of Dearborn and Ohio Counties*, 116-18. A Senate bill to form a new county out of Dearborn was introduced early in the session but was superseded by the House bill. *Senate Journal*, 1843-44, pp. 51, 123, 156.

rise to another contest. The first move was the introduction of a House bill on December 13, 1843, creating the county of Cicero. On December 18 an amendment changed the name to Tipton and the bill went to a select committee.[2] Eight days later another House bill was introduced attaching part of the Miami Reserve to Miami County, and enlarging Fulton, probably at the expense of Miami County. After second reading this bill was referred to the same committee which had the formation of Tipton under consideration.[3] The committee on January 6 reported a bill as an amendment to the original bill concerning Tipton, and reported the Miami-Fulton bill without recommendation. Both were recommitted to the select committee. In the meantime, a third bill, to organize the new county of Whitcomb, had been introduced and referred to the committee.[4]

On January 10 a divided committee report was presented. The majority recommended the organization of Tipton and Richardville counties; the minority argued that this would create two counties in "territory containing but little more than the constitutional quantity required for one county," that Richardville would include territory which rightfully belonged to Miami County, and that the new counties would be of awkward shape. They recommended the enactment of the bill enlarging Miami and Fulton counties. Nevertheless, the bill creating Tipton and Richardville was eventually passed in an amended form. It was approved on January 15, 1844.[5]

[2] *House Journal*, 1843-44, pp. 111, 156.
[3] *Ibid.*, 234-35, 359.
[4] *Ibid.*, 289-90, 446.
[5] The record appears in *ibid.*, 404, 460-61, 462; *Senate Journal*, 1843-44, pp. 487, 544-46, 562. A defeated House amendment proposed the name Whitcomb. Pershing, M. W., *History of Tipton County Indiana* . . ., 58 ff. (Indianapolis, 1914); Blanchard, Charles (ed.), *Counties of Howard and Tipton, Indiana* . . ., pt. 2:43 ff. (Richardville); pt. 3:1 ff. (Tipton) [Chicago, 1883]; Morrow, Jackson, *History of Howard County Indiana*, 1:55 ff. (Indianapolis, n. d.).

Following the rejection of the bill enlarging Miami and Fulton counties, a new bill was introduced and passed, which gave to Fulton a small projection of Miami County north of the line dividing townships 29 and 30 north.[6]

Citizens of Carroll and Clinton counties, three hundred of whom had petitioned on December 28 for the erection of a new county out of Carroll, Clinton, and the Miami Reserve, saw their project blocked by the act creating Tipton and Richardville. Two days before the latter bill became a law the Carroll-Clinton petition was unfavorably reported upon, on the ground that the counties were too small to admit of further reduction.[7]

In the meantime, Warrick County was protesting to the General Assembly of 1843-44 against her exclusion by the law of 1843 from the territory which had been in dispute between her and Gibson. On December 9 a bill was introduced in the House repealing the provisions of the 1843 law, and establishing the Gibson-Warrick line according to the county-boundary act of February 10, 1831.[8] This simply reopened the question of jurisdiction, for the law of 1831 repeated the ambiguity of the law of 1824 which had begun the difficulty. The report of the Senate committee on the bill attempted a justification of the course:[9]

"A difference in the construction of the act of 1831, between the counties of Gibson and Warrick, has placed about twenty-six sections of territory in dispute; over which territory, or the greater part thereof, the county of Warrick has, for the most part of the time, exercised jurisdiction. By reference to the act of 1831, abundant reasons are found for that difference of construction, and the dispute and controversy which has necessarily grown

[6] *House Journal*, 1843-44, pp. 466, 602. See map, Fulton County V.
[7] *House Journal*, 1843-44, pp. 265, 551.
[8] *Ibid.*, 69, 188.
[9] *Senate Journal*, 1843-44, pp. 229-30.

out of it. By the revision of the county boundaries of the last session, the boundary in dispute was clearly defined in such a manner as to remove all ambiguity and to settle the dispute, but excluding Warrick county from the whole of the disputed territory. The then and now delegation of Warrick county insist that the law of the last session was passed without their knowledge or that of their constituents, and is a violation of their rights. The delegation of Gibson insist that the law of the last session makes no change in the boundary, but only makes clear and certain what before was ambiguous. . . . your committee think, in justice to Warrick county, she should be restored to the condition in which she was placed by the law of 1831, and the settlement of the controversy be deferred to a time when the parties interested can be fully and fairly heard."

The bill was tabled, but was again taken up in January, 1844. An amendment reserving to Gibson County jurisdiction over nine sections in the northwest corner of township 4 south, range 9 west, was defeated, and the bill passed in its original form.[10]

Knox County also protested indignantly against the transfer to Sullivan of a narrow strip of territory in range 10 west, charging that the alteration made by the *Revised Statutes* of 1842-43 had been carried through without the knowledge of Knox County representatives. On December 8 a resolution was offered asking an investigation of the change and, "if deemed right" the reporting of a bill to reënact "the former description of Knox county boundaries, so that said county shall be restored the strip of territory and population so improperly attached to Sullivan county." Such a bill was reported on January 1, but its passage was vigorously opposed and finally blocked.[11]

[10] *Senate Journal*, 1843-44, pp. 369-70; *Laws of Indiana*, 1843-44 (general), p. 87.

[11] *Senate Journal*, 1843-44, pp. 40-41, 54-55, 227, 243, 404, 419-20.

BOUNDARY LEGISLATION

An act approved on January 15, 1844, appointed commissioners to run and mark the boundary line between Clark and Floyd. Their report of April 23, 1844, made a small alteration in the existing line.[12]

Two bills were introduced, one in the House and one in the Senate, asking a clear definition of Rush County's eastern boundary line, but the point in question was held to be covered by section 90 of the county-boundary act of 1843, and neither bill became law.[13]

Half a dozen other proposed changes failed. They are listed in the order in which the petitions made their appearance. Citizens of St. Joseph desired attachment to La Porte, and part of Sullivan wished to be transferred to Vigo County.[14] Blackford County continued her efforts to secure more territory from Grant County. Because Blackford was one of the smallest counties of the state and because there was "much waste and unorganized territory west of Grant county," a bill enlarging Blackford was reported out, but it was killed on second reading.[15] A petition from citizens of Warrick and Spencer "in relation to the boundary line between Spencer and Gibson" was tabled, as was a memorial asking that part of Spencer be attached to Warrick.[16] The last of these unsuccessful petitions had to do with the boundaries of Elkhart, but the nature of the proposed change does not appear from the title of the document.[17]

1844-45. The citizens of Ohio County had secured their organization by a meticulous compliance with the state law concerning the formation of new counties from old ones. At the formation of Ohio, Dearborn County had been left her full quota of four hundred square miles. Having fulfilled the letter of the law at some expense

[12] See map, Floyd County IV.
[13] See page 81.
[14] St. Joseph-La Porte, *House Journal*, 1843-44, pp. 210-11, 256; Sullivan-Vigo, *ibid.*, 266, 322.
[15] *Ibid.*, 294, 384, 415.
[16] *Ibid.*, 419, 476.
[17] *Ibid.*, 449.

and with considerable difficulty, Ohio evidently felt no responsibility toward upholding its spirit, and with the opening of a new session, began a fight for more territory. In this she was strongly supported by citizens of Dearborn County living south of Laughery Creek. The first petition for change came from that district on December 5; two days later Ohio County petitioned for the addition, and on December 16 a House bill was reported attaching certain territory to Ohio County. This bill was tabled on December 27, while remonstrances against its enactment continued to pour in.[18]

This action did not dispose of the question, however. A bill extending Ohio County west to the 1795 treaty line and north to Laughery Creek, had passed the Senate, and on December 28 came before the House.

Both branches of the General Assembly opposed an amendment proposing to leave the question of transfer to the voters of the two counties, and the Senate refused to accept a House amendment regulating the apportionment of representatives from that district. The Senate bill, in its original form, was passed by a close vote and was approved on January 7, 1845. By this change Ohio and Dearborn counties reached their present form.[19] Another law, supplying an omission in the description of Dearborn as given in the *Revised Statutes* of 1842-43 was enacted without controversy.[20]

Two other corrective measures were adopted at this session. Richardville's boundaries were amended to include a strip of territory one section wide and nine long, lying adjacent to Carroll County, which had been overlooked when the new county was laid out in 1844.[21] The

[18] *House Journal*, 1844-45, pp. 34, 49-50, 137, 282. See also pages 245, 283, and 322.

[19] *Senate Journal*, 1844-45, pp. 123, 218-19, 227-28, 238, 248-49; *House Journal*, 1844-45, pp. 294-97, 415, 417-18. See map, Ohio County II.

[20] *Laws of Indiana*, 1844-45 (local), p. 136.

[21] *Ibid.*, 151. Verbal errors in this law were in turn corrected by a law of the next session. *Ibid.*, 1845-46 (local), p. 260.

second correction rectified a verbal error in the law of 1844 which attached part of Miami to Fulton County.[22]

The southeast township of Fulton County and the southwest township of Kosciusko County had petitioned in December for attachment to Wabash County. Their interests, they pointed out, would benefit by an arrangement which would enable them to transact their county business where their commercial interests lay, along the Wabash and Erie Canal. School interests too would gain if the congressional township in which the applicants lived lay within one county, instead of distributed among three.

While there was sufficient sympathy with this plea to cause a divided committee report, the majority of the committee opposed it. For one thing it would "throw all the counties interested into an ill shape"; for another, remonstrators against the transfer outnumbered petitioners, although sentiment in the territory actually involved favored the change. The majority report derived additional support from the failure of the petitioners to give sufficient notice of their intention, and a bill reported out by the minority of the select committee was tabled on second reading.[23]

Encouraged by the formation of three new counties in 1843-44, several groups of citizens petitioned the Twenty-ninth General Assembly for separate county organization. One such group, from the surplus territory of Parke, Putnam, and Montgomery, secured the introduction of a Senate bill for the erection of Gallatin County. This was on December 16, 1845. On December 18, 20, 23, 24, and 25 remonstrances were registered against the formation, and on December 25 Senator Godlove S. Orth, of Tippecanoe County, laid before the Senate a communication "proposing to bestow a pecuniary reward of a certain amount upon Mr. Orth, should he use his influence

[22] *Ibid.*, 1844-45 (local), p. 191.
[23] *House Journal*, 1844-45, pp. 134, 246, 478-80, 545.

to obtain the passage" of the act.[24] Two days later engrossment of the bill was refused; it was brought up for consideration again, however, and the name Polk suggested as a substitute for Gallatin. On the same day, January 4, 1845, the bill was finally disposed of by an adverse vote on the question of engrossment.[25]

New counties to be called Hart and Smith were proposed by citizens of Bartholomew and Decatur counties, and by citizens of Posey County, respectively, but no bill was introduced for either project. This failure was inevitable in view of the small area available.[26]

Plans for other changes of boundary were laid before the legislature. An alteration between Clinton and Richardville was proposed. Pike County asked to have her original western boundary restored, and the attachment of part of Perry to Crawford was advocated. Blackford made another unsuccessful plea for enlargement, no doubt considering her cause quite as constitutional and no less important than that of Ohio County. A bill altering the Marion-Hendricks line was tabled on second reading.[27]

The legislature made another attempt in 1844-45 to save succeeding assemblies from the burden of hastily concocted petitions for county-boundary changes. Since 1841 a public notice of thirty days had been required before the circulation of petitions for the change of county seats or county boundaries. Under this system, it was still possible for a petition to be circulated and introduced after the General Assembly had met.[28] By a law of January 13, 1845, the requirement was stiffened to exclude

[24] *Senate Journal*, 1844-45, p. 232.

[25] *Ibid.*, 274-75, 422-23.

[26] Hart County, *House Journal*, 1844-45, pp. 151, 212, 320; Smith County, *ibid.*, 177.

[27] Clinton-Richardville, *ibid.*, 369, 484; Pike-Gibson, *ibid.*, 49, 207, 228-29; Perry-Crawford, *ibid.*, 134, 151, 203, 254; Blackford-Grant, *ibid.*, 60-61, 370; Marion-Hendricks, *ibid.*, 254, 533.

[28] See, for example, the account of a transfer from Starke County to La Porte, page 80.

any petition for which public notice had not been published or posted ninety days previous to the meeting of the legislature.[29]

1845-46. The session of 1845-46 saw the final transfer from Kosciusko to Fulton of the northeast quarter of township 30 north, range 4 east, which had been shuttled back and forth between them since 1840. The territory in question had belonged originally to Kosciusko County. Its first attachment to Fulton was for school purposes only, but a year later it became an actual part of Fulton County. By an error in the county-boundary act of 1843 it was included within Kosciusko County. This unintentional change apparently went unnoticed for several years, with Fulton maintaining jurisdiction over the quarter township in question, and with an associate judge who lived in that particular area still serving in the Fulton County Court. At the spring term of court in 1845 the matter came to light, and the General Assembly which met in December was asked to, and did, correct the law of 1843, restoring the territory to Fulton County.[30] A petition asking the attachment of part of Kosciusko and Fulton counties to Wabash was dropped as "inexpedient."[31] Neither county has since made any changes.

Clark and Washington counties continued to question their common boundary, which in 1843, for the first time, had been set out by line and measurement. Apparently the result proved as unsatisfactory as the indefinite boundary of earlier years, for on December 20 a bill was introduced in the House repealing the provision of 1843 and putting into effect once more the boundary line of

[29] *Laws of Indiana*, 1844-45 (general), p. 53.

[30] *Ibid.*, 1845-46 (general), pp. 87-88; see also *House Journal*, 1845-46, pp. 221-22. See maps of Fulton and Kosciusko counties for texts of laws.

Another belated correction of the 1843 county-boundary law was made at this session. It concerned Carroll, but made no change. *Laws of Indiana*, 1845-46 (local), p. 264.

[31] *House Journal*, 1845-46, pp. 450, 525-26.

1831 along the "extreme height" of the Silver Creek Knobs. It was enacted without change and approved January 14, 1846.[32]

Ohio County was still a center of controversy. Strong feeling against the creation of the county and its subsequent enlargement resulted in the presentation of a petition on December 24, 1845, asking for the repeal of the Ohio formation law. On the opposite side of the question appeared a second petition, filed two weeks later, which asked that Posey Township of Switzerland County, lying adjacent to Ohio County along the Ohio River, be added to Ohio. Both memorials were dismissed following unfavorable committee reports of January 10, 1846.[33]

The question of new counties made its customary appearance. Parke, Putnam, and Montgomery repeated their plea for the erection of an additional county in their contiguous territory, but the activities of the opposition prevented the introduction of a bill. Citizens of Knox, Daviess, and Greene also petitioned for a new county, but apparently no committee report was made on the memorial.[34]

Eight transfers of territory were asked for, in addition to the changes already mentioned. First to be presented was a petition advocating the attachment of part of Adams County to Wells. No report was made on this memorial. Committees reported unfavorably on proposed transfers from Jackson to Lawrence, and from Delaware to Madison. Legislation on a petition to transfer part of Perry to Crawford was denied because the required public notice had not been given the petition. Later in the session a Senate bill was introduced enlarging Crawford from Harrison County, but it failed of engrossment after a troubled course to that point. On December 15

---

[32] *Laws of Indiana*, 1845-46 (general), pp. 111-12.

[33] *House Journal*, 1845-46, pp. 254, 374, 435; for the petition concerning Posey Township, see *ibid.*, 415, 434.

[34] Parke-Putnam-Montgomery, *ibid.*, 212, 213, 235, 279, 290; Knox-Daviess-Greene, *ibid.*, 380.

BOUNDARY LEGISLATION

a bill was introduced nominally intended "to fix and establish the northern boundary line of Union County," but it is evident from the protests of Wayne County citizens that part of their territory was threatened. This measure died in committee. Blackford County, in a bill presented December 20, made a similar attempt to add to her very limited territory but was also unsuccessful. Marion County failed to secure new territory along the Hendricks boundary.[35]

1846-47. Upon the General Assembly of 1846-47 fell the necessity of dealing with several county-boundary squabbles which had vexed preceding legislatures. Among the more robustly waged disputes was the one between Warrick and Gibson counties. At this session an attempt was made to quiet contention by a law which divided the disputed territory between the two counties, and defined their common boundary precisely.[36]

Another familiar problem was the marking of the Clark-Washington boundary line. A bill was introduced to abolish the act of January 14, 1846, relating to this line; its passage would have restored the boundary marked out in 1843, but later in the session, action was indefinitely postponed.[37]

The Switzerland-Ohio-Dearborn controversy dragged on throughout the session. On December 14, 1846, Posey Township of Switzerland County again petitioned the Senate for annexation to Ohio County. On January 20,

[35] Adams-Wells, *House Journal*, 1845-46, p. 75; Jackson-Lawrence, *ibid.*, 115, 397-98; Delaware-Madison, *Senate Journal*, 1845-46, pp. 491, 576. That part of Delaware County in range 8 east was the territory under question. Perry-Crawford, *House Journal*, 1845-46, pp. 213, 353; Crawford-Harrison, *Senate Journal*, 1845-46, pp. 176, 258-59, 265, 433, 467, 521-22; Union-Wayne, *House Journal*, 1845-46, pp. 154, 159, 380; Blackford-Grant, *ibid.*, 204, 228, 514; Marion-Hendricks, *ibid.*, 235, 434, 483, 532.

[36] See account of the session of 1843-44 for a history of this dispute. See also *House Journal*, 1846-47, pp. 68, 190, 200, 202; *Laws of Indiana*, 1846-47 (local), p. 272; maps, Gibson County XII, Warrick County IX.

[37] *House Journal*, 1846-47, pp. 590-91, 617-18.

no report on the Senate petition having been made, a similar petition was laid before the House. The select committee of the House favored granting the request, but, because of the lack of time for proper investigation, asked to be discharged from further consideration of the matter. The Senate committee reported unfavorably on January 25, supporting its decision by two formidable reasons: the petitioners "although numerous and respectable" were "greatly exceeded" by the remonstrators; the constitutionality of the law creating the county of Ohio was being contested before the Supreme Court of Indiana, and knowledge of the outcome was important before adding more territory to the county.[38]

In the meantime there had come to the Senate a demand from Dearborn County for the reattachment of Ohio County, and to the House a petition from citizens of Dearborn asking to be attached to Ohio. Neither was favorably acted upon, and the session ended without either gain or loss of territory for Ohio County.[39]

The boundaries of Harrison County likewise emerged intact, although threatened during the session by a House bill for the creation of a new county out of Washington, Harrison, and Crawford, and by a Senate bill attaching part of Harrison to Crawford County.[40]

This Assembly was not sympathetic toward county formation movements. Petitions appeared in December and January asking for a new county out of Knox, Greene, and Sullivan. The first was reported upon adversely, the second, tabled.[41] Pleas for a new county from the contiguous territory of Carroll, Richardville, Cass, and Clinton persisted at short intervals during December, 1846, and were finally referred to a select com-

[38] *Senate Journal*, 1846-47, pp. 56, 101, 115, 204, 605; *House Journal*, 1846-47, pp. 567, 591-92. No record of the case before the Supreme Court has been found.

[39] *Senate Journal*, 1846-47, pp. 142, 175; *House Journal*, 1846-47, pp. 493, 537.

[40] *Ibid.*, 294, 320, 406; *Senate Journal*, 1846-47, pp. 264, 321, 352, 521-22.

[41] *House Journal*, 1846-47, pp. 260, 273, 347, 493.

mittee of the House which reported against the formation, referring the constitutionality of the question to the Judiciary Committee. Their report of December 31 showed that only Clinton, of the four counties concerned, had any territorial surplus over four hundred square miles, and that but twenty square miles. Nevertheless, as late as January 20, 1847, citizens from Clinton County laid before the House a last petition for a new organization.[42]

There is mention in the *Senate Journal* of a petition from Fountain County relating to a new county, but it was apparently allowed to die in committee.[43]

Following the failure to organize a new county in the neighborhood of Carroll, two attempts were made to redistribute part of the area by transfers. On January 9 a Senate bill was introduced attaching part of Howard County to Carroll. It was finally tabled on third reading. On January 26, 1847, a House committee added to its adverse report on a proposed transfer from Carroll to Cass, its opinion that "it is inexpedient to pass any law taking from any county in this State any of its territory."[44]

Blackford County did not fail to request enlargement, with Grant County promptly protesting at the possible loss of a three-mile strip of territory. A compromise transfer of a strip one and a half miles wide was suggested by the minority of the House committee, and a bill based on this figure was introduced on January 6, 1847; on second reading it was referred to the Judiciary Committee, and did not appear for further action.[45]

[42] *Ibid.*, 68-69, 79, 110, 190. See *ibid.*, 171 and 227 for remonstrances, *ibid.*, 165, 213, and 261-62 for committee action, and *ibid.*, 567-68 for the final petition.

[43] *Senate Journal*, 1846-47, p. 239.

[44] The name Richardville had been changed to Howard by act of December 28, 1846. *Laws of Indiana*, 1846-47 (local), p. 261. For action on the Senate bill, see *Senate Journal*, 1846-47, pp. 361, 397, 567-68, 619-20; on the House petition, see *House Journal*, 1846-47, pp. 501, 704.

[45] *Ibid.*, 324-25, 348, 390.

A bill to alter the La Porte-St. Joseph boundary was designed to accommodate petitioners separated from their county seat by marshes and compelled to travel from fifteen to eighteen miles over bad roads, but the House rejected the measure. Martin County citizens petitioning for attachment to Dubois, and Jackson County citizens petitioning for attachment to Lawrence were likewise unsuccessful.[46]

1847-48. Little county-boundary legislation disturbed the Thirty-second General Assembly. On December 8, 1847, citizens of Shelby and Decatur counties petitioned the Senate for the transfer of part of Shelby to Decatur, and on December 9 the House was petitioned for a transfer from Jackson to Lawrence. Dearborn County, on January 14, 1848, made another demand for the repeal of the act moving her county seat to Lawrenceburg, and creating Ohio County. Later in the month, Washington Township of Carroll County asked to be attached to Cass. Action for annexation of part of Benton County to Tippecanoe was begun on the same day, January 25, but met a counter movement which would have given Benton County all that part of Tippecanoe lying west of the Wabash River. Only two of these projects were reported in bill form and neither passed the originating house.[47]

1848-49. County-boundary legislation continued to play a comparatively minor role during the next session. The most determined fight for change originated in Blackford County. A bill attaching territory not specified in the *Journal* account passed the House January 6. The Senate committee on the bill reported an amendment striking out the original text and inserting an amendment taking from northern Delaware County a

[46] La Porte-St. Joseph, *House Journal*, 1846-47, pp. 294, 409; Martin-Dubois, *Senate Journal*, 1846-47, p. 323; Jackson-Lawrence, *House Journal*, 1846-47, pp. 535, 704.

[47] Shelby-Decatur, *Senate Journal*, 1847-48, pp. 20, 85, 117, 129; Jackson-Lawrence, *House Journal*, 1847-48, pp. 32, 50-51; Ohio-Dearborn, *ibid.*, 155, 178; Carroll-Cass, *Senate Journal*, 1847-48, pp. 239-40; Benton-Tippecanoe, *ibid.*, 239, 275, 465.

BOUNDARY LEGISLATION

strip of territory two miles wide and fifteen long. An amendment to the amendment, adding territory from both Jay and Wells counties, failed of adoption. On January 12 the bill passed the Senate in a form which left the decision of the question to a vote of the electors in the part of Delaware County concerned. This amendment failed of acceptance in the House, and the bill was eventually tabled in the Senate.[48]

Unrest in the Dearborn-Ohio area showed itself at this session in a petition from 349 citizens of the two counties asking for the straightening of their common boundary. A bill was reported out on January 11, but further action was indefinitely postponed two days later.[49]

Presentation of a petition from citizens of Jackson County asking attachment to Lawrence resulted in the introduction of a House bill on January 6 to straighten the line between the counties. When the measure came up for second reading, a dissenting member from Jackson County proposed an amendment which would have satisfied the ostensible purpose of the bill—to straighten the county boundary—but which would have made the alteration at the expense of Lawrence instead of Jackson County by restoring the line of 1822. The amendment failed and the bill itself was subsequently dropped.[50]

In the meantime, 149 citizens of St. Joseph County, separated by the Kankakee River and marshes from their county seat, were requesting transfer to La Porte County. A bill for this purpose passed the House on January 13, and on January 16 passed the Senate in an amended form which made the attachment conditional upon the vote of the county commissioners of St. Joseph County. At their June term, 1849, finding the sentiment of the citizens of St. Joseph against the transfer, they inscribed

[48] *House Journal*, 1848-49, pp. 172, 237-38, 353, 566-67; *Senate Journal*, 1848-49, pp. 343, 364-66, 373-74, 378-79, 425, 544-45.
[49] *House Journal*, 1848-49, pp. 193, 443-44, 535.
[50] *Ibid.*, 227, 341, 529-30, 594-95.

on their records an order that "said territory shall not be set off as a part of the territory of La Porte County."[51]

1849-50. December 14, 1849, found the familiar Blackford-Delaware dispute once more demanding attention. On that day some sixty residents of Delaware County asked for the annexation of part of Delaware to Blackford. A bill making the attachment, conditional upon a favorable vote of the legally qualified voters in the territory to be attached, was immediately reported out of committee, only to be followed on December 17 by remonstrances of more than two hundred citizens against the transfer. On second reading the bill was referred to an enlarged committee which asked on December 29 to be discharged. This was not granted.[52] The committee report of January 5 labeled the proposed legislation as inexpedient for two reasons: "the establishment of the precedent . . . of taking territory from one county and adding it to another, because that other happens to contain a less number of square miles would be extremely dangerous to the well being of a large majority of the counties in this State; 2d, because a large and respectable majority of the voters of the territory proposed to be attached, have respectfully and solemnly remonstrated against legislative action on this subject."

The Senate nevertheless refused to concur in the report, and two days later passed the bill by a vote of 23 to 19, after tabling several proposed amendments dealing with the form of elections to settle the contested question.[53]

On January 9, after second reading, the bill went to a select committee of the House. On January 10 a petition for the attachment to Blackford and two formidable remonstrances, one with 90 and one with 115 names, were

[51] *House Journal*, 1848-49, p. 527; *Senate Journal*, 1848-49, pp. 543-44; *Laws of Indiana*, 1848-49 (local), p. 32; Howard, *History of St. Joseph County*, 1:179.

[52] *Senate Journal*, 1849-50, pp. 125, 136-37, 149-50, 166-67, 299.

[53] *Ibid.*, 403-8, 443-46.

BOUNDARY LEGISLATION

referred to the same committee. A favorable report was made by the majority of the committee four days later. The strong minority report pointed out that the number of remonstrators outnumbered the petitioners, and urged that the "vexed question" be pushed no further. They also brought to light the eminently practical consideration that Delaware County had subscribed for $13,000 worth of stock in the Indianapolis and Bellefontaine Railroad, payment for three-fourths of which was still due from the taxpayers of the county. Should one section of the county be allowed to transfer itself to some adjoining county, any section of Delaware could avoid the tax by a similar process.[54]

Two amendments to the bill were adopted. The first of these, providing that nothing in the act should prevent the treasurer of Delaware County from collecting the railroad tax that might become due from that territory to meet the subscription already made, met considerable objection, but the second, providing that no further legislation be had upon any petition to attach territory to Blackford County until a majority of the citizens living in such territory should have signed the petition, was agreed to unanimously. The amended bill passed the House on January 17, but further action was blocked upon its return to the Senate.[55]

Half a dozen other boundary measures had gone down to defeat during this protracted struggle. One was a House bill, introduced on December 29, 1849, "to straighten the line" between Dearborn and Ohio counties.

The majority of a select committee reported that "common justice, and the interests and necessities" of persons who lived along the dividing line "imperatively" demanded the enactment of the bill. The minority report was more specific in its contentions: first, that the citizens of Dearborn and Ohio counties had not petitioned for

[54] *House Journal*, 1849-50, pp. 571, 579, 685-87.
[55] *Ibid.*, 688-89, 801-2; *Senate Journal*, 1849-50, pp. 737-38, 754-55.

the change outlined in the bill, and that thirty-five hundred voters of Dearborn County opposed it; second, that Ohio County was already indebted to Dearborn for her entire territory and was violating a contract by attempting to extend her jurisdiction beyond Laughery Creek; third, that the form of the bill made it possible for the commissioners of Ohio County to interpret as they liked petitions from the territory in question; and, fourth, that the title of the bill did not express its actual purpose—to detach a large portion of territory from Dearborn County.

In spite of this broadside, the bill passed the House by a vote of 53 to 23. After second reading the Senate placed it in the hands of a select committee. It was returned without recommendation on January 16, the committee admitting their inability to agree upon any report. The troublesome matter was ended for the session by a vote against ordering the bill to third reading.[56]

House bills to attach part of Jackson County to Lawrence, and altering the Fountain-Warren county line both failed in the originating house.[57] Petitions relating to the Clark-Washington line, and a proposed transfer from Morgan to Monroe County were unfavorably received, and a select House committee reported adversely upon a petition from citizens of Posey County asking for the formation of a county to be called Cynthiana.[58]

The Senate in the meantime had tabled a bill creating a new county out of Parke, Putnam, and Montgomery. They also refused to support the proposed transfer of a large part of Owen to Clay.[59]

[56] *House Journal*, 1849-50, pp. 389, 476-77, 673; *Senate Journal*, 1849-50, pp. 657, 658, 665-66.

[57] Jackson-Lawrence, *House Journal*, 1849-50, pp. 340, 414-15, 700; Fountain-Warren, *ibid.*, 558, 737.

[58] Clark-Washington, *ibid.*, 438, 478; Morgan-Monroe, *ibid.*, 657-58, 782; Posey, *ibid.*, 453, 597. The town of Cynthiana, in northeastern Posey County, doubtless hoped to become a county seat.

[59] Parke-Putnam-Montgomery, *Senate Journal*, 1849-50, pp. 305, 377, 410-11, 649; Owen-Clay, *ibid.*, 377, 407, 426, 606.

BOUNDARY LEGISLATION

A solitary boundary measure, authorizing a transfer from St. Joseph to La Porte County, was duly enacted. The law so altered the provisions of an act passed by the preceding Assembly as to deprive St. Joseph County of any voice in the question of cession, while empowering the commissioners of La Porte County to attach the territory in question at their next regular term or subsequently. The law became effective on July 4, 1850, and on July 10 the commissioners made the addition to La Porte.[60]

Starke County, which had been laid out by the act of February 7, 1835, had not heretofore had a separate county organization. This it received by an act of January 15, 1850, effective upon passage.[61]

1850-51. Boundary changes made by the Thirty-fifth Assembly were slight. On February 10, 1851, an act was approved defining the northern boundary of La Porte, Porter, and Lake counties as the north line of the state.[62] Three days later the governor signed a second act transferring half a section of land from Jefferson to Scott County, a change requested by the proprietors of the half section in question.[63] These two counties have made no further changes.

Blackford County continued to work for an enlargement of territory, its representative introducing two bills during the session "describing" the boundaries of Blackford County. From the tone of remonstrances and proposed amendments, it appears that Blackford still hoped to acquire a part of Delaware County. One bill was withdrawn, and the other failed to pass.[64]

A bill "defining" the boundaries of Tipton County was

[60] *Laws of Indiana*, 1849-50 (general), pp. 114-15; Howard, *History of St. Joseph County*, 1:179; *History of La Porte County*, 442-43.

[61] *Laws of Indiana*, 1849-50 (general), pp. 213-14.

[62] *Ibid.*, 1850-51 (general), p. 58.

[63] *Ibid.*

[64] *House Journal*, 1850-51, pp. 184, 268, 578, 608-9, 684; *ibid.*, 555, 586.

recommended for passage in the House, but by a close vote further action was indefinitely postponed. Nothing in the *Journal* indicates the content of the bill.[65]

From citizens of Jackson County came a petition relative to the Jackson-Lawrence boundary, which received an adverse report. The consolidation of La Grange and Noble counties was also petitioned for, but remonstrances from Noble County against either a change of boundary or consolidation with La Grange County resulted in an unfavorable committee report.[66]

[65] *House Journal*, 1850-51, pp. 643, 667-68.

[66] Jackson-Lawrence, *ibid.*, 245, 270; La Grange-Noble, *ibid.*, 636, 694.

CHANGES UNDER THE SECOND CONSTITUTION

WHILE specific county-boundary measures were under discussion in the Assembly of 1850-51, general provisions regulating the formation of new counties and alterations in old ones were being considered in the Constitutional Convention then in session. The convention Committee on County and Township Organization, on October 29, 1850, reported a section providing that the General Assembly should reduce no county to a less extent than four hundred square miles. A minority report, arguing that such a limitation was antirepublican and not properly a constitutional matter, proposed a section which avoided all mention of the area of counties, but provided that no new county be made without the approval of a majority of the voters from the county or counties affected.[1]

No less than eight amendments were offered: the more radical included a provision authorizing the General Assembly to alter county boundaries whenever the public good might demand; a provision that no county contain over four hundred square miles, and that excess territory thus arising be attached to adjacent small counties; a provision that no county be reduced in population, by division of territory, below the representative ratio. The one amendment adopted provided that no county under four hundred square miles in area be further reduced. With this amendment the section was engrossed for third reading.[2] On December 3 the convention voted to recommit the section with instructions to add an exception in cases where two or more counties desired the formation of a new county, and where, after the dimensions were laid off, the proposed change was approved by a majority vote of each county separately. The next day

[1] *Journal of the Convention of the People of the State of Indiana, to Amend the Constitution* . . . *1850*, 151 (Indianapolis, 1851).
[2] *Ibid.*, 314-18.

the vote to recommit was reconsidered and the section passed third reading. It was reported by the Committee on Revision and Arrangement on February 10, 1851, and appeared as section 7, Article 15, of the new Constitution.[3]

Late in January the Committee on Miscellaneous Provisions reported a special article permitting the erection of a new county out of Spencer and Perry, equal territory, as nearly as possible, to be taken from each county, and the proposal submitted to the voters of the counties at a general election. Should a favorable vote result, it would devolve upon the General Assembly to create the new county.

An attempt to amend this proposal to include any two or more contiguous counties having been defeated, a second amendment was offered, permitting the legislature to act upon petitions from Dearborn, Ohio, Switzerland, Delaware, Grant, and Blackford for alteration, whenever a majority of the citizens of the counties affected should agree. An additional section was proposed, allowing the consolidation of Dearborn and Ohio counties upon approval by a majority of the voters in a joint election. Both amendment and new section were tabled. With an amendment limiting the amount of territory to be taken from Perry and Spencer to a third of each, the article was passed on February 1, and on February 9 was reported out of the Committee on Revision and Arrangement. It appeared as the fifteenth section of the Schedule of the 1851 Constitution.[4]

1851-52. During the first half of the divided session of 1851-52, which met from December 1, 1851, to March 10, 1852, and again from April 20 to June 21, 1852, and which was engaged in a revision of the laws, several proposals were made for boundary changes.

The Senate adopted a resolution on December 3, 1851, referring all existing laws relating to state and county

[3] *Journal of the Convention, 1850*, 340-42, 344-45, 984-85.
[4] *Ibid.*, 732, 842-43, 856-57, 876, 978.

BOUNDARY LEGISLATION 105

boundaries to the Committee on Federal Relations, to be checked for confirmation with the new Constitution.[5] The same day a petition was presented in the House asking the attachment of part of Knox County to Pike. The area which asked to be transferred included part of township 1 north, range 8 west, and sections 31 to 36 of township 2 north, in the same range. A bill making the attachment was reported on December 30, but was allowed to die in committee after second reading.[6] On February 12 a bill was introduced attaching to Pike part of Gibson County. The object of the measure was completely reversed when it was referred to a select committee with instructions to divide Pike County between Knox, Gibson, Daviess, and Dubois counties. On recommendation of the committee the bill was tabled on February 20.[7]

Perry and Spencer counties had presented a petition to the House on January 3, 1852, relative to the formation of a new county, but the plan submitted took more territory from Perry than from Spencer County and was declared unconstitutional. On the ninth of March a new petition came before the House, presumably correcting the irregularity of its predecessor. A bill was reported on April 27, submitting the matter of a county formation to the voters of the two counties. It passed the House on May 10, the Senate, in an amended form, on May 13, and was approved on May 27, 1852,[8] but was subsequently voted down locally.[9]

[5] *Senate Journal*, 1851-52, p. 110.
[6] *House Journal*, 1851-52, vol. 1:39, 298, 358-59, 422.
[7] *Ibid.*, 848, 873, 980.
[8] See the record in *ibid.*, vol. 1:344, 879-80; vol. 2:1241, 1368, 1562, 1736-37; *Laws of Indiana*, 1851-52 (special and local), pp. 132-34.
[9] De la Hunt, *Perry County*, 157-58. The election was held on October 11, 1852. Perry County voted 1041 against, to 311 for, the formation. De la Hunt, Thomas J., Pocket Periscope, in *Evansville Courier & Journal*, April 24, 1927. The boundaries laid out for the proposed county were as follows: "Commencing in the county of Perry, at the Ohio river, at a point one mile west

In the face of the new constitutional provision regarding the size of counties, citizens of Delaware, Grant, and Madison petitioned for the formation of a new county. Grant and Madison each contained more than four hundred square miles of territory, but Delaware had but 392 square miles, and the petition was tabled.[10]

April 20, 1852, the first day of the second half of the session, saw the introduction of a general act defining the boundaries of all counties. The House passed the bill in its original form on May 12; the Senate amended the sections dealing with Blackford, Floyd, and Harrison, and passed the bill on May 25. It was approved as passed by the Senate, on June 7. Two changes were incorporated in the measure. One made a slight alteration, a matter of a fractional section, between Floyd and Harrison counties. The second alteration revised the Gibson-Warrick common boundary to its present form.[11] Floyd, Harrison, Gibson, and Warrick have made no alterations since that date.

1853. Gibson County made a strenuous effort to regain the territory lost to Warrick by the act of June 7, 1852. Warrick County countered with a proposal to attach four more sections from Gibson. The House bill to "more

of the line dividing ranges two and three west, being the southwest corner of fractional section thirteen (13), in township number seven (7,) of range three (3) west; thence running due north with the section line, until said line strikes the township line dividing townships number four (4) and five (5;) thence west with said township line one mile; thence due north until it strikes the line dividing the counties of Perry and Dubois; thence due west with said county line to the north west corner of Perry county; thence south with the line dividing Perry and Dubois counties, three miles to the north east corner of the county of Spencer; thence west with the line dividing Spencer and Dubois counties, until said line strikes the range line dividing ranges number four (4) and five (5;) thence south with said range line to the Ohio river; thence up the Ohio river . . . to the place of beginning." *Laws of Indiana,* 1851-52 (local), p. 133.

[10] *Senate Journal,* 1851-52, pp. 215, 482.

[11] See maps, Floyd County IV, Gibson County XIII, Warrick County X.

BOUNDARY LEGISLATION 107

particularly define the boundary line between the counties of Gibson and Warrick" which had been introduced on January 24, was at this point referred to a select committee. An amendment reported by the committee reassigned to Gibson twelve of the disputed twenty-four sections. This amendment was adopted and the bill was engrossed for third reading, but on three successive trials failed to pass.[12] A verbal error in the description of the Warrick-Spencer boundary was corrected by a law of March 1, 1853, which passed without objection.[13]

Certain citizens of Knox County renewed their plea for attachment to Pike. Their petition received an unfavorable report on January 25, but the same day a bill was introduced on leave, to attach township 1 north, range 8 west, and sections 31 to 36 in town 2 north, range 8 west, to Pike County. It passed the House by a vote of 53 to 29, and was received by the Senate on February 1. The committee to which it was referred made a detailed report on February 22, advising indefinite postponement of the bill. The situation was similar to that which had arisen between Delaware and Blackford counties in 1849-50. Knox County had subscribed heavily to the Ohio and Mississippi Railroad Company; to reduce her taxable property by thousands of acres before the obligation could be discharged would put an unjust burden upon the remaining territory. Nor did the committee feel that the advantage to the petitioners of having their county seat at Petersburg instead of at Vincennes was proportionate to the lesser distance they would have to travel, for an intervening river and chain of hills discounted the shortening of mileage. There was, furthermore, no guarantee that the county seat of Pike County would not be moved to a point as distant as Vincennes.[14] In spite of this report the bill was engrossed

[12] *House Journal*, 1853, pp. 230, 254-55, 296-97, 324, 462, 597-98.
[13] *Laws of Indiana*, 1853, p. 15.
[14] That same day a bill was introduced in the House to relocate the county seat of Pike County. *House Journal*, 1853, p. 691.

for third reading, but on February 25 it was defeated by a vote of 18 to 20.[15]

Starke County made an effort in 1853 to secure the return of the large tract of land north and west of the Kankakee River which had been transferred to La Porte County in 1842. Because the transfer had been made before the organization of Starke County, and because Starke contained less than four hundred square miles and La Porte considerably more, the bill introduced on February 22 by Brown, of Starke, received a favorable committee report. Representative Walker, of La Porte, immediately moved that bill and report be tabled until a petition be received on the subject, and this motion was carried by a vote of 41 to 39.[16]

A House bill "to provide for a more uniform mode of changing county boundaries" was presented in February, amended on second reading, and defeated on March 1. The provisions of the bill are not indicated.[17] On March 1 a Senate bill was introduced, amending the county-boundary act of 1852. It was allowed to die after first reading in the House.[18]

1855. First to appear among pleas for boundary changes in the General Assembly of 1855 was a petition from citizens of Jasper and Pulaski asking for the formation of a new county along the Kankakee. Its presentation on January 11, 1855, was followed by remonstrances from Pulaski, La Porte, and Starke counties, indicating that the two last-named counties were concerned as well as Pulaski and Jasper in a possible cession of territory. The Senate tabled the petition on February 26.[19]

Gibson County was not yet content to accept her recent loss of territory to Warrick, and on January 22 a bill was

[15] *House Journal*, 1853, pp. 263, 271, 320; *Senate Journal*, 1853, pp. 222-23, 419-20, 492.
[16] *House Journal*, 1853, pp. 691, 725, 845.
[17] *Ibid.*, 443, 805-6, 853.
[18] *Senate Journal*, 1853, pp. 542-43, 547-48; *House Journal*, 1853, p. 901.
[19] *Senate Journal*, 1855, pp. 68, 193, 293, 497, 562.

BOUNDARY LEGISLATION   109

introduced to recover possession of the contested area. Petitions appeared for and against the bill, which remained in committee from January 29 until February 28. A favorable committee report of that date attempted to show that the change brought about in 1852 had been unintentional, but the House tabled the bill without discussion. Citizens from Pike County had meantime asked to be attached to Warrick. Their petition was denied on the ground of unconstitutionality, for Pike County contained only 338 square miles.[20]

Two other boundary bills were disposed of in February. The Senate tabled a measure making an unspecified change in the line between Decatur and Shelby, and the House killed a bill declaring certain statutes a misprint and attaching territory to Fulton County.[21]

1857. No boundary change was contemplated in the House bill introduced on January 16, 1857, to amend the 1852 description of Harrison County boundaries. The bill was purely corrective and passed the House by a unanimous vote on February 14. In the Senate it was ordered to third reading on March 3, but did not again appear.[22]

The Gibson-Warrick controversy came before the House in a bill to more particularly define their common boundary, but was dismissed with an unfavorable committee report.[23]

Of real importance in the history of county-boundary legislation was an act "to authorize the formation of new counties, and to change county boundaries." Its purpose was to expedite county formations and transfers by taking the authority to make such changes out of the hands of the General Assembly and delegating it to the voters in the territory concerned. Boards of county commis-

[20] Gibson-Warrick, *House Journal*, 1855, pp. 195, 275, 420, 609, 717-18; Pike-Warrick, *ibid.*, 609, 659.
[21] Decatur-Shelby, *Senate Journal*, 1855, p. 617; Fulton, *House Journal*, 1855, p. 709.
[22] *Ibid.*, 1857, pp. 139-40, 568; *Senate Journal*, 1857, p. 625.
[23] *House Journal*, 1857, pp. 200, 336, 1067.

sioners and commissioners to be appointed by them were intrusted with the technicalities of records and boundaries. The bill was not introduced until February 23, and was hurried through both branches of the legislature without amendment, passing the House on March 5 by a vote of 58 to 13, and the Senate on March 7 by a vote of 28 to 6. It reiterated the constitutional provisos against reducing any county below four hundred square miles, or further reducing any county already below that area. It carried an additional provision that any new county must contain four hundred square miles. This limitation was certain to bring opposition; so were carelessly drawn sections of the act. It failed to provide any machinery for organizing counties formed under its provisions, and it gave counties affected by new formations or by transfers no chance to vote as a whole. Full power of decision rested with the area desiring organization or transfer.[24]

[24] Because of the objections to the act, and because the constitutionality of both first and second sections was later attacked, the provisions of the two sections are quoted in full:

"*Be it enacted* . . . That whenever a majority of the legal vote[r]s to be effected thereby in any district embracing an area of not less than four hundred square miles, shall desire the formation of a new county, and by written request, petition the board of commissioners of the several counties to be effected by the formation of said new county, and shall designate . . . the name of said new county, the boundaries of such proposed county—and which shall be in the form of a square as nearly as the character of the territory . . . will permit—and which petition, and the qualifications of the signers thereto, shall be verified by the oath or oaths of competent witnesses, the said boards shall appoint each, a committee of three resident freeholders in each county of the district embraced in such change, who shall form a board of commissioners to lay off and establish the boundaries of the proposed county, conforming to the lines and boundaries named in said petition, and shall report the same to such boards of commissioners of the several counties affected . . . at the next or some subsequent session, and upon said report being made, the boards of commissioners of the said several counties . . . shall enter upon their order books respectively, an order establishing the boundaries of said new county, shall be by them filed in the office of the Secretary of

Immediately after the passage of the law of March 7, citizens living in the western half of Jasper County made an attempt to secure the formation of a new county under its provisions. They were spurred to action by fear that the northern part of the county, along the Kankakee, might secure a transfer to Starke County, thereby reducing the chances for further division.

A petition for division was circulated and presented at the September meeting of the county board of commissioners; the rival faction petitioned at the same time that the five northeastern townships be conveyed to Starke

State; a majority of the commissioners so appointed as aforesaid, shall constitute a quorum to transact business . . . under this act; *Providing, however,* That no county now organized, which shall contain a greater area than four hundred square miles, shall be reduced below the area of four hundred square miles, and no county now organized, which shall contain an area of less than four hundred square miles, shall be further reduced. And upon the establishment of the boundaries of said new county, the Governor shall appoint three commissioners to locate a county seat . . . and from the time said boundaries are established, said new county shall be, to all intents and purposes, an organized county, with all the rights and privileges, that . . . appertain to organized counties.

SEC. 2. Whenever a majority of the legal voters, who shall reside in the territory whose jurisdiction it is proposed to be changed, shall desire to change the boundaries of two or more organized counties that may lay contiguous, and shall petition the board of commissioners of the said counties whose boundaries it is proposed to change, by a written petition verified by the oath or oaths of competent witnesses, as to the residence and qualification of such petitioners, designating in such petition the line or lines of said proposed change, the said boards shall file said petitions, and continue the same until the next regular meeting of said boards, at which time they shall enter upon their order books respectively, an order changing the boundaries of their several counties so as to conform to the line or lines designated in said petition, and shall forward to the Secretary of State a copy of such order . . .; and such change shall take effect from the date of such order: *Provided,* In any such change, no organized county that shall have an area of over four hundred square miles, shall be reduced below that quantity, and no organized county that shall have an area of less than four hundred square miles, shall be further reduced in area." *Laws of Indiana,* 1857, pp. 25-27.

County: this petition was approved, while the petition for division was dismissed on the ground that signatures had been obtained for it before the law of March 7 took effect. In a desperate effort to push the organization through, the petitioners scoured the county that night and the next day, and in twenty-four hours had another petition ready, but when they came to present it, they found an insufficient number of commissioners to act upon it.

At the December term of court the position of the two factions was reversed. The petitioners for a western county succeeded in obtaining the approval of the Board of Commissioners, while the northern group were doubly defeated in having their remonstrance against the new county rejected, and in having their own petition for attachment to Starke County refused by the commissioners of that county. They made another attempt to prevent the erection of Newton County, appealing the question to the circuit court; here the decision of the commissioners was overruled, but upon appeal to the Supreme Court, the legality of the erection of Newton County was upheld. The order defining the boundaries of Newton County was recorded on December 8, 1859.[25]

1858. Others than disgruntled citizens of Jasper County joined battle against the county-boundary measure of 1857. On the third day of the special session of 1858, a Senate bill was presented to repeal the act. A week later, November 29, the House voiced its opposition in a bill to repeal the second section, which dealt with transfers of territory between counties. An amendatory

[25] Commissioners' Records, Jasper and Starke counties, September and December terms, 1857. The difficulties which beset the petitioners are sympathetically described by one of their number, John Ade, in his history, *Newton County* . . ., 57-61 (Indianapolis, 1911). For the decision of the Supreme Court, see 13 *Indiana*, 235-45. The court held that the legislature might delegate the power to organize counties, and that a single county containing the requisite area, might be divided under the act, by its own board of commissioners, acting through a single committee of freeholders.

House bill was introduced on November 30. The bill repealing section 2 passed the House by a vote of 54 to 30 on December 9. Its passage was recommended by a Senate committee but bill and report were tabled the same day. Neither of the other bills passed its originating house.[26]

1859. No sooner had the Fortieth General Assembly completed its organization than a bombardment of the 1857 boundary act was begun. House and Senate together produced six different bills, all aimed at amending, repealing, or supplementing one or the other of its main provisions. In the order of their appearance they were: House Bill No. 6, introduced January 10, to amend the second section; Senate Bill No. 54, January 15, to amend the act; House Bill No. 96, January 22, to repeal the second section; Senate Bill No. 208, February 12, to amend the first section; House Bill No. 257, February 12, to provide for organization, representation, and administration of justice in counties formed under provisions of section one; Senate Bill No. 249, February 24, to amend and supplement section one.[27] As if this situation were not sufficiently confusing, complications were multiplied by extensive amendments to several of the bills. As one representative remarked in the midst of heated argument: "The title of the statute of 1857 should have been, 'An act for the purpose of getting people by the ears.'"[28]

Senate Bill No. 208, considerably amended, was the

[26] Senate Bill No. 2, *Senate Journal*, 1858 (special session), pp. 17, 35, 73; House Bill No. 11, *House Journal*, 1858 (special session), pp. 64, 135, 155; *Senate Journal*, 1858 (special session), pp. 213, 294; House Bill No. 14, *House Journal*, 1858 (special session), pp. 76, 86-87, 170.

[27] House Bill No. 6, *House Journal*, 1859, pp. 35-36, 449-52, 727-28; Senate Bill No. 54, *Senate Journal*, 1859, pp. 154, 245; House Bill No. 96, *House Journal*, 1859, pp. 195, 233; Senate Bill No. 208, *Senate Journal*, 1859, pp. 480, 693, 880; *House Journal*, 1859, pp. 979, 1024-25, 1031, 1062, 1083-84; House Bill No. 257, *ibid.*, 529, 544, 790, 885-87, 999, 1037; Senate Bill No. 249, *Senate Journal*, 1859, pp. 701-2, 847-48, 870-71, 932.

[28] *Brevier Legislative Reports*, 1859, p. 156.

only measure to become law. It decreased the necessary content of a new county to two hundred square miles, and it set up a procedure for the organization and representation of newly formed counties.[29] One important amendment which was ordered to be made did not appear in the printed act. It was intended to require the consent of a majority of the qualified voters in the county or counties affected to secure the formation of a new county.[30]

The section relating to transfers of territory between counties remained unchanged, although there was strong feeling against it in the counties which were likely to be exploited under its provisions. A committee report summarizes the objections to it:

"The undersigned has not been able to find any law, on any statute book, that furnishes the same facility for a portion of a county, to transfer itself without notice, and without having ascertained the wish of the voters of one or the other of the counties to be affected thereby, severing corporations with the wish only of the minority expressed, diminishing or increasing the jurisdiction of county officers, making counties liable to be added to or diminished to suit the whims of politicians or others, destroying vested rights and deranging land titles."[31]

While the fate of the 1857 law and its amendatory offspring was still in question, proceedings under its provisions were instituted by several dissatisfied border districts desiring transfer from one county to another. The northeast corner of Clinton County, Honey Creek Township, was the first tract to change its allegiance. Two petitions for attachment to Howard County were disapproved, one because it divided school districts, the other because it included too much territory. The third petition was laid before the county commissioners at their December session, 1858, and was granted at the March

[29] *Laws of Indiana*, 1859, pp. 60-63.
[30] See *post*, 116, 117.
[31] *House Journal*, 1859, pp. 449-52.

BOUNDARY LEGISLATION

session, 1859. The change was recorded by the commissioners of Howard County on March 3, and a copy of the order directed to be sent to the secretary of state.[32]

The next transfer, between Jackson and Lawrence counties, became a test case on the validity of the second section of the 1857 law. A petition with fifty-three signatures was put before the commissioners of Lawrence County at their March term, 1859, asking the attachment of part of Jackson County. A remonstrance was also filed. On June 8, 1859, the change was ordered, but an appeal was taken to the circuit court. The court held that the act of 1857 was unconstitutional and the proceedings for transfer consequently void. Another appeal brought the case before the Indiana Supreme Court at its May term, 1860, and there the validity of the law was upheld as it had been in the suit growing out of the formation of Newton County.[33]

The third transfer made in 1859 attached to Whitley County twelve sections from the south side of Washington Township, Noble County. The change was proposed at the March term of the Board of County Commissioners and recorded on June 11. Whitley and Noble have made no further boundary alterations.[34] Clinton, Howard, Jackson, and Lawrence also reached their present form by the territorial readjustments of that year. Newton and Jasper have made no alteration except in connection with the dredging operations along the Kankakee River.[35]

Sullivan County had no difficulty in securing the passage of an act correcting an error in the description of

[32] Woody, H. G., history of "Honey Creek Township," in *Combination Atlas Map of Howard County, Indiana* (Kingman Brothers, 1877); Record of Howard County Commissioners, 3:33. See maps, Clinton County II, and Howard County III.

[33] Commissioners' Record E, 174-75, Lawrence County; 14 *Indiana*, 299-300. See maps, Jackson County XI, and Lawrence County III.

[34] Commissioners' Record, Whitley County. See maps, Whitley County II, and Noble County II.

[35] For an account of Newton's formation from Jasper, see above, pp. 111-12.

her boundaries as given in the county-boundary act of June 7, 1852.[36]

From Spencer and Perry counties came a petition asking for the formation of a new county from their contiguous territory. Apparently the proposal was made more as a gesture against the town of Cannelton, in a three-sided county-seat war with Rome and Troy, than with any hope of securing a new county. The petition was referred to a select committee but was not reported out.[37]

1861. By 1861 dissatisfaction with the new system of county formations and transfers reached a high point. With the constitutionality of the unpopular law of 1857 attested by two Supreme Court decisions, the larger counties were forced to face the likelihood of losing their border townships without so much as an opportunity to protest. Any hope they may have held that the amendatory law of 1859 would eliminate this particular objection faded when the printed act appeared, minus the expected amendment on this point. Accusations of fraud were made freely in the House,[38] and petitions for repeal of both laws poured in throughout the session.[39] Legislation on the subject became almost as involved and even more excited in tone than it had been in 1859. Senate Bill No. 6, introduced on January 12, to repeal the act of March 7, 1857, was tabled on third reading. Senate Bill No. 43, presented on January 18, proposed a new law and the repeal of all conflicting acts. An attempt to exclude from the provisions of the bill any proceedings already pending, resulted in a wrangle which obstructed

[36] *Laws of Indiana*, 1859, p. 43.

[37] De la Hunt, *Perry County*, 161; *House Journal*, 1859, p. 452.

[38] See *ante*, 114; *Senate Journal*, 1861, p. 79; *Brevier Legislative Reports*, 1861, pp. 106 ff., 176-78, 224-25, 229.

[39] Clinton, Daviess, Dubois, Lake, Lawrence, Montgomery, Orange, Parke, Porter, Pulaski, Ripley, St. Joseph, and Sullivan, all large counties, petitioned for repeal of the act. Warren County, with an area of 368 square miles, and Starke, with but 305 square miles, were also represented. Various petitions came in from unspecified districts.

BOUNDARY LEGISLATION 117

action until February 26, when Senate Bill No. 43 and its amendment were tabled. Senate Bill No. 56, introduced on January 18 to amend the act of 1857 "so as to allow new counties to be formed out of territories of less than four hundred square miles, and prescribing how the number of qualified voters shall be ascertained," passed the Senate on February 5 by a vote of 40 to 1. On second reading in the House it was referred to the Committee on County and Township Business, which was already considering House Bill No. 39 on the same subject. Senate Bill No. 84, to amend section 2 of the act of 1857, was not introduced until January 25, and did not pass the Senate.[40]

House Bill No. 39, mentioned above, had been before the House since January 15. Like the amendatory law of 1859 it put the territorial requirement for a new county at two hundred square miles. It eliminated two of the main objections to its predecessors by requiring public notice to be given before the presentation of petitions to county boards, and by making the outcome of movements for county formation dependent upon a majority vote taken in the counties affected. Practically the same procedure was outlined for transfers of territory. Both the act of March 7, 1857, and the act of March 5, 1859, were repealed.

These two last-named measures were not without their adherents. More than one ambitious town had seen in their provisions the path to position as a county seat, and had set about building up a new county unit of which it might be the center. Michigan City wanted the formation of a new county from La Porte and Porter, though to secure the necessary mileage it would have to include the part of Lake Michigan in Porter County, and in spite of the fact that the formation would cut off four rail-

[40] Senate Bill No. 6, *Senate Journal*, 1861, pp. 31, 46, 78-80, 142; Senate Bill No. 43, *ibid.*, 110-11, 273-75, 283-87, 621; Senate Bill No. 56, *ibid.*, 113, 154, 268; *House Journal*, 1861, pp. 399, 600-1, 1041; Senate Bill No. 84, *Senate Journal*, 1861, pp. 163, 312.

roads from Porter County.[41] On the other side of La Porte County other interests were working for the formation of a county out of La Porte and St. Joseph, with New Carlisle as the county seat.[42] Putnam, Montgomery, and Parke counties were threatened with the loss of sufficient territory for a new county to be called Bourbon.[43]

In addition to county formation projects, numerous transfers were under consideration. Whitley County wanted part of Allen, and charged bluntly that Allen County had managed her finances badly and that the section of territory in question was eager for the transfer.[44] Elkhart cast a greedy eye on one of Starke's best townships; Bartholomew faced a possible division; and Martin and Daviess were at law on the question of a two-mile wide strip between them.[45]

In some of these cases proceedings had been instituted under the provisions of the 1857 or 1859 acts. Their promoters, naturally enough, objected heartily to the passage of House Bill No. 39, which would certainly delay and probably prevent the carrying out of their plans. An attempt was made, first in the House and later in the Senate, to add a provision allowing all such initiated movements to be carried through.[46] This was finally modified by a Senate amendment providing that nothing in the law "be so construed as to affect any county now fully organized under existing laws." Although the wording of this proviso is open to various interpretations, it is likely that it was meant to ratify the organization of Newton County. On February 26 the bill passed the Senate by a vote of 73 to 14; two days later the House concurred in the Senate amendment, and on March 1,

[41] *Brevier Legislative Reports*, 1861, p. 107.
[42] *Ibid.*, 178.
[43] *Ibid.*, 107, 177.
[44] *Ibid.*, 107.
[45] *Ibid.*, 108.
[46] A specific attempt was made on behalf of the movement for "Bourbon" County. For thirty-five years this district had struggled for organization. *House Journal*, 1861, p. 688.

BOUNDARY LEGISLATION   119

1861, the act was approved. An emergency clause made it effective from passage.[47]

Several petitions for boundary changes were made directly to the legislature during the session of 1861. Part of Franklin Township of Kosciusko County asked attachment to Fulton, and a change between Dubois and Orange was also proposed. No action was taken on the petitions.[48]

Morgan and Putnam counties succeeded in effecting a change by the passage of an act amending sections 54 and 66 of the county-boundary law of June 7, 1852. The bill was not introduced until March 5. Under suspension of the rules it was passed in the Senate the same day, and it emerged from the House on March 9. It gave Putnam County the triangular tract along Mill Creek in range 2 west, completing the development of that county to date.[49]

[47] *Ibid.*, 78, 191-93, 340-42, 467-68, 687-88, 689; *Laws of Indiana*, 1861, pp. 99-103. A part of section 1 runs as follows: "Whenever a majority of the legal voters to be effected thereby in any district embracing an area of not less than 200 square miles shall desire the formation of a new county, and after having given twenty days' notice, by publication by three insertions in some weekly newspaper, published in each county affected thereby, if any there be, or by one notice posted in each of all the townships of such counties to be affected thereby, such notices to be verified . . ., may petition the board of commissioners of the several counties to be affected by the formation of said new county." Upon the report of a board appointed to lay off county boundaries, the boards of commissioners of the several counties affected "shall order the question of such formation to be submitted to the legal voters of the several counties to be affected thereby at their next general election, and notice thereof shall be included in the notice of said election . . ., and if . . . the voters of the said counties shall by a majority of the votes cast in each severally, decide in favor of such formation of such new county, the boards of county commissioners shall enter upon their order books respectively an order establishing the boundaries of said new county . . . and shall forward to the Secretary of State a copy of such orders to be by him filed in his office." *Laws of Indiana*, 1861, pp. 99-100.

[48] Kosciusko-Fulton, *Senate Journal*, 1861, p. 550; Orange-Dubois, *House Journal*, 1861, pp. 170, 455.

[49] *Senate Journal*, 1861, pp. 796, 799-800, 971; *Laws of Indiana*, 1861, pp. 98-99. See maps, Morgan County II, Putnam County V.

The right of part of a county to secede from the parent county was not the only local secession issue before the legislators. At a so-called "Union" meeting held at Cannelton, Perry County, on January 1, 1861, the following resolution was adopted by a vote of 99 to 55:

"Resolved, That if no concessions and compromises can be obtained and a disunion shall be unfortunately made between the Northern and Southern States, then the commercial, manufacturing and agricultural interests of the people of this county require us to say that we can not consent that the Ohio River shall be the boundary line of the contending nations, and we earnestly desire that if a line is to be drawn between the North and the South that line shall be found north of us."

An editorial in the *Indianapolis Daily Journal* for January 9, 1861, scored this action of the "Democracy of Perry County," and quoted a letter written at Cannelton on January 2, protesting that the meeting did not show the true feeling of the county, but that the passage of the resolution had been forced through by coal and cotton interests controlled by southern men. The implication of this and a subsequent editorial was that not only Perry but other southern counties considered the possibility of joining themselves to Kentucky, in the event of a division between North and South.

There was no legislation on the matter, but it was mentioned in legislative debate more than once during the session.[50]

1863. The law of March 1, 1861, had the immediate effect of decreasing the amount of boundary legislation. In 1863 it was confined to one unsuccessful bill. Blackford asked an amendment to her boundaries as given in the *Revised Statutes* of 1852, to secure six border sections in township 24 north, range 12 east. Her claim was based on the discrepancy between the formation law of February 15, 1838, and the law of 1852, and on the fact

[50] De la Hunt, *Perry County*, pp. 207-9; *Indianapolis Daily Journal*, 1861, January 9, 11; *Brevier Legislative Reports*, 1861, pp. 5-6, 107.

BOUNDARY LEGISLATION 121

that the six sections in question had "been taxed by and considered a portion of the county of Blackford, a greater part of the time since the passage of the said act in 1852."

Promoters of the bill ignored the incorrect and ambiguous wording of the formation law, and the fact that the description of 1852 is precisely like that of 1843. The bill passed the Senate by a vote of 31 to 16, but was received in the House late in the session, and was not acted upon.[51]

1865. Blackford's appeal for a boundary alteration came before the succeeding General Assembly as Senate Bill No. 140. Although a committee report favoring its passage was concurred in, no further action was taken during the regular session. At the special session which began in November, 1865, the bill passed the Senate by an uncontested vote on December 18. It was pushed to third reading in the House but failed to pass by a vote of 34 to 57.[52]

During the regular session of 1865, a Senate bill was introduced to amend the descriptions of Jackson and Lawrence counties as given in the county-boundary law of 1852, incorporating the change made by commissioners' report in 1859. The bill passed the Senate with but one dissenting vote. No action was then taken on it in the House, but it was revived during the special session and referred to the Committee on Rights and Privileges where it remained during the rest of the session.[53]

[51] See text with map, Blackford County; *Laws of Indiana*, 1837-38 (local), pp. 290-91; 1838-39 (general), p. 65; *Revised Statutes*, 1842-43, p. 86; 1852, vol. 1: 170; *Senate Journal*, 1863, pp. 183-84, 530-31, 545-46, 606; *House Journal*, 1863, p. 687. The irregularity of the surveys in range 12 west probably had something to do with the ambiguous wording of the original law. Townships 22 and 23, range 12, are but five sections wide, while township 24 is the regulation width of six sections.

[52] *Senate Journal*, 1865 (regular session), pp. 271, 287, 405; (special session), 92, 114, 165, 246, 477; *House Journal*, 1865 (special session), pp. 584, 599, 681-83.

[53] *Senate Journal*, 1865 (regular session), pp. 204, 285, 345, 399; *House Journal*, 1865 (regular session), p. 544; (special session), **pp. 157, 741; original Senate Bill No. 127.**

1867. No changes were made during the legislative session of 1867, although there were two attempts to amend the county-boundary law of 1852. The introduction of Senate Bill No. 198, proposing an exchange of territory between Warren and Fountain counties, was followed by an outbreak of protests from Warren, the last of which represented one thousand voters. In spite of this opposition, the bill passed the Senate by a vote of 26 to 11. It was less fortunate in the House, remaining in the hands of the Judiciary Committee until the last day of the session.[54]

The second proposed alteration concerned the town of St. Paul, divided by the Shelby-Decatur boundary line, and consequently unable to establish satisfactory municipal and school systems. It was proposed to extend the boundaries of Decatur County to include the entire town. In an unfavorable report of March 6, the committee dwelt at some length on the usurpation of legislative time caused by attempts to secure boundary changes by legislation instead of under the procedure set up for that specific purpose. A minority report favoring the change was tabled.[55]

1868. Morgan County in 1868 transferred to Hendricks County a strip of territory along her north boundary, east of Mill Creek and west of the second principal

[54] *Senate Journal*, 1867, pp. 591, 609, 620, 625, 726, 771-72; *House Journal*, 1867, pp. 1062, 1198. It was proposed to run the line between the counties from the half-mile stake on the west line of fractional section 27, township 21 north, range 10 west, east with the middle line of that tier of sections across the Wabash River to the half-mile stake on the east boundary of section 29, range 7 west; thence north on the section line to the half-mile stake on the east line of section 20, township 21 north, range 7 west; east through sections 21 and 22 to the half-mile stake in the east boundary of section 22; north with the east boundary of section 22, 157⅓ rods; east, parallel with the north boundary of section 23 to the line running north through the center of section 23 and north with the surveys to the center of section 14; east on the middle line of that tier of sections to the line running through the center of range 6 west. Original Senate Bill No. 198.

[55] *House Journal*, 1867, pp. 822, 995-96.

BOUNDARY LEGISLATION 123

meridian. Some twenty-one sections were involved. The change was made by the boards of commissioners of the two counties, at their March and June terms, 1868, apparently according to the procedure laid down in the law of March 7, 1857, instead of under the law of March 1, 1861. The petition asking for the transfer makes this plain: "your petitioners respectfully ask your honors to . . . make such orders in the premises as may be right and proper according to the Act of the 7th of March 1857, and the law in such case made and provided." The order for the boundary change reads: "the Board being satisfied of the sufficiency of said petition, and that it is signed by a majority of the legal voters living in the territory, proposed to be annexed to the County of Hendricks, and the facts as required by law being verified by the affidavit of competent witnesses, the Board orders that the territory described . . . be . . . attached to the County of Hendricks." There is nothing in the record to indicate that the transfer was voted on by the two counties, as required in the law of 1861.[56] No evidence has appeared, however, to show that the legality of this procedure has ever been questioned.[57]

1869-73. In the adjoining areas of Warren and Fountain counties, the desire persisted for a rearrangement of their common boundary. In spite of previous failures a bill was introduced in 1869, asking that the question be submitted to the voters of the two counties, but following an unfavorable committee report the bill was tabled. A House bill with the same title was introduced late in the session of 1873, but was withdrawn from the files four days later.[58] Neither Fountain nor Warren contained four

[56] Commissioners' Record No. 10, pp. 250, 251, 252, and 336, Auditor's office, Morgan County.

[57] Mr. A. M. Smith, who lived in Adams Township at the time, says the transfer was not voted on at a general election, and that he has never heard any talk of its possible illegality. Letter of J. W. Clark, auditor of Morgan County, September 25, 1930.

[58] *Senate Journal*, 1869, pp. 535, 603; *House Journal*, 1873, pp. 704, 828.

hundred square miles, and any change lessening the area of either would have been illegal.

In 1871 Starke County for the second time petitioned for the restoration of her original northern and western boundary, and secured the introduction of a bill making the alteration. The movement was begun late in the session, however, and the measure did not come up for second reading.[59]

Clark and Washington counties, in 1871, began campaigning for the correction and redefining of their common boundary. House Bill No. 358 of that year did not progress beyond first reading. During the special session of 1872, Senate Bill No. 50, for the same purpose, was recommended for enactment, but did not pass before the end of the session. This bill, which defined the boundary, was brought up early in the session of 1873 and passed without amendment, receiving the governor's approval on March 7, 1873.[60]

Jennings County, in 1873, made a movement to amend its boundaries as stated in the county-boundary law of 1852, to include several fractional sections north of the Muscatatuck River in township 4 north, range 8 east. Passage of the bill was recommended, but no further action was taken.[61]

1875. The General Assembly of 1875, in a law of March 10, once more reconstructed the machinery for making county-boundary changes.[62] The new act was

[59] *House Journal*, 1871, pp. 845, 958; original House Bill No. 366. Starke County had made a similar attempt at the session of 1853.

[60] *Laws of Indiana*, 1873, pp. 105-6. See maps, Clark County XVI, and Washington County IX.

[61] *Senate Journal*, 1873, pp. 748, 875. Beginning on the old boundary, where the line dividing ranges 7 and 8 crossed the Muscatatuck, the proposed boundary was to continue easterly with the river to a point in the south line of the northeast quarter of section 4, township 4 north, range 8 east, where the river intersected the Jennings boundary, then continue on the old line. Original Senate Bill No. 338.

[62] *Laws of Indiana*, 1875, pp. 9-12. Senate Bill No. 273 on the same subject was introduced on February 8, 1875, but failed to pass. *Senate Journal*, 1875, pt. 1:448, 506.

considerably more specific in its requirements than its predecessor. It permitted the presentation of a petition for change signed by fifty resident freeholders of the territory concerned, required boards of commissioners to submit the question to the interested counties at a special election within thirty days from their first meeting after presentation of the petition, and put a limit on the time for making returns and ordering the change if favorably voted upon. As a safeguard against immediate renewal of unsuccessful pleas, the act provided that a vote should not be taken under its provision oftener than once in three years. Section 4 of the act was intended to do away with transfers actuated by the tax-dodging impulse. Any district transferred from one county to another was required to continue contributing its share to the payment of such indebtedness in the parent county as existed at the time of the transfer.[63]

Scott County presented the only bill of this session asking a specific boundary change. She hoped to attach all that part of Washington County east and north of a line beginning on the Muscatatuck at the center section line of range 5 east, running thence south to the line between townships 2 and 3 north, and east with that line

[63] Section 4 of the act reads:
"It shall be the duty of the Board or Boards of Commissioners of the said county or counties, if any indebtedness exist in either or both, that the said boards shall levy, from year to year, a tax upon the detached territory, by such a per centage upon all the taxable property within such district so detached, as shall be necessary to liquidate and pay the indebtedness of the county, from which such territory was detached, until the said indebtedness be fully paid, which rate per cent. shall not be in excess of that levied upon the county so indebted, and when such assessment shall be made by said boards, it shall be the duty of the Auditor of each of said counties to certify the rate per cent. so levied, to the Auditor of the county to which said territory was attached, which Auditor shall place such rate per cent. on the tax duplicate of said county, and it shall be the duty of the Treasurer of said county to collect the same, and upon demand of the Treasurer of the proper county, he shall pay over the same as other monies are paid out." *Laws of Indiana*, 1875, p. 11.

to the Scott boundary. This would have given her a tract of land four miles wide and from six to eight miles long. The bill did not pass, however.[64]

1877-85. Two county-boundary bills, one specific in purpose, and one of a general nature, were introduced during the session of 1877. Both received unfavorable committee reports and failed to pass. The first proposed the amendment of the Jennings boundary which had failed of adoption in the session of 1873; the second proposed an amendment to that part of the general act of March 1, 1861, relating to transfers of territory from one county to another.[65]

During the succeeding session, 1879, still less attention was devoted to county boundaries. The only bill on the subject was framed for the benefit of the town of Wolcottville, which extended across the county line dividing La Grange from Noble County. The proposal to include the town in La Grange County by annexing the northwest quarter of section 3, township 35 north, range 10 east, was not carried through.[66]

In 1883, for the first time since 1865, Blackford County attempted to enlarge her territory. Early in the session her representative introduced a House bill to amend section 1 and repeal section 2 of the county-boundary law of March 10, 1875. The amendment would have restored the process of territorial transfers laid down in the law of March 7, 1857, under which Blackford's chances of making an attachment would have been greatly increased. The bill carried an emergency clause. On second reading it was referred to the Committee on County and Township Business, and did not reappear during the session.[67] On February 8 and February 19 bills were introduced in

[64] *Senate Journal*, 1875, pt. 1:447-48, 498, 554; original Senate Bill No. 269.

[65] *House Journal*, 1877, pp. 447-48, 809; original House Bill No. 445; *House Journal*, 1877, pp. 426, 474, 748-49.

[66] *Ibid.*, 1879, pp. 662, 667, 770; original House Bill No. 616.

[67] *House Journal*, 1883, pp. 203, 251; original House Bill No. 210.

the Senate and House respectively to amend the boundaries of Blackford, Grant, Scott, and Washington. Blackford was to have the easternmost tier of sections from Grant; Scott would have taken from Washington a tract of territory three sections wide, bounded on the north by the Muscatatuck River, and on the south by a line running east from the southwest corner of section 2, township 2 north, range 5 east to the old Scott boundary. There is no record of any action on either of these bills.[68]

Scott County repeated her request for an addition from Washington at the next session—1885—limiting the area this time to the three easternmost tiers of sections in Washington County, between the Muscatatuck River and the line dividing townships 2 and 3 north.[69] The bill was returned to the House without recommendation and no further action was taken.

1887-97. On January 13, 1887, a House bill with the same provisions was introduced. The bill was followed by a favorable petition, signed by twenty-two citizens from the area of Washington County which it was proposed to attach, ostensibly because the distance to Scottsburg was but half that to Salem; Scottsburg was the most accessible railroad point for produce; and the road to Scottsburg avoided the Knobs, and was much easier to travel. One more petition was filed in favor of the bill, but the remonstrators greatly outnumbered the petitioners, and some of those who had first favored the change, later opposed it, having discovered that not only were the tax rate and county debt higher in Scott County, but that they would be obliged to continue payment on their share of the existing Washington County debt. The Committee on County and Township Business recommended indefinite postponement.[70]

[68] *House Journal*, 1883, p. 691; *Senate Journal*, 1883, p. 467; original House Bill No. 427. Original Senate Bill No. 253 is missing from the file in the Indiana State Library.

[69] Original House Bill No. 503; *House Journal*, 1885, pp. 881, 1046.

[70] Original House Bill No. 59, 1887, and accompanying petitions and remonstrances.

A bill to revise the method of altering county boundaries was once more introduced by the representative of Adams, Jay, and Blackford counties in 1887. Like House Bill No. 210, introduced in 1883, this bill would have deprived the county, as a unit, from voting on a proposed secession; it would have made change obligatory upon presentation of a petition signed by the majority of legal voters from the area desiring detachment. The new measure retained the provision of the 1875 law making any detached area responsible for its share of such indebtedness of the parent county as existed at the time of transfer. A minority report of the committee recommended passage with an amendment requiring the signatures of two-thirds of the legal voters upon the petition, but the majority report was for indefinite postponement.[71] In 1889 another attempt was made to enact a law of this type, but the bill was buried in committee.[72] The county-boundary question did not come before the legislature again until 1895, when an amendment to section 2 of the act of 1875 was proposed in Senate Bill No. 154. Where the existing law made four hundred square miles the area below which no county could be further reduced, the proposed bill set the limit at 350 square miles. This contravened a constitutional provision, and the bill did not pass the originating house.[73]

1899-1933. For over twenty years legislative sessions were entirely free from bills relating to specific county-boundary alterations or to the method of making transfers. The several changes that have been made in the period from 1920 to the present time have all taken place in the northwestern counties which border on the Kankakee River and consist of modifications of the existing boundaries to follow the new channel of the river, resulting from extensive drainage operations. In 1921 Jasper County tried to secure an amendment of this

[71] Original House Bill No. 301; *House Journal*, 1887, p. 458.
[72] *Ibid.*, 1889, pp. 153-54.
[73] Original Senate Bill No. 154; *Senate Journal*, 1895, pp. 143, 465, and 687.

nature, but the bill did not come up for third reading. At the next session a law was enacted redefining the boundaries of Newton, Jasper, Lake, and Porter counties to follow the line of the Marble Powers and Williams dredge ditches. In 1925 the common water boundary of La Porte and Starke counties was declared to be along the Dixon W. Place ditch, and in 1929 an attempt was made to alter the description of St. Joseph and La Porte counties along the river, but the Senate bill was crowded out at the end of the session.[74] A Senate bill making this change was passed at the 1931 session.[75]

The completion of a cycle in the history of county boundaries was forecast by several bills presented in the regular sessions of 1931 and 1933, and in the special session of 1932. From the formation of the first territorial counties in the late 1700's to the middle of the next century, the line of progress was steadily toward the creation of more counties. During the next fifty years, legislative effort was directed toward the prevention of ill-considered boundary changes and the protection of existing units from damaging losses to contiguous counties.

By 1930 a new point of view was making itself apparent. The physical factors which had dictated the formation of early counties—long distances, unbridged rivers, unsurveyed forests—had long since either ceased to exist, or lost their importance in an era of rapid transportation. With the cry for lowered taxes and economy in government growing in volume and intensity, there was a natural legislative move to consider the advisability of combining counties, in the hope of simplification and economy. Various methods of making the desired reduction have been proposed.

[74] Jasper, *House Journal*, 1921, pp. 367, 425-26, 609; Newton-Jasper-Lake-Porter, *Laws of Indiana*, 1923, pp. 464-67; La Porte-Starke, *ibid.*, 1925, p. 123; St. Joseph-La Porte, *Senate Journal*, 1929, pp. 348, 628; *House Journal*, 1929, pp. 591, 628, 799.

[75] *Senate Journal*, 1931, pp. 73-74, 101, 134-35, 224-25, 909; *House Journal*, 1931, pp. 993-94, 1043.

Senate Joint Resolution No. 1, introduced on January 14, 1931, proposed the creation of a commission of seven members to make a critical study of the structure and resources of counties, "To study the problem of consolidating counties and to propose tentative rearrangements and consolidations of the existing counties, which, in the judgment of the commission, will subserve the best interests of the citizens concerned and . . . enable county governments to operate more economically." The Committee on Finance recommended passage on January 29, and the resolution was adopted without amendment on February 5. In the House it was referred to the Committee on Ways and Means, but was never reported upon.[76]

Three measures dealing with this problem were introduced in the Senate in July, 1932. Senate Bill No. 348 provided three possible ways for the formation of new counties: the consolidation of two or more contiguous counties; the consolidation of one county and a part or parts of one or more contiguous counties; the consolidation of two or more adjoining counties and a part or parts of one or more contiguous counties, if approved by a majority of the electors of all the counties affected, voting at an election for which the bill also provided. This measure passed the Senate on July 15, by a vote of 40 to 5. Passage was recommended by the House Committee on Rights and Privileges, and the bill came up for third reading on August 2, but failed to receive a constitutional majority. On August 15 it was put on passage again and was voted down.[77] This measure was introduced in the 1933 session as Senate Bill No. 36, but did not pass the originating house.

Senate Joint Resolution No. 4, duplicating Senate Joint Resolution No. 1, which failed to pass in the 1931 session, was introduced on July 11, 1932, and adopted by the

[76] Senate Joint Resolution No. 1; *Senate Journal*, 1931, pp. 64-65, 199, 246, 292-93; *House Journal*, 1931, pp. 328, 340.

[77] Original Senate Bill No. 348; *Senate Journal*, 1932 (special session), pp. 20, 24, 59, 92-93; *House Journal*, 1932 (special session), pp. 84, 99, 310, 355, 389-90, 610-11.

BOUNDARY LEGISLATION 131

Senate on July 22, by a vote of 26 to 14. On August 4 the House voted for indefinite postponement of further action.[78]

The third bill mentioned was Senate Bill No. 457, introduced on July 26 under the title, "A Bill for an Act creating a state committee on economy, providing for compensation for its services and prescribing its rights, powers and duties." Section 2 provided for a study of the "structure and functions of state, county, township, city and town governments," and authorized the committee "to initiate methods to reorganize, consolidate or abolish the number of units . . . where it can be done effectively." Like Senate Bill No. 348 and Senate Joint Resolution No. 4, this measure failed of enactment. It passed the Senate on a reconsidered vote of 27 to 21 on August 4, 1932, but was indefinitely postponed in the House six days later. Creation of a nonpartisan state committee to make such an examination of governmental units was authorized by the Assembly of 1933, in Concurrent Resolution No. 6, filed February 21, 1933.[79]

One House bill, No. 764, introduced on July 21, 1932, proposed to amend section 10 of the county-boundary act of 1861, requiring that petitions for transfer of territory be submitted to the board of commissioners of the county to which attachment was desired, as well as to the board of commissioners in the county from which the transfer was to be made. The bill was immediately reported back from the committee with a recommendation for indefinite postponement, and the report was adopted.[80]

[78] *Senate Journal*, 1932 (special session), pp. 30-31, 79, 123, 177-78; *House Journal*, 1932 (special session), pp. 196, 212, 310, 356, 444-45.

[79] *Senate Journal*, 1932 (special session), pp. 218-19, 276, 293, 343, 355; *House Journal*, 1932 (special session), pp. 463, 464, 468-69, 524-25. *Laws of Indiana*, 1933, pp. 1242-43.

[80] Original House Bill No. 764.

MAPS
TERRITORY, STATE, AND COUNTY

ILLINOIS COUNTY
[Commonwealth of Virginia]

DECEMBER 9, 1778: Formation by statute, effective December 12, 1778.

BOUNDARIES: "All the citizens of this commonwealth who are already settled, or shall hereafter settle, on the western side of the Ohio . . . shall be included in a distinct county, which shall be called Ilinois county." Hening, William W. (ed.), *The Statutes at Large: being a collection of all the laws of Virginia, from the first session of the legislature, in the year 1619*, 9:553 (Richmond, 1821).

"This new territory . . . stretched from the Ohio to the Illinois River and up the Wabash towards Detroit to an indefinite boundary. Ouiatanon was certainly under the jurisdiction of Virginia, but beyond that post and the Illinois River there is no proof of her exercising jurisdiction. The land lying between this northern boundary and the lakes was disputed territory and was traversed by Virginia and British troops at various times." Alvord, Clarence W. (ed.), *Cahokia Records, 1778-1790*, lii ff., and 9 n. (*Collections of the Illinois State Historical Library*, vol. 2, Springfield, 1907).

Ouiatanon was a post not far from the present Lafayette, Indiana. The act was to be in effect for one year, and until the end of the next session of the Assembly. In May, 1780, it was renewed for a like period, but expired at the adjournment of the Assembly on January 5, 1782. Hening (ed.), *op cit.*, 9:555 and 10:303-4; Alvord (ed.), *op cit.*, cxviii-cxix.

NORTHWEST TERRITORY

JULY 13, 1787: Formation by ordinance of the Continental Congress, effective on passage.

BOUNDARIES: "The Territory of the United States, north-west of the river Ohio." *Journals of the American Congress*, 4:752.

The boundaries of the Northwest Territory were not specifically given in the Ordinance of 1787. The Pennsylvania state line formed the eastern boundary; the northwest boundary followed the line established by the Treaty of Paris, signed on September 3, 1783, running through the middle of Lake Erie, "until it arrives at the water communication between that lake and lake Huron; thence along the middle of said water communication into the lake Huron; thence through the middle of said lake to the water communication between that lake and lake Superior; thence through lake Superior northward of the isles, Royal and Philipeaux, to the long lake; thence through the middle of said long lake and the water communication between it and the lake of the Woods, to the said lake of the Woods; thence through the said lake to the most north-western point thereof, and from thence on a due west course to the river Mississippi; thence by a line to be drawn along the middle of the said river Mississippi." *Ibid.*, 324.

The line "on a due west course" from the Lake of the Woods to the Mississippi was impossible, as the map shows.

SEAT OF GOVERNMENT: The governor and judges met once in Marietta, once in Vincennes, and six times in Cincinnati for lawmaking sessions, from 1788 to 1799. No one of these towns was designated by law as the capital city.

NORTHWEST TERRITORY BOUNDARIES 137

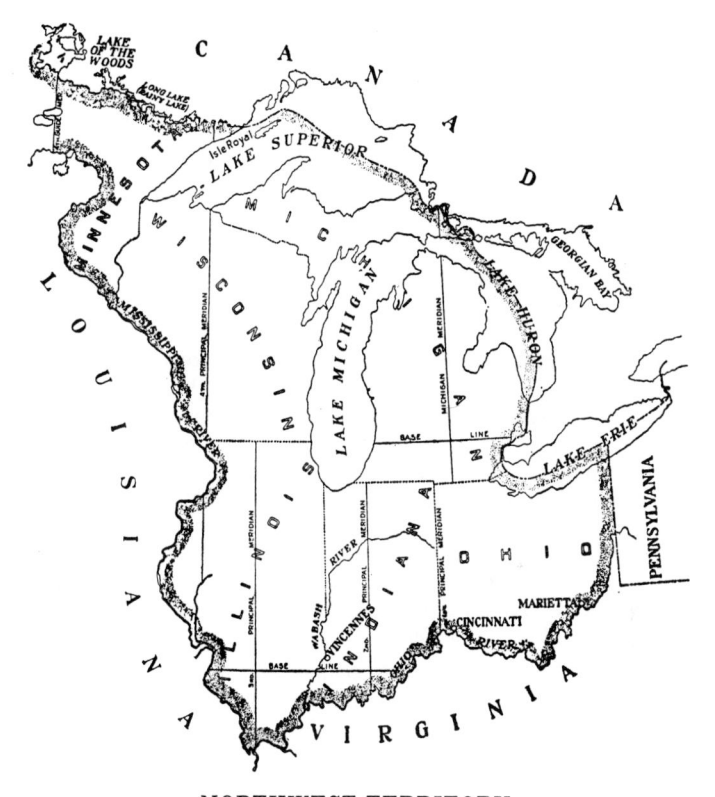

NORTHWEST TERRITORY

[Ordinance of Continental Congress: July 13, 1787, effective on passage]

INDIANA TERRITORY I

MAY 7, 1800: Formation by act of Congress, dividing the Northwest Territory, effective July 4, 1800.

BOUNDARIES: "All that part of the Territory of the United States Northwest of the Ohio river, which lies to the westward of a line beginning at the Ohio, opposite to the mouth of Kentucky river, and running thence to Fort Recovery, and thence north until it shall intersect the territorial line between the United States and Canada." *Annals*, 6 Congress, 1 session, 1498.

The act provided that "whenever that part of the Territory of the United States which lies to the eastward of a line beginning at the mouth of the Great Miami river, and running thence due north to the territorial line between the United States and Canada, shall be erected into an independent State, and admitted into the Union . . ., thenceforth said line shall become and remain permanently the boundary line between such State and the Indiana Territory." *Ibid.*, 1499-1500.

SEAT OF GOVERNMENT: Vincennes was made the seat of government at the organization of the territory. *Ibid.*, 1500.

INDIANA TERRITORY BOUNDARIES 139

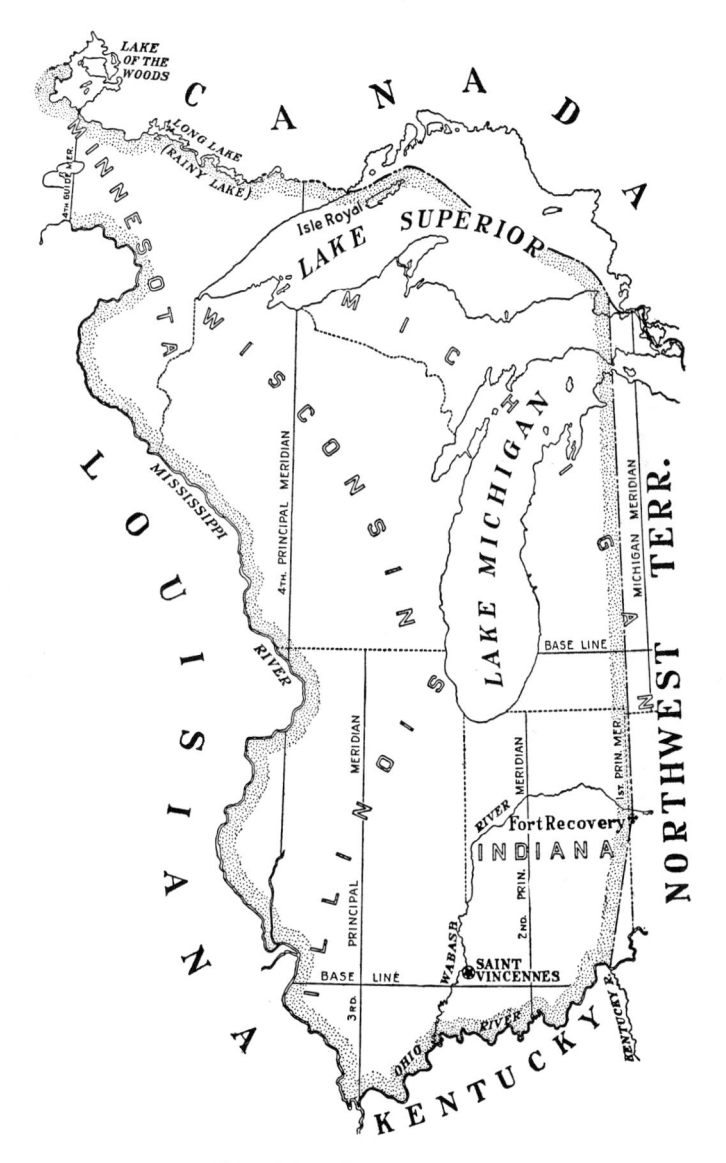

INDIANA TERRITORY I

[Act of Congress: May 7, 1800, effective July 4, 1800]

INDIANA TERRITORY II

APRIL 30, 1802: Alteration by Enabling Act for the formation of the State of Ohio, effective upon the admission of Ohio.

BOUNDARY CHANGE: The west and north boundary of Ohio was established along a "line drawn due north from the mouth of the Great Miami" until intersected "by an east and west line, drawn through the southerly extreme of Lake Michigan, running east after intersecting the due north line aforesaid, from the mouth of the Great Miami, until it shall intersect Lake Erie, or the territorial line, and thence with the same through Lake Erie to the Pennsylvania line." The law provided that "all that part of the Territory of the United States Northwest of the river Ohio, heretofore included in the eastern division of said Territory, and not included within the boundary herein prescribed" for the state of Ohio, be attached to Indiana Territory. *Annals*, 7 Congress, 1 session, 1349.

The west boundary of Ohio was between a mile and a half and two miles west of the former line running north from Fort Recovery. See *ante*, 4-5, for a statement as to the date upon which the act became effective.

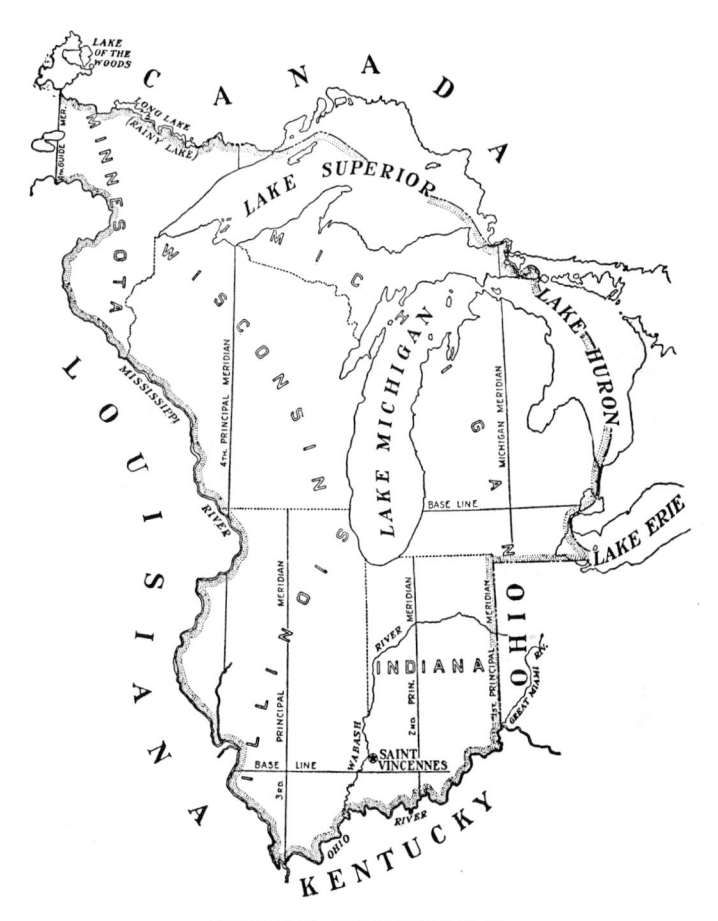

INDIANA TERRITORY II

[Act of Congress: Apr. 30, 1802, effective Mar. 1, 1803]

INDIANA TERRITORY III

JANUARY 11, 1805: Alteration by act of Congress forming Michigan Territory, effective June 30, 1805.

BOUNDARY CHANGE: All that part of Indiana Territory lying "north of a line drawn east from the southerly bend, or extreme, of Lake Michigan, until it shall intersect Lake Erie, and east of a line drawn from the said southerly bend through the middle of said lake to its northern extremity, and thence due north to the northern boundary of the United States" was transferred to Michigan Territory. *Annals,* 8 Congress, 2 session, 1659.

It is impossible to determine just what point was considered the northern extremity of Lake Michigan. See, however, Larzelere, Claude S., "The Boundaries of Michigan," in *Michigan Historical Collections,* 30:14-16 (Lansing, 1906).

INDIANA TERRITORY BOUNDARIES 143

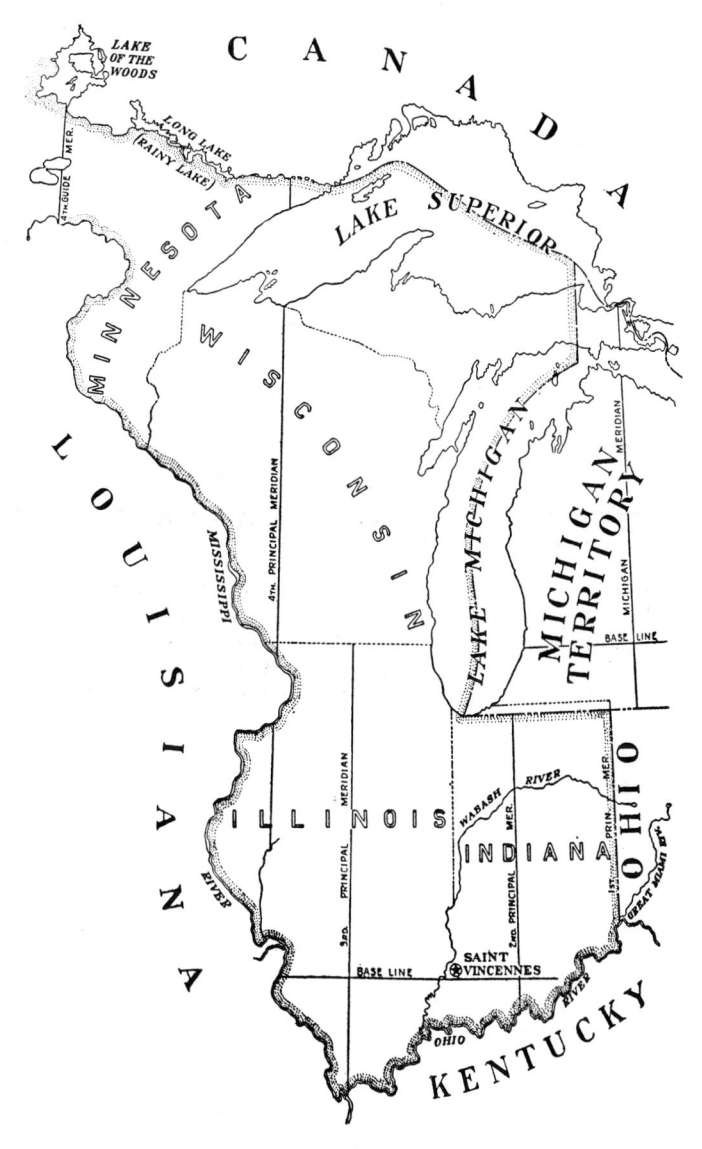

INDIANA TERRITORY III

[Act of Congress: Jan. 11, 1805, effective June 30, 1805]

INDIANA TERRITORY IV

FEBRUARY 3, 1809: Alteration by act of Congress forming Illinois Territory, effective March 1, 1809.

BOUNDARY CHANGE: "All that part of the Indiana Territory which lies west of the Wabash river, and a direct line drawn from the said Wabash river and Post Vincennes, due north to the territorial line between the United States and Canada," was formed into Illinois Territory. *Annals*, 10 Congress, 2 session, 1808.

INDIANA TERRITORY IV
[Act of Congress: Feb. 3, 1809, effective Mar. 1, 1809]

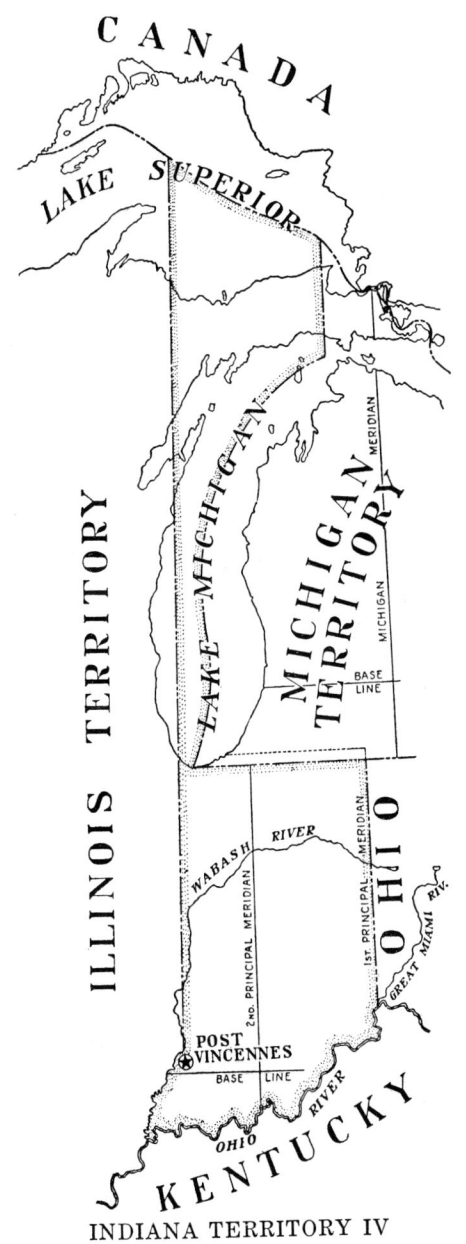

INDIANA I

This map shows county boundaries as they appeared prior to the admission of Indiana to the Union on December 11, 1816. Knox County maps IV to X show the formation of counties before the legislative session of 1816-17.

INDIANA I

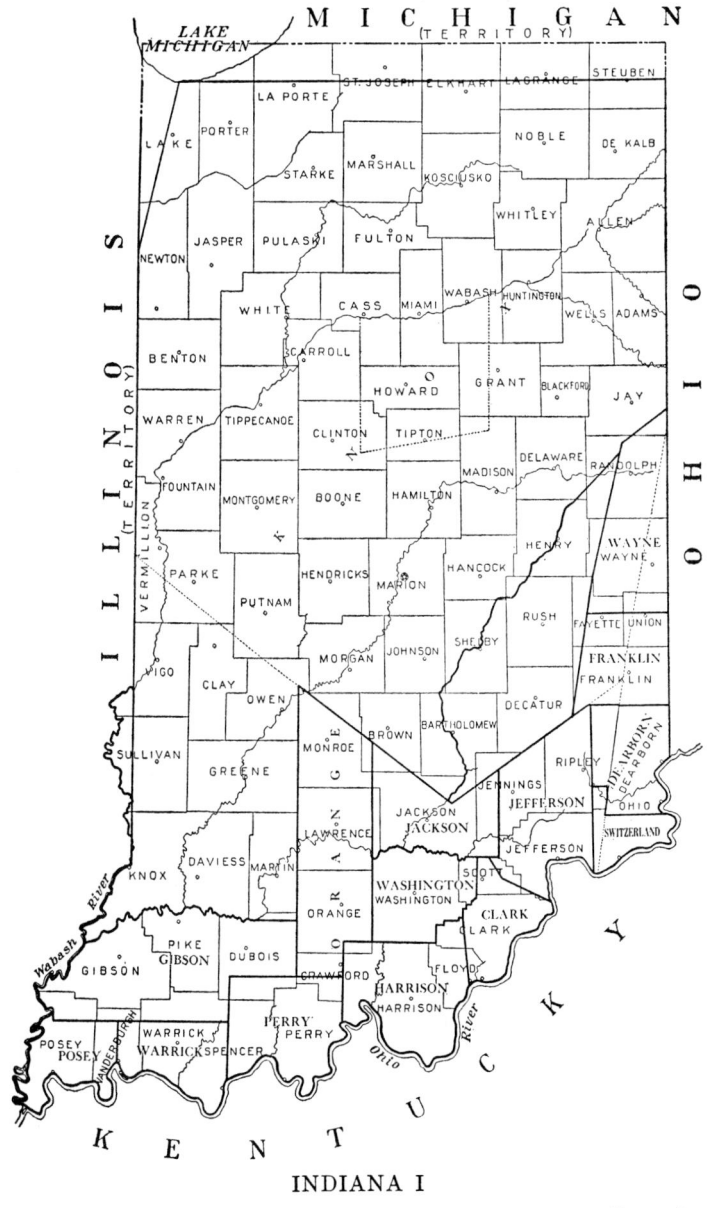

[Counties prior to the admission of Indiana to the Union, December 11, 1816]

INDIANA II

New Counties

Pike.	December 21, 1816
Daviess.	December 24, 1816
Jennings.	December 27, 1816
Ripley.	December 27, 1816
Sullivan.	December 30, 1816

Transfers and Additions

Perry.	Loss to Pike, December 21, 1816
Gibson.	Loss to Pike, December 21, 1816. Loss to Posey, January 1, 1817
Knox.	Loss to Daviess, December 24, 1816. Loss to Sullivan, December 30, 1816
Dearborn.	Loss to Ripley, December 27, 1816
Jackson.	Loss to Jennings, December 27, 1816
Jefferson.	Loss to Jennings and Ripley, December 27, 1816
Posey.	Addition from Gibson, January 1, 1817

INDIANA BOUNDARIES 149

INDIANA II

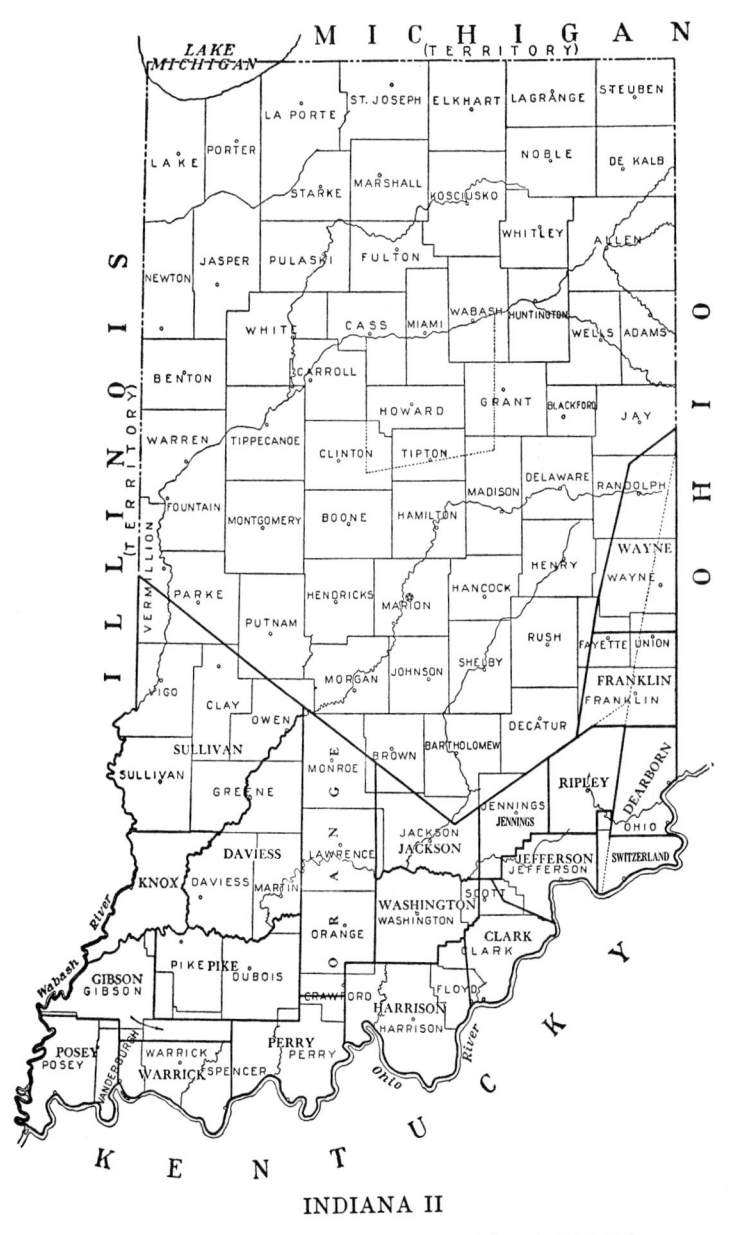

[As changed by the General Assembly of 1816-17]

INDIANA III

New Counties

Dubois.	December 20, 1817
Lawrence.	January 7, 1818
Vanderburgh.	January 7, 1818
Randolph.	January 10, 1818
Spencer.	January 10, 1818
Monroe.	January 14, 1818
Vigo.	January 21, 1818
Crawford.	January 29, 1818

Transfers and Additions

Pike.	Loss to Dubois, December 20, 1817
Gibson.	Loss to Vanderburgh, January 7, 1818
Posey.	Loss to Vanderburgh, January 7, 1818
Warrick.	Loss to Vanderburgh, January 7, 1818. Loss to Spencer, January 10, 1818
Orange.	Loss to Lawrence, January 7, 1818. Loss to Monroe, January 14, 1818. Loss to Crawford, and addition from Harrison, January 29, 1818
Harrison.	Loss to Perry, January 10, 1818. Loss to Crawford and Orange, January 29, 1818
Perry.	Addition from Harrison, and loss to Spencer, January 10, 1818. Loss to Crawford, and addition from Dubois, January 29, 1818
Wayne.	Loss to Randolph, January 10, 1818
Sullivan.	Loss to Vigo, January 21, 1818
Dubois.	Loss to Perry, January 29, 1818

INDIANA III

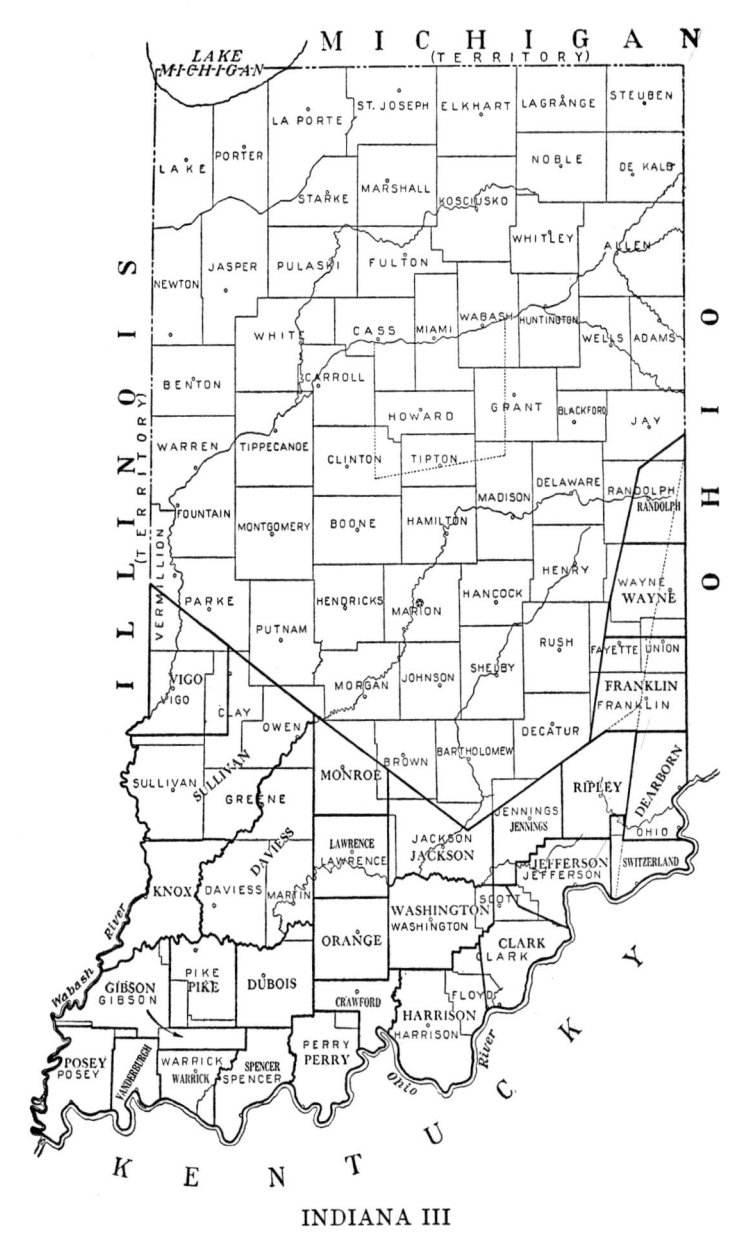

[As changed by the General Assembly of 1817-18]

INDIANA IV

New Counties

Owen.   December 21, 1818
Fayette. December 28, 1818
Floyd.   January 2, 1819

Transfers and Additions

Jackson.   Addition from New Purchase, October 2-6, 1818
Daviess.   Loss to Owen, December 21, 1818
Sullivan. Loss to Owen, December 21, 1818. Loss to Vigo, January 1, 1819
Franklin. Loss to Fayette, December 28, 1818
Wayne.   Loss to Fayette, and addition from unorganized territory, December 28, 1818
Vigo.   Addition from Sullivan, January 1, 1819
Clark.   Loss to Floyd, January 2, 1819
Harrison. Loss to Floyd, January 2, 1819

INDIANA IV

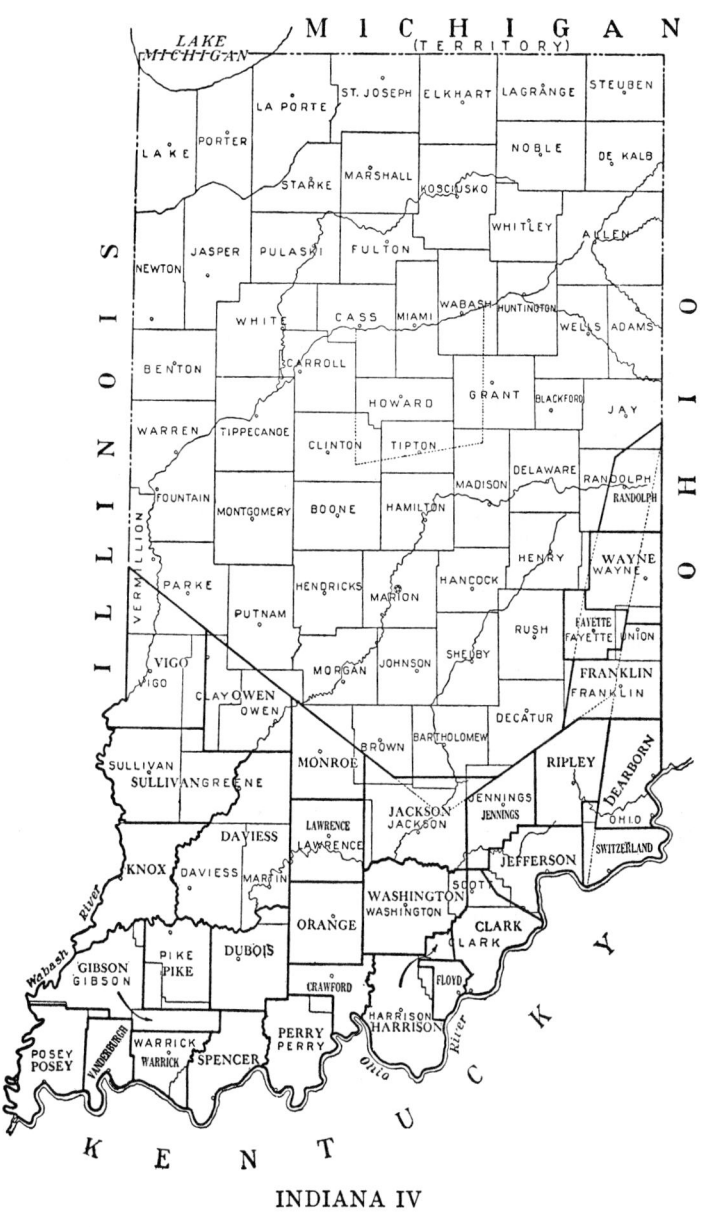

[As changed by the General Assembly of 1818-19]

INDIANA V

New Counties

Scott.	January 12, 1820
Martin.	January 17, 1820
Delaware.	January 20, 1820
Wabash.	January 20, 1820. Wabash and Delaware counties were not given separate organization, but were placed under the jurisdiction of bounding counties.

Transfers and Additions

Clark.	Loss to Scott, January 12, 1820
Jefferson.	Loss to Scott, January 12, 1820
Washington.	Loss to Scott, January 12, 1820
Jackson.	Loss to Scott, January 12, 1820. Loss to Jennings, January 20, 1820
Jennings.	Loss to Scott, January 12, 1820. Addition from Jackson and New Purchase, January 20, 1820
Dubois.	Loss to Martin, January 17, 1820
Daviess.	Loss to Martin, January 17, 1820. Alteration of northern boundary, January 21, 1820
Franklin.	Addition from New Purchase, January 20, 1820
Randolph.	Addition from New Purchase, January 20, 1820

INDIANA BOUNDARIES 155

INDIANA V

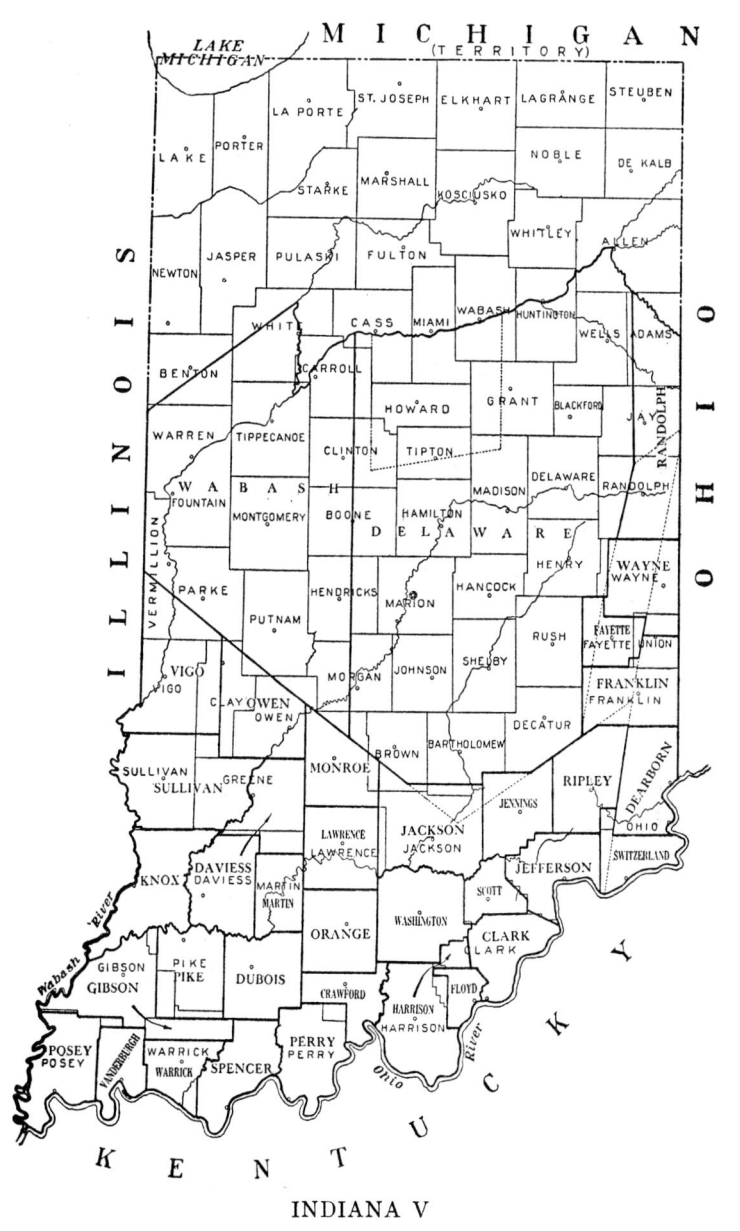

[As changed by the General Assembly of 1819-20]

INDIANA VI

New Counties

Greene.	January 5, 1821
Union.	January 5, 1821
Bartholomew.	January 8, 1821. Given jurisdiction over Delaware, January 9, 1821
Parke.	January 9, 1821

Transfers and Additions

Randolph.	Extension north, December 23, 1820
Scott-Washington.	Transfer, December 26, 1820
Daviess.	Loss to Greene, January 5, 1821
Sullivan.	Loss to Greene, January 5, 1821
Fayette.	Loss to Union, January 5, 1821
Franklin.	Loss to Union, January 5, 1821
Wayne.	Loss to Union, and addition from New Purchase, January 5, 1821
Jackson.	Loss to Bartholomew, January 8, 1821
Vigo.	Loss to Parke, January 9, 1821
Monroe.	Given jurisdiction over Wabash, January 9, 1821

INDIANA VI

[As changed by the General Assembly of 1820-21]

INDIANA VII

New Counties

Decatur.	December 31, 1821
Henry.	December 31, 1821
Marion.	December 31, 1821. Attachment same date
Morgan.	December 31, 1821
Putnam.	December 31, 1821. Attachment, January 2, 1822
Rush.	December 31, 1821
Shelby.	December 31, 1821

Transfers and Additions

Vigo.	Loss to Putnam, December 31, 1821
Owen.	Loss to Putnam, and addition from **Monroe** and Wabash, December 31, 1821
Monroe.	Addition from Wabash and Delaware; loss to Owen, December 31, 1821
Gibson-Posey.	Transfer, December 31, 1821
Ripley-Switzerland.	Transfer, December 31, 1821
Parke.	Attachment, January 2, 1822

INDIANA BOUNDARIES

INDIANA VII

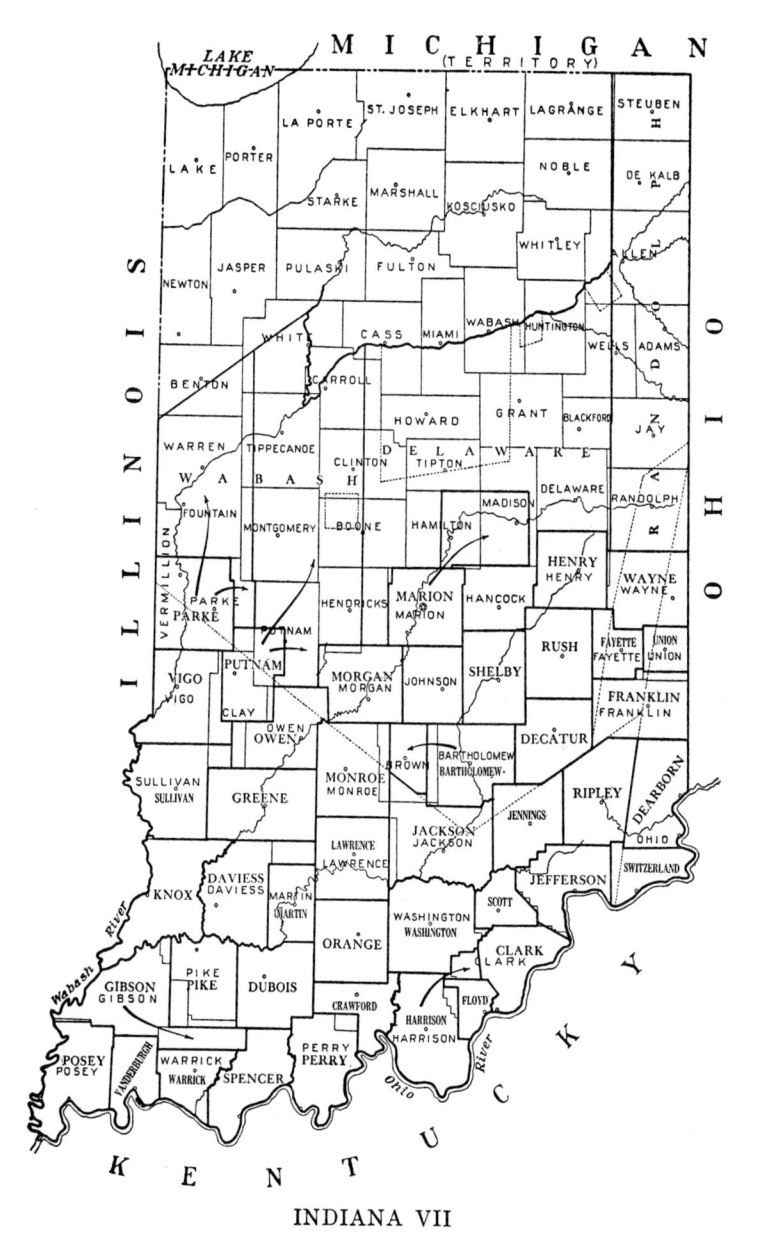

[As changed by the General Assembly of 1821-22]

INDIANA VIII

New Counties

Montgomery.	December 21, 1822
Johnson.	December 31, 1822
Madison.	January 4, 1823
Hamilton.	January 8, 1823

Transfers and Additions

Owen.	Addition from Putnam, December 21, 1822
Putnam.	Loss to Owen and Vigo, and addition from Wabash, December 21, 1822. Note that the boundaries of Putnam are entirely changed.
Vigo.	Addition from Putnam, December 21, 1822
Lawrence-Jackson.	Transfer, December 31, 1822
Posey-Gibson.	Transfer, January 6, 1823
Harrison-Floyd.	Transfer, January 10, 1823
Wayne-Henry.	Transfer, January 11, 1823

INDIANA VIII

[As changed by the General Assembly of 1822-23]

INDIANA IX

New Counties

Allen.	December 17, 1823. Attachment same date
Hendricks.	December 20, 1823
Vermillion.	January 2, 1824. Attachment same date

Transfers and Additions

Randolph.	Loss to Allen, and attachment, December 17, 1823. Boundaries redefined, January 31, 1824
Montgomery.	Loss to Parke, January 2, 1824
Putnam.	Loss to Parke, January 2, 1824
Parke.	Loss to Vermillion, and addition from Putnam and Montgomery, January 2, 1824
Wayne-Henry.	Transfer, January 22, 1824
Madison.	North boundary defined, January 26, 1824
Pike.	Loss to and addition from Gibson, January 26, 1824
Gibson.	Loss to and addition from Pike, January 26, 1824. Loss to Warrick, January 31, 1824
Warrick.	Addition from Gibson, January 31, 1824
Clark-Harrison.	Transfer, January 31, 1824
Jackson.	North boundary altered, January 31, 1824

INDIANA IX

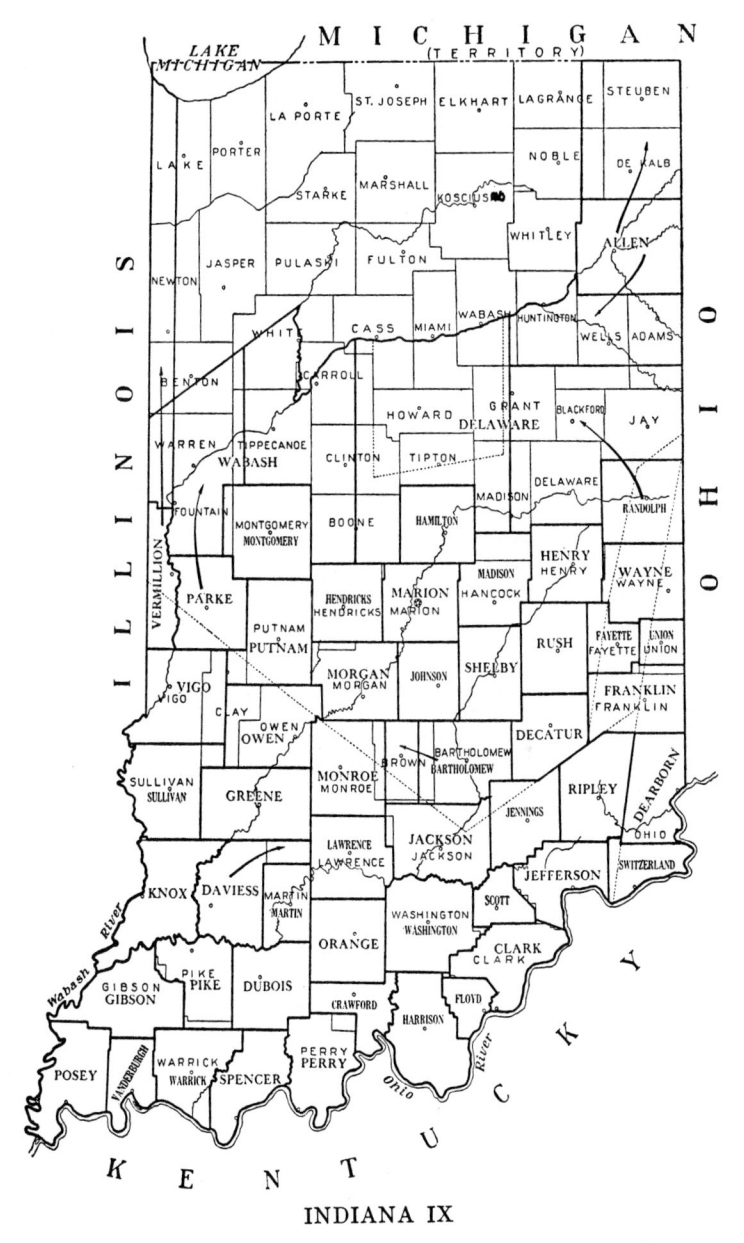

[As changed by the General Assembly of 1823-24]

INDIANA X

New Counties

Clay. February 12, 1825

Transfers and Additions

Gibson-Pike.   Transfer, February 3, 1825
Spencer-Warrick. Transfer, February 10, 1825
Marion.   Attachment, February 12, 1825
Owen.   Loss to Clay, February 12, 1825
Putnam.   Loss to Clay, February 12, 1825
Sullivan.   Loss to Clay, February 12, 1825
Vigo.   Loss to Clay, February 12, 1825

INDIANA BOUNDARIES

INDIANA X

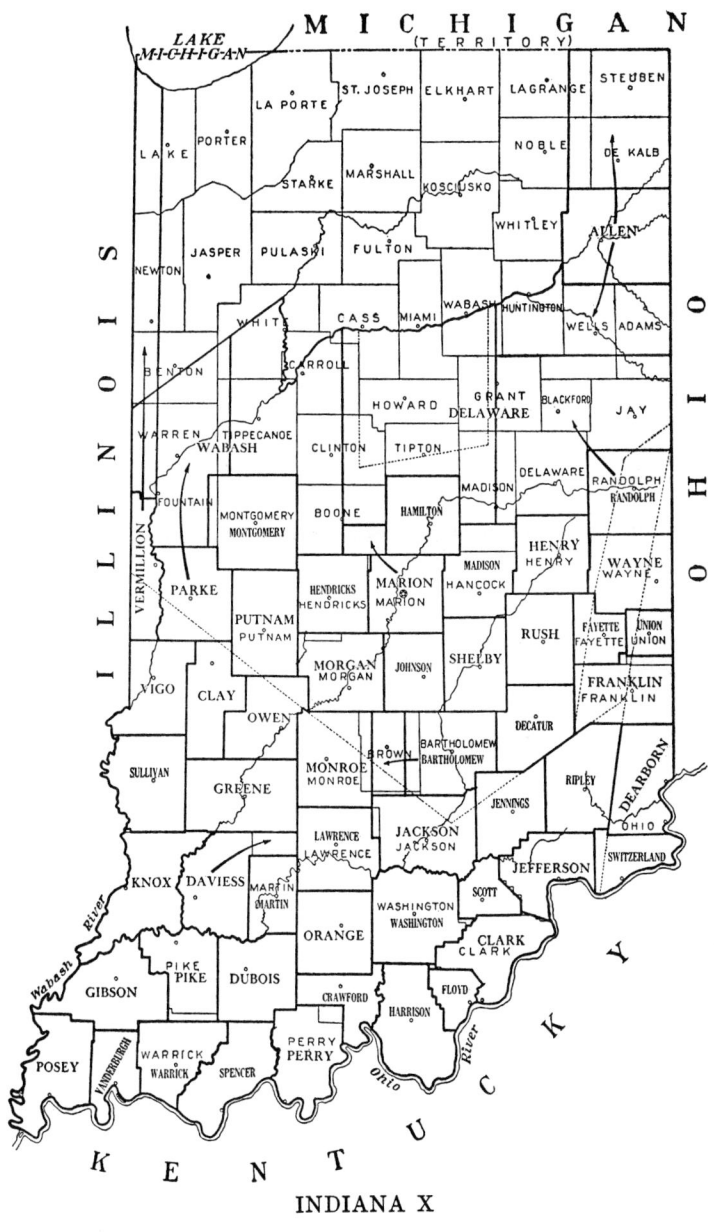

[As changed by the General Assembly of 1825]

INDIANA XI

New Counties
Fountain.   December 30, 1825.   Attachment same date
Tippecanoe.   January 20, 1826

Transfers and Additions
Montgomery.   Loss to Fountain, December 30, 1825
Hamilton.   Attachment, January 13, 1826
Fayette.   Addition from Franklin, January 16, 1826
Franklin.   Loss to Fayette and Union, January 16, 1826
Union.   Addition from Franklin, January 16, 1826
Pike-Warrick.   Transfer, January 20, 1826

INDIANA XI

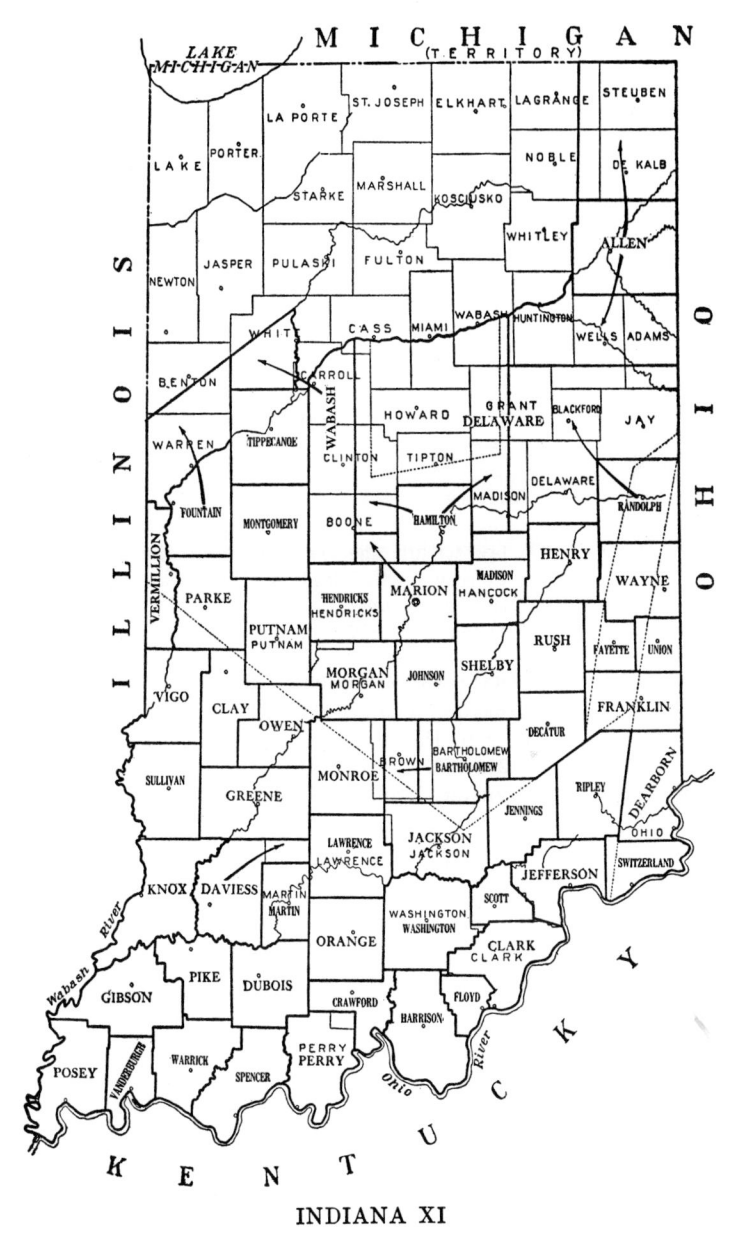

[As changed by the General Assembly of 1825-26]

INDIANA XII

New Counties

Warren. January 19, 1827
Delaware. January 26, 1827. Though this Delaware County lay within the boundaries of the Delaware County formed in 1820, there was no connection in organization.
Hancock. January 26, 1827

Transfers and Additions

Crawford-Perry. Transfer, January 23, 1827
Madison. Loss to Hancock and extension north, January 26, 1827
Henry-Wayne. Transfer, January 26, 1827

INDIANA BOUNDARIES 169

INDIANA XII

[As changed by the General Assembly of 1826-27]

INDIANA XIII

New Counties

Carroll. January 7, 1828. Attachments, January 24, 1828

Transfers and Additions

Floyd. Addition of open territory, January 5, 1828
Bartholomew. Addition from attached territory, January 16, 1828
Monroe. Addition from Bartholomew attachment, January 16, 1828
Jackson. Addition from Bartholomew attachment, January 16, 1828
Daviess-Martin. Transfer, January 24, 1828
Allen. Attachment, January 24, 1828
Delaware. Attachment, January 24, 1828
Hendricks. Attachment, January 24, 1828
Tippecanoe. Attachment, January 24, 1828

INDIANA BOUNDARIES

INDIANA XIII

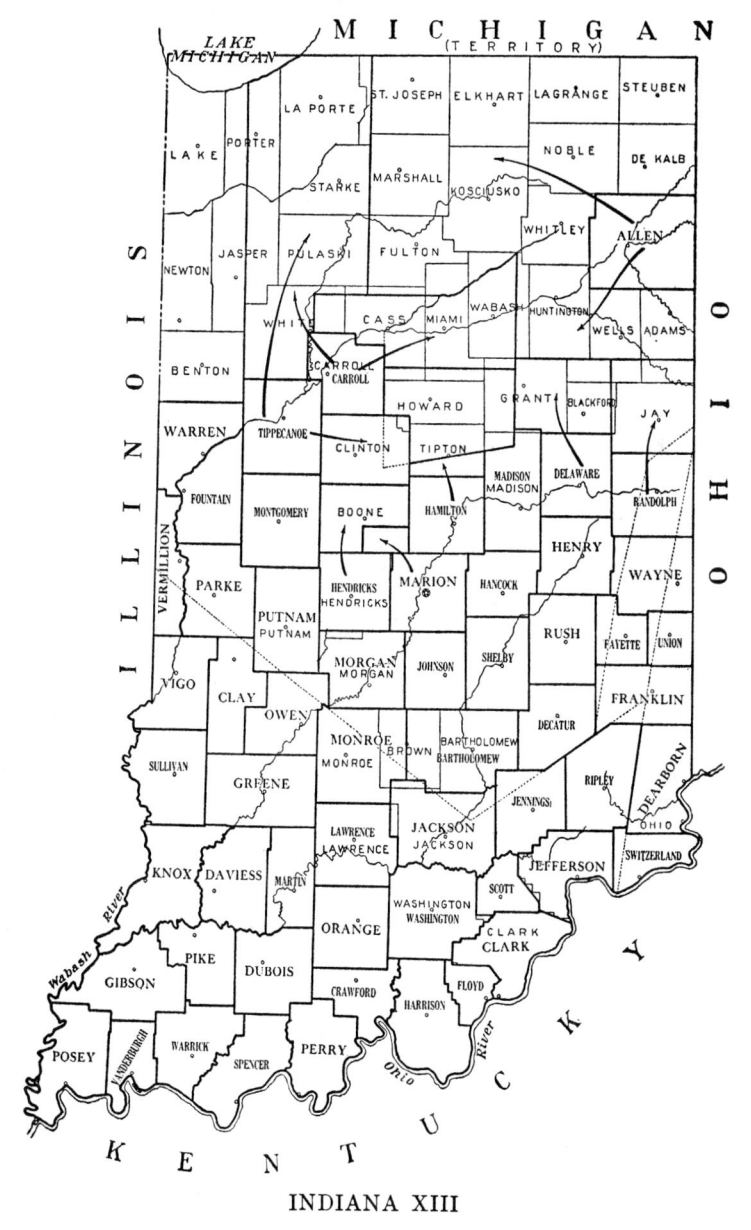

[As changed by the General Assembly of 1827-28]

INDIANA XIV
New County
Cass. December 18, 1828. Attachment, January 19, 1829

INDIANA XIV

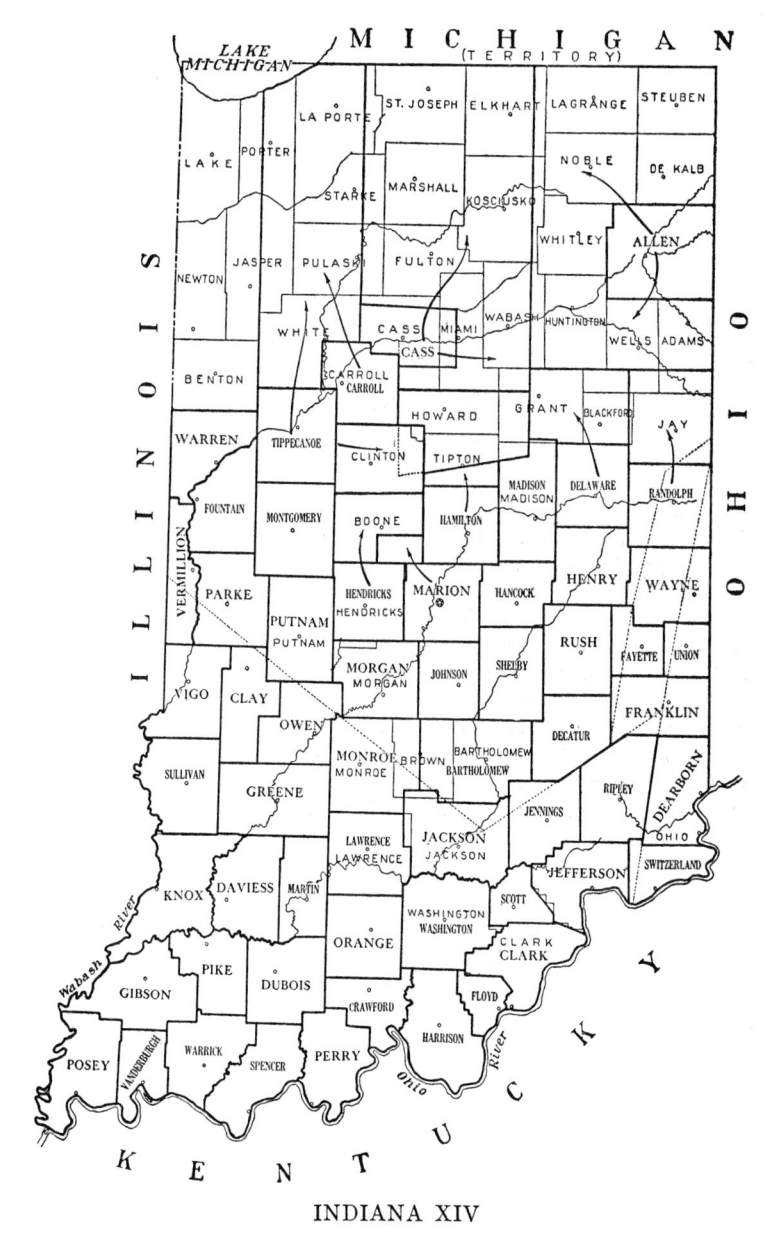

[As changed by the General Assembly of 1828-29]

INDIANA XV

New Counties

Boone.   January 29, 1830
Clinton.   January 29, 1830
Elkhart.   January 29, 1830. Attachment same date
St. Joseph. January 29, 1830. Attachment same date

Transfers and Additions

Scott.   Addition from Jefferson, January 22, 1830
Jefferson. Loss to Scott, January 22, 1830. Loss to Jennings, January 25, 1830
Jennings. Addition from Jefferson, January 25, 1830
Hamilton. Attachment redefined, January 29, 1830
Carroll.   Attachment redefined, January 30, 1830
Warren.   Attachment, January 30, 1830

INDIANA BOUNDARIES

INDIANA XV

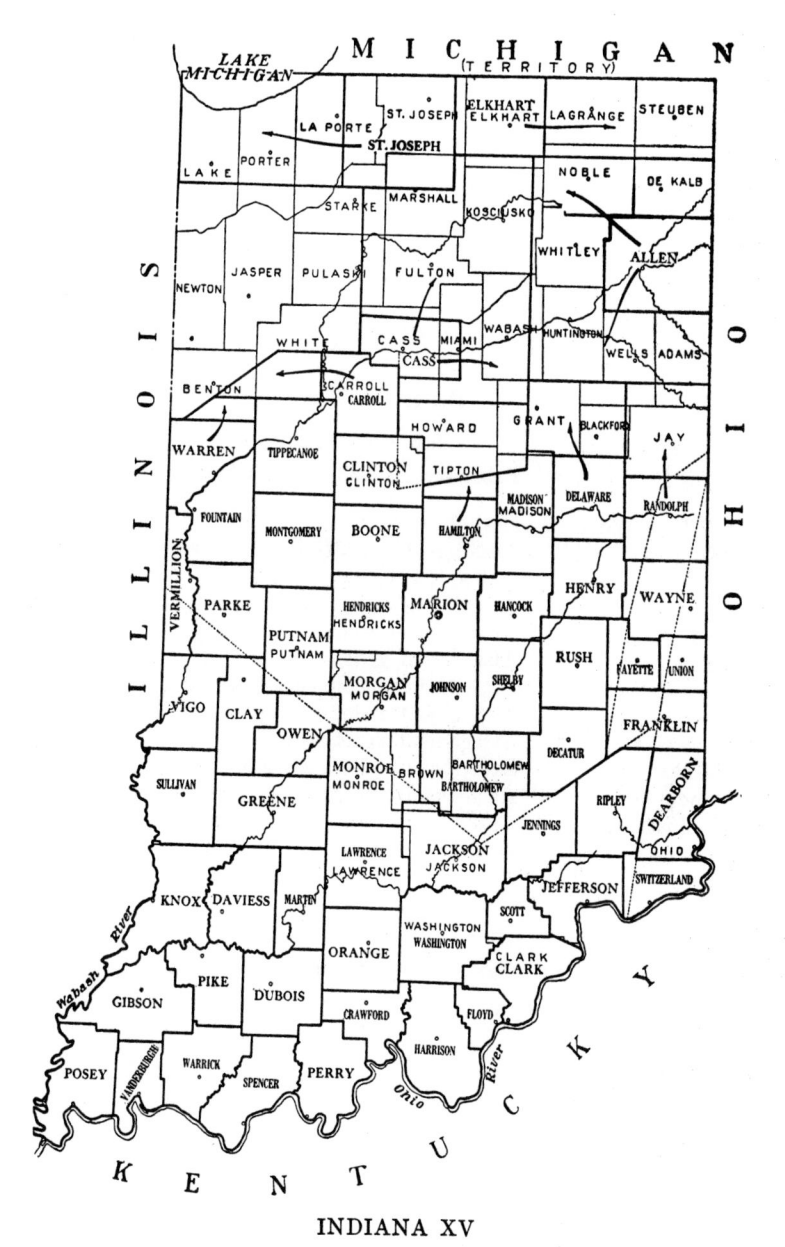

[As changed by the General Assembly of 1829-30]

INDIANA XVI

New County
Grant. February 10, 1831. Attachment same date

Transfers and Additions
Madison. Addition from Miami Reserve and loss to Grant, February 10, 1831
Monroe. Addition of open territory, February 10, 1831
Hendricks-Marion. Transfer, February 10, 1831
Allen. Attachment redefined, February 10, 1831
Carroll. Attachment redefined, February 10, 1831
Cass. Attachment redefined, February 10, 1831
Delaware. Attachment redefined, February 10, 1831
Elkhart. Attachment redefined, February 10, 1831
Randolph. Attachment redefined, February 10, 1831
St. Joseph. Attachment redefined, February 10, 1831
Warren. Attachment redefined, February 10, 1831

INDIANA BOUNDARIES 177

INDIANA XVI

[As changed by the General Assembly of 1830-31]

INDIANA XVII

NEW COUNTIES

La Porte.	January 9, 1832
Huntington.	February 2, 1832
La Grange.	February 2, 1832. Attachment same date
Miami.	January 30, 1833
Wabash.	January 30, 1833. The preceding legislature had laid out boundaries for Miami and Wabash counties, but ambiguities in the descriptions made a new law necessary for their formation.

TRANSFERS AND ADDITIONS

St. Joseph.	Loss to La Porte, January 9, 1832. Addition from Elkhart, January 31, 1832
Elkhart.	Loss to St. Joseph, January 31, 1832. Addition from attachment, February 2, 1832
Cass.	Addition from Miami Reserve, February 2, 1832. Loss to Miami, January 30, 1833

INDIANA XVII

[As changed by the General Assemblies of 1831-32, 1832-33]

INDIANA XVIII

New County
White. February 1, 1834. Attachment same date

Transfers and Additions
Cass.   Loss to Miami, January 2, 1834
Miami. Addition from Cass and attachment, January 2, 1834

INDIANA BOUNDARIES 181

INDIANA XVIII

[As changed by the General Assembly of 1833-34]

INDIANA XIX

New Counties

Adams.	February 7, 1835
De Kalb.	February 7, 1835
Fulton.	February 7, 1835
Jasper.	February 7, 1835
Jay.	February 7, 1835
Kosciusko.	February 7, 1835
Marshall.	February 7, 1835
Newton.	February 7, 1835
Noble.	February 7, 1835
Porter.	February 7, 1835
Pulaski.	February 7, 1835
Starke.	February 7, 1835
Steuben.	February 7, 1835
Wells.	February 7, 1835
Whitley.	February 7, 1835

Transfers and Additions

Cass.	Attachment redefined, December 24, 1834
White.	Attachment redefined, December 24, 1834
Jefferson-Jennings.	Transfer, February 6, 1835
St. Joseph.	Loss to Marshall and Starke, February 7, 1835

INDIANA XIX

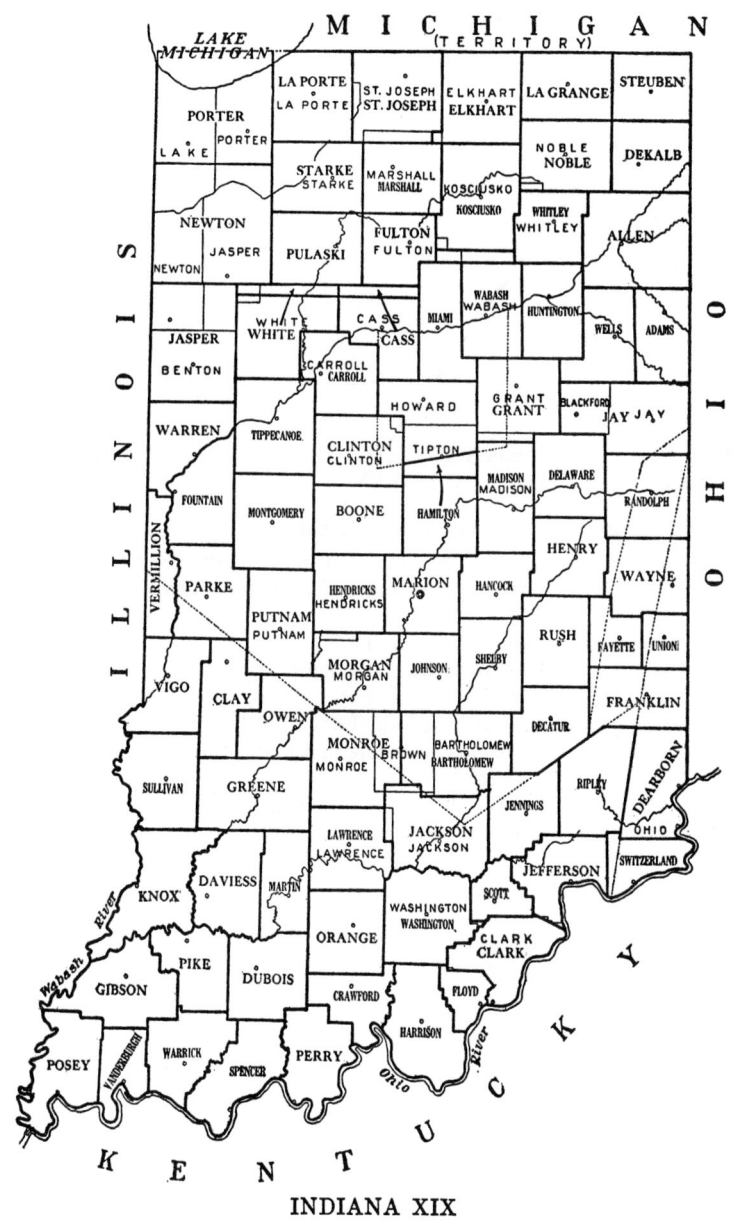

[As changed by the General Assembly of 1834-35]

INDIANA XX

New Counties
Lake. January 28, 1836
Brown. February 4, 1836

Transfers and Additions
Newton. Loss to Lake and Porter, January 28, 1836
Porter. Loss to Lake, and addition from Newton, January 28, 1836
Bartholomew. Loss to Brown, February 4, 1836
Jackson. Loss to Brown, February 4, 1836
Monroe. Loss to Brown, February 4, 1836
Elkhart. Loss to Marshall, February 4, 1836
Marshall. Additions from Elkhart and St. Joseph, February 4, 1836
St. Joseph. Loss to Marshall, February 4, 1836
Clark-Jefferson. Transfer, February 8, 1836

INDIANA XX

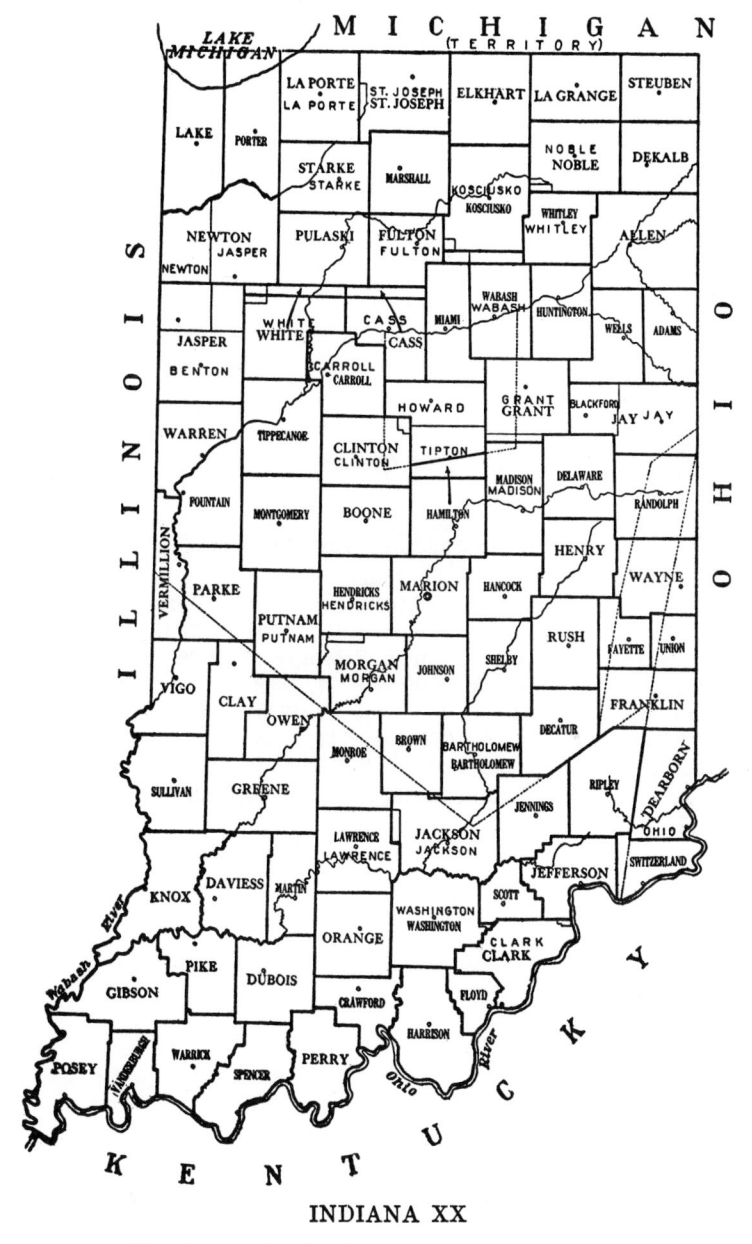

[As changed by the General Assembly of 1835-36]

INDIANA XXI

New County
Blackford. February 15, 1838

Transfers and Additions
Clark-Jefferson. Transfer, February 2, 1837
Jay. Loss to Blackford, February 15, 1838
Bartholomew. Boundaries redefined, February 17, 1838
Cass. Extended north, February 17, 1838
Fulton. Addition, February 17, 1838
Miami. Addition, February 17, 1838
Grant-Madison. Transfer, February 17, 1838
Wabash. Extended north, February 17, 1838
White. Extended north, February 17, 1838

INDIANA XXI

[As changed by the General Assemblies of 1836-37, 1837-38]

INDIANA XXII

TRANSFERS AND ADDITIONS

Carroll-White.	Transfer, February 14, 1839
Scott-Clark-Washington.	Transfer, February 16, 1839
Carroll.	Attachment, February 16, 1839
Cass.	Attachment, February 16, 1839
Hamilton.	Attachment, February 16, 1839
Miami.	Attachment, February 16, 1839
Grant.	The law of February 16, 1839, dividing the remainder of the Miami Reserve, provided that any territory not otherwise attached should be attached to Grant County. No such territory remained.
Jasper-Newton.	Consolidation, June (?), 1839

INDIANA BOUNDARIES 189

INDIANA XXII

[As changed by the General Assembly of 1838-39]

INDIANA XXIII

NEW COUNTY

Benton. February 18, 1840

TRANSFERS AND ADDITIONS

Jasper. Loss to Benton, February 18, 1840
Fulton-Kosciusko. Transfer, February 24, 1840

INDIANA XXIII

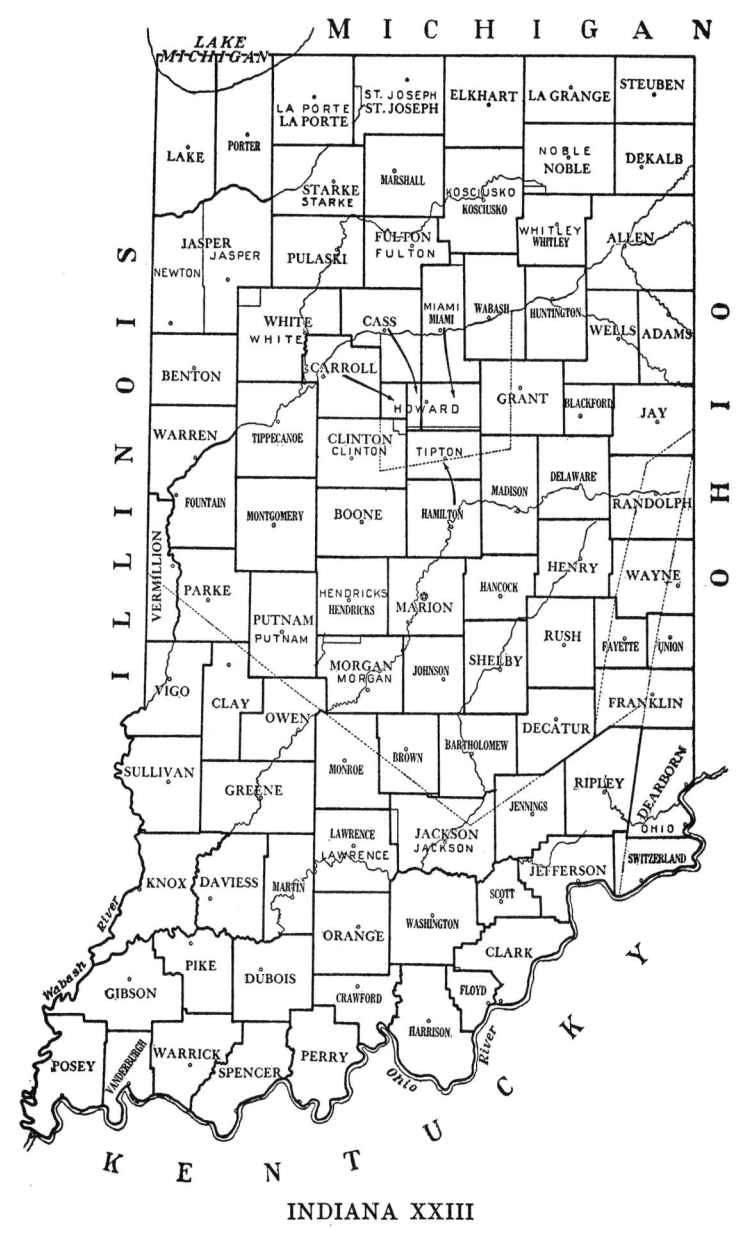

[As changed by the General Assembly of 1839-40]

INDIANA XXIV

Transfers

Jasper-White.   Transfer, February 10, 1841
La Porte-Starke. Transfer, January 29, 1842

INDIANA XXIV

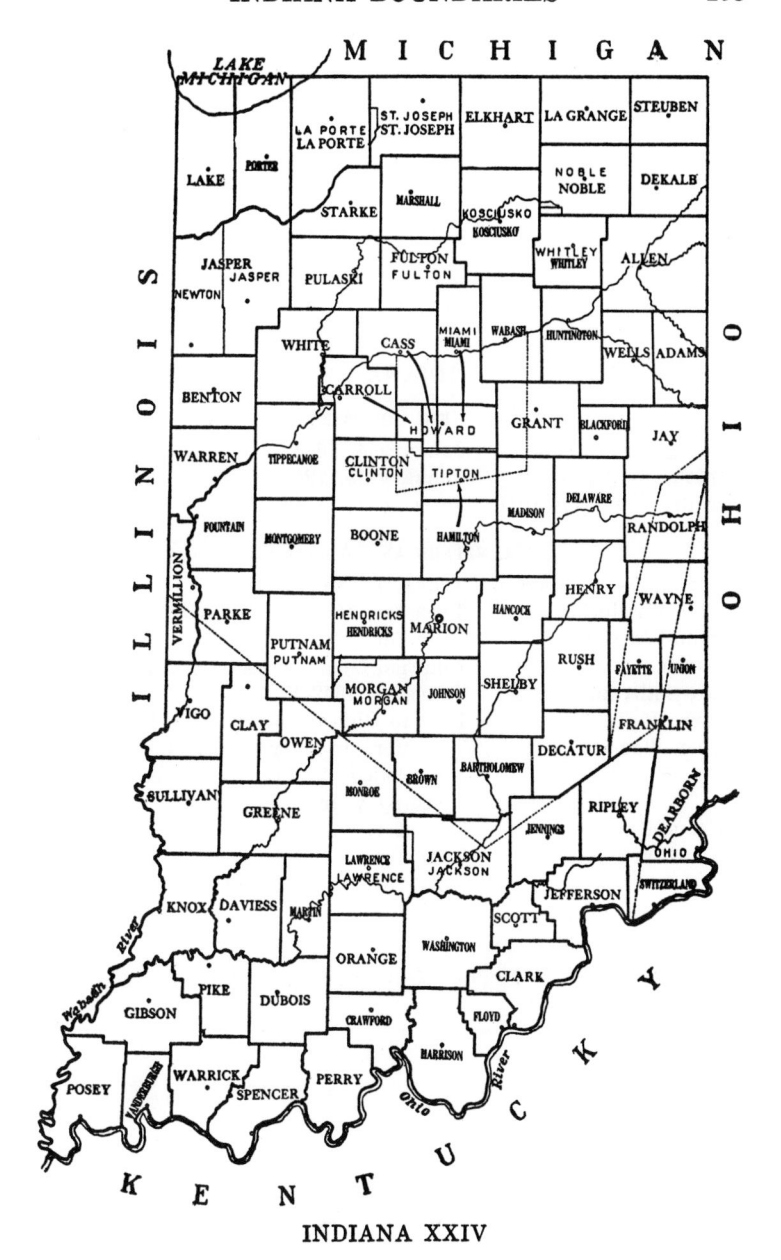

[As changed by the General Assemblies of 1840-41, 1841-42]

INDIANA XXV

New Counties
Ohio   January 4, 1844
Tipton.   January 15, 1844
Richardville (Howard).   January 15, 1844

Transfers and Additions
Scott-Clark-Washington.   Transfer, 1842-43
Fulton-Kosciusko.   Transfer, 1842-43
Gibson-Warrick.   Transfer, 1842-43
Jackson.   Addition from open territory, 1842-43
Knox-Sullivan.   Transfer, 1842-43
Dearborn.   Loss to Ohio, January 4, 1844
Gibson-Warrick.   Transfer, January 13, 1844. This law cancelled the transfer made the preceding year.
Fulton-Miami.   Transfer, January 15, 1844
Floyd-Clark.   Transfer. Commissioners' report, April 23, 1844, under act of January 15, 1844

INDIANA XXV

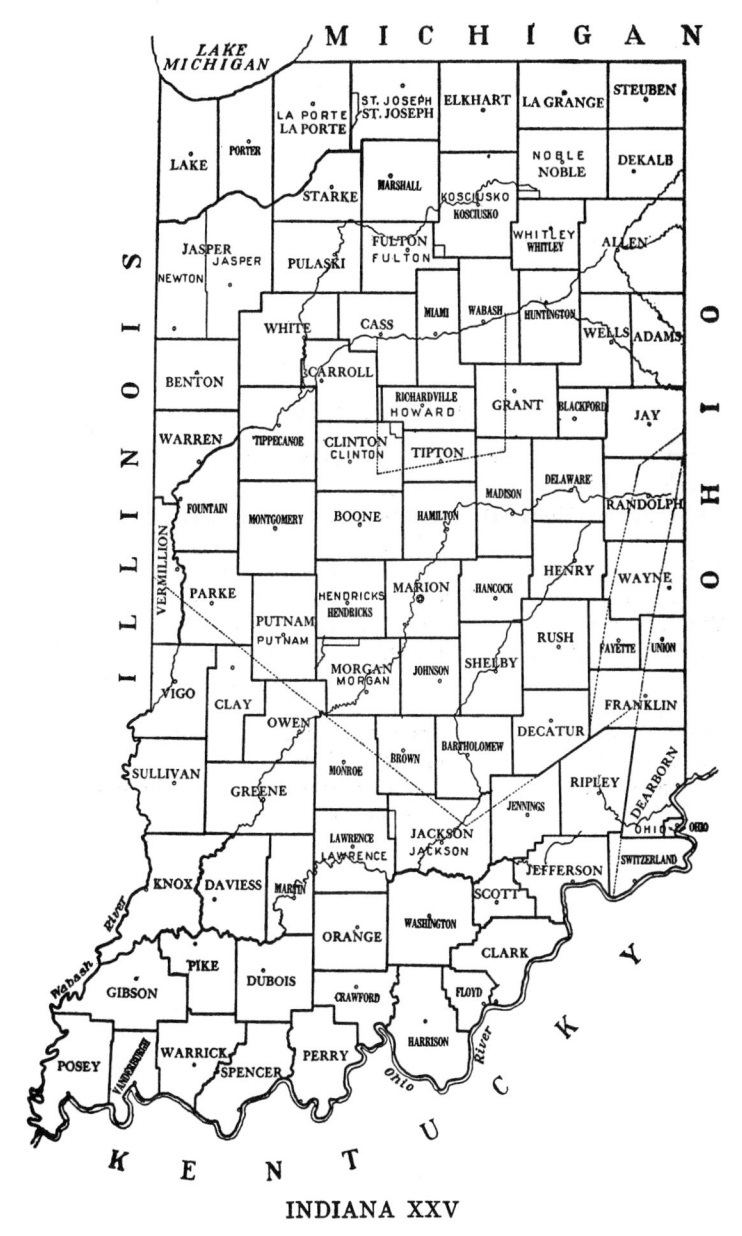

[As changed by the General Assemblies of 1842-43, 1843-44]

INDIANA XXVI

Transfers and Additions

Dearborn-Ohio.	Transfer, January 7, 1845
Richardville (Howard).	Addition from open territory, January 13, 1845
Fulton-Kosciusko.	Transfer, January 13, 1846
Clark-Washington.	Transfer, January 14, 1846
Gibson-Warrick.	Transfer, January 18, 1847
La Porte-St. Joseph.	Transfer. Commissioners' report, July 10, 1850, under act of January 14, 1850
Jefferson-Scott.	Transfer, February 13, 1851
Floyd-Harrison.	Transfer, June 7, 1852
Gibson-Warrick.	Transfer, June 7, 1852, reversing transfer of 1847

INDIANA XXVI

[As changed by the General Assemblies of 1844-45 to 1851-52]

INDIANA XXVII

NEW COUNTY

Newton. Reorganization, December 8, 1859

TRANSFERS

Clinton-Howard. Transfer, March 3, 1859
Jackson-Lawrence. Transfer, June 8, 1859
Noble-Whitley. Transfer, June 11, 1859
Jasper. Loss to Newton, December 8, 1859
Morgan-Putnam. Transfer, March 11, 1861
Hendricks-Morgan. Transfer, June, 1868
Clark-Washington. Transfer, March 7, 1873

INDIANA XXVII

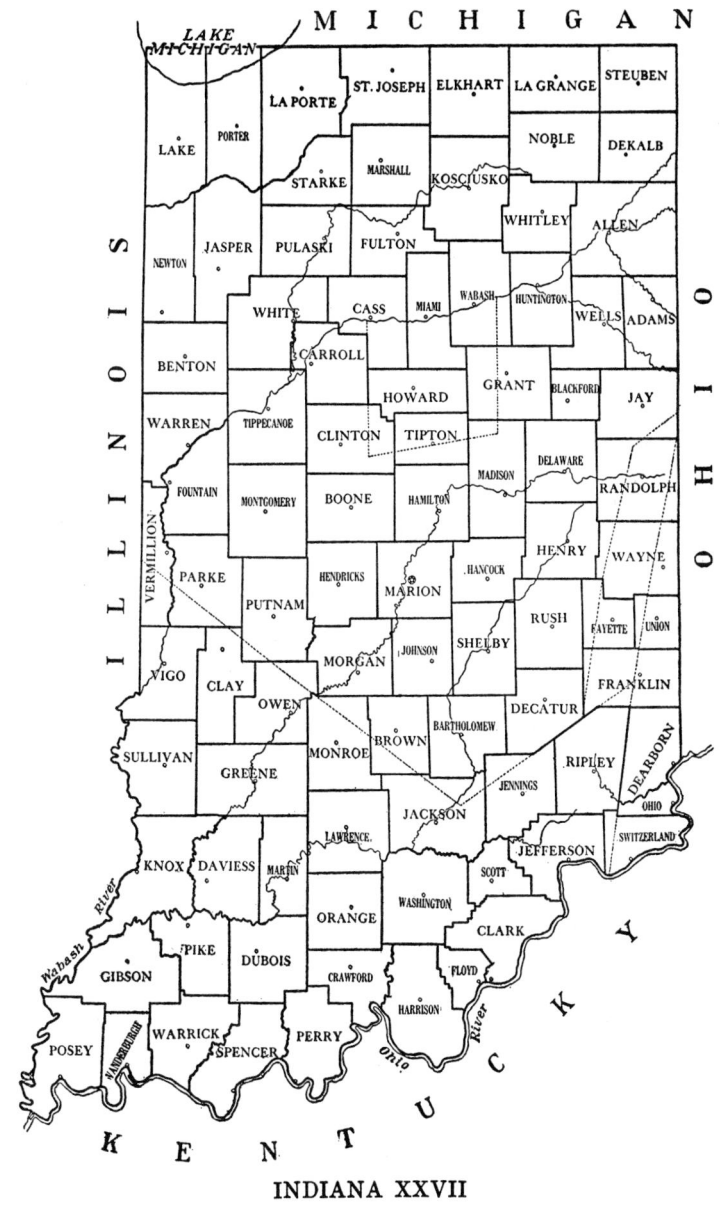

[As changed by county commissioners' reports and statutes, 1859 to 1873]

INDIANA XXVIII

TRANSFERS

Lake-Newton-Porter-Jasper. Transfer, March 8, 1923
La Porte-Starke. Transfer, March 2, 1925
La Porte-St. Joseph. Transfer, March 9, 1931

INDIANA XXVIII

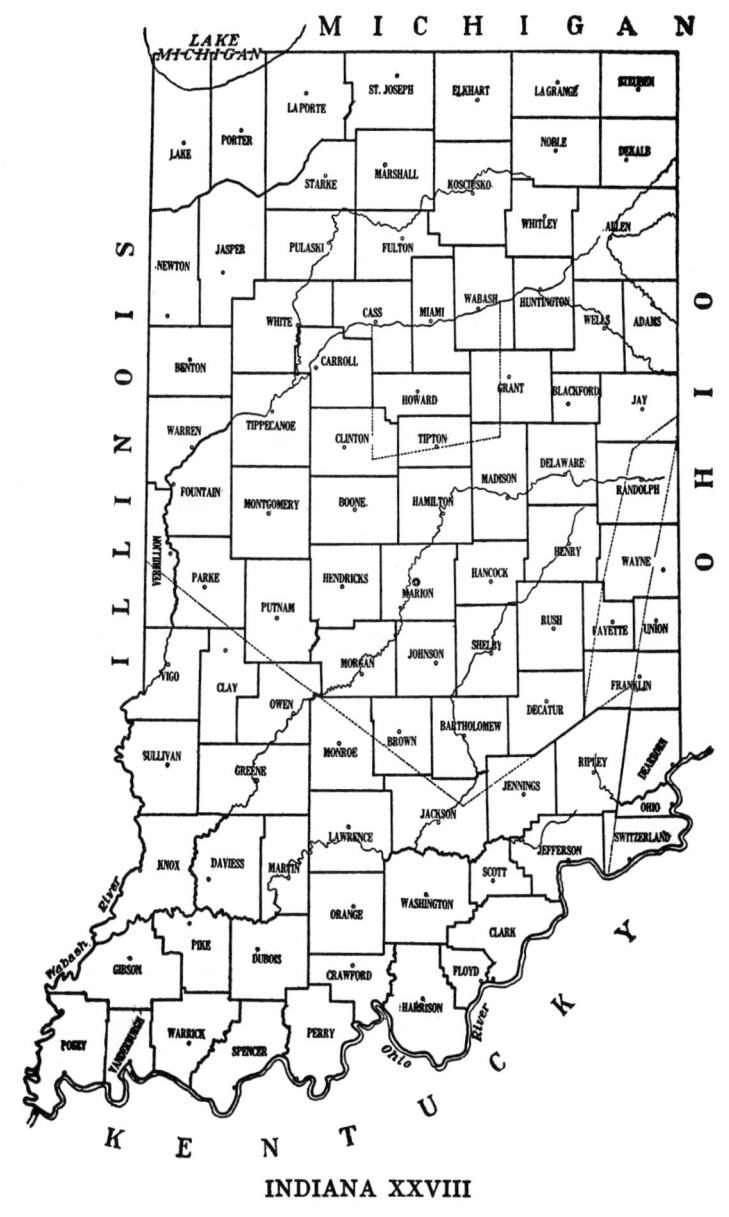

[As changed by the General Assemblies of 1923, 1925, 1931]

RANDOLPH COUNTY I
[Northwest Territory]

OCTOBER 5, 1795: Formation by proclamation, affecting St. Clair County.

BOUNDARIES: "Beginning at the Cave Spring, a little south of the new design, and running from thence due east to the line of the county of Knox, and thence with that line to the Ohio River; thence with the Ohio to the Mississippi; thence with the Mississippi to the parallel of the said Cove Spring; and thence to the place of beginning." Smith (ed.), *St. Clair Papers*, 2:345 n.

Some copies of the *St. Clair Papers* show two variations from the reading given above. Instead of "Cave" Spring, they read "Cove" Spring, and the phrase "thence with that line to the Ohio River," reads, "thence west with that line to the Ohio River."

There has been some question as to the location of Cave, or Cove Spring. After a recent investigation of the locality, Mr. J. Nick Perrin, of Belleville, Illinois, and Mr. Rufus W. Gardner, surveyor of Monroe County, Illinois, state their conclusion that Cave Spring was situated in section 31, township 3 south, range 9 west. The location has also been given as section 10, township 4 south, range 10 west. Emmerson, Louis L. (comp.), *Counties of Illinois* . . ., 6 (Springfield, 1920). See, however, notes on the boundary line between Randolph and St. Clair counties, with maps, Randolph County II and III.

New Design was a settlement about four miles south of the present town of Waterloo, Illinois. Woollen, W. W., Howe, D. W., and Dunn, J. P. (eds.), *Executive Journal of Indiana Territory, 1800-1816*, 99 n. (*Indiana Historical Society Publications*, 3:no. 3, Indianapolis, 1900).

COUNTY SEAT: With the division of St. Clair County, Kaskaskia became the county seat for the newly formed Randolph County. See Allinson, May, "The Government of Illinois, 1790-1799," in *Transactions of the Illinois State Historical Society*, 1907, p. 290 (Springfield, 1908).

RANDOLPH COUNTY, NORTHWEST TERRITORY I
[Proclamation: Oct. 5, 1795]

RANDOLPH COUNTY II
[Indiana Territory]

FEBRUARY 3, 1801: Alteration by proclamation.

BOUNDARIES: Beginning "on the Ohio River at a Place called the Great Cave, below the Saline Lick, thence by a direct north line until it intersects an East and West line running from the Mississippy through the Sink hole spring, thence along the said line to the Mississippy thence down the Mississippi to the mouth of the Ohio and up the Ohio to the place of beginning." Territorial *Executive Journal*, 98.

Great Cave was located on section 13, township 12 south, range 9 east, near the present village of Cave-in-Rock, Hardin County, Illinois. Emmerson (comp.), *Counties of Illinois*, 6.

According to this same source, Sink Hole Spring was identical with Cave Spring, and the north boundary of Randolph County was merely extended further east; other authorities believe that Sink Hole Spring was somewhat north of the Cave Spring, and that Randolph County's whole north boundary was therefore changed. According to Mr. J. Nick Perrin, and Mr. Gardner, surveyor of Monroe County, Sink Hole Spring was situated in section 13, township 3 south, range 10 west. See text with preceding and following maps for further comment on the boundary between Randolph and St. Clair counties.

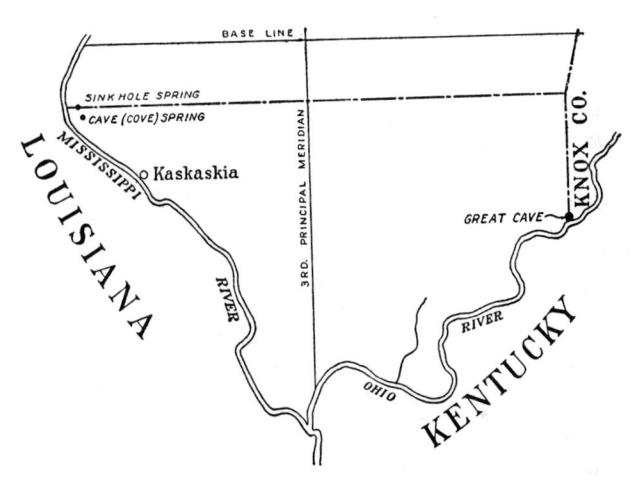

RANDOLPH COUNTY, INDIANA TERRITORY II
[Proclamation: Feb. 3, 1801]

RANDOLPH COUNTY III
[Indiana Territory]

MARCH 25, 1803: Alteration by proclamation, effective May 1, 1803.

BOUNDARY CHANGE: "The line seperating the Counties of Randolph and St. Clair shall begin on the Mississippi River four miles and thirty two Chains south of the point, where the present division line intersects the Mississippi Bottom, thence by a direct line to the Sink hole Springs, thence by a line north sixty degrees East until it intersects a north line running from the great Cave on the Ohio River." Territorial *Executive Journal*, 118.

It is explained that the beginning of the boundary between St. Clair and Randolph counties was moved 4 miles and 32 chains south to restore to St. Clair County part of the small settlement of New Design, which had been originally within St. Clair County, but which the change of boundary in 1801 had transferred to Randolph County. Territorial *Executive Journal*, 99 n. This explanation depends upon the acceptance of the theory that Cave Spring and Sink Hole Spring were several miles apart. See preceding Randolph County maps for further comment on this boundary line.

RANDOLPH COUNTY BOUNDARIES 207

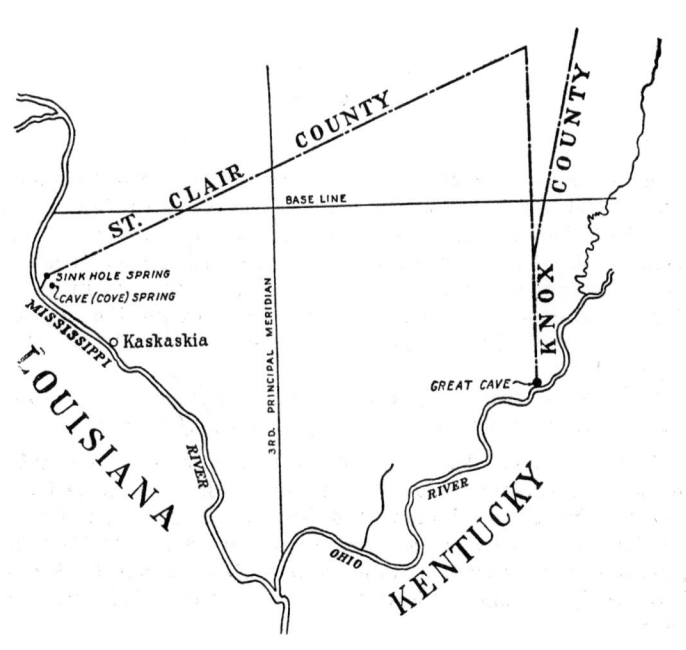

RANDOLPH COUNTY, INDIANA TERRITORY III
[Proclamation: Mar. 25, 1803, effective May 1, 1803]

ST. CLAIR COUNTY I
[Northwest Territory]

APRIL 27, 1790: Formation by proclamation.

BOUNDARIES: "Beginning at the mouth of the Little Michilmacinack River, running thence southerly in a direct line to the mouth of the little river above Ft. Massac, on the Ohio River; thence with Ohio to its junction with the Mississippi: thence up the Mississippi to the mouth of the Illinois River, and so up the Illinois River to the place of beginning, with all the adjacent islands of the said Illinois and Mississippi Rivers." *St. Clair Papers*, 2:165 n.

The "little river" mentioned in the description is now called Massac Creek. Emmerson (comp.), *Counties of Illinois*, 6.

COUNTY SEAT: There was no seat of justice for the entire county. Courts were held in three judicial districts, centering at Cahokia, Prairie du Rocher, and Kaskaskia. *St. Clair Papers*, 2:165 n; *The Laws of the Northwest Territory, 1788-1800*, 154 (*Collections of the Illinois State Historical Library*, vol. 17, Springfield, 1925); Allinson, "Government of Illinois, 1790-1799," pp. 284-85.

ST. CLAIR COUNTY BOUNDARIES

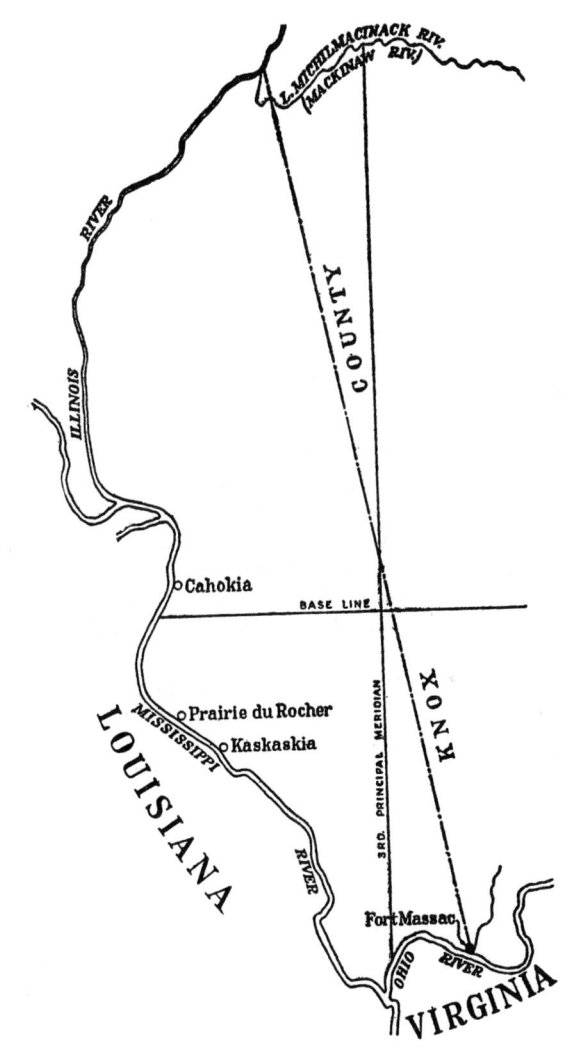

ST. CLAIR COUNTY, NORTHWEST TERRITORY I
[Proclamation: Apr. 27, 1790]

ST. CLAIR COUNTY II
[Northwest Territory]

OCTOBER 5, 1795: Alteration by proclamation forming Randolph County, Northwest Territory.

BOUNDARY CHANGE: By the proclamation of October 5, 1795, that part of St. Clair County south of a line "beginning at the Cave Spring, a little south of the new design, and running from thence due east" to the eastern boundary of St. Clair County, was transferred to Randolph County. *St. Clair Papers*, 2:345 n.

For a note on Cave Spring and the "new design," see text with map of Randolph County, Northwest Territory I.

COUNTY SEAT: Cahokia became the county seat of St. Clair County, upon the formation of Randolph County. See Allinson, "Government of Illinois, 1790-1799," p. 290.

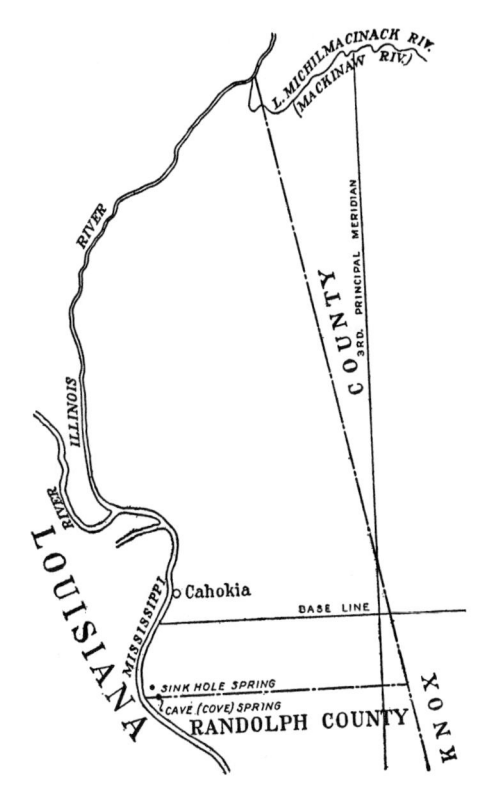

ST. CLAIR COUNTY, NORTHWEST TERRITORY II
[Proclamation: Oct. 5, 1795]

ST. CLAIR COUNTY III
[Indiana Territory]

FEBRUARY 3, 1801: Alteration by proclamation.

BOUNDARIES: "The County of St. Clair shall be bounded on the South by the beforementioned East and West line, running from the Mississippi through the Sink hole Spring to the intersection of the North line running from the great cave aforesaid, thence from the said point of intersection by a direct line to the mouth of the great Kennoumic River falling into the Southerly bend of Lake Michigan, thence by a direct north east line to the division line between the Indiana and North Westrn Territorys, thence along the said line to the Territorial Boundary of the United States, and along the said Boundary line to the Intersection thereof with the Mississippi and down the Mississippi to the place of beginning." Territorial *Executive Journal*, 98-99.

For a location of Great Cave and Sink Hole Spring, see text with map of Randolph County, Indiana Territory II.

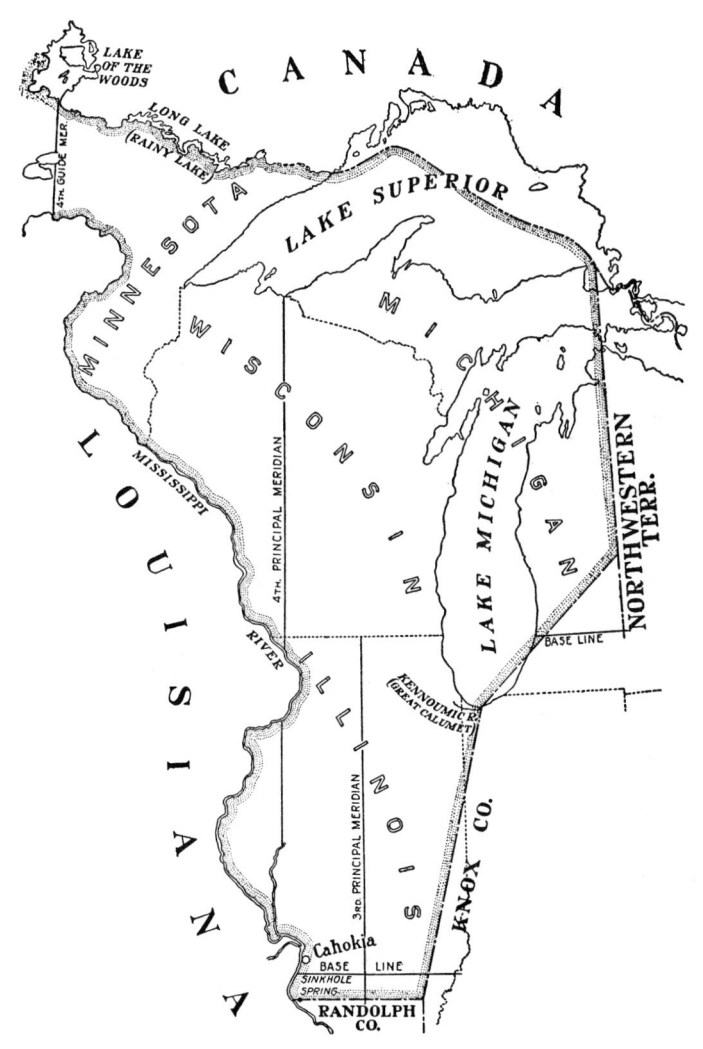

ST. CLAIR COUNTY, INDIANA TERRITORY III
[Proclamation: Feb. 3, 1801]

ST. CLAIR COUNTY IV
[Indiana Territory]

JANUARY 24, 1803: Alteration by proclamation forming Wayne County, Indiana Territory, effective upon admission of Ohio to the Union.

BOUNDARY CHANGE: By the proclamation of January 24, 1803, that part of St. Clair County lying north and east of a line beginning at "the Southerly Extreame of Lake Michigan," running thence due west until it "would intersect a North and South line passing through the most westerly bend of the said Lake, and thence north along the last mentioned line to the Territorial Boundary of the United States," was transferred to Wayne County. Territorial *Executive Journal*, 115.

MARCH 25, 1803: Alteration by proclamation extending Randolph County, effective May 1, 1803.

BOUNDARY CHANGE: "The line seperating the Counties of Randolph and St. Clair shall begin on the Mississippi River four miles and thirty two Chains south of the point, where the present division line intersects the Mississippi Bottom, thence by a direct line to the Sink hole Springs, thence by a line north sixty degrees East until it intersects a north line running from the great Cave on the Ohio River." Territorial *Executive Journal*, 118.

See map of Randolph County, Indiana Territory III, for note on this alteration.

When Illinois Territory was formed in 1809, St. Clair County was cut off from Indiana Territory.

ST. CLAIR COUNTY BOUNDARIES 215

ST. CLAIR COUNTY, INDIANA TERRITORY IV

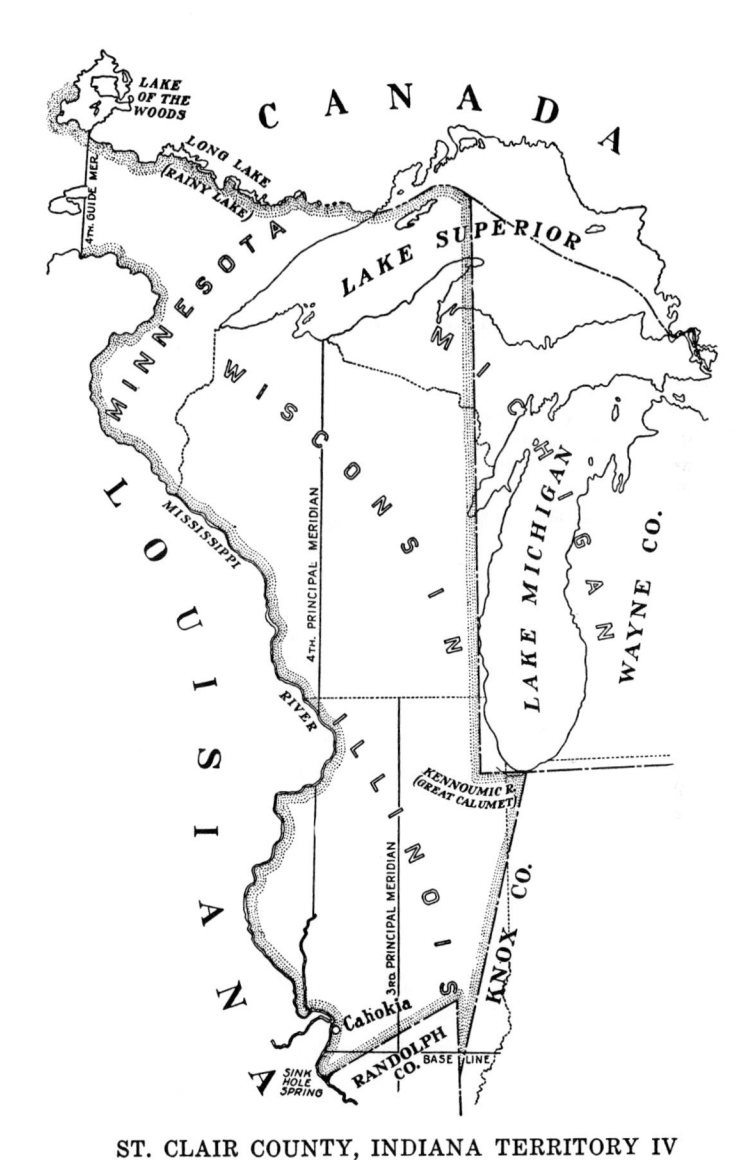

[Proclamations: Jan. 24, 1803, effective on admission of Ohio; Mar. 25, 1803, effective May 1, 1803]

WAYNE COUNTY I
[Northwest Territory]

AUGUST 15, 1796: Formation by proclamation, affecting Knox County.

BOUNDARIES: "Beginning at the mouth of Cuyahoga river, upon Lake Erie, and with the said river to the portage, between it and the Tuscarawas branch of the Muskingum; thence down the said branch to the forks, at the carrying place above Fort Lawrence (Laurens); thence by a west line, to the eastern boundary of Hamilton county, (which is a due north line from the lower Shawnee town upon the Scioto river); thence by a line west-northerly to the southern part of the portage, between the Miamis of the Ohio and the St. Marys river; thence by a line also west-northerly, to the southwestern part of the portage, between the Wabash and the Miamis of Lake Erie, where Fort Wayne now stands; thence by a line west-northerly, to the most southern part of Lake Michigan; thence along the western shores of the same, to the northwest part thereof, (including the lands upon the streams emptying into said lake); thence by a due north line to the territorial boundary in Lake Superior, and through the said boundary through lakes Huron, Sinclair, and Erie, to the mouth of the Cuyahoga river, the place of beginning." Laning, J. F., "The Evolution of Ohio Counties," in *Ohio Archaeological and Historical Publications*, 5:333 (Columbus, 1900).

The boundary along Lake Michigan is too vaguely defined for representation.

The formation of Indiana Territory in 1800 split this county almost in two. The part remaining in the Northwest Territory continued to function as a county, and upon the formation of Ohio in 1803 was reorganized. See following map, and maps of Indiana Territory I, and Knox County IV.

COUNTY SEAT: Courts were held at Detroit. See Laning, *op. cit.*, 5:350.

WAYNE COUNTY BOUNDARIES 217

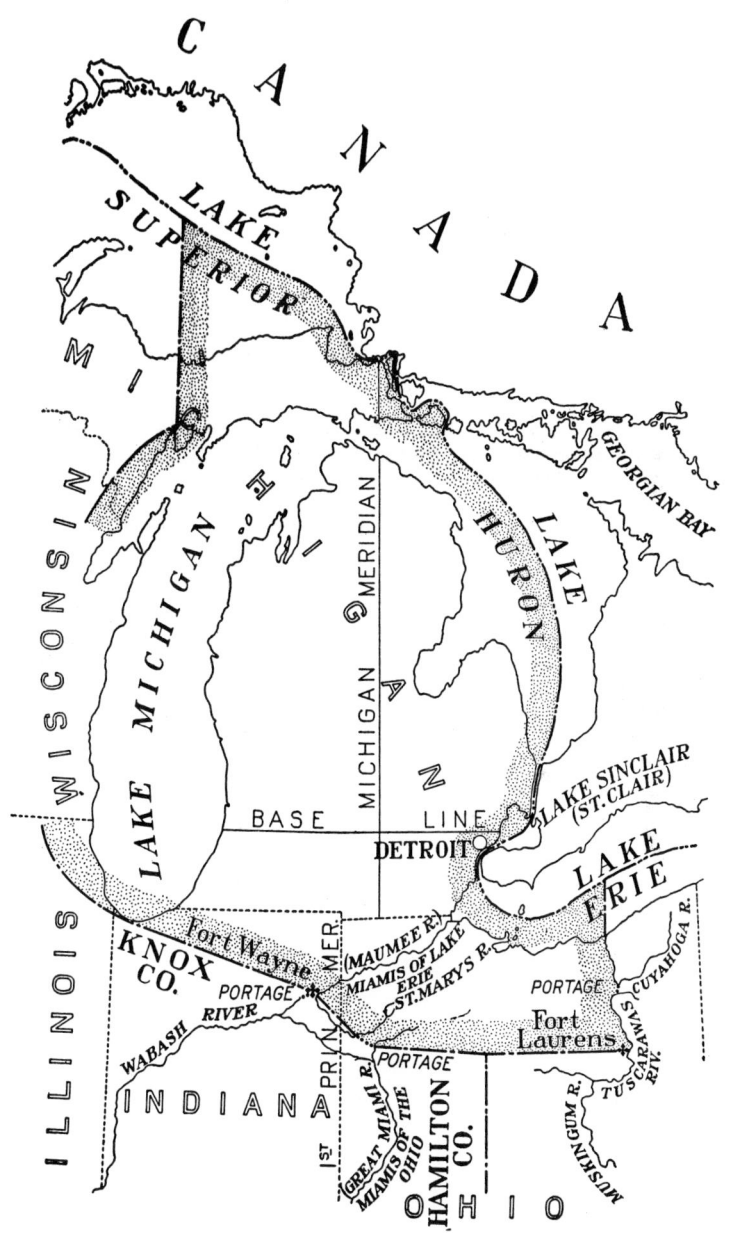

WAYNE COUNTY, NORTHWEST TERRITORY I

[Proclamation: Aug. 15, 1796]

WAYNE COUNTY II
[Indiana Territory]

JANUARY 24, 1803: Reorganization by proclamation, effective upon admission of Ohio to the Union. The formation affected Knox and St. Clair counties.

BOUNDARIES: "Beginning at a point where an East and west line passing through the Southerly Extreame of Lake Michigan would intersect a North and South line passing through the most westerly bend of the said Lake, and thence north along the last mentioned line to the Territorial Boundary of the United States thence along the said boundary line to a point where a due east and west line passing through the Southerly extreme of Lake Michigan would intersect the same thence west along the last mentioned line to the place of begining." Territorial *Executive Journal*, 115.

The county was cut off from Indiana Territory by the formation of Michigan Territory in 1805. See maps of Indiana Territory, II and III.

COUNTY SEAT: Courts were to be held at Detroit. Territorial *Executive Journal*, 115.

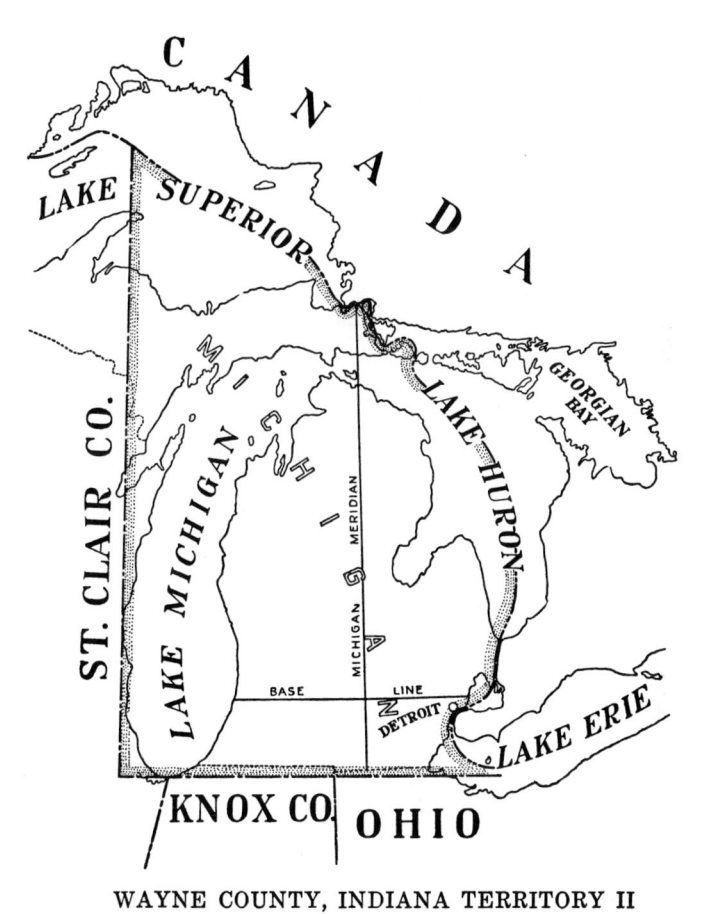

WAYNE COUNTY, INDIANA TERRITORY II
[Proclamation: Jan. 24, 1803, effective on admission of Ohio]

WABASH COUNTY
[New Purchase]

JANUARY 20, 1820: Formation by statute making provision for the New Purchase.

BOUNDARIES: Wabash County was formed as "all that part of the said new purchase, lying west of the second principal meridian." *Laws of Indiana*, 1819-20, p. 96.

The New Purchase included that territory ceded by the Indians at the Treaty of St. Mary's, October 2-6, 1818.

COUNTY SEAT: Jurisdiction in civil cases within Wabash County was held concurrently by the bounding counties of Vigo, Owen, and Monroe. Wabash County had, therefore, no county seat. On January 9, 1821, jurisdiction over the county was given to Monroe County, but on January 2, 1822, this act was repealed. Wabash was put under the jurisdiction of Parke and Putnam counties. *Ibid.*, 96; 1820-21, p. 84; 1821-22, p. 119.

WABASH COUNTY BOUNDARIES 221

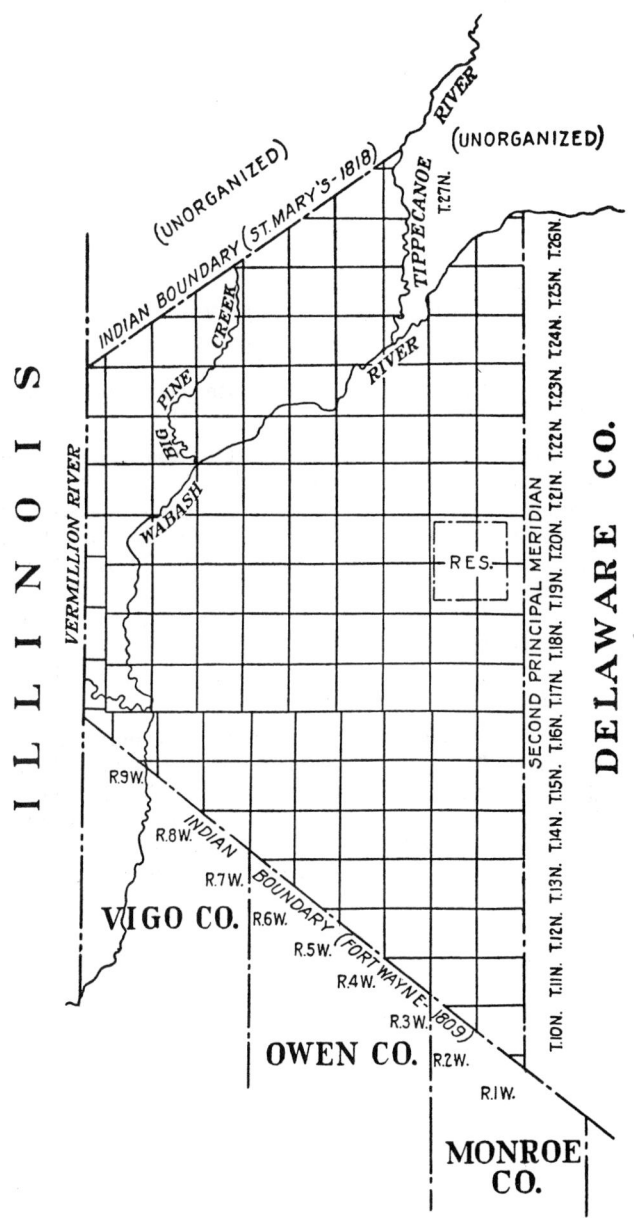

WABASH COUNTY, NEW PURCHASE
[Law: Jan. 20, 1820]

DELAWARE COUNTY
[New Purchase]

JANUARY 20, 1820: Formation by statute making provision for the New Purchase.

BOUNDARIES: "All the remaining part of the said new purchase, lying east of the second principal meridian, except so much of it as has been attached to the counties of Fayette, Jackson, and Wayne by former laws, and except so much of it as is attached by the first section of this act, to the counties named therein." *Laws of Indiana*, 1819-20, p. 96.

The counties mentioned in the first section of the act are Randolph and Franklin.

The New Purchase was that territory ceded by the Indians at the Treaty of St. Mary's, October 2-6, 1818.

COUNTY SEAT: Delaware County had no county seat, the bounding counties of Jackson, Jennings, Ripley, Franklin, Fayette, Wayne, and Randolph, having concurrent jurisdiction over civil cases. By an act of January 9, 1821, Delaware County was placed under the jurisdiction of Bartholomew County. This law was repealed January 2, 1822. *Laws of Indiana*, 1819-20, p. 96; 1820-21, p. 84; 1821-22, p. 119.

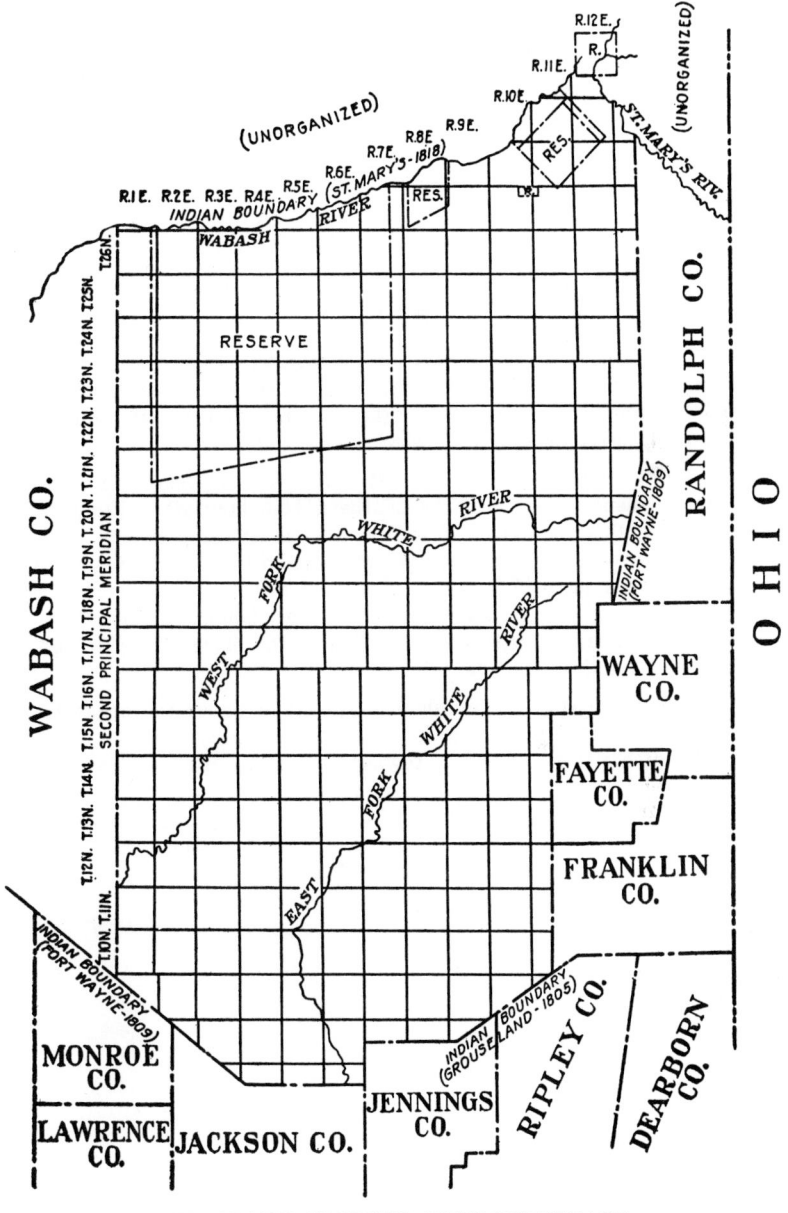

DELAWARE COUNTY, NEW PURCHASE
[Law: Jan. 20, 1820]

ADAMS COUNTY

FEBRUARY 7, 1835: Formation by statute, effective on publication. The formation affected territory attached to Allen and Randolph counties. Adams was organized under an act of January 23, 1836, effective March 1, 1836.

BOUNDARIES: "Commencing at the south east corner of Allen county, thence west with the southern boundary of said county, to the north east corner of section five in township twenty eight range thirteen, thence south with the section lines to the township line between townships twenty four and twenty five, thence east with the said township line to the eastern boundary line of the state, thence north with the state line to the place of beginning." *Laws of Indiana*, 1834-35 (general), p. 44.

COUNTY SEAT: Commissioners appointed under the organization act reported to county commissioners on May 18, 1836, their choice of a site in section 3, township 27 north, range 14 east of the second principal meridian, where Decatur now stands. *Ibid.*, 1835-36 (general), p. 46; Tyndall and Lesh (eds.), *Standard History of Adams and Wells Counties*, 1:54-55; *Biographical and Historical Record of Adams and Wells Counties*, 197-98.

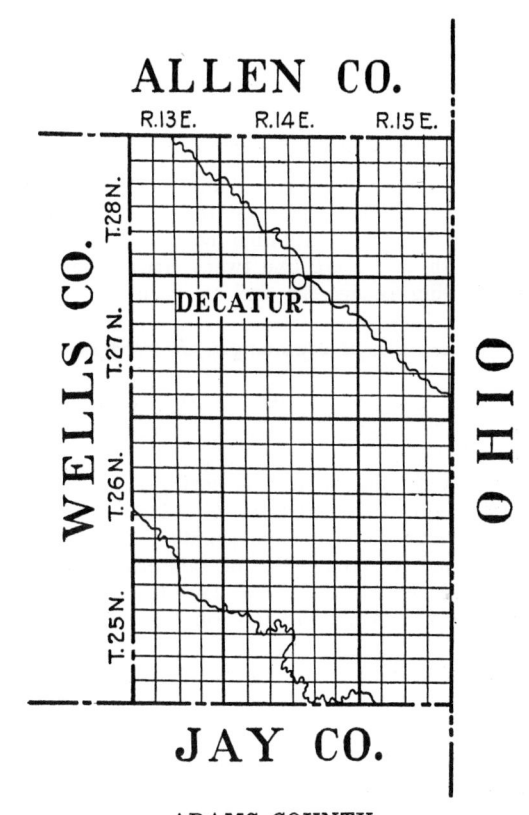

ADAMS COUNTY

[Law: Feb. 7, 1835, effective on publication]

ALLEN COUNTY

DECEMBER 17, 1823: Formation by statute, effective April 1, 1824. The formation affected Randolph and Delaware counties.

BOUNDARIES: "Beginning at a point on the line dividing this state and the state of Ohio, where the township line dividing townships twenty-eight and twenty-nine north, intersects the same; thence north with said state line twenty-four miles; thence west to the line dividing ranges ten and eleven east; thence south to the line dividing townships twenty-eight and twenty-nine north, thence east to the place of beginning." *Revised Laws of Indiana*, 1823-24, p. 109.

The same act attached to Allen County, for civil and criminal jurisdiction "all that part of the new purchase lying south of the . . . county of Allen, and north of the township line, dividing townships twenty-five and twenty-six north, so far west as the line dividing ranges seven and eight east, and also that part of the new purchase, lying north of said county . . . including all that territory contained within the line of said county, and the northern boundary of the state." *Ibid.*, 110-11. An act of January 24, 1828, attached to Allen "all the country . . . east of the second principal meridian line, and north to the northern line of the state." *Laws of Indiana*, 1827-28, p. 14. A fourth attachment, made on February 10, 1831, included all the territory north of the line dividing townships 25 and 26, and "east of range nine, to the northern line of the state." *Ibid.*, 1830-31 (special), p. 18.

COUNTY SEAT: Fort Wayne was made the county seat in May, 1824, by commissioners appointed under the act forming the county. *Revised Laws of Indiana*, 1823-24, p. 109.

ALLEN COUNTY BOUNDARIES 227

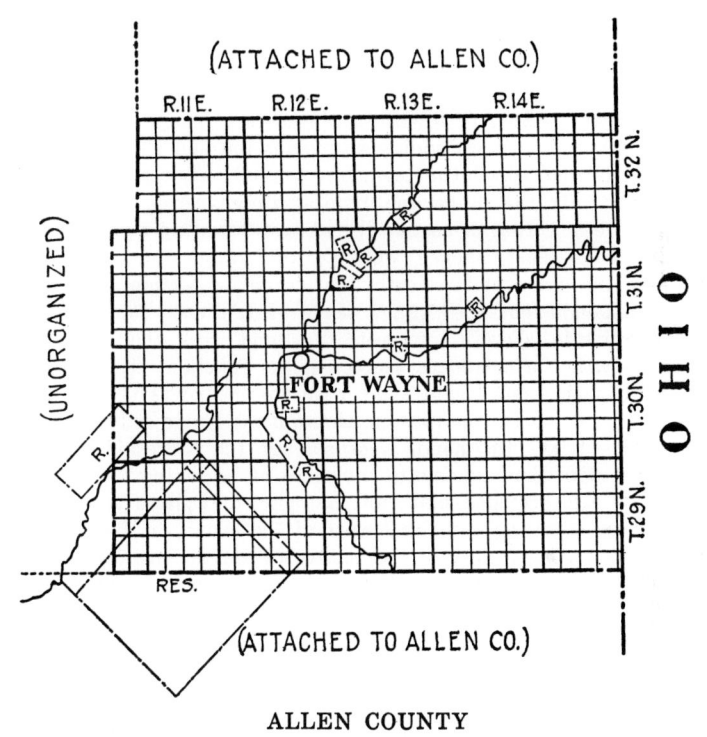

ALLEN COUNTY

[Law: Dec. 17, 1823, effective Apr. 1, 1824]

BARTHOLOMEW COUNTY I

JANUARY 8, 1821: Formation by statute effective February 12, 1821. The formation affected Jackson County and Delaware. The county was organized by act of January 9, 1821, effective February 12, 1821.

BOUNDARIES: "Beginning at the south west corner of section eighteen in township seven north of range four east, thence north to the northwest corner of township ten north of range four east, thence east with the line dividing townships ten and eleven north to the north east corner of township ten of range seven east, thence south with the range line dividing ranges seven and eight to the south east corner of section thirteen, in township eight north of range seven east, thence west to the range line dividing ranges six and seven at the north west corner of section nineteen in township eight north of range seven east, thence south with said range line to where it intersects Big Sand creek, thence down said creek with the meanders thereof to its junction with Driftwood river, thence down said river with the meanders thereof to where an east and west line running through the centre of township seven north strikes the north west side of the aforesaid river, thence west with the said line to the place of beginning."

The law also provided that "all that part of Delaware county lying east of Monroe county and west of the county of Bartholomew . . . be . . . attached to the county of Bartholomew temporarily, for the purpose of exercising jurisdiction only." *Laws of Indiana*, 1820-21, pp. 79-80, 82-83.

By the organizing act of January 9, 1821, Bartholomew was given jurisdiction over all of Delaware County. This act was repealed January 2, 1822. *Ibid.*, pp. 83-84; 1821-22, p. 119.

COUNTY SEAT: Commissioners appointed under the act forming the county reported on February 15, 1821, their selection of part of sections 24 and 25, township 9 north, range 5 east of the second principal meridian as the site for a county seat. The name Tiptona was suggested, but on March 20, the name Columbus was adopted. The county seat has never been removed. *Ibid.*, 1820-21, p. 80; *History of Bartholomew County*, 314, 317; Shockley, "County Seat Wars in Indiana," in *Indiana Magazine of History*, 10:no.1:23.

DELAWARE CO.

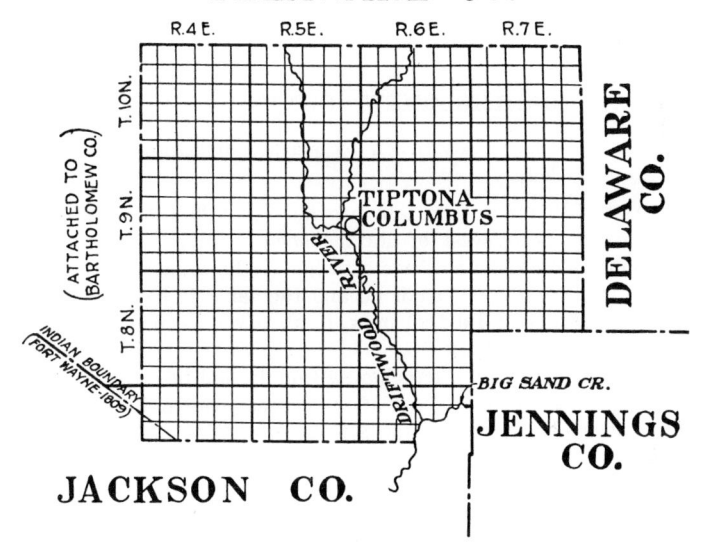

BARTHOLOMEW COUNTY I

[Law: Jan. 8, 1821, effective Feb. 12, 1821]

BARTHOLOMEW COUNTY II

JANUARY 16, 1828: Alteration by statute attaching territory to Bartholomew County.

BOUNDARY CHANGE: The law provided that "all the residue of the territory lying west of Bartholomew county and east of Monroe county which has not been attached to the counties of Jackson or Monroe by this act, shall be and the same is hereby made a part of the county of Bartholomew, to all intents and purposes." *Laws of Indiana*, 1827-28, p. 15.

The west boundary of Bartholomew County had been the range line dividing ranges 3 and 4 east of the second principal meridian. See descriptions with maps, Jackson County VIII, and Monroe County III.

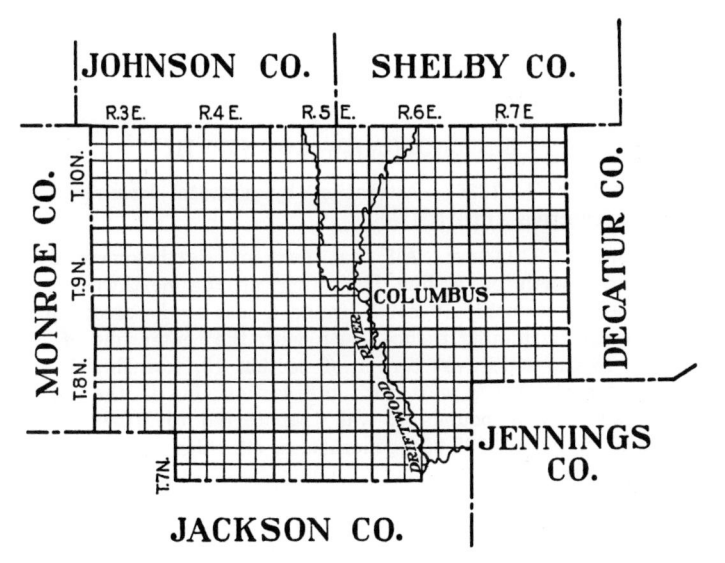

BARTHOLOMEW COUNTY II
[Law: Jan. 16, 1828]

BARTHOLOMEW COUNTY III

FEBRUARY 4, 1836: Alteration by statute forming Brown County, effective April 1, 1836.

BOUNDARY CHANGE: All that part of Bartholomew County west and north of a line beginning at the northwest corner of section 3, township 10 north, range 4 east of the second principal meridian, running thence south with the center line of range 4 east to the southwest corner of section 10, township 7 north, range 4 east, thence west with the section line to the old Bartholomew County boundary, was transferred to Brown County. *Laws of Indiana,* 1835-36 (general), p. 52. See text of law with map, Brown County.

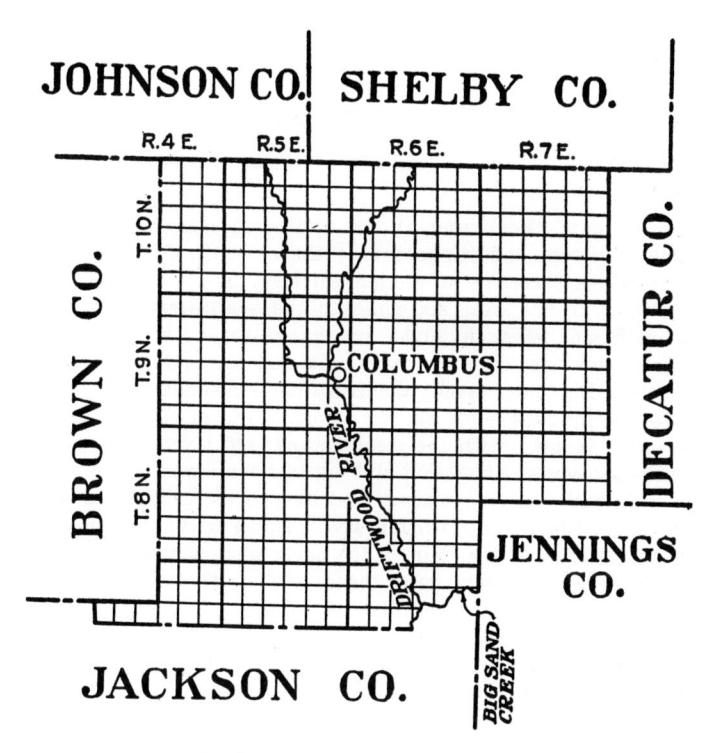

BARTHOLOMEW COUNTY III
[Law: Feb. 4, 1836, effective Apr. 1, 1836]

BARTHOLOMEW COUNTY IV

FEBRUARY 17, 1838: Alteration by statute defining county boundaries.

BOUNDARIES: "Beginning at the north-east corner of section one, township ten, and range seven; thence south fifteen miles, to the south-east corner of section thirteen, in town eight and range seven; thence west six miles to the south-west corner of section eighteen, township eight and range seven; thence south with the range line, dividing ranges six and seven, to where the same crosses Big Sand creek; thence with the meandering of said creek to its junction with the Driftwood fork of White river; thence north [south] with the meanders of said river, to or near the south-east corner of section sixteen, in town seven, range six; thence west with the government land line, to the south-west corner of section fifteen, in township seven, range four; then on the centre line dividing range four, to the north-west corner of section three, township ten, range four; thence east on the township line dividing ten and eleven, to the place of beginning." *Laws of Indiana,* 1837-38 (local), pp. 253-54.

The territory marked (a) on the map was left unassigned by the above act. It later became part of Jackson County. See map, Jackson County X.

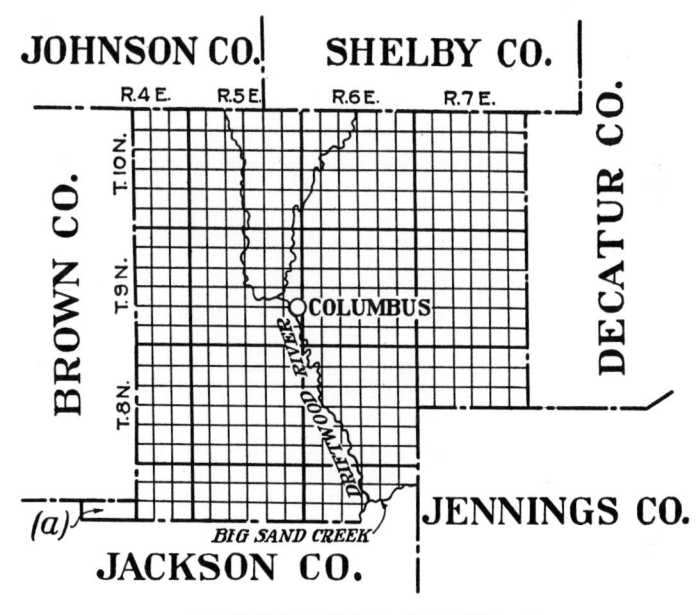

BARTHOLOMEW COUNTY IV
[Law: Feb. 17, 1838]

BENTON COUNTY

FEBRUARY 18, 1840: Formation by statute, effective on passage. The formation affected Jasper County.

BOUNDARIES: "All that part of Jasper county south of the line between township twenty-six (26) and twenty-seven (27) north." *Laws of Indiana*, 1839-40 (general), p. 62. See map, Jasper County II.

COUNTY SEAT: The law forming the county did not provide commissioners to locate a county seat, but stipulated that courts be held at the home of Basil Justus, a short distance south of the present town of Oxford. An act of January 31, 1843, appointed commissioners to select a county seat. Their choice was a part of sections 18 and 20 in township 24 north, range 7 west. The town's first name, Milroy, was changed to Oxford in the same year. In 1874, after a long struggle between contending factions, the county seat was removed to Fowler, where it has since remained. *Laws of Indiana*, 1839-40 (general), p. 63; 1842-43 (local), pp. 123-24; Shockley, "County Seat Wars," *op. cit.*, 10:no.1:39-40; *Counties of Warren, Benton, Jasper and Newton, Indiana* . . ., 227, 233-34, 241-51.

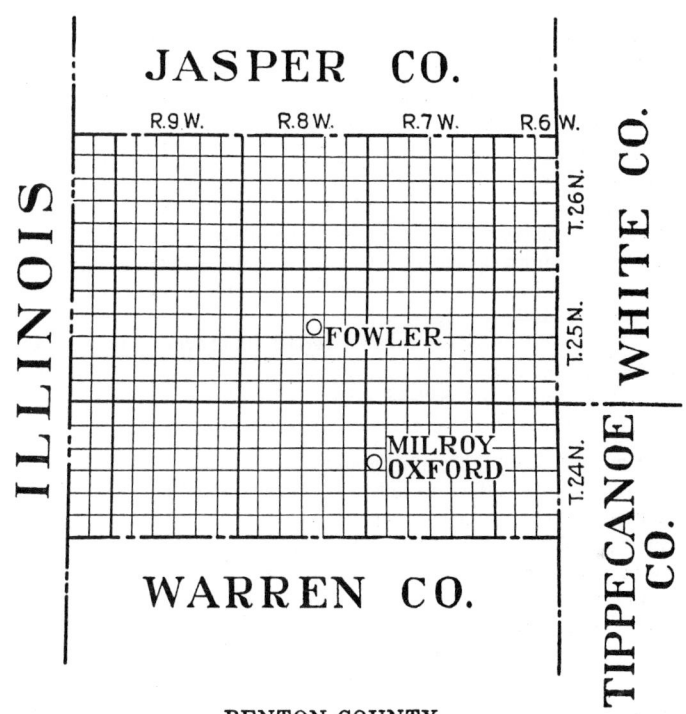

BENTON COUNTY BOUNDARIES 237

BENTON COUNTY
[Law: Feb. 18, 1840, effective on passage]

BLACKFORD COUNTY

FEBRUARY 15, 1838: Formation by statute, effective April 2, 1838. The formation affected Jay County. Blackford was organized by an act of January 29, 1839, effective on passage.

BOUNDARIES: "Beginning at the north-east [northwest] corner of section number five in township number twenty-four, range number twelve east; thence west on the south boundary of Wells county, to the east boundary of Grant county; thence south with the eastern boundary of said county, to the north boundary of Delaware county; thence east to the south-east [northeast] corner of section eight, township twenty-two, range twelve east; thence north on the nearest section line, to the place of beginning." *Laws of Indiana*, 1837-38 (local), p. 290.

The second of the errors corrected in brackets above was corrected by the organizing act; the other was apparently overlooked until the session of 1842-43. *Laws of Indiana*, 1838-39 (general), p. 65; *Revised Statutes of Indiana*, 1842-43, p. 86.

COUNTY SEAT: Commissioners appointed under the law forming the county failed to act. A second set of commissioners appointed under the organizing act selected a site, probably that of Hartford City, which was unsatisfactory, but none of the subsequent acts for relocating a county seat appear to have made an actual change. Commissioners appointed under an act of February 4, 1841, filed the report on June 10 of their selection of the site in section 11, township 23 north, range 10 east. The town was first called Hartford. *Laws of Indiana*, 1837-38 (local), p. 291; 1838-39 (general), pp. 64-65; 1839-40 (general), pp. 42-43; 1840-41 (local), p. 202; Shockley, "County Seat Wars," *op cit.*, 10:no.1:38-39; *Biographical and Historical Record of Jay and Blackford Counties, Indiana* . . ., 725; Shinn, Benjamin G., *Biographical Memoirs of Blackford County, Indiana* . . ., 224-30 (Chicago, 1900).

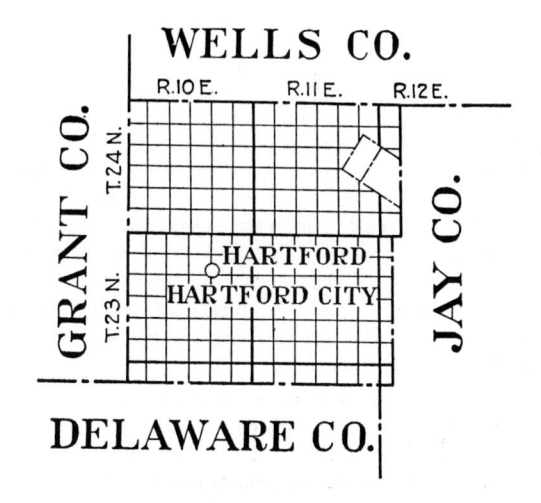

BLACKFORD COUNTY BOUNDARIES 239

BLACKFORD COUNTY
[Law: Feb. 15, 1838, effective Apr. 2, 1838]

BOONE COUNTY

JANUARY 29, 1830: Formation by statute, effective April 1, 1830. The formation affected territory attached to Hendricks and Marion.

BOUNDARIES: "Beginning at the south west corner of the county of Hamilton; thence north with the line dividing ranges two and three, seventeen and a half miles, to the centre stake of section thirteen, township twenty, range three [two] east; thence westwardly, twenty-four miles, to the centre stake on the west side of section eighteen, township twenty, range two west; thence south with the line dividing ranges two and three west, seventeen and a half miles, to the north west corner of the county of Hendricks; thence east with the northern boundary of the counties of Hendricks and Marion, to the place of beginning." *Laws of Indiana*, 1829-30, p. 31.

COUNTY SEAT: Commissioners appointed under the act forming the county selected Jamestown as the first county seat of Boone County, but its location did not meet approval, and a law of January 26, 1832, appointed commissioners to make a relocation within two miles of the center of the county. The commissioners met at the center of the county on May 1, 1831, and selected that spot as the county seat. The removal to the new site, which was called Lebanon, was made in 1833. *Ibid.*, 32; 1831-32, pp. 114-15; Crist, *History of Boone County*, 1:114-15.

BOONE COUNTY

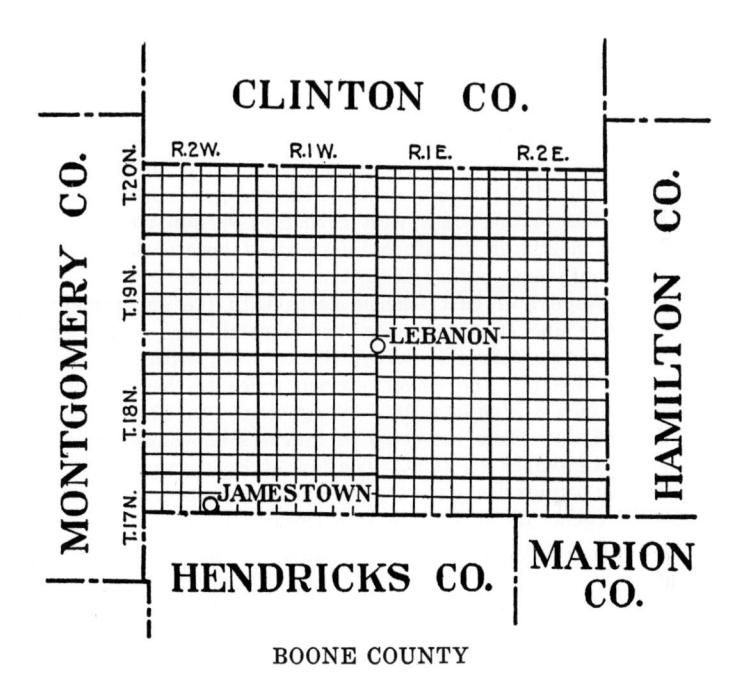

[Law: Jan. 29, 1830, effective Apr. 1, 1830]

BROWN COUNTY

FEBRUARY 4, 1836: Formation by statute, effective April 1, 1836. This formation affected Bartholomew, Jackson, and Monroe counties.

BOUNDARIES: "Beginning at the north west conner of section one, in township ten north, of range one west [east] of the second principal meredian; thence south, with the government land line twenty miles to the south west corner of section twelve, in township seven north, of the aforesaid range; thence east sixteen miles to the south east corner of section nine in the last named township, in range four east; thence north with the government land line twenty one [twenty] miles to the north east corner of section four, in township ten north; thence west, with the line dividing townships ten and eleven sixteen miles to the place of beginning." *Laws of Indiana*, 1835-36 (general), p. 52.

The first of the errors corrected in brackets above was rectified by act of December 20, 1836. The law of February 17, 1838, defining county boundaries, gave the complete description correctly. *Ibid.*, 1836-37 (general), p. 100; 1837-38 (local), p. 260.

COUNTY SEAT: Commissioners appointed in the law forming the county, on August 11, 1836, selected a site in the town of Jacksonburg; the name was changed to Nashville by a law of February 6, 1837. The county seat has never been moved. *Ibid.*, 1835-36 (general), pp. 52-53; 1836-37 (local), p. 320; Shockley, "County Seat Wars," *op. cit.*, 10:no.1:34; Blanchard (ed.), *Counties of Morgan, Monroe and Brown, Indiana*, 683, 727.

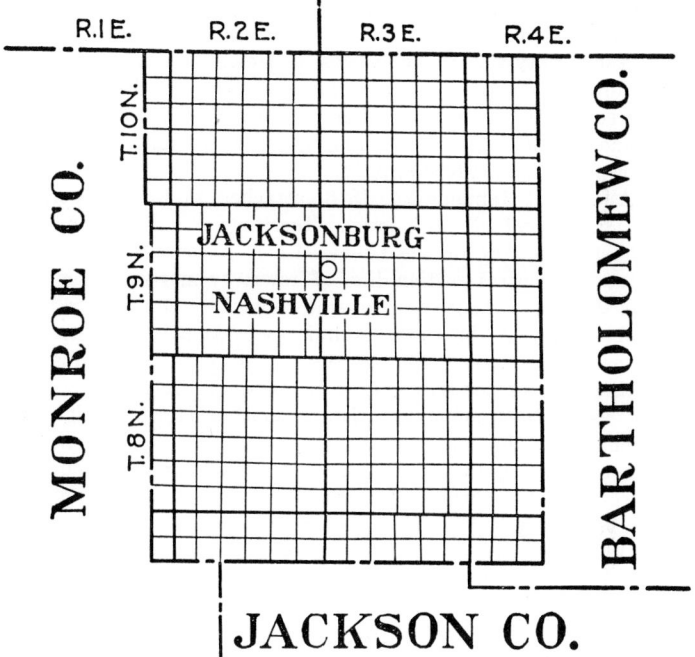

BROWN COUNTY

[Law: Feb. 4, 1836, effective Apr. 1, 1836]

CARROLL COUNTY I

JANUARY 7, 1828: Formation by statute, effective May 1, 1828.

BOUNDARIES: "Beginning at the north west corner of township numbered twenty-four north, range two west . . .; thence south nine miles to the centre of township numbered 23; thence east 17 miles to the western boundary of the great Miami reservation; thence north with said boundary eighteen miles to the centre of township numbered twenty-six; thence west eight miles to the south-east corner of section sixteen, range one west; thence north three miles to the township line dividing townships twenty-six and twenty-seven; thence west thirteen miles to the section line, dividing sections four and five, range three west; thence south with said sectional line, twelve miles to the northern boundary of Tippecanoe county; thence east four miles to the place of beginning." *Laws of Indiana*, 1827-28, p. 21.

An act of January 24, 1828, attached to Carroll County for civil and criminal jurisdiction "territory . . . Beginning on the western boundary of the Great Miami reservation, at the point where the central section line of town. twenty-five, north, intersects the same; thence east on said central section line, to the eastern boundary of the Great Miami reservation; thence north, with the eastern boundary line of the . . . reservation, and a line in continuation of the same, to a point where such line will intersect the Indian boundary; thence south-westerly, with the said boundary, to the centre of range three, west . . .; thence south, with the central line of said range, to the northern boundary of Carroll county; thence with the boundary of said county to the . . . beginning." The law also provided that "all the country north of the counties of Tippecanoe and Carroll, and west of the second principal meridian, to the northern boundary of the state, and not otherwise attached . . . be attached to the counties of Tippecanoe and Carroll, with concurrent civil and criminal jurisdiction." *Ibid.*, 14.

An act of January 30, 1830, attached to Carroll County "all that part of the county of Wabash, that lies west of Carroll." *Ibid.*, 1829-30, p. 26. The attachment made in 1830 was altered by an act of February 10, 1831, to include that territory north of Tippecanoe and Carroll, to the line dividing townships 30 and 31 north. *Ibid.*, 1830-31 (special), p. 18.

COUNTY SEAT: Commissioners appointed under the act forming the county reported May 15, 1828, their selection of a site in section 29, township 25 north, range 2 west, to be called Carrollton. The name was changed to Delphi within the month. *Ibid.*, 1827-28, p. 21; Stewart, *Early Settlement of Carroll County*, 21-22; *Historical Atlas of Indiana*, 261.

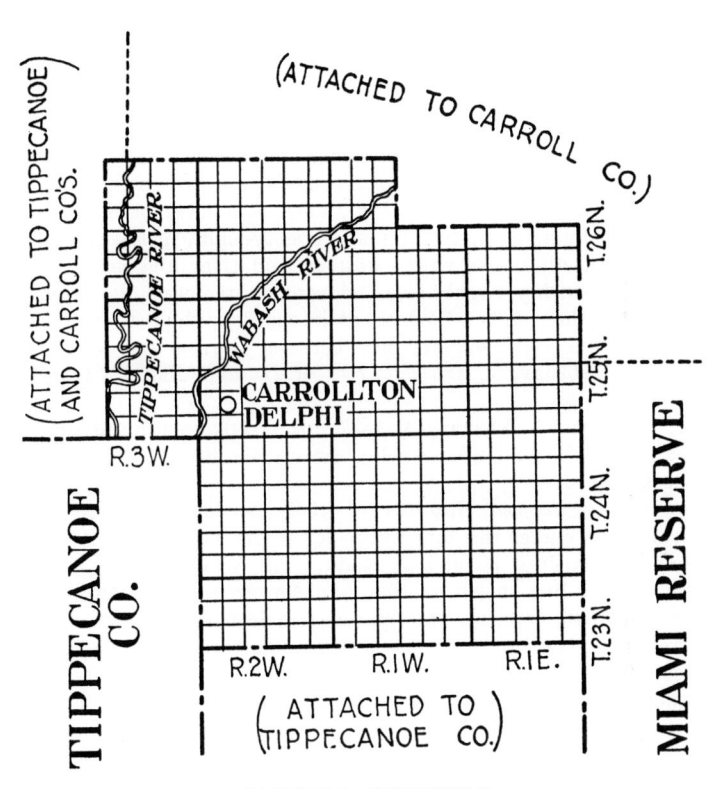

CARROLL COUNTY I

[Law: Jan. 7, 1828, effective May 1, 1828]

CARROLL COUNTY II

FEBRUARY 14, 1839: Alteration by statute to change the boundary line of the counties of Carroll and White, effective on passage.

BOUNDARY CHANGE: "Hereafter the Tippecanoe river shall be the western boundary of Carroll county, from where the north line of said county strikes the river, until said river strikes the section line dividing thirty-three and twenty-eight, in township twenty-six, and all the territory west of said river and north of said line in township twenty-six, and range three west, is hereby attached to the county of White, as intended by the act, entitled, 'an act to alter the boundary line between Carroll and White,' approved, February 4, 1837." *Laws of Indiana*, 1838-39 (general), p. 93.

The law of February 4, 1837, incorrectly mentioned township six north, instead of township twenty-six north. *Ibid.*, 1836-37 (local), p. 379.

In the *Revised Statutes* of 1843 the law describing county boundaries makes the Tippecanoe River the west boundary of Carroll in townships 25 and 26 north. The White County boundary follows the line shown on this map, however, and a law of January 13, 1846, confirms this reading: "So much of section thirty-three in township twenty-six north, range three west, and sections four, nine, sixteen, and twenty-one in township twenty-five north, range three west, as lies west of Tippecanoe river, . . . is hereby made a part of Carroll county." *Revised Statutes of Indiana*, 1842-43, pp. 84, 89-90; *Laws of Indiana*, 1845-46 (local), p. 264.

A law of February 16, 1839, attached to Carroll for jurisdictional purposes "so much of the great Miami reservation [as lies] south of Cass county, and north of Clinton, and west of the range line dividing ranges two and three east." *Ibid.*, 1838-39 (general), p. 75.

CARROLL COUNTY BOUNDARIES 247

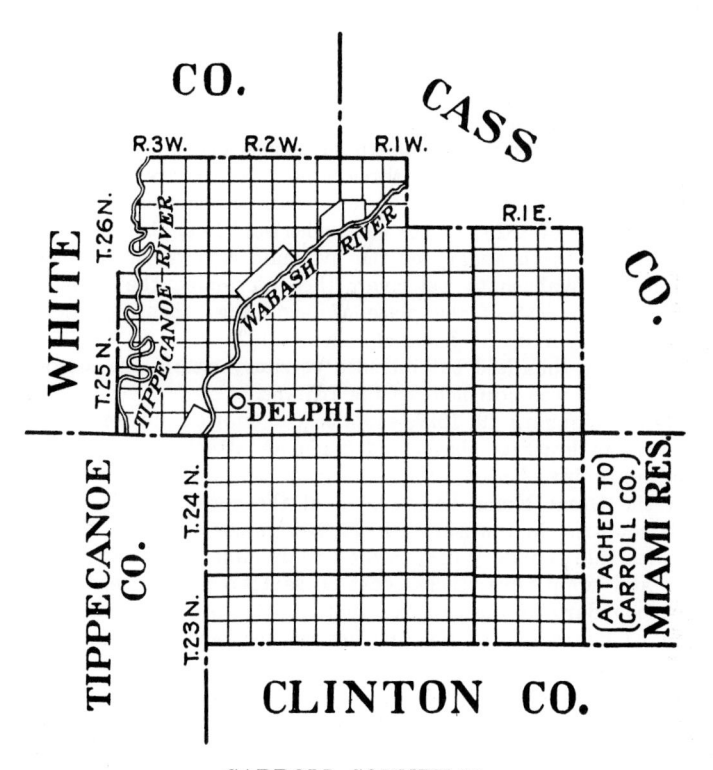

CARROLL COUNTY II

[Law: Feb. 14, 1839, effective on passage]

CASS COUNTY I

DECEMBER 18, 1828: Formation by statute, effective April 14, 1829. The formation affected territory attached to Carroll County.

BOUNDARIES: "Beginning on the west boundary line of the great Miami reservation at the intersection of the township line, dividing townships twenty-five and twenty-six; thence north three miles, thence west eight miles to the south west corner of section fifteen, township twenty-six, north of range one west; [thence north three miles] thence west three miles to the range line dividing ranges one and two west; thence north to the boundary line of the purchase of 1826; thence east, with said line, about twenty eight miles to the boundary of the five mile reservation, extending from the Wabash to Eel river; thence crossing the Wabash to a point due east of the place of beginning: thence west to the place of beginning." *Laws of Indiana*, 1828-29, p. 26.

The county thus laid out included territory within the Miami Reserve, which was still held by the Indians.

A law of January 19, 1829, supplied the omitted phrase of the law, given in brackets above, and made an attachment for civil and criminal jurisdiction: "beginning on the western boundary line of the Great Miami reservation, at the corner of Cass and Carroll counties, in township twenty-five, range one east, thence south with said boundary line, to the line dividing townships twenty-four and twenty-five; thence east on said township line, to the eastern boundary of the said reservation; thence north, with the eastern boundary line of the said reservation, and in a line due north in continuation thereof, to the state line; thence on the line of the state, west to a point, where a due south line will strike the western boundary line of the said county of Cass; thence south to the line of Cass county; and thence east and with the lines of said county of Cass to the place of beginning." *Ibid.*, 28.

COUNTY SEAT: Commissioners appointed under the act forming the county announced their selection of a site in Logansport as the county seat, in a report of August 12, 1829. The county seat has never been removed. Helm (ed.), *History of Cass County*, 268-69; Powell (ed.), *History of Cass County*, 1:60.

CASS COUNTY BOUNDARIES 249

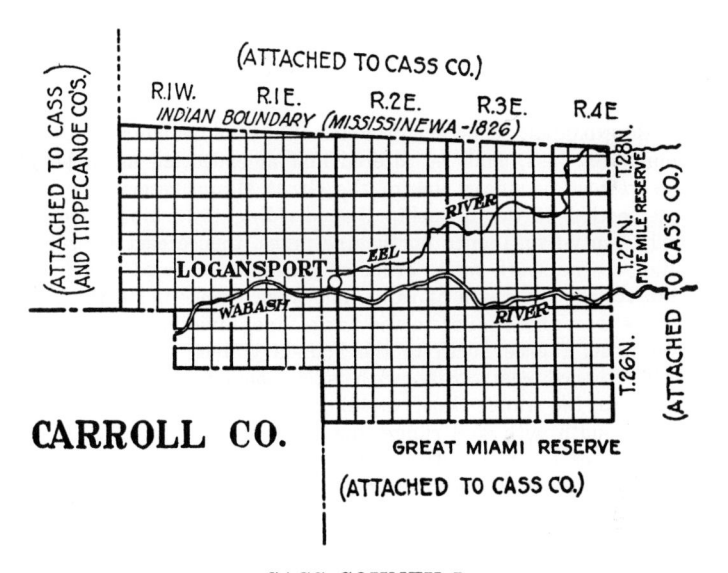

CASS COUNTY I

[Law: Dec. 18, 1828, effective Apr. 14, 1829]

CASS COUNTY II

FEBRUARY 2, 1832: Alteration by statute forming Miami County, effective April 2, 1832, and extending Cass County, effective on passage.

BOUNDARIES: The act provided that "the boundary lines of the county of Cass, shall be altered and amended, so as to begin at the western boundary line of the Great Miami reservation, at the intersection of the township line, dividing townships twenty-four and twenty-five, thence north nine miles, thence east [west] eight miles, to the south west corner of section number fifteen, in township twenty-six, north of range one west, thence north three miles, thence west three miles to the range line, dividing ranges one and two west; thence north to the boundary line of the purchase of 1826; thence eastwardly with said boundary line, twenty-four miles to the range line, dividing ranges three and four east, thence south with said range line, crossing the Wabash, to a point due east of the place of beginning, thence west to place of beginning." *Laws of Indiana*, 1831-32, pp. 113-14.

The boundary is given as corrected in the law of January 30, 1833, which defines the boundaries of Miami, Wabash, and Cass counties. *Ibid.*, 1832-33, p. 39.

A law of February 10, 1831, limited the district attached to Cass County for jurisdiction to "all the territory north of Cass county and the great Miami reservation to the line" dividing townships 30 and 31. *Ibid.*, 1830-31 (special), p. 18.

CASS COUNTY BOUNDARIES 251

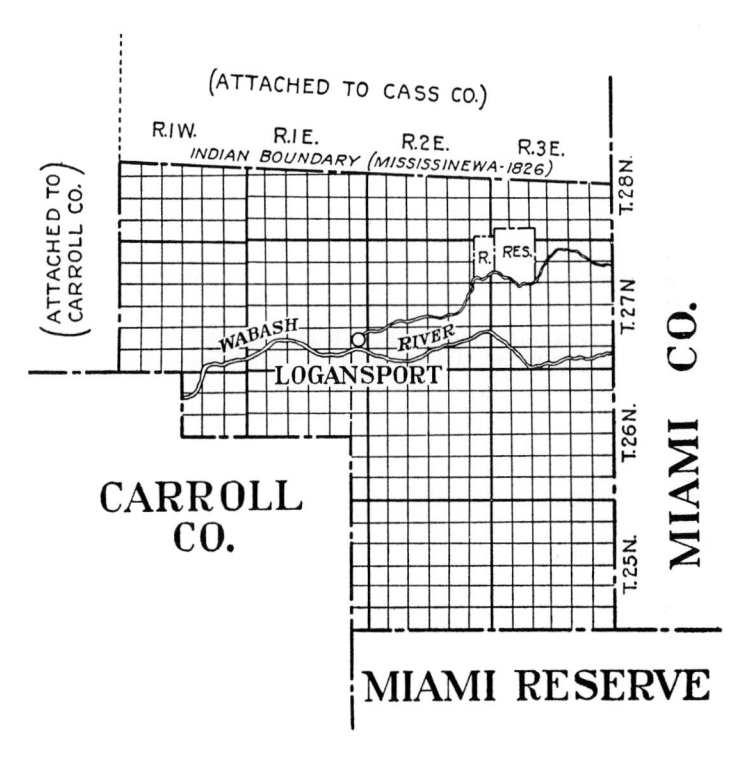

CASS COUNTY II

[Law: Feb. 2, 1832, effective Apr. 2, 1832, and on passage]

CASS COUNTY III

JANUARY 2, 1834: Alteration by statute organizing Miami County, effective March 1, 1834.

BOUNDARY CHANGE: The act attached to Miami County that part of Cass County, and territory attached to Cass County, included in the following boundaries: "beginning at the south west corner of the county of Miami, running thence west two miles, thence north with the section lines thirty miles, to the north east corner of section three, in township twenty nine, and in range three, thence east two miles on the line dividing townships twenty-nine and thirty, to the north west corner of the county of Miami." *Laws of Indiana*, 1833-34, p. 65.

White County was formed by an act of February 1, 1834, effective April 1, 1834.

By a law of December 24, 1834, the attachment to Cass was redefined to include "all the territory lying north of the county of Cass to the line dividing townships thirty two and thirty three north," for judicial and representative purposes. *Ibid.*, 1834-35 (general), p. 77.

CASS COUNTY BOUNDARIES 253

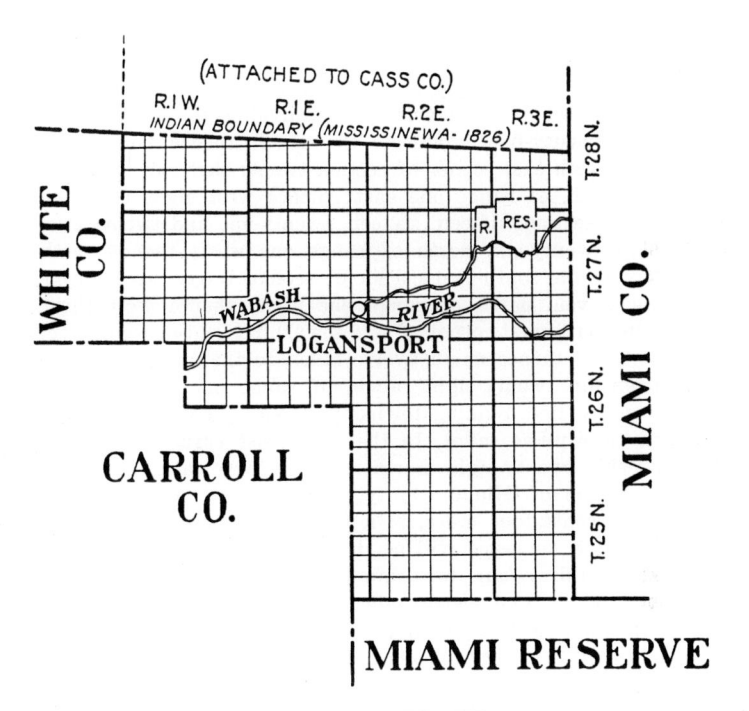

CASS COUNTY III

[Law: Jan. 2, 1834, effective Mar. 1, 1834]

CASS COUNTY IV

FEBRUARY 17, 1838: Alteration by statute defining county boundaries.

BOUNDARIES: "Beginning on the west side of the great Miami reservation line where the township line, dividing townships twenty-four and twenty-five intersects the same; thence north nine miles to the north east corner of section twenty-three, in township twenty-six north, of range one east; thence west eight miles, to the corner of sections fifteen, sixteen, twenty-one and twenty-two, in township twenty-six, north of range one west; thence north three miles, to the south-east corner of section thirty-three, township twenty-seven, north of range one west; thence west three miles, to the south-west corner of said township twenty-seven north, range one west; thence north twelve miles, to the north-west corner of township twenty-eight north, of range one west; thence on the township line dividing townships twenty-eight and twenty-nine east, twenty-two miles, to the north-east corner of section three, township twenty-eight, north of range three east, that being the western line of Miami county; thence south on the Miami county line, twenty-four miles, to a point in the great Miami reserve, when it is surveyed will be the south-west [southeast] corner of section thirty-four, township [twenty-five] north, of range three east; thence west eleven miles, to the place of beginning." *Laws of Indiana*, 1837-38 (local), p. 256.

By a law of February 16, 1839, so much of the Great Miami Reserve as lay "south of Cass county, and north of the township line dividing townships twenty-two and twenty-three," and was "bounded on the west" by the range line dividing ranges 2 and 3 east, was attached to Cass County for jurisdiction. *Ibid.*, 1838-39 (general), p. 75.

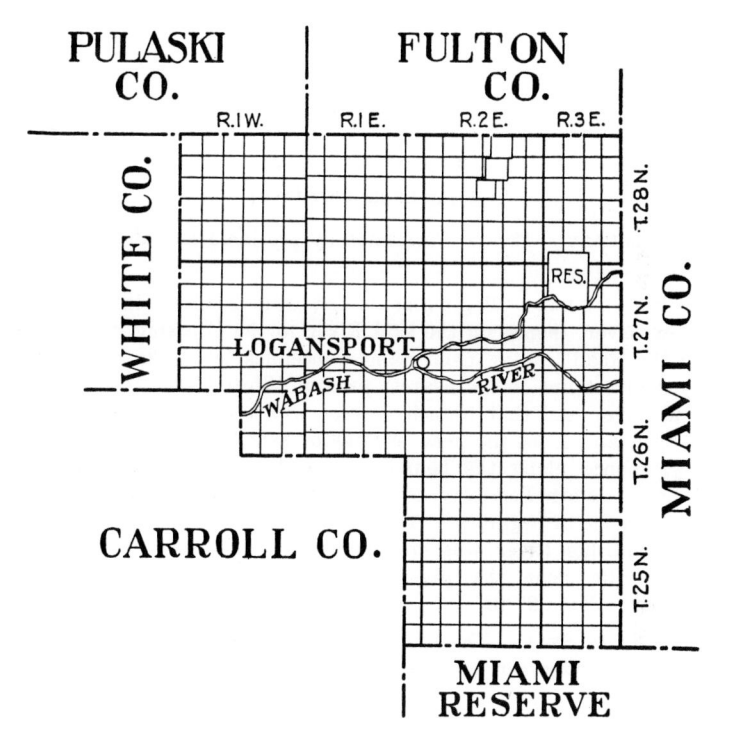

CASS COUNTY IV

[Law: Feb. 17, 1838]

CLARK COUNTY I
[Indiana Territory]

FEBRUARY 3, 1801: Formation by proclamation, affecting Knox County.

BOUNDARIES: "Beginning at the Ohio river at the mouth of Blew River, thence up the said River to the Crossing of the same by the Road leading from Saint Vincennes to Clarks ville, thence by a direct line to the nearest part of White River thence up the said River and that branch thereof which runs toward Fort Recovery, and from the head springs of said branch to Fort Recovery, thence along the boundary line Between the Indiana, and North Western Territory, to the Ohio, thence down the same River to the place of begining." Territorial *Executive Journal*, 97.

The Blue River was crossed by the road from Vincennes to Clarksville near the present northern boundary of Harrison County. *Ibid.*, 97 n.

COUNTY SEAT: The proclamation forming the county directed that the first session of courts be held at Springville. *Ibid.*, 97.

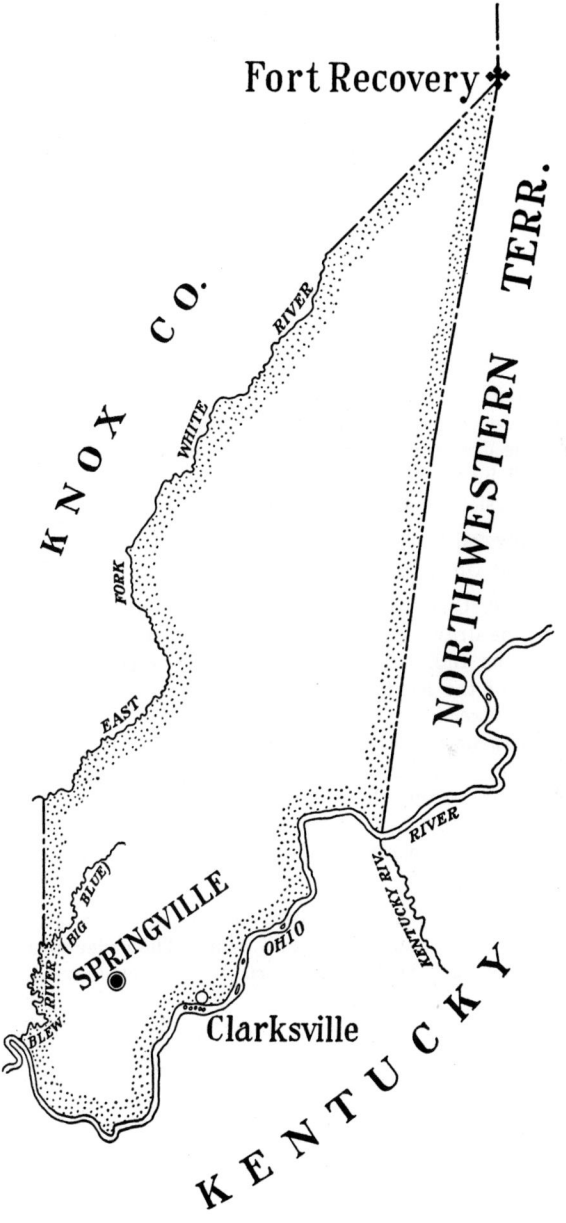

CLARK COUNTY I
[Proclamation: Feb. 3, 1801]

CLARK COUNTY II
[Indiana Territory]

APRIL 30, 1802: Alteration by Ohio Enabling Act, effective upon admission of Ohio.

BOUNDARY CHANGE: The tiny northeastern peak of Clark County between Fort Recovery, the Greenville Treaty line of 1795, and a "line drawn due north from the mouth of the Great Miami" was cut off by the formation of the state of Ohio. *Annals*, 7 Congress, 1 session, 1349.

JANUARY 24, 1803: Alteration by proclamation, effective upon admission of Ohio.

BOUNDARY CHANGE: "That tract of Country included between a North line drawn from the mouth of the Big miamie River, the Ohio and the Indian boundary line running from a point opposite the mouth of the Kentucky River," was attached to Clark County. Territorial *Executive Journal*, 115.

This attachment was made pursuant to the Ohio Enabling Act of April 30, 1802, before Governor Harrison had "Sufficient Information respecting the settlements below the great miamie, to Enable him to form [a government] in that tract." For a comment on the controversy as to the date of Ohio's admission to the Union, see pages 4-5.

COUNTY SEAT: By ordinance of the governor, June 9, 1802, Jeffersonville was made the county seat. The order was to become effective August 1, 1802. Territorial *Executive Journal*, 109.

CLARK COUNTY BOUNDARIES 259

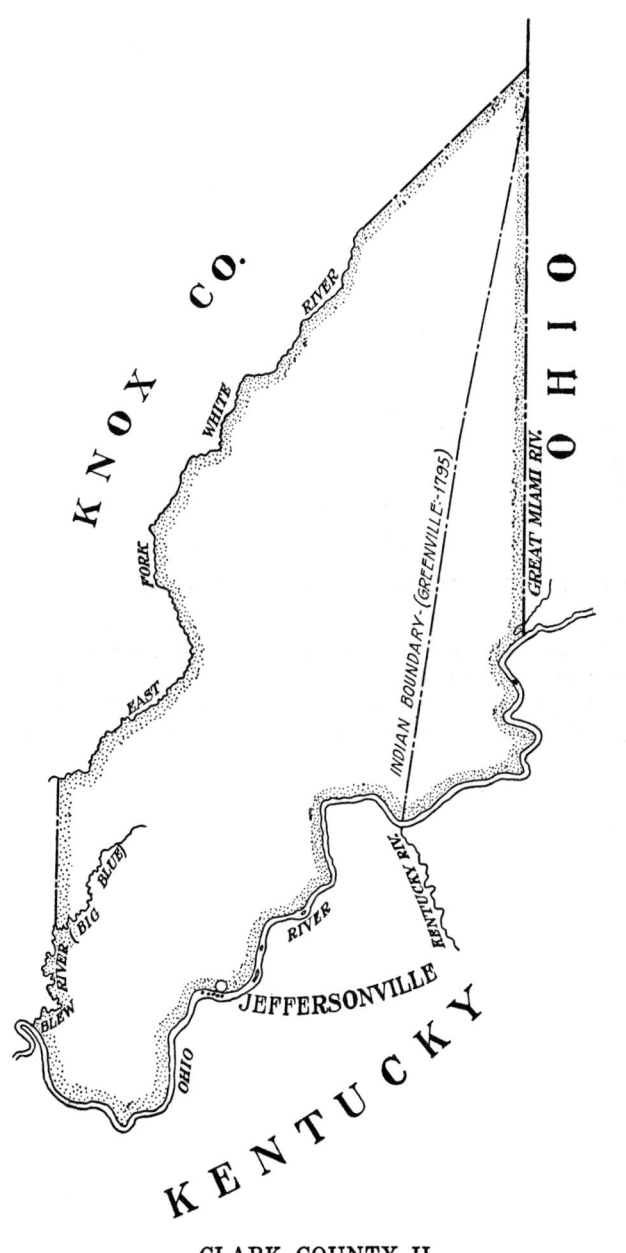

CLARK COUNTY II

[Act of Congress: Apr. 30, 1802, and Proclamation: Jan. 24, 1803, effective on admission of Ohio]

CLARK COUNTY III
[Indiana Territory]

MARCH 7, 1803: Alteration by proclamation forming Dearborn County.

BOUNDARY CHANGE: All that part of Clark County southeast of "the Indian Boundary line runing from a point opposite the mouth of the River Kentucky" was transferred to Dearborn County. Territorial *Executive Journal*, 116. See map, Dearborn County I.

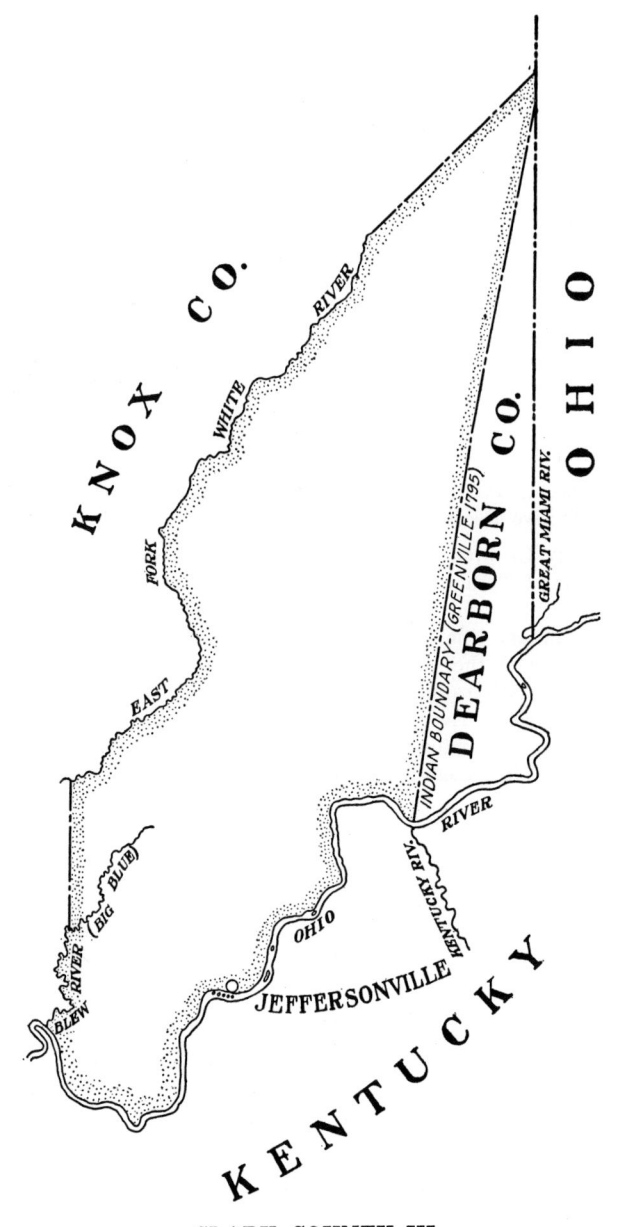

CLARK COUNTY III
[Proclamation: Mar. 7, 1803]

CLARK COUNTY IV
[Indiana Territory]

OCTOBER 11, 1808: Alteration by statute forming Harrison County, effective December 1, 1808.

BOUNDARY CHANGE: All that part of Clark County, south of the Grouseland Treaty line of 1805 and west of "the line which divides the fourth and fifth ranges east, thence with the latter to the . . . boundary line, between the Jeffersonville, and Vincennes districts, and with the same to the intersection of the line dividing the fifth and sixth ranges, thence with the said range line until it strikes the Ohio river," was transferred to Harrison County. *Acts of Indiana Territory*, 1808, p. 3. For a note on the Jeffersonville and Vincennes districts see text with map, Harrison County I.

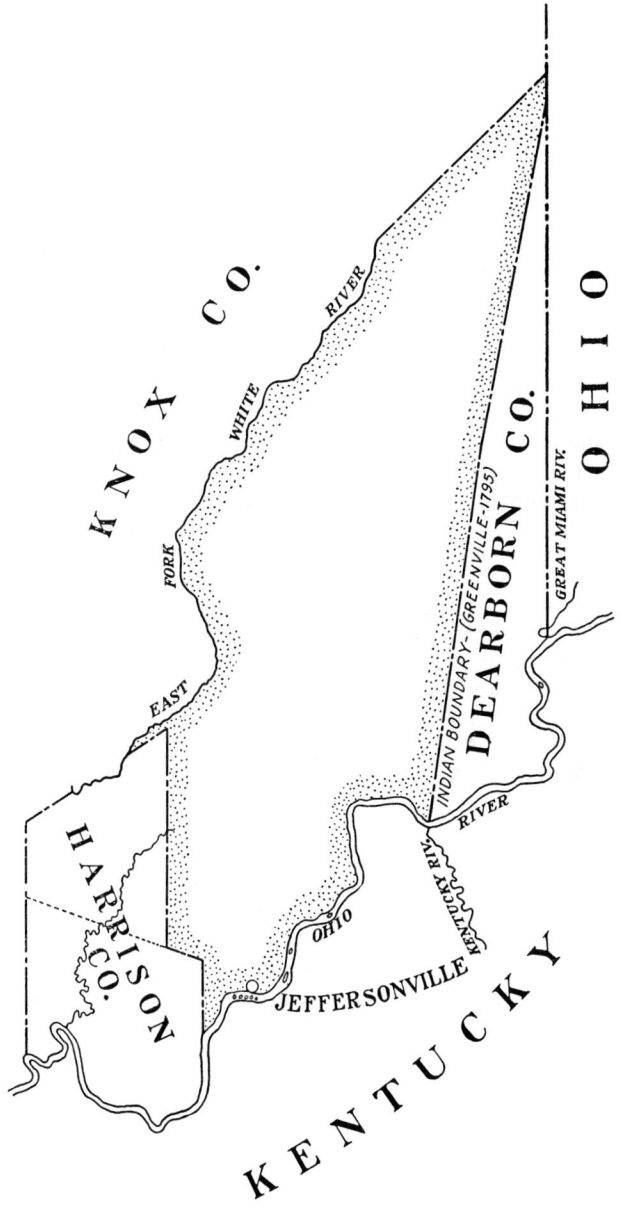

CLARK COUNTY IV

[Law: Oct. 11, 1808, effective Dec. 1, 1808]

CLARK COUNTY V
[Indiana Territory]

NOVEMBER 23, 1810: Alteration by statute forming Jefferson County, Indiana Territory, effective January 1, 1811.

NOVEMBER 27, 1810: Alteration by statute forming Franklin and Wayne counties, Indiana Territory, effective January 1, 1811.

DECEMBER 10, 1810: Alteration by statute extending Harrison County, Indiana Territory, effective on passage.

BOUNDARIES: Clark County, as the result of these three acts, was reduced within an entirely new set of boundaries. A part of the original county lying between the Grouseland Treaty line of 1805 and the East Fork of White River was cut off from the organized area by these changes and lost its identity as part of Clark County.

The new boundaries began at a point on the Indian boundary of 1805, where the range line dividing ranges 5 and 6 east crossed the same, running thence on a direct line to the northeast corner of Clark's Grant, thence by a direct line to the Ohio River at the lower line of township 2 north, range 10 east, thence with the Ohio River westwardly to the mouth of Falling Run, thence by a direct line to the beginning. See descriptions with maps, Jefferson County I, Franklin County I, Wayne County I, and Harrison County II.

The line between Jefferson and Clark counties was ordered to be run by commissioners appointed under a law of January 1, 1817, effective on March 1, 1817. *Laws of Indiana*, 1816-17, p. 200.

COUNTY SEAT: The removal of the county seat from Jeffersonville to Charlestown, following an act of December 14, 1810, was legalized by an act of December 5, 1811. *Acts of Indiana Territory*, 1810, pp. 56-59; 1811, pp. 10-11.

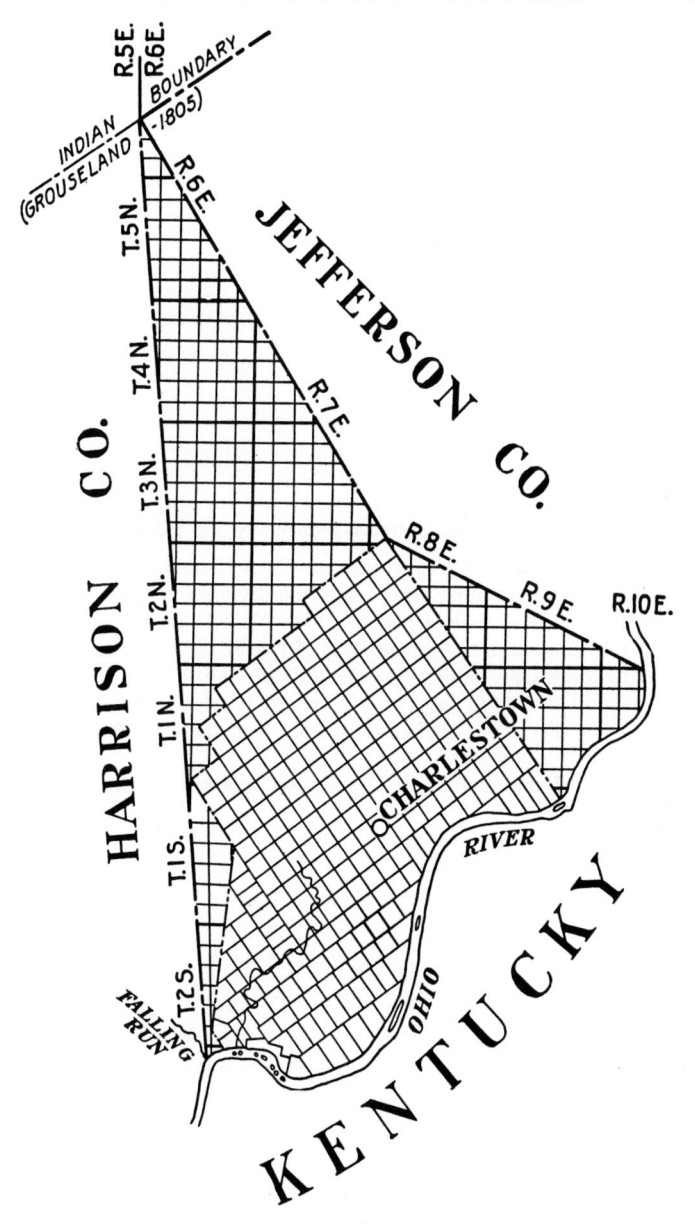

CLARK COUNTY V

[Laws: Nov. 23, 1810, effective Jan. 1, 1811; Nov. 27, 1810, effective Jan. 1, 1811; Dec. 10, 1810, effective on passage]

CLARK COUNTY VI
[Indiana Territory]

DECEMBER 21, 1813: Alteration by statute forming Washington County, Indiana Territory, effective January 17, 1814.

BOUNDARY CHANGE: All that part of Clark County lying west and north of a line beginning where the line dividing ranges 6 and 7 east crossed the Clark-Jefferson boundary line, running thence south with the range line to "the summit of the Silver creek knobs," thence southwestwardly along the height of the Knobs to the Clark-Harrison boundary, was transferred to Washington County. *Acts of Indiana Territory*, 1813-14, p. 91. See map, Washington County I.

The line along the summit of the Knobs was not at this time definitely fixed.

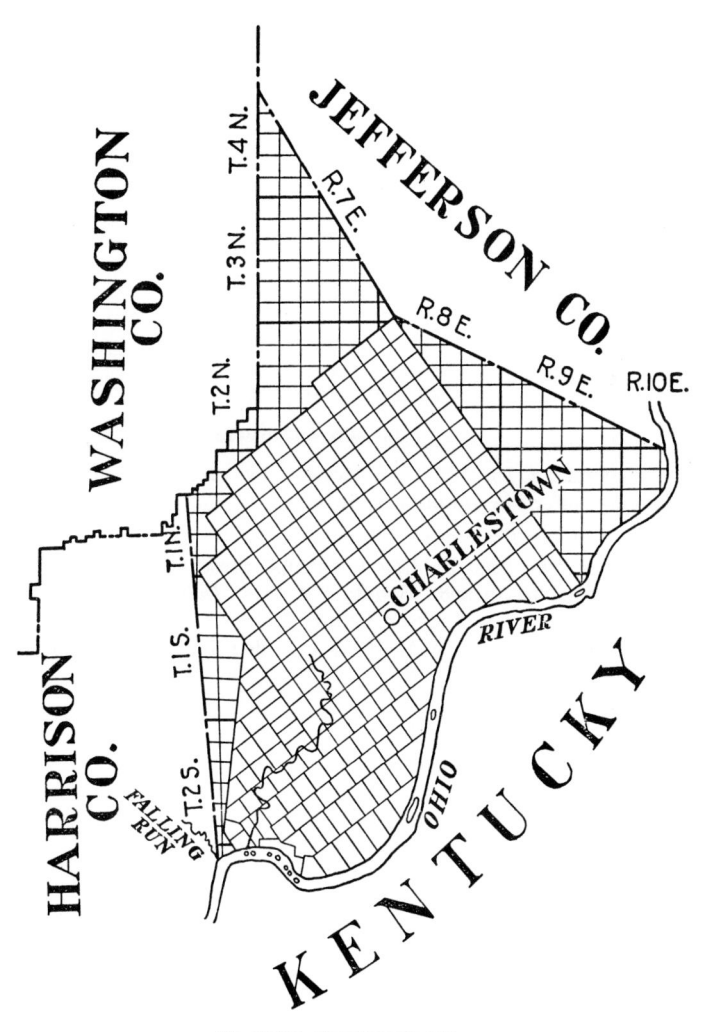

CLARK COUNTY VI

[Law: Dec. 21, 1813, effective Jan. 17, 1814]

CLARK COUNTY VII
[Indiana Territory]

DECEMBER 18, 1815: Alteration by statute forming Jackson County, effective January 1, 1816.

BOUNDARY CHANGE: A small triangular area of Clark County north of "the line dividing townships three and four north" was transferred to Jackson County. *Acts of Indiana Territory*, 1815, pp. 3-4. See map, Jackson County I.

A law of January 1, 1817, provided for the running of the Clark-Jefferson line. *Laws of Indiana*, 1816-17, p. 200.

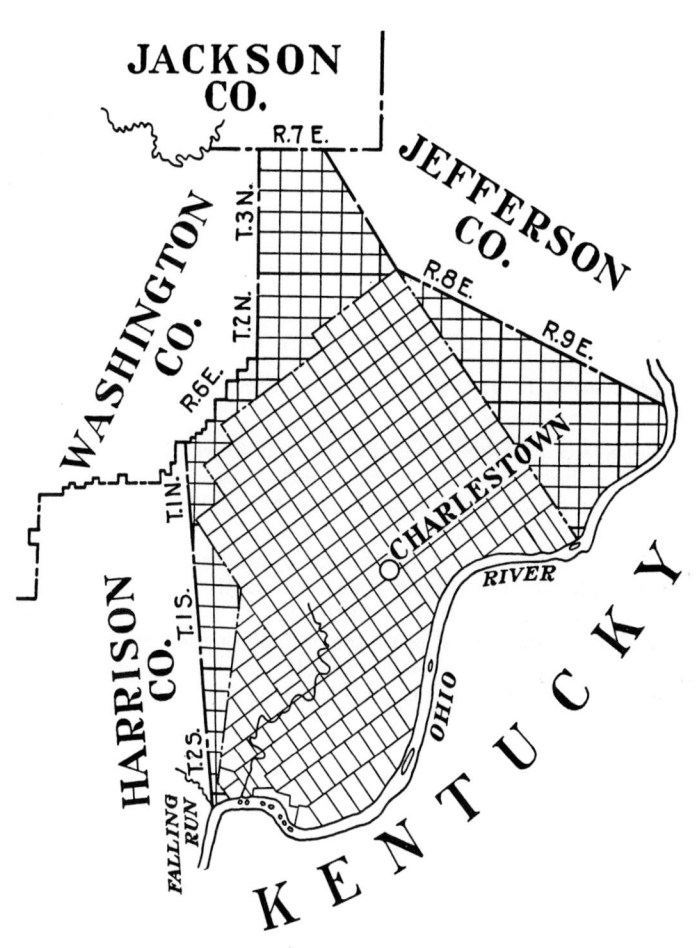

CLARK COUNTY VII

[Law: Dec. 18, 1815, effective Jan. 1, 1816]

CLARK COUNTY VIII

JANUARY 2, 1819: Alteration by statute forming Floyd County, effective February 1, 1819.

BOUNDARY CHANGE: All that part of Clark County south and west of a line beginning on the Clark-Harrison boundary at its intersection by a line dividing sections 22 and 27, township 1 south, range 6 east of the second principal meridian, running with said line "east to the Illinois grant line in the county of Clark . . . thence with the said Illinois grant line south forty east to Silver Creek in said Grant, on the south side of lot number sixty six, thence down said Creek, with the meanders thereof, on the west side of the same, to the mouth thereof," was transferred to Floyd County. *Laws of Indiana*, 1818-19, p. 100. See map, Floyd County I.

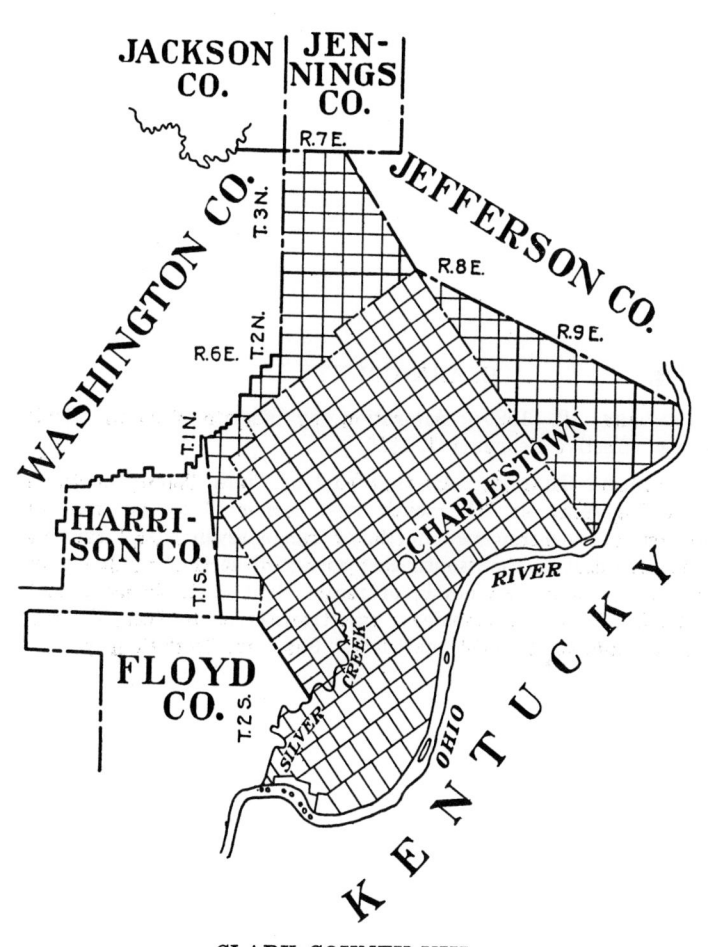

CLARK COUNTY VIII

[Law: Jan. 2, 1819, effective Feb. 1, 1819]

CLARK COUNTY IX

JANUARY 12, 1820: Alteration by statute forming Scott County, effective February 1, 1820.

BOUNDARY CHANGE: All that part of Clark County north of a line beginning at "the south west corner of section number eighteen, of township two north, of range seven east," running thence due east to the "south east corner of section number thirteen, in township two north, of range eight east, thence north" to the Clark County boundary, was transferred to Scott County. *Laws of Indiana*, 1819-20, pp. 51-52. See map, Scott County I.

CLARK COUNTY IX

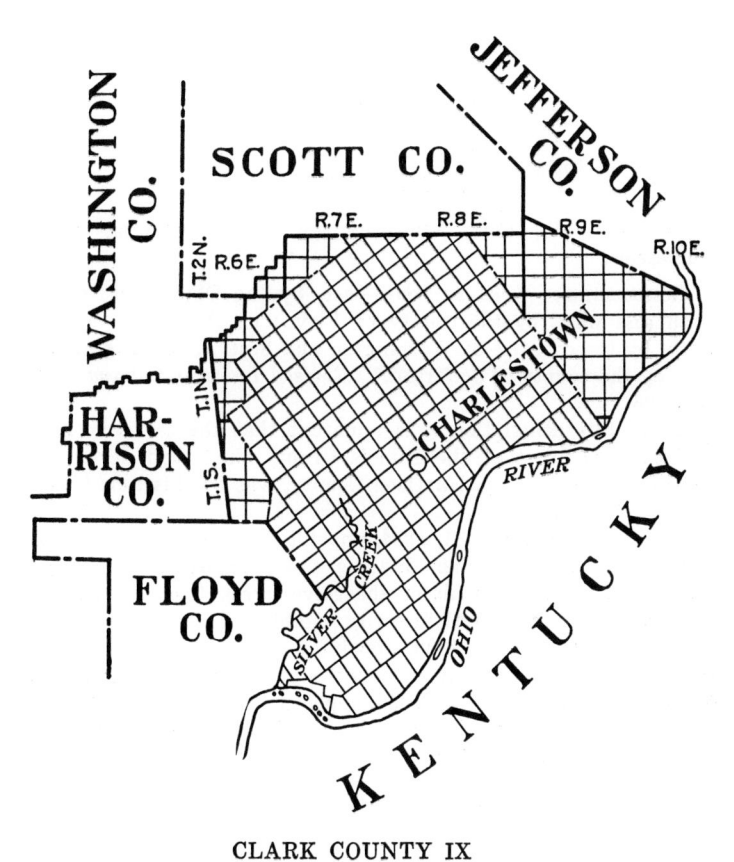

[Law: Jan. 12, 1820, effective Feb. 1, 1820]

CLARK COUNTY X

JANUARY 31, 1824: Alteration by statute defining county boundaries.

BOUNDARIES: "On the south-east, by the Ohio river; on the south and west, by the county of Floyd; on the north-west and north, by the counties of Washington and Scott; and on the north-east, by the county of Jefferson." *Revised Laws of Indiana*, 1823-24, p. 96.

From this description it is apparent that the territory north of Floyd and west of the Illinois Grant, which had never been formally detached from Harrison County, was by this time treated as part of Clark County.

The law of January 31, 1824, appointed commissioners to "designate and mark the line, dividing the counties of Washington and Clark, on the summit of the Silver-creek knobs." The line was not, apparently, satisfactorily established at that time, for an act of December 19, 1828, appointed commissioners to "survey and mark the line dividing the counties of Washington and Clark." A third law, of January 12, 1829, appointed commissioners to "survey and mark the line dividing the counties of Clark and Scott." *Laws of Indiana*, 1828-29, pp. 16, 17.

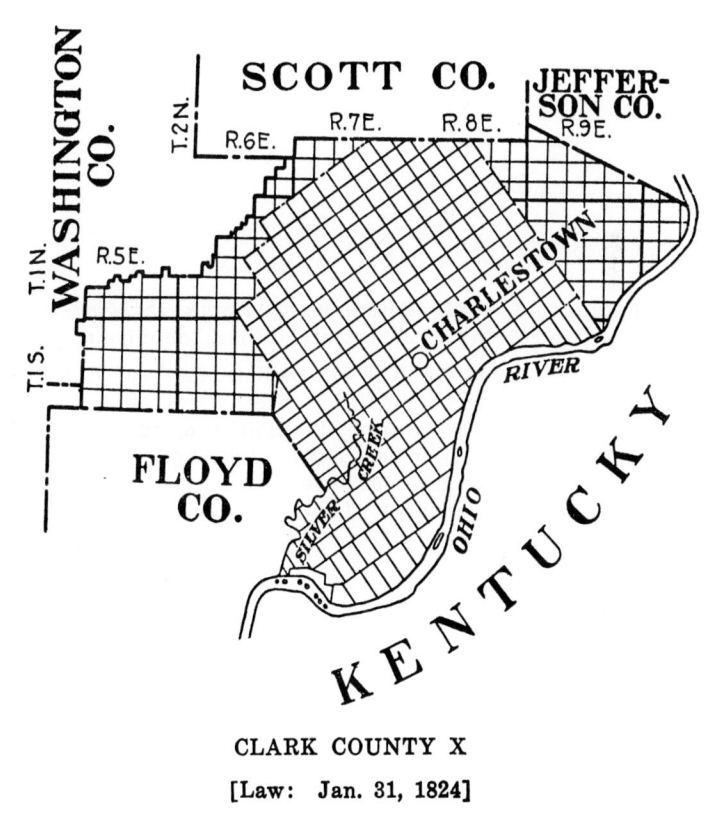

CLARK COUNTY X
[Law: Jan. 31, 1824]

CLARK COUNTY XI

FEBRUARY 8, 1836: Alteration by statute changing the line dividing the counties of Jefferson and Clark, effective on passage.

BOUNDARY CHANGE: The act outlined the new boundary as follows: "Beginning on the Ohio river, where the line dividing sections eighteen and nineteen, township two, range ten, strikes the same; thence west on the sectional lines to the south east corner of section thirteen, township two, range eight, being the south east corner of Scott county." *Laws of Indiana*, 1835-36 (general), p. 80.

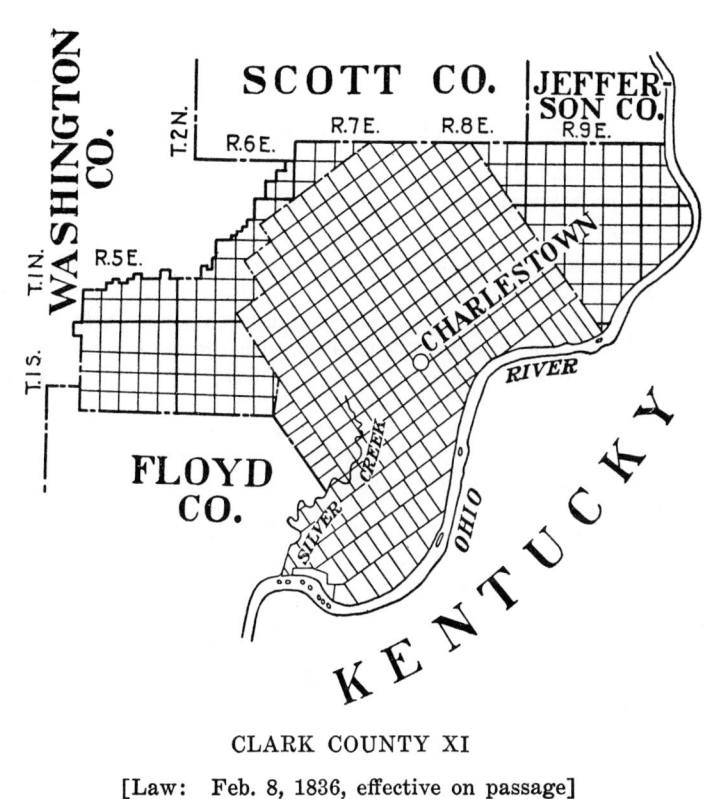

CLARK COUNTY XI

[Law: Feb. 8, 1836, effective on passage]

CLARK COUNTY XII

FEBRUARY 2, 1837: Alteration by statute permanently fixing the line between the counties of Jefferson and Clark, effective on passage.

BOUNDARY CHANGE: The act described the following permanent boundary between the two counties: "Beginning at the south-east corner of section thirteen, township two north of range eight east, and running thence east with the section line dividing sections eighteen and nineteen to the north-east corner of section twenty-two in town two north, of range nine east, thence south one mile to the south-east corner of said section twenty-two, thence east one mile to south-east corner of section twenty-three, thence south on the line dividing sections twenty-five and twenty-six one half mile to the open line running through section twenty-five, in town two range nine, thence east with said open line through sections twenty-five, thirty and twenty-nine to the Ohio river." *Laws of Indiana*, 1836-37 (general), p. 98.

An act of February 15, 1839, appointed commissioners to determine that part of the Clark-Floyd boundary which ran along the height of the Knobs. No record of action has been discovered. *Ibid.*, 1838-39 (general), p. 89.

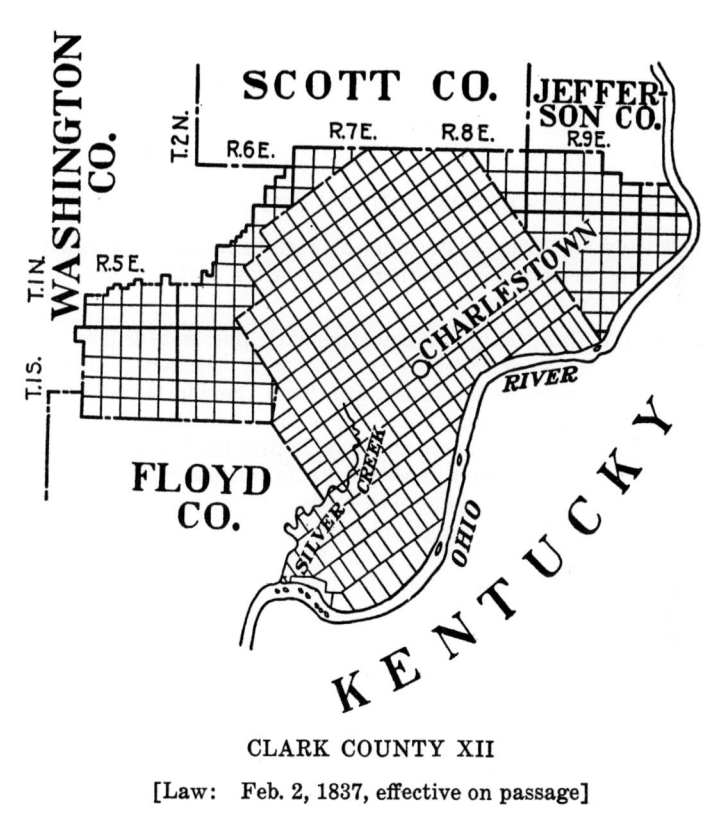

CLARK COUNTY XII

[Law: Feb. 2, 1837, effective on passage]

CLARK COUNTY XIII

FEBRUARY 16, 1839: Alteration by statute "more particularly defining the western and southern boundaries of the county of Scott," effective on passage.

BOUNDARY CHANGE: The new boundary line was defined as beginning at the intersection of the old Clark boundary with the line dividing townships 1 and 2 north, "and running thence eastwardly upon said township line . . . to the south-west corner of section thirty-six; thence north with said section line one mile to the south-west corner of section twenty-five; thence east with said section line one mile to the range line dividing ranges six and seven; thence north with said range line two miles to the south-west corner of section eighteen, township two, north of range seven east, intersecting at this point the line heretofore dividing the counties of Scott and Clark, running thence east with said county line as heretofore." *Laws of Indiana*, 1838-39 (local), pp. 323-24.

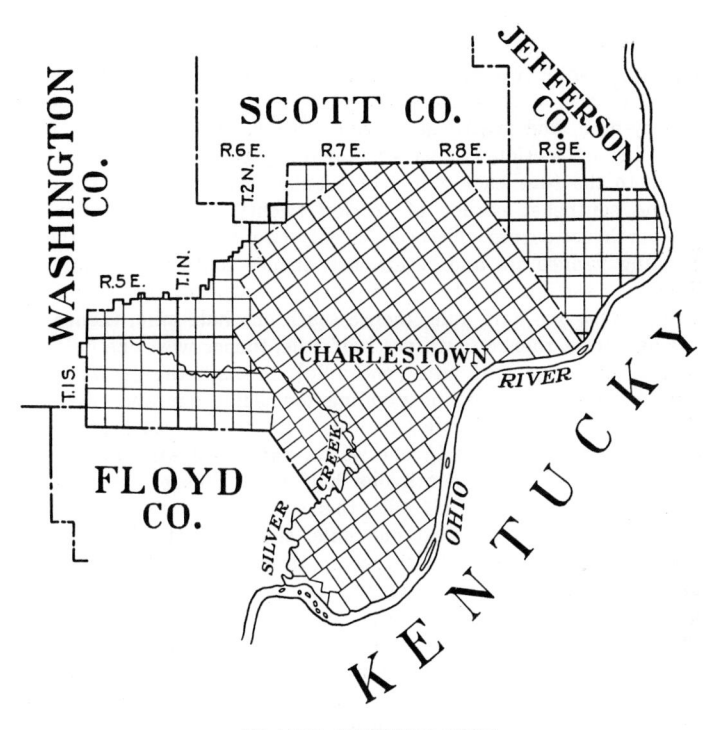

CLARK COUNTY XIII

[Law: Feb. 16, 1839, effective on passage]

CLARK COUNTY XIV

1842-43: Alteration by statute defining county boundaries.

BOUNDARIES: "Beginning on the Ohio river at a point where an east and west line dividing fractional section number twenty-nine, township two south [north], of range ten east, strikes the same, thence west through the centre of said fractional section twenty-nine, and fractional sections thirty, and twenty-five, to the east line of section twenty-six, township two, range nine, thence north to the southeast corner of section twenty-three, thence west to the southeast corner of section twenty-two, thence north to the northeast corner of section twenty-two, thence west to the line dividing ranges six and seven east, thence south to the northeast corner of section twenty-five, township two north, range six east, thence west one half mile, thence south one half mile, thence west one half mile, thence south one half mile, thence west one half mile, thence south one half mile [one mile], through the centre of section thirty-five, to the line dividing townships one and two north, thence west one half mile, thence south to the southeast corner of section three, township one north, range six east, thence west one half mile, thence south one half mile, thence west one half mile, thence south one half mile, thence west one mile, thence south one half mile, thence west one mile, thence south one half mile, thence west one half mile, thence south one half mile, thence west to the centre of section twenty-three, township one north, range five east, thence south one half mile, thence west one mile, thence south one half mile, thence west one mile and a half, thence south one half mile, thence west one half mile, thence south to the south line of section five, township one south, range five east, thence west one half mile, thence south to the southwest corner of section twenty-three [twenty], east [from this point], to the southeast corner of section twenty-three, township one south, range six east, thence southeastward to the south corner of lot sixty-six, in Clark's grant, on Silver creek, thence down said creek to the Ohio river, thence up said river to the place of beginning." *Revised Statutes of Indiana*, 1842-43, pp. 75-76.

The errors corrected in brackets above were never rectified by statute.

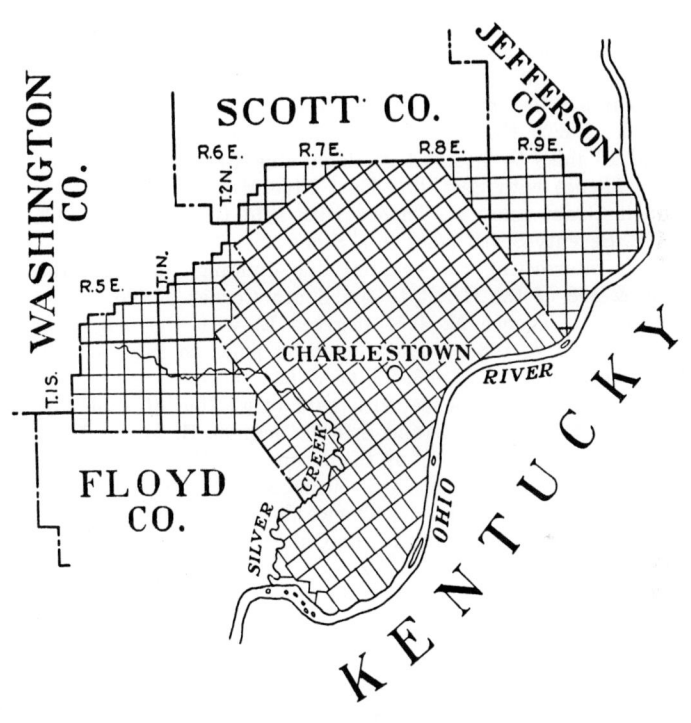

CLARK COUNTY XIV
[Law: 1842-43]

CLARK COUNTY XV

APRIL 23, 1844: Alteration by report of commissioners appointed by an act of January 15, 1844, relating to the boundary line between the counties of Clark and Floyd.

BOUNDARY CHANGE: The new boundary between Clark and Floyd counties followed a line "Beginning at a stone corner of sections numbers 17, 18, 19, & 20 in township one south of range five east . . . Running thence South one half mile . . . Thence East One mile and a half to the *center* of Sect. 21 . . . Thence South One half mile to the Sectional line . . . Thence with said line E. Three miles and a half to the town-ship line between ranges Nos. 5 & 6 East . . . Thence with said line South Seven Poles and 16 links to intersect sectional line (There being an off set) . . . Thence with Sect. line East Five Miles and 18 poles to the Illinois Grant line . . . Thence with said Grant Line S. 1½ degrees E. Seventy-Seven poles to a Stone . . . Thence S. 40¼ degrees East intersecting the original line dividing Nos. 127, 128, 107, 109, & 108 of the Grant to the South Corner of No. 108 of said Grant . . . Thence N. 49½ degrees E. with the orig'l line between Nos. 86 & 108 of said Grant 30 poles to intersect the orig'l line between Nos. 86, 88, 87, 65 & 66—there being an offset between the lines . . . Thence with said orig'l line of said Nos. 86, 88, 87, 65 & 66 of the Grand S. 40¼ degrees E. to the South Corner of No. Sixty six (66) of the Grant . . . Thence with the orig'l line between Nos. 47 & 65 S. 50 degrees W. 60 poles to the West Bank of Silver Creek . . . Thence down said creek with its Meanderings of the West Bank to the Ohio River." Floyd County Records, Deed Book Q, pp. 125-26.

For a note on earlier attempts to fix this line, see Floyd County map, same date.

JANUARY 14, 1846: Alteration by statute defining the boundaries between the counties of Clark and Washington, effective on publication.

BOUNDARY CHANGE: The Clark-Washington boundary, established in the *Revised Statutes* of 1842-43, was altered by the provision that "so much of the revised statutes of 1831 as defines the boundary line between said counties . . . is hereby revived and declared to be in full force." *Laws of Indiana*, 1845-46 (general), pp. 111-12.

The law of 1831 mentioned above defined the Clark-Washington boundary as it was drawn at the formation of Washington County, December 21, 1813, along the "extreme heighth" of the Silver Creek Knobs.

CLARK COUNTY BOUNDARIES 285

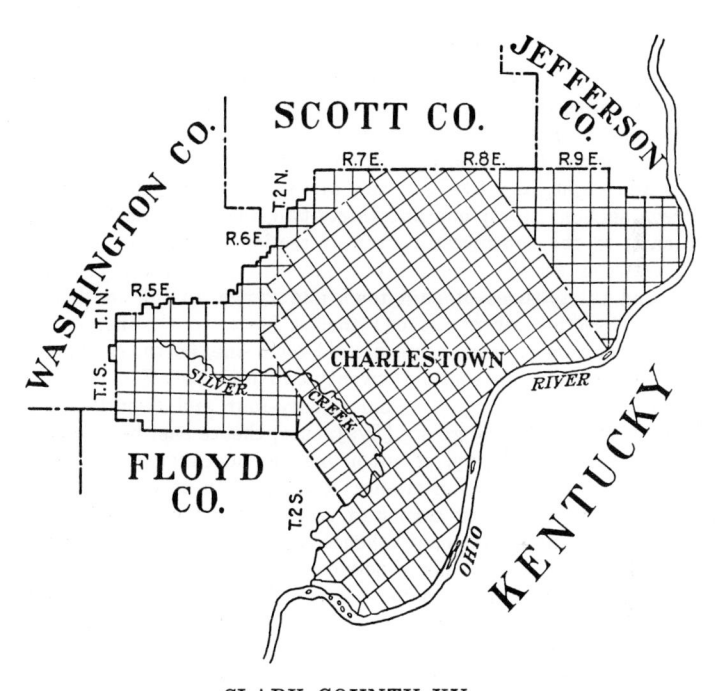

CLARK COUNTY XV

[Commissioners' Report: Apr. 23, 1844; Law: Jan. 14, 1846,
effective on publication]

CLARK COUNTY XVI

MARCH 7, 1873: Alteration by statute changing the Clark-Washington County boundary, effective on passage.

BOUNDARY CHANGE: The boundary between Clark and Washington counties is defined as "Commencing at the southwest corner of section seventeen, town one, south of range five, east, thence north along the line dividing sections seventeen and eighteen, and seven and eight, and five and six, to the base line; thence north between sections thirty-one and thirty-two, town one, north, range five east, to the southwest corner of section twenty-nine; thence east between section twenty-nine and thirty two, and twenty-eight and thirty-three of said town and range, to the south-west corner of section twenty-seven; thence north to the north-west corner of section twenty-seven, in said town one, north, range five, east; thence between sections twenty-two and twenty-seven, and twenty-three and twenty-six, and twenty-four and twenty-five in said town one, north, range six [five], east; thence east between sections nineteen and thirty, of town one, north, range six, east, to southwest corner of section twenty; thence north between nineteen and twenty, to southwest corner of section seventeen in said town one, north of range six, east; thence east to southwest corner of [section] sixteen; thence north between sections sixteen and seventeen, and eight and nine, to the northwest corner of nine, of said town and range; thence east between four and nine, to southwest corner of section three; thence north between three and four in said town one, north, range six, east, to Scott county line." *Laws of Indiana*, 1873, pp. 105-6.

COUNTY SEAT: After a bitter struggle the county seat was removed from Charlestown to Jeffersonville in October, 1878, following an order of September 23. Shockley, "County Seat Wars," *op cit.*, 10:no.1:2; Baird, *History of Clark County*, 120-21.

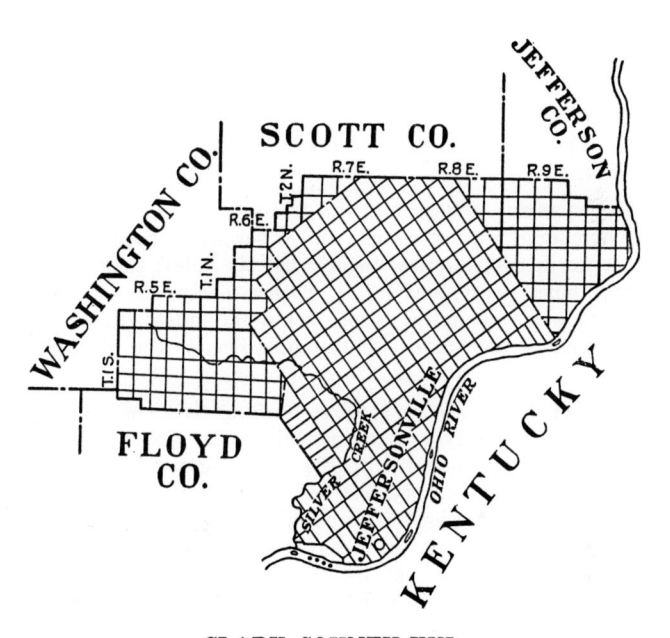

CLARK COUNTY XVI

[Law: Mar. 7, 1873, effective on passage]

CLAY COUNTY

FEBRUARY 12, 1825: Formation by statute, effective April 1, 1825. The formation affected Owen, Putnam, Vigo, and Sullivan counties.

BOUNDARIES: "Beginning at the south west corner of township numbered nine, of range number seven; thence east ten miles; thence north twelve miles; thence east six miles; thence north nine miles; thence west four miles; thence north nine miles; thenee [thence] west ten miles; thence south six miles; thence west two miles; and thence south twenty-four miles, to the place of beginning." *Laws of Indiana*, 1825, p. 17.

COUNTY SEAT: In May, 1825, Bowling Green was made the location of the county seat by commissioners appointed under the act forming the county. In 1843 and again in 1853, Bowling Green retained the county seat in spite of acts providing for elections or for commissioners to relocate the seat of government.

In 1871 a petition was granted by county commissioners for removing the county seat to Brazil. The records were not removed until the completion of a building in 1877. *Ibid.*, 17; 1842-43 (local), p. 120; 1853, pp. 27-28; Shockley, "County Seat Wars," *op cit.*, 10:no.1:25; Blanchard, *Counties of Clay and Owen*, 55-61.

CLAY COUNTY BOUNDARIES 289

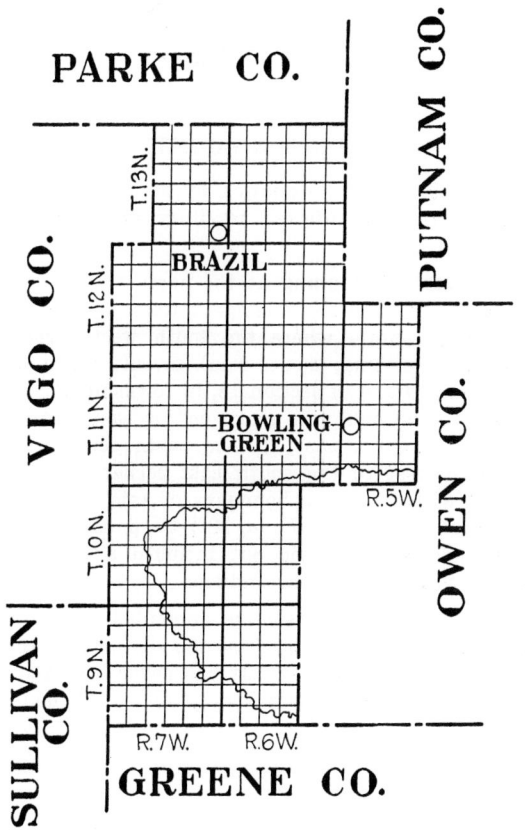

CLAY COUNTY

[Law: Feb. 12, 1825, effective Apr. 1, 1825]

CLINTON COUNTY I

JANUARY 29, 1830: Formation by statute, effective March 1, 1830. The formation affected territory attached to Tippecanoe County.

BOUNDARIES: "Beginning at the north west corner of section 19, in township 23, north of range 2 west, on the east boundary of Tippecanoe county, where the south west corner of Carroll county strikes the same; thence south seventeen and one half miles to the half mile stake in section 18, in township 20, range 2 west; thence east to the half mile stake on the east side of section 13, township 20, range 2 east; thence north seventeen and a half miles; thence west to the south east corner of Carroll county; thence west with the south boundary of said county, to the place of beginning." *Laws of Indiana*, 1829-30, p. 33.

The boundaries thus laid out included a part of the Miami Reserve not yet ceded by the Indians.

COUNTY SEAT: Commissioners appointed under the act forming the county, in May, 1830, chose the site of the present town of Frankfort as the county seat. It has never been removed. *Ibid.*, 33-34; Shockley, "County Seat Wars," *op cit.*, 10:no.1:28; *History of Clinton County*, 339-40.

CLINTON COUNTY BOUNDARIES 291

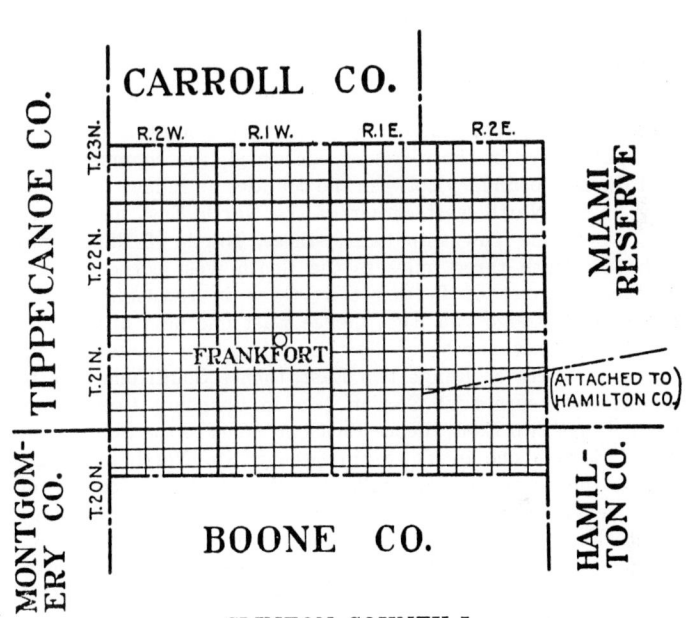

CLINTON COUNTY I

[Law: Jan. 29, 1830, effective Mar. 1, 1830]

CLINTON COUNTY II

MARCH 3, 1859: Alteration by report of county commissioners transferring a part of the county of Clinton to Howard County.

BOUNDARY CHANGE: Acceding to the petition of a majority of the legal voters in the territory concerned, the commissioners outlined the new boundary between the counties as follows: "Commencing at the North west corner of the North East quarter of Section twenty-one Township twenty-three, North of Range two East thence South three miles to the South west corner of the South East Quarter of Section thirtythree in township twenty three North of Range two East thence East one mile and a half to the South East corner of Section thirty-four in town ship twenty-three North of Range two East, thence South one mile to the South west corner of Section two in township twenty-two, North of Range two East, thence East two miles to the South East corner of Section one in Township twenty-two, North of Range two East, thence north four miles to the Northeast corner of Section twenty four in Township twenty-three, North of Range two East, taking from the territory and jurisdiction of the County of Clinton and adding and attaching to the territory and jurisdiction of the County of Howard, the East half of sections 21, 28 and 33 and all of Sections 22, 27, 34, 35, 26, 23, 24 25 & 36 all in township twenty-three North of Range two East and Sections one and two in township twenty-two, North of Range two East." Record of Howard County Commissioners, 3:33.

CLINTON COUNTY BOUNDARIES 293

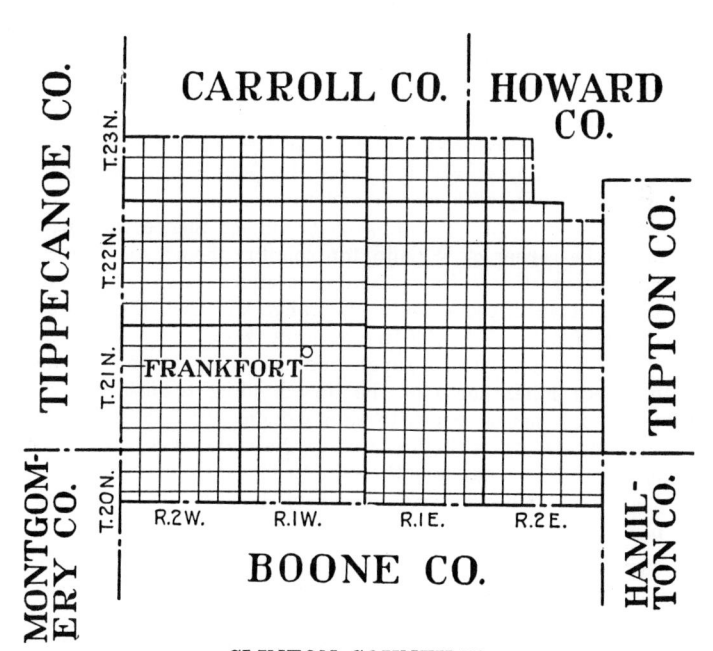

CLINTON COUNTY II

[Commissioners' Report: Mar. 3, 1859]

CRAWFORD COUNTY I

JANUARY 29, 1818: Formation by statute, effective March 1, 1818. The formation affected Harrison, Orange, and Perry counties.

BOUNDARIES: "Beginning on the [O]hio river at the mouth of Big Blue river; thence up the same with the meanders thereof, until it strikes the line dividing sections twenty six and twenty seven, in township three south and range two east; thence north with said sectional line until it strikes Big Blue river; thence up said Big Blue river, with the meanders thereof, until it strikes the line of Harrison and Washington Counties; thence west with said line to the corner of Washington county; thence south to an east and west sectional line, dividing sections twenty-nine and thirty two, in township one south and range two east, thence west with said sectional line to the line dividing ranges two and three west; thence south with said range line nine miles to an east and west line, four miles north of the line dividing townships three and four south; thence east with said sectional line to the meridian line; thence south with the same to the Ohio river; thence up the same, with the meanders thereof, to the mouth of Big Blue river the place of beginning." *Laws of Indiana*, 1817-18 (special), p. 27.

COUNTY SEAT: Commissioners appointed in the act forming the county met in April, 1818, to select a county seat. They chose a site in section 33, township 2 south, range 1 east. The plat of the town, which was called Mount Sterling, was recorded on November 11, 1818. An act of December 24, 1821, provided for a relocation. Commissioners thus appointed accepted a site in Fredonia, in section 10, township 4 south, range 1 east, the deed for which was recorded on December 16, 1822. *Ibid.*, 27-28; 1821-22, pp. 9-12; Pleasant, *History of Crawford County*, 4-6, 31-34.

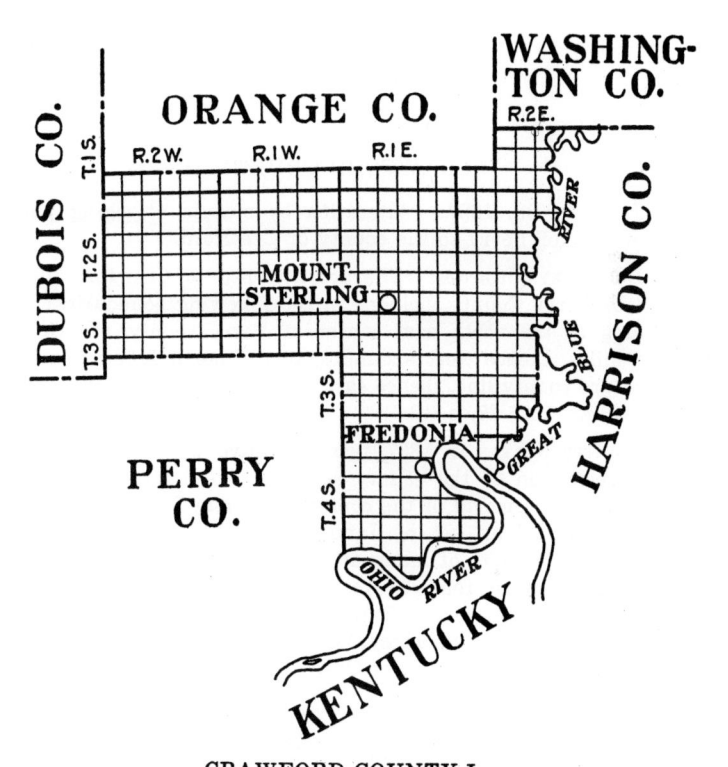

CRAWFORD COUNTY I
[Law: Jan. 29, 1818, effective Mar. 1, 1818]

CRAWFORD COUNTY II

JANUARY 23, 1827: Alteration by statute attaching part of the county of Perry to the county of Crawford.

BOUNDARY CHANGE: The act attached to Crawford all that part of Perry County included in the following boundaries: "Beginning at the north east corner of Perry county, thence south four miles, thence west six miles, thence north four miles to the Crawford county line, thence east to the place of beginning." *Laws of Indiana*, 1826-27, p. 12.

COUNTY SEAT: In 1827, two legislative acts dealt with a possible relocation of the county seat, but no change was made at the time. A removal of the county seat from Fredonia to Leavenworth followed an act of January 4, 1843. This remained the county seat in spite of many attempts at change, until 1894, when the records were removed to English. This has remained the county seat. *Ibid.*, 1821-22, pp. 9-12; 1826-27, pp. 86-87; 1842-43 (local), pp. 122-23; Shockley, "County Seat Wars," *op cit.*, 10:no. 1:11-15; Pleasant, *History of Crawford County*, 31-34, 65-66, 105-7, 343-47, 405-9.

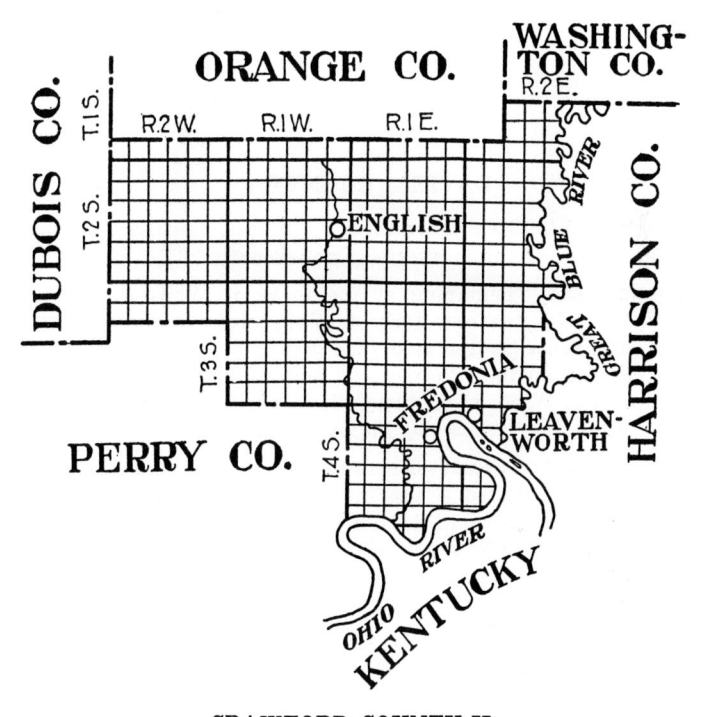

CRAWFORD COUNTY II

[Law: Jan. 23, 1827]

DAVIESS COUNTY I

DECEMBER 24, 1816: Formation by statute, effective February 15, 1817. The formation affected Knox County.

BOUNDARIES: "Beginning at the forks of White river, running thence with the east fork of White river to the mouth of Lick creek, thence up the said Lick creek, to the line of Orange county, thence north with the said line to where it strikes the west branch of White river, thence down the said west fork to the place of beginning." *Laws of Indiana*, 1816-17, p. 192.

COUNTY SEAT: Commissioners appointed under the act forming the county selected a site in the town of Liverpool as the county seat. On March 18, 1817, the town was renamed Washington. *Ibid.*, 192-93; *History of Knox and Daviess Counties*, 607-8; Shockley, "County Seat Wars," *op cit.*, 10:no.1:9.

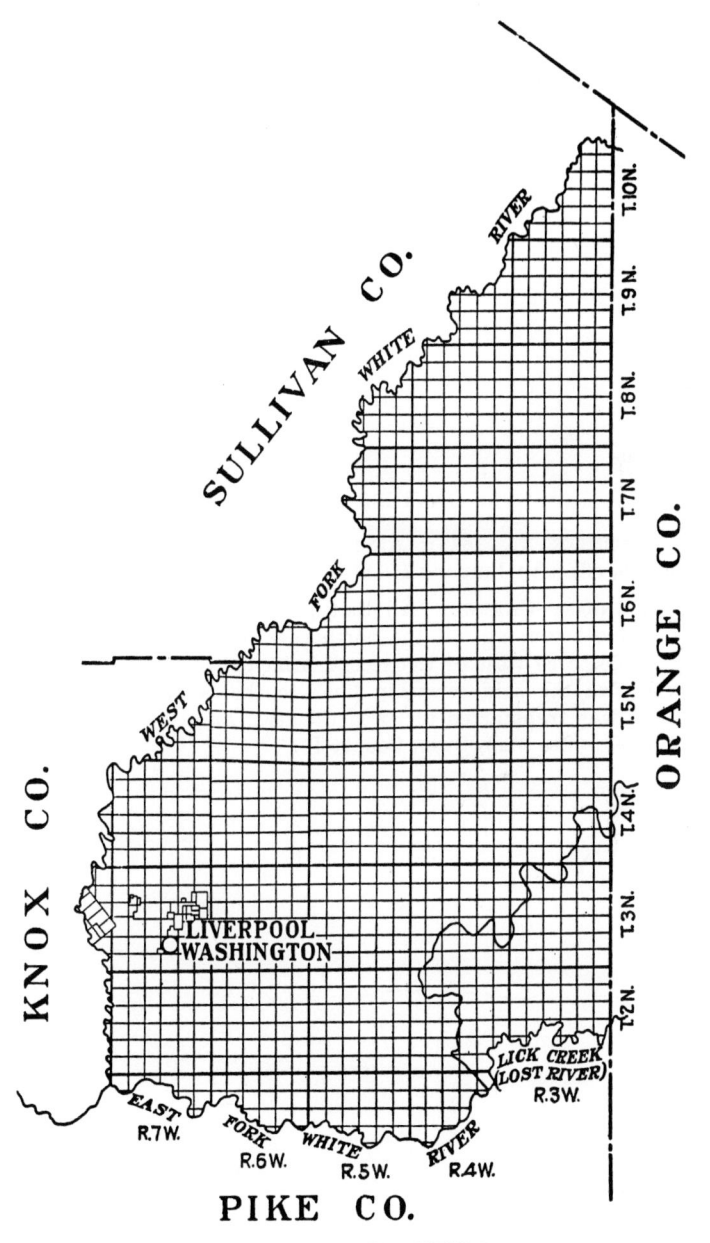

DAVIESS COUNTY I

[Law: Dec. 24, 1816, effective Feb. 15, 1817]

DAVIESS COUNTY II

DECEMBER 21, 1818: Alteration by statute forming Owen County, effective January 1, 1819.

BOUNDARY CHANGE: All that part of Daviess County north of a line beginning "at the north east corner of township eight of range three west of the second principal meridian line, thence west with the said township line" to the West Fork of White River, was transferred to Owen County. *Laws of Indiana*, 1818-19, p. 96. See map, Owen County I.

DAVIESS COUNTY BOUNDARIES

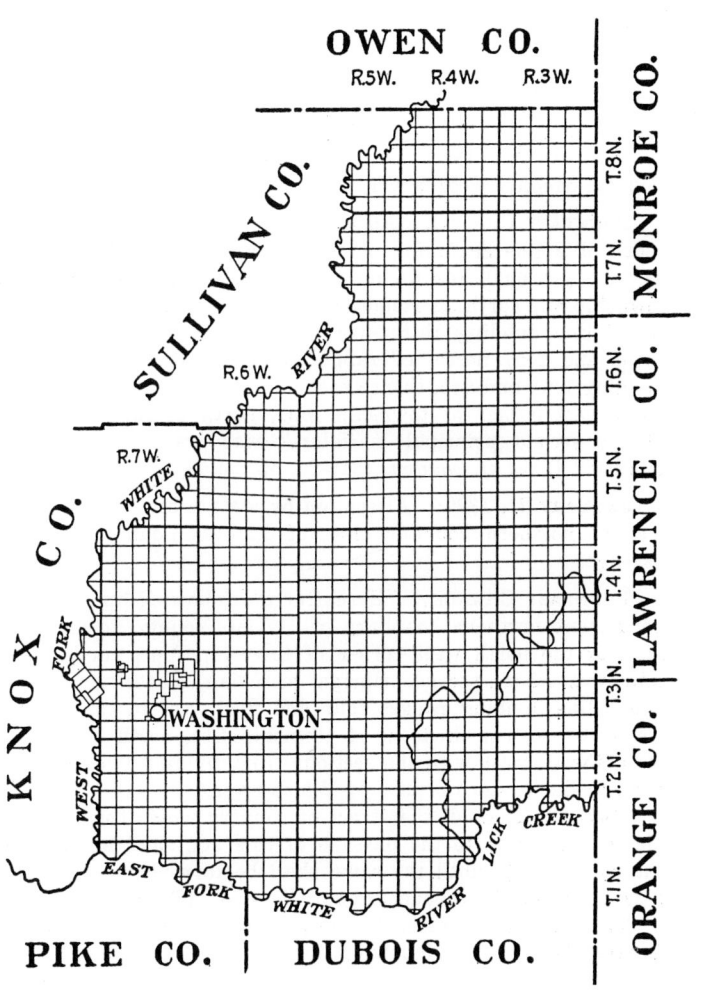

DAVIESS COUNTY II

[Law: Dec. 21, 1818, effective Jan. 1, 1819]

DAVIESS COUNTY III

JANUARY 17, 1820: Alteration by statute forming Martin County, effective February 1, 1820.

BOUNDARY CHANGE: All that part of Daviess County east and south of a line beginning on the eastern branch of White River at "the sectional line dividing twenty-three and twenty-four, of township one north, of range five west, thence north with said sectional line dividing thirty-five and thirty-six, in township two, three and four north, of range five west, to the township line dividing four and five, thence east with said township line" to "the north east corner of township four, north of range three, west of the second principal meridian," was transferred to Martin County. *Laws of Indiana*, 1819-20, pp. 54-55.

JANUARY 21, 1820: Alteration by statute establishing the permanent northern boundary line of Daviess County, effective on passage.

BOUNDARY CHANGE: "Hereafter the following line shall be the permanent northern boundary of Daviess county, to wit: beginning at the north west corner of township four, north of range four, west of the second principal meredian, thence north with the range line dividing ranges four and five, west to the north east corner of section thirteen, of township five, north of range five west, thence west with the sectional line dividing twelve and thirteen, to the western branch of White river.

"Sec. 2. That all that tract of country which belonged to Davies county prior to the passage of this act, shall be attached to the said county, until the same shall be formed and organized in a separate and independent county." *Ibid.*, 125-26.

This act was repealed in the act of January 5, 1821, forming Greene County. See following map.

DAVIESS COUNTY BOUNDARIES 303

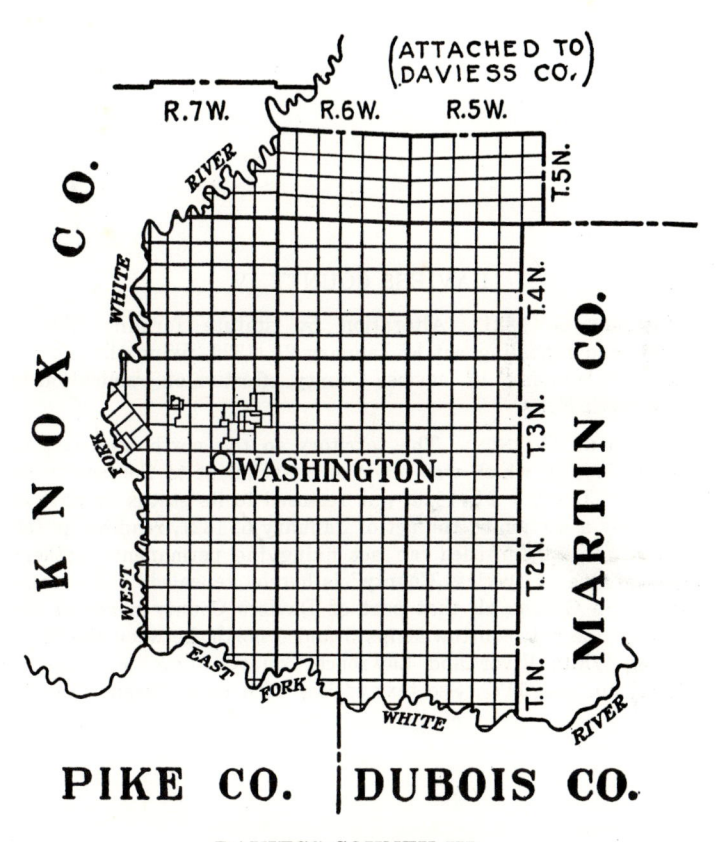

DAVIESS COUNTY III

[Law: Jan. 17, 1820, effective Feb. 1, 1820; Jan. 21, 1820, effective on passage]

DAVIESS COUNTY IV

JANUARY 5, 1821: Alteration by statute forming Greene County, and repealing act of January 21, 1820, fixing the permanent north boundary of Daviess County, effective on publication in the *Western Sun*.

BOUNDARY CHANGE: The territory to the north and east of Daviess County, which was made an attachment to the county by the law of January 21, 1820, was restored to its status as part of Daviess by a section of the act of January 5, 1821, reading as follows: "The act, entitled 'an act fixing the permanent northern boundary line of Daviess County,' is hereby repealed." The same act gave to Greene all that part of Daviess County north of the township line between townships 5 and 6 north, between the West Fork of White River and Lawrence County. *Laws of Indiana*, 1820-21, pp. 114, 117. See text of law with map, Greene County.

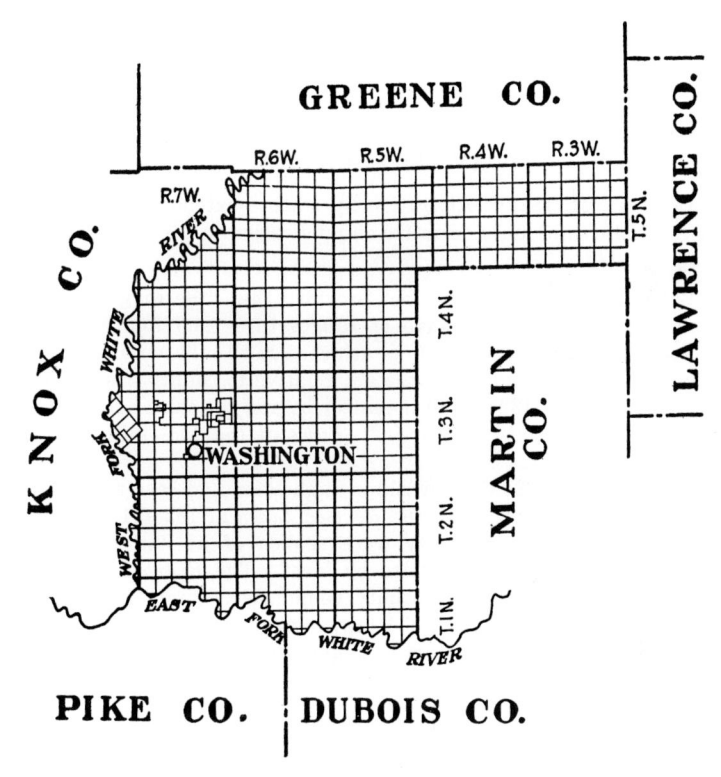

DAVIESS COUNTY IV

[Law: Jan. 5, 1821, effective on publication in *Western Sun*]

DAVIESS COUNTY V

JANUARY 24, 1828: Alteration by statute extending the boundaries of Martin County, effective on publication in the *Indianapolis Daily Gazette*.

BOUNDARY CHANGE: The act provided that "the congressional townships numbered five north of ranges three and four west of the second principal meridian, as attached until otherwise directed by law to Daviess county, by the act relative to county boundaries approved, Jan. 31, 1824, shall hereafter be and the same are hereby attached to the county of Martin." *Laws of Indiana*, 1827-28, pp. 17-18.

From 1821 to 1824 the townships in question had been a regular part of Daviess County. In the *Revised Laws* of 1823-24, as indicated in the text above, they were spoken of as "attached" to Daviess "until otherwise directed by law." The *Revised Laws* of 1830-31, in the law defining county boundaries, simply repeat the description as given in the 1824 law, disregarding this statute of January 24, 1828. The Martin County boundaries, however, as given in the 1831 law, include the two townships. *Revised Laws of Indiana*, 1823-24, p. 104; 1830-31, p. 117.

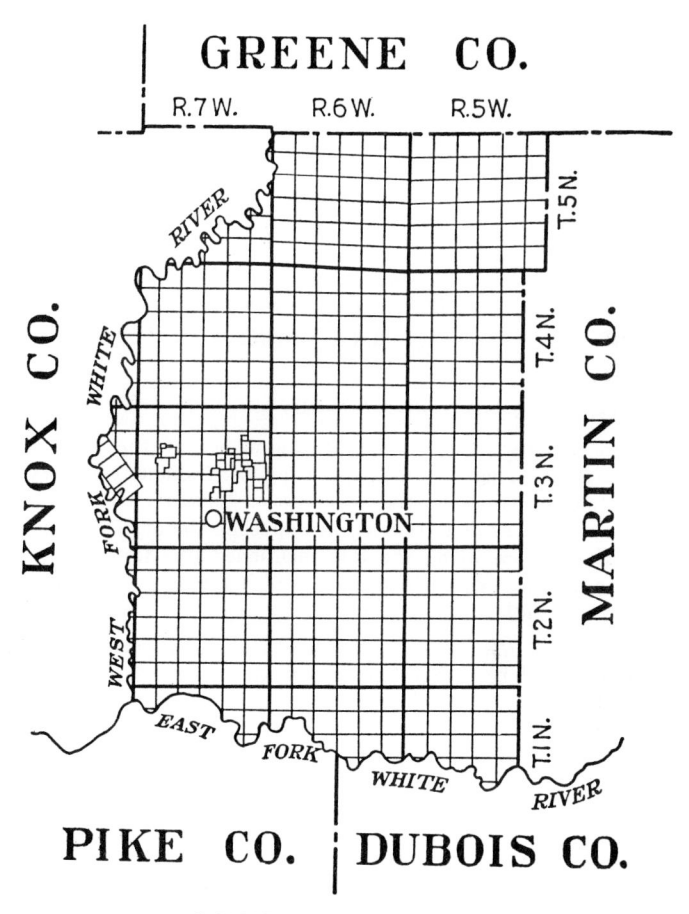

DAVIESS COUNTY V

[Law: Jan. 24, 1828, effective on publication in *Indianapolis Daily Gazette*]

DEARBORN COUNTY I
[Indiana Territory]

MARCH 7, 1803: Formation by proclamation, affecting Clark County.

BOUNDARIES: "Beginning at the mouth of the great Miami thence north along the line seperating the Indiana Territory from the State of Ohio, to the Intersection thereof with the Indian Boundary line runing from a point opposite the mouth of the River Kentucky thence along the last mentioned line to the Ohio river and up the said River to the place of begining." Territorial *Executive Journal*, 116.

COUNTY SEAT: It was provided that until a permanent seat of justice should be established, court was to be held at Lawrenceburg. *Ibid.*, 116.

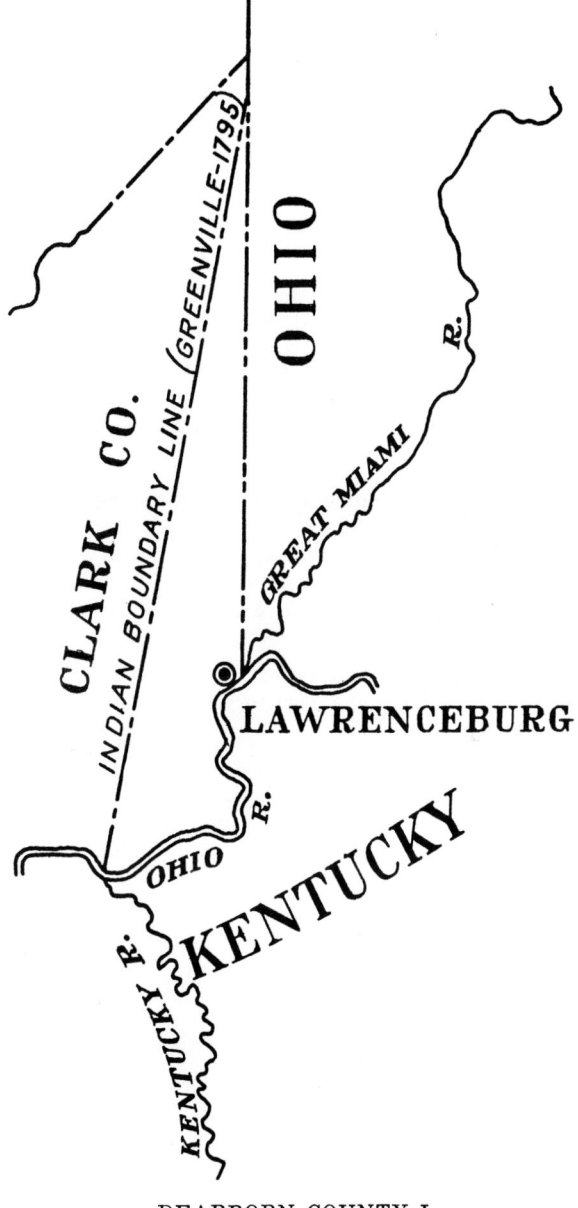

DEARBORN COUNTY I
[Proclamation: Mar. 7, 1803]

DEARBORN COUNTY II
[Indiana Territory]

NOVEMBER 23, 1810: Alteration by statute forming Jefferson County, Indiana Territory, effective January 1, 1811.

BOUNDARY CHANGE: All that part of Dearborn County, south and west of a line "beginning at the mouth of Log Lick creek, on the bank of the river Ohio, thence to the corner of sections five and eight, town four, range three, thence north[wardly] to the Indian boundary line," was transferred to Jefferson County. *Acts of Indiana Territory*, 1810, pp. 14, 114. See map, Jefferson County I.

NOVEMBER 27, 1810: Alteration by statute forming Franklin and Wayne counties, Indiana Territory, effective January 1, 1811.

BOUNDARY CHANGE: All that part of Dearborn County north of the line dividing townships 7 and 8, from the Ohio boundary to the Indian boundary line of 1795, was transferred to Wayne and Franklin counties. *Acts of Indiana Territory*, 1810, pp. 19-20, 114. See text with maps, Franklin County I, and Wayne County I.

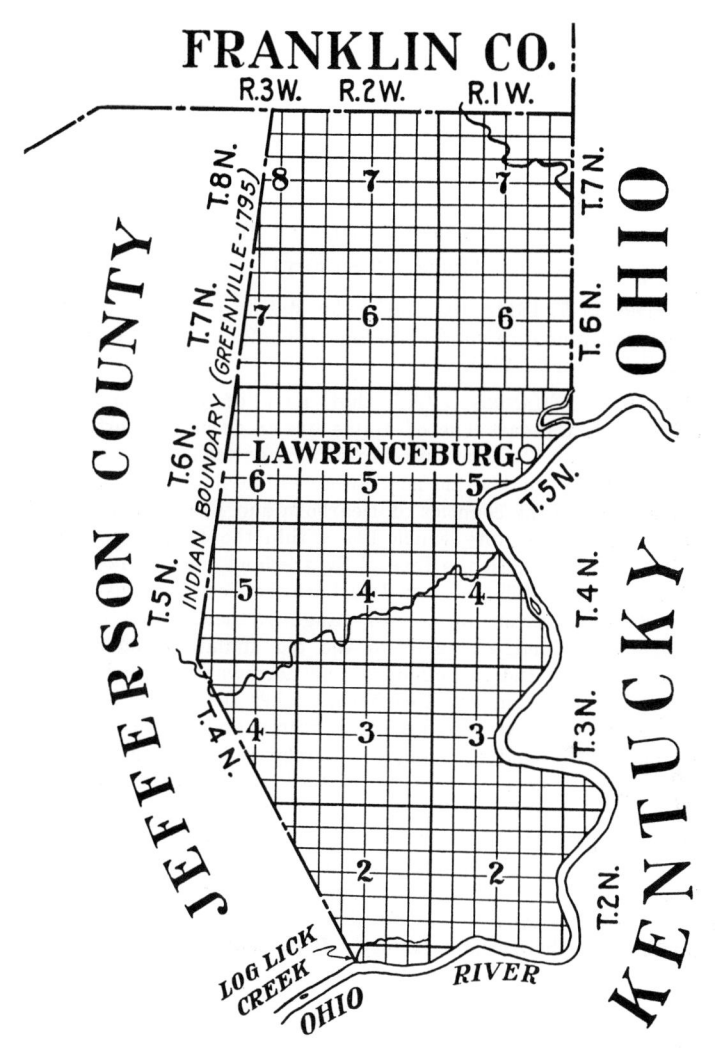

DEARBORN COUNTY II

[Laws: Nov. 23, 1810, effective Jan. 1, 1811; Nov. 27, 1810, effective Jan. 1, 1811]

DEARBORN COUNTY III
[Indiana Territory]

SEPTEMBER 7, 1814: Alteration by statute attaching territory to Dearborn and forming Switzerland County, Indiana Territory, effective October 1, 1814.

BOUNDARY CHANGES: "All that part of Jefferson county which lies on the east side of a line drawn from the north west corner of section four, in township six, range twelve, and running due north so far that a due north line, will strike the west end of the line dividing the counties of Dearborn and Franklin; also that part of Jefferson county which lies within the following bounds, to wit, beginning where the line of Switzerland county crosses the old line, between Jefferson and Dearborn, between sections twenty two and twenty seven, in town 4, range 3; thence west with the line of Switzerland aforesaid to the old Indian boundary line, thence with said Indian boundary line northwardly to where the line between Jefferson and Dearborn, strikes the old Indian boundary line, thence with said line of Jefferson and Dearborn to the begining shall be and the same are hereby added and attached to the county of Dearborn." *Acts of Indiana Territory*, 1814, pp. 34-35.

All that part of Dearborn County south of a line "beginning at a point between fractional sections number twenty two and twenty seven, on the Ohio river, in town three range one, west," and running thence due west to the old Jefferson County boundary was transferred to Switzerland County. *Ibid.*, 30-31.

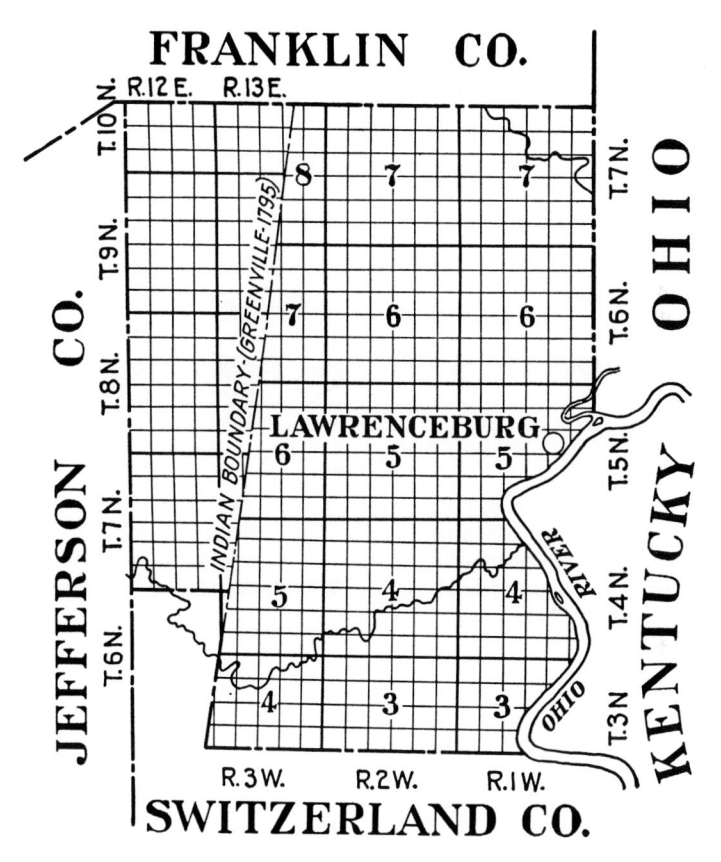

DEARBORN COUNTY III

[Law: Sep. 7, 1814, effective Oct. 1, 1814]

DEARBORN COUNTY IV

DECEMBER 27, 1816: Alteration by statute forming Ripley County.

BOUNDARY CHANGE: All that part of Dearborn County west of the Greenville Treaty line of 1795 was transferred to Ripley County. *Laws of Indiana*, 1816-17, p. 199. For text of the law, see map, Ripley County I.

This territory remained under the jurisdiction of Dearborn County until the organization of Ripley County by a law of January 14, 1818, effective February 1, 1818. *Laws of Indiana*, 1816-17, p. 199; 1817-18 (special), pp. 32-34.

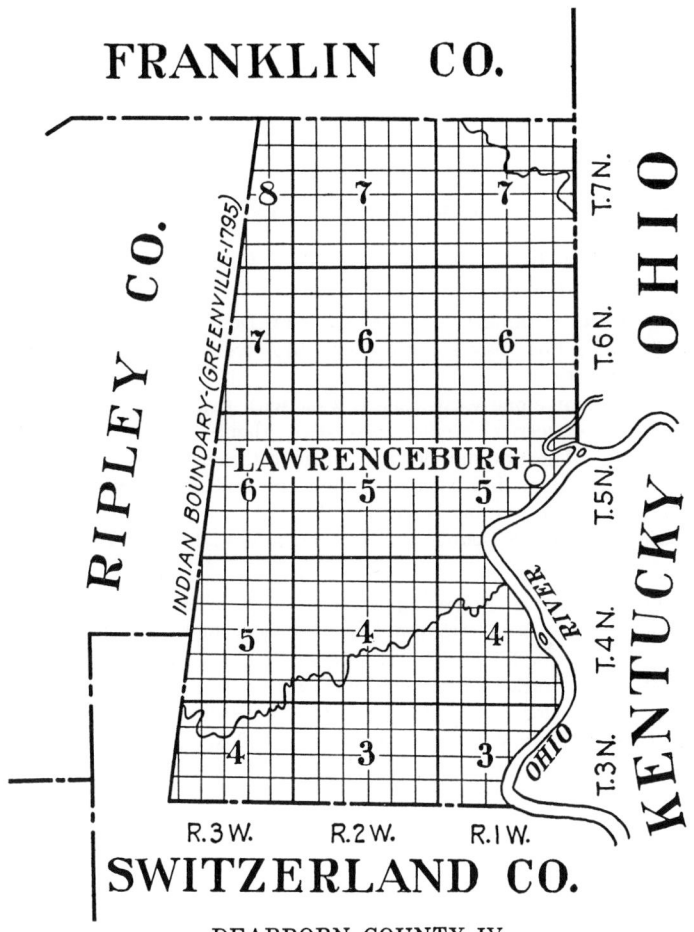

DEARBORN COUNTY IV
[Law: Dec. 27, 1816]

DEARBORN COUNTY V

JANUARY 4, 1844: Alteration by statute forming Ohio County, effective March 1, 1844.

BOUNDARY CHANGE: All that part of Dearborn County south and east of a line "beginning on the Ohio river on the section line, between fractional sections number twenty-five and thirty-six, in town four, range one west, thence west with said line to the north west corner of section number thirty-two; thence south to the north west corner of section number five, in town three, range one; thence west to the range line between range one and range two; thence south to the line dividing Switzerland and Dearborn counties," was transferred to Ohio County. *Laws of Indiana*, 1843-44 (general), p. 7.

COUNTY SEAT: Following an act of February 6, 1835, the county seat had been removed from Lawrenceburg to Wilmington on September 26, 1836. The act forming Ohio County moved the seat of justice back to Lawrenceburg, where it has since remained. *Ibid.*, 1834-35 (local), pp. 169-70; 1843-44 (general), p. 9; Shockley, "County Seat Wars," *op. cit.*, 10:no.1:2-3; *History of Dearborn and Ohio Counties*, 116-17; Shaw (ed.), *History of Dearborn County*, 133-34.

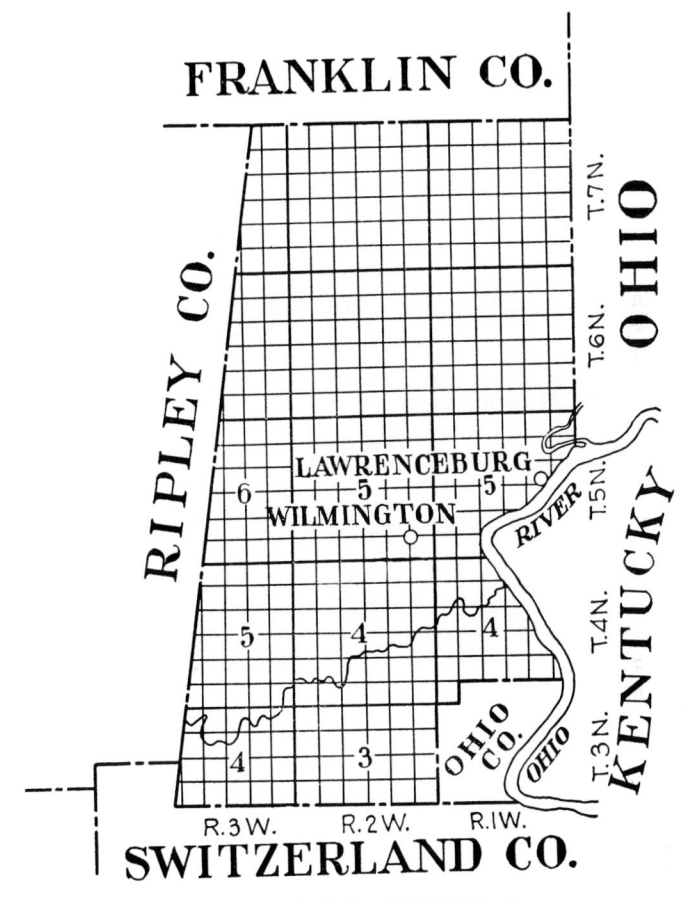

DEARBORN COUNTY V

[Law: Jan. 4, 1844, effective Mar. 1, 1844]

DEARBORN COUNTY VI

JANUARY 7, 1845: Alteration by statute attaching additional territory to the county of Ohio, effective on publication in the *Indiana Blade*, of Rising Sun.

BOUNDARY CHANGE: "All the territory which now belongs to Dearborn county, and which lies south of the main channel of Laughery Creek . . . is hereby attached to the county of Ohio, and shall form a part of said county of Ohio." *Laws of Indiana*, 1844-45 (local), p. 225.

A law of January 13, 1845, effective on passage, supplied omissions in the description of Dearborn County as given in the *Revised Statutes* of 1843. *Revised Statutes of Indiana*, 1842-43, p. 68; *Laws of Indiana*, 1844-45 (local), p. 136.

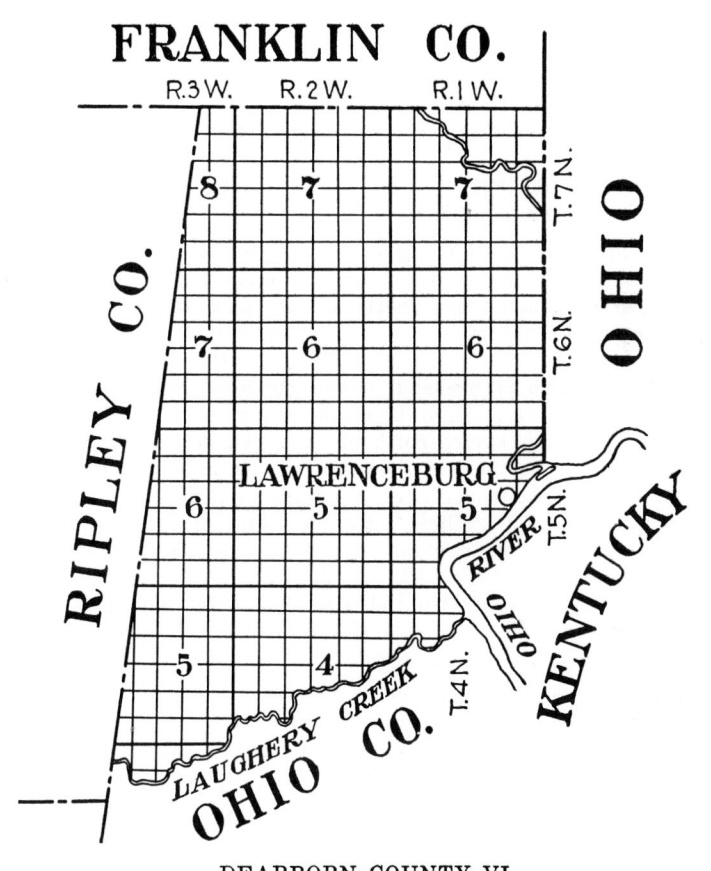

DEARBORN COUNTY VI

[Law: Jan. 7, 1845, effective on publication in *Indiana Blade*]

DECATUR COUNTY

DECEMBER 31, 1821: Formation by statute, effective March 4, 1822. The formation affected Delaware County, New Purchase.

BOUNDARIES: "Beginning at the south-west corner of section eighteen in township eight north of range eight east of the second principal meridian, thence north fifteen miles to the south-west [north-west] corner of section six, in township ten north of range eight east, thence east three miles to the south-east corner of section thirty-three in township eleven north of range eight east, thence north seven miles to the north-west corner of section thirty-four in township twelve north of range eight east, thence east eighteen miles to the west boundary of Franklin county, thence south with said boundary to the north line of Ripley county, thence with the old boundary line to the north line of Jennings county, thence west with the Jennings county line to the place of beginning." *Laws of Indiana*, 1821-22, pp. 57-58.

The error in description, indicated by brackets above, was corrected by an act of January 24, 1828. *Ibid.*, 1827-28, p. 13.

COUNTY SEAT: Commissioners appointed in the act forming the county, decided upon the site of Greensburg for the county seat. It became the seat of government for the county on June 12, 1822. *Ibid.*, 1821-22, pp. 57-58; Harding (ed.), *History of Decatur County*, 73; Shockley, "County Seat Wars," *op. cit.*, 10:no. 1:23.

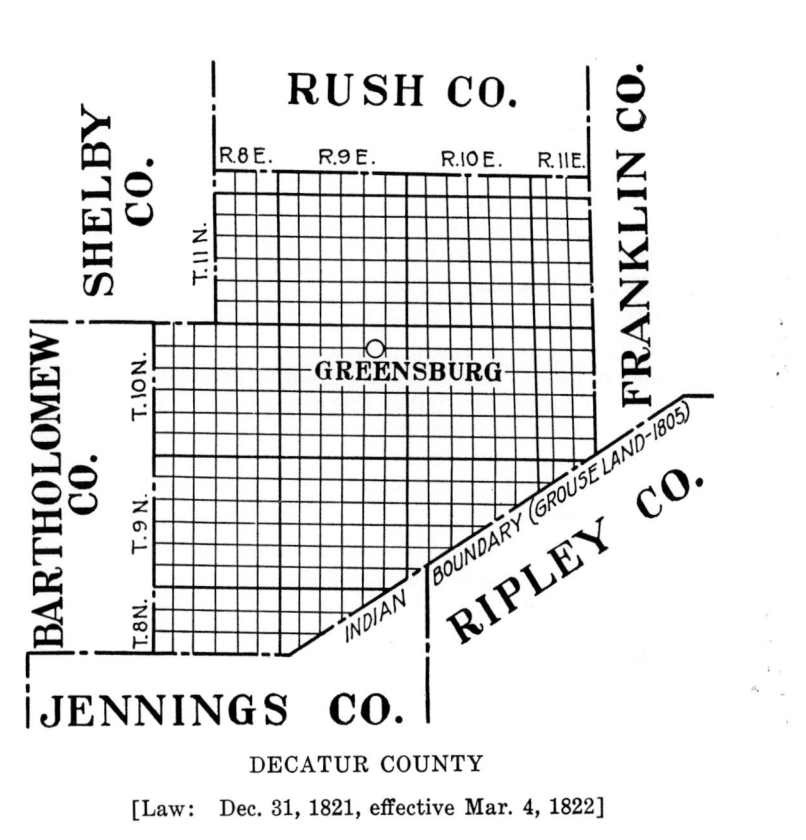

DECATUR COUNTY
[Law: Dec. 31, 1821, effective Mar. 4, 1822]

DE KALB COUNTY

FEBRUARY 7, 1835: Formation by statute, effective on publication. The formation affected territory attached to Allen and La Grange counties. De Kalb was organized by an act of January 14, 1837, effective May 1, 1837.

BOUNDARIES: "Beginning at the south west corner of township thirty three north of range twelve east, thence east with the line of Allen county to the line of the State of Ohio thence north with said state line eighteen miles, thence west with the line dividing townships thirty five and thirty six to the line dividing ranges eleven and twelve east, thence south with said range line eighteen miles to the place of beginning," *Laws of Indiana*, 1834-35 (general), pp. 44-45.

COUNTY SEAT: Commissioners appointed under the act organizing the county located the county seat at Auburn, where it has since remained. *Ibid.*, 1836-37 (general), pp. 57-58; *History of De Kalb County, Indiana* . . ., 269 (Inter-State Publishing Co., Chicago, 1885); *History of De Kalb County, Indiana* . . ., 77-78 (B. F. Bowen & Company, Indianapolis, 1914).

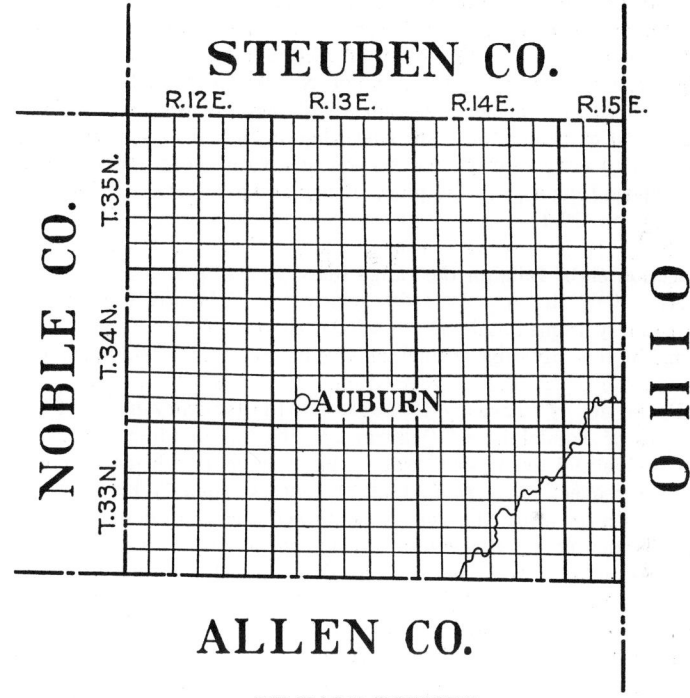

DE KALB COUNTY

[Law: Feb. 7, 1835, effective on publication]

DELAWARE COUNTY

JANUARY 26, 1827: Formation by statute, effective April 1, 1827. The formation affected that part of the old Delaware County attached to Randolph.

BOUNDARIES: "Beginning at the north east corner of Henry county, thence due north with the western boundary of Randolph to the north east [west] corner of section numbered eight, township No. twenty-two, north of range No. twelve east, thence west to the north east corner of section No. eleven, township No. twenty-two, north of range No. eight east, thence south to the north west corner of Henry county, and thence east with the northern boundary of said county, to the place of beginning." *Laws of Indiana,* 1826-27, pp. 12-13.

Range 12 is only five sections wide, and the northwest corner of section eight falls on the range line.

An act of January 24, 1828, attached to Delaware County "all the country immediately north of the county of Delaware, to the township line dividing townships twenty-five and twenty-six, and west to the Great Miami reservation." *Ibid.*, 1827-28, p. 14.

By an act of February 10, 1831, "all the territory north of the counties of Randolph and Delaware, to the line dividing townships twenty-five and twenty-six" was declared to be attached to the two counties respectively. *Ibid.*, 1830-31 (special), pp. 17-18.

The act forming the county contained the provision that "all that district of country heretofore known as the county of Delaware, yet unorganized, be hereafter called and known by the name of the county of Adams." *Ibid.*, 1826-27, p. 14. This district did not have a county organization, and there was no connection between it and the Adams County formed later.

COUNTY SEAT: Commissioners appointed under the act organizing the county met on June 11, 1827, to select a county seat. A few days later they chose a site near the geographical center of the county, which was called Munseytown, Muncietown, or Muncie Town. The name was changed to Muncie in 1845 by an act of January 13. *Ibid.*, 1826-27, p. 13; 1844-45 (local), p. 247; Shockley, "County Seat Wars," *op. cit.*, 10:no. 1:27; Kemper (ed.), *History of Delaware County,* 1:58-59.

(ATTACHED TO RANDOLPH CO.)

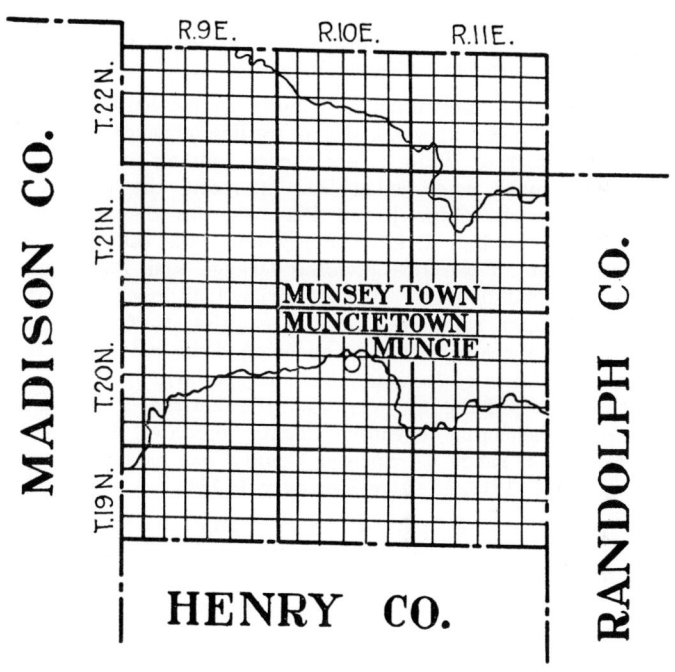

MADISON CO.

RANDOLPH CO.

HENRY CO.

MUNSEY TOWN
MUNCIETOWN
MUNCIE

DELAWARE COUNTY

[Law: Jan. 26, 1827, effective Apr. 1, 1827]

DUBOIS COUNTY I

DECEMBER 20, 1817: Formation by statute, effective February 1, 1818. The formation affected Pike County.

BOUNDARIES: "Beginning at a point on the bank of the east fork of White river, at which the centre line of range six shall intersect said fork of White river; thence running south with said centre line, until said centre line intersects the present line, dividing Warrick [Gibson] and Pike counties thence east with said line, to the line dividing Perry and Pike counties; thence with said line to the line dividing Orange and Pike counties; thence with said line until it shall strike Lick creek; and thence meandering down said creek until it empties itself into the east fork of White river; thence meandering down said river to the beginning." *Laws of Indiana*, 1817-18 (special), pp. 16-17.

The framers of the law overlooked the fact that a narrow strip of territory belonging to Gibson County separated Warrick from Pike County in range 6. Spencer County was created by an act of January 10, 1818, effective February 1, 1818.

COUNTY SEAT: Commissioners were appointed under the act forming the county to select a county seat, but failed to act. A new set of commissioners, appointed by the county commissioners, selected a site on the East Fork of White River. Their proceedings were legalized by the next Assembly. The town was named Portersville, and remained the county seat until 1830. *Ibid.*, 17; 1818-19, p. 90; Wilson, *History of Dubois County*, 32-33; *History of Pike and Dubois Counties*, 488; Shockley, "County Seat Wars," *op. cit.*, 10:no.1:10.

DUBOIS COUNTY BOUNDARIES 327

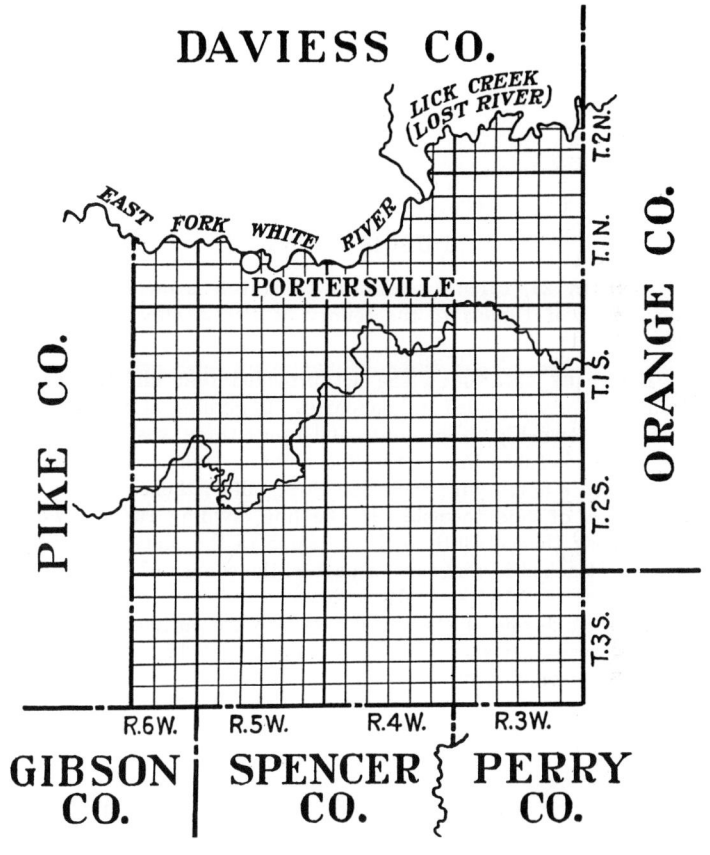

DUBOIS COUNTY I
[Law: Dec. 20, 1817, effective Feb. 1, 1818]

DUBOIS COUNTY II

JANUARY 29, 1818: Alteration by statute attaching a part of the county of Dubois to the county of Perry, effective February 15, 1818.

BOUNDARY CHANGE: The act provided that all that part of Dubois County included in boundaries "Beginning at the south east corner of township three south, and range three west; thence west with said township line to the line dividing ranges three and four west; thence north with the same three miles; thence east through the centre of said township to the line dividing ranges two and three west; thence south with the same to the place of beginning . . . be attached to and form a part of the county of Perry." *Laws of Indiana*, 1817-18 (special), p. 26.

The boundaries of Crawford County were outlined in the same act; its formation was effective on March 1, 1818. *Ibid.*, 27. See map, Crawford County I.

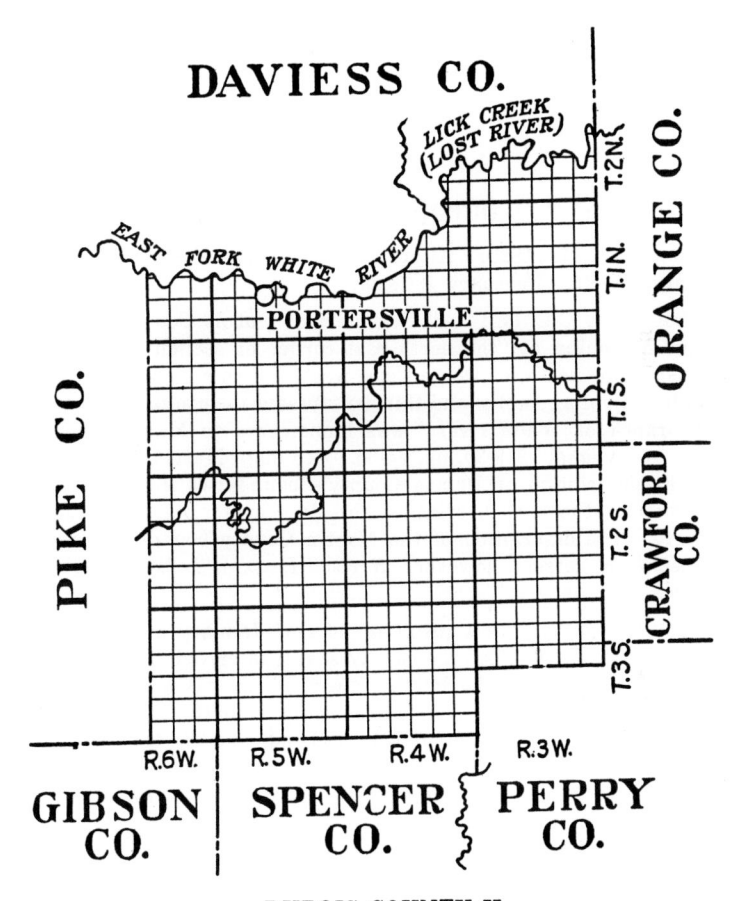

DUBOIS COUNTY II

[Law: Jan. 29, 1818, effective Feb. 15, 1818]

DUBOIS COUNTY III

JANUARY 17, 1820: Alteration by statute forming Martin County, effective February 1, 1820.

BOUNDARY CHANGE: All that part of Dubois County north of a line beginning at "the north east corner of section thirteen, in township one north, of range three west, thence west with the section line dividing twelve and thirteen, in said township, to the eastern branch of White river," was transferred to Martin County. *Laws of Indiana*, 1819-20, pp. 54-55. See map, Martin County I.

The description of Dubois County's boundaries in the 1823-24 Revision of the laws overlooked this loss of territory to Martin County. The description of the Martin County boundaries in the Revision are correct, however. *Revised Laws of Indiana*, 1823-24, p. 104.

COUNTY SEAT: As a result of acts of January 19, 1829, and January 21 and 30, 1830, the county seat was moved from Portersville to a new site on the Patoka River, which was named Jasper. The location was in section 35, township 1 south, range 5 west. *Laws of Indiana*, 1828-29, p. 131; 1829-30, pp. 38, 41; Shockley, "County Seat Wars," *op. cit.*, 10:no. 1:10-11; *History of Pike and Dubois Counties*, 489; Wilson, *History of Dubois County*, 154-62.

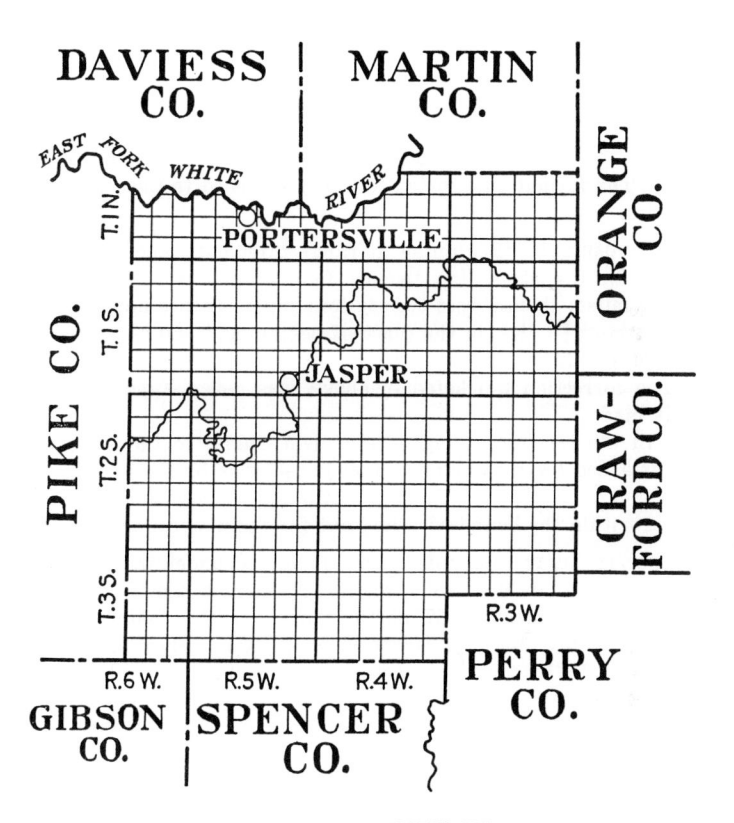

DUBOIS COUNTY III

[Law: Jan. 17, 1820, effective Feb. 1, 1820]

ELKHART COUNTY I

JANUARY 29, 1830: Formation by statute, effective April 1, 1830. The formation affected territory attached to Cass and Allen counties.

BOUNDARIES: "Beginning at range three east, and thence running with the state line twenty four miles east; thence south twenty miles; thence west twenty-four miles; thence north twenty-four [twenty] miles, to the place of beginning." *Laws of Indiana*, 1829-30, pp. 29-30.

The correction bracketed in above, was never, apparently, formally made.

"All the territory lying east of said county to the state line" was attached for civil and criminal jurisdiction by the law forming the county. *Ibid.*, 31. Territory still under Indian title was included within the boundaries laid out for the new county.

COUNTY SEAT: Commissioners appointed under the law forming the county, in May, 1830, selected a site now known as Dunlap, in section 24, township 37 north, range 5 east. County officers, meeting in July, filed the report without action. By a law of February 10, 1831, commissioners were appointed to relocate the county seat, and on May 26 they reported their selection of a site in section 9, township 36 north, range 6 east. Their recommendation that the town be named Goshen was accepted. *Ibid.*, 30; 1830-31 (special), pp. 22-23; Shockley, "County Seat Wars," *op. cit.*, 10:no. 1:29; Weaver (ed.), *History of Elkhart County*, 1:72-73, 74-75; *History of Elkhart County*, 370-71.

MICHIGAN TERRITORY

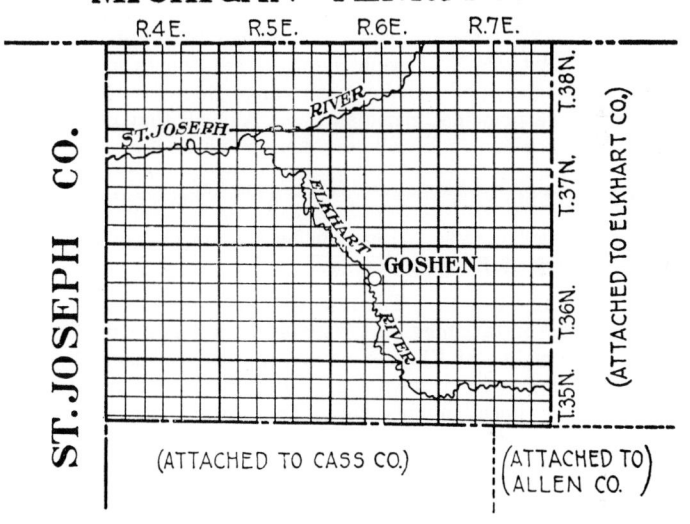

ELKHART COUNTY I

[Law: Jan. 29, 1830, effective Apr. 1, 1830]

ELKHART COUNTY II

JANUARY 31, 1832: Alteration by statute changing the boundary line between Elkhart and St. Joseph counties, effective on passage.

BOUNDARY CHANGE: The act provided that the boundary between Elkhart and St. Joseph counties "be a north and south line, three miles east, and parallel with range line, number three, east of the second principal meridian line. And all that portion of territory so stricken off of Elkhart county, be . . . attached to, and . . . constitute a part of St. Joseph county." *Laws of Indiana*, 1831-32, p. 114.

FEBRUARY 2, 1832: Alteration by statute changing the southern boundary of Elkhart County.

BOUNDARY CHANGE: The law attached to Elkhart County, "all that portion of territory . . . situated between the present southern boundary line of Elkhart county, and the township line, dividing the congressional townships, thirty-four and thirty-five, between range lines, number three and seven, east of the second principal meridian." *Ibid.*, 112.

That part of Elkhart County south of the Carey Mission Treaty line was not ceded by the Indians until October, 1832.

By the law of February 10, 1831, "all the territory east of the line dividing ranges three and four east, not otherwise attached," had been attached to Elkhart for jurisdiction. *Ibid.*, 1830-31 (special), p. 18.

La Grange County was formed by an act of February 2, 1832, effective April 1, 1832.

MICHIGAN TERRITORY

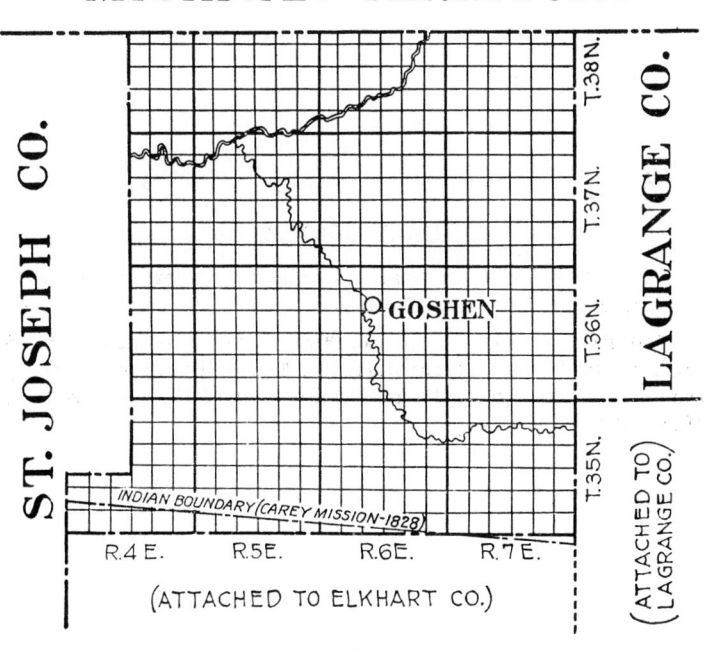

ELKHART COUNTY II

[Laws: Jan. 31, 1832, effective on passage; Feb. 2, 1832]

ELKHART COUNTY III

FEBRUARY 4, 1836: Alteration by statute organizing the county of Marshall, effective April 1, 1836.

BOUNDARY CHANGE: The southwest quarter of township 35 north, range 4 east was transferred to Marshall County. *Laws of Indiana*, 1835-36 (general), p. 50. For text of the law, see map, Marshall County II.

ELKHART COUNTY BOUNDARIES 337

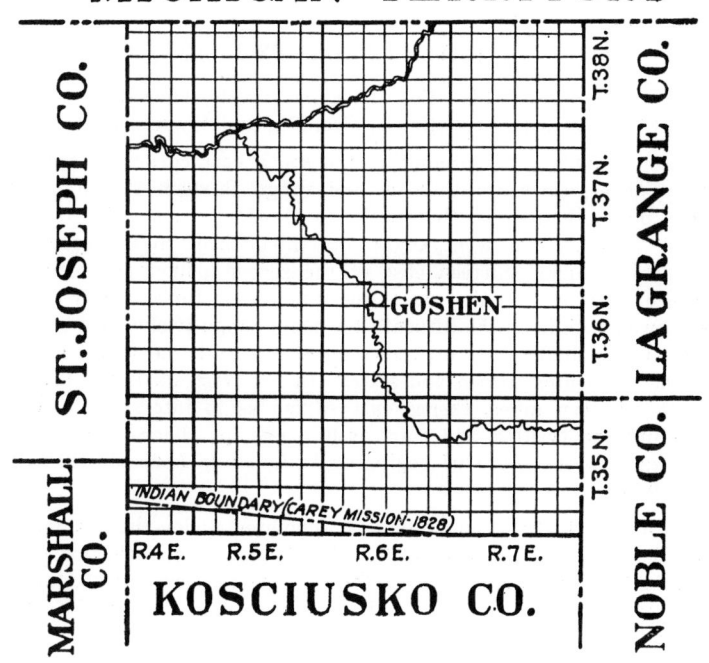

ELKHART COUNTY III

[Law: Feb. 4, 1836, effective Apr. 1, 1836]

FAYETTE COUNTY I

DECEMBER 28, 1818: Formation by statute, effective January 1, 1819. The formation affected Franklin and Wayne counties.

BOUNDARIES: "Beginning at the south east corner of section thirty-three, township thirteen and range thirteen thence north three miles, thence east three miles to the old boundary line thence north to fractions twenty-eight and thirty-three in the fifteenth township, range fourteen east of the second principal meridian, thence west on said line, to a line dividing sections twenty-seven and twenty eight in the fifteenth township range twelve east of the second principal meridian, thence north on said line to a line dividing townships fifteen and sixteen thence west six miles, thence south eighteen miles, thence east so far as to intersect the line dividing the twelfth and thirteenth townships thence along said line east to the place of beginning." *Laws of Indiana*, 1818-19, pp. 103-4.

COUNTY SEAT: Commissioners appointed under the act forming the county, on February 17, 1819, reported their selection of a site in Connersville, on the northwest corner of section 25, township 14 north, range 12 east. Barrows (ed.), *History of Fayette County*, 161.

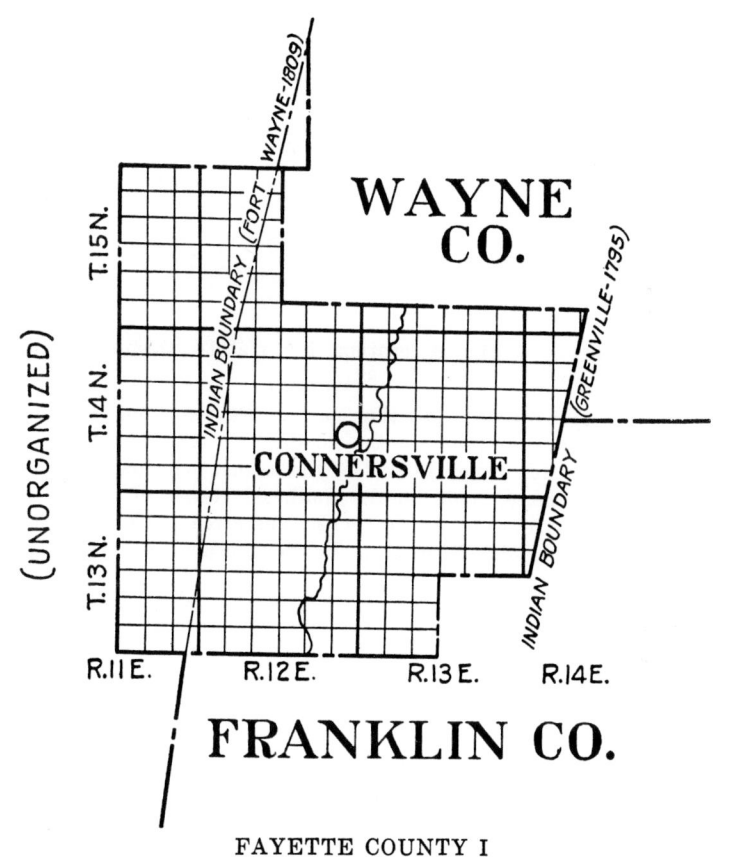

FAYETTE COUNTY I
[Law: Dec. 28, 1818, effective Jan. 1, 1819]

FAYETTE COUNTY II

JANUARY 5, 1821: Alteration by statute forming Union County, effective February 1, 1821.

BOUNDARY CHANGE: All that part of Fayette County east of the section line beginning at the northeast corner of section 35, township 15 north, range 13 east of the second principal meridian, and running thence south to the southeast corner of section 14, township 13 north, range 13 east, was transferred to Union County. *Laws of Indiana*, 1820-21, p. 127. For text of law, see map, Union County I.

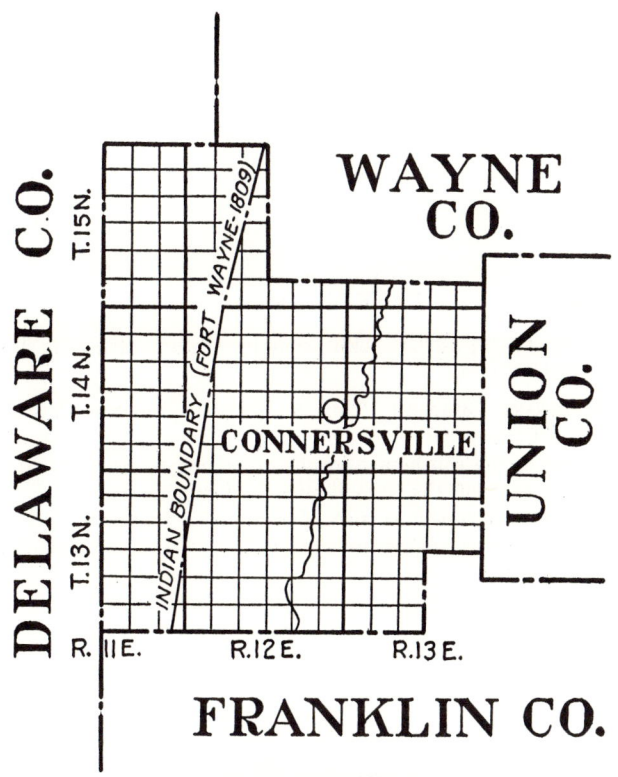

FAYETTE COUNTY II

[Law: Jan. 5, 1821, effective Feb. 1, 1821]

FAYETTE COUNTY III

JANUARY 16, 1826: Alteration by statute attaching territory to Fayette County.

BOUNDARY CHANGE: This act gave to Fayette County from Franklin County "all that district of country lying north of a line drawn from the south-east corner of section 33, in township 13, in range 13 east of the second principal meridian; thence running east to the south-east corner of section 35, in township 13, range 13 east of the second principal meridian." *Laws of Indiana,* 1825-26, pp. 11-12.

FAYETTE COUNTY BOUNDARIES 343

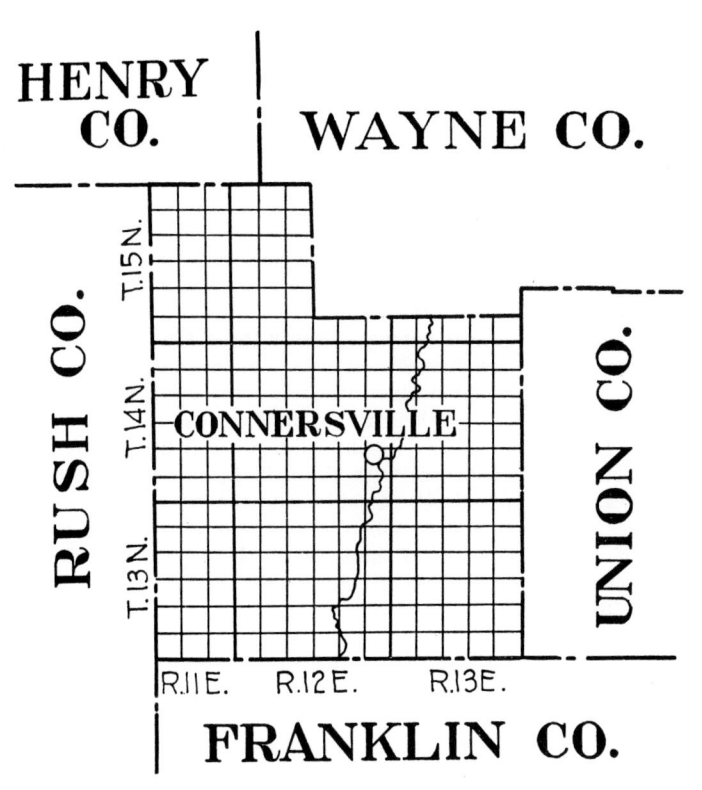

FAYETTE COUNTY III
[Law: Jan. 16, 1826]

FLOYD COUNTY I

JANUARY 2, 1819: Formation by statute, effective February 1, 1819. The formation affected Clark and Harrison counties.

BOUNDARIES: "Beginning on the Ohio river, where the sectional line dividing fractional sections six and seven strikes the same in township four south of range five [six] east, thence west with said line to the south west corner of section three, in the town and range aforesaid [township four south, range five east], thence north with the sectional line dividing sections numbers three and four to the township line dividing town number one and two, thence west with said township line to the south west corner of section thirty six, in town one south of range four east, thence north with the said sectional line dividing sections thirty four [five] and thirty six to the corner of sections numbers twenty three, twenty four, twenty five and twenty six, thence east from said last mentioned corner with sectional line dividing sections twenty four and twenty five in town number one south in range number four east, thence with the said sectional line east to the Illinois grant line in the county of Clark aforesaid, thence with the said Illinois grant line south forty east to Silver Creek in said Grant, on the south side of lot number sixty six, thence down said Creek, with the meanders thereof, on the west side of the same, to the mouth thereof, thence down the Ohio to the place of beginning." *Laws of Indiana,* 1818-19, p. 100.

For a note concerning that portion of Harrison County to the north of Floyd, see text with map, Harrison County VI.

A law of January 9, 1821, attached to Floyd County "all that part of the county of Clark lying south and west of the lines dividing Harrison and Floyd counties." *Laws of Indiana,* 1820-21, p. 111. No satisfactory interpretation of this law seems possible.

COUNTY SEAT: Commissioners appointed under the act forming the county reported on March 4, 1819, their selection of four lots in New Albany for the county seat. It has never been removed. *Ibid.,* 1818-19, p. 101; *History of the Ohio Falls Cities and their Counties,* 2:85-86.

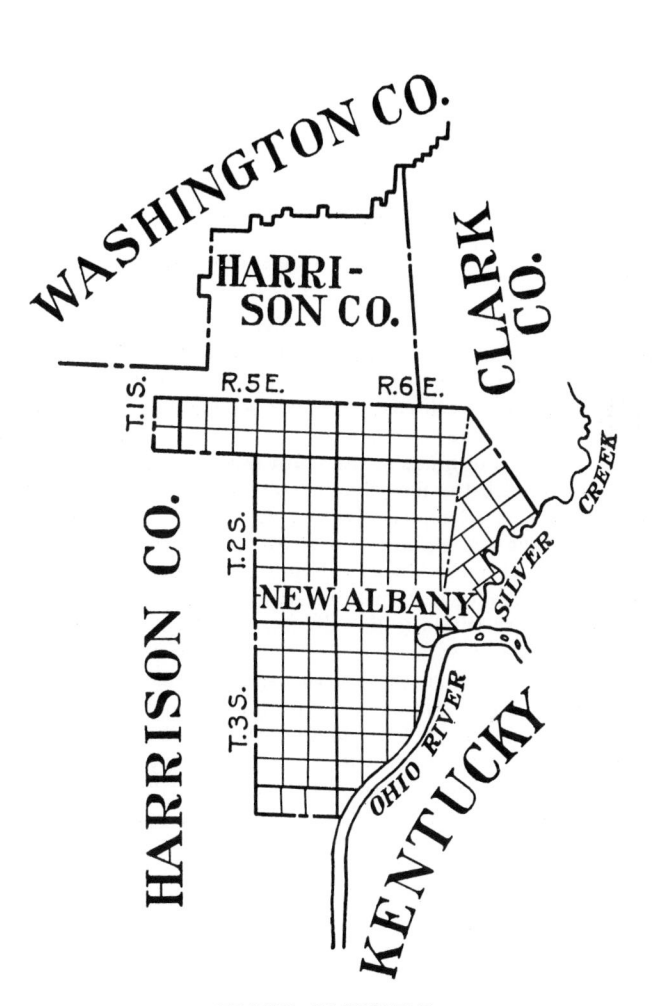

FLOYD COUNTY I

[Law: Jan. 2, 1819, effective Feb. 1, 1819]

FLOYD COUNTY II

JANUARY 10, 1823: Alteration by statute attaching part of the county of Harrison to the county of Floyd.

BOUNDARY CHANGE: The act provided that "all that part of the county of Harrison, contained in the following boundary, to wit: commencing on the line dividing the said counties of Harrison and Floyd, at the north east corner of section sixteen, in township three, south of range five east, thence west with the line dividing sections sixteen and nine; to the south west corner of section nine; thence north, with the line dividing sections eight and nine, to the south east corner of section five; thence west, with the line dividing sections five and eight, to the south west corner of section five; thence north with the line dividing sections five and six, to the north west corner of section thirty two, in township two, in range five; thence west with the line dividing sections thirty and thirty one, to the south west corner of section thirty; thence north with the range line, to the south west corner of section eighteen; thence west with the line dividing sections thirteen and twenty four, in township two, in range four, to the south west corner of section thirteen; thence north with the line dividing sections thirteen and fourteen, in said range, to the south west [north west] corner of Floyd county . . . be attached to, and form a part of the county of Floyd." *Laws of Indiana*, 1822-23, pp. 77-78.

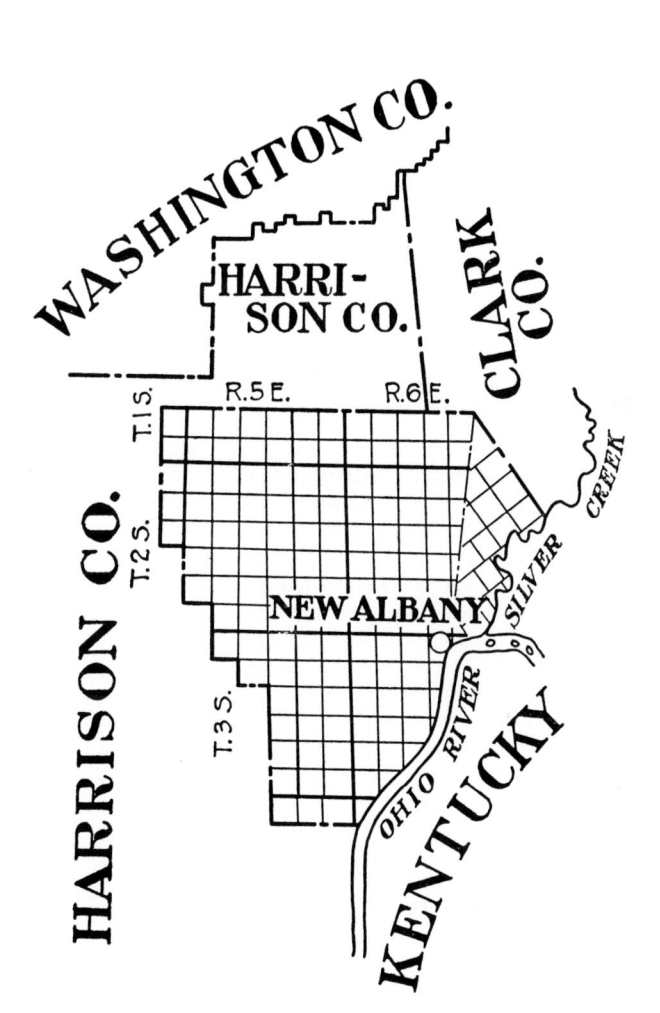

FLOYD COUNTY II
[Law: Jan. 10, 1823]

FLOYD COUNTY III

JANUARY 5, 1828: Alteration by statute attaching a portion of vacant territory to Floyd County, effective on passage.

BOUNDARY CHANGE: The act attached to Floyd the two sections described as follows: "All that territory which is included in the following lines, viz: beginning at the corner of sections numbered twenty-three, twenty-four, twenty-five and twenty-six, in township numbered one, south of range numbered four, east, in the district of land sold at Jeffersonville; thence north one mile, to the corner of sections numbered thirteen, fourteen, twenty-three and twenty-four; thence east, according to the true meridian, on the exterior line of the county of Washington, to the exterior line of the county of Clark; thence with said line of Clark county, southward, to the intersection thereof with the northern boundary of the county of Floyd, and with the said last mentioned boundary to the place of beginning." *Laws of Indiana*, 1827-28, p. 12.

These two sections had been unattached since 1824. See map, Harrison County VIII.

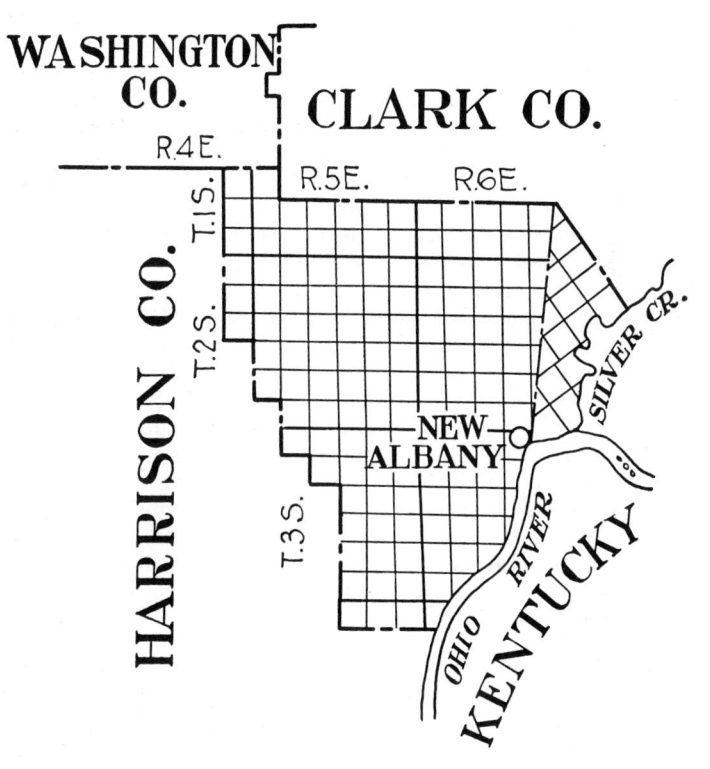

FLOYD COUNTY III

[Law: Jan. 5, 1828, effective on passage]

FLOYD COUNTY IV

APRIL 23, 1844: Alteration by report of commissioners appointed by an act of January 15, 1844, relating to the boundary line between the counties of Clark and Floyd.

BOUNDARY CHANGE: The new boundary between Clark and Floyd County followed a line "Beginning at a stone corner of sections numbers 17, 18, 19, & 20 in township one south of range five east . . . Running thence South one half mile . . . Thence East One mile and a half to the *center* of Sect. 21 . . . Thence South One half mile to the Sectional line . . . Thence with said line E. Three miles and a half to the town-ship line between ranges Nos. 5 & 6 East . . . Thence with said line South Seven Poles and 16 links to intersect sectional line (There being an off set) . . . Thence with Sect. line East Five Miles and 18 poles to the Illinois Grant line . . . Thence with said Grant Line S. 1½ degrees E. Seventy-Seven poles to a Stone . . . Thence S. 40¼ degrees East intersecting the original line dividing Nos. 127, 128, 107, 109, & 108 of the Grant to the South Corner of No. 108 of said Grant . . . Thence N. 49½ degrees E. with the orig'l line between Nos. 86 & 108 of said Grant 30 poles to intersect the orig'l line between Nos. 86, 88, 87, 65 & 66—there being an offset between the lines . . . Thence with said orig'l line of said Nos. 86, 88, 87, 65 & 66 of the Grant S. 40¼ degrees E. to the South Corner of No. Sixty six (66) of the Grant . . . Thence with the orig'l line between Nos. 47 & 65 S. 50 degrees W. 60 poles to the West Bank of Silver Creek . . . Thence down said creek with its Meanderings of the West Bank to the Ohio River." Floyd County Records, Deed Book Q, pp. 125-26.

At least two unsuccessful attempts to determine this line had preceded the law of January 15, 1844. By an act of February 15, 1839, and again by an act of January 25, 1841, commissioners had been appointed to fix the line. No record of action has been found. *Laws of Indiana*, 1838-39 (general), p. 89; 1840-41 (general), pp. 147-48.

JUNE 7, 1852: Alteration by statute defining county boundaries.

BOUNDARY CHANGE: The only change was the transfer to Floyd County of fractional section 7, township 4 south, range 6 east. This area is marked (a) on the map. *Revised Statutes of Indiana*, 1851-52, vol. 1:174-75.

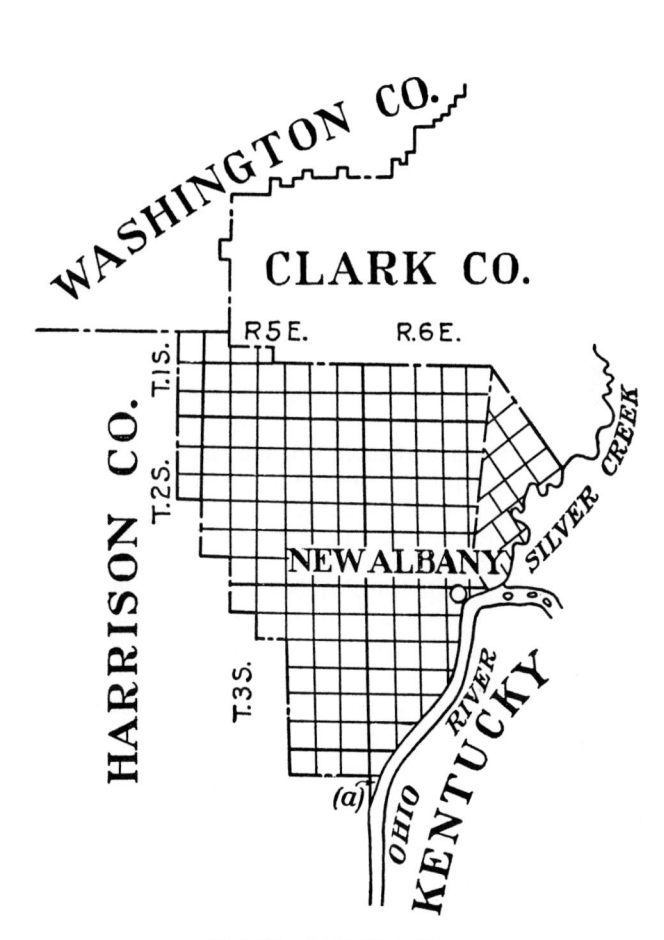

FLOYD COUNTY IV
[Commissioners' Report: Apr. 23, 1844; Law: June 7, 1852]

FOUNTAIN COUNTY

DECEMBER 30, 1825: Formation by statute, effective April 1, 1826. The formation affected Montgomery County and territory attached to Parke.

BOUNDARIES: "Beginning where the line dividing townships seventeen and eighteen crosses the channel of the Wabash river; thence east to the line running through the centre of range six, west of the second principal meridian; thence north to where the said line strikes the main channel of the Wabash river; thence running down with the meanderings of said river, to the place of beginning." *Laws of Indiana*, 1825-26, p. 13.

The same act attached to Fountain County for jurisdiction "all that part of the county of Wabash lying north and west of the said county." *Ibid.*, 14.

COUNTY SEAT: Commissioners appointed under the act forming the county located the county seat at the site of Covington in July, 1826. The county seat has never been moved, although numerous attempts have been made to change it. *Ibid.*, 13; *Historical Atlas of Indiana*, 310; Shockley, "County Seat Wars," *op. cit.*, 10:no. 1:25-26.

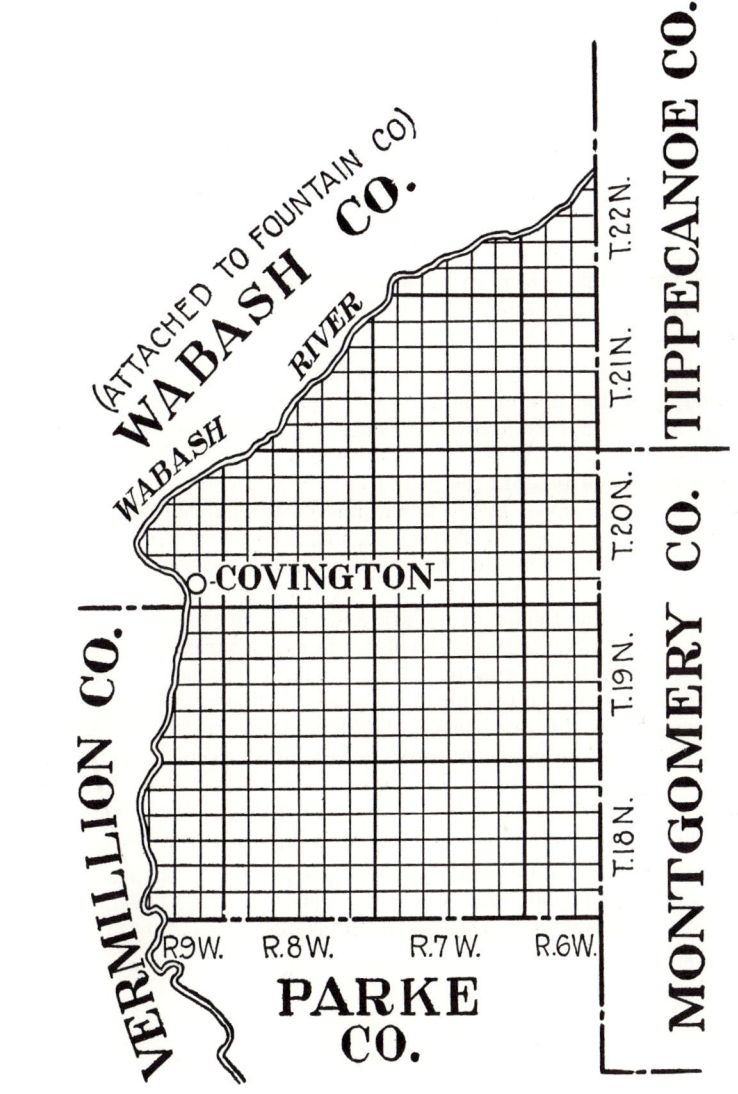

FOUNTAIN COUNTY BOUNDARIES 353

FOUNTAIN COUNTY
[Law: Dec. 30, 1825, effective Apr. 1, 1826]

FRANKLIN COUNTY I
[Indiana Territory]

NOVEMBER 27, 1810: Formation by statute, effective January 1, 1811. The formation affected Jefferson, Clark, and Dearborn counties.

BOUNDARIES: "Beginning at the corner of townships number 7 and 8, on the line of the state of Ohio, thence north, until the same arrives at fort Recovery, thence, from fort Recovery southwardly, with the line of the western boundary of the purchase made at fort Wayne, in the year one thousand eight hundred and nine, until the same intersects the line of the northern boundary of the purchase made at Grouseland, thence northwardly, with the line of the last mentioned purchase until the same arrives at a point from which a due east and west line will strike the corner of town seven and eight on the aforesaid state of Ohio line.

". . . The same is hereby divided into two separate and distinct counties by a line beginning at the corner of townships number eleven and twelve, on the line of the state of Ohio, and from thence due west until the same intersects the line of the western boundary of the before mentioned purchase of fort Wayne . . . the tract of country falling within the southern division thereof shall be known and designated by the name and style of the county of Franklin." *Acts of Indiana Territory*, 1810, pp. 19-20, 114.

COUNTY SEAT: Commissioners were appointed in the same act to fix a county seat. An act of December 5, 1811, effective on passage, confirmed the selection of Brookville. *Ibid.*, 20-21; 1811, pp. 11-12.

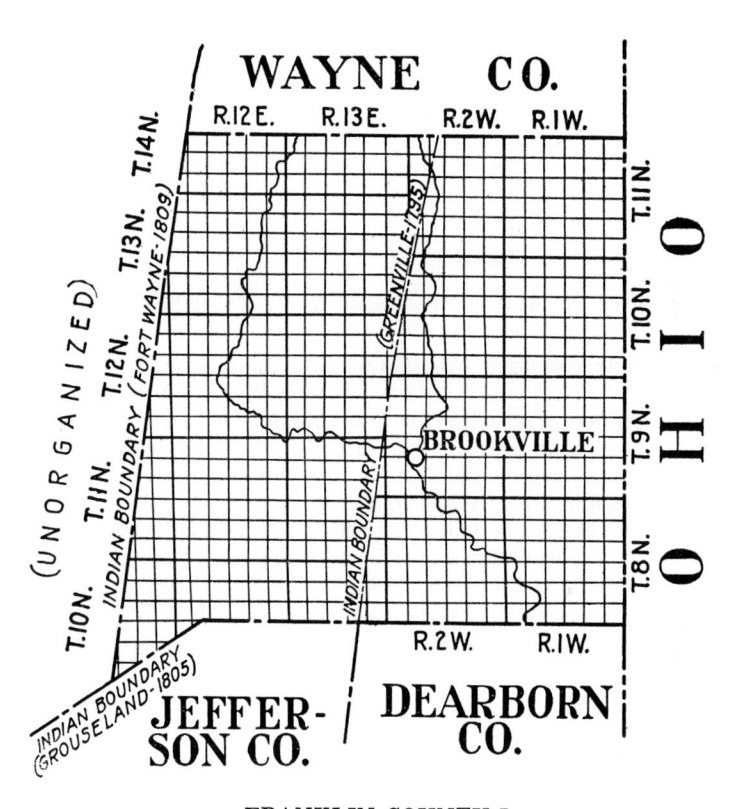

FRANKLIN COUNTY I
[Law: Nov. 27, 1810, effective Jan. 1, 1811]

FRANKLIN COUNTY II

DECEMBER 28, 1818: Alteration by statute forming Fayette County, effective January 1, 1819.

BOUNDARY CHANGE: All that part of Franklin County north and west of a line beginning on the Fort Wayne Treaty line of 1809 at its intersection by the township line between townships 12 and 13 north, in range 11 east of the second principal meridian, running thence east to "the south east corner of section thirty-three, township thirteen and range thirteen thence north three miles, thence east three miles to the old boundary line thence north" with the Indian boundary to the line dividing townships 11 and 12 north, ranges 1 and 2 west of the first principal meridian, was transferred to Fayette County. *Laws of Indiana,* 1818-19, pp. 103-4. See map, Fayette County I.

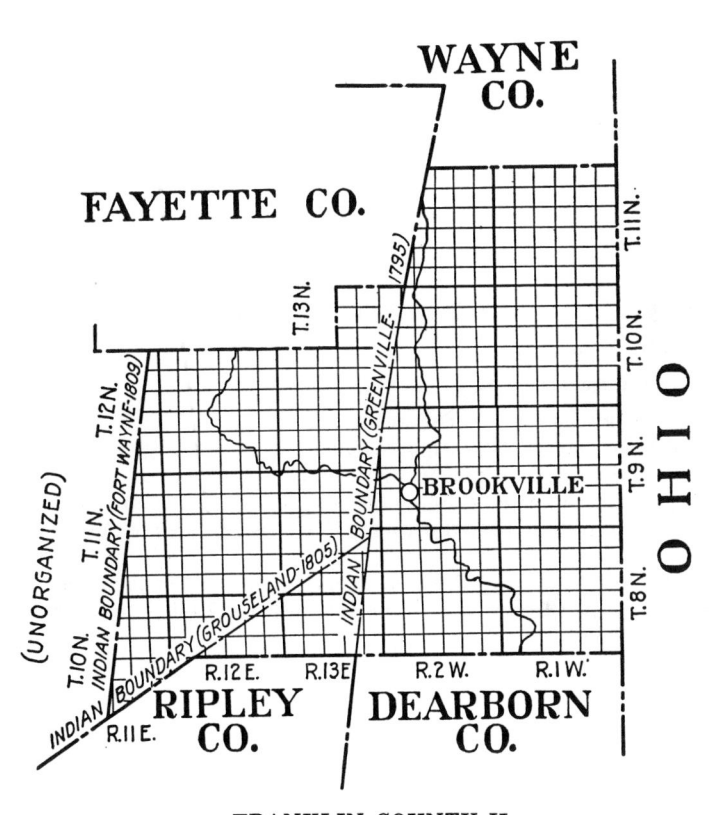

FRANKLIN COUNTY II
[Law: Dec. 28, 1818, effective Jan. 1, 1819]

FRANKLIN COUNTY III

JANUARY 20, 1820: Alteration by statute making provision for the New Purchase.

BOUNDARY CHANGE: The act provided that "all that part of the new purchase, lately acquired from the Indians, lying east of a line drawn due north, from the south west corner of Franklin county, until it intersects the southern boundary of Fayette county, be . . . attached to Franklin county." *Laws of Indiana*, 1819-20, p. 95.

Franklin County, by this act, acquired concurrent jurisdiction over Delaware County, with Randolph, Wayne, Ripley, and other bounding counties.

FRANKLIN COUNTY BOUNDARIES 359

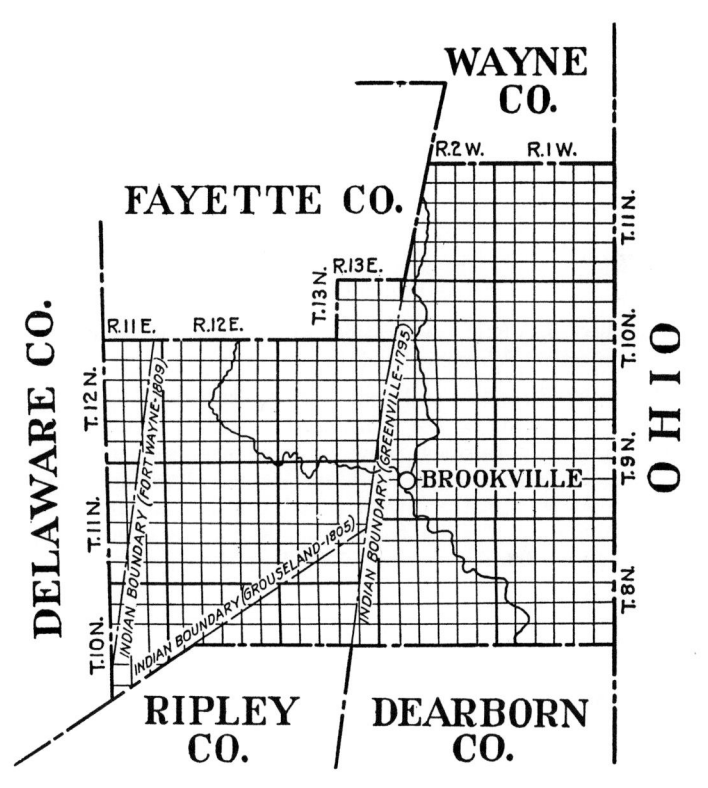

FRANKLIN COUNTY III
[Law: Jan. 20, 1820]

FRANKLIN COUNTY IV

JANUARY 5, 1821: Alteration by statute, forming Union County, effective February 1, 1821.

BOUNDARY CHANGE: All that part of Franklin County north of a line "beginning at the south west corner of section twenty-four in township thirteen range thirteen east second principal meridian, thence east to the south east corner of section one town ten range one west of the first principal meridian, it being the line dividing the state of Ohio from this state;" was transferred to Union County. *Laws of Indiana*, 1820-21, p. 127.

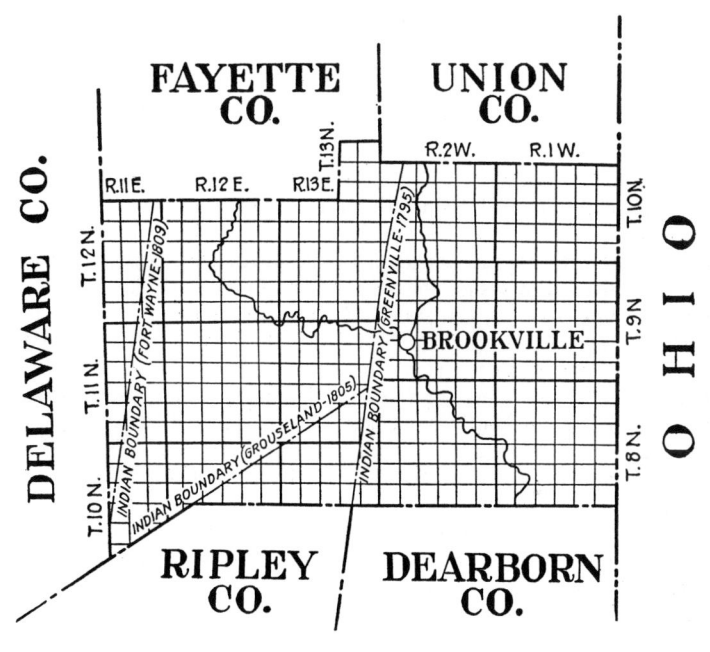

FRANKLIN COUNTY IV

[Law: Jan. 5, 1821, effective Feb. 1, 1821]

FRANKLIN COUNTY V

JANUARY 16, 1826: Alteration by statute detaching territory from Franklin County.

BOUNDARY CHANGE: All that part of Franklin County north of a line beginning "at the south west corner of section thirty-six, in township 13, range 13 east of the second principal meridian; thence east with the section line, to the south east corner of section 13, town 10, in range one west, of the first principal meridian, being the line dividing the states of Ohio and Indiana" was transferred to Union County. "All that district of country lying north of a line drawn from the south-east corner of section 33, in township 13, in range 13 east of the second principal meridian; thence running east to the south-east corner of section 35, in township 13, range 13 east of the second principal meridian" was attached to Fayette County. *Laws of Indiana,* 1825-26, pp. 11-12.

The north boundary of Franklin County as given in the *Revised Laws* of 1830-31, does not agree with the boundary as shown in this map, but the south boundaries of Fayette and Union counties, as given there, follow the line shown here. *Revised Laws of Indiana,* 1830-31, pp. 110-11, 113.

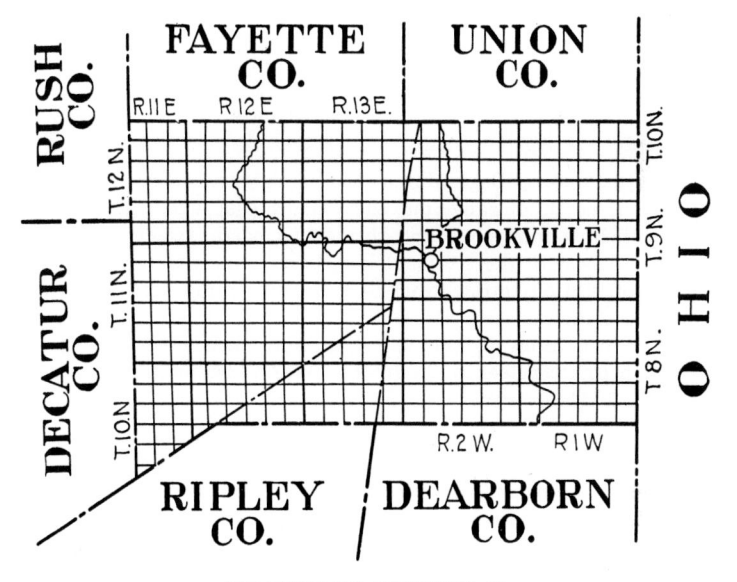

FRANKLIN COUNTY V

[Law: Jan. 16, 1826]

FULTON COUNTY I

FEBRUARY 7, 1835: Formation by statute, effective on publication. The formation affected territory attached to Cass and St. Joseph counties. Fulton was organized by an act of January 23, 1836, effective April 1, 1836.

BOUNDARIES: "Beginning at the north west corner of township thirty one north, of range one east, thence east with the line dividing townships thirty one and thirty two north, twenty one miles, thence south with the sectional line, twelve miles to the south east corner of section thirty three in township thirty north, of range four east, thence west five miles, thence south six miles, thence west sixteen miles to the meridian line, thence north with the meridian line eighteen miles to the place of beginning." *Laws of Indiana*, 1834-35 (general), pp. 45-46.

COUNTY SEAT: Commissioners to select a county seat, appointed under the organizing act, met on June 13, 1836. After considering the various sites, they reported that they had fixed the seat of justice at Rochester. The county seat has never been removed. *Ibid.*, 1835-36 (general), p. 48; Shockley, "County Seat Wars," *op. cit.*, 10:no. 1:34; Barnhart (ed.), *Account of Fulton County from its Organization*, 3:37-38.

FULTON COUNTY BOUNDARIES 365

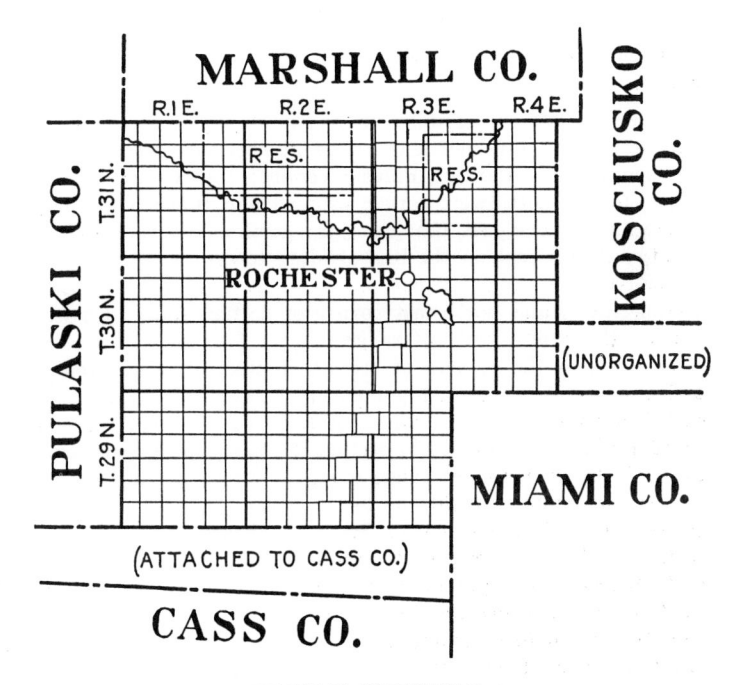

FULTON COUNTY I

[Law: Feb. 7, 1835, effective on publication]

FULTON COUNTY II

FEBRUARY 17, 1838: Alteration by statute defining county boundaries.

BOUNDARIES: "Beginning at the south-west corner of township number twenty-nine, north of range number one east, that being the south-east corner of Pulaski county; thence north eighteen miles, to the north-west corner of township thirty-one, north of range number one east, that being the north east corner of Pulaski county; thence east on the line dividing townships thirty one and thirty-two north, twenty one miles, to the north west corner of section three, and north-east corner of section four, in township number thirty-one, north of range number four east; thence south nine miles, to the corners of sections fifteen, sixteen, twenty-one and twenty-two, in township number thirty north, of range four east, being the south-west corner of Kosciusko county; thence east three miles, to the corners of sections thirteen and twenty four, in township thirty north, of range number four east, and the corners of sections number eighteen and nineteen, in township number thirty north, of range number five east; thence south three miles, to the south-east corner of township thirty north, of range four east; thence west eight miles, to the south-east corner of section thirty-four and south-west corner of section thirty-five, in township thirty north, of range number three east; thence south six miles, to the south-east corner of section thirty-four, and the south-west corner of section thirty-five, in township number twenty-nine north, of range number three east, being the north-east corner of Cass county; thence west sixteen miles, to the place of beginning." *Laws of Indiana*, 1837-38 (local), pp. 261-62.

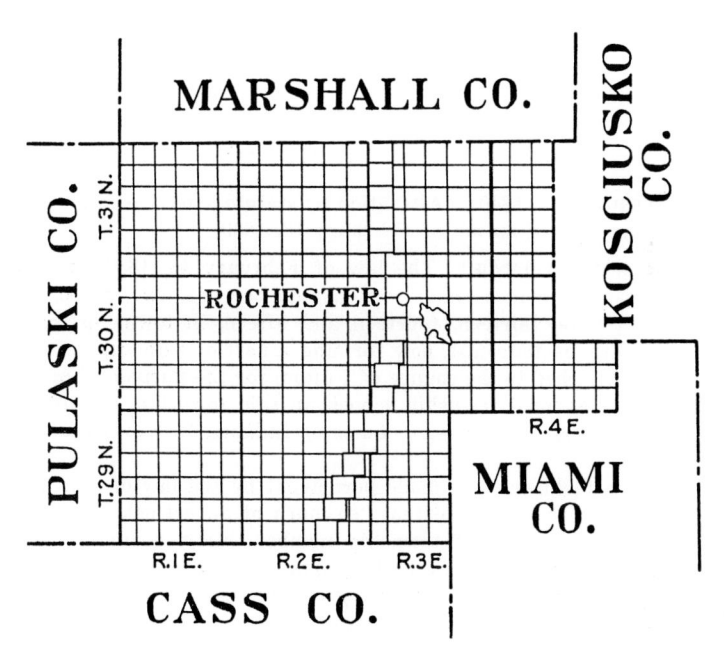

FULTON COUNTY II
[Law: Feb. 17, 1838]

FULTON COUNTY III

FEBRUARY 24, 1840: Alteration by statute, effective on passage, repealing part of an act of February 18, 1839.

BOUNDARY CHANGE: The law of February 18, 1839, effective on passage, provided that "sections number one, two, three, ten, eleven, twelve, thirteen, fourteen and fifteen, in township thirty, north of range four east, now forming a part of Kosciusko county, be . . . attached to the county of Fulton, for the purpose of organizing congressional township schools in said township, and for no other purposes whatsoever." *Laws of Indiana*, 1838-39 (local), p. 336.

This attachment was made permanent by the law of February 24, 1840, which stipulated that "so much of an act entitled an act to attach one-fourth of township number thirty, north of range four east, to the county of Fulton, approved February 18, 1839, as says for the purpose of organizing congressional township schools and for no other purpose whatsoever, be . . . repealed." *Ibid.*, 1839-40 (local), p. 229.

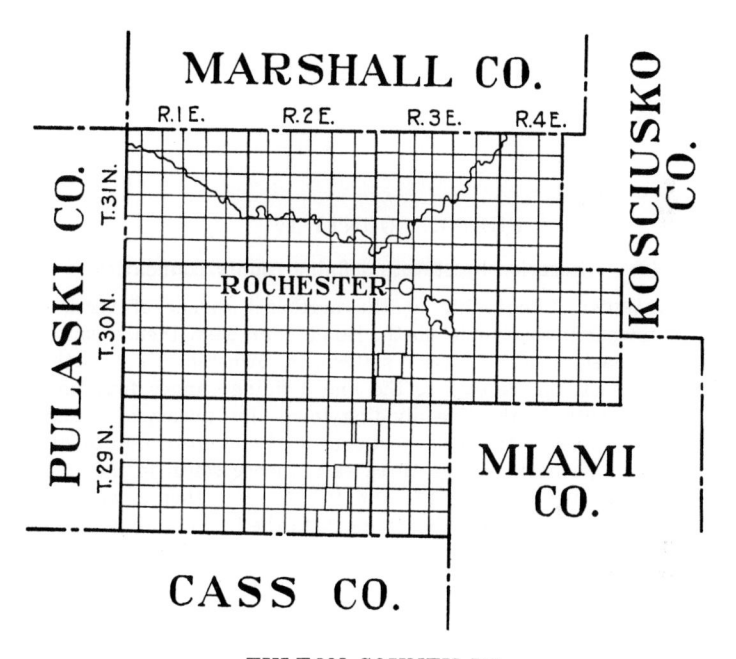

FULTON COUNTY III

[Law: Feb. 24, 1840, effective on passage]

FULTON COUNTY IV

1842-43: Alteration by statute defining county boundaries.

BOUNDARIES: "Beginning at the northeast corner of section four, in township thirty-one north, range four east, thence south to the southeast corner of section sixteen, in township thirty north, range four east, thence east to the line dividing ranges four and five, thence south to the line dividing townships twenty-nine and thirty, thence west to the northwest corner of section two, in township twenty-nine north, range three east, thence south to the line dividing townships twenty-eight and twenty-nine, thence west to the principal meridian line, thence north to the line dividing townships thirty-one and thirty-two, thence east to the place of beginning." *Revised Statutes of Indiana*, 1842-43, p. 89.

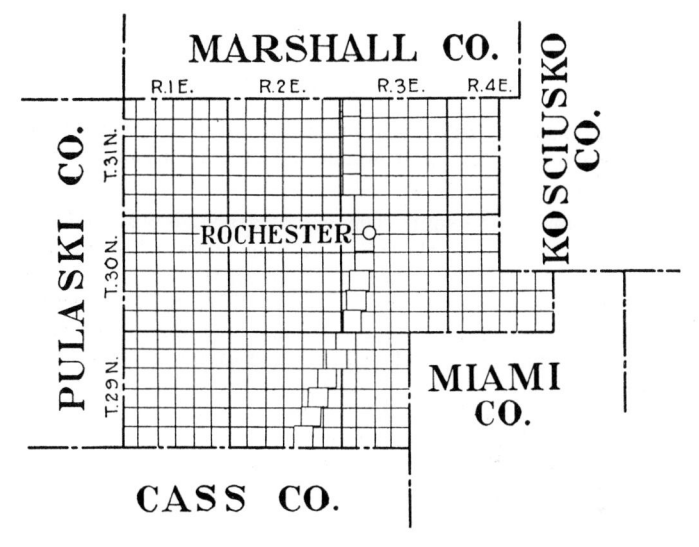

FULTON COUNTY IV

[Law: 1842-43]

FULTON COUNTY V

JANUARY 15, 1844: Alteration by statute to detach certain territory from the county of Miami and attach the same to the county of Fulton, effective on passage.

BOUNDARY CHANGE: The act attached to Fulton County the territory included in the following boundaries: "Beginning at the north west corner of section nineteen, in township thirty north, of range five east; thence east to the south east [north east] corner of section twenty-two, same township and range; thence south to the south east corner of section thirty-four, same township and range; thence west to the south west corner of section thirty-one, same township and range; thence north to the place of beginning." *Laws of Indiana*, 1843-44 (general), p. 73.

The error corrected in brackets above was rectified by an amendatory law of January 13, 1845. *Ibid.*, 1844-45 (general), p. 191.

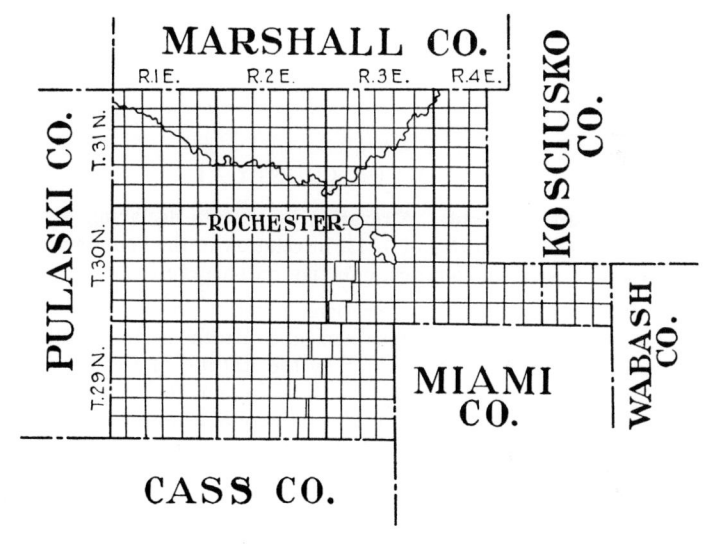

FULTON COUNTY V

[Law: Jan. 15, 1844, effective on passage]

FULTON COUNTY VI

JANUARY 13, 1846: Alteration by statute declaring a mistake in the *Revised Statutes* of 1843, in relation to the boundary of Fulton and Kosciusko counties, effective on passage.

BOUNDARY CHANGE: "Sections number one, two, three, ten, eleven, twelve, thirteen, fourteen, and fifteen, in township thirty, north of range four east, which by the statutes of 1843, is included in the boundaries of Kosciusko . . . is hereby declared to be a mistake, and . . . said territory . . . is hereby attached to the county of Fulton." *Laws of Indiana*, 1845-46 (general), pp. 87-88.

FULTON COUNTY BOUNDARIES 375

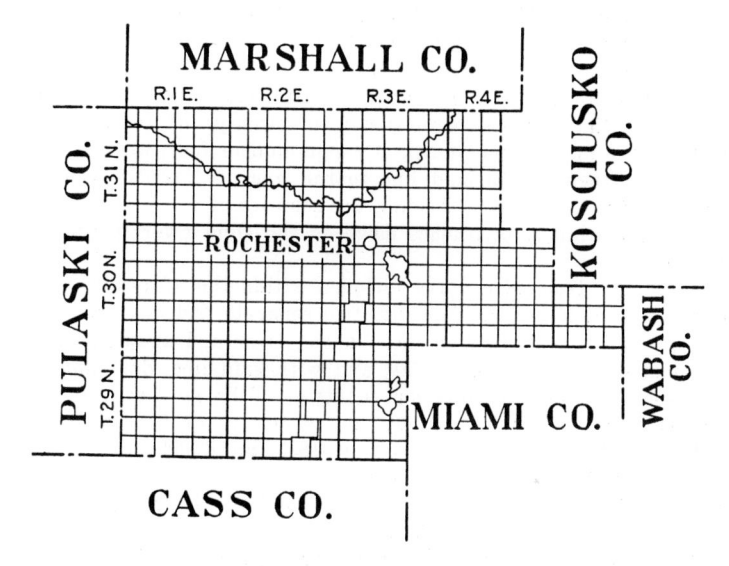

FULTON COUNTY VI
[Law: Jan. 13, 1846, effective on passage]

GIBSON COUNTY I
[Indiana Territory]

MARCH 9, 1813: Formation by statute, effective April 1, 1813. The formation affected Knox County.

BOUNDARIES: "Beginning at the mouth of the Wabash, thence up the same with the meanders thereof to the mouth of White river, thence up White river with the meanders thereof to the forks of White river, thence up the East Fork of White river to where the line between sections number twenty and twenty nine, in township number one, north, of range number four, west, strikes the same, thence with said line to the line of Harrison county, thence with the said line dividing the counties of Knox and Harrison to the Ohio river, thence down to the Ohio river to the beginning.

". . . the tract of country included within the aforesaid boundaries . . . is hereby divided into two separate and distinct counties by a line beginning on the Wabash river and known . . . by the name of Rector's base line, and with said line East until it intersects the line of Harrison county . . . the northern division thereof shall be known . . . by the name . . . of the county of Gibson." *Acts of Indiana Territory*, 1813, pp. 67-68.

Rector's base line was surveyed by William Rector on the line between townships 4 and 5 south, from New Harmony toward Alton, Indiana, and became locally known as "Rector's Base Line." Letter from G. R. Wilson to George Pence, June 9, 1927. For confirmative evidence on the location of the line, see text with maps of Posey County II and III.

COUNTY SEAT: By an act of December 14, 1813, commissioners were appointed to fix a county seat. They reported on February 14, 1814, their choice of a site in the northeast quarter of section 7, township 2 south, range 10 west. The name Princeton was chosen on February 16. *Acts of Indiana Territory*, 1813-14, p. 74; Stormont, *History of Gibson County*, 67-68.

GIBSON COUNTY BOUNDARIES

GIBSON COUNTY I

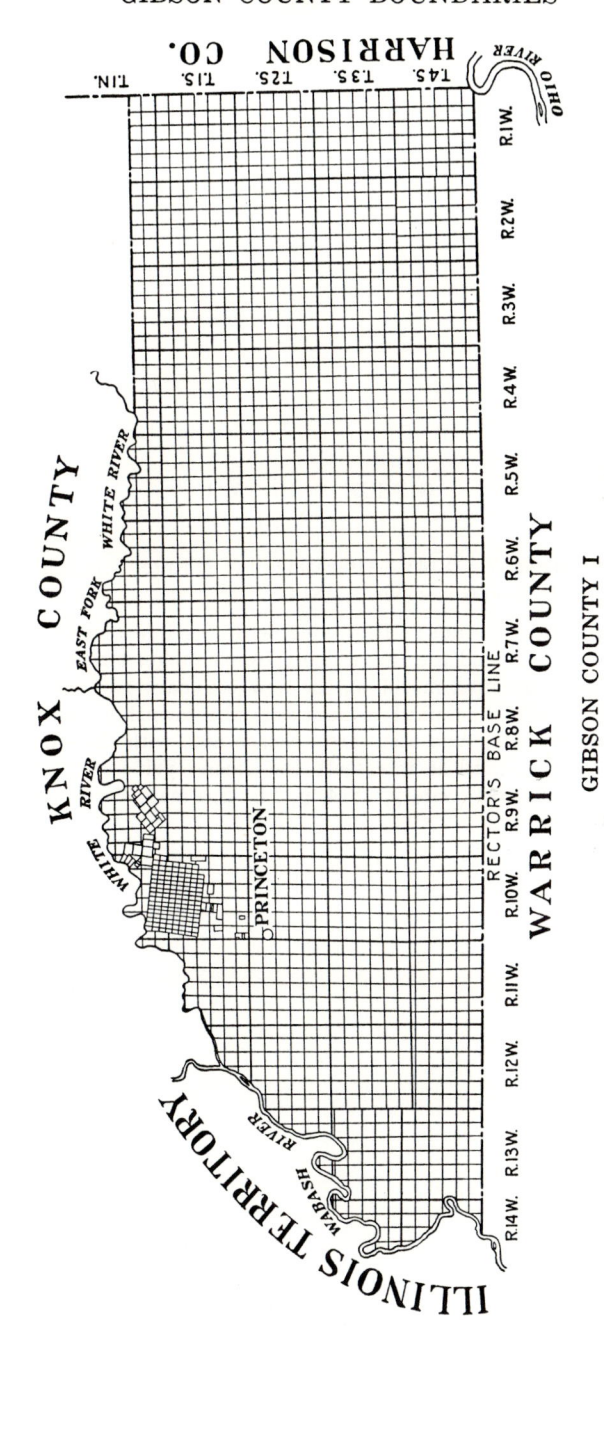

[Law: Mar. 9, 1813, effective Apr. 1, 1813]

GIBSON COUNTY II
[Indiana Territory]

SEPTEMBER 7, 1814: Alteration by statute forming Perry County, effective November 1, 1814.

BOUNDARY CHANGE: Beginning with the intersection of Rector's Base Line and the range line between ranges 5 and 6 west of the second principal meridian, the new boundary ran "north with the said range line until it intersects the township line passing between township two and three, thence east with the said township line . . . until it intersects the second principal meridian." *Acts of Indiana Territory*, 1814, p. 19. See map, Perry County I.

GIBSON COUNTY BOUNDARIES 379

GIBSON COUNTY II

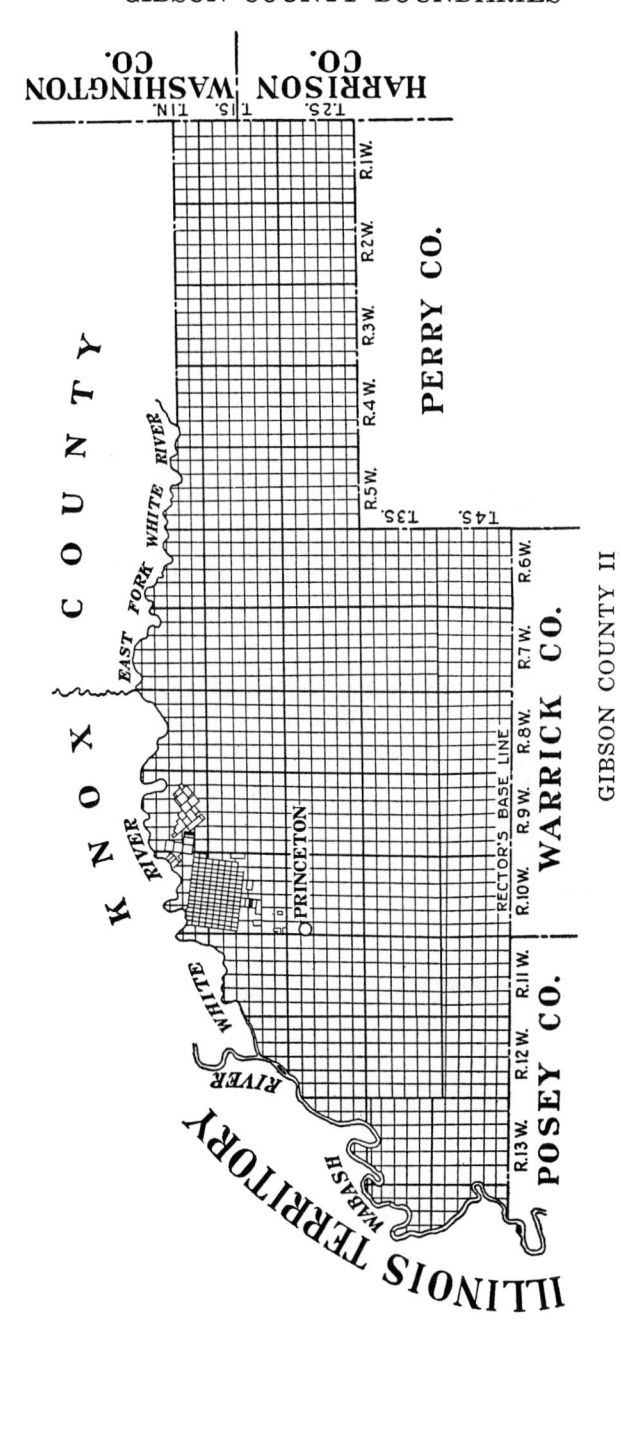

[Law: Sep. 7, 1814, effective Nov. 1, 1814]

GIBSON COUNTY III
[Indiana Territory]

DECEMBER 26, 1815: Alteration by statute forming Orange County, effective February 1, 1816.

BOUNDARY CHANGE: All that part of Gibson County east of "the range line dividing ranges two and three west of the second principal meridian" was transferred to Orange County. *Acts of Indiana Territory*, 1815, pp. 57-58. See text with map, Orange County I.

DECEMBER 18, 1815: Alteration by statute attaching part of Gibson County to Posey County, effective March 1, 1816.

BOUNDARY CHANGE: A small triangular area of Gibson County, bounded by the range line dividing ranges 13 and 14 west of the second principal meridian, the township line dividing townships 4 and 5 south, and the Wabash River, was transferred to Posey County. *Acts of Indiana Territory*, 1815, pp. 7-8. See text with map, Posey County II.

GIBSON COUNTY III

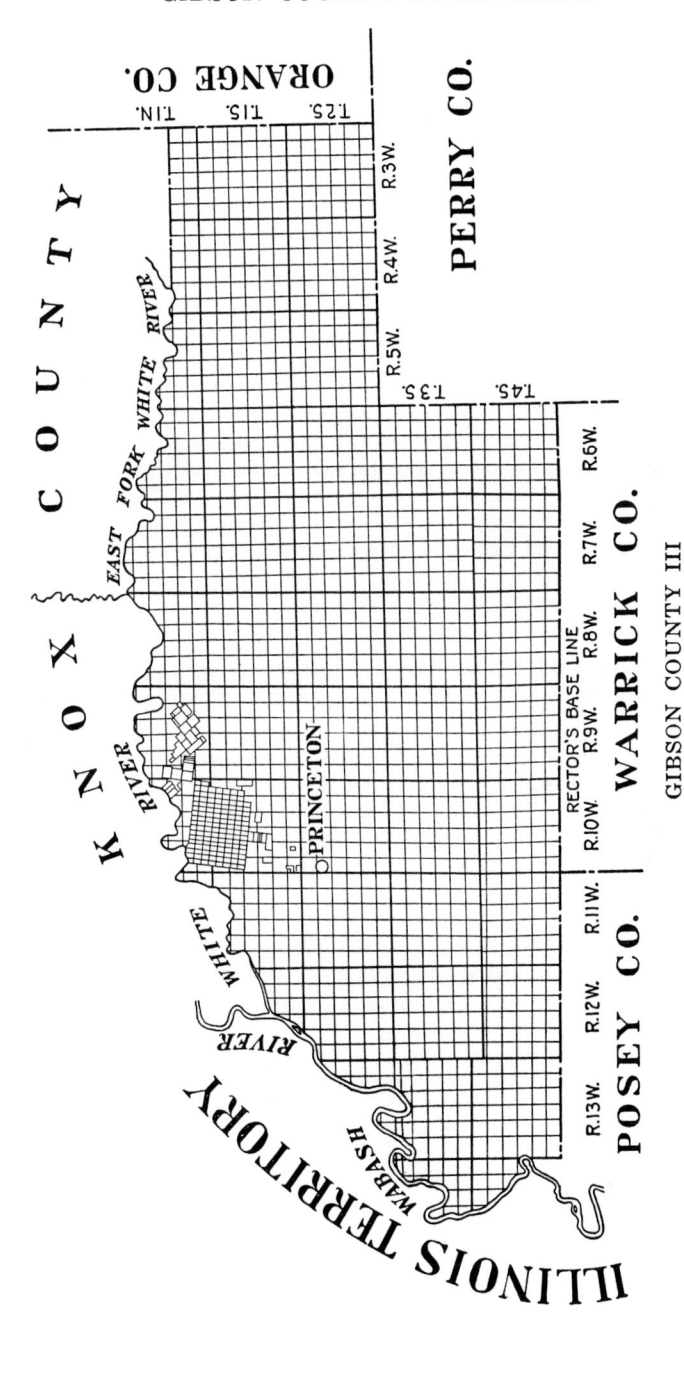

[Laws: Dec. 26, 1815, effective Feb. 1, 1816; Dec. 18, 1815, effective Mar. 1, 1816]

GIBSON COUNTY IV

DECEMBER 21, 1816: Alteration by statute forming Pike County, effective February 1, 1817.

BOUNDARY CHANGE: All that part of Gibson County east and north of a line "begining at a point on White river where the line dividing sections nine and ten in range nine, town one north of Buckingham's base line strikes the same, thence south with said line to the township line dividing townships three and four south, thence with said township line" to the line dividing ranges 5 and 6 west of the second principal meridian, thence north to the line dividing townships 2 and 3 south, thence east to the Orange County line, was transferred to Pike County. *Laws of Indiana*, 1816-17, p. 208. See map, Pike County I.

JANUARY 1, 1817: Alteration by statute to attach part of the county of Gibson to the county of Posey, effective February 1, 1817.

BOUNDARY CHANGE: Townships 4 south, in ranges 11, 12, 13, and 14 west of the second principal meridian were transferred to Posey County. *Laws of Indiana*, 1816-17, pp. 202-3. See text with map, Posey County III.

The act of December 24, 1816, effective February 15, 1817, which formed Daviess County, provided that "all that part of the county of Knox, which lies east of the east fork of White river, and south of Lick creek, be added to and constitute a part of of Gibson county." The creation of Pike, effective February 1, 1817, nullified this provision, as the territory in question was included within the new Pike County. *Laws of Indiana*, 1816-17, pp. 193, 208.

GIBSON COUNTY BOUNDARIES 383

GIBSON COUNTY IV

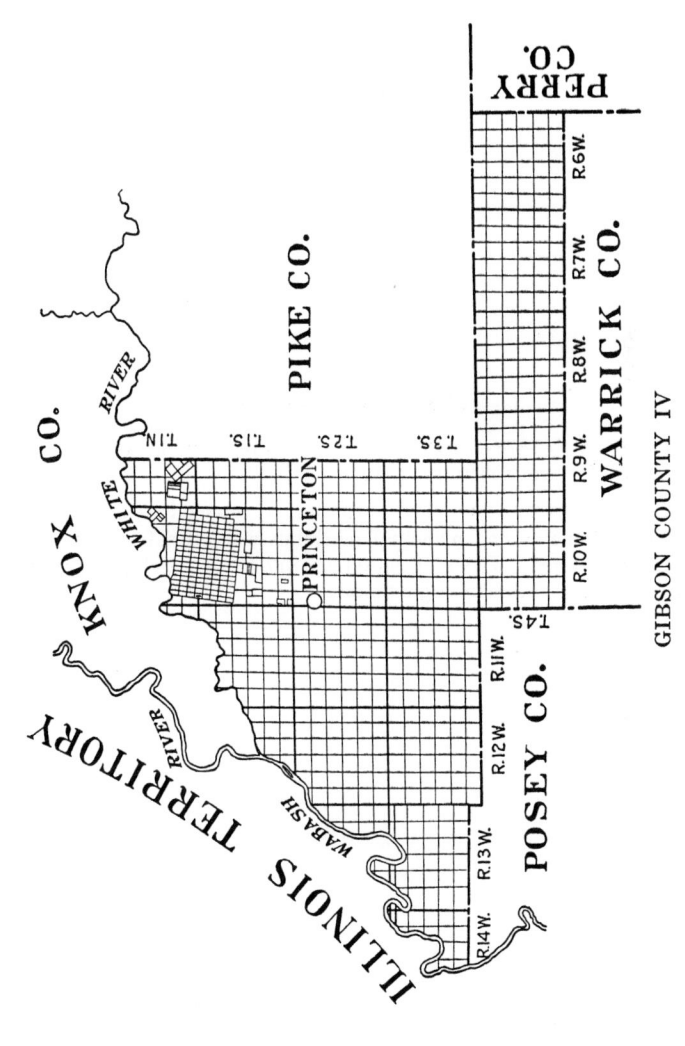

[Laws: Dec. 21, 1816, effective Feb. 1, 1817; Jan. 1, 1817, effective Feb. 1, 1817]

GIBSON COUNTY V

JANUARY 7, 1818: Alteration by statute forming Vanderburgh County, effective February 1, 1818.

BOUNDARY CHANGE: The south half of township 4 south, range 10 west of the second principal meridian was transferred to Vanderburgh County. *Laws of Indiana*, 1817-18 (special), p. 22. See text with map, Vanderburgh County.

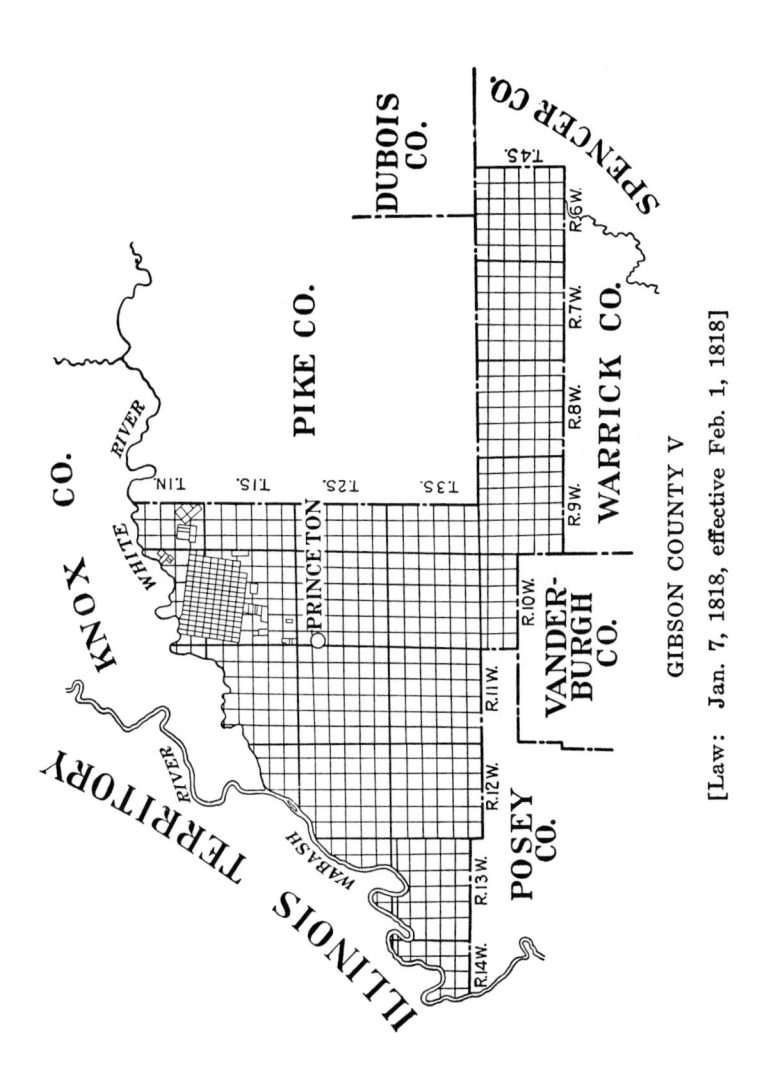

GIBSON COUNTY V

[Law: Jan. 7, 1818, effective Feb. 1, 1818]

GIBSON COUNTY VI

DECEMBER 31, 1821: Alteration by statute attaching part of the county of Posey to Gibson County, effective February 1, 1822.

BOUNDARY CHANGE: The act provided that "all that part of the county of Posey that lies in township four south of Buckingham's base line, in range eleven west be separated from said county of Posey and attached to the county of Gibson." *Laws of Indiana*, 1821-22, p. 120.

Buckingham's base line was named for its surveyor, Ebenezer Buckingham, Jr. The base line and meridian were run in connection with the survey of the Vincennes Tract. See Wilson, *Early Indiana Trails and Surveys*, 414 ff.

GIBSON COUNTY BOUNDARIES 387

GIBSON COUNTY VI

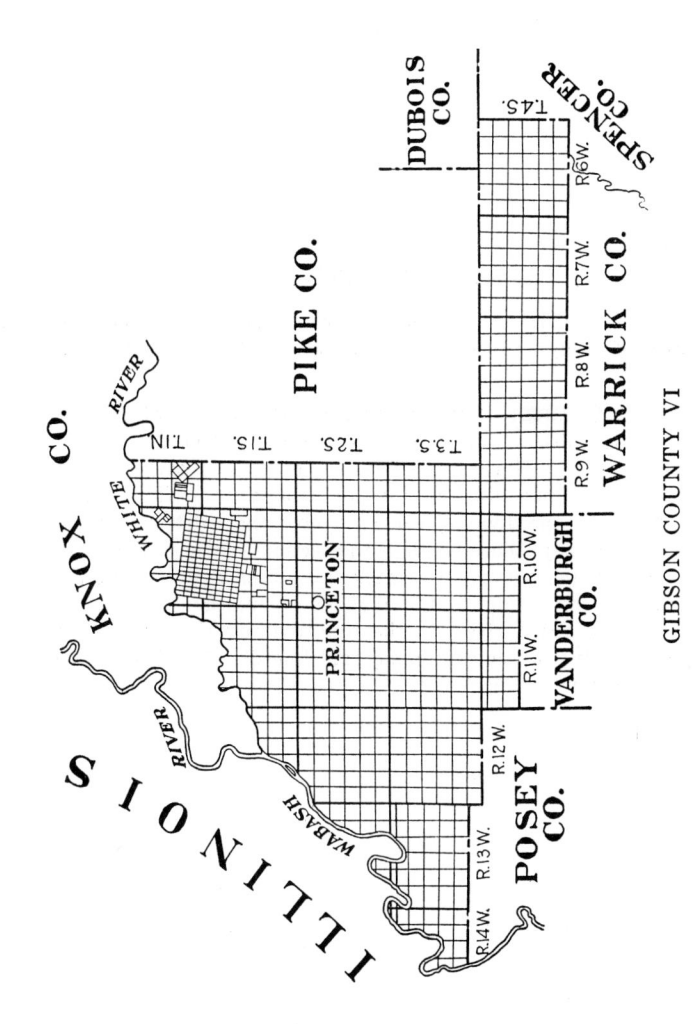

[Law: Dec. 31, 1821, effective Feb. 1, 1822]

GIBSON COUNTY VII

JANUARY 6, 1823: Alteration by statute to attach a part of the county of Gibson to the county of Posey, effective January 1, 1823.

BOUNDARY CHANGE: The law provided that "all that part of the county of Gibson . . . within the following bounds, be . . . attached to, and . . . form a part of the county of Posey, to wit: beginning on the line dividing the said counties of Gibson and Posey, where the line dividing ranges twelve and thirteen, crosses the said county line; thence north to the section line, one mile north of the line dividing the counties aforesaid; thence west with the section line, to the middle of the Wabash river; thence down the middle of the Wabash river, to the line dividing the counties of Gibson and Posey; thence east along said line dividing Gibson and Posey, to the place of beginning." *Laws of Indiana*, 1822-23, p. 116.

GIBSON COUNTY BOUNDARIES 389

GIBSON COUNTY VII

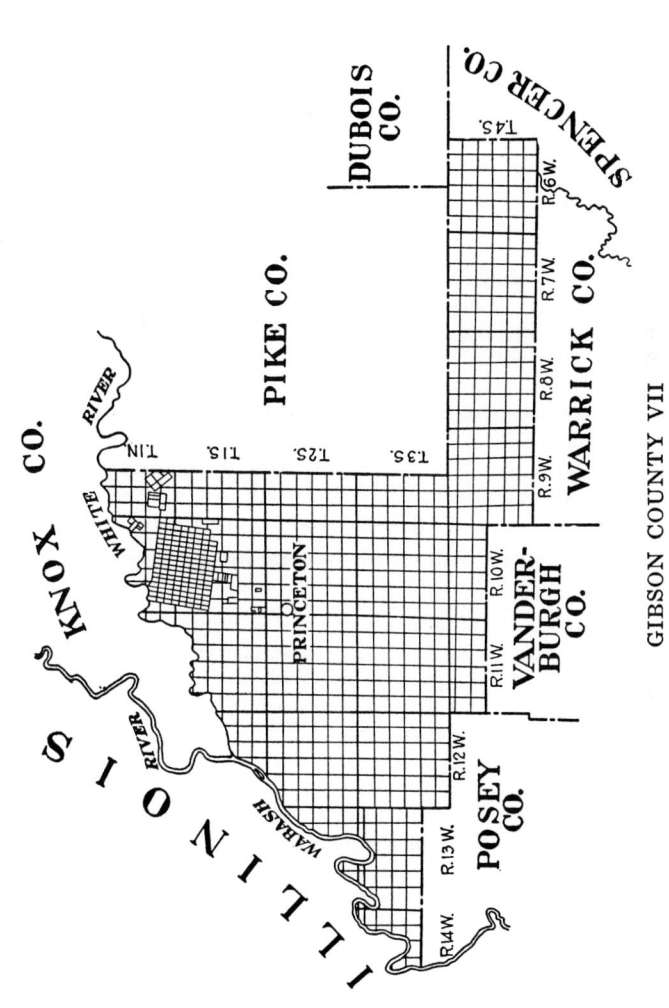

[Law: Jan. 6, 1823, effective Jan. 1, 1823]

GIBSON COUNTY VIII

JANUARY 26, 1824: Alteration by statute attaching part of the county of Gibson to the county of Pike, effective March 1, 1824.

BOUNDARY CHANGE: The act attached to Pike County all that part of Gibson within the following boundaries: "Beginning on White River, where the range line dividing ranges nine and ten strikes the same; thence south with said range line, to the river Patoka; thence up the said last named river, to the present line dividing the said counties of Pike and Gibson; thence north with said county line to White River, and thence down the same to the beginning."

It also provided that "all that part of Pike county contained within the following bounds, be . . . attached to . . . the county of Gibson, to wit: Beginning on the river Patoka, where the present line dividing the counties of Pike and Gibson crosses the same; thence up said river, with the meanders thereof, to the line dividing sections four and five, in township one [two] south, of range eight west; thence south with said section line, to the line dividing the counties of Pike and Warrick; thence west to the present line of Gibson and Pike counties; and thence north to the place of beginning." *Revised Laws of Indiana*, 1823-24, pp. 115-16.

JANUARY 31, 1824: Alteration by statute defining county boundaries.

BOUNDARIES: "Beginning at a point on the White River, where the line dividing ranges nine and ten west, strikes the same; thence down the same, to its junction with the Wabash; thence down the said last named river, to the line of Posey county; thence with the line of Posey county, south and east, to the line of Vanderburgh county; thence east with the same, to the line of Warrick county; thence continuing east, with the Warrick county line, to the line dividing sections thirty-two and thirty-three, in town three south, of range eight west, of the second principal meridian; thence north with the said sectional line, to the river Patoka; thence down the same, with the meanders thereof, to the range line dividing ranges nine and ten; and thence with said line north to the place of beginning." *Ibid.*, 107.

The ambiguity of the above description of the line between Gibson and Warrick was carried through the revision of 1837-38. In 1843 the line was specifically defined. See later maps of Warrick and Gibson.

GIBSON COUNTY BOUNDARIES 391

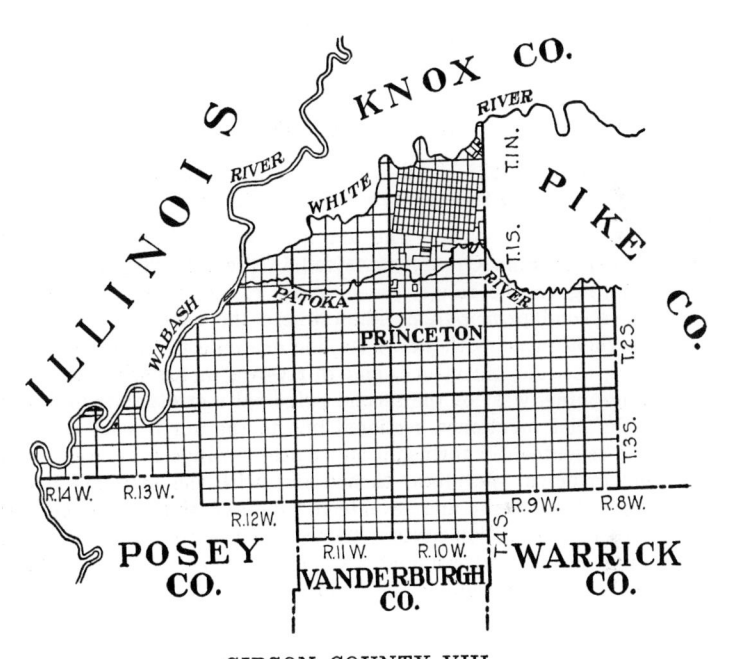

GIBSON COUNTY VIII

[Laws: Jan. 26, 1824, effective Mar. 1, 1824; Jan. 31, 1824]

GIBSON COUNTY IX

FEBRUARY 3, 1825: Alteration by statute to attach part of the county of Pike to the county of Gibson, effective on passage.

BOUNDARY CHANGE: The act attached to Gibson County all that part of Pike County contained in the following boundaries: "Beginning on the range line dividing ranges nine, and ten west of the second principal meridian where the base line crosses the same; thence east with said base line one mile to the sectional line dividing sections thirty-one, and thirty-two in township one north of range nine, west of the second principal meridian; thence south with the last mentioned sectional line to the north west corner of section seventeen in township one south of range nine, west of the second principal meridian; thence east with the sectional line dividing sections eight and seventeen, nine and sixteen, to the north west corner of section fifteen; thence south with the sectional line dividing sections fifteen and sixteen, until it crosses the Patoka River." *Laws of Indiana*, 1825, pp. 15-16.

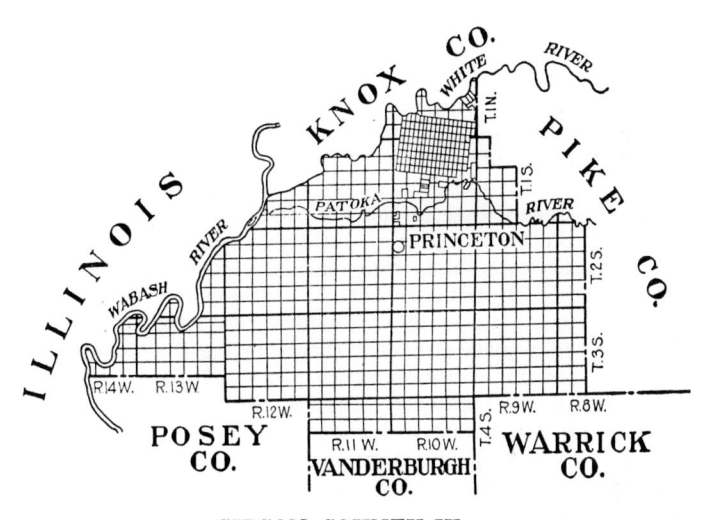

GIBSON COUNTY IX

[Law: Feb. 3, 1825, effective on passage]

GIBSON COUNTY X

1842-43: Alteration by statute defining county boundaries.

BOUNDARIES: "Beginning on White river where the line dividing ranges nine and ten crosses the same, thence down the said river to the junction with the Wabash river, thence down the same to where the line dividing sections twenty-eight and thirty-three, township three south, range fourteen west, strikes the same, thence east to the line dividing ranges twelve and thirteen west, thence south to the line dividing townships three and four south, range twelve west, thence east to the line dividing ranges eleven and twelve west, thence south to the southwest corner of section eighteen, in township four south, range eleven west, thence east to the southeast corner of section seventeen, township four south, range eight west, thence north to the Patoka river, thence down the same, with the meanders thereof, thence to the line dividing sections three and four, township two south, of range nine west, thence north to the northeast corner of section sixteen, township one, range nine west, thence west to the southwest corner of section eight, in said township, thence north to the line dividing townships one north and one south, thence west to the line dividing ranges nine and ten, thence north to the place of beginning." *Revised Statutes of Indiana*, 1842-43, pp. 80-81.

This act definitely assigned to Gibson County twenty-four sections of land in township 4 south, ranges 8 and 9 west, which had been in dispute between Gibson and Warrick since 1824. See note 66, page 42.

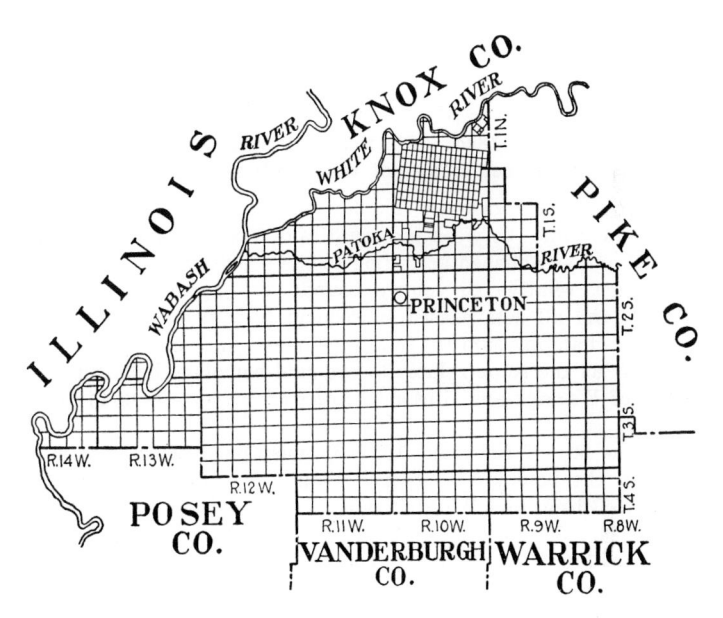

GIBSON COUNTY X

[Law: 1842-43]

GIBSON COUNTY XI

JANUARY 13, 1844: Alteration by statute, effective on passage, regulating the boundaries of the counties of Warrick and Gibson.

BOUNDARY CHANGE: The law of January 13 provided that "the boundary lines between the counties of Warrick and Gibson be . . . fixed and established according to the provisions of the act entitled 'An act relative to county boundaries,' approved February 10, 1831, and all acts passed subsequent to said mentioned act, altering or changing said act in any manner whatever, be . . . repealed, so far as the same relates to the said boundary between the counties of Warrick and Gibson." *Laws of Indiana*, 1843-44 (general), p. 87.

The law of February 10, 1831, mentioned above, was a law defining the boundaries of each county, in which the boundary between Gibson and Warrick remained as given in the *Revised Laws* of 1824. See map of that date. *Revised Laws of Indiana*, 1830-31, pp. 116, 120. This act reopened the question of jurisdiction in disputed territory in townships 4 south, ranges 8 and 9 west.

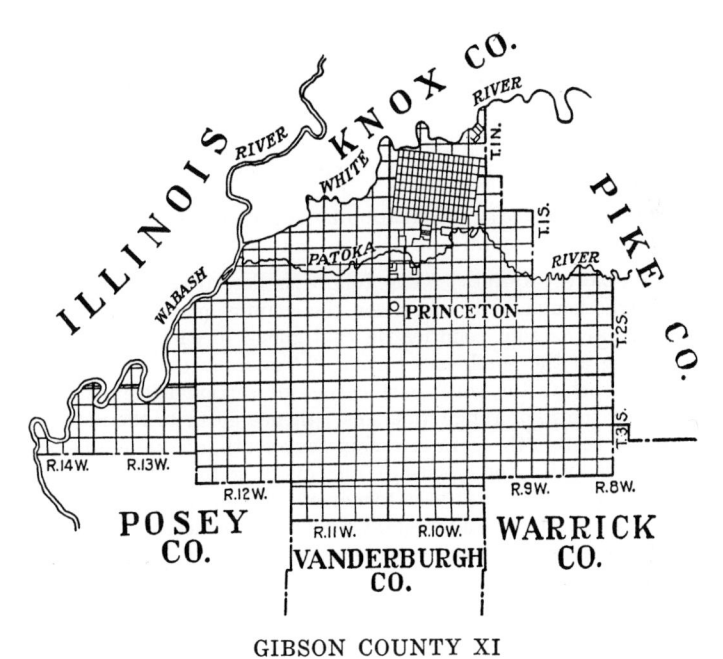

GIBSON COUNTY XI

[Law: Jan. 13, 1844, effective on passage]

GIBSON COUNTY XII

JANUARY 18, 1847: Alteration by statute defining the boundary line between the counties of Gibson and Warrick.

BOUNDARY CHANGE: "The following described line shall form and be the boundary line between the counties of Gibson and Warrick, so far as said counties lie contiguous to each other, to-wit: Beginning at the north-east corner of Vanderburgh county; thence running east to the south-east corner of section fifteen, in township four south, of range nine west; thence north to the north-east corner of section three, in township four south, of range nine west; thence east with the township line dividing townships three and four south, to the south east corner of section thirty-two, in township three south, of range eight west; thence north to the northwest corner of section twenty-one, in township three south, of range eight west." *Laws of Indiana*, 1846-47 (local), p. 272.

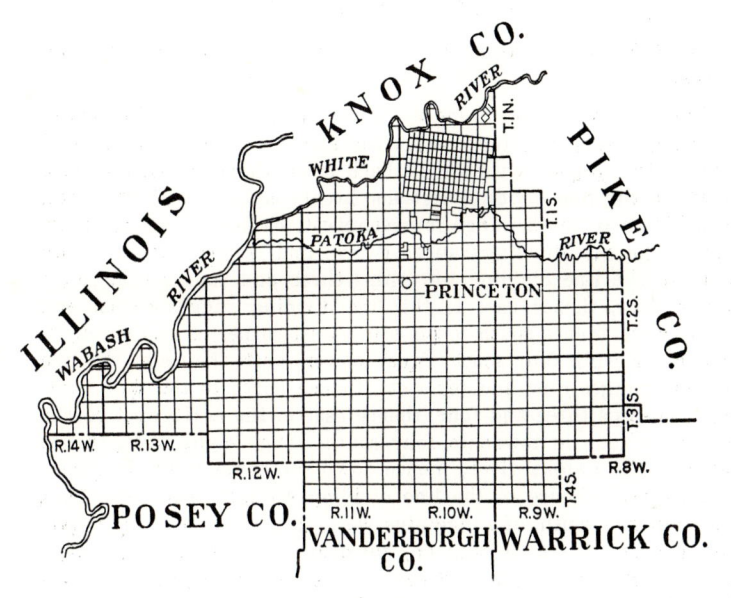

GIBSON COUNTY XII
[Law: Jan. 18, 1847]

GIBSON COUNTY XIII

JUNE 7, 1852: Alteration by statute defining county boundaries:

BOUNDARIES: "Beginning on White river where the line dividing ranges nine and ten crosses the same, thence down the said river to its junction with the Wabash river, thence down the same to where the line dividing sections twenty-eight and thirty-three, township three south, range fourteen west, strikes the same, thence east to the line dividing ranges twelve and thirteen west, thence south to the line dividing townships three and four south, range twelve west, thence east to the line dividing ranges eleven and twelve west, thence south to the south-west corner of section eighteen, in township four south, range eleven west, thence to the line dividing ranges nine and ten west, thence north to the line dividing townships three and four, thence east to the north-west corner of section four in township four south, range eight west, thence north to the Patoka river, thence down the same, with the meanders thereof, thence to the line dividing sections three and four, township two south, of range nine west, thence north to the northeast corner of section sixteen, township one, range nine west, thence west to the south-west corner of section eight, in said township, thence north to the line dividing townships one north, and one south, thence west to the line dividing ranges nine and ten, thence north to the place of beginning." *Revised Statutes of Indiana*, 1851-52, vol. 1:176.

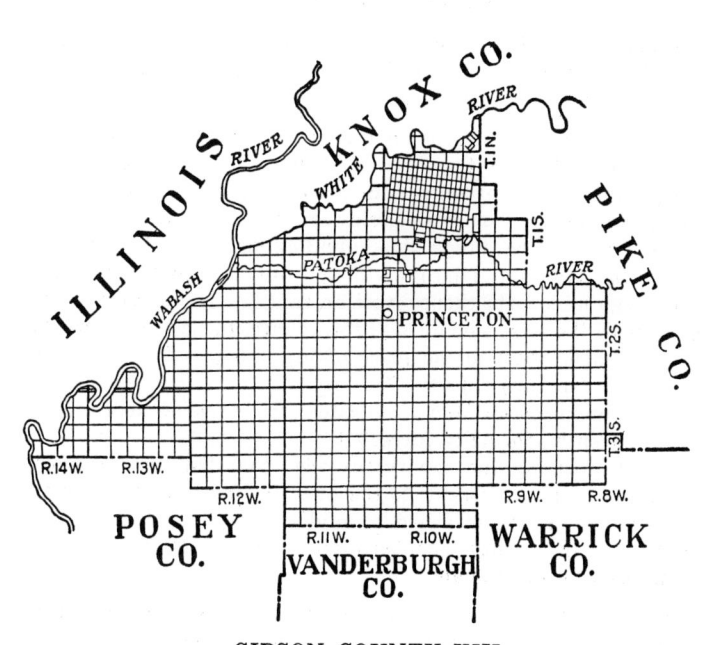

GIBSON COUNTY XIII
[Law: June 7, 1852]

GRANT COUNTY I

FEBRUARY 10, 1831: Formation by statute, effective April 1, 1831. The formation affected Madison County and territory attached to Delaware and Cass counties.

BOUNDARIES: "Beginning on the line dividing the counties of Madison and Delaware, three miles north of the township line, dividing townships twenty-one and twenty-two, in range 8 east; thence north to the corner of Delaware county; thence east six [seven] miles to the range line, dividing nine and ten; thence north to the township [line] dividing townships twenty-five and six, in range nine east; thence west on said line to intersect a line ranging with the west side of Madison county, thence south twenty one miles; thence east to the place of beginning." *Laws of Indiana*, 1830-31 (special), pp. 16-17.

The error in description, indicated by brackets above, was never, apparently, formally corrected.

The law forming the county provided that "all the territory north of the county of Grant, to the line dividing townships thirty and thirty-one . . . be attached to said county." *Ibid.*, 18. The boundaries of the county included territory in the Miami Reserve, not yet ceded by the Indians.

COUNTY SEAT: Commissioners appointed under the act forming the county, in a report of May 20, 1831, announced their selection of a site in section 6, township 24 north, range 8 east of the second principal meridian. In September it was named Marion by the county commissioners. *Ibid.*, 17; *History of Grant County*, 272-73, 542.

GRANT COUNTY BOUNDARIES 403

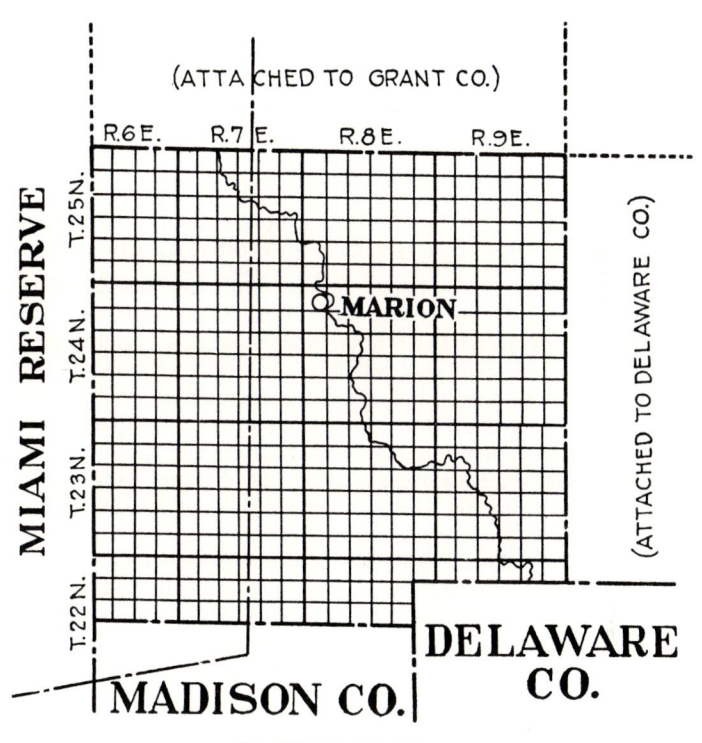

GRANT COUNTY I
[Law: Feb. 10, 1831, effective Apr. 1, 1831]

GRANT COUNTY II

FEBRUARY 17, 1838: Alteration by statute to alter and define the boundary lines of Grant County, effective on passage.

BOUNDARIES: "Beginning at the south east corner of section one, of township twenty-two, north of range nine east, on the north line of Delaware county; thence west on said line to the north west corner of said county of Delaware; thence west on the same sectional line, till it shall intersect a line drawn from the north east corner of Hamilton county to the south east corner of Miami county; thence north on said line to the south boundary of Wabash county; thence east to the line dividing ranges nine and ten; thence south on said line to the place of beginning." *Laws of Indiana*, 1837-38 (local), pp. 266-67.

A law of February 16, 1839, attached to Grant County so much of the Great Miami Reserve as lay west of Grant County, and was not attached to Miami County, but no land remained open for such an attachment. *Ibid.*, 1838-39 (general), p. 75.

GRANT COUNTY II

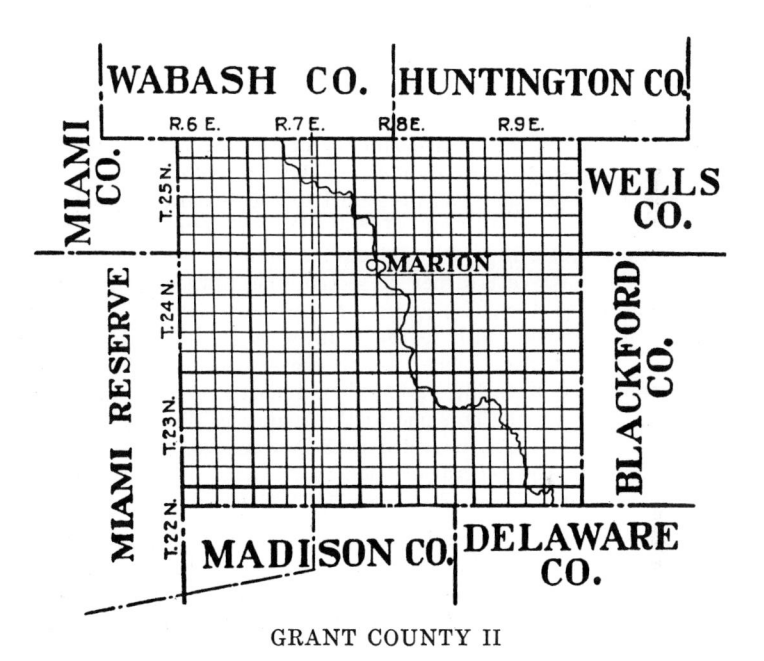

[Law: Feb. 17, 1838, effective on passage]

GREENE COUNTY

JANUARY 5, 1821: Formation by statute, effective February 5, 1821. The formation affected Daviess and Sullivan counties.

BOUNDARIES: "Beginning at the north east corner of township eight north of range three west of the second principal meridian; thence south to the south east corner of township six north of range three west; thence west to the south west corner of township six north of range seven west; thence north to the north west corner of township eight north of range seven west; thence east to and with the south boundary of Owen county to the place of beginning." *Laws of Indiana*, 1820-21, p. 114.

In 1838 a petition was presented to the General Assembly requesting that body to "cut off from the . . . county of Green, a strip three miles in width and twelve miles in length, commencing at the north-east corner of section one, township eight, north of range three west, thence west to the northwest corner of section three, thence south to the south-west [southeast] corner of section thirty-three, thence east to the south-east corner of section thirty-six, township seven, thence north to the place of beginning, and attach the same to the county of Monroe." An act of February 17, 1838, provided that this question be voted on in the county, at the general election in August. The territory was not transferred. *Laws of Indiana*, 1837-38 (local), p. 432.

COUNTY SEAT: Commissioners appointed in the act forming the county, on March 10, 1821, reported their selection of a site in sections 9 and 10, township 7 north, range 5 west of the second principal meridian for a county seat. The town was called Burlington. *Ibid.*, 1820-21, pp. 114-15; *History of Greene and Sullivan Counties*, 37.

By an act of December 17, 1823, commissioners were appointed to make a relocation of the county seat. In February, 1824, Bloomfield was made the seat of government. *Ibid.*, 43-45; *Laws of Indiana*, 1823-24 (special), pp. 48-49; Shockley, "County Seat Wars," *op. cit.*, 10:no. 1:21-22.

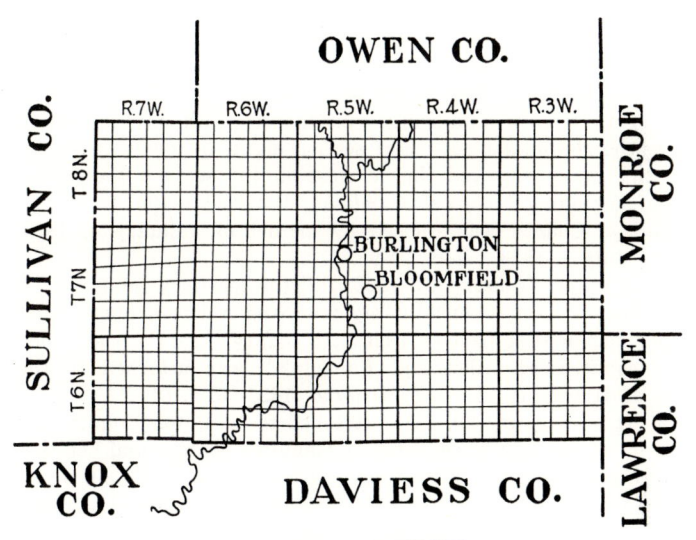

GREENE COUNTY

[Law: Jan. 5, 1821, effective Feb. 5, 1821]

HAMILTON COUNTY

JANUARY 8, 1823: Formation by statute, effective April 7, 1823. The formation affected Delaware County and the attachment to Marion County.

BOUNDARIES: "Beginning on the range line dividing ranges two and three, east of the second principal meridian, at the south west corner of section seven, in township seventeen and range three, thence running north on the said range line, to the township line dividing townships twenty and twenty one, thence east on the said township line, to the north east corner of section five, in township twenty, and range six, thence south on the section line, to the south east corner of section eight, in township seventeen, and range six, and thence west on the section line to the place of beginning." *Laws of Indiana*, 1822-23, p. 100.

Madison County was formed by an act of January 4, 1823, effective July 1, 1823. *Ibid.*, 94-95.

By an act of January 13, 1826, "all the territory lying north" of the line dividing townships eighteen and nineteen north "and not included in that part of Delaware county heretofore attached to the counties of Allen and Randolph," was attached to the county of Hamilton. *Laws of Indiana*, 1825-26, p. 81.

An act of January 29, 1830, attached to Hamilton County "all that tract of country lying north of Hamilton county, and between the same and the great Miami reservation." *Ibid.*, 1829-30, p. 22.

Nine years later, an act of February 16, 1839, attached so much of the Great Miami Reservation to Hamilton County as was "north of the county of Hamilton, and south of the township line dividing townships twenty-two and twenty-three." *Ibid.*, 1838-39 (general), pp. 75-76. By an act of January 15, 1844, this provision was repealed. *Ibid.*, 1843-44 (general), p. 12.

COUNTY SEAT: Commissioners appointed under the act forming the county, on March 4, 1824, selected a site on part of section 31, township 19 north, range 5 east, and section 36, township 19, range 4 east. Noblesville has remained the county seat. *Ibid.*, 1822-23, p. 101; Haines, *History of Hamilton County*, 123.

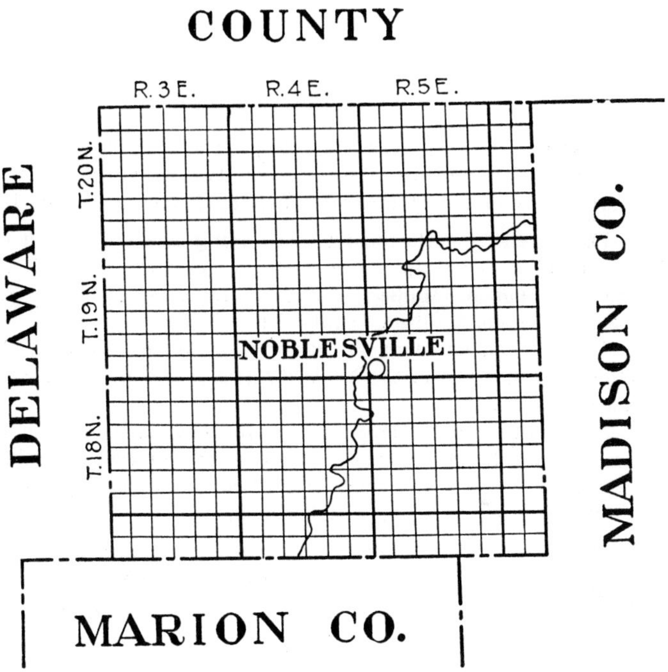
COUNTY
R. 3 E.
R. 4 E.
R. 5 E.
T. 20 N.
T. 19 N.
T. 18 N.
DELAWARE
MADISON CO.
NOBLESVILLE
MARION CO.

HAMILTON COUNTY

[Law: Jan. 8, 1823, effective Apr. 7, 1823]

HANCOCK COUNTY

JANUARY 26, 1827: Formation by statute, effective on passage. The formation affected Madison County. Hancock County was organized by an act of December 24, 1827, effective March 1, 1828.

BOUNDARIES: "All the territory lying one mile south of the line dividing township seventeen and eighteen, and within the former bounds of Madison county." *Laws of Indiana*, 1826-27, p. 85. See map, Madison County III.

There is an error in the description of the Hancock County boundaries as given in the *Revised Laws of Indiana*, 1830-31. This was not corrected.

A law of June 15, 1833, defines the boundary between Henry County and the counties of Madison and Hancock as "the first section line west of the range line dividing ranges eight and nine east." *Laws of Indiana*, 1832-33, p. 20.

COUNTY SEAT: Commissioners appointed under the act organizing the county reported their choice of Greenfield on April 11, 1828. It has never been removed. *Ibid.*, 1827-28, p. 19; Richman, *History of Hancock County*, 67-68.

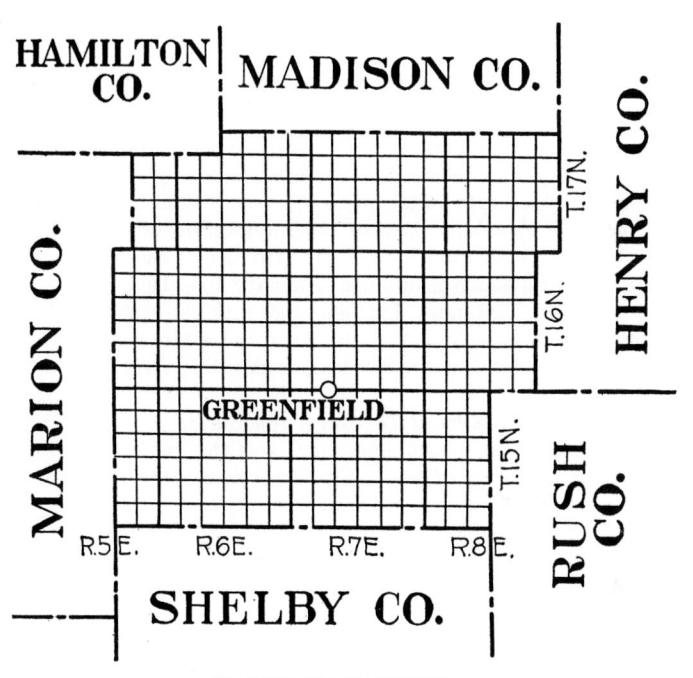

HANCOCK COUNTY

[Law: Jan. 26, 1827, effective on passage]

HARRISON COUNTY I
[Indiana Territory]

OCTOBER 11, 1808: Formation by statute, effective December 1, 1808. The formation affected Knox and Clark counties.

BOUNDARIES: "Beginning at the point on the river Ohio, where the meredian line from which the ranges take number, strikes the same, thence due north to the present Indian boundary line, thence with the said boundary line, to the intersection of the same by the line which divides the fourth and fifth ranges east, thence with the latter to the above mentioned boundary line, between the Jeffersonville, and Vincennes districts, and with the same to the intersection of the line dividing the fifth and sixth ranges, thence with the said range line until it strikes the Ohio river, and thence down the same, with the meanders thereof, to the place of beginning." *Acts of Indiana Territory*, 1808, p. 3.

The "present Indian boundary line" was the line established by the Grouseland Treaty of 1805. The line between the Jeffersonville and Vincennes land districts at this time followed the line established by the treaty made at Vincennes in 1804. See acts of March 3, 1805, and March 3, 1807, in United States *Statutes at Large*, 2:343-44, 448 (Boston, 1845). An act of April 30, 1810, provided that after June 1 of that year the boundary between the Jeffersonville and Vincennes districts should run along the second principal meridian. *Ibid.*, 590.

COUNTY SEAT: Corydon was made the county seat by the act which formed the county. *Acts of Indiana Territory*, 1808, p. 5.

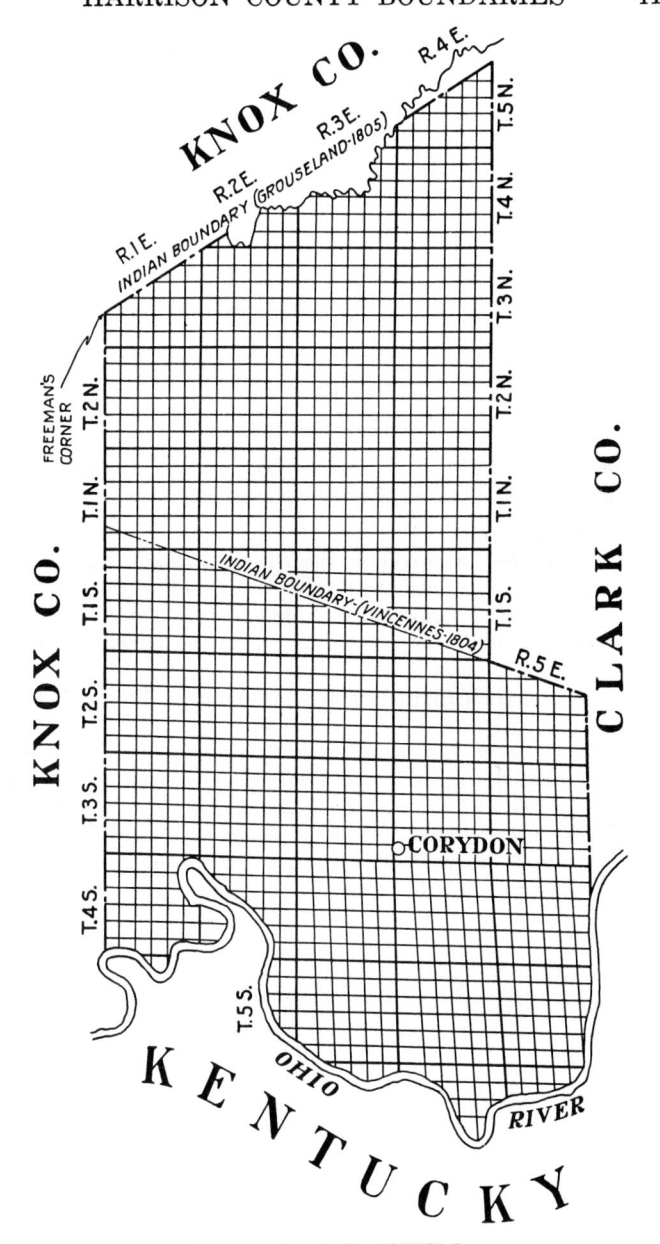

HARRISON COUNTY I

[Law: Oct. 11, 1808, effective Dec. 1, 1808]

HARRISON COUNTY II
[Indiana Territory]

DECEMBER 10, 1810: Alteration by statute extending the bounds of Harrison County, effective on passage.

BOUNDARY CHANGE: A transfer of territory "to begin at the intersection of the line dividing the fifth and sixth ranges with the river Ohio, thence with the meanders thereof to the mouth of Falling run, thence a straight line to the intersection of the range line between the fifth and sixth ranges, on the boundary of the Delaware purchase, thence with that line to the place of beginning," was made from Clark to Harrison County. *Acts of Indiana Territory*, 1810, p. 40.

The annexation to Harrison County failed to make any disposition of the land in range 5, between the Grouseland, or Delaware, Treaty line of 1805 and the Vincennes Treaty line of 1804. There was apparently no correction of this oversight. The greater part of the area in question was included in the formation of Washington County in 1813.

HARRISON COUNTY BOUNDARIES 415

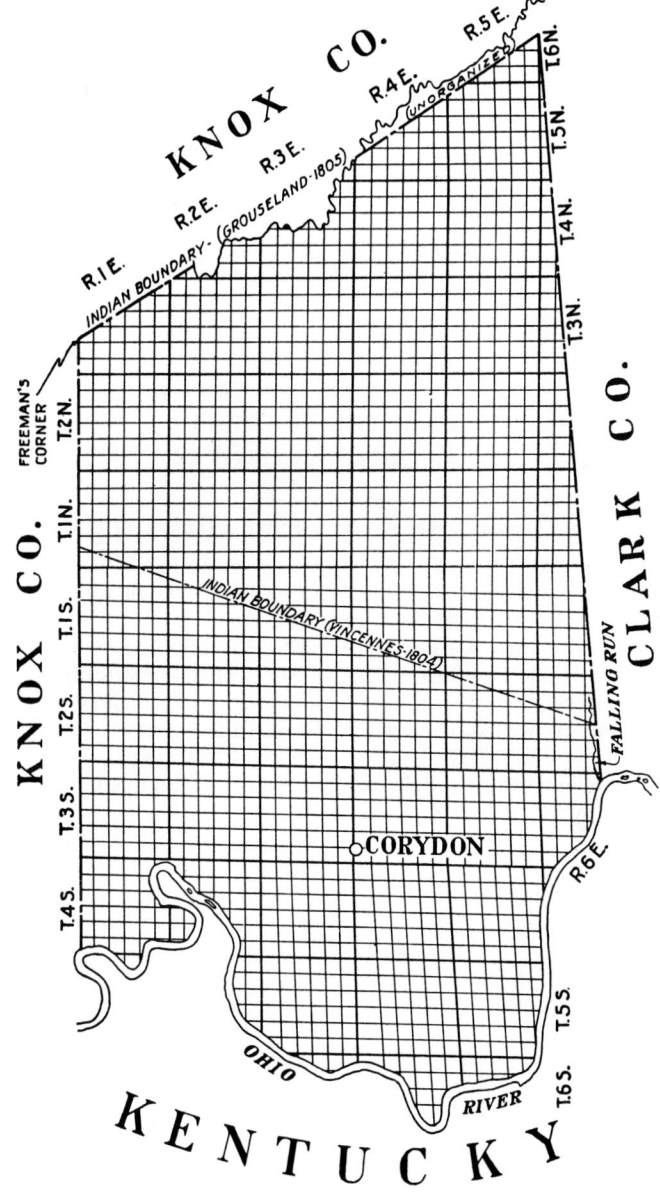

HARRISON COUNTY II

[Law: Dec. 10, 1810, effective on passage]

HARRISON COUNTY III
[Indiana Territory]

DECEMBER 21, 1813: Alteration by statute forming Washington County, Indiana Territory, effective January 17, 1814.

BOUNDARY CHANGE: All that part of Harrison County north of an east and west line beginning on the meridian where it is intersected by "an east and west line running through the centre of township one south; thence with the same eastwardly to the summit of the Silver creek knobs; thence north-eastwardly with the extreme heighth of the same" to the eastern boundary of Harrison County, was transferred to Washington County. *Acts of Indiana Territory*, 1813-14, p. 91. See map, Washington County I.

The line along the height of the Knobs was not definitely drawn for many years.

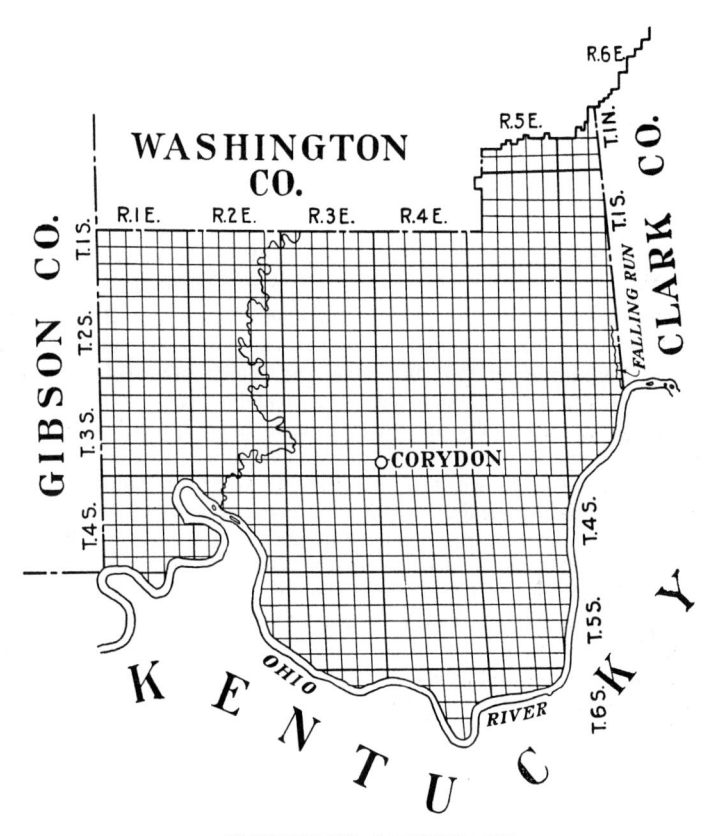

HARRISON COUNTY III

[Law: Dec. 21, 1813, effective Jan. 17, 1814]

HARRISON COUNTY IV

JANUARY 10, 1818: Alteration by statute attaching a part of Harrison County to Perry County, effective February 1, 1818.

BOUNDARY CHANGE: It was provided "That . . . all that part of Harrison county, which lies within the following boundary, to wit: Beginning on the Ohio river, at the mouth of Little Blue river; thence up the same with the meanders thereof to the line dividing sections thirty and thirty-one, in town 3, south and range one, east; thence with the last mentioned line to the second principal meridian, the western boundary of Harrison county; thence south with said meridian to the Ohio river; thence up the same to the place of beginning, be separated from the county of Harrison and attached to and form a part of the said county of Perry." *Laws of Indiana*, 1817-18 (special), p. 29.

The irregular boundary between Washington and Harrison counties in ranges 5 and 6 east of the second principal meridian, had not yet been definitely run. The law provided that it follow the height of the Silver Creek Knobs.

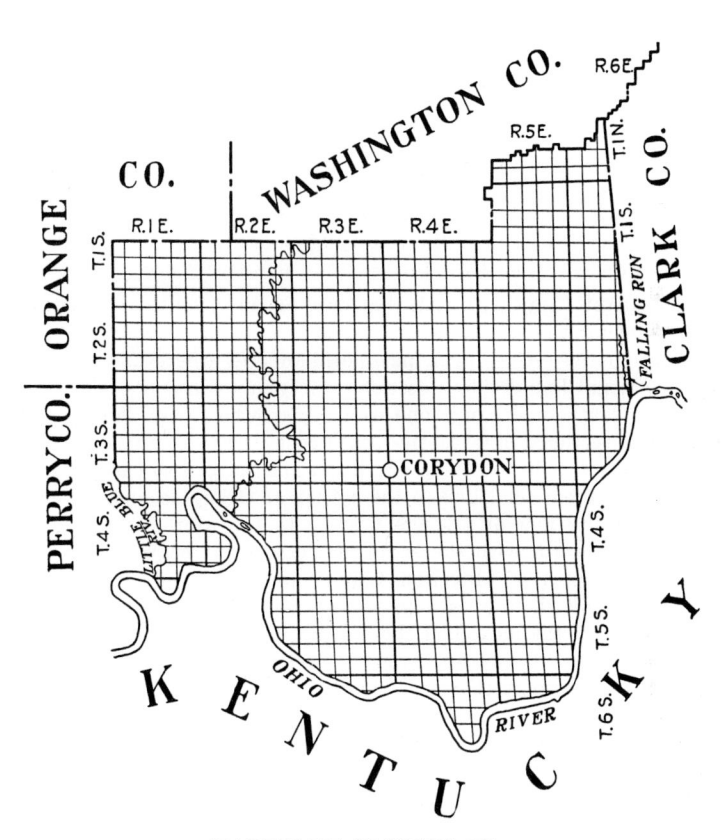

HARRISON COUNTY IV
[Law: Jan. 10, 1818, effective Feb. 1, 1818]

HARRISON COUNTY V

JANUARY 29, 1818: Alteration by statute attaching a part of the county of Harrison to the county of Orange, effective February 15, 1818, and forming Crawford County, effective March 1, 1818.

BOUNDARY CHANGES: All that part of Harrison County within the following boundaries was attached to Orange County: "Beginning on the second principal meridian line, where an east and west sectional line dividing sections thirty and thirty one, in township one south, and range one east strikes the same; thence east with said sectional line to the south-east corner of section number twenty nine, in township one south and range two east; thence north with a sectional line to the corner of Orange county; thence west with the line of Orange County to the aforesaid meridian line; thence south with the same to the place of beginning."

All that part of Harrison County west of a line "beginning on the [O]hio river at the mouth of Big Blue river; thence up the same with the meanders thereof, until it strikes the line dividing sections twenty six and twenty seven, in township three south and range two east; thence north with said sectional line until it strikes Big Blue river; thence up said Big Blue river, with the meanders thereof, until it strikes the line of Harrison and Washington Counties," was transferred to Crawford County. *Laws of Indiana,* 1817-18 (special), pp. 25-26, 27.

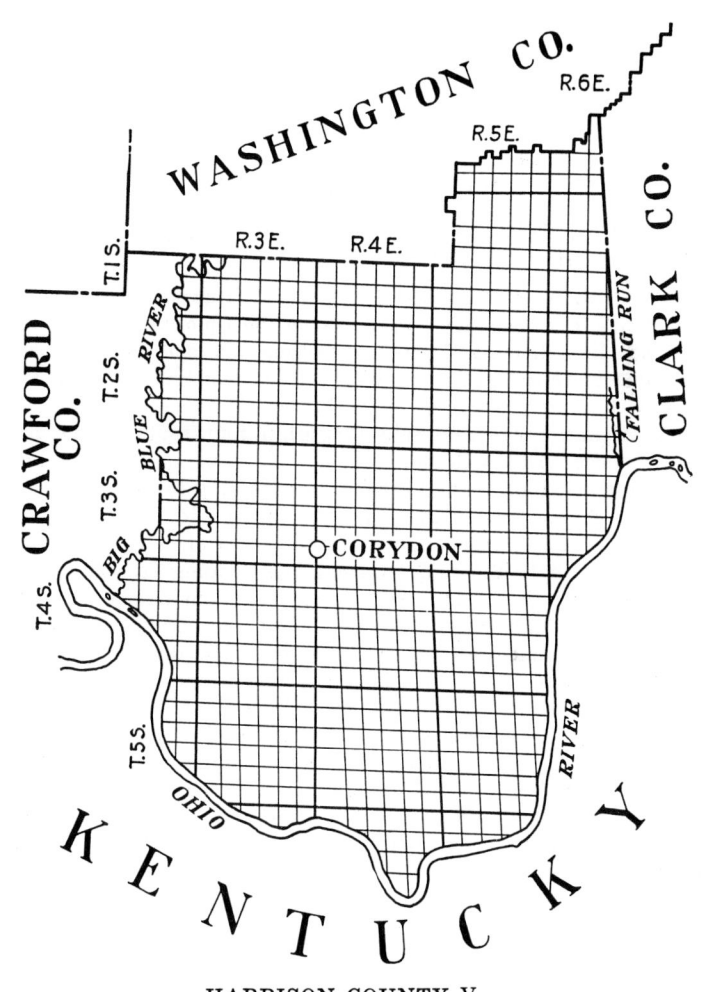

HARRISON COUNTY V

[Law: Jan. 29, 1818, effective Feb. 15 and Mar. 1, 1818]

HARRISON COUNTY VI

JANUARY 2, 1819: Alteration by statute forming Floyd County, effective February 1, 1819.

BOUNDARY CHANGE: All that part of Harrison County included within a boundary "beginning on the Ohio river, where the sectional line dividing fractional sections six and seven strikes the same in township four south of range five [six] east, thence west with said line to the south west corner of section three, in the town and range aforesaid [township four south, range five east], thence north with the sectional line dividing sections numbers three and four to the township line dividing town number one and two, thence west with said township line to the south west corner of section thirty six, in town one south of range four east, thence north with the said sectional line dividing sections thirty four [five] and thirty six to the corner of sections numbers twenty three, twenty four, twenty five and twenty six, thence east from said last mentioned corner with sectional line dividing sections twenty four and twenty five in town number one south in range number four east, thence with the said sectional line east to the Illinois grant line in the county of Clark aforesaid," was transferred to Floyd County. *Laws of Indiana*, 1818-19, p. 100.

The portion of Harrison County left to the north of Floyd County was treated as a part of Clark County in the *Revised Laws* of 1823-24, though never allotted to Clark from Harrison County. See map, Clark County X.

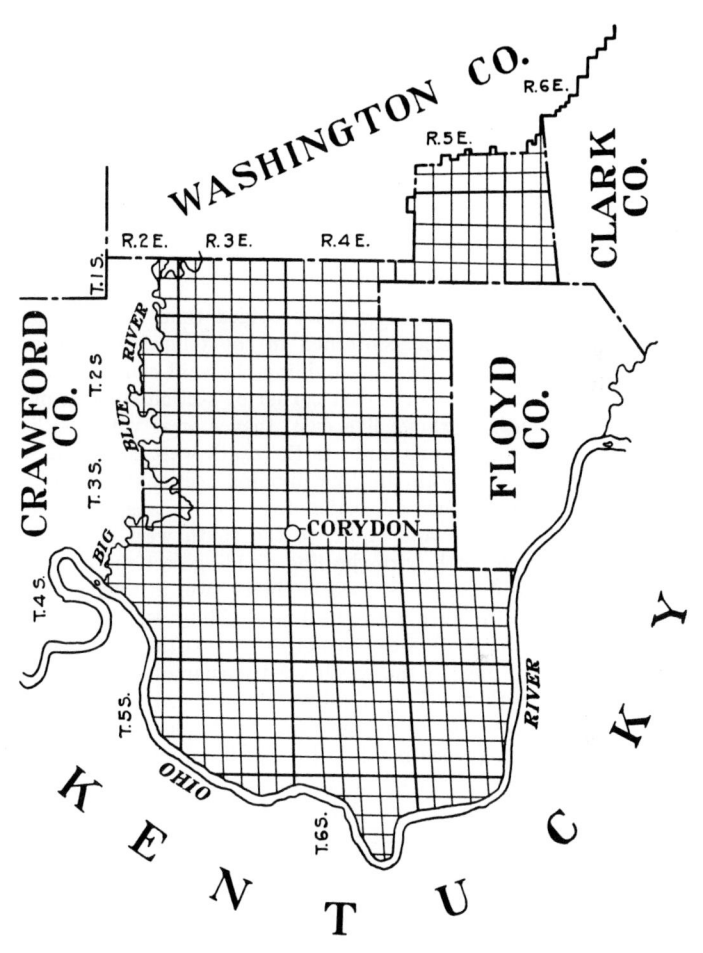

HARRISON COUNTY VI
[Law: Jan. 2, 1819, effective Feb. 1, 1819]

HARRISON COUNTY VII

JANUARY 10, 1823: Alteration by statute attaching part of the county of Harrison to the county of Floyd.

BOUNDARY CHANGE: The act provided that "all that part of the county of Harrison, contained in the following boundary, to wit: commencing on the line dividing the said counties of Harrison and Floyd, at the north east corner of section sixteen, in township three, south of range five east, thence west with the line dividing section sixteen and nine; to the south west corner of section nine; thence north, with the line dividing sections eight and nine, to the south east corner of section five; thence west, with the line dividing sections five and eight, to the south west corner of section five; thence north with the line dividing sections five and six, to the north west corner of section thirty two, in township two, in range five; thence west with the line dividing sections thirty and thirty one, to the south west corner of section thirty; thence north with the range line, to the south west corner of section eighteen; thence west with the line dividing sections thirteen and twenty four, in township two, in range four, to the south west corner of section thirteen; thence north with the line dividing sections thirteen and fourteen, in said range, to the south west [north west] corner of Floyd county . . . be attached to, and form a part of the county of Floyd." *Laws of Indiana*, 1822-23, pp. 77-78.

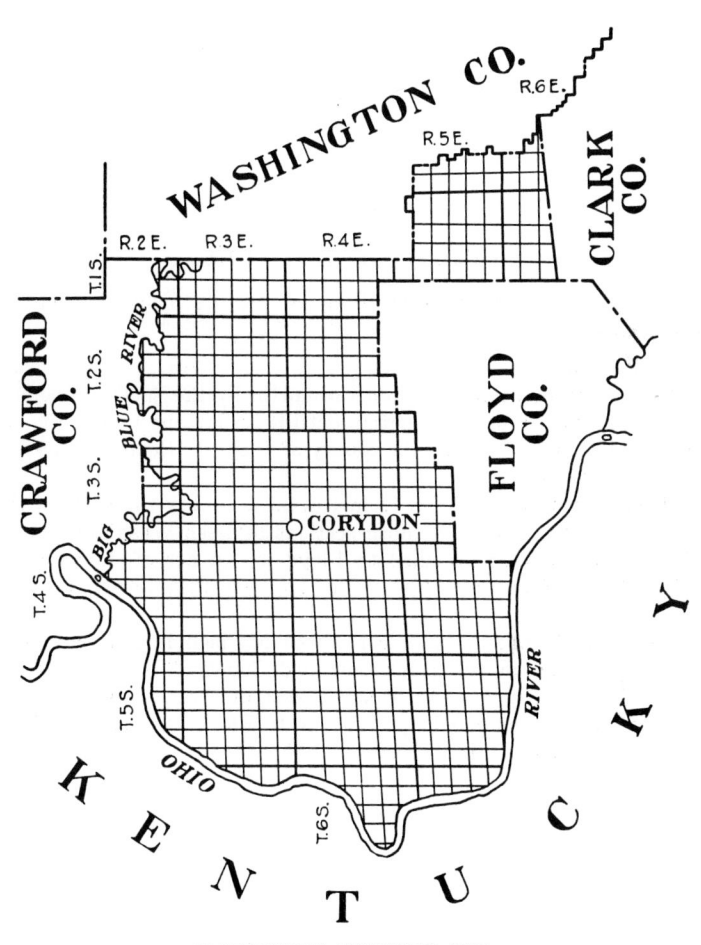

HARRISON COUNTY VII
[Law: Jan. 10, 1823]

HARRISON COUNTY VIII

JANUARY 31, 1824: Alteration by statute defining county boundaries.

BOUNDARIES: "On the south by the Ohio river, on the west, by the Crawford county line, on the north, by the southern boundary of the county of Washington, until it strikes the line of Floyd county, and on the east, by the county of Floyd." *Revised Laws of Indiana*, 1823-24, p. 96.

This description excludes from Harrison County the area north of Floyd County. The two open sections between Washington and Floyd counties were attached to Floyd by an act of January 5, 1828. *Laws of Indiana*, 1827-28, p. 12. See map, Floyd County III.

The law of June 7, 1852, defining county boundaries, made one slight alteration in the Harrison-Floyd County line. Fractional section 7, township 4 south, range 6 east of the second principal meridian was transferred by that law to Floyd County. *Revised Statutes of Indiana*, 1851-52, vol. 1:177.

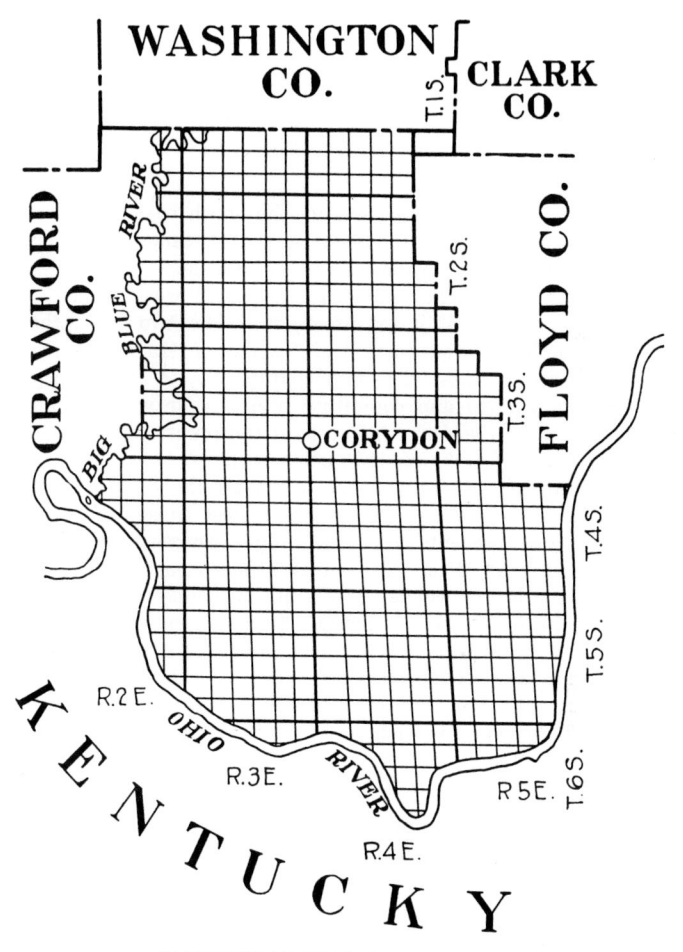

HARRISON COUNTY VIII

[Laws: Jan. 31, 1824; June 7, 1852]

HENDRICKS COUNTY I

DECEMBER 20, 1823: Formation by statute, effective April 1, 1824. The formation affected Delaware County and a part of Wabash attached to Putnam.

BOUNDARIES: "Beginning at the south east corner of section twenty, in township fourteen north, of range two east, thence west, twenty miles to the east line of Putnam county, thence north with said line twenty miles, to the north west corner of section eighteen, in township seventeen, in range two west, thence east twenty miles, to the north west corner of Marion county, thence south twenty miles with said county line, to the place of beginning, shall form and constitute a new county, to be known and designated by the name and style of the county of Hendricks." *Revised Laws of Indiana*, 1823-24, p. 111.

By an act of January 24, 1828, all the territory included in boundaries beginning "at the north-west corner of section eighteen, in town seventeen north, range two west, being the north west corner of Hendricks county; thence east twenty-four miles, to the south-west corner of Hamilton county; thence north, with the western boundary thereof, to the centre of town twenty; thence west, with the central section line of said town, to the eastern boundary of Montgomery county; thence south, with said boundary, to the place of beginning" was attached to Hendricks County, "except so much as is already attached to the county of Marion, for civil and criminal jurisdiction." *Laws of Indiana*, 1827-28, p. 13. See text with map, Marion County I.

COUNTY SEAT: Commissioners appointed under the act forming the county, on July 12, 1824, made their selection of Danville as the county seat. It has never been removed. *Revised Laws of Indiana*, 1823-24, p. 112; *History of Hendricks County*, 276-78; Hadley (ed.), *History of Hendricks County*, 44-46.

HENDRICKS COUNTY BOUNDARIES 429

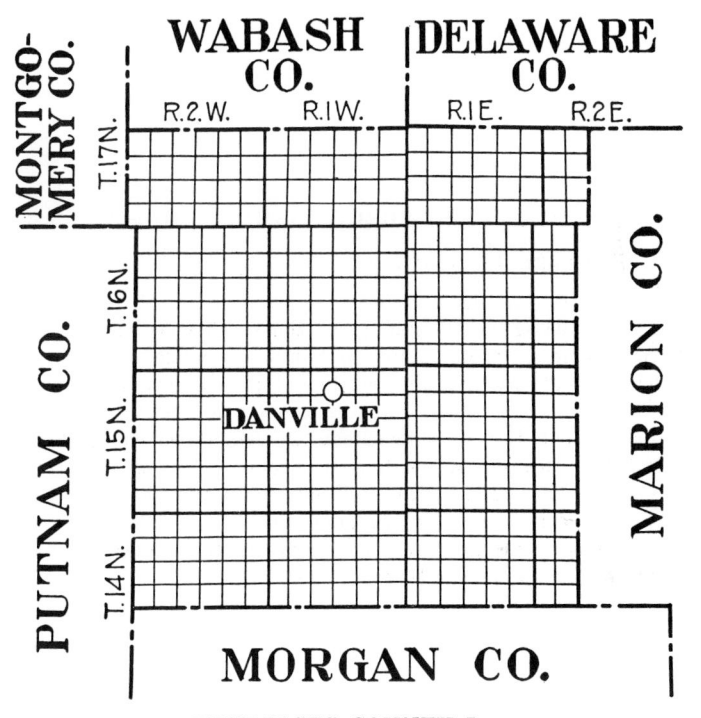

HENDRICKS COUNTY I

[Law: Dec. 20, 1823, effective Apr. 1, 1824]

HENDRICKS COUNTY II

FEBRUARY 10, 1831: Alteration by statute defining county boundaries.

BOUNDARIES: "Beginning at the south east corner of section twenty, in township fourteen north, of range two east; thence west, twenty miles to the east line of Putnam county; thence north with said line twenty miles, to the north west corner of section eighteen, in township seventeen, in range two west; thence east twenty miles, to the north west corner of Marion County; thence south twenty miles with said county line, to the place of beginning." *Revised Laws of Indiana*, 1830-31, pp. 121-22.

See text with map, Marion County II, for a more exact description of the Hendricks-Marion boundary.

HENDRICKS COUNTY II
[Law: Feb. 10, 1831]

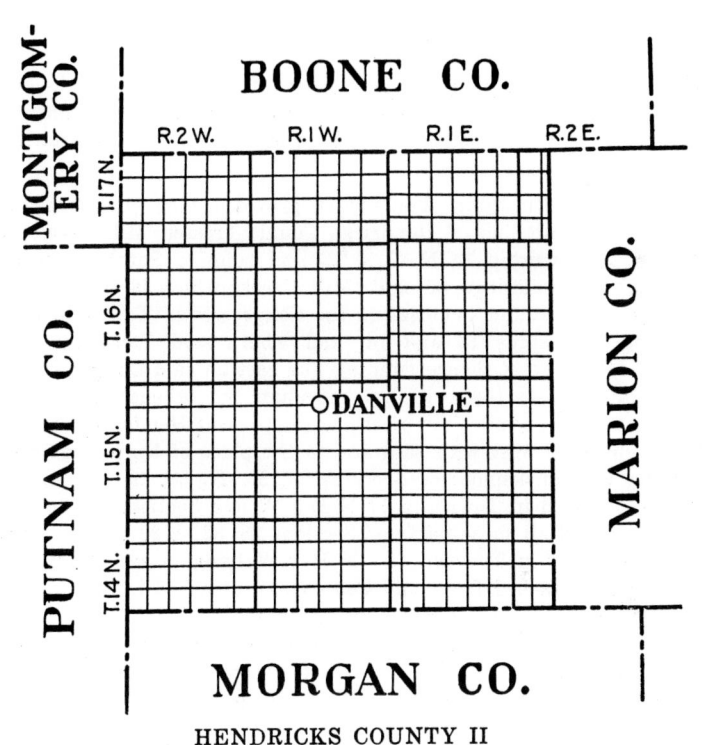

HENDRICKS COUNTY III

JUNE, 1868: Alteration by report of county commissioners changing the boundary between Hendricks and Morgan counties, in accordance with a petition presented March 3, 1868, and granted at the June term.

BOUNDARY CHANGE: The report provided that "Commencing where the South line of Hendricks County crosses 'Mill Creek in Section 28 Township 14 N. R. 2 W and running South westerly along the meanderings of said 'Mill Creek' which is the line of Morgan and Putnam Counties to the Congressional Township line dividing Townships 13 and 14, and where said Township line crosses 'Mill Creek' thence running due east on said Congressional Township line to the principal meridian line, thence with said meridian line two miles due north to the present Hendricks County line thence due west with said line to the place of beginning: embracing in said boundaries Sections 25, 26, 27, 28, 29, 30, 31, 32, 33, 34, 35, & 36 in Township 14 N R 1 W and Sections 25, 26, 27, 34, 35, 36 and all those parts of Sections 28, 32, & 33 that lie east of 'Mill Creek' in Township 14 N R 2 W lying in the County of Morgan be detached from said County and attached to the County of Hendricks, all in the State of Indiana: And . . . further ordered that the boundaries of the County of Hendricks be changed so as to include in its area the territory described above." Commissioners' Record 10, Auditor's Office, Morgan County.

HENDRICKS COUNTY III

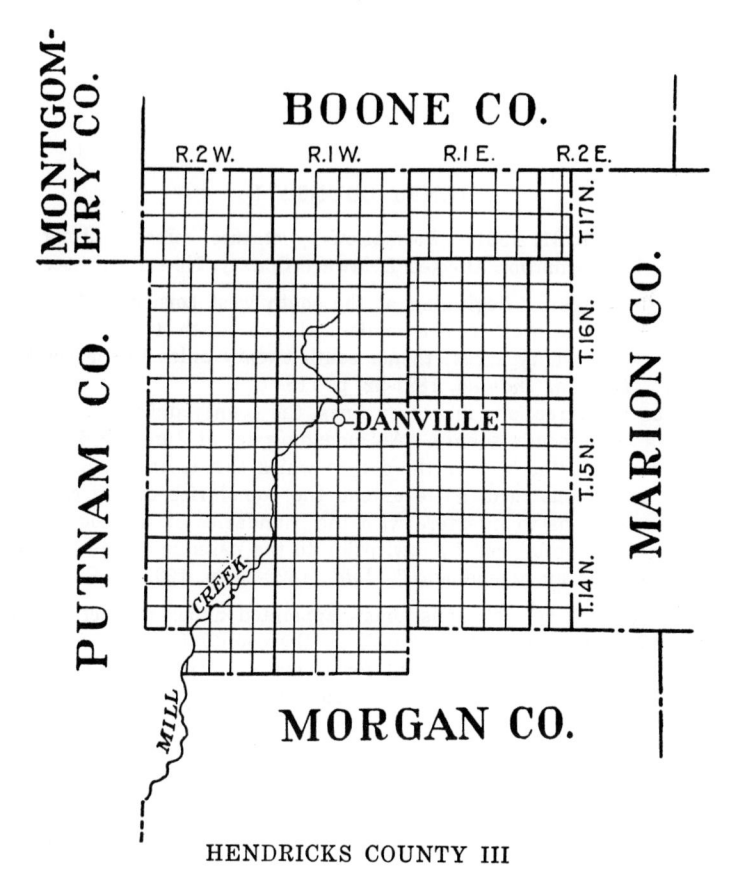

[Commissioners' Report: Mar. 3, 1868, granted June, 1868]

HENRY COUNTY I

DECEMBER 31, 1821: Formation by statute, effective June 1, 1822. The formation affected Delaware County, New Purchase.

BOUNDARIES: "Beginning at the south west corner of Wayne county; thence west twenty miles; thence north twenty miles; thence east twenty miles; thence south twenty miles to the beginning." *Laws of Indiana*, 1821-22, p. 115.

Due to corrections in survey lines, the county did not actually form a twenty-mile square. An amending act of January 6, 1823, provided that "nothing in the act, to which this is an amendment, shall be so construed, as to extend the boundaries of the county of Henry, so as to interfere with the boundaries of the county of Fayette, as established by law, prior to the passage of the act, to which this is an amendment." *Ibid.*, 1822-23, p. 123.

COUNTY SEAT: Commissioners appointed under the act forming the county chose New Castle as the county seat. It has remained the seat of government for Henry County. *Ibid.*, 1821-22, p. 116; *History of Henry County*, 295-96.

HENRY COUNTY BOUNDARIES 435

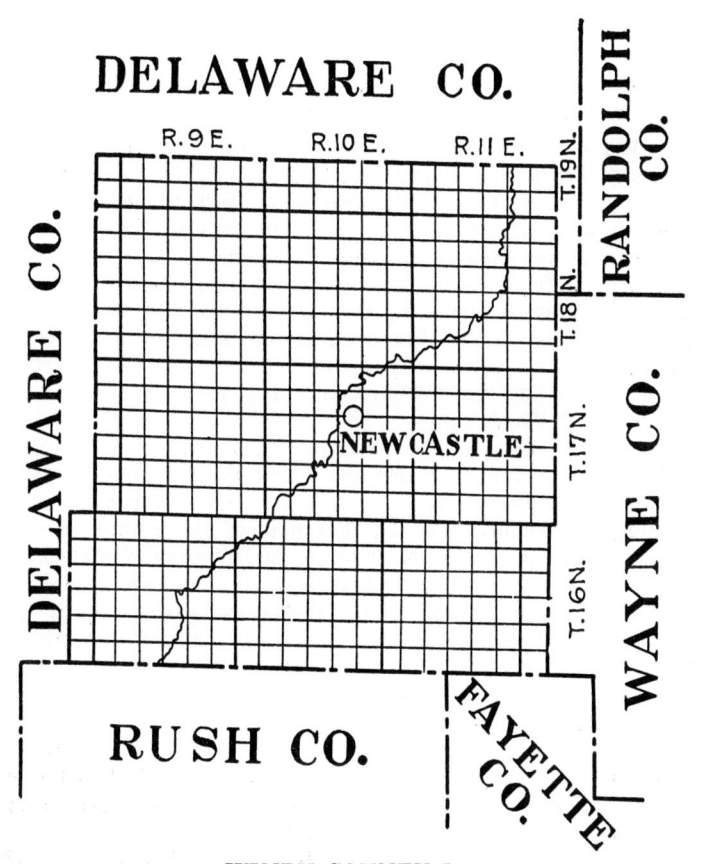

HENRY COUNTY I
[Law: Dec. 31, 1821, effective June 1, 1822]

HENRY COUNTY II

JANUARY 11, 1823: Alteration by statute changing the western boundary line of Wayne County.

BOUNDARY CHANGE: The act provided that "the said line, dividing Wayne and Henry counties, as fixed by the General Assembly of this state, in the year A. D. 1819, be and the same is hereby altered; the said boundary line, dividing the said counties of Wayne and Henry, to commence at the south west corner of section thirty four, in township sixteen, range twelve, east of the second principal meridian; thence north on said section line, to the [point where the] line dividing towns sixteen and seventeen, crosses the said line; thence east to the section line dividing sections thirty three and thirty four; thence due north, to the north boundary line of Wayne county.

"SEC. 2. *Be it further enacted,* That hereafter all that part of Henry county, falling by this line, within the said county of Wayne, be and the same is hereby attached to, and made a part of the county of Wayne. And all that part of the county of Wayne, which may fall by the said line, in the boundary of the county of Henry, be and the same is hereby attached to, and made a part of the county of Henry." *Laws of Indiana,* 1822-23. pp. 138-39.

The line between Wayne and Henry counties was originally fixed by an act of December 31, 1821, instead of in 1819.

Note that due to the irregularity of the survey lines, the map cannot exactly coincide with the description. Range 12 east of the second principal meridian in township 17 north, is only five sections wide, and the line dividing section 33 and 34 in that township is a continuation of the line beginning at the southwest corner of section 34, in township 16, range 12.

Madison County was formed by an act of January 4, 1823, effective July 1, 1823. *Ibid.,* 94-95.

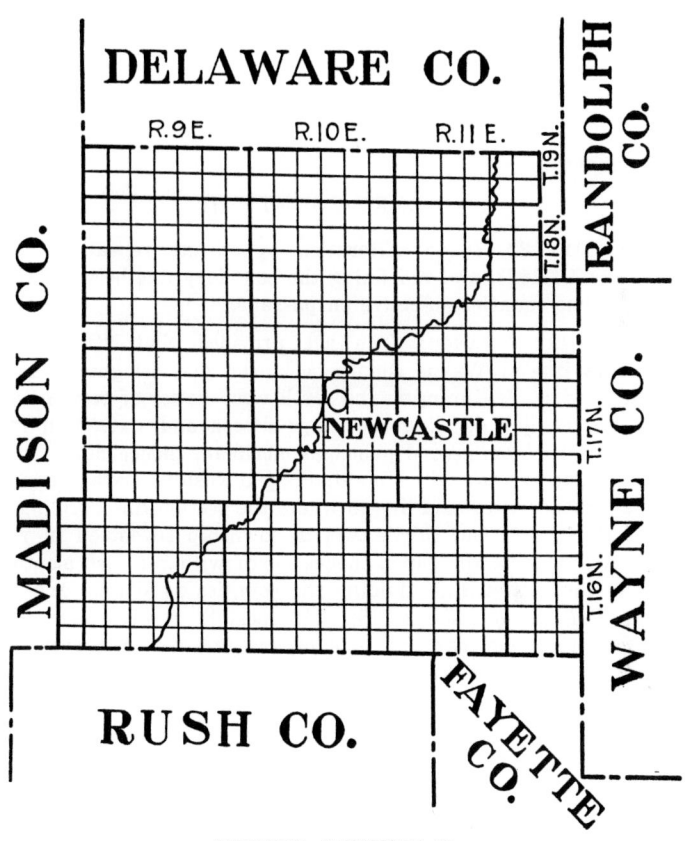

HENRY COUNTY II
[Law: Jan. 11, 1823]

HENRY COUNTY III

JANUARY 22, 1824: Alteration by statute repealing act of January 11, 1823, and redefining the boundary line between Henry and Wayne counties, effective on passage.

BOUNDARY CHANGE: The act provided that "the western boundary line of Wayne county be known and designated as follows, to wit: Beginning at the south west corner of section thirty two, on the line dividing townships fifteen and sixteen in range twelve east of the second principal meridian, thence north on the said line, to the township line dividing townships sixteen and seventeen, thence with said line to where the section line dividing sections thirty one and thirty two, in township seventeen in range twelve, intersects the same, thence north with the last mentioned line to the section line dividing the counties of Wayne and Randolph." *Laws of Indiana*, 1823-24 (special), p. 52.

See preceding map for note on irregularity of survey lines, which explains the apparent discrepancy between map and description.

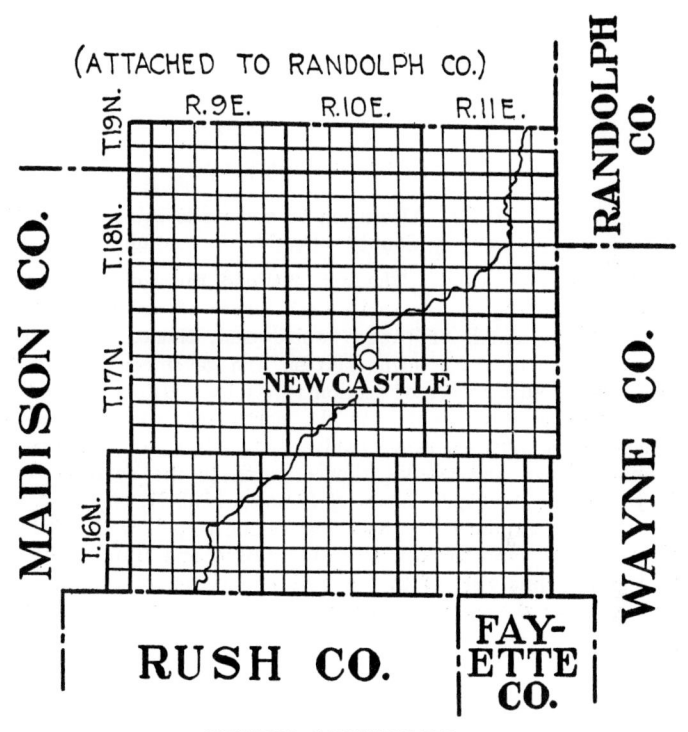

HENRY COUNTY III
[Law: Jan. 22, 1824, effective on passage]

HENRY COUNTY IV

JANUARY 26, 1827: Alteration by statute to establish the eastern boundary of Henry County, effective on passage.

BOUNDARY CHANGE: The act outlined the boundary as follows: "Beginning at the south west corner of section thirty-two, town sixteen, north of range twelve east, thence north to the township line dividing towns sixteen and seventeen, thence east to the south east corner of section thirty-two, township seventeen, range twelve, thence north to the north east corner of section twenty, town eighteen, range twelve, thence west to the range line dividing eleven and twelve, thence north to the northern boundary of Henry county." *Laws of Indiana*, 1826-27, pp. 11-12.

A law of January 15, 1833, defines the boundary line between Henry County and the counties of Madison and Hancock as "the first section line west of the range line dividing ranges eight and nine east" of the second principal meridian. *Ibid.*, 1832-33, p. 20.

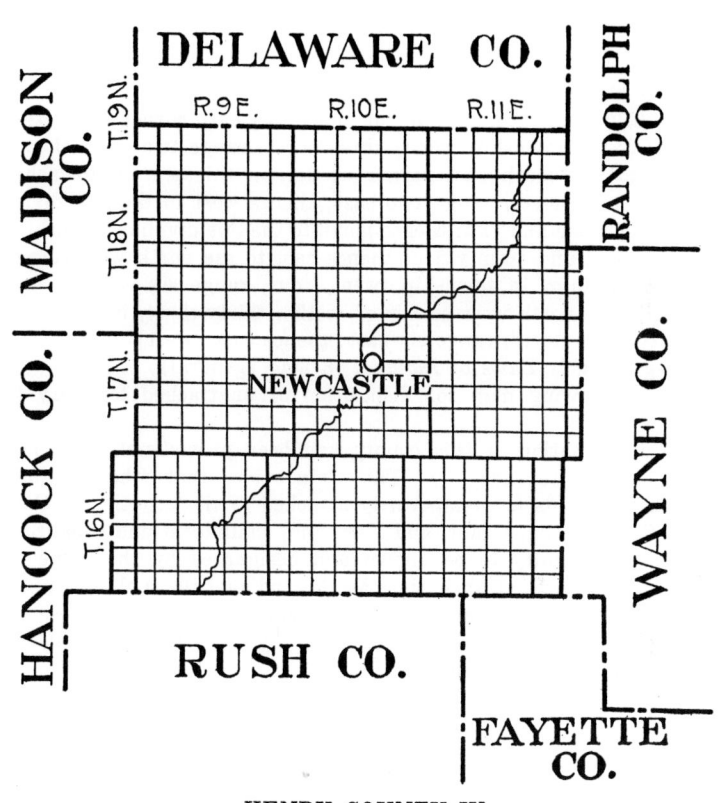

HENRY COUNTY IV

[Law: Jan. 26, 1827, effective on passage]

RICHARDVILLE [HOWARD] COUNTY I

JANUARY 15, 1844: Formation by statute, effective on passage. The organization of Richardville County was provided for by this law, to be effective May 1, 1844.

BOUNDARIES: "Beginning at the north east corner of section thirty-six, in township twenty-three north, range two east; thence north to the south east corner of section thirteen, in township twenty-three north, range two east; thence west to the line dividing ranges one and two; thence north to the line dividing townships twenty-four and twenty-five; thence east to the north west corner of section four, in township twenty-four, range six east; thence south to the north west corner of section thirty-three, in township twenty three north, range six east; thence east [west] to the place of beginning." *Laws of Indiana*, 1843-44 (general), p. 10.

See following map for disposition of unattached territory to the west.

The formation of this county had been provisionally outlined in an act of February 16, 1839. It provided that "the territory which is by this act temporarily attached to the counties of Carroll, Cass, Miami, Grant, and Hamilton, shall form and constitute a separate county to be known and designated by the name of Richardville, and at such time as the Indian title shall be extinguished and the population within the same will warrant, the said county shall be organized as a separate county." *Laws of Indiana*, 1838-39 (general), p. 76.

The attachments mentioned included not only the territory formed into Richardville by the law of January 15, 1844, quoted above, but also the territory out of which Tipton was formed. See map, Tipton County.

COUNTY SEAT: Commissioners appointed under the act forming the county met in May, 1844, and on August 17, 1844, reported their selection of a site within the present town of Kokomo. *Laws of Indiana*, 1843-44 (general), p. 11; Morrow, *History of Howard County*, 1:56-58.

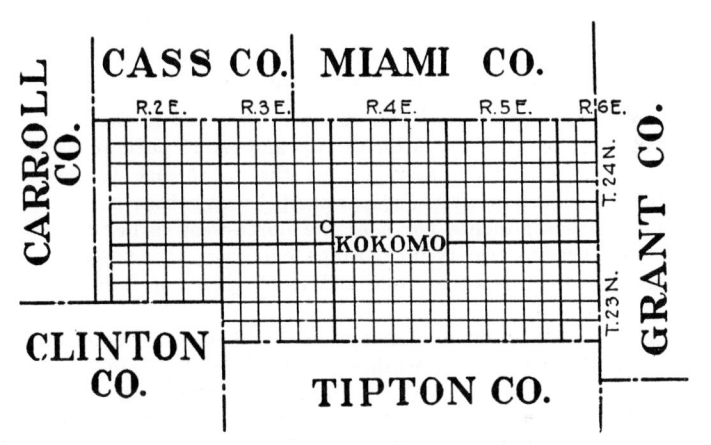

RICHARDVILLE [HOWARD] COUNTY I
[Law: Jan. 15, 1844, effective on passage]

RICHARDVILLE [HOWARD] COUNTY II

JANUARY 13, 1845: Alteration by statute correcting the boundary line of Richardville County, effective on passage. Corrected by act of January 13, 1846, effective on passage.

BOUNDARY CHANGE: "The territory included in the following boundary . . . is hereby attached to, and made part of Richardville county, to-wit: Beginning at the north-east [south-east] corner of section fourteen, in township twenty-three north, range two [one] east; thence north to the north-west corner of section one, in township twenty-four, range one east; thence east to the range line dividing ranges one and two." *Laws of Indiana,* 1844-45 (local), p. 151.

The corrective act of January 13, 1846, read: "Sections one, twelve and thirteen, in township twenty-three north, of range one east, and sections one, twelve, thirteen, twenty-four, twenty-five and thirty-six, in township twenty-four north, of range one east . . . are hereby attached to and made a part of the county of Richardville." *Ibid.,* 1845-46 (local), p. 260.

The name of the county was changed to Howard by a legislative act of December 28, 1846. The organization of the county was in no way affected. *Ibid.,* 1846-47 (local), p. 261.

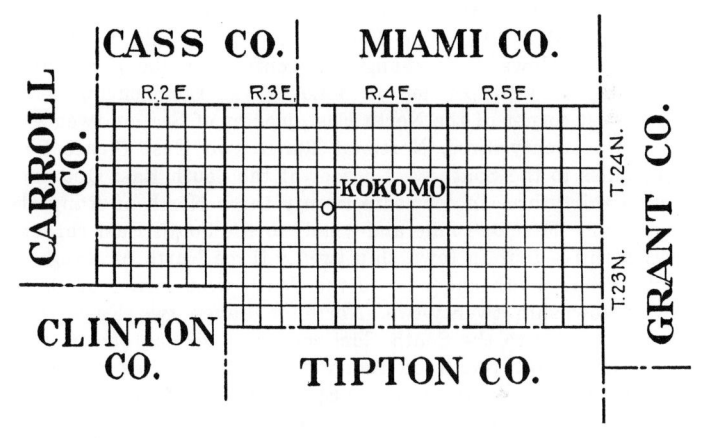

RICHARDVILLE [HOWARD] COUNTY II
[Law: Jan. 13, 1845, effective on passage]

446   INDIANA HISTORICAL COLLECTIONS

HOWARD COUNTY III

MARCH 3, 1859: Alteration by report of county commissioners, changing the boundary line between Howard and Clinton counties.

BOUNDARY CHANGE: The report of the commissioners granting the petition of the majority of legal voters in the territory concerned orders "that the Boundaries of the said Counties of Clinton and Howard, be changed to conform to the [boundaries] designated in said petition as follows, vis, Commencing at the North west corner of the North East quarter of Section twenty-one Township twenty-three, North of Range two East thence South three miles to the South west corner of the South East Quarter of Section thirtythree in township twenty three North of Range two East thence East one mile and a half to the South East corner of Section thirty-four in town ship twenty-three North of Range two East, thence South one mile to the South west corner of Section two in township twenty-two, North of Range two East, thence East two miles to the South East corner of Section one in Township twenty-two, North of Range two East, thence north four miles to the Northeast corner of Section twenty four in Township twenty-three, North of Range two East, taking from the territory and jurisdiction of the County of Clinton and adding and attaching to the territory and jurisdiction of the County of Howard, the East half of sections 21, 28 and 33 and all of Sections 22, 27, 34, 35, 26, 23, 24 25 & 36 all in township twenty-three North of Range two East and Sections one and two in township twenty-two, North of Range two East, and the Auditor is directed to forward a certified copy of this order to the Secretary of State." Record of Howard County Commissioners, 3:33.

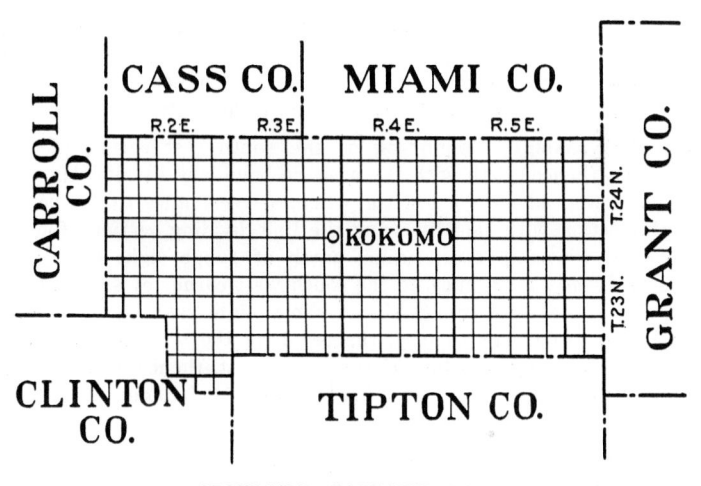

HOWARD COUNTY III
[Commissioners' Report: Mar. 3, 1859]

HUNTINGTON COUNTY

FEBRUARY 2, 1832: Formation by statute, effective on passage. The formation affected territory attached to Grant and Allen counties. The county was organized by an act of February 1, 1834, effective after publication in the *Indiana Journal*.

BOUNDARIES: "Beginning at the south-west corner of Allen county, thence north with the western boundary thereof, six miles; thence west along the township line, sixteen miles to the point of intersection with said line, and the line dividing sections four and five, of township twenty-nine, north of range eight east, thence south twenty-four miles, to the south west corner of section thirty-three, in township twenty-six, of range eight east, on the northern boundary of Grant County, thence along the township line, to its intersection with the line of range ten east, thence north eighteen miles to the place of beginning." *Laws of Indiana*, 1831-32, pp. 112-13.

COUNTY SEAT: In the act organizing the county, commissioners were appointed for the location of a county seat. Lands offered by General John Tipton on the site of Huntington were selected and the town laid out. It has remained the county seat. *Ibid.*, 1833-34, pp. 65-66; Shockley, "County Seat Wars," *op. cit.*, 10:no. 1:30; *History of Huntington County*, 321-22, 402.

HUNTINGTON COUNTY BOUNDARIES 449

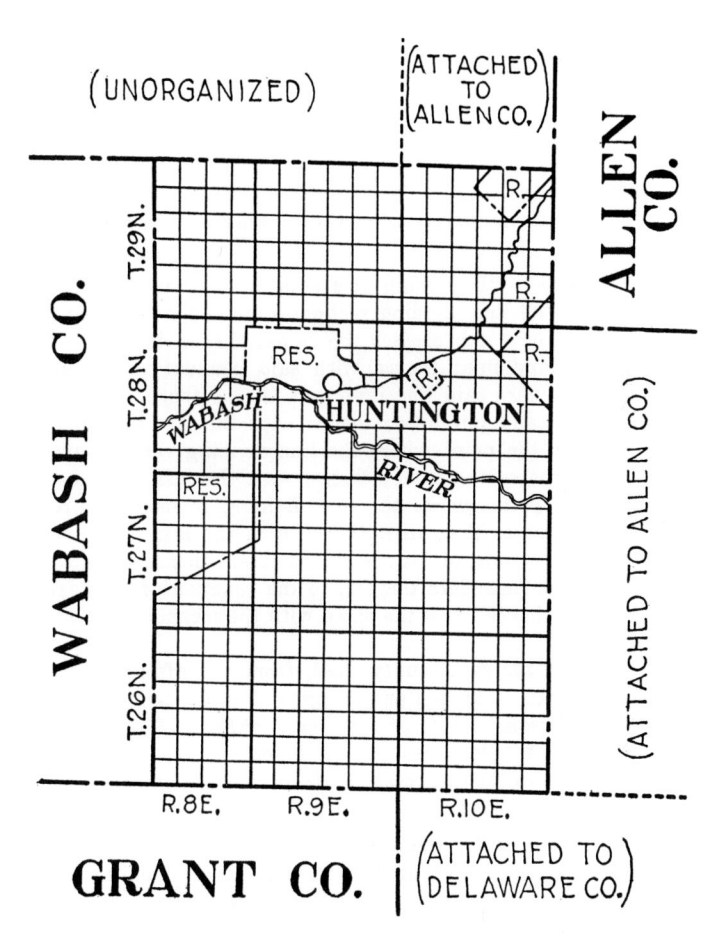

HUNTINGTON COUNTY

[Law: Feb. 2, 1832, effective on passage]

JACKSON COUNTY I
[Indiana Territory]

DECEMBER 18, 1815: Formation by statute, effective January 1, 1816. The formation affected Clark, Jefferson, and Washington counties.

BOUNDARIES: "Beginning at a point on the east fork of White River where the line dividing sections four and five, in range two east, town three north crosses the same; thence due north to the Indian boundary line; thence with said boundary line eastward to the point where said line intersects the northern boundary line of the Grouseland purchase; thence with the last mentioned line eastwardly to the point where the line dividing ranges seven and eight east, crosses the same; thence with the last mentioned line south, to the point where the line dividing townships three and four north, crosses the same; thence with the last mentioned line west, to the east fork of Muscacketuck river; thence down the said river, with the meanders thereof, to the junction of Drift fork of White river; thence down the same with the meanders to the place of beginning.

". . . That the said county shall, from and after the first day of January next, be known and designated by the name . . . of the county of Jackson." *Acts of Indiana Territory*, 1815, pp. 3-4.

This law provided also for an extension of Jackson County northward, when further cessions from the Indians should be secured. *Ibid.*, 5-6. See map, Jackson County III.

COUNTY SEAT: By the act forming the county, "Velonia" was made a temporary seat of justice, until the commissioners appointed under the same act should select a county seat. *Acts of Indiana Territory*, 1815, p. 5.

JACKSON COUNTY I

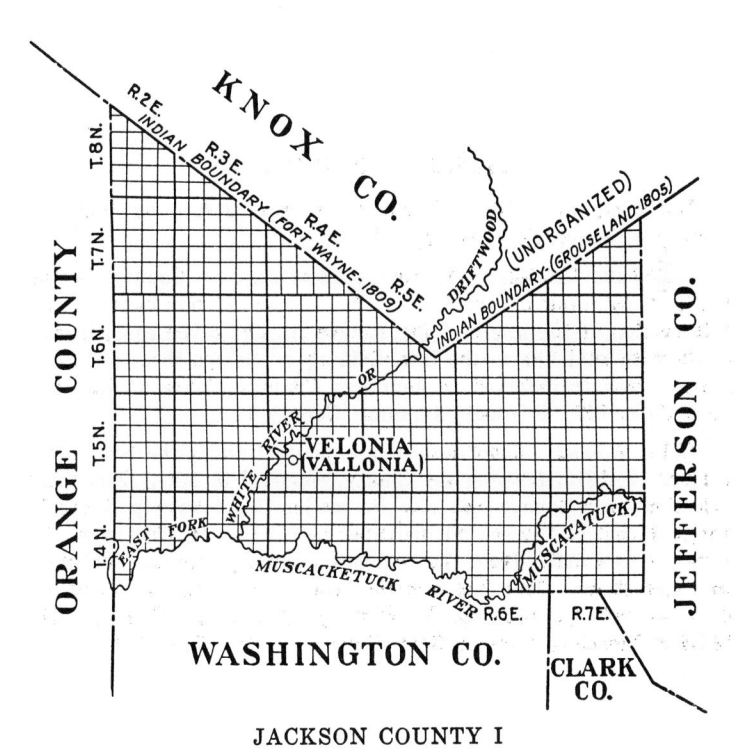

[Law: Dec. 18, 1815, effective Jan. 1, 1816]

JACKSON COUNTY II

DECEMBER 27, 1816: Alteration by statute forming Jennings County, effective February 1, 1817.

BOUNDARY CHANGE: All that part of Jackson County east of a line "beginning on the line of the Grousland purchase, at the intersection of the line dividing ranges six and seven east; thence south with said line to the line dividing townships three and four north;" was transferred to Jennings County. *Laws of Indiana*, 1816-17, p. 197. See map, Jennings County I.

COUNTY SEAT: Commissioners appointed under the act of December 18, 1815, forming the county, reported in May, 1816, their selection of a county-seat site in section 14, township 5 north, range 4 east of the second principal meridian. In November the removal was made from the temporary county seat at "Velonia" to Brownstown. This has remained the county seat. *Laws of Indiana Territory*, 1815, p. 5; *History of Jackson County*, 328, 341-42; Shockley, "County Seat Wars," *op. cit.*, 10:no. 1:9.

JACKSON COUNTY II

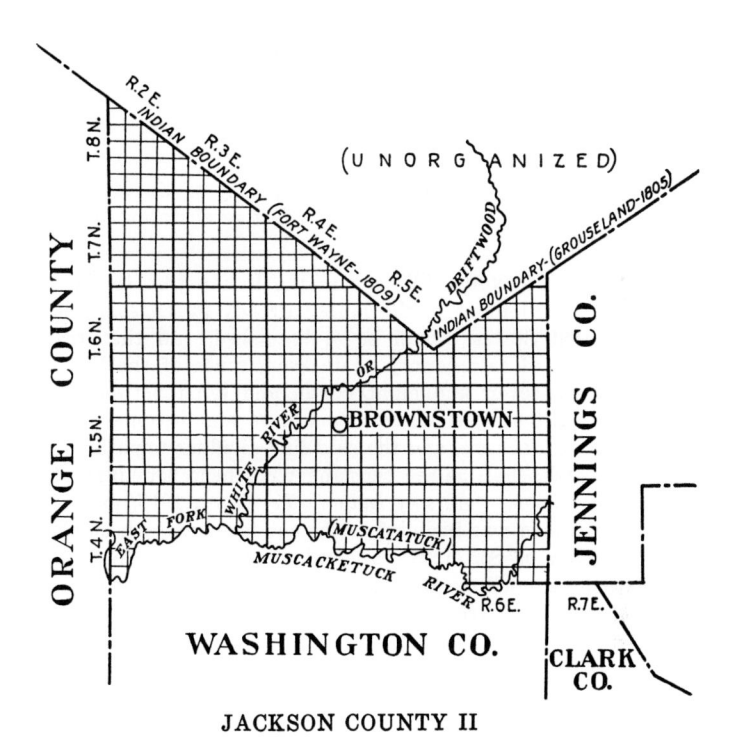

[Law: Dec. 27, 1816, effective Feb. 1, 1817]

JACKSON COUNTY III

OCTOBER 2-6, 1818: Alteration by Treaty of St. Mary's, proclaimed January 7-15, 1819, making effective a statute of December 18, 1815.

BOUNDARY CHANGE: "Whenever the Indian title to the lands, north of and adjoining to the lands, already purchased, and sold by the United States, [shall be extinguished,] all that tract of country, north of said county of Jackson, south of the line dividing townships seven and eight north, and lying between ranges three and eight east, shall be attached to and become a part of said county of Jackson, and the said line dividing townships seven and eight north, shall be the permanent northern boundary of said county of Jackson." *Acts of Indiana Territory*, 1815, pp. 5-6.

This provision was included in the act forming Jackson County.

The Treaty of St. Mary's secured to the United States a vast area extending north to the St. Mary's River, the Wabash, and a line north of, and parallel to, the Wabash west of the Tippecanoe River. For treaties with the Wea, Delaware, and Miami, see Kappler (ed.), *Indian Affairs. Laws and Treaties*, 2:168-74.

JACKSON COUNTY BOUNDARIES 455

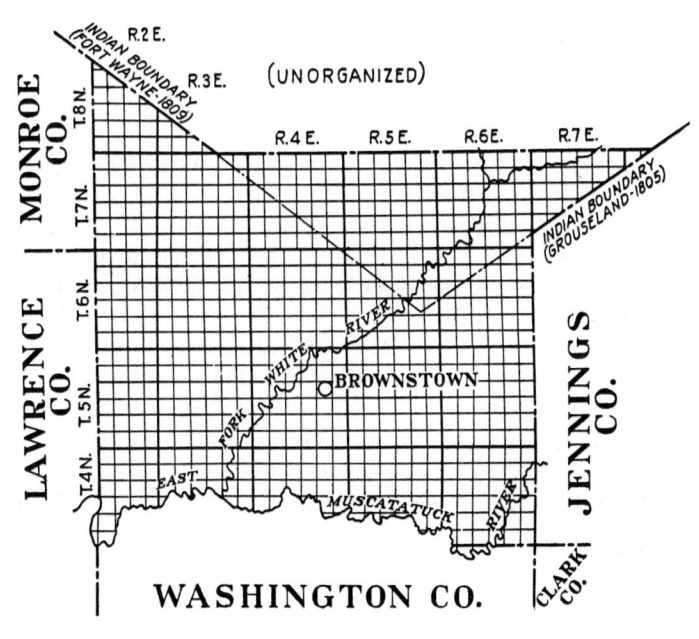

JACKSON COUNTY III

[Treaty of St. Mary's: Oct. 2-6, 1818, proclaimed Jan. 7-15, 1819, making effective law of Dec. 18, 1815]

JACKSON COUNTY IV

JANUARY 12, 1820: Alteration by statute forming Scott County, effective February 1, 1820.

BOUNDARY CHANGE: All that part of Jackson County, bounded by the Muscatatuck River, the line dividing ranges 6 and 7 east of the second principal meridian, and the line dividing townships 3 and 4 north, was transferred to Scott County. *Laws of Indiana,* 1819-20, pp. 51-52. See map, Scott County I.

JANUARY 20, 1820: Alteration by statute attaching territory to Jennings County.

BOUNDARY CHANGE: All that part of Jackson County in township 7 north, ranges 7 and 8 east of the second principal meridian, was transferred to Jennings County. *Laws of Indiana,* 1819-20, pp. 95-96.

Jackson County, by this same law, was given concurrent jurisdiction over Delaware County with Jennings, Ripley, and other bounding counties. *Ibid.,* 96.

JACKSON COUNTY BOUNDARIES 457

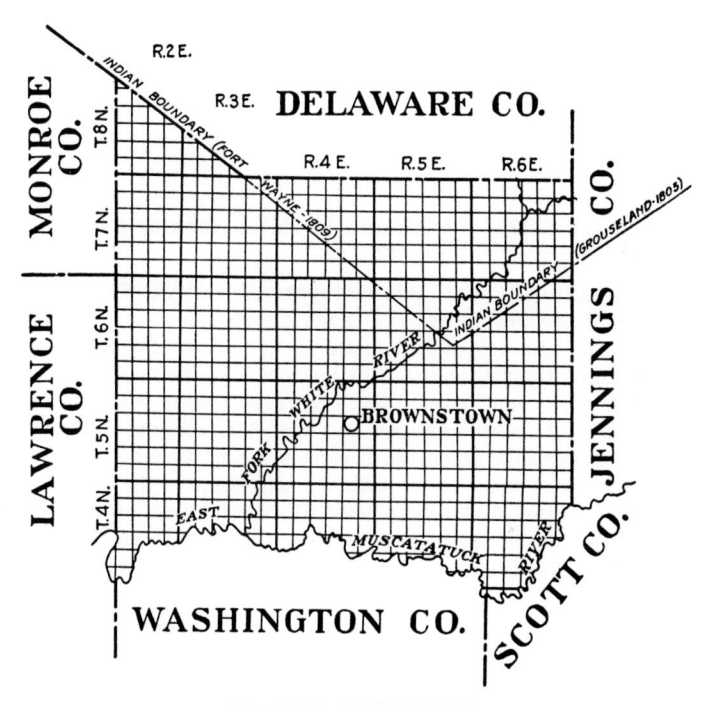

JACKSON COUNTY IV

[Laws: Jan. 12, 1820, effective Feb. 1, 1820; Jan. 20, 1820]

JACKSON COUNTY V

JANUARY 8, 1821: Alteration by statute forming Bartholomew County, effective February 12, 1821.

BOUNDARY CHANGE: All that part of Jackson County north of a line beginning where the range line dividing ranges 6 and 7 east of the second principal meridian "intersects Big Sand creek, thence down the said creek with the meanders thereof to its junction with Driftwood river, thence down said river with the meanders thereof to where an east and west line running through the centre of township seven north strikes the north west side of the aforesaid river, thence west with the said line," to the "south west corner of section eighteen in township seven north of range four east" was transferred to Bartholomew County. *Laws of Indiana*, 1820-21, pp. 79-80.

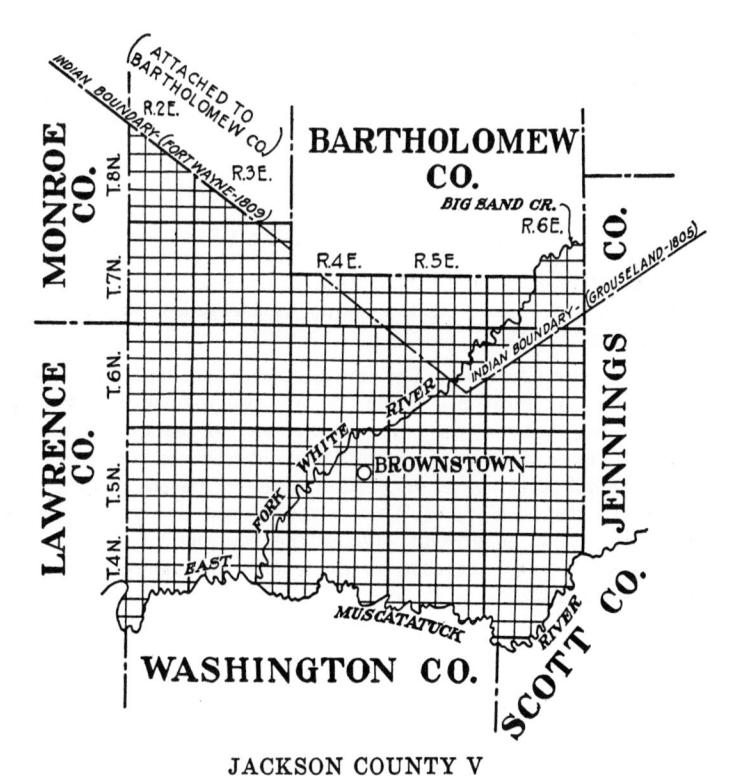

JACKSON COUNTY V

[Law: Jan. 8, 1821, effective Feb. 12, 1821]

JACKSON COUNTY VI

DECEMBER 31, 1822: Alteration by statute attaching part of the county of Jackson to the county of Lawrence, effective January 1, 1823.

BOUNDARY CHANGE: The law provided that "all that part of the county of Jackson, included within the following boundaries, to wit: beginning at the north west corner of section number sixteen, in range two east, in town five north; thence east two miles, to the north east corner of section number fifteen; thence south to the Driftwood Fork of White river; thence down said river to the line which at present divides the counties of Jackson and Lawrence; be . . . attached to the county of Lawrence." *Laws of Indiana*, 1822-23, p. 27.

JACKSON COUNTY BOUNDARIES 461

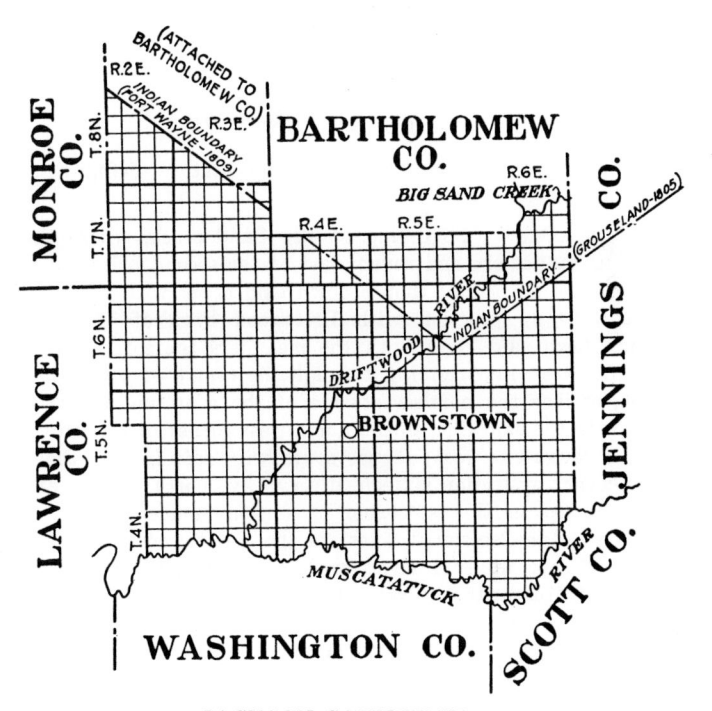

JACKSON COUNTY VI

[Law: Dec. 31, 1822, effective Jan. 1, 1823]

JACKSON COUNTY VII

JANUARY 31, 1824: Alteration by statute defining county boundaries.

BOUNDARIES: "Beginning at Big Sand creek, where the line dividing ranges six and seven, east of the second principal meridian, crosses the same; thence down said creek with the meanders thereof, to its junction with Driftwood Fork of White River; thence down said river with the meanders thereof, to where an east and west line running through the centre of township seven north, strikes the north-west side of the aforesaid river; thence west with the said line, to the north-west corner of section twenty-one, in range two east; thence south with said line, to the north-west corner of section sixteen, in town five north; thence east two miles, to the north-east corner of section number fifteen; thence south with the sectional lines, to the Driftwood Fork of White River; thence up said river, with the meanders thereof, to the mouth of Muscatituck river; thence up the last mentioned river to the forks thereof; thence up the South Fork to where the line dividing ranges six and seven crosses the same, and from thence north with said range line to the place of beginning." *Revised Laws of Indiana*, 1823-24, pp. 97-98.

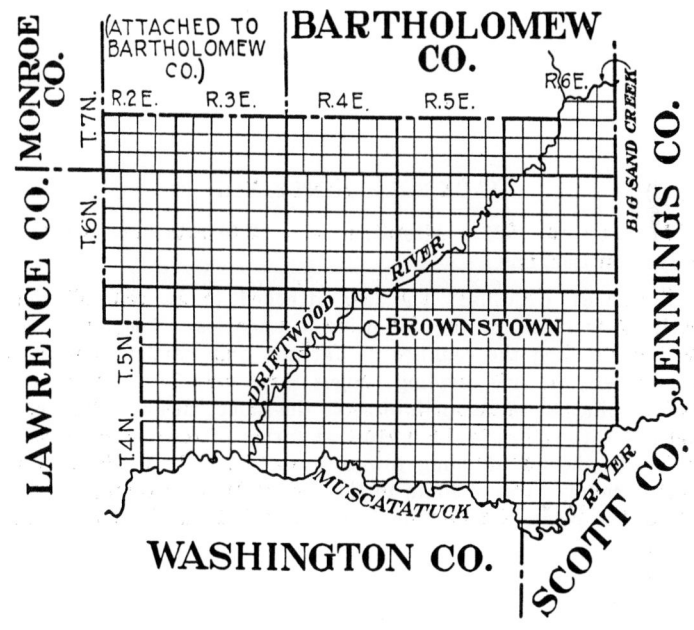

JACKSON COUNTY VII

[Law: Jan. 31, 1824]

JACKSON COUNTY VIII

JANUARY 16, 1828: Alteration by statute attaching territory to Jackson County.

BOUNDARY CHANGE: The law attached to Jackson all that territory included in the following boundaries: "beginning on the line dividing the counties of Jackson and Bartholomew at a point where the line dividing ranges three and four, east of the second principal meridian intersects the same, thence north with said line three miles to the north-east corner of town seven, thence west with the line dividing towns seven and eight to the line of Monroe county; thence south to the line of Jackson county, thence east to the place of beginning." *Laws of Indiana*, 1827-28, p. 15.

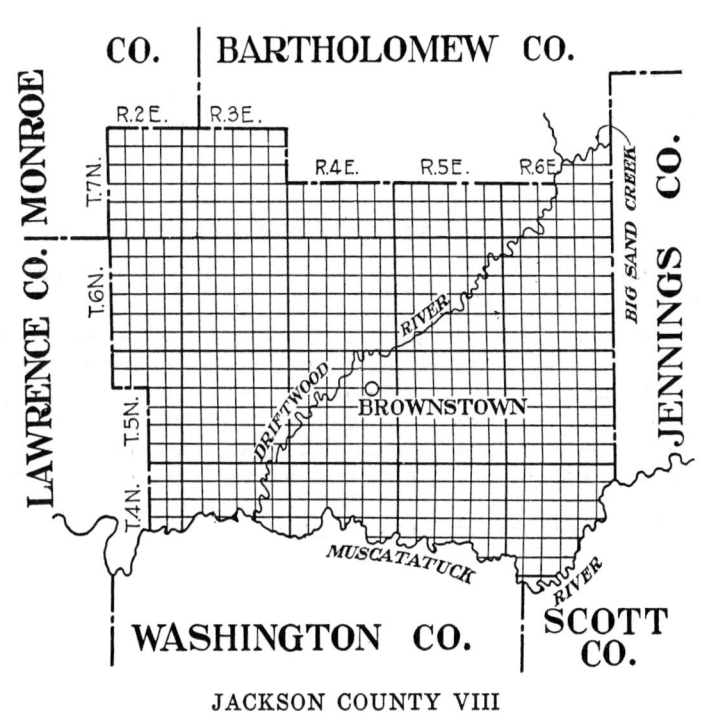

JACKSON COUNTY VIII
[Law: Jan. 16, 1828]

JACKSON COUNTY IX

FEBRUARY 4, 1836: Alteration by statute forming Brown County, effective April 1, 1836.

BOUNDARY CHANGE: All that part of Jackson County north of a line beginning at the northeast corner of section 13, township 7 north, range 3 east of the second principal meridian, and running thence with the section line west to the northwest corner of section 16, township 7 north, range 2 east, was transferred to Brown County. This was a strip of territory ten miles long and two miles wide. *Laws of Indiana*, 1835-36 (general), p. 52. See text of the law with map of Brown County.

JACKSON COUNTY IX

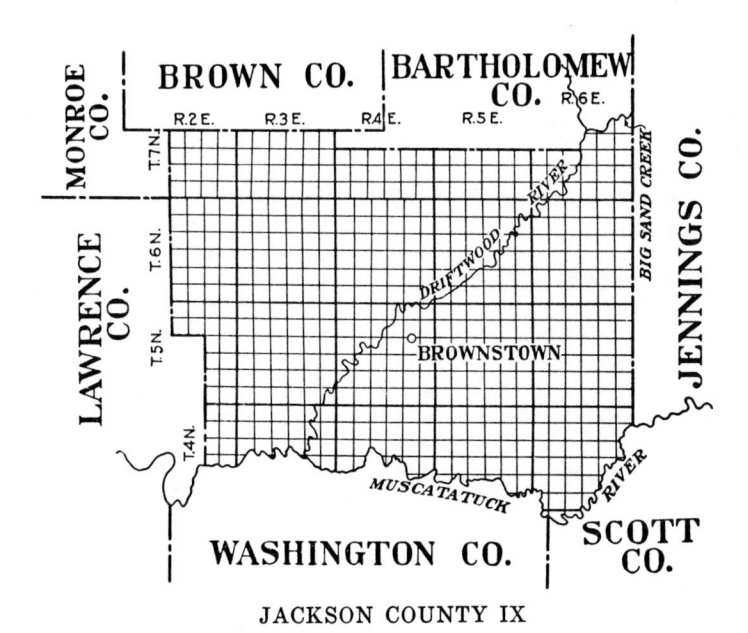

[Law: Feb. 4, 1836, effective Apr. 1, 1836]

JACKSON COUNTY X

1842-43: Alteration by statute defining county boundaries.

BOUNDARIES: "Beginning at Big Sand creek where the line dividing ranges six and seven east crosses the same, thence down said creek, with the meanders thereof, to its junction with the drift wood fork of White river, thence down the same to where an east and west line, running through the centre of township seven north, strikes the northwest side of the aforesaid river, thence west to where it crosses the line dividing sections fifteen and sixteen, in range four, thence north with said line to the northeast corner of section sixteen, township seven, range four, thence west to the northwest corner of section sixteen, township seven, range two east, thence south to the northwest corner of section sixteen, in township five north, range two east, thence east to the northeast corner of section fifteen, in the same range and township, thence south to the drift wood fork of White river, thence up said river, with the meanders thereof, to the mouth of the Muscatituck river, thence up the said last mentioned river to the forks thereof, thence up the south fork to where the line dividing ranges six and seven, crosses the same, thence north with said range line to the place of beginning." *Revised Statutes of Indiana*, 1842-43, pp. 74-75.

The only change made was the addition of sections 16, 17, and 18, township 7 north, range 4 east of the second principal meridian, which had been left unassigned since detached from Bartholomew County by the act of February 17, 1838.

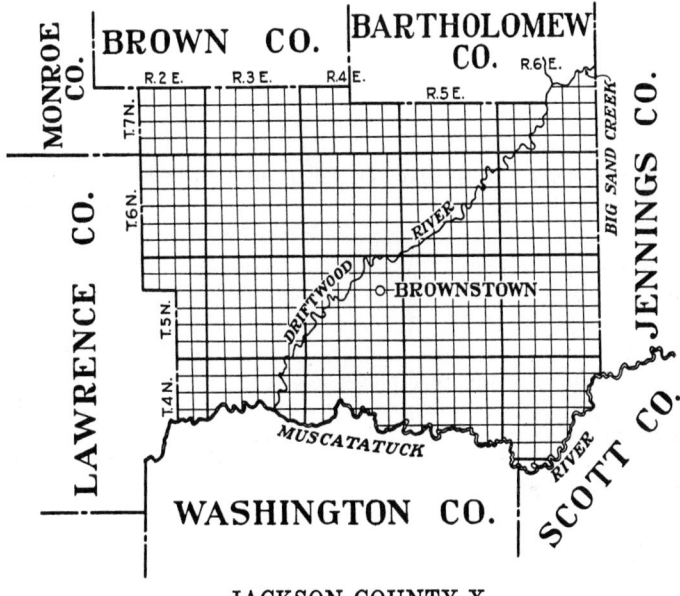

JACKSON COUNTY X

[Law: 1842-43]

JACKSON COUNTY XI

JUNE 8, 1859: Alteration by report of county commissioners, changing the boundary line between Jackson and Lawrence counties.

BOUNDARY CHANGE: The changed Lawrence County line was run as follows: "Beginning at the Northwest corner of Section 4, in Township 6 North, Range 2 East, thence due East to the Northeast corner of Section 3, in Township 6 North, Range 2 East, and running thence directly South to White River," taking from Jackson County a strip of territory two miles wide and eight miles long. Lawrence County Commissioners' Record E.

See *ante*, 115, for a statement concerning opposition to this change.

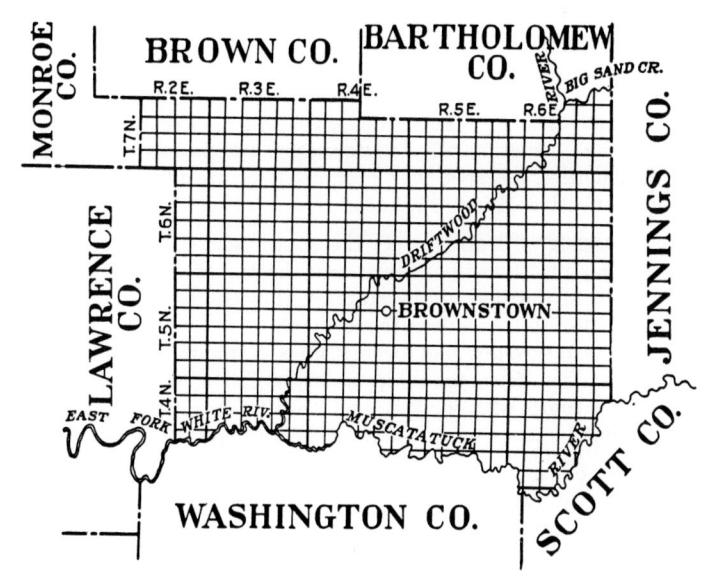

JACKSON COUNTY XI
[Commissioners' Report: June 8, 1859]

JASPER COUNTY I

FEBRUARY 7, 1835: Formation by statute, effective on publication. The formation affected territory attached to White and Warren counties. Jasper was organized by an act of February 17, 1838, effective March 15, 1838.

BOUNDARIES: "Beginning at the south east corner of section thirty three, in township twenty four north, of range six west, thence west to the line of the state of Illinois, thence north with the state line thirty miles, thence east with the line dividing townships twenty eight and twenty nine north, to the north east corner of section four, township twenty eight north, of range six west, thence south with the sectional lines thirty miles to the place of beginning." *Laws of Indiana*, 1834-35 (general), p. 46.

COUNTY SEAT: Parish Grove and Spitler's Cabin were temporary seats of justice. With the reorganization of the county in 1839, a permanent county seat was chosen. See following map. Hamilton and Darroch (eds.), *History of Jasper and Newton Counties*, 1:47.

JASPER COUNTY I

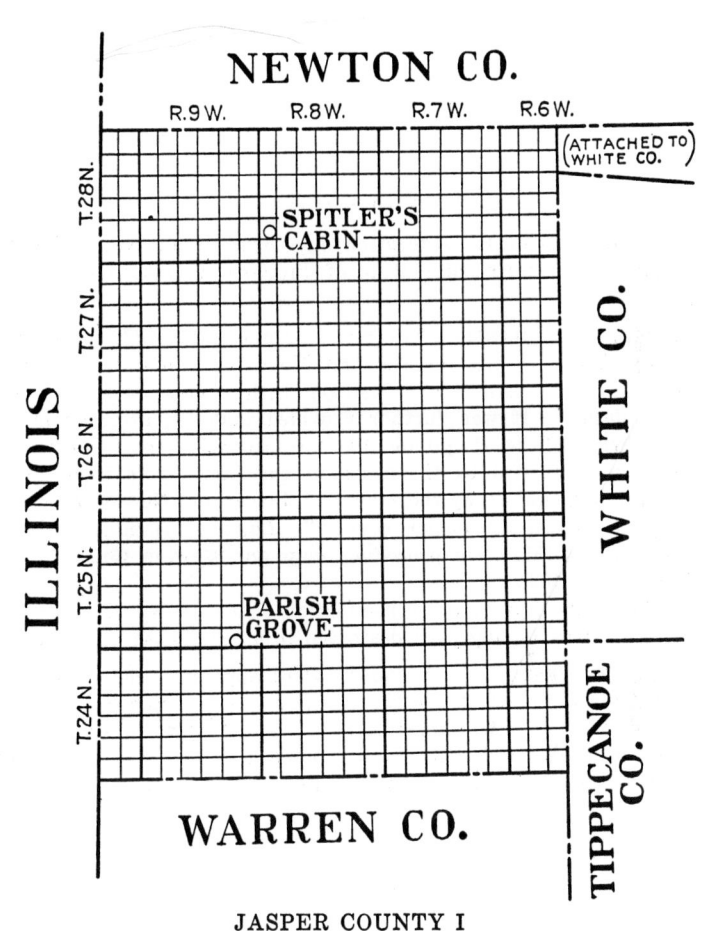

[Feb. 7, 1835, effective on publication]

JASPER COUNTY II

JUNE [?], 1839: Alteration by consolidation with Newton County, under terms of statute of January 29, 1839, effective on passage.

BOUNDARY CHANGE: The law of January 29, 1839, appointed commissioners to meet on the first Monday of June, "to examine the counties of Jasper and Newton, with a view of their being consolidated." It was further provided that "if, after examination, they shall be of opinion that the interest of the two counties would be promoted by the union of the same, from thenceforth the territory, known by the names of Jasper and Newton counties, shall be known as Jasper county." *Laws of Indiana*, 1838-39 (general), p. 83. See preceding map and Newton County map, January 28, 1836.

The exact date of the consolidation is not known, the commissioners' report having been destroyed in a courthouse fire of 1865.

COUNTY SEAT: Commissioners were appointed under this act to locate a county seat. If the two counties were consolidated the county seat was to be named Newton. The Jasper county seat has never been removed, though the name was changed. *Laws of Indiana*, 1838-39 (general), p. 83. See following map.

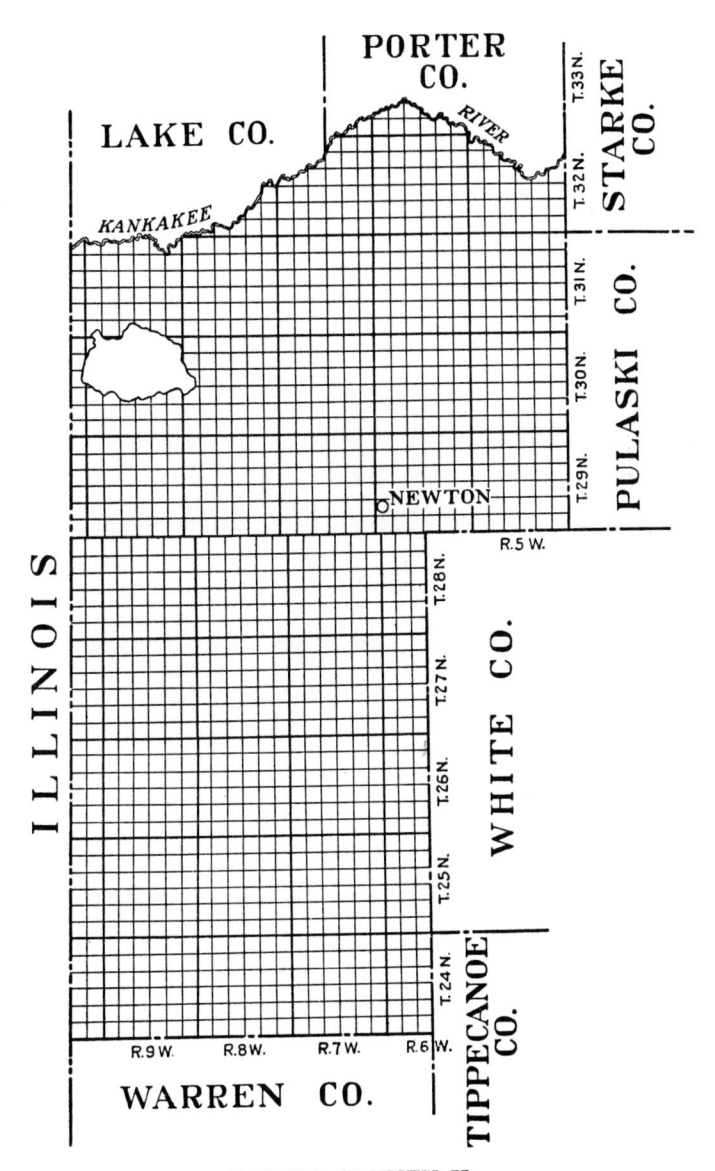

JASPER COUNTY II

[Commissioners' Report: June (?), 1839]

JASPER COUNTY III

FEBRUARY 18, 1840: Alteration by statute forming Benton County, effective on passage.

BOUNDARY CHANGE: "All that part of Jasper county south of the line between township twenty-six (26) and twenty-seven (27) north" was formed into Benton County. *Laws of Indiana*, 1839-40 (general), p. 62.

By an act of the same date, the name of the county seat was changed from Newton to Rensselaer. *Ibid.* (local), p. 240.

JASPER COUNTY III

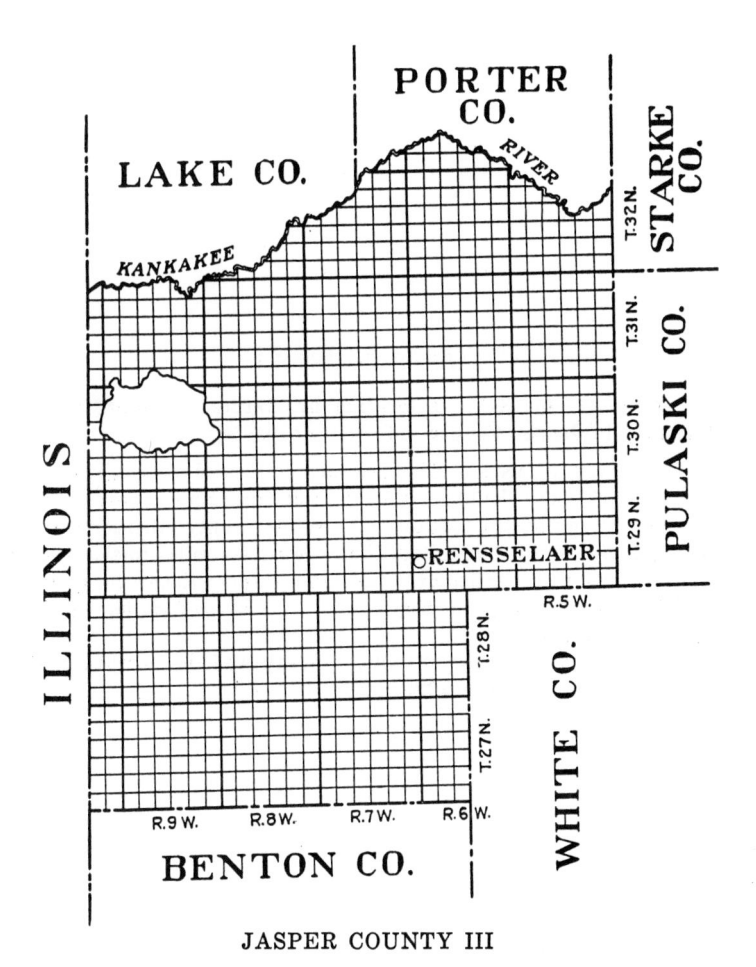

[Law: Feb. 18, 1840, effective on passage]

JASPER COUNTY IV

FEBRUARY 10, 1841: Alteration by statute, attaching certain territory to Jasper County, effective on passage.

BOUNDARY CHANGE: The law attached to Jasper County all that part of White County within the following boundaries: "Commencing at the northwest corner of White county; thence east six miles; thence south five miles; thence west six miles to the county line dividing the counties of White and Jasper; thence north with said line to the place of beginning." *Laws of Indiana,* 1840-41 (general), p. 135.

The northwest corner of White County was the northwest corner of section 3, township 28 north, range 6 west.

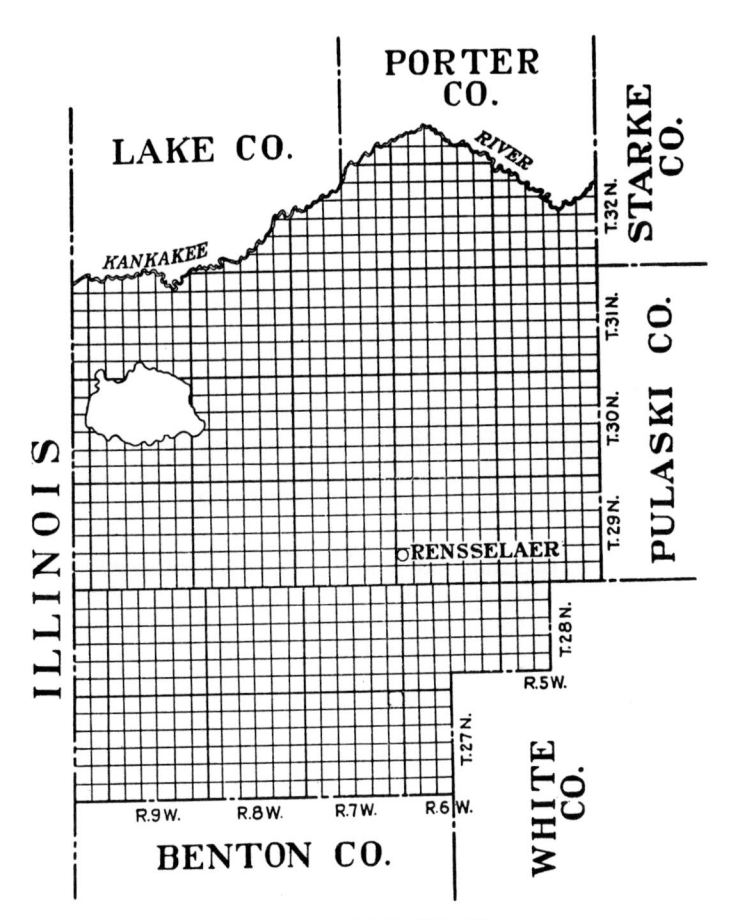

JASPER COUNTY IV

[Law: Feb. 10, 1841, effective on passage]

JASPER COUNTY V

DECEMBER 8, 1859: Alteration by commissioners' report of February 27, 1858, dividing Jasper County, made effective by the decision of the Indiana Supreme Court, and recorded December 8, 1859.

BOUNDARY CHANGE: All that part of Jasper County west of the range line between ranges 7 and 8 west of the second principal meridian was reorganized as Newton County. For text and comment, see map, Newton County III.

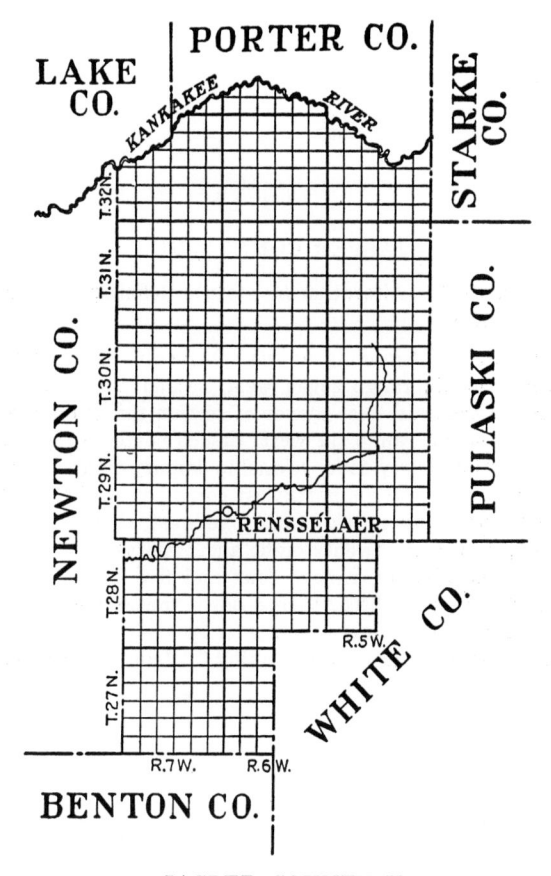

JASPER COUNTY V

[Commissioners' Report: Feb. 27, 1858, recorded Dec. 8, 1859]

JASPER COUNTY VI

MARCH 8, 1923: Alteration by statute defining the boundaries of Jasper County.

BOUNDARIES: "Beginning at the southwest corner of township twenty-seven north, range seven west, second principal meridian, thence east to the southwest corner of section thirty-four, township twenty-seven north, range six west, thence north to the northwest corner of section thirty-four, township twenty-eight north, range six west, thence east to the northwest corner of section thirty-four, township twenty-eight north, range five west, thence north to the line dividing townships twenty-eight and twenty-nine north, thence east to the line dividing ranges four and five west, thence north to the Marble Powers ditch, thence down the middle of the channel of the same to the line dividing ranges seven and eight west, thence south to the place of beginning." *Laws of Indiana*, 1923, p. 464.

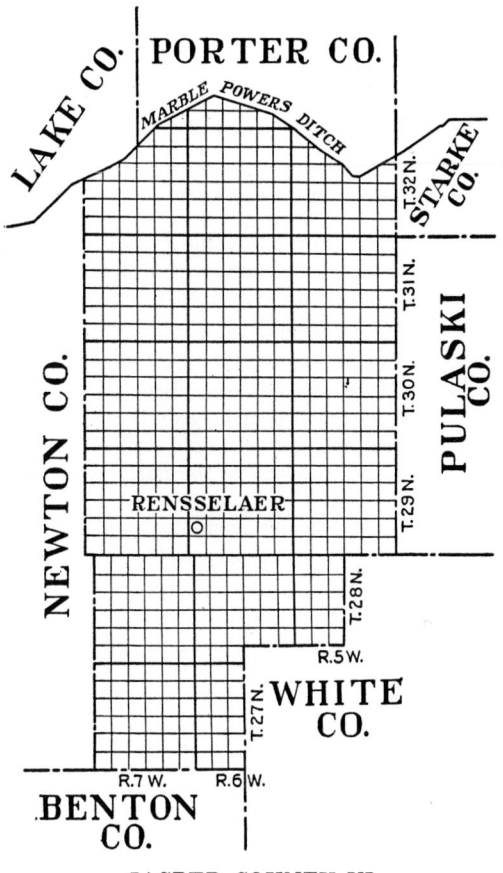

JASPER COUNTY VI

[Law: Mar. 8, 1923]

JAY COUNTY I

FEBRUARY 7, 1835: Formation by statute, effective on publication. The formation affected territory attached to Delaware and Randolph counties. Jay was organized by an act of January 30, 1836, effective March 1, 1836.

BOUNDARIES: "Beginning at the south east corner of Adams county, thence west to the eastern boundary of Grant county, thence south to the northern boundary of Delaware county, thence east with the northern boundary of said county, to the north east corner of the same, thence south to the north west corner of Randolph county, thence east with the northern boundary of said county to the state line, thence north to the place of beginning." *Laws of Indiana,* 1834-35 (general), p. 44.

COUNTY SEAT: Commissioners appointed under the organizing act, in June, 1836, decided upon the site of Portland, which received its name on December 5, 1836. It has remained the county seat. *Ibid.*, 1835-36 (general), p. 47; Jay, Milton T. (ed.), *History of Jay County, Indiana* . . ., 1:84-86 (Indianapolis, 1922); *Biographical and Historical Record of Jay and Blackford Counties,* 199-201; Shockley, "County Seat Wars," *op. cit.,* 10:no. 1:31-32.

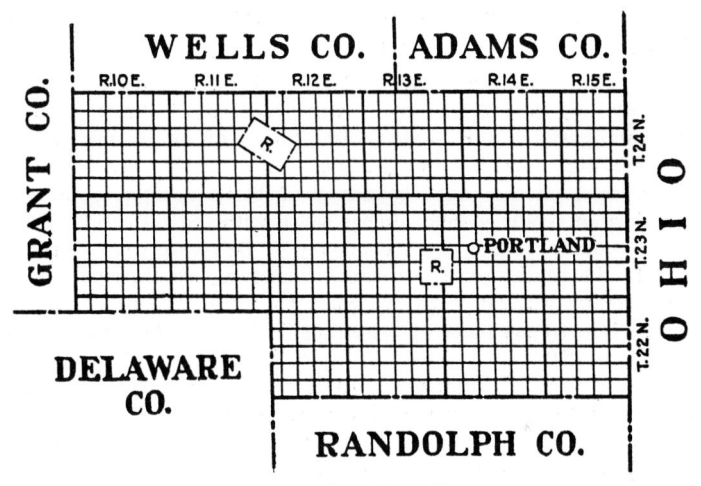

JAY COUNTY I

[Law: Feb. 7, 1835, effective on publication]

JAY COUNTY II

FEBRUARY 15, 1838: Alteration by statute forming Blackford County, effective April 2, 1838.

BOUNDARY CHANGE: All that part of Jay County included in the following boundaries was transferred to Blackford County: "Beginning at the north-east [west] corner of section number five in township number twenty-four, range number twelve east; thence west on the south boundary of Wells county, to the east boundary of Grant county; thence south with the eastern boundary of said county, to the north boundary of Delaware county; thence east to the south-east [northeast] corner of section eight, township twenty-two, range twelve east; thence north on the nearest section line, to the place of beginning." *Laws of Indiana*, 1837-38 (local), p. 290.

The law of February 17, 1838, defining county boundaries, overlooked the formation of Blackford County in describing the boundaries of Jay County. This error was corrected by the law of February 20, 1840, which provided that "all that district of country which was included within the boundaries of Jay county, before the formation of the county of Blackford, be, and the same is hereby declared to be within the county of Jay, except so much as is included within the county of Blackford." *Ibid.*, 265; 1839-40 (general), p. 79.

JAY COUNTY BOUNDARIES 487

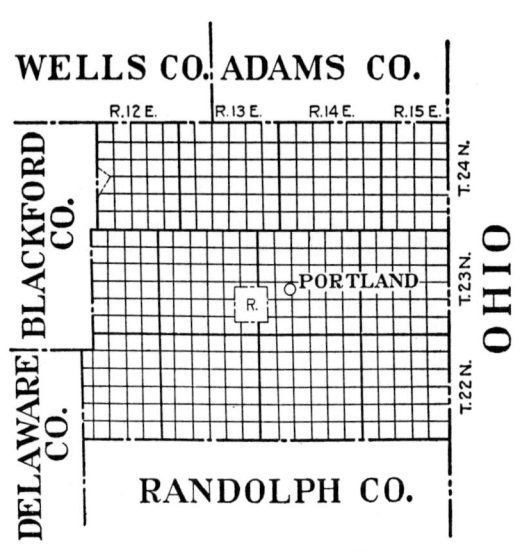

JAY COUNTY II

[Law: Feb. 15, 1838, effective Apr. 2, 1838]

JEFFERSON COUNTY I
[Indiana Territory]

NOVEMBER 23, 1810: Formation by statute, effective January 1, 1811. The formation affected Dearborn and Clark counties.

BOUNDARIES: "Beginning at the mouth of Log Lick creek, on the bank of the river Ohio, thence to the corner of sections five and eight, town four, range three, thence north[wardly] to the Indian boundary line, thence with the same [northwardly and] westwardly to a point opposite the north-east corner of Clark's grant, thence on a direct line to the said corner of the said grant, thence a direct line to the Ohio river at the lower line of town two, north, range ten, east, thence up the Ohio river with the meanders thereof to the beginning." *Acts of Indiana Territory,* 1810, pp. 14, 114.

The most plausible reading of this ambiguous description seems to be a line running from the corner of sections 5 and 8, town 4, range 3, thence northwestwardly to the Greenville Treaty line of 1795, thence with that line northwardly to its intersection by the Grouseland Treaty line of 1805, and with that line westwardly to a point opposite Clark's Grant.

The boundaries of Jefferson County at no time completely followed the lines thus laid out. A law for the formation of Franklin County, passed five days later, but effective on the same date as the Jefferson County law, altered the northern boundary of Jefferson. See below. In a law of January 1, 1817, effective March 1, 1817, commissioners were appointed to run the boundary line between Clark and Jefferson counties. The boundary is not repeated in that law.

NOVEMBER 27, 1810: Alteration by statute forming Franklin County, effective January 1, 1811.

BOUNDARY CHANGE: The southern boundary of Franklin County as established in this law ran with the Grouseland Treaty line of 1805 from the point of its intersection with the west boundary of the Fort Wayne purchase of 1809, northeastwardly to a point from which a due east line would strike the Ohio boundary at the corner of townships 7 and 8, thence with said due east line to that point on the Ohio boundary. *Acts of Indiana Territory,* 1810, pp. 19-20, 114. See map, Franklin County I.

COUNTY SEAT: Madison was made the county seat in the act which formed the county.

JEFFERSON COUNTY BOUNDARIES   489

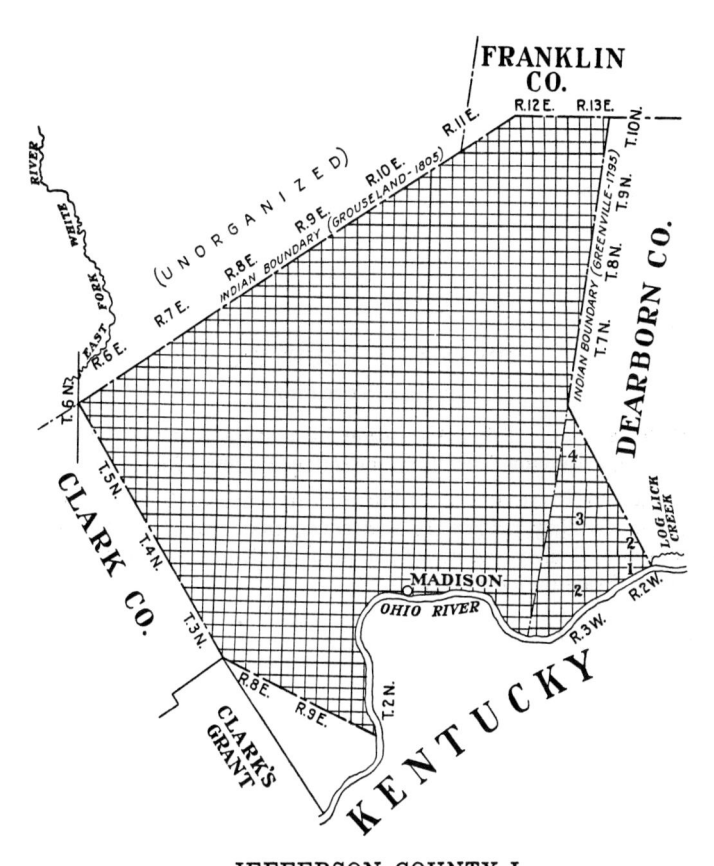

JEFFERSON COUNTY I

[Laws: Nov. 23, 1810, effective Jan. 1, 1811; Nov. 27, 1810, effective Jan. 1, 1811]

JEFFERSON COUNTY II
[Indiana Territory]

DECEMBER 21, 1813: Alteration by statute forming Washington County, Indiana Territory, effective January 17, 1814.

BOUNDARY CHANGE: All that part of Jefferson County west of "the line dividing ranges six and seven east" was transferred to Washington County. *Acts of Indiana Territory*, 1813-14, p. 91. See map, Washington County I.

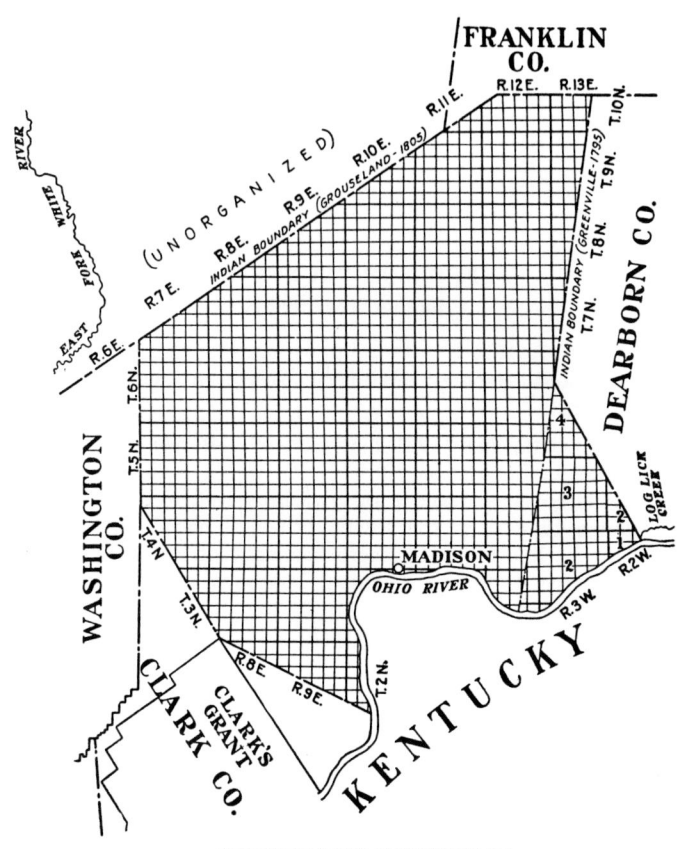

JEFFERSON COUNTY II
[Law: Dec. 21, 1813, effective Jan. 17, 1814]

JEFFERSON COUNTY III
[Indiana Territory]

SEPTEMBER 7, 1814: Alteration by statute forming Switzerland County and attaching territory to Dearborn County, effective October 1, 1814.

BOUNDARY CHANGES: All that part of Jefferson County east of a line beginning on the Ohio River where a due north line would divide sections 4 and 5 in townships 3, 4, 5, 6, 7, 8, and 9 north, range 12 east of the second principal meridian, and running with that line to the southern boundary of Franklin County, was transferred to Switzerland and Dearborn counties. *Acts of Indiana Territory*, 1814, pp. 30-31, 34-35. See maps, Dearborn County III, and Switzerland County I.

JEFFERSON COUNTY BOUNDARIES 493

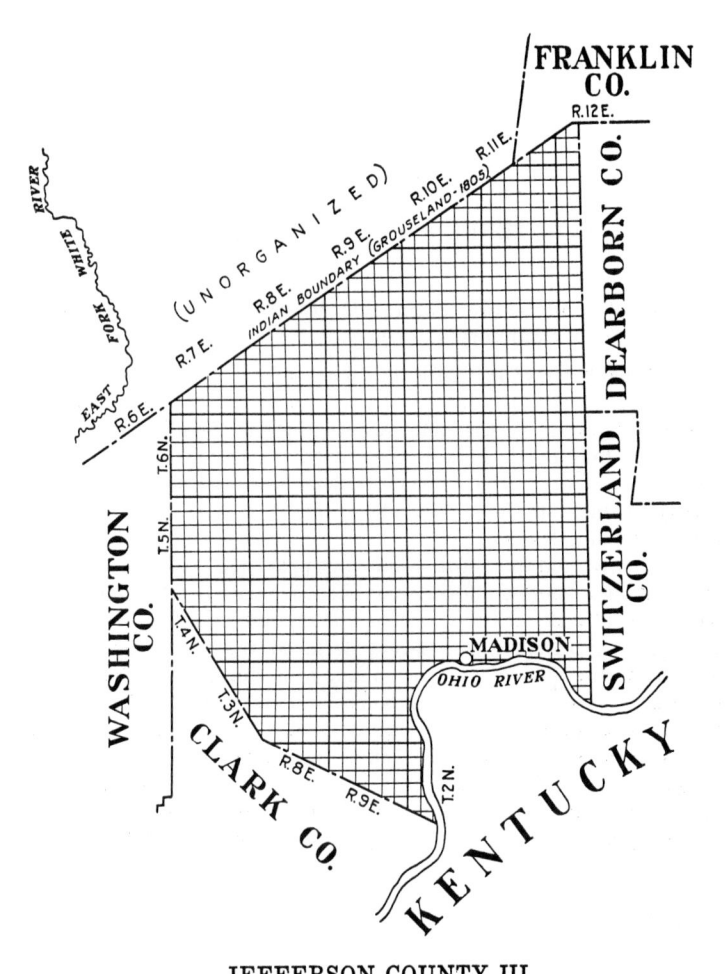

JEFFERSON COUNTY III

[Law: Sep. 7, 1814, effective Oct. 1, 1814]

JEFFERSON COUNTY IV
[Indiana Territory]

DECEMBER 18, 1815: Alteration by statute forming Jackson County, effective January 1, 1816.

BOUNDARY CHANGE: All that part of Jefferson County west and north of a "line dividing ranges seven and eight east . . . thence . . . south, to the point where the line dividing townships three and four north, crosses the same; thence with the last mentioned line west" to the Clark-Jefferson boundary line was transferred to Jackson County. *Acts of Indiana Territory*, 1815, pp. 3-4. See map, Jackson County I.

This law contained the following provision, enacted "to prevent future disputes, and in some measure to quiet the solicitudes which usually attend the settlement of new counties, respecting fixing county seats, &c. it is hereby declared, that the future permanent northern boundary of the county of Jefferson shall be an east and west line dividing townships five and six north; and whenever the inhabitants north of said east and west line, determined as the future northern boundary of Jefferson county, and lying between ranges seven and twelve east, amount to two hundred rank and file on the muster roll, they shall be entitled to the privileges of becoming a new county." *Acts of Indiana Territory*, 1815, p. 6.

JEFFERSON COUNTY BOUNDARIES 495

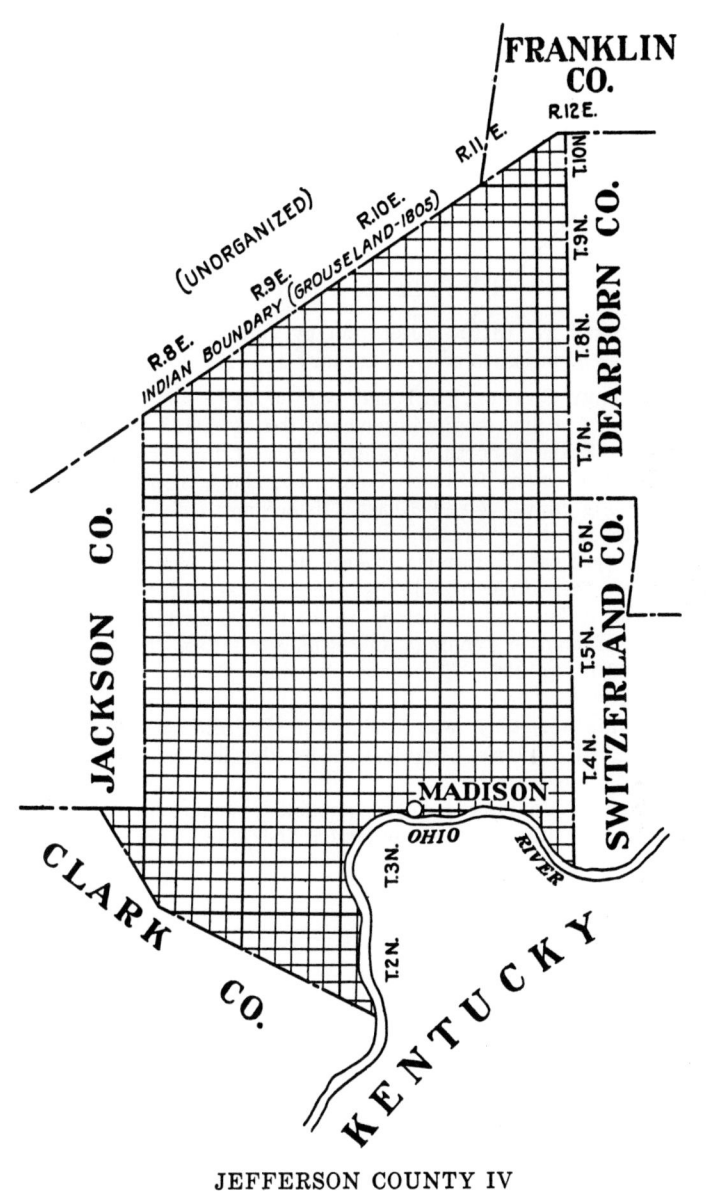

JEFFERSON COUNTY IV
[Law: Dec. 18, 1815, effective Jan. 1, 1816]

JEFFERSON COUNTY V

DECEMBER 27, 1816: Alteration by statute forming Jennings and Ripley counties, effective February 1, 1817.

BOUNDARY CHANGE: All that part of Jefferson County north and west of a line beginning where the township line dividing townships 3 and 4 north in range 7 east of the second principal meridian crosses the Jefferson County boundary, thence east to the line dividing ranges 7 and 8 east, "thence north six miles; thence east with another township line four miles; thence north two miles; thence east two miles; thence north two miles; thence east two miles; thence north two miles; thence east with the line dividing township five and six north," to the line of Switzerland County was transferred to Jennings and Ripley counties. *Laws of Indiana*, 1816-17, p. 197. See maps, Jennings County I and Ripley County I.

All this territory was under the jurisdiction of Jennings County until Ripley's organization by the law of January 14, 1818.

An act of January 1, 1817, appointed commissioners to run the boundary line between Jefferson and Clark counties. *Laws of Indiana*, 1816-17, p. 200.

JEFFERSON COUNTY BOUNDARIES

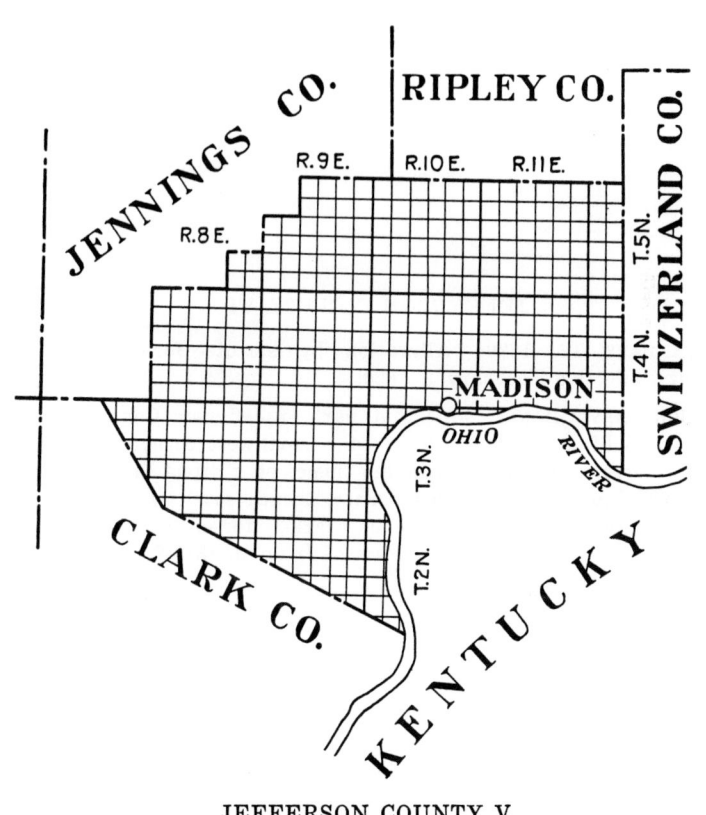

JEFFERSON COUNTY V

[Law: Dec. 27, 1816, effective Feb. 1, 1817]

JEFFERSON COUNTY VI

JANUARY 12, 1820: Alteration by statute forming Scott County, effective February 1, 1820.

BOUNDARY CHANGE: All that part of Jefferson County west and south of a line beginning at the northwest corner of township 3 north, range 8 east, running thence on a direct line through the township to its southeast corner, thence south with the line dividing ranges 8 and 9 east to the Clark-Jefferson boundary, was transferred to Scott County. *Laws of Indiana*, 1819-20, pp. 51-52. See map, Scott County I.

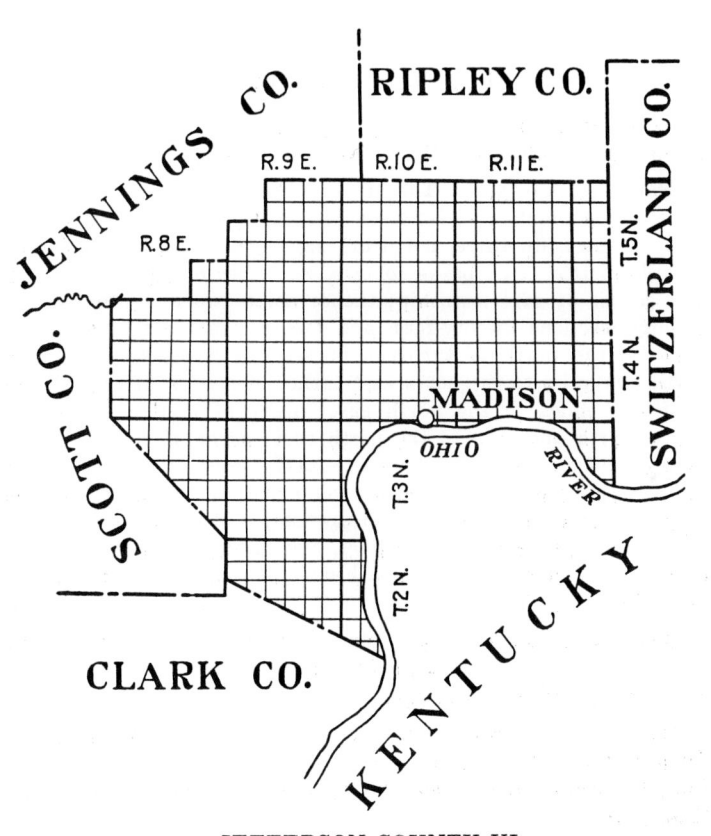

JEFFERSON COUNTY VI
[Law: Jan. 12, 1820, effective Feb. 1, 1820]

JEFFERSON COUNTY VII

JANUARY 22, 1830: Alteration by statute changing the line dividing the counties of Jefferson and Scott, effective on passage.

BOUNDARY CHANGE: The act provided that "the dividing line between the counties of Jefferson and Scott, where the same runs through township three, north of range eight east, in the Jeffersonville district, . . . be as follows, viz: Beginning at the south east corner of said township; thence north two miles to the line dividing sections twenty-four and twenty-five; thence west two miles to the north east corner of section twenty-seven; thence north two miles to the north east corner of section fifteen; thence west two miles to the north east corner of section seventeen; thence north one mile to the north east corner of section eight; thence west one mile to the north east corner of section seven; thence north one mile, to the township line; thence west one mile to the north west corner of said township: And that all the territory south and west of said lines, and formerly belonging to the county of Jefferson, be . . . attached to the county of Scott." *Laws of Indiana*, 1829-30, p. 21.

JANUARY 25, 1830: Alteration by statute attaching part of the town of Paris, which lies in Jefferson County, to the county of Jennings, effective on passage.

BOUNDARY CHANGE: The territory attached to Jennings County was "a part of the north east quarter of section number four, township number four north, in range number eight east." *Ibid.*, p. 20.

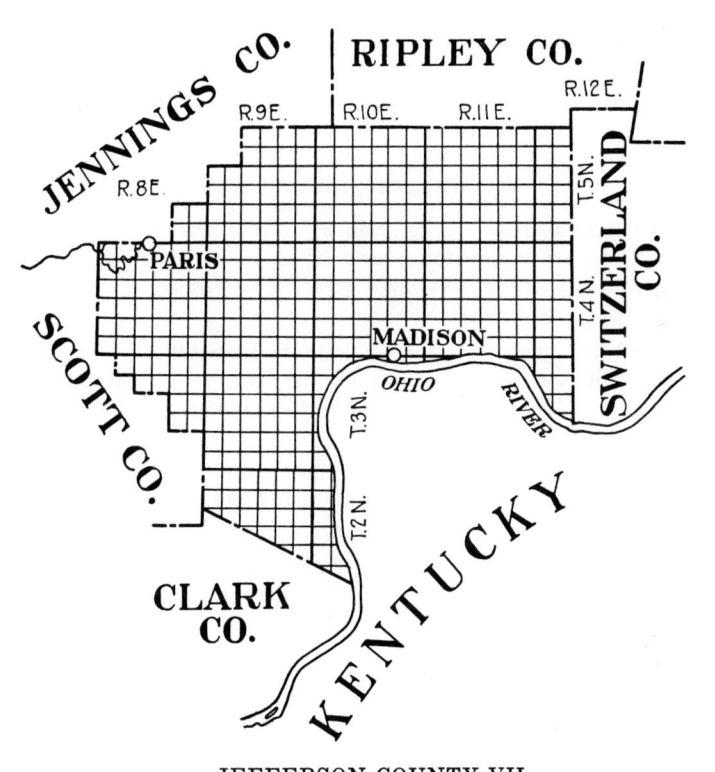

JEFFERSON COUNTY VII

[Laws: Jan. 22, 1830, effective on passage; Jan. 25, 1830, effective on passage]

JEFFERSON COUNTY VIII

FEBRUARY 6, 1835: Alteration by statute attaching the northeast quarter of section four, township four, north of range eight east, to the county of Jennings, effective on passage.

BOUNDARY CHANGE: The act provided that "all that part of the northeast quarter of section four, in township four north, of range eight east, in the county of Jefferson, be . . . attached to . . . the county of Jennings." *Laws of Indiana*, 1834-35 (general), p. 78.

FEBRUARY 8, 1836: Alteration by statute changing the line dividing the counties of Jefferson and Clark, effective on passage.

BOUNDARY CHANGE: The act described the new line between Jefferson and Clark as follows: "Beginning on the Ohio river, where the line dividing sections eighteen and nineteen, township two, range ten, strikes the same; thence west on the sectional lines to the south east conrrer of section thirteen, township two, range eight, being the south east corner of Scott county." *Ibid.*, 1835-36 (general), p. 80.

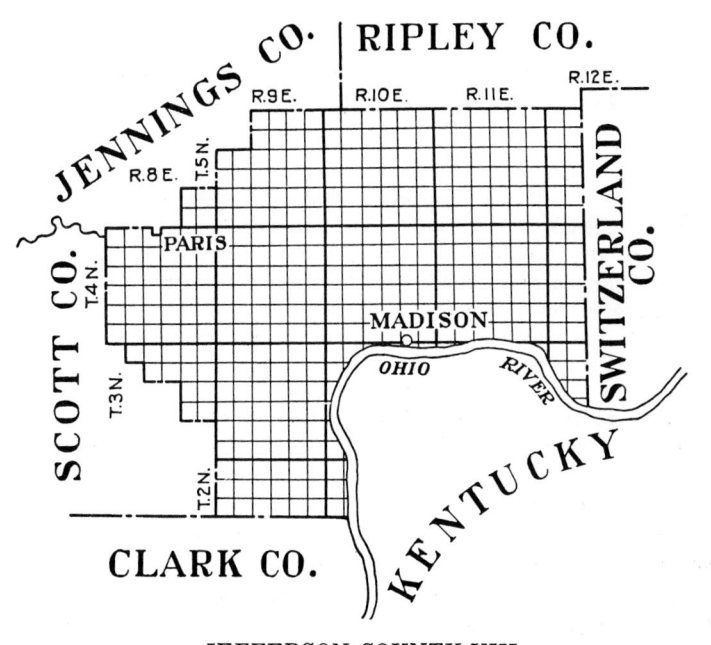

JEFFERSON COUNTY VIII

[Laws: Feb. 6, 1835, effective on passage; Feb. 8, 1836, effective on passage]

JEFFERSON COUNTY IX

FEBRUARY 2, 1837: Alteration by statute permanently fixing the line between the counties of Jefferson and Clark, effective on passage.

BOUNDARY CHANGE: The law described the permanent boundary between the two counties as follows: "Beginning at the south-east corner of section thirteen, township two north of range eight east, and running thence east with the section line dividing sections eighteen and nineteen to the north-east corner of section twenty-two in town two north, of range nine east, thence south one mile to the south-east corner of said section twenty-two, thence east one mile to south-east corner of section twenty-three, thence south on the line dividing sections twenty-five and twenty-six one half mile to the open line running through section twenty-five, in town two range nine, thence east with said open line through sections twenty-five, thirty and twenty-nine to the Ohio river." *Laws of Indiana,* 1836-37 (general), p. 98.

FEBRUARY 13, 1851: Alteration by statute detaching territory from Jefferson County, effective on passage.

BOUNDARY CHANGE: This law provided that "the south half of section five, in township number three north, of range eight east, in the county of Jefferson, be . . . attached to the county of Scott." This area is marked (a) on the map. *Ibid.,* 1850-51 (general), p. 58.

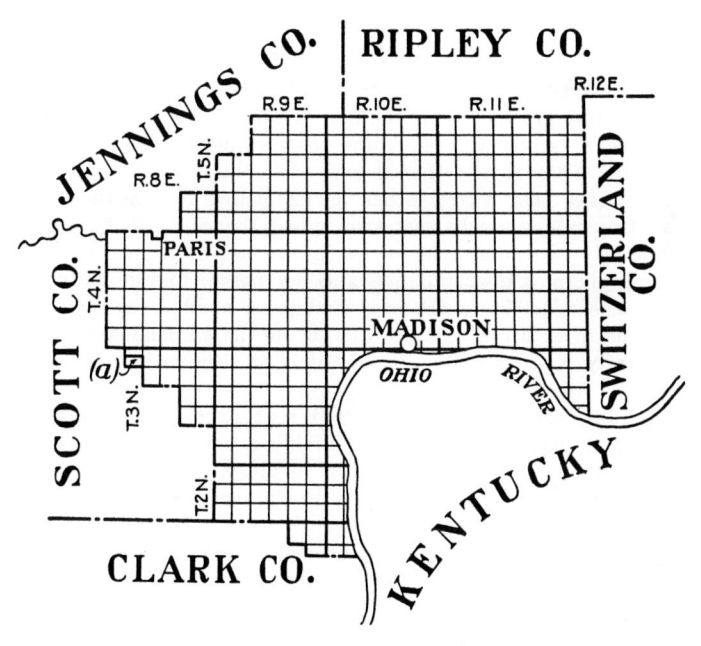

JEFFERSON COUNTY IX

[Laws: Feb. 2, 1837, effective on passage; Feb. 13, 1851, effective on passage]

JENNINGS COUNTY I

DECEMBER 27, 1816: Formation by statute, effective February 1, 1817. The formation affected Jefferson and Jackson counties.

BOUNDARIES: "Beginning on the line of the Grousland purchase, at the intersection of the line dividing ranges six and seven east; thence south with said line to the line dividing townships three and four north; thence east six miles; thence north six miles; thence east with another township line four miles; thence north two miles; thence east two miles; thence north two miles; thence east two miles; thence north two miles; thence east with the line dividing township five and six north, to the south east corner of section thirty one in township six north, range ten east; thence north with the sectional line to the Indian boundary; thence westwardly with said line to the place of beginning." *Laws of Indiana*, 1816-17, p. 197.

The law also provided that "all that part of the county of Jefferson, lying north of the line dividing townships five and six north, and east of the county hereby established; shall be attached to the county by this act formed, until the legislature think proper to erect said district into a separate county." *Ibid.*, 199. A law of January 14, 1818, organizing Ripley County, removed this territory from Jennings County's jurisdiction. See map, Ripley County I, and accompanying text.

COUNTY SEAT: Commissioners appointed in the act forming the county selected the site of Vernon as the county seat. It has never been moved, though there have been attempts to secure a relocation. *Laws of Indiana*, 1816-17, p. 198; *Biographical and Historical Souvenir for the Counties of Clark . . . Jennings . . .*, 225-26; Shockley, "County Seat Wars," *op. cit.*, 10:no.1:9.

JENNINGS COUNTY BOUNDARIES 507

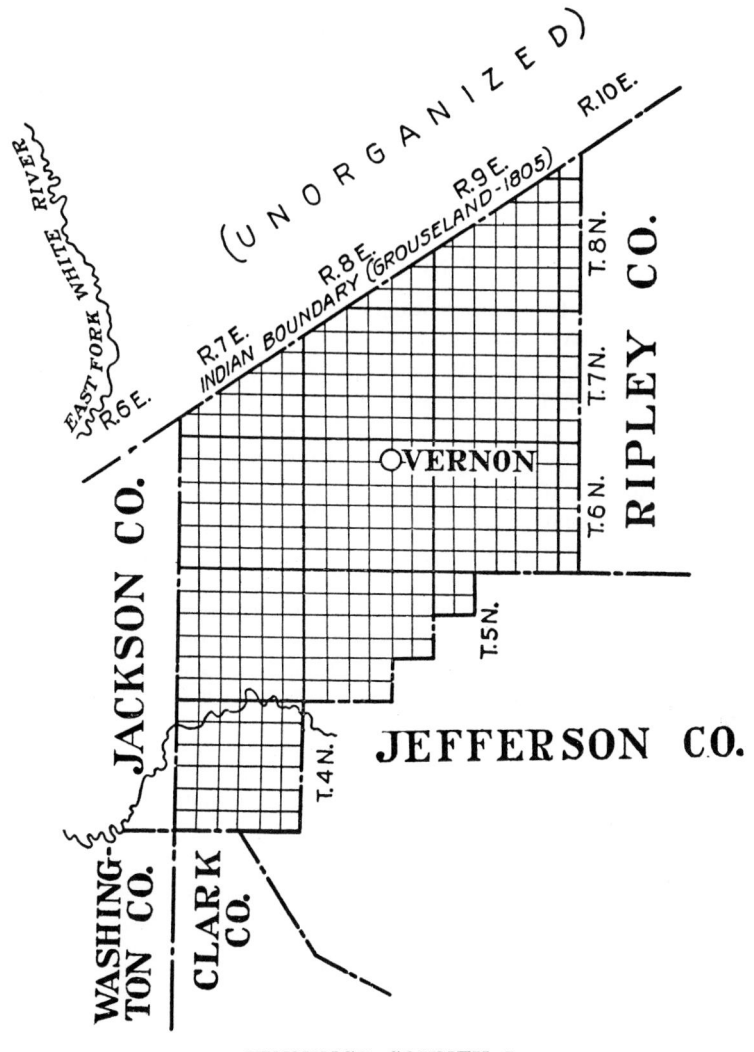

JENNINGS COUNTY I
[Law: Dec. 27, 1816, effective Feb. 1, 1817]

JENNINGS COUNTY II

JANUARY 12, 1820: Alteration by statute forming Scott County, effective February 1, 1820.

BOUNDARY CHANGE: All that part of Jennings County south of the Muscatatuck River in range 7 east of the second principal meridian, was transferred to Scott County. *Laws of Indiana*, 1819-20, pp. 51-52. See map, Scott County I.

JANUARY 20, 1820: Alteration by statute, attaching territory to Jennings County.

BOUNDARY CHANGE: The act attached to Jennings County "all that part of the . . . new purchase, lying south of a line drawn due west, from the line dividing the Grouseland purchase, from the said new purchase, through the centre of town eight, until it intersects the range line dividing ranges six and seven, (east of the second principal meridian) and east of said range line." *Laws of Indiana*, 1819-20, pp. 95-96.

By the law of January 20, 1820, concurrent jurisdiction over Delaware County was given to Jennings County, along with Jackson, Ripley, Franklin, and other counties bounding Delaware County. *Laws of Indiana*, 1819-20, p. 96.

JENNINGS COUNTY BOUNDARIES 509

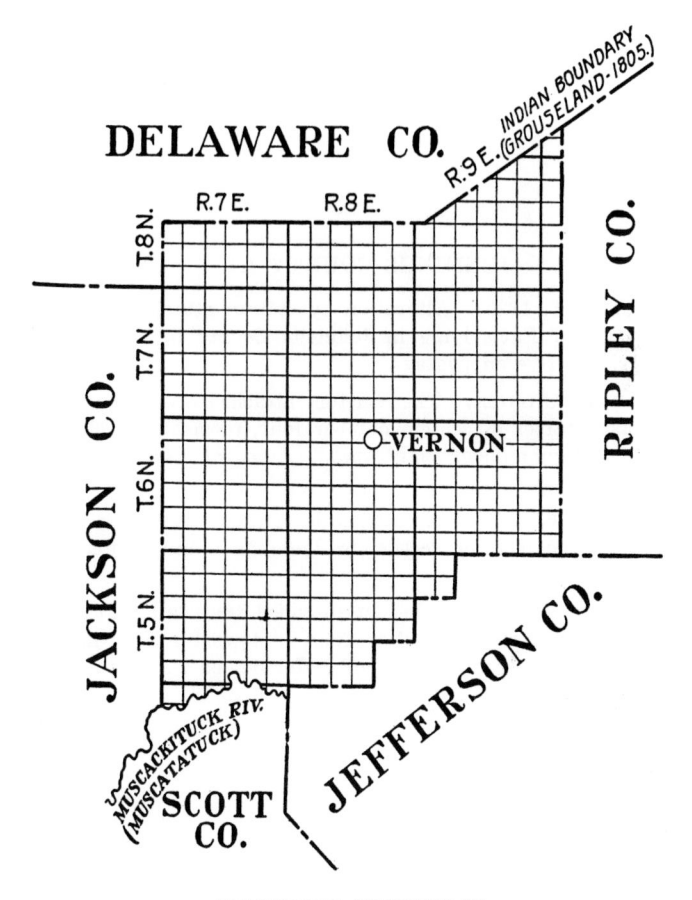

JENNINGS COUNTY II

[Laws: Jan. 12, 1820, effective Feb. 1, 1820; Jan. 20, 1820]

JENNINGS COUNTY III

JANUARY 25, 1830: Alteration by statute attaching that part of the town of Paris lying in Jefferson County to the county of Jennings, effective on passage.

BOUNDARY CHANGE: The territory attached was "a part of the north east quarter of section number four, township number four north, in range number eight east." *Laws of Indiana*, 1829-30, p. 20.

FEBRUARY 6, 1835: Alteration by statute attaching the remainder of the quarter section to Jennings County, effective on passage.

BOUNDARY CHANGE: The act provided that "all that part of the northeast quarter of section four, in township four north, of range eight east, in the county of Jefferson, be . . . attached to" Jennings County. *Ibid.*, 1834-35 (general), p. 78.

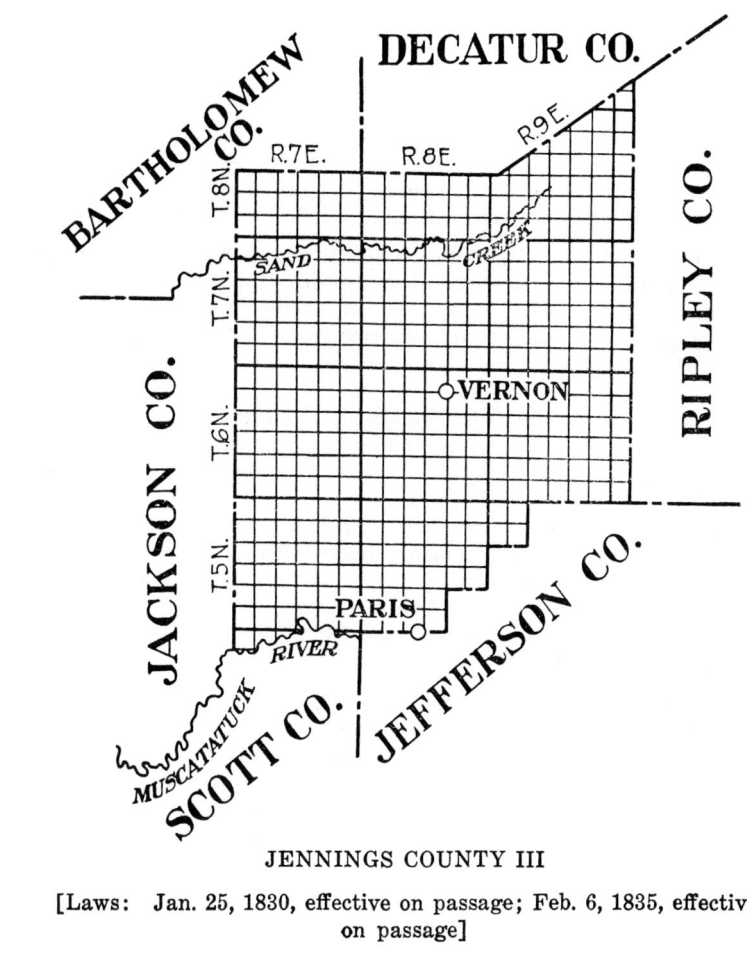

JENNINGS COUNTY III

[Laws: Jan. 25, 1830, effective on passage; Feb. 6, 1835, effective on passage]

JOHNSON COUNTY

DECEMBER 31, 1822: Formation by statute, effective May 5, 1823. The formation affected Delaware County, New Purchase.

BOUNDARIES: "Beginning at the south west [east] corner of section thirty four, in town eleven, north of range five east, the same being the south west corner of Shelby county: thence running north with the line of said county, to the south east corner of Marion county; thence west to the north east corner of Morgan county; thence south with the line of said county, to the township line dividing townships ten and eleven; thence east with said line to the place of beginning, shall constitute and form a new county, which shall be called, and designated by the name of Johnson." *Laws of Indiana*, 1822-23, p. 22.

The error in the description, corrected above in brackets, was repeated in the county boundary description as given in the *Revised Laws* for 1824 and 1831. A law of February 2, 1832, made the necessary correction, and restated the entire boundaries. *Revised Laws of Indiana*, 1823-24, p. 98; 1830-31, p. 123; *Laws of Indiana*, 1831-32, p. 267.

COUNTY SEAT: Commissioners appointed under the act forming the county met in May, 1823, and selected the site of Franklin as the county seat. It has never been removed. *Ibid.*, 1822-23, p. 22; Branigin, *History of Johnson County*, 524; *History of Johnson County*, 682-83; Banta, D. D., *Historical Sketch of Johnson County, Indiana*, 31 (Chicago, 1881).

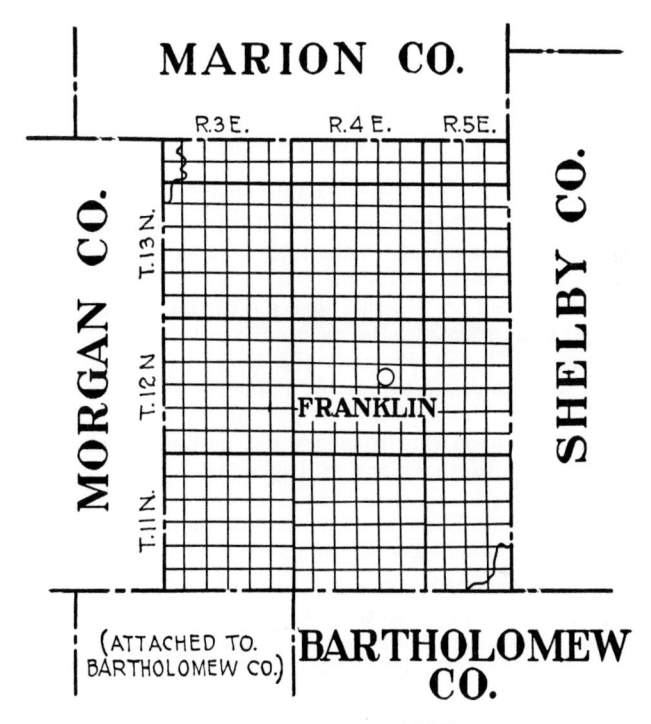

JOHNSON COUNTY BOUNDARIES 513

JOHNSON COUNTY
[Law: Dec. 31, 1822, effective May 5, 1823]

KNOX COUNTY I
[Northwest Territory]

JUNE 20, 1790: Formation by proclamation.

BOUNDARIES: "Beginning at the standing stone Forks of the Great Miami River and down the said river to the confluence with the Ohio River, thence with the Ohio River to the small stream or rivulet above Fort Massac, thence with the eastern boundary line of St. Clair county to the mouth of the Little Michilmacinack, thence up the Illinois River to the Forks or confluence of the Theokiki and Chicago; thence by a line to be drawn due north to the boundary line of the Territory of the United States, and so far easterly upon said boundary line as that a due south line may be drawn to the place of beginning." *St. Clair Papers*, 2:166 n.

Standing Stone Forks is at the site of the village of Loramie, Shelby County, Ohio. Emmerson (comp.), *Counties of Illinois*, 6.

COUNTY SEAT: When this area was part of the County of Illinois, under the commonwealth of Virginia, courts had been established at Vincennes. They continued to be held there after the formation of Knox County. See *History of Knox and Daviess Counties*, 168-70.

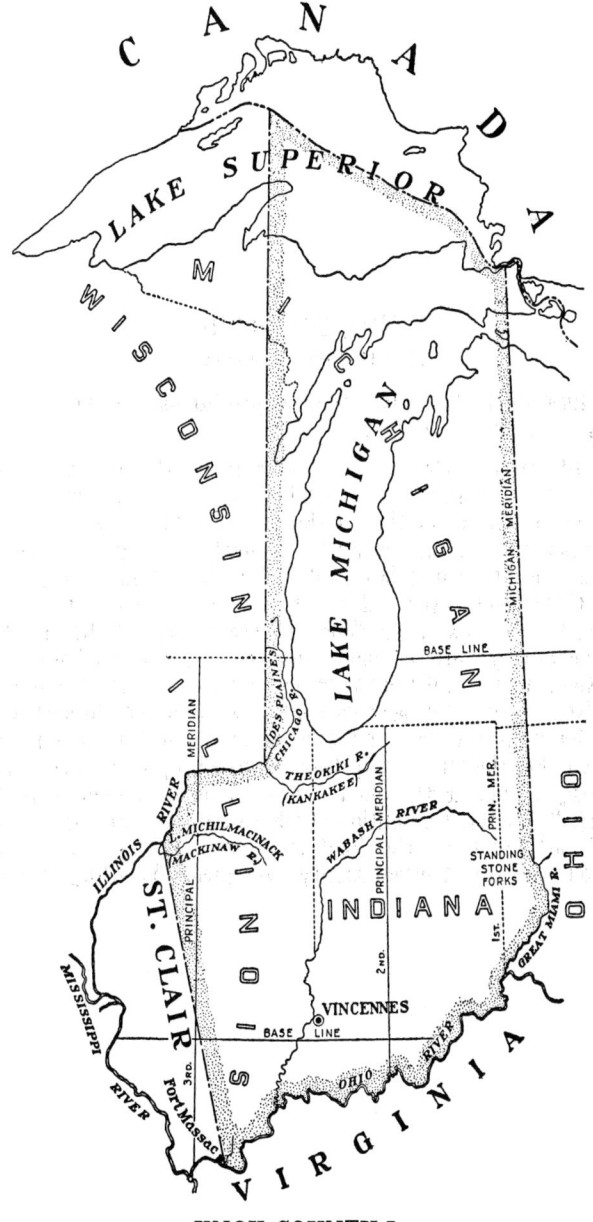

KNOX COUNTY I

[Proclamation: June 20, 1790]

KNOX COUNTY II
[Northwest Territory]

AUGUST 15, 1796: Alteration by proclamation forming Wayne County, Northwest Territory.

BOUNDARY CHANGE: The proclamation of August 15, 1796, gave to Wayne County all that part of Knox County east and north of a line drawn from the southernmost part of Lake Michigan southeastwardly to the southwestern part of the portage between the Wabash and the Miamis of Lake Erie, where Fort Wayne stood; thence southeastwardly to the southern part of the portage between the Miamis of the Ohio and the St. Mary's River; thence southeastwardly until it would intersect the eastern boundary of Knox County; also all that territory north and east of a line running from "the most southern part of Lake Michigan; thence along the western shores of the same, to the northwest part thereof, (including the lands upon the streams emptying into said lake); thence by a due north line to the territorial boundary in Lake Superior." Laning, "Evolution of Ohio Counties," in *Ohio Archaeological and Historical Publications*, 5:333. For text of the proclamation, see map, Wayne County, Northwest Territory, page 217.

KNOX COUNTY BOUNDARIES 517

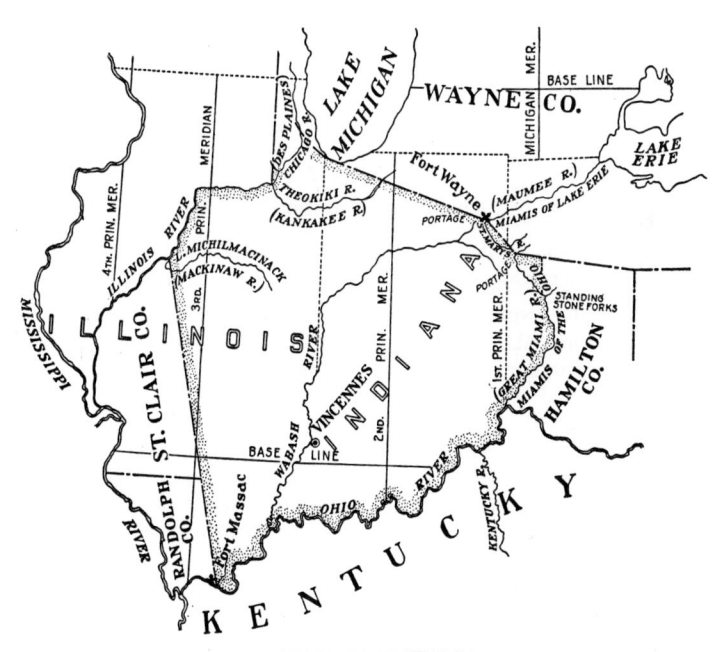

KNOX COUNTY II

[Proclamation: Aug. 15, 1796]

KNOX COUNTY III
[Northwest Territory]

JUNE 22, 1798: Alteration by proclamation extending Hamilton County, Northwest Territory.

BOUNDARY CHANGE: All that part of Knox County east of a line drawn from "the spot, on the bank of the Ohio river where the general boundary line of the United States and the Indian tribes, established at Greenville the third day of August, 1795, intersects the bank of that river," and running "with that general boundary line to Fort Recovery, and from thence by a line to be drawn due north from Fort Recovery, until it intersects the southern boundary line of the county of Wayne" was given to Hamilton County. Laning, "Evolution of Ohio Counties," *op. cit.*, 5:337.

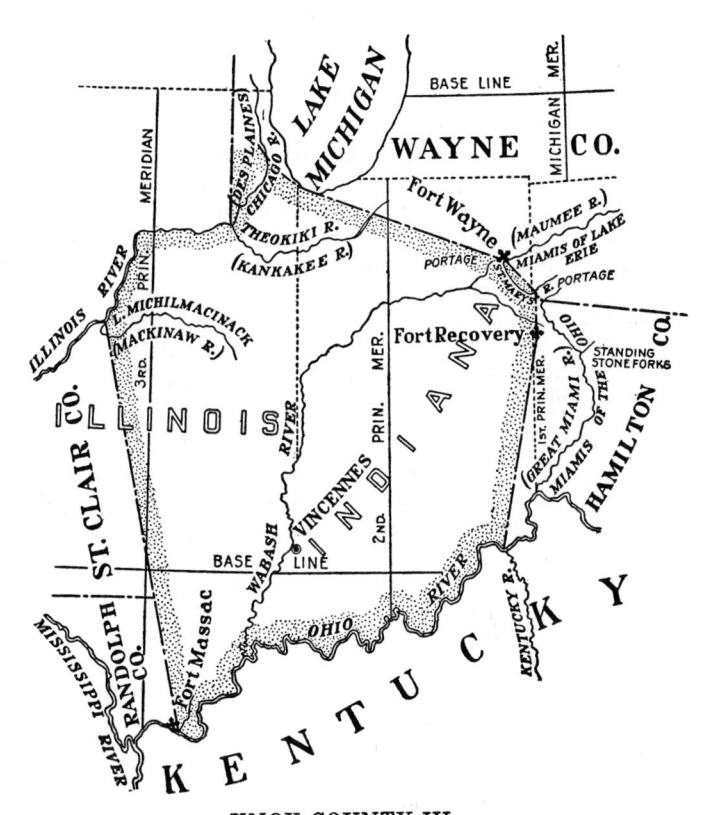

KNOX COUNTY III

[Proclamation: June 22, 1798]

KNOX COUNTY IV
[Indiana Territory]

FEBRUARY 3, 1801: Alteration by proclamation forming Clark County, Indiana Territory.

BOUNDARY CHANGE: All that part of Knox County east of a line "beginning at the Ohio river at the mouth of Blew River, thence up the said River to the Crossing of the same by the Road leading from Saint Vincennes to Clarks ville, thence by a direct line to the nearest part of White River thence up the said River and that branch thereof which runs toward Fort Recovery, and from the head springs of said branch to Fort Recovery," was transferred to Clark County. Territorial *Executive Journal*, 97.

For location of the crossing of Blue River, see text with map, Clark County I.

FEBRUARY 3, 1801: Alteration by proclamation.

BOUNDARIES: "The County of Knox shall be bounded by the Ohio from the great Cave above mentioned to the mouth of blue River, thence up the said River and along the lines and boundaries seperating the said County of Knox from the County of Clarke, in their whole extent to Fort Recovery, thence along the line seperating the Indiana from the North Westrn Territory, until it will intersect a line drawn North East from the mouth of the great Kennoumic River aforesaid and along the said Line to the mouth of the Great Kennoumic River thence by a line running from the mouth of said River so as to strike the point of Intersection formed by a line drawn due east through the sink Hole spring above mentioned and a line drawn due north from the great cave above mentioned and along the last mentioned line to the said great Cave the place of Beginning." Territorial *Executive Journal*, 99-100.

For location of Great Cave and Sink Hole Spring, see page 204.

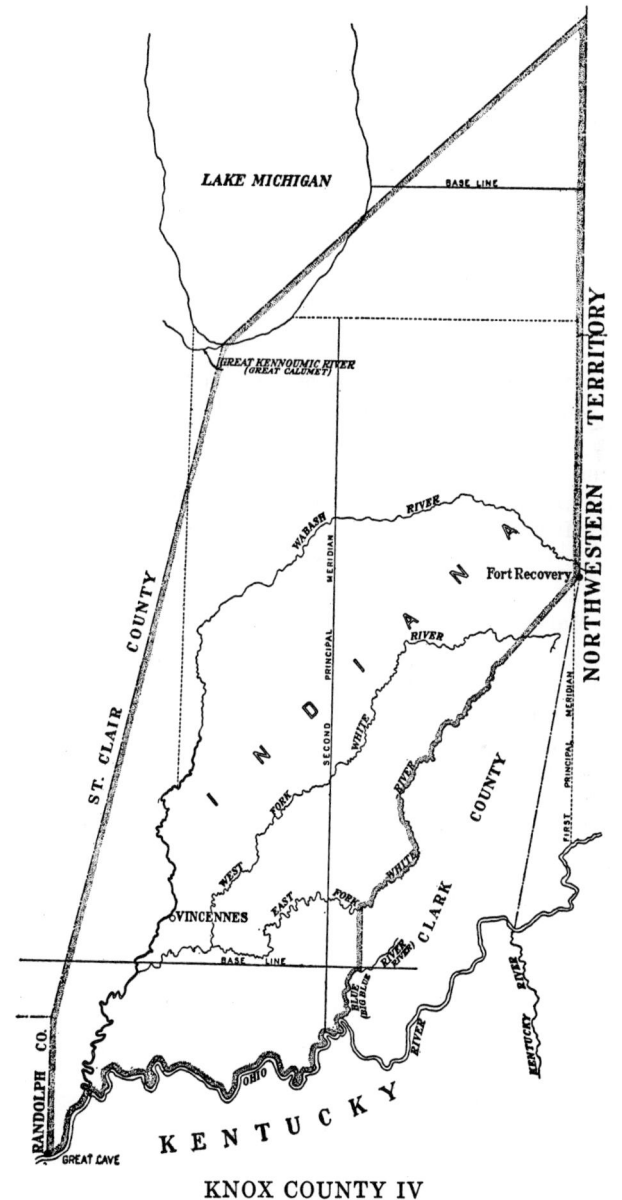

KNOX COUNTY IV

[Proclamation: Feb. 3, 1801]

KNOX COUNTY V
[Indiana Territory]

JANUARY 24, 1803: Alteration by proclamation forming Wayne County, Indiana Territory, effective upon admission of Ohio to the Union.

BOUNDARY CHANGE: All that part of Knox County north of "an East and west line passing through the Southerly Extreame of Lake Michigan" was transferred to Wayne County, Indiana Territory. Territorial *Executive Journal*, 115.

APRIL 20, 1802: Alteration by formation of the State of Ohio, effective March 1, 1803.

BOUNDARY CHANGE: All that part of Knox County east of "a line drawn due north from the mouth of the Great Miami" and south of the boundary of Wayne County was transferred to the State of Ohio. *Annals*, 7 Congress, 1 session, 1349.

This transfer moved the eastern boundary of Knox County between one and a half and two miles west of Fort Recovery. For a statement concerning the date of Ohio's formation, see pages 4-5.

KNOX COUNTY BOUNDARIES 523

KNOX COUNTY V

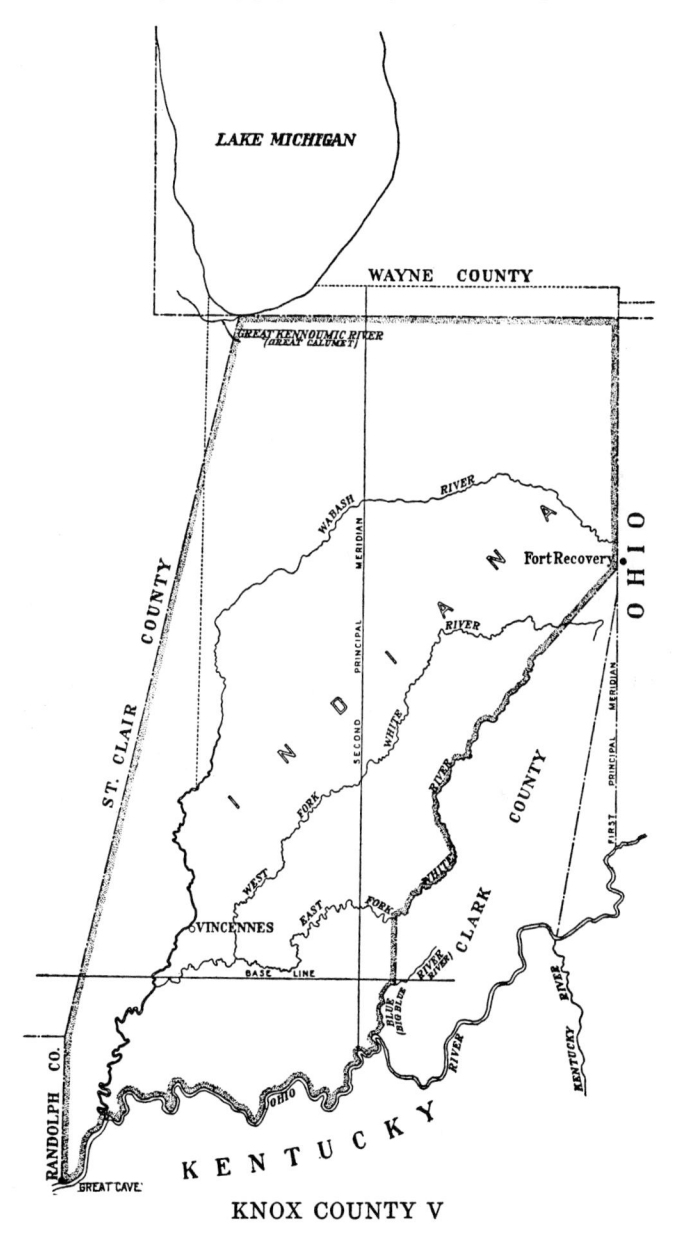

[Proclamation: Jan. 24, 1803, effective upon admission of Ohio to the Union; Act of Congress, Apr. 20, 1802, effective Mar. 1, 1803]

KNOX COUNTY VI
[Indiana Territory]

OCTOBER 11, 1808: Alteration by statute forming Harrison County, Indiana Territory, effective December 1, 1808.

BOUNDARY CHANGE: All that part of Knox County south and east of a line beginning "at the point on the river Ohio, where the meredian line from which the ranges take number, strikes the same, thence due north to the present Indian boundary line, thence with the said boundary line" to the old Clark County boundary, was transferred to Harrison County. *Acts of Indiana Territory*, 1808, p. 3. See map, Harrison County I.

The line of the Grouseland Treaty, 1805, is the Indian boundary mentioned.

KNOX COUNTY VI

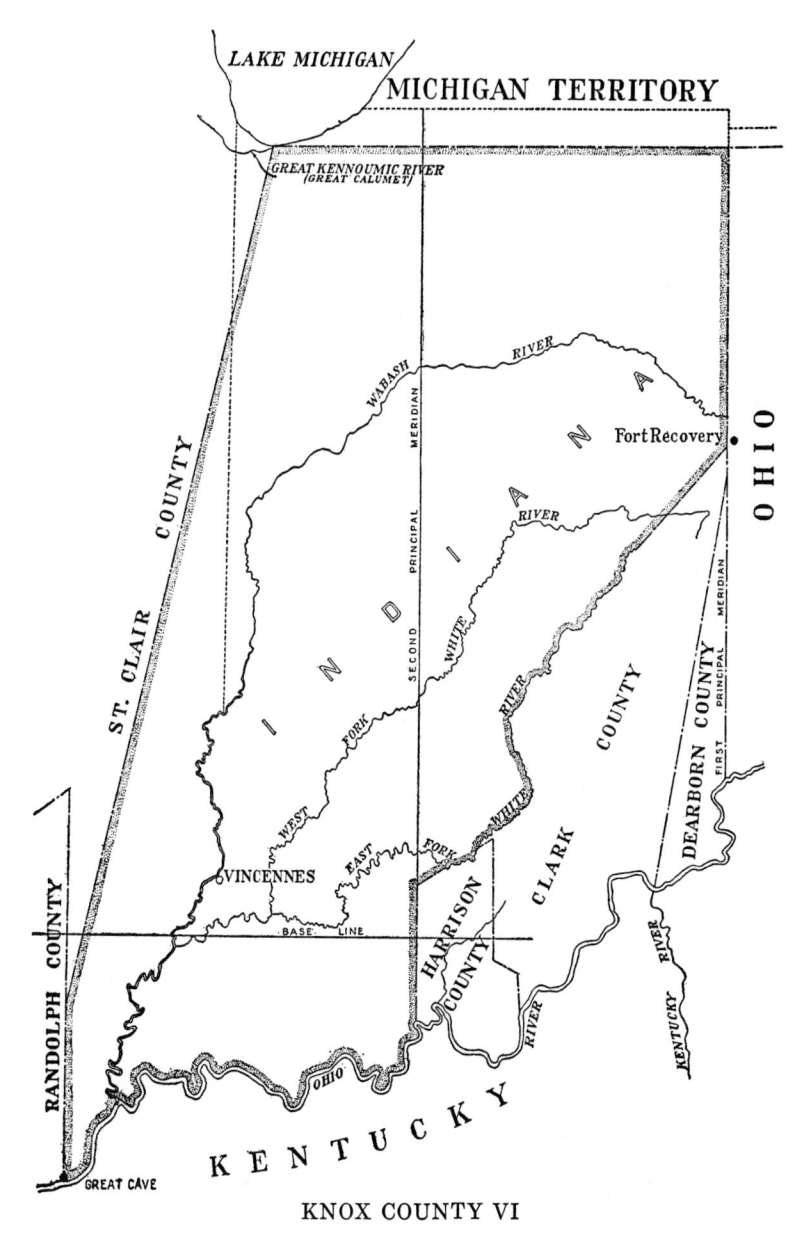

[Law: Oct. 11, 1808, effective Dec. 1, 1808]

KNOX COUNTY VII
[Indiana Territory]

FEBRUARY 3, 1809: Alteration by act of Congress forming Illinois Territory, effective March 1, 1809.

BOUNDARY CHANGE: All that part of Knox County lying "west of the Wabash river, and a direct line drawn from the Wabash river and Post Vincennes, due north to the territorial line between the United States and Canada," was transferred to Illinois Territory. *Annals,* 10 Congress, 2 session, 1808.

KNOX COUNTY BOUNDARIES 527

KNOX COUNTY VII

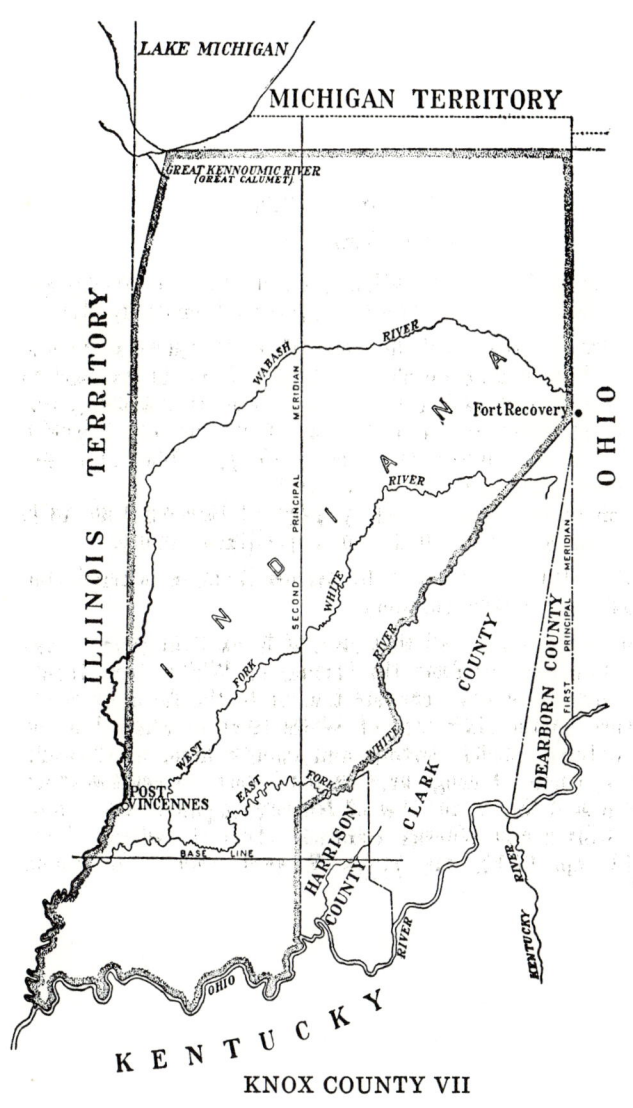

[Act of Congress: Feb. 3, 1809, effective Mar. 1, 1809]

KNOX COUNTY VIII
[Indiana Territory]

NOVEMBER 27, 1810: Alteration by statute forming Wayne and Franklin counties, Indiana Territory, effective January 1, 1811.

BOUNDARY CHANGE: All that part of Knox County south and east of the Twelve Mile Purchase boundary from its intersection with the Ohio boundary line to the Clark County boundary, was removed from Knox at the formation of Wayne and Franklin counties. *Acts of Indiana Territory*, 1810, pp. 19-20, 114. See maps, Franklin County I, Wayne County I.

Jefferson County was formed by a law of November 23, 1810, effective January 1, 1811. It did not affect Knox County.

MARCH 9, 1813: Alteration by statute forming Warrick and Gibson counties, Indiana Territory.

BOUNDARY CHANGE: All that part of Knox County south and east of a line running from the "mouth of White river, thence up White river with the meanders thereof to the forks of White river, thence up the East fork of White river to where the line between sections number twenty and twenty nine, in township number one, north, of range number four, west, strikes the same, thence with said line to the line of Harrison county," was transferred to Gibson and Warrick counties. *Acts of Indiana Territory*, 1813, pp. 67-68. See maps, Warrick County I, Gibson County I.

KNOX COUNTY VIII

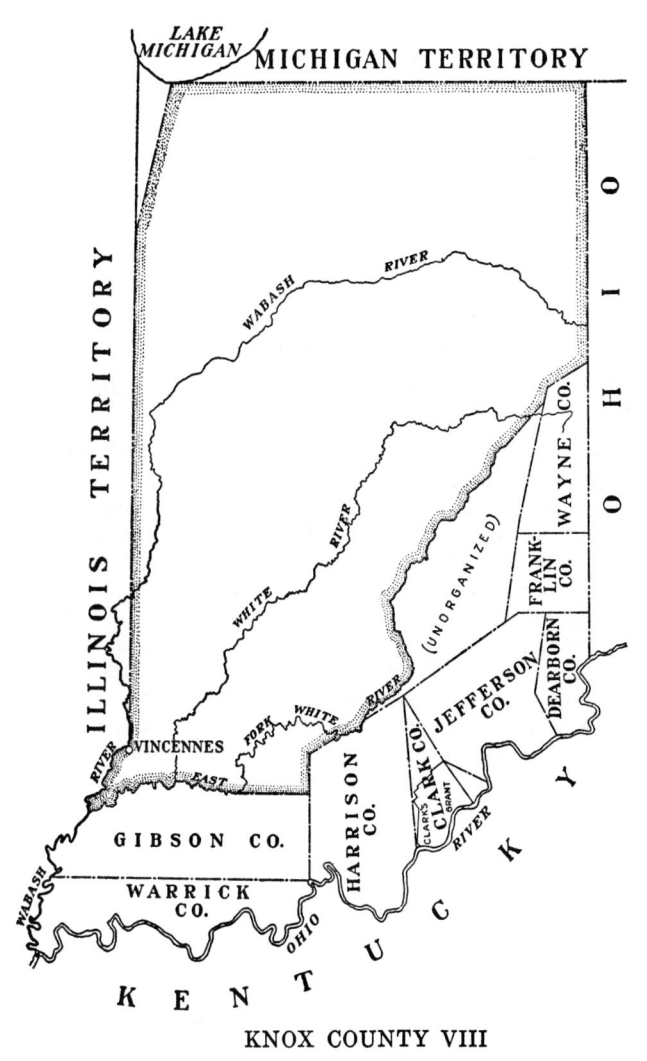

[Laws: Nov. 27, 1810, effective Jan. 1, 1811; Mar. 9, 1813]

KNOX COUNTY IX
[Indiana Territory]

SEPTEMBER 1, 1814: Alteration by statute extending the bounds of Washington County.

BOUNDARY CHANGE: All that part of Knox County "begining at Freeman's corner on the meridian line, thence north to the present Indian boundary line, thence with said Indian boundary to the line established by the treaty of Grousland, thence with said line to the place of beginning," was transferred to Washington County. *Acts of Indiana Territory*, 1814, p. 15.

The county of Washington had been formed by a law of December 21, 1813; its formation did not affect Knox County, however. Freeman's corner, mentioned above, was the northeast corner of the Vincennes purchase, made at Fort Wayne in 1803. The corner was named for Thomas Freeman, who made the survey. The "present Indian boundary line" referred to was the north boundary of the purchase made at Fort Wayne on September 30, 1809.

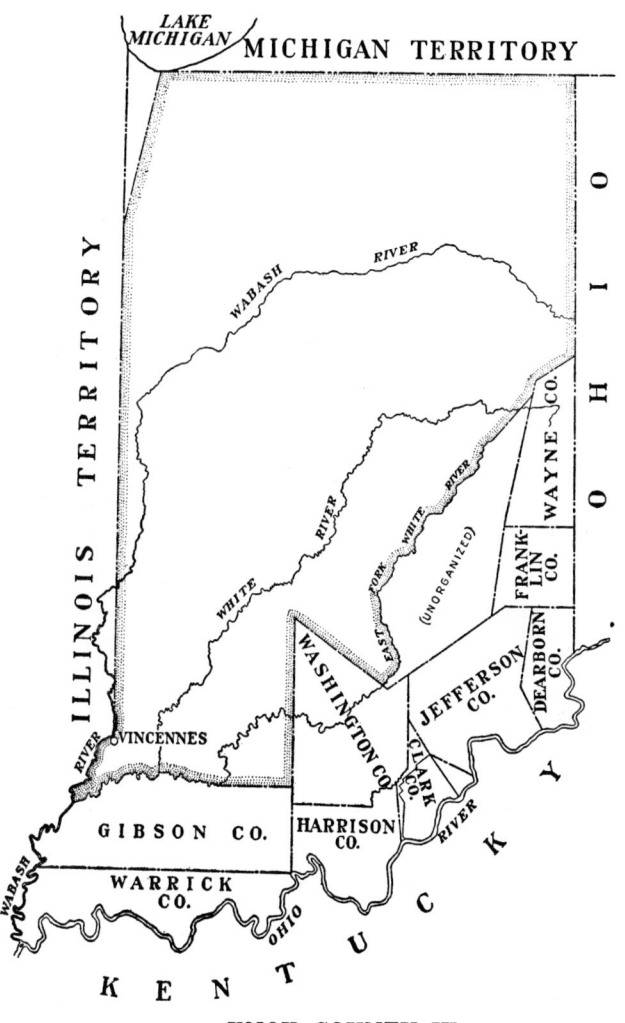

KNOX COUNTY IX
[Law: Sep. 1, 1814]

KNOX COUNTY X
[Indiana Territory]

DECEMBER 26, 1815: Alteration by statute forming Orange County, Indiana Territory, effective February 1, 1816.

BOUNDARY CHANGE: All that part of Knox County to the east and south of a line beginning where the northern boundary of Gibson County is intersected by "the range line dividing ranges two and three west of the second principal meridian," running thence north with the range line to the Fort Wayne Treaty line of 1809, thence with the treaty line southeastwardly to the second principal meridian, was transferred to Orange County. *Acts of Indiana Territory*, 1815, pp. 57-58. See map, Orange County I.

Knox County was not affected by the formation of Switzerland County, September 7, 1814, effective October 1, 1814, of Perry and Posey counties on September 7, 1814, effective November 1, 1814, or of Jackson County, December 18, 1815, effective January 1, 1816.

KNOX COUNTY X

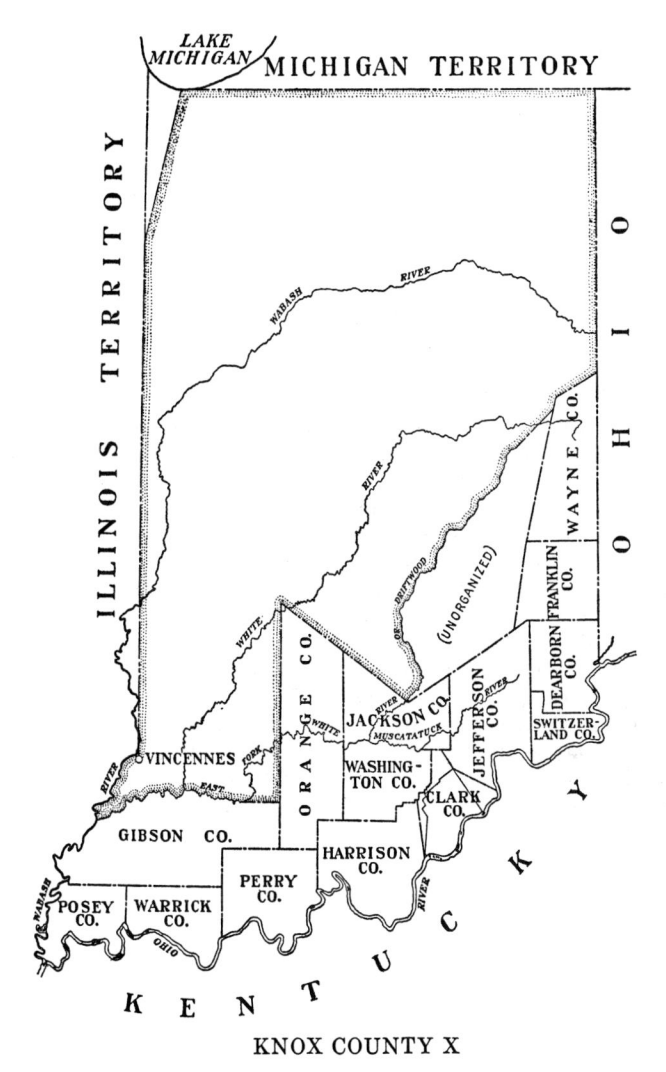

[Law: Dec. 26, 1815, effective Feb. 1, 1816]

KNOX COUNTY XI

DECEMBER 30, 1816: Alteration by statute forming Sullivan County, effective January 15, 1817.

BOUNDARY CHANGE: All that part of Knox County within the following boundaries was transferred to Sullivan County: "Beginning on the Wabash river, where the line dividing township five, and six, crosses the same; running thence east, with said line, until it strikes the west fork of White river; thence up the said west fork of said river, to the Orange county line; thence with said line, to the Indian boundary line; thence with said boundary line, crossing the Wabash river, to the line dividing the state of Indiana, and the Illinois territory; thence with said line south, to the Wabash river; thence down the said river, with the meanders thereof to the place of beginning." *Laws of Indiana*, 1816-17, p. 205.

Sullivan County cut a large block of territory out of the middle of the old Knox County, leaving two disjoined areas both of which had belonged to the original Knox County. The county organization persisted only in the southern area.

KNOX COUNTY XI

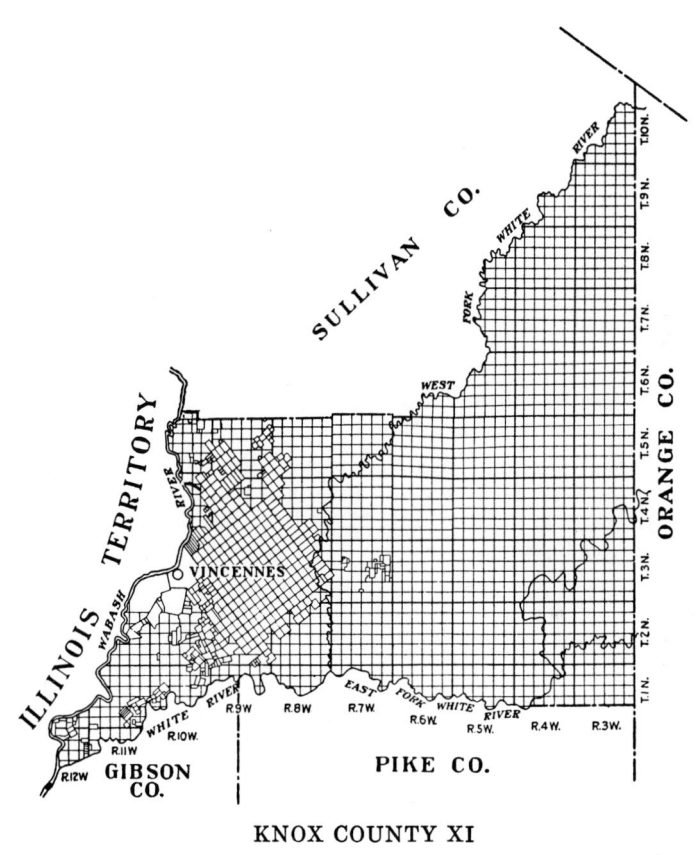

[Law: Dec. 30, 1816, effective Jan. 15, 1817]

KNOX COUNTY XII

DECEMBER 24, 1816: Alteration by statute forming Daviess County, effective February 15, 1817.

BOUNDARY CHANGE: All that part of Knox County east and south of the West Fork of White River was transferred to Daviess County. *Laws of Indiana*, 1816-17, p. 192. See text of law, with map, Daviess County I.

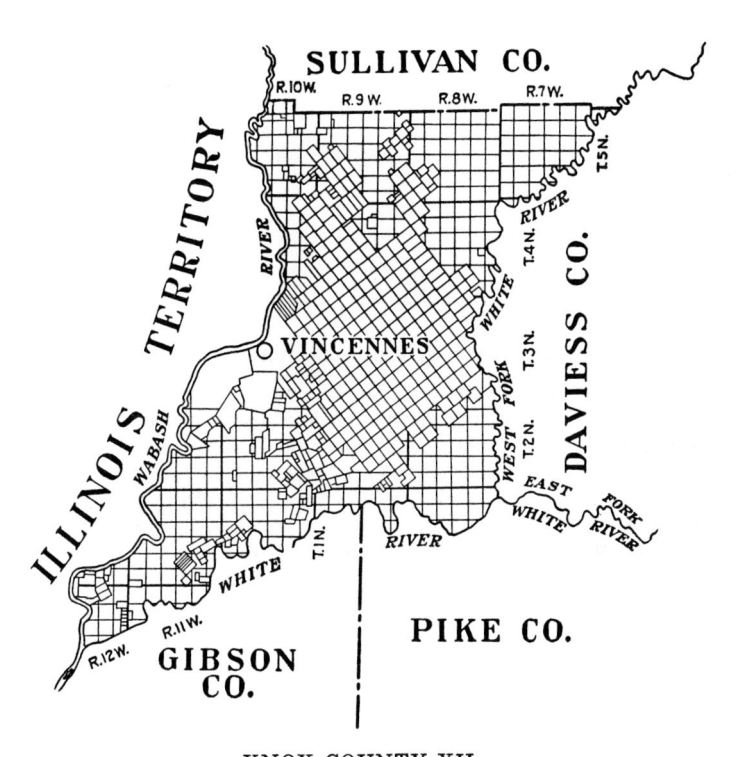

KNOX COUNTY XII

[Law: Dec. 24, 1816, effective Feb. 15, 1817]

KNOX COUNTY XIII

1842-43: Alteration by statute defining county boundaries.

BOUNDARIES: "Beginning at the west branch of White river where the line dividing townships five and six north crosses the same, thence west with said township line to the line dividing ranges nine and ten west, thence due west to the Wabash river, with the meanders thereof, to the mouth of White river, then up the same, with the meanders thereof, to the place of beginning." *Revised Statutes of Indiana*, 1842-43, p. 81.

KNOX COUNTY XIII
[Law: 1842-43]

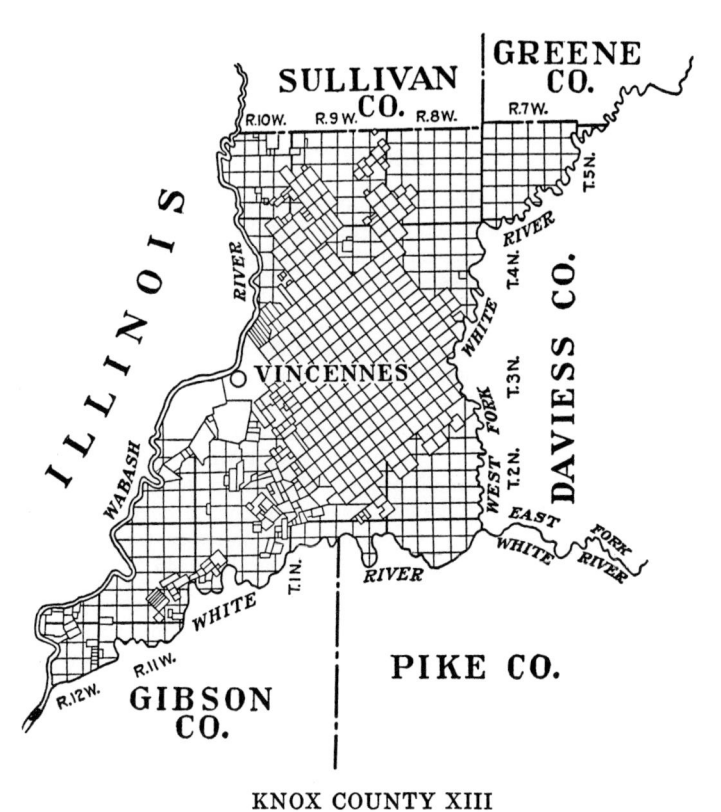

KOSCIUSKO COUNTY I

FEBRUARY 7, 1835: Formation by statute, effective on publication. The formation affected territory attached to Cass and Elkhart counties. Kosciusko was organized by a law of February 4, 1836, effective June 1, 1836.

BOUNDARIES: "Beginning at the north west corner of section three in township thirty four north, of range four east, thence east with the line dividing townships thirty four and thirty five north, twenty one miles, thence south twenty seven miles, to the south east corner of section thirteen, township thirty north, of range seven east, thence west through the centre of township thirty north, to the south east corner of section sixteen in township thirty north, of range four east twenty one miles, thence north through the middle of range four east twenty seven miles to the place of beginning." *Laws of Indiana*, 1834-35 (general), p. 45.

COUNTY SEAT: Commissioners appointed in the act organizing the county selected a site in the center of the county as the seat of government. The town of Warsaw was laid out. Previous to its selection, courts had been held at the town of Leesburg, about six miles north of Warsaw. *Ibid.*, 1835-36 (general), pp. 55-56; Royse (ed.), *History of Kosciusko County*, 1:116-17.

KOSCIUSKO COUNTY BOUNDARIES 541

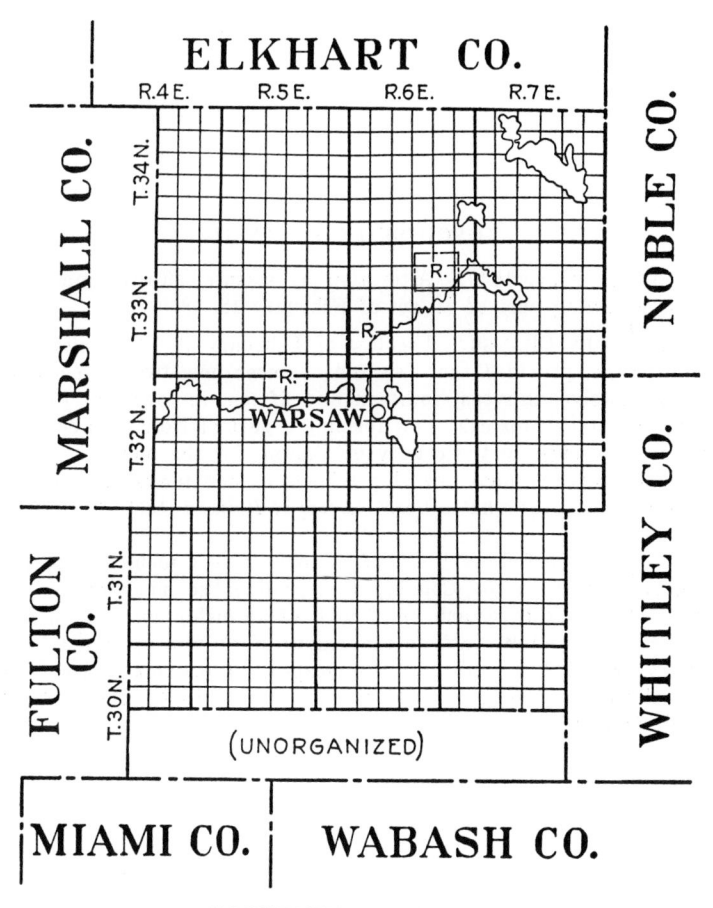

KOSCIUSKO COUNTY I

[Law: Feb. 7, 1835, effective on publication]

KOSCIUSKO COUNTY II

FEBRUARY 24, 1840: Alteration by statute, effective on passage, repealing part of an act of February 18, 1839.

BOUNDARY CHANGE: The law of February 18, 1839, effective on passage, provided that "sections number one, two, three, ten, eleven, twelve, thirteen, fourteen and fifteen, in township thirty, north of range four east, now forming a part of Kosciusko county, be . . . attached to the county of Fulton, for the purpose of organizing congressional township schools in said township, and for no other purposes whatsoever." *Laws of Indiana*, 1838-39 (local), p. 336.

The law of February 24, 1840, made this attachment an integral part of Fulton County, by repealing "so much of an act entitled an act to attach one-fourth of township number thirty, north of range four east, to the county of Fulton, approved February 18, 1839, as says for the purpose of organizing congressional township schools and for no other purpose whatsoever." *Ibid.*, 1839-40 (local), p. 229.

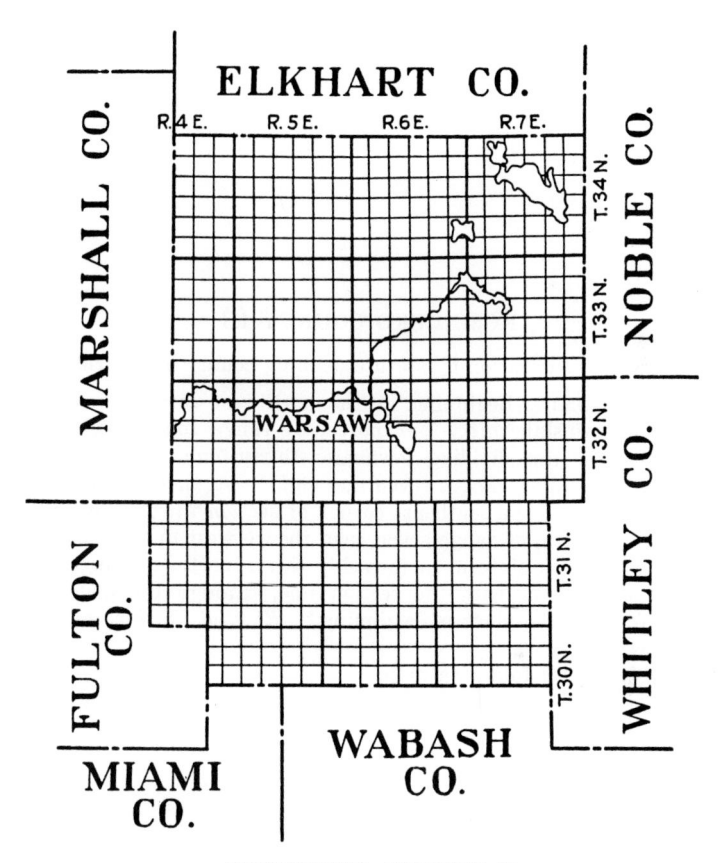

KOSCIUSKO COUNTY II

[Law: Feb. 24, 1840, effective on passage]

KOSCIUSKO COUNTY III

1842-43: Alteration by statute defining county boundaries.

BOUNDARIES: "Beginning at the northwest corner of section three, in township thirty-four north, of range four east, thence east with the line dividing townships thirty-four and thirty-five, to the line dividing ranges seven and eight east, thence south with the range line to the southeast corner of section thirteen, in township thirty north, of range seven east, thence west to the southeast corner of section sixteen, in township thirty north, of range four east, thence north with the section line, through the middle of range four, to the place of beginning." *Revised Statutes of Indiana*, 1842-43, p. 88.

See text with following map.

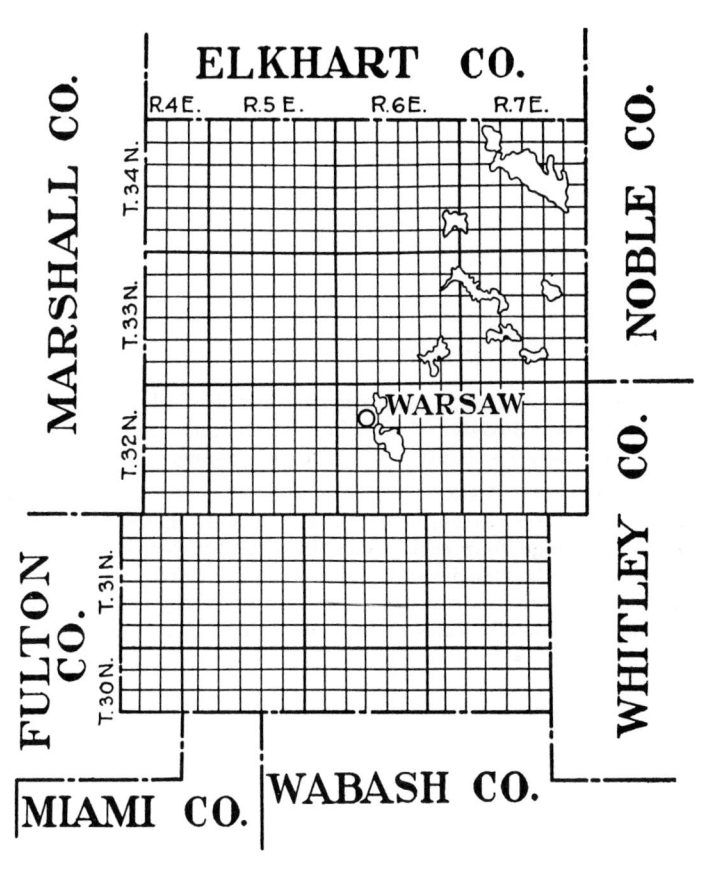

KOSCIUSKO COUNTY III
[Law: 1842-43]

KOSCIUSKO COUNTY IV

JANUARY 13, 1846: Alteration by statute declaring a mistake in the *Revised Statutes* of 1843 in relation to the boundary of Fulton and Kosciusko counties, effective on passage.

BOUNDARY CHANGE: "Sections number one, two, three, ten, eleven, twelve, thirteen, fourteen, and fifteen, in township thirty, north of range four east, which by the statutes of 1843, is included in the boundaries of Kosciusko . . . is hereby declared to be a mistake, and . . . said territory . . . is hereby attached to the county of Fulton." *Laws of Indiana*, 1845-46 (general), pp. 87-88.

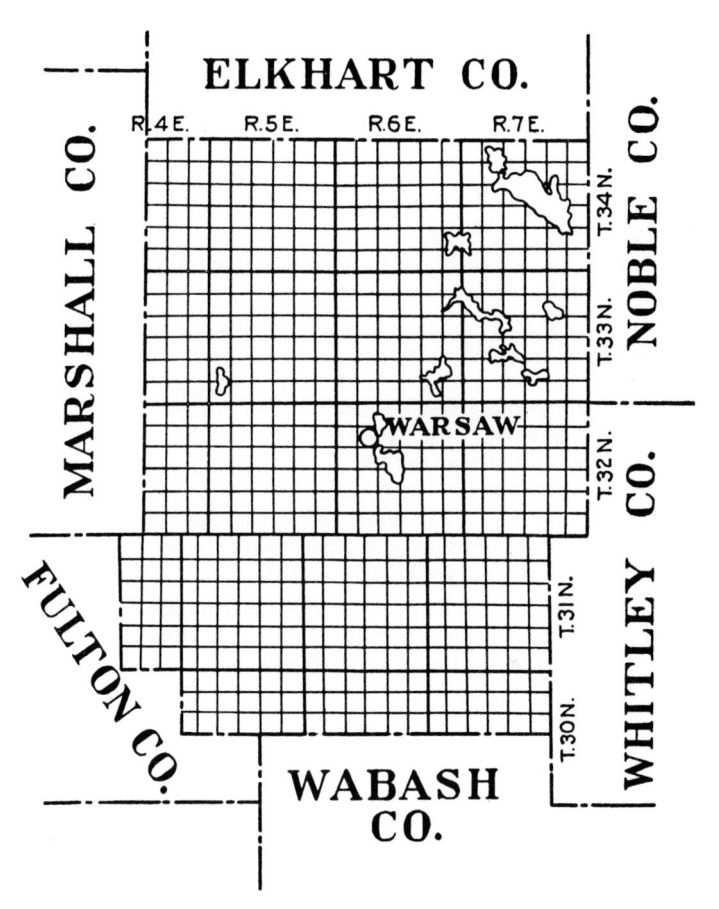

KOSCIUSKO COUNTY IV
[Law: Jan. 13, 1846, effective on passage]

LA GRANGE COUNTY

FEBRUARY 2, 1832: Formation by statute, effective April 1, 1832. The formation affected territory attached to Elkhart and Allen counties.

BOUNDARIES: "Beginning at the north east corner of Elkhart county, thence running east with their northern boundary, to the range line, between eleven and twelve, thence south sixteen and a half miles, thence west to the eastern boundary of Elkhart county, thence north with said boundary, to the place of beginning." *Laws of Indiana*, 1831-32, pp. 110-11.

The law forming the county attached for jurisdiction "all the territory lying east of the county of Lagrange, to the state line, and south of said territory and said county, to the township line dividing townships thirty-three and thirty-four." *Ibid.*, 111.

COUNTY SEAT: Commissioners appointed under the act forming the county chose the site of an old Indian village called Mongoquinong for the location of the county seat. It was given the name Lima. By an act of February 13, 1840, commissioners were appointed to choose a new county seat. A more central location was desired and the site of La Grange was chosen. The removal was made in 1844. Shockley, "County Seat Wars," *op. cit.*, 10:no. 1:29-30; *Laws of Indiana*, 1831-32, p. 111; 1839-40 (general), pp. 47-48; *Counties of La Grange and Noble*, 37-38.

LA GRANGE COUNTY BOUNDARIES 549

MICHIGAN TERRITORY

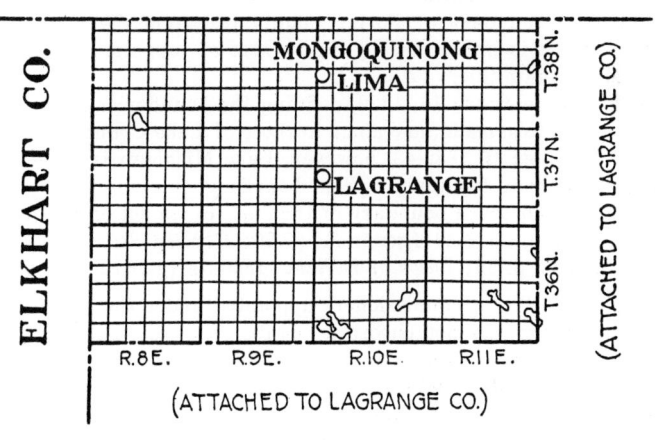

ELKHART CO.

MONGOQUINONG
LIMA
LAGRANGE

T.38N.
T.37N.
T.36N.

(ATTACHED TO LAGRANGE CO.)

R.8E.   R.9E.   R.10E.   R.11E.

(ATTACHED TO LAGRANGE CO.)

LA GRANGE COUNTY
[Law: Feb. 2, 1832, effective Apr. 1, 1832]

LAKE COUNTY I

JANUARY 28, 1836: Formation by statute, effective February 1, 1836. This formation affected Newton and Porter counties. Lake was organized by an act of January 18, 1837, effective February 15, 1837.

BOUNDARIES: "All that part of the country that lies north of the Kankakee river, and west of the county of Porter, within the State of Indiana." *Laws of Indiana*, 1835-36 (general), p. 51.

The west boundary of Porter County ran from the Kankakee River where it is intersected by the "centre of range seven, thence north to the state line." *Ibid.*

A law of February 16, 1839, defining the boundaries of several northern counties, made no change in those of Lake County. In the *Revised Statutes* of 1842-43, however, Lake Michigan is made the county's northern boundary. This boundary was specifically extended to the northern boundary of the state by an act of February 10, 1851. *Ibid.*, 1838-39 (general), p. 70; *Revised Statutes of Indiana*, 1842-43, p. 89; *Laws of Indiana*, 1850-51 (general), p. 58.

COUNTY SEAT: Commissioners appointed under the act organizing the county did not choose a county seat. On February 17, 1838, the legislature in one act established a temporary courthouse at the home of Milo Robinson, and in another, provided for the location of a permanent county seat. Still no action was taken. On February 14, 1839, a new set of commissioners was appointed. They selected Liverpool, but their choice proved unpopular. Commissioners appointed under an act of February 13, 1840, in June established the permanent county seat on the site of the first temporary location. The name Lake Court House proving awkward, the name Crown Point was selected. *Ibid.*, 1836-37 (general), pp. 55-56; 1837-38 (local), pp. 388-89; 1838-39 (local), pp. 303-4; 1839-40 (general), pp. 67-68; Shockley, "County Seat Wars," *op. cit.*, 10:no.1:34-35; Ball (ed.), *Encyclopedia of Genealogy and Biography of Lake County*, 34-35.

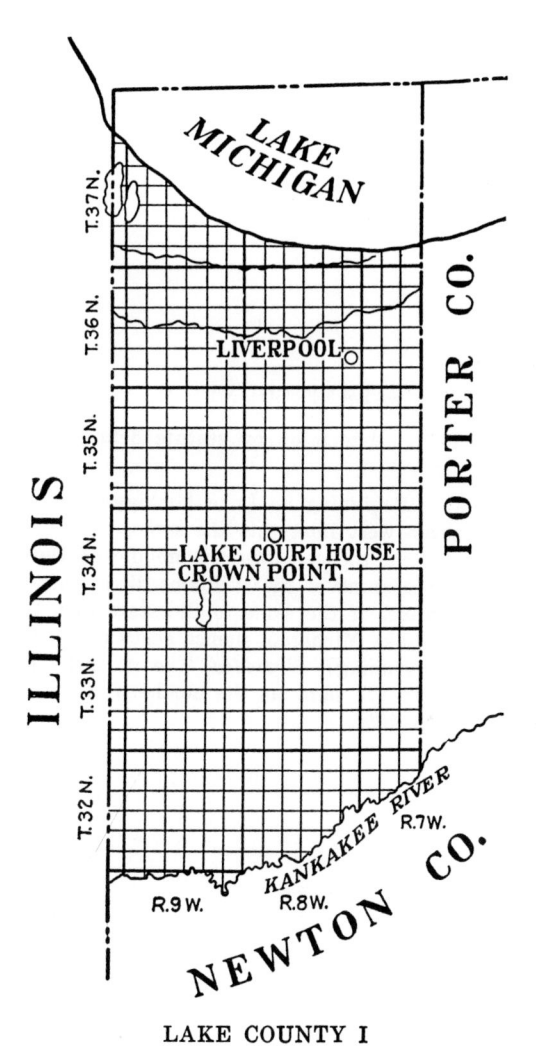

LAKE COUNTY I

[Law: Jan. 28, 1836, effective Feb. 1, 1836]

LAKE COUNTY II

MARCH 8, 1923: Alteration by statute defining Lake County boundaries.

BOUNDARIES: "Beginning on Lake Michigan where the center line of range seven west intersects the same, thence south to the Marble Powers ditch, thence down the middle of the channel of the same to the beginning of the Williams ditch, thence down the middle of the channel of the same to the state line, thence north with the same to Lake Michigan, thence eastwardly with the lake to the place of beginning: *Provided*, The northern boundary of said county shall be the same as the northern state line." *Laws of Indiana*, 1923, p. 465.

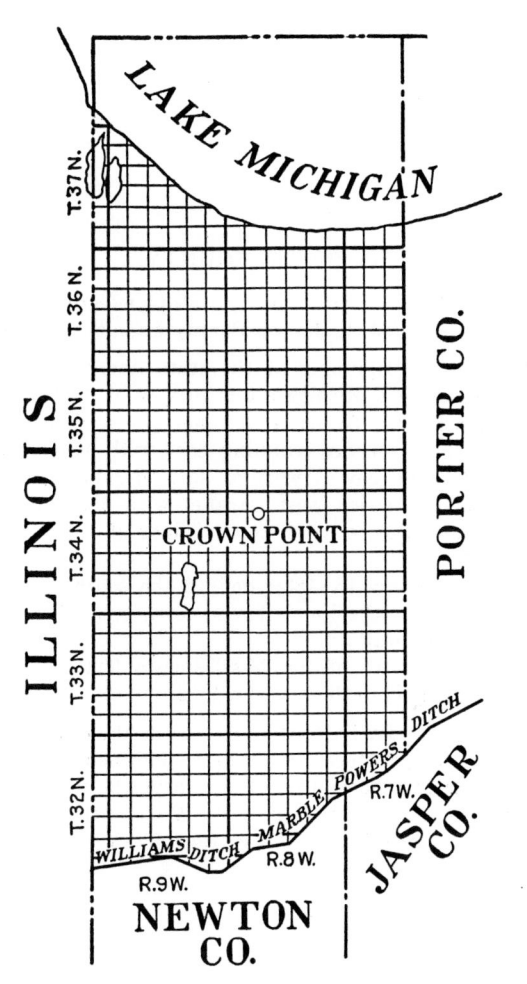

LAKE COUNTY II
[Law: Mar. 8, 1923]

LA PORTE COUNTY I

JANUARY 9, 1832: Formation by statute, effective April 1, 1832. The formation affected St. Joseph County and attached territory.

BOUNDARIES: "Beginning at the state line, which divides the state of Indiana and Michigan territory, and at the north-west corner of township No. 38, north of range No. 4, west of the second principal meridian; thence, running east with said state line, to the centre of range No. 1, west of said meridian; thence south, twenty-two miles, thence west parallel with the said state line, twenty-one miles, thence north to the place of beginning." *Laws of Indiana*, 1831-32, p. 9.

A law of February 16, 1839, defined the southern boundary of La Porte County as the line between townships 34 and 35 north. *Ibid.*, 1838-39 (general), p. 70.

The territory south of the Mississinewa Treaty line was not ceded by the Indians until October, 1832.

COUNTY SEAT: La Porte was selected as the county seat in late September or early October, 1832, by commissioners appointed under the act forming the county. It has never been changed, though there have been attempts to remove it. *Ibid.*, 1831-32, p. 9; Daniels, *History and Biographical Record of La Porte County*, 33-34, 39-42.

LA PORTE COUNTY BOUNDARIES 555

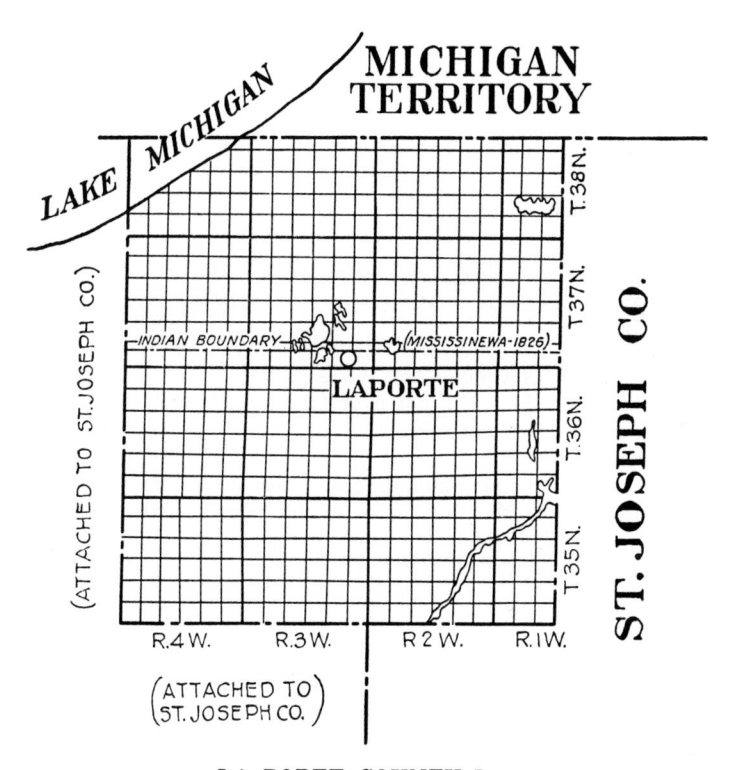

LA PORTE COUNTY I
[Law: Jan. 9, 1832, effective Apr. 1, 1832]

LA PORTE COUNTY II

JANUARY 29, 1842: Alteration by statute attaching a part of Starke County to the county of La Porte, effective on passage.

BOUNDARY CHANGE: The law provided that "all that part of Stark county which lies north of the Kankakee river be . . . attached permanently to the county of Laporte." *Laws of Indiana*, 1841-42 (general), p. 152.

In the law defining county boundaries in the *Revised Statutes* of 1842-43, Lake Michigan is made the boundary, where it touches the county. By a law of February 10, 1851, the northern boundary was "extended to the northern line of this state." *Revised Statutes of Indiana*, 1842-43, pp. 88-89; *Laws of Indiana*, 1850-51 (general), p. 58.

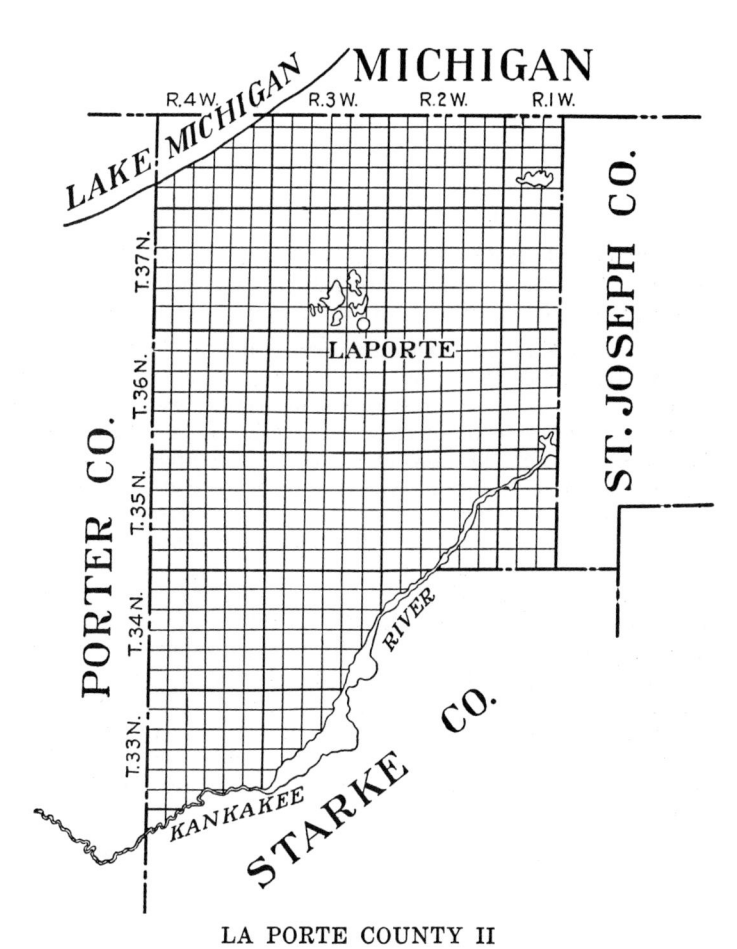

LA PORTE COUNTY II

[Law: Jan. 29, 1842, effective on passage]

LA PORTE COUNTY III

JANUARY 14, 1850: Alteration under provisions of statute of January 14, 1850, in force from July 4, 1850, made effective by order of commissioners of La Porte County, July 10, 1850.

BOUNDARY CHANGE: The act provided that all that part of St. Joseph County described as follows: "beginning at the present county line, at the north-west corner of section twenty-two, township thirty seven north, of range one west, thence with the north line of said section, and that of section twenty-three, to the northeast corner of said section twenty-three, thence south with the section line, until it shall strike the Great Kankakee river, thence with said river to the present county line, may be attached to the county of La Porte." The board doing county business in and for the county of La Porte was authorized, "at their first or any subsequent meeting, after the taking effect of this act, to attach the said territory to any of the townships in the said county of Laporte." By an order of July 10, 1850, the Board of Commissioners of La Porte County divided the territory described between Wills and Pleasant townships, La Porte County. Lincoln Township, in which part of this territory now lies, was not organized until 1866. *Laws of Indiana*, 1849-50 (general), pp. 114-15; *History of La Porte County*, 442-43, 446.

LA PORTE COUNTY III

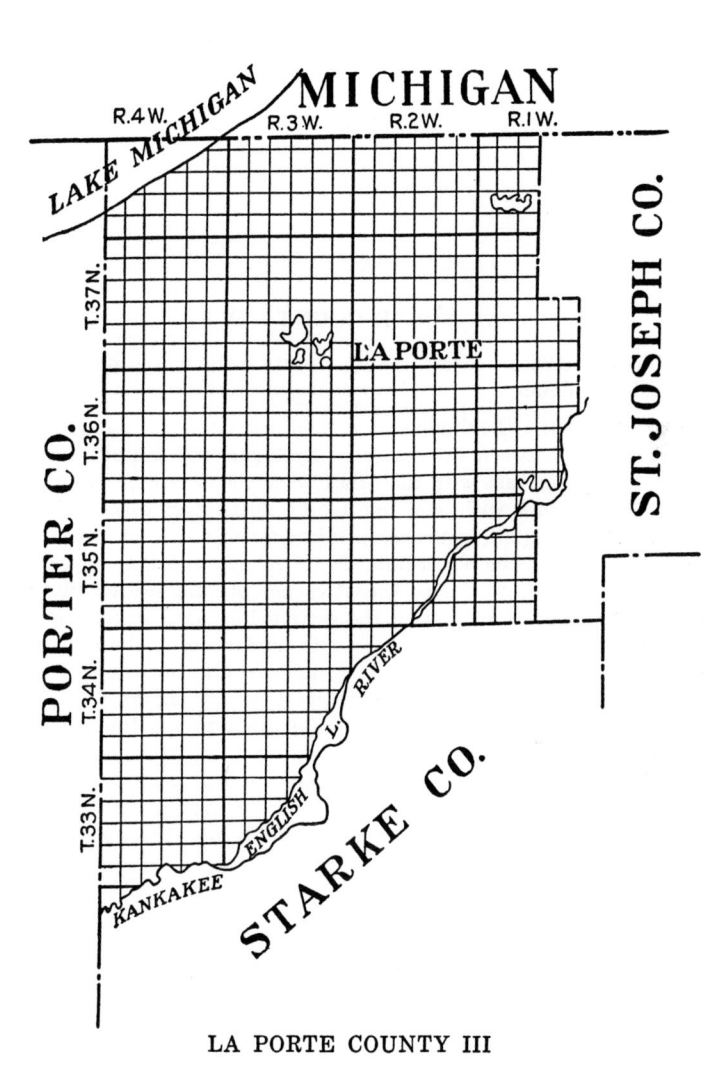

[Law: Jan. 14, 1850, in force July 4, 1850, made effective by commissioners' order, July 10, 1850]

LA PORTE COUNTY IV

MARCH 2, 1925: Alteration by statute defining the boundaries of La Porte County.

BOUNDARIES: "Beginning at a point on Lake Michigan where the state line between the states of Michigan and Indiana strikes the same, thence east with the said line to the centre of range one west, thence south with said line to the north-west corner of section twenty-two (22) in township thirty-seven north, of range one west, thence with the north line of said section and that of section twenty-three (23) to the northeast corner of said section twenty-three (23), thence south with the section line until it shall strike the great Kankakee river, thence with said river to the centre of range one west, thence south to the line dividing townships thirty-four and thirty-five north, thence west to the Dixon W. Place ditch, thence down the middle of said ditch to the line dividing ranges four and five west, thence north to Lake Michigan, thence with the same eastwardly to the place of beginning: *Provided*, that the northern boundary shall extend to, and be the same as the northern line of the state." *Laws of Indiana*, 1925, pp. 122-23.

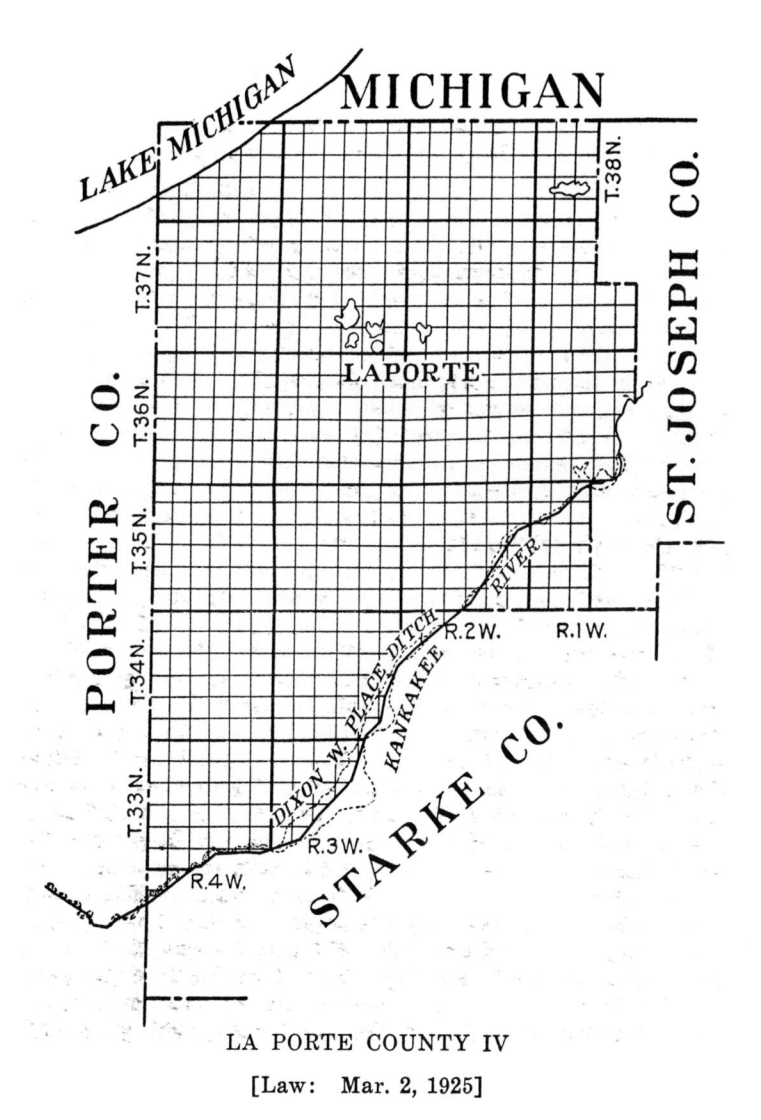

LA PORTE COUNTY IV
[Law: Mar. 2, 1925]

LA PORTE COUNTY V

MARCH 9, 1931: Alteration by statute defining the boundaries of La Porte and St. Joseph counties, effective on passage.

BOUNDARIES: "Beginning at a point on Lake Michigan where the state line between the state of Michigan and Indiana strikes the same, thence east with the said state line to the center of range one (1) west of the second principal meridian, thence south with said line to the northwest corner of section twenty-two (22) in township thirty-seven (37) north, of range one (1) west, thence east along the north line of sections twenty-two (22) and twenty-three (23), township thirty-seven (37) north, range one (1) west to the northeast corner of section twenty-three (23) township thirty-seven (37) north, range (1) west, thence south and along the east lines of sections twenty-three (23), twenty-six (26) and thirty-five (35), township thirty-seven (37) north, range one (1) west, and sections two (2), eleven (11) and fourteen (14), township thirty-six (36) north, range one (1) west, to the center of the Dixon W. Place ditch, thence down the center of the said Dixon W. Place ditch to a point where a line protracted due north from the center of the channel of the beginning of the east branch of the Horace Miller ditch would intersect with the center of the channel of said Dixon W. Place ditch, thence south along said line to said center of the channel of said Horace Miller ditch, thence down the center of said Horace Miller ditch to the intersection with the center line of Mud Lake Channel of the Dixon W. Place ditch, thence on the center line of said Mud Lake Channel of the Dixon W. Place ditch to the center line of range one (1) west, thence south along said center line of range one (1) west to the south line of township thirty-five (35) north, thence west to the center of the Dixon W. Place ditch, thence down the middle of said ditch to the line dividing ranges four (4) and five (5) west, thence north along the said line to Lake Michigan, thence with the same northeasterly to the place of beginning: *Provided*, That the northern boundary shall extend to, and be the same as the northern line of the State of Indiana." *Laws of Indiana*, 1931, pp. 450-51.

LA PORTE COUNTY BOUNDARIES 563

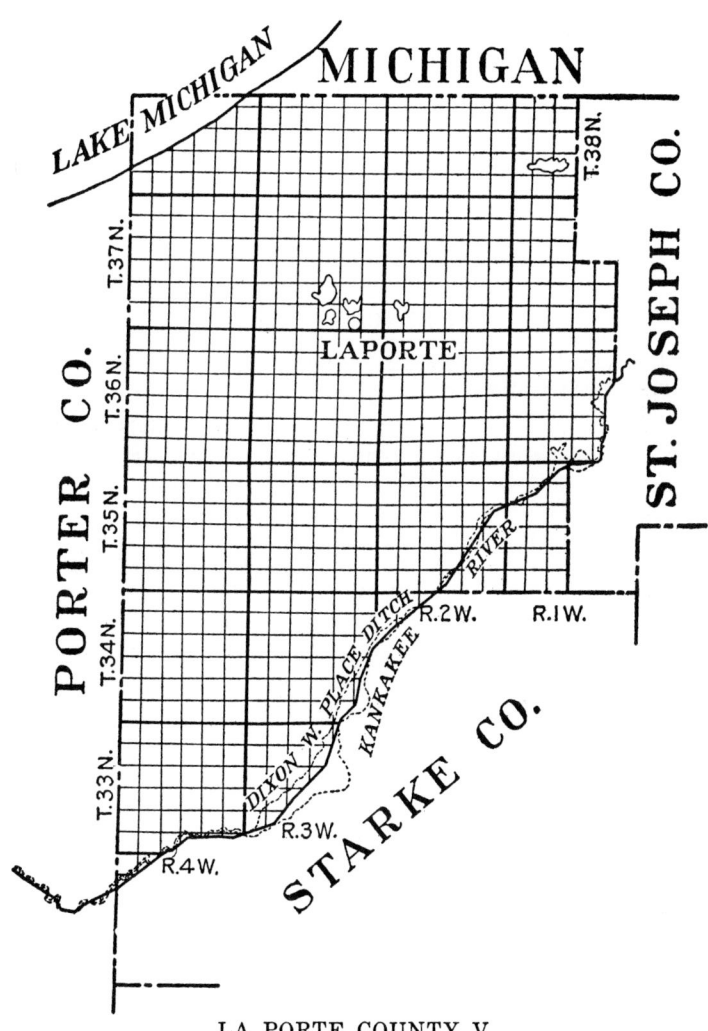

LA PORTE COUNTY V
[Law: Mar. 9, 1931, effective on passage]

LAWRENCE COUNTY I

JANUARY 7, 1818: Formation by statute, effective **March 16, 1818**. The formation affected Orange County.

BOUNDARIES: "Beginning at the range line dividing ranges two and three west, at the centre of town three north, and running thence east to the line dividing the counties of Washington, Orange and Jackson, thence north with said line to the line dividing townships six and seven north, thence west with said line [to the line] dividing ranges two and three west, thence south with said range line to the place of beginning." *Laws of Indiana*, 1817-18 (special), p. 12.

COUNTY SEAT: Commissioners appointed under the act forming the county reported on March 21 their selection of a county-seat site on the meridian line. It was called Palestine. *Ibid.*, 13; *History of Lawrence and Monroe Counties*, 67-68.

LAWRENCE COUNTY BOUNDARIES 565

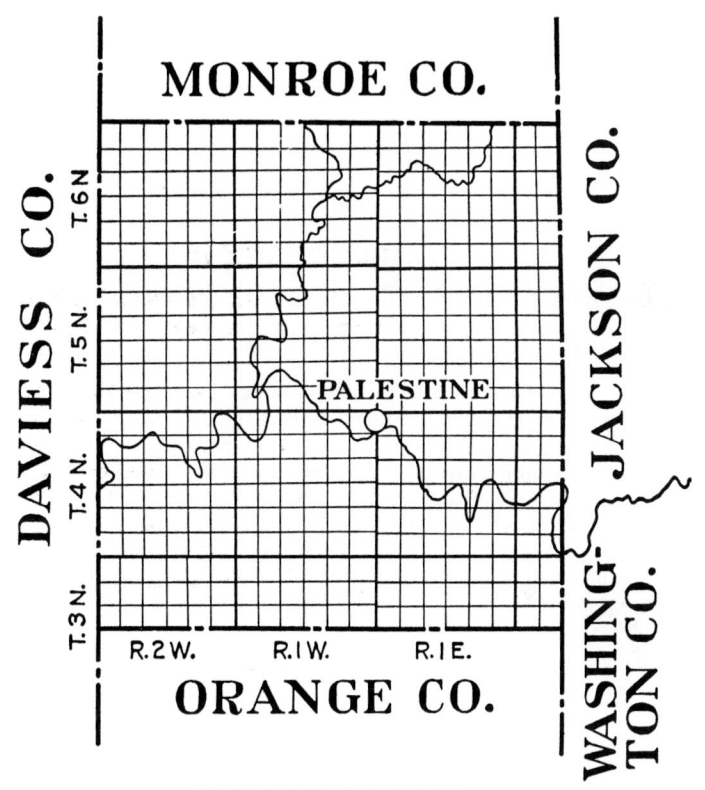

LAWRENCE COUNTY I
[Law: Jan. 7, 1818, effective Mar. 16, 1818]

LAWRENCE COUNTY II

DECEMBER 31, 1822: Alteration by statute attaching part of the county of Jackson to the county of Lawrence, effective January 1, 1823.

BOUNDARY CHANGE: The law provided that "all that part of the county of Jackson, included within the following boundaries, to wit: beginning at the north west corner of section number sixteen, in range two east, in town five north; thence east two miles, to the north east corner of section number fifteen; thence south to the Driftwood Fork of White river; thence down said river to the line which at present divides the counties of Jackson and Lawrence; be . . . attached to the county of Lawrence." *Laws of Indiana*, 1822-23, p. 27.

LAWRENCE COUNTY BOUNDARIES 567

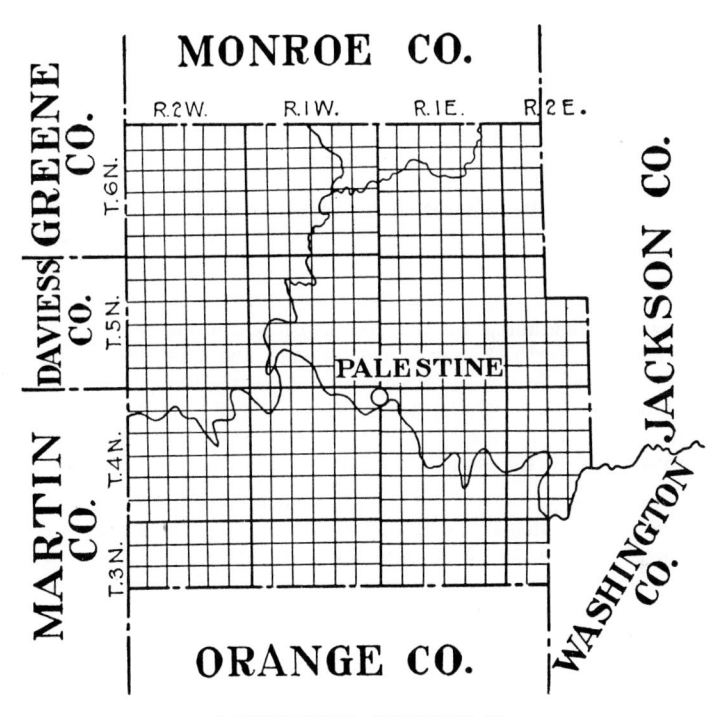

LAWRENCE COUNTY II
[Law: Dec. 31, 1822, effective Jan. 1, 1823]

LAWRENCE COUNTY III

JUNE 8, 1859: Alteration by report of county commissioners changing the boundary line between Lawrence and Jackson counties.

BOUNDARY CHANGE: The line between the counties was run as follows: "Beginning at the Northwest corner of Section 4, in Township 6 North, Range 2 East, thence due East to the Northeast corner of Section 3, in Township 6 North, Range 2 East, and running thence directly South to White River." Lawrence County Commissioners' Record E. See page 115 for comment on the constitutionality of the change.

COUNTY SEAT: Under an act of February 9, 1825, commissioners were appointed to relocate the county seat. On March 9 they reported their choice of a site in the northeast corner of section 23, township 5 north, range 1 west. The name Bedford was selected. This has remained the county seat. *History of Lawrence, Orange and Washington Counties*, 69-73; *Laws of Indiana*, 1825, pp. 88-90.

LAWRENCE COUNTY BOUNDARIES

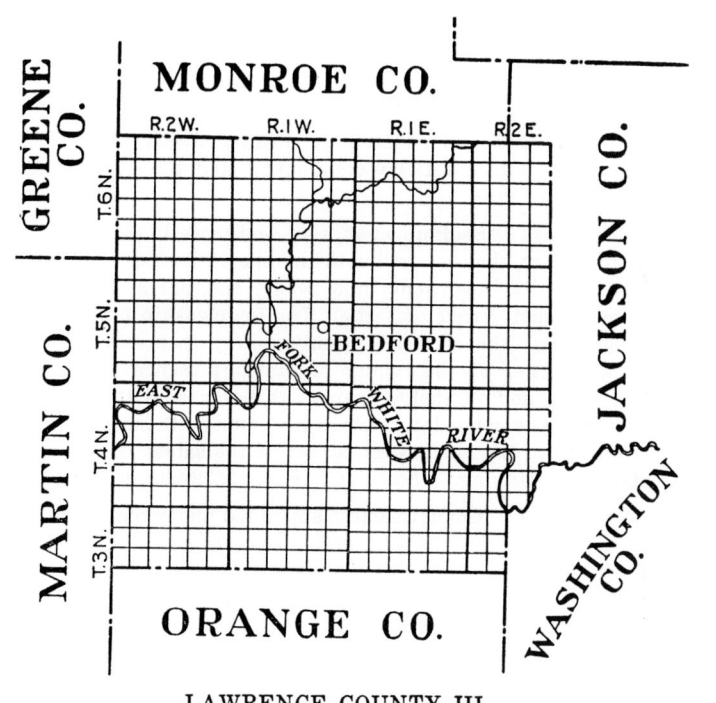

LAWRENCE COUNTY III

[Commissioners' Report: June 8, 1859]

MADISON COUNTY I

JANUARY 4, 1823: Formation by statute, effective July 1, 1823. The formation affected Delaware County, and the attachment to Marion County.

BOUNDARIES: "Beginning at the south west corner of the county of Henry, thence north with the line of the same, and to the township line dividing twenty and twenty one, north; thence west, to the north east corner of section five, in township twenty north, range six east; thence south twenty miles; thence west, to the north east corner of the county of Marion; thence south to the north west corner of Shelby county; thence east with the line of Shelby, until the same intersects Rush county; thence north with Rush county, to the north west corner of the same; thence east to the place of beginning." *Laws of Indiana*, 1822-23, pp. 94-95.

COUNTY SEAT: Commissioners appointed under the act forming the county considered a site at Andersontown, but did not come to a definite decision. Courts were to be held temporarily at a house within the limits of the present Pendleton, according to the formation act. *Ibid.*, 95; Shockley, "County Seat Wars," *op. cit.*, 10:no. 1:24; Forkner and Dyson, *Historical Sketches of Madison County*, 26, 29.

MADISON COUNTY BOUNDARIES 571

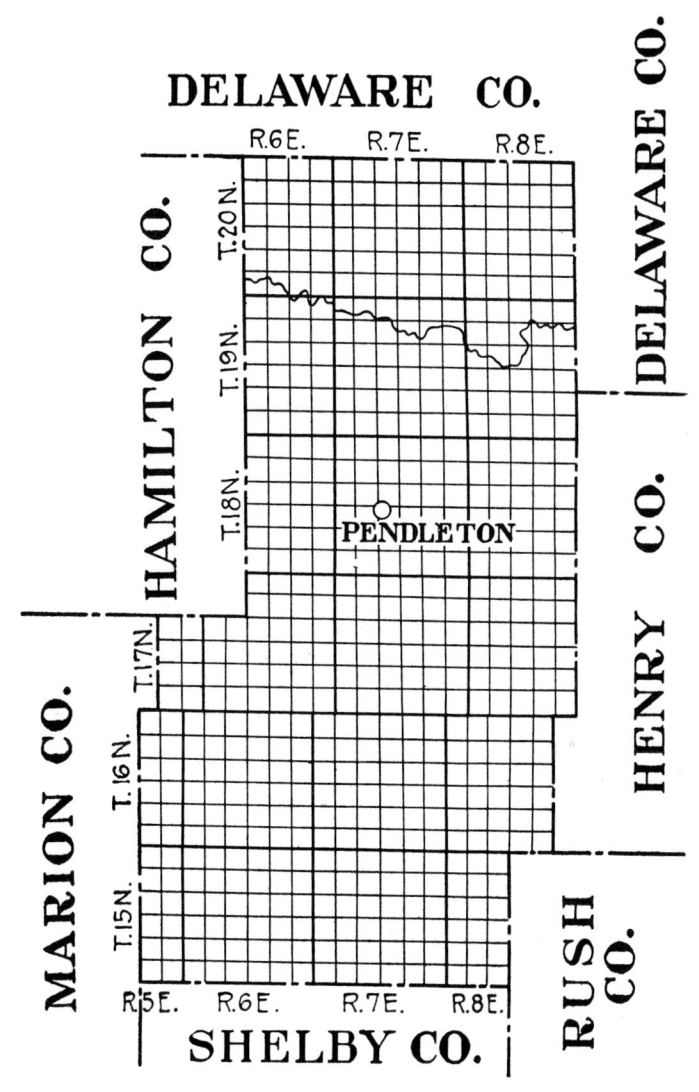

MADISON COUNTY I

[Law: Jan. 4, 1823, effective July 1, 1823]

MADISON COUNTY II

JANUARY 26, 1824: Alteration by statute, altering the north boundary line of Madison County, effective on passage.

BOUNDARY CHANGE: The law provided "That from and after the passage of this act, the line dividing townships eighteen and nineteen north, shall form and constitute the north boundary of the county of Madison." *Laws of Indiana*, 1823-24 (special), p. 51.

A law of January 31, 1824, in defining the boundaries of Madison County, erroneously mentions "the north-west corner of section four, in township seventeen, range five east," instead of the north-west corner of section 14, in the same township and range. *Revised Laws of Indiana*, 1823-24, p. 99.

MADISON COUNTY BOUNDARIES 573

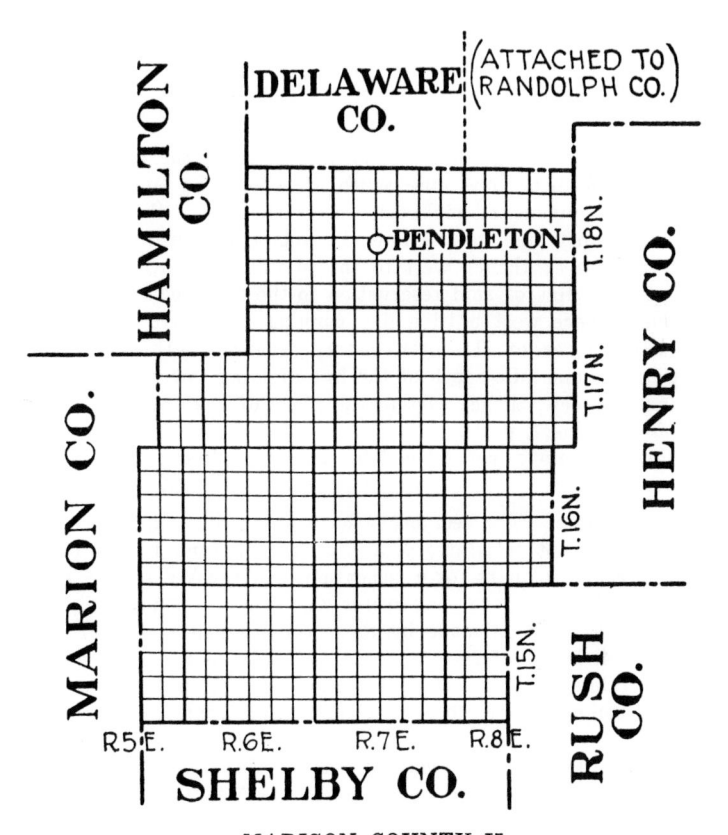

MADISON COUNTY II
[Law: Jan. 26, 1824, effective on passage]

MADISON COUNTY III

JANUARY 26, 1827: Alteration by statute for the relocation of the seat of justice of the county of Madison, and for the formation of the county of Hancock, effective on passage.

BOUNDARIES: "Beginning on the line dividing the counties of Henry and Madison, one mile south of where the line dividing townships seventeen and eighteen crosses the same; thence north with said county line, to the line dividing townships twenty-two and twenty-three; thence west to the Miami reservation; thence south with the line of said reservation to the south east corner of the same; thence west until a line running south will strike the north east corner of Hamilton county; thence south with said county line to one mile south of the line dividing townships seventeen and eighteen; thence east to the place of beginning." *Laws of Indiana*, 1826-27, p. 85.

Delaware County was formed by an act of January 26, 1827, effective April 1.

COUNTY SEAT: The temporary location of the county seat at Pendleton was not satisfactory, and an act of January 13, 1826, appointed commissioners for a relocation, and revoked earlier proceedings with regard to Andersontown. There seems to be no record of the selection made by these commissioners, but an act of January 4, 1827, refers to a town of Bedford as the county seat not yet established. An act of January 26, 1827, however, again appointed commissioners to relocate the county seat, and a site in Andersontown was chosen in May, 1827. The county seat has not been removed, but the name was later shortened. *Laws of Indiana*, 1825-26, pp. 80-81; 1826-27, pp. 65, 84-85; 1847-48 (local), p. 300; Shockley, "County Seat Wars," *op. cit.*, 10:no.1:24; Forkner and Dyson, *Historical Sketches of Madison County*, 29-31; Netterville (ed.), *Centennial History of Madison County*, 1:92-95.

MADISON COUNTY BOUNDARIES 575

MIAMI RESERVE

(ATTACHED TO RANDOLPH CO.)

(ATTACHED TO HAMILTON CO.)

HAMILTON CO.

ANDERSONTOWN

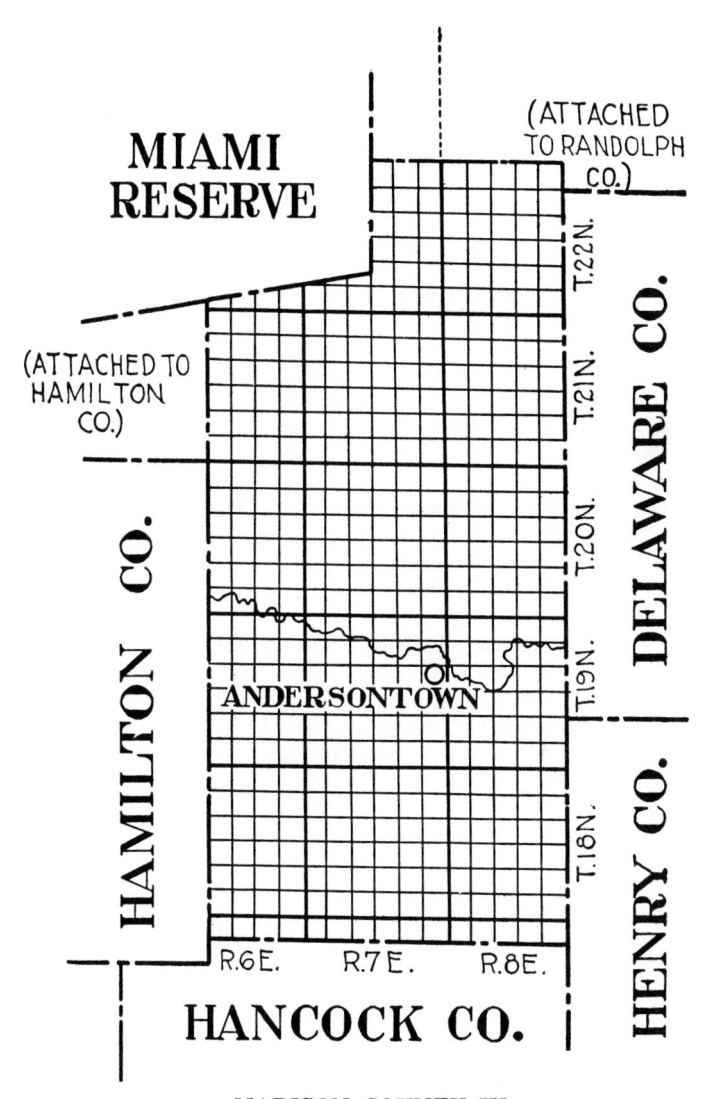

T.22N.
T.21N.
T.20N.
T.19N.
T.18N.

R.6E. R.7E. R.8E.

HANCOCK CO.

DELAWARE CO.

HENRY CO.

MADISON COUNTY III
[Law: Jan. 26, 1827, effective on passage]

MADISON COUNTY IV

FEBRUARY 10, 1831: Alteration by statute forming Grant County, effective April 1, 1831.

BOUNDARY CHANGE: This law transferred from Madison to Grant County all her territory north of a line beginning "on the line dividing the counties of Madison and Delaware, three miles north of the township line, dividing townships twenty-one and twenty-two, in range 8 east" thence running west with the section line through the center of township 22 north to the northwest corner of section 21, township 22 north, range 6 east of the second principal meridian. *Laws of Indiana*, 1830-31 (special), pp. 16-17. See Grant County map, same date.

The law attached to Madison County "the strip of land lying between the north line of the county of Madison, and the south line of the . . . county of Grant." *Laws of Indiana*, 1830-31 (special), p. 17. The territory thus added was still a part of the Miami Reserve.

The definition of the Madison County boundaries, as given in the law of February 10, 1831, does not take cognizance of the change made by Grant's formation. The boundaries of the county are outlined precisely as they appear on the map of January 26, 1827. Jurisdiction over the strip of territory disputed by Madison and Grant counties was given to Madison in a law of February 17, 1838. See Madison and Grant County maps for that date. *Revised Laws of Indiana*, 1830-31, p. 123; *Laws of Indiana*, 1837-38 (local), pp. 254, 265.

By a law of June 15, 1833, the boundary between Madison and Hancock counties and the county of Henry was defined as "the first section line west of the range line dividing ranges eight and nine east." *Ibid.*, 1832-33, p. 20.

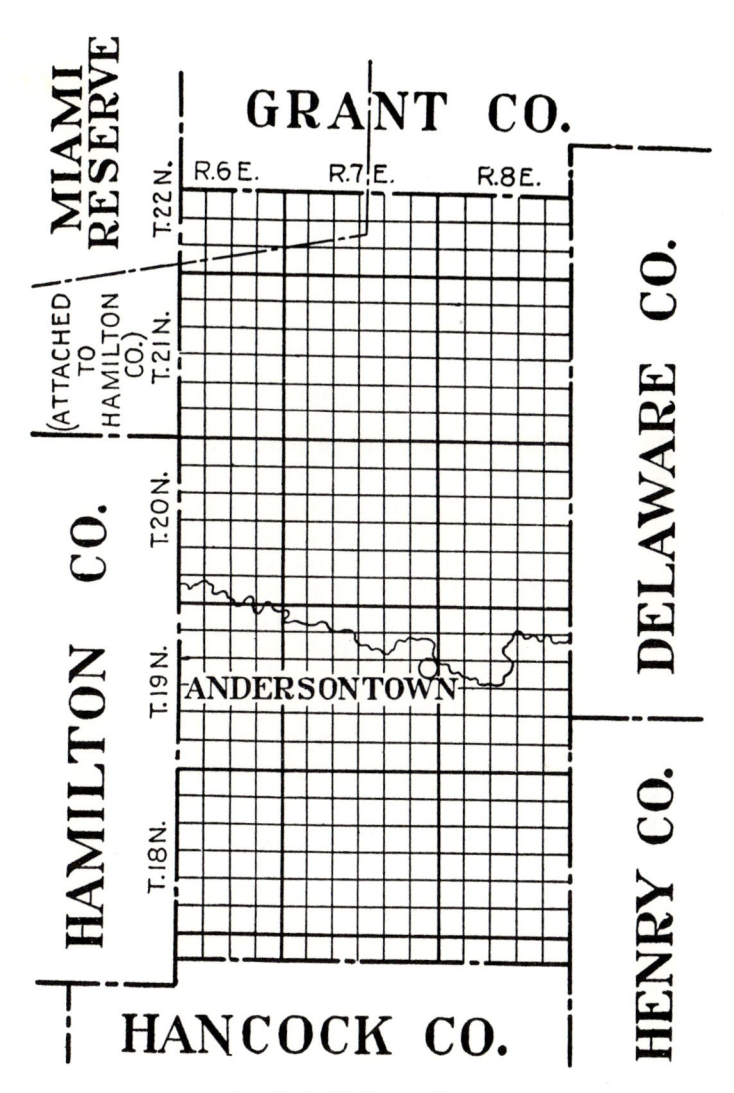

MADISON COUNTY IV

[Law: Feb. 10, 1831, effective Apr. 1, 1831]

MADISON COUNTY V

FEBRUARY 17, 1838: Alteration by statute to alter and define the boundary lines of Grant County, effective on passage.

BOUNDARY CHANGE: The south boundary of Grant County was defined as "beginning at the south east corner of section one, of township twenty-two, north of range nine east, on the north line of Delaware county; thence west on said line to the north west corner of said county of Delaware; thence west on the same sectional line, till it shall intersect a line drawn from the north east corner of Hamilton county to the south east corner of Miami county." *Laws of Indiana*, 1837-38 (local), pp. 266-67.

COUNTY SEAT: An act of February 16, 1848, changed the name Andersontown to Anderson. *Ibid.*, 1847-48 (local), p. 300.

MADISON COUNTY BOUNDARIES 579

GRANT CO.

MIAMI RESERVE

[ATTACHED TO HAMILTON CO.]

R.6 E.   R.7 E.   R.8 E.

T.22N.
T.21N.
T.20N.
T.19N.
T.18N.

HAMILTON CO.

DELAWARE CO.

ANDERSONTOWN
ANDERSON

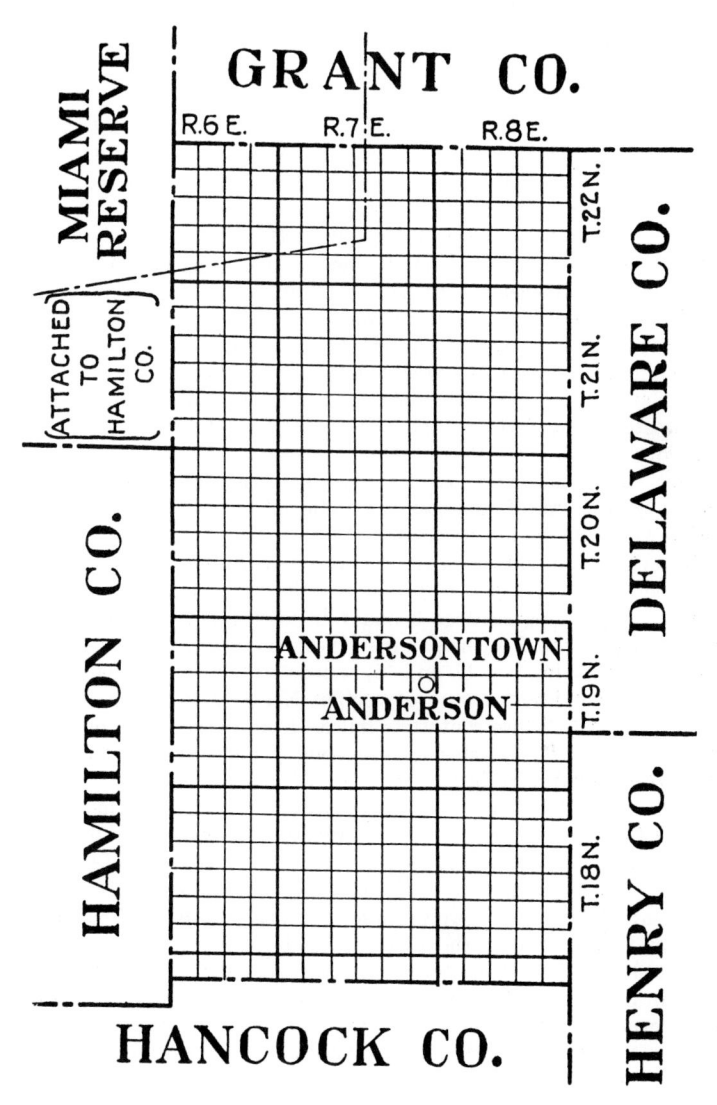

HENRY CO.

HANCOCK CO.

MADISON COUNTY V
[Law: Feb. 17, 1838, effective on passage]

MARION COUNTY I

DECEMBER 31, 1821: Formation by statute, effective April 1, 1822. The formation affected Delaware County.

BOUNDARIES: "Beginning at the north-east corner of section numbered fifteen in township seventeen north of range five east of the second principal meridian line, in the district of Public Lands sold at Brookville; thence south twenty miles to the south-east corner of section twenty two in township fourteen north of range five east; thence west twenty miles to the south-west corner of section twenty-one, in township fourteen north of range two east; thence north twenty miles to the north west corner of section sixteen in township seventeen north of range two cast [east] thence east to the beginning." *Laws of Indiana*, 1821-22, pp. 135-36.

An amendatory act of January 7, 1824, redefined the eastern and western boundaries to indicate that they followed the corrections in survey lines. *Ibid.*, 1823-24 (special), pp. 52-53.

The law forming the county provided that "all that tract of county lying north of said county of Marion of the following boundaries, viz: Beginning at the line dividing sections No. 9 and 10 in township 17 in range 4 east, thence north along said line to the line dividing townships No. 20 and 21, thence east along said line to the line dividing sections 3 and 4 in township No. 20 in range No. 8 east of the 2 principal meridian; thence south to the line dividing townships No. 17 and 18, thence north [west] along said line to the northwest corner of section No. 6 in township No. 17 in range 5 east, thence south two miles, thence west to the place of beginning, be . . . attached to the said county of Marion until otherwise provided by law." *Ibid.*, 1821-22, p. 138.

In a law of February 12, 1825, the following attachment to Marion County was described: "Beginning on the county lines of Marion county . . . at the south west corner of . . . Hamilton county; thence north to the line dividing townships eighteen and nineteen; thence west twelve miles; thence south to Hendricks county; thence east to the place of beginning, shall be, and the same is hereby attached to the county of Marion for all purposes of civil, and criminal jurisdiction." *Ibid.*, 1825, p. 15. The southwest corner of Hamilton County was the northwest corner of section 18, township 17 north, range 3 east. The north line of Hendricks County was a continuation of the north line of Marion. See following map.

COUNTY SEAT: The act forming the county provided that square 58 in the town of Indianapolis should be the county seat. *Ibid.*, 1821-22, p. 136.

MARION COUNTY BOUNDARIES 581

COUNTY (ATTACHED TO MARION CO.)

DELAWARE — T.17N., T.16N., T.15N., T.14N.

INDIANAPOLIS

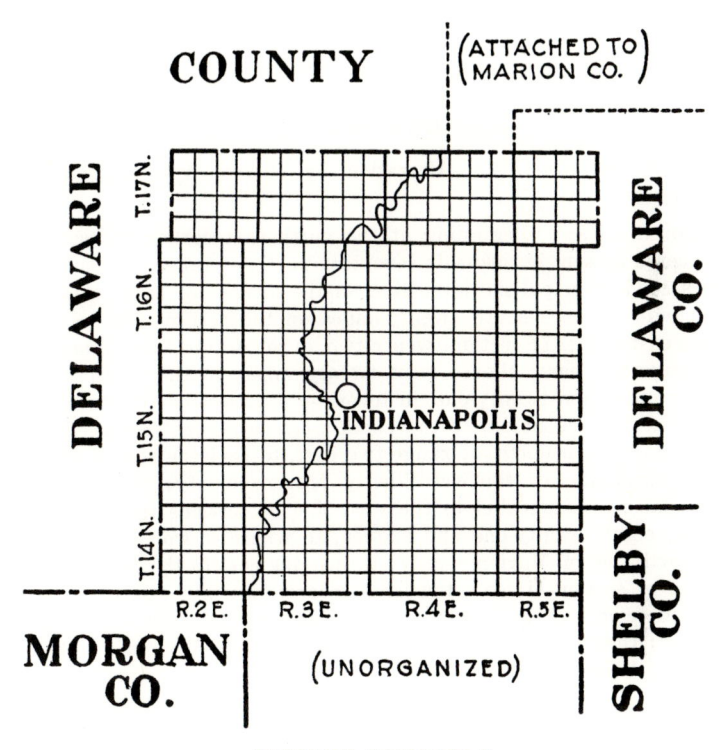

DELAWARE CO.

R.2E. R.3E. R.4E. R.5E.

MORGAN CO.

(UNORGANIZED)

SHELBY CO.

MARION COUNTY I
[Law: Dec. 31, 1821, effective Apr. 1, 1822]

MARION COUNTY II

FEBRUARY 10, 1831: Alteration by statute defining county boundaries.

BOUNDARIES: "Beginning at the north east corner of section numbered fifteen, in township seventeen north, of range five east of the second principal meridian line, in the district of lands sold at Brookville; thence south twenty miles on the section line to the south east corner of section twenty-two, in township fourteen north, of range five east; thence west twenty miles, to the south west corner of section twenty-one, in township fourteen north, of range two east; thence north, to the north west corner of section four, township sixteen north, of range two east, to [of] the second principal meridian, . . . the west line of Marion county; thence running due north, parallel to the west line of sections thirty-three, twenty-eight, twenty-one and sixteen, to where it would intersect the north line of Marion county; thence due east to the north west corner of section sixteen, township seventeen, north of range two east, to where it strikes the north boundary of said county of Marion; thence east to the place of beginning." *Revised Laws of Indiana*, 1830-31, p. 126.

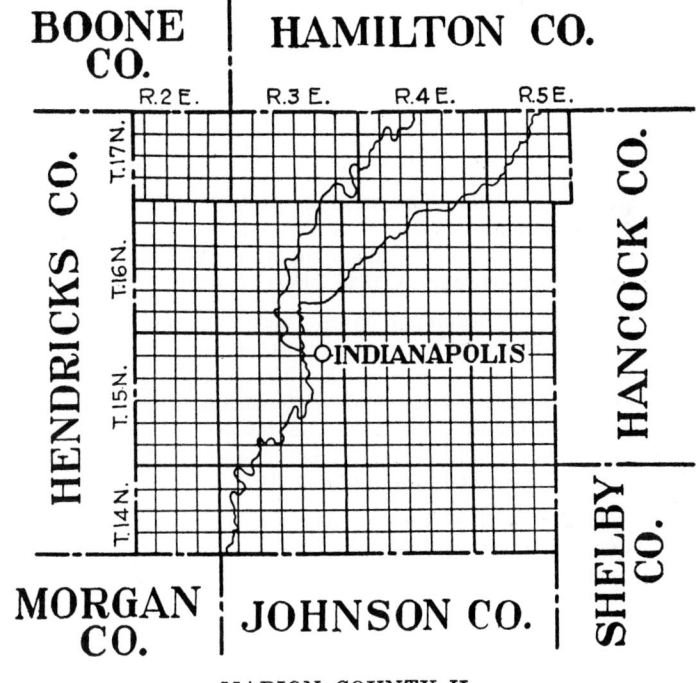

MARION COUNTY II
[Law: Feb. 10, 1831]

MARSHALL COUNTY I

FEBRUARY 7, 1835: Formation by statute, effective on publication. The formation affected St. Joseph County and territory attached to St. Joseph and Elkhart counties. Marshall was organized by an act of February 4, 1836, effective April 1, 1836.

BOUNDARIES: "Beginning on the meridian line, at the south west corner of township thirty two north, of range one east, thence east twenty one miles, thence north with the sectional lines to the north-east corner of section four in township thirty four north, eighteen miles, thence west with the township line twenty one miles, thence south with the meridian line eighteen miles to the place of beginning." *Laws of Indiana*, 1834-35 (general), p. 46.

COUNTY SEAT: The selection of a county seat followed the organization of the county. See text with following map.

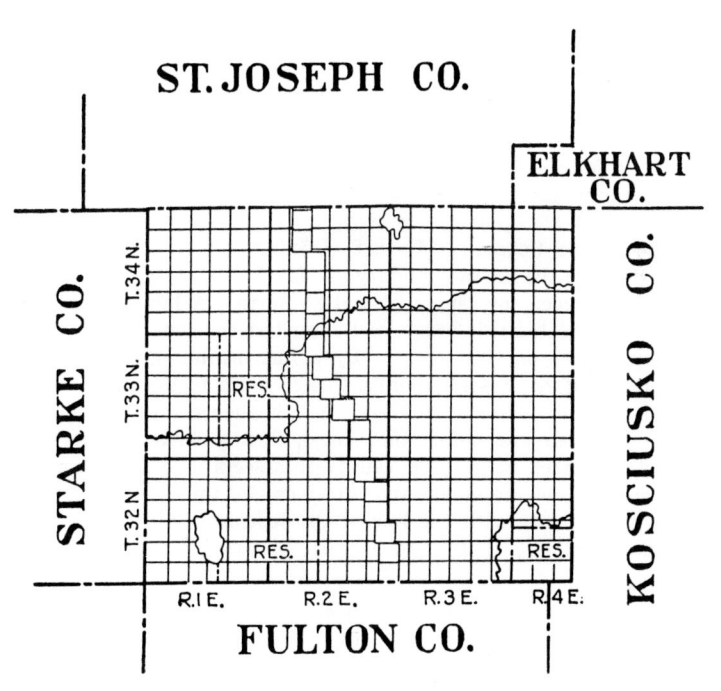

MARSHALL COUNTY I
[Law: Feb. 7, 1835, effective on publication]

MARSHALL COUNTY II

FEBRUARY 4, 1836: Alteration by statute organizing the county of Marshall, effective April 1, 1836.

BOUNDARY CHANGE: "The northern boundary line of the county of Marshall shall be extended to an east and west line running through the centre of township thirty-five north." *Laws of Indiana*, 1835-36 (general), p. 50.

The law of February 17, 1838, defining county boundaries, incorrectly gave the north boundary of Marshall County as the township line between townships 34 and 35 north. A law of February 16, 1839, corrected this error, and described the county boundaries as they appear on this map: "By a line beginning at the south east corner of St. Joseph county, thence south to the line between townships thirty-one and thirty-two north, thence west on said line to the meridian line before mentioned, thence north to where the boundary line of St. Joseph county intersects said meridian line between sections eighteen and nineteen in township thirty-five north, thence east with the line of St. Joseph county to the place of beginning." *Ibid.*, 1837-38 (local), p. 262; 1838-39 (general), p. 70.

COUNTY SEAT: Commissioners appointed under the act organizing the county, on July 20, 1836, reported their selection of Plymouth as the county seat. It has never been removed. Shockley, "County Seat Wars," *op. cit.*, 10:no.1:34; McDonald (ed.), *History of Marshall County*, 1:83-84.

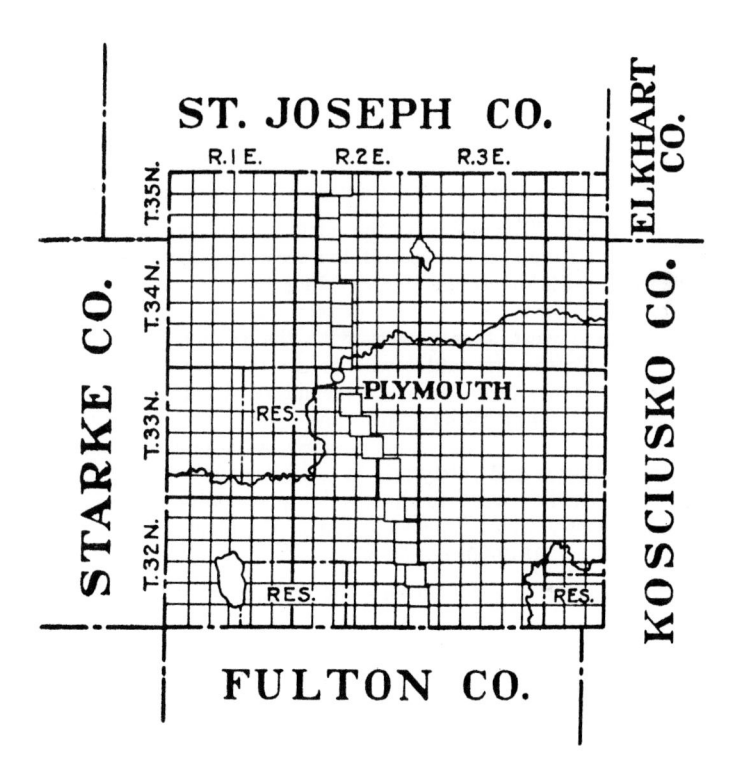

MARSHALL COUNTY II
[Law: Feb. 4, 1836, effective Apr. 1, 1836]

MARTIN COUNTY I

JANUARY 17, 1820: Formation by statute, effective February 1, 1820. The formation affected Daviess and Dubois counties.

BOUNDARIES: "Beginning at the north east corner of township four, north of range three, west of the second principal meridian, thence south with the range line dividing two and three west, to the north east corner of section thirteen, in township one north, of range three west, thence west with the section line dividing twelve and thirteen, in said township, to the eastern branch of White river, thence down with the meanders of said river, to the sectional line dividing twenty-three and twenty-four, of township one north, of range five west, thence north with said sectional line dividing thirty-five and thirty-six, in township two, three and four north, of range five west, to the township line dividing four and five, thence east with said township line to the place of beginning." *Laws of Indiana*, 1819-20, pp. 54-55.

COUNTY SEAT: Hindostan was chosen county seat by commissioners appointed under the act forming the county. *Ibid.*, 55-56; Shockley, "County Seat Wars," *op. cit.*, 10:no.1:18. The county seat was changed several times. See following map.

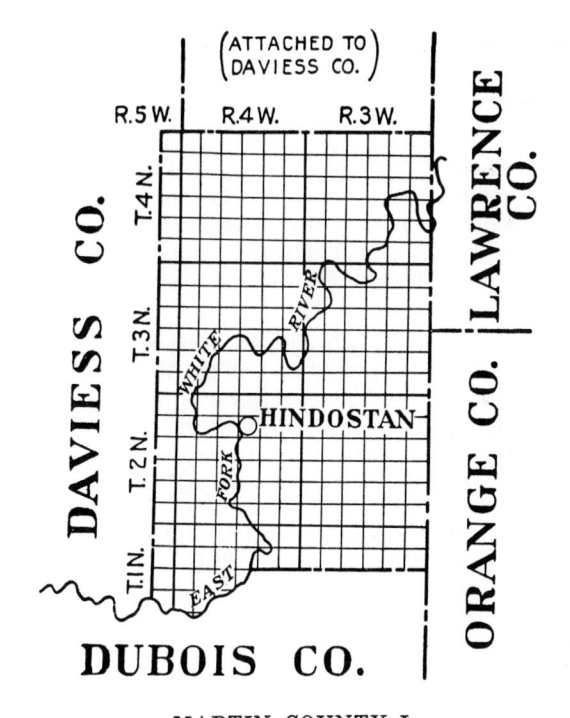

MARTIN COUNTY I

[Law: Jan. 17, 1820, effective Feb. 1, 1820]

MARTIN COUNTY II

JANUARY 24, 1828: Alteration by statute extending the boundaries of Martin County, effective on publication in the *Indianapolis Daily Gazette*.

BOUNDARY CHANGE: The act provided that "the congressional townships numbered five north of ranges three and four west of the second principal meridian, as attached until otherwise directed by law to Daviess county, by the act relative to county boundaries approved, Jan. 31, 1824, shall hereafter be and the same are hereby attached to the county of Martin." *Laws of Indiana*, 1827-28, pp. 17-18.

COUNTY SEAT: Following the act of January 24, 1828, commissioners relocated the county seat at Mt. Pleasant. It remained here for sixteen years before its removal to the new town of Memphis, chosen by commissioners appointed under an act of January 13, 1844. This location was unsatisfactory, and the following autumn the county seat was moved to Harrisonville. Here it remained less than a year. A new relocation under an act of January 11, 1845, resulted in a removal to Hillsborough. The name Hillsborough was changed to Dover Hill by a law of February 11, 1848. After nineteen years, an order changing the county seat to Loogootee was issued by county commissioners on September 23, 1867. This order was rescinded. No action followed a subsequent order making Harrisonville again the county seat. A final change, in December, 1869, transferred the seat of government to West Shoals, across the river from the site of Memphis, one of the earlier county seats. West Shoals is now incorporated with the town of Shoals under the latter name. *Ibid.*, 16-17; 1843-44 (local), p. 158; 1844-45 (local), pp. 79-81; 1847-48 (local), p. 460; Shockley, "County Seat Wars," *op. cit.*, 10:no.1:18 ff.

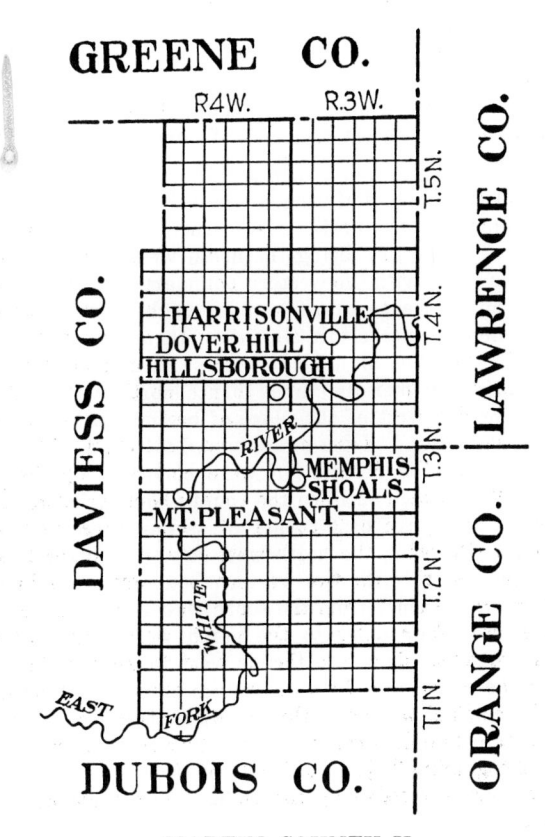

MARTIN COUNTY II

[Law: Jan. 24, 1828, effective on publication in *Indianapolis Daily Gazette*]

MIAMI COUNTY I

FEBRUARY 2, 1832: Formation by statute, effective April 2, 1832, corrected by statute of January 30, 1833, effective on publication. The formation affected Cass County and attached territory. Miami was organized by a law of January 2, 1834, effective March 1, 1834.

BOUNDARIES: The description in the original act of formation read: "beginning at the north west corner of section five, town twenty-nine, of range five, being the north west corner of Wabash county, thence south with the western boundary line of said county, twenty-four miles, thence east five miles to the north west corner of Grant county, thence south six miles, thence west, to a point due south of range line dividing townships three and four east of the second principal meridian line, thence north with said range line, to a point due west of the place of beginning, thence east to the place of beginning." *Laws of Indiana*, 1831-32, p. 113.

Ambiguities in the description were corrected by the act of January 30, 1833, which outlined the county boundaries as follows: "beginning at the north east corner of section three in township twenty-nine north, being the north west corner of Wabash county, running thence south with the western boundary of said county twenty-four miles, thence from the south west corner of the county of Wabash, east four miles to the north west corner of Grant county, thence south six miles, thence west fourteen miles, thence north with the range line dividing ranges three and four east of the second principal meredian thirty miles, thence east ten miles on the township line dividing townships twenty-nine and thirty to the place of beginning." *Ibid.*, 1832-33, pp. 38-39.

Territory not yet ceded by the Indians was included in these boundaries.

COUNTY SEAT: No county seat was chosen until after the organization of the county. See text with following map.

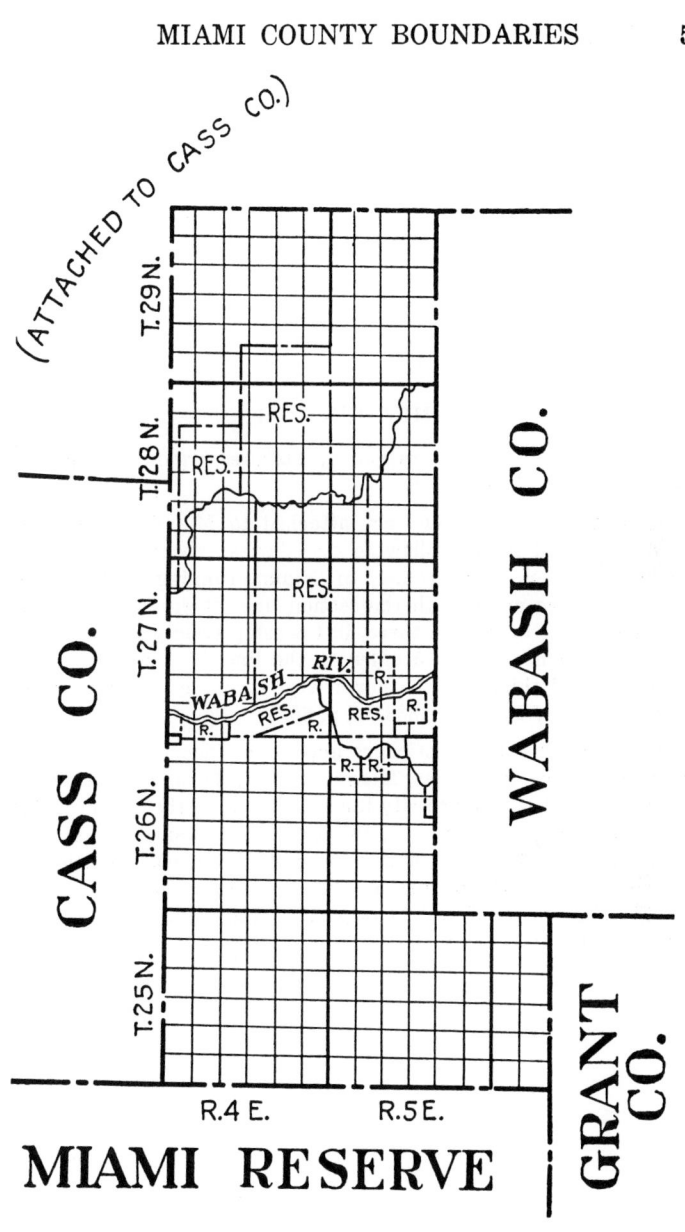

MIAMI COUNTY I

[Law: Feb. 2, 1832, effective Apr. 2, 1832, as corrected Jan. 30, 1833, effective on publication]

MIAMI COUNTY II

JANUARY 2, 1834: Alteration by statute, organizing Miami County, effective March 1, 1834.

BOUNDARY CHANGE: The act attached to Miami County the territory included in the following boundaries: "beginning at the south west corner of the county of Miami, running thence west two miles, thence north with the section lines thirty miles, to the north east corner of section three, in township twenty nine, and in range three, thence east two miles on the line dividing townships twenty-nine and thirty, to the north west corner of the county of Miami." *Laws of Indiana*, 1833-34, p. 65.

COUNTY SEAT: Commissioners appointed under this act hesitated between two town sites, Miamisport and Peru, both of which are now included within the city limits of Peru, in their choice of a county seat. Peru was chosen, though county business was done at Miamisport before the newer town of Peru was sufficiently established. *Ibid.*, 64; Bodurtha (ed.), *History of Miami County*, 1:157-58; *History of Miami County*, 274; Shockley, "County Seat Wars," *op. cit.*, 10:no.1:30.

MIAMI COUNTY BOUNDARIES 595

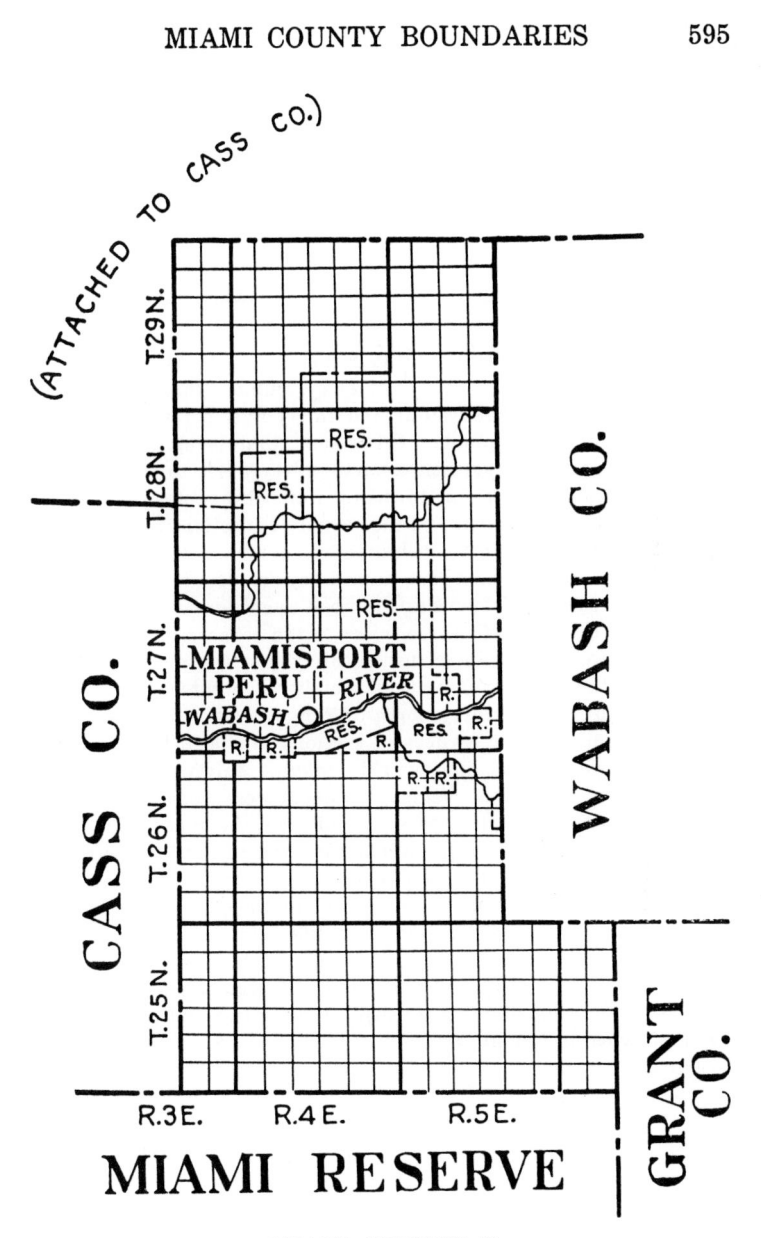

MIAMI COUNTY II

[Law: Jan. 2, 1834, effective Mar. 1, 1834]

MIAMI COUNTY III

FEBRUARY 17, 1838: Alteration by statute defining county boundaries.

BOUNDARIES: "Beginning at corners of sections two and three in township twenty-four north of range number three east, and the corners of sections thirty-four and thirty-five in township twenty-five north of range number three east, that being the south-east corner of Cass county; thence north thirty miles to the corners of sections two and three in township number twenty-nine north of range number three east, and the corners of sections number thirty-four and thirty-five in township thirty north of range three east; on the line dividing said last named townships, eight miles to the north-east corner of township number twenty-nine north of range four east; thence north three miles to the corners of sections thirteen and twenty-four in township thirty north, range number four east, and the corners of sections numbered eighteen and nineteen in township number thirty north of range number five east; thence east four miles to the corners of sections fourteen, fifteen, twenty-two and twenty-three in township number thirty north of range number five east, that being the north-west corner of Wabash county; thence south twenty-seven miles to the corners of sections two and three in township twenty-five, and of sections thirty-four and thirty-five in township twenty-six of range five east," [east four miles, south six miles, and west to the place of beginning]. *Laws of Indiana,* 1837-38 (local), p. 264.

By a law of February 16, 1839, so much of the Great Miami Reservation "as is south of the county of Miami, and north of the . . . township line dividing township twenty-two and twenty-three," was attached to Miami County for judicial purposes. *Ibid.*, 1838-39 (general), p. 75.

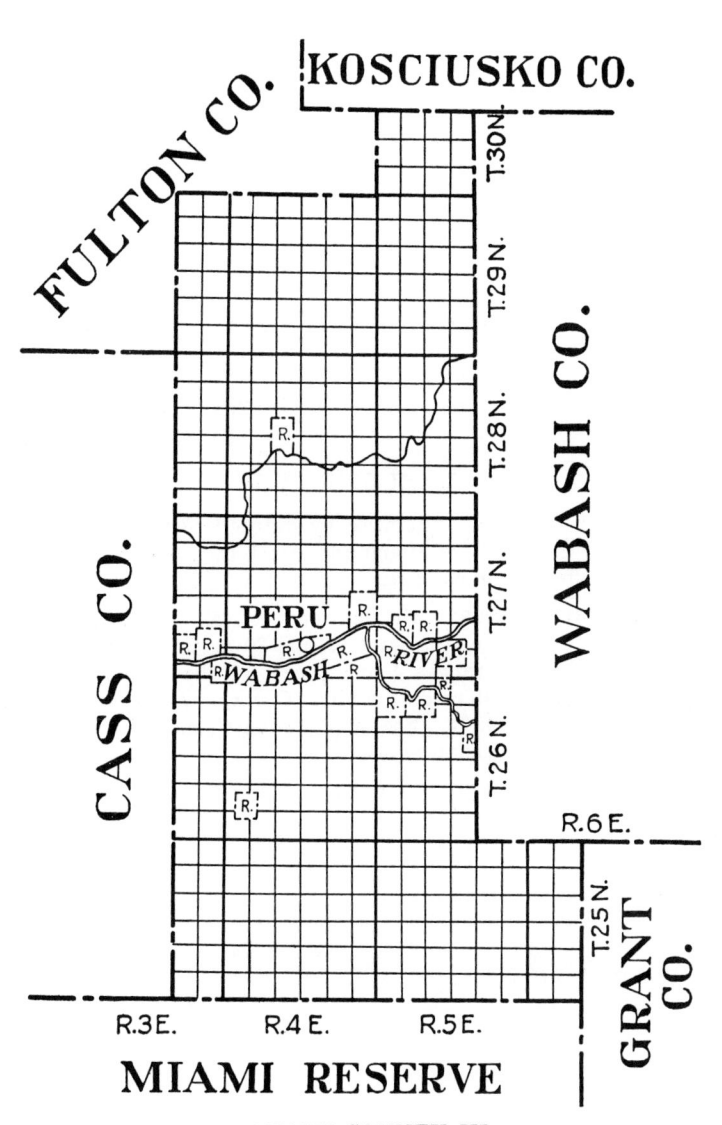

MIAMI COUNTY III
[Law: Feb. 17, 1838]

MIAMI COUNTY IV

JANUARY 15, 1844: Alteration by statute to detach certain territory from the county of Miami and attach the same to the county of Fulton, effective on passage.

BOUNDARY CHANGE: All that part of Miami north of the township line dividing townships 29 and 30 north, and east of the range line dividing ranges 4 and 5 east of the second principal meridian, was transferred to Fulton County. *Laws of Indiana*, 1843-44 (general), p. 73. See map, Fulton County V, for text of law and note on amendatory act.

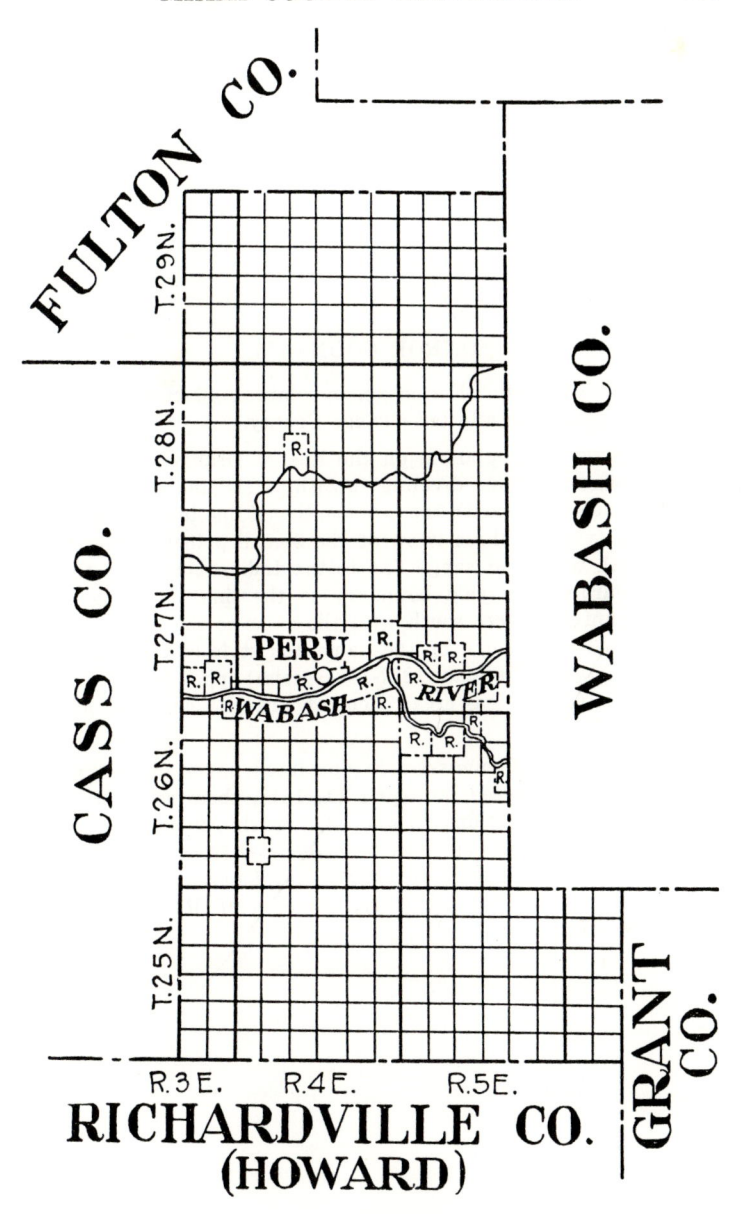

MIAMI COUNTY IV

[Law: Jan. 15, 1844, effective on passage]

MONROE COUNTY I

JANUARY 14, 1818: Formation by statute, effective April 10, 1818. The formation affected Orange County.

BOUNDARIES: "Beginning on the line of Orange and Jackson counties, where the line dividing townships six and seven crosses the same, thence west with the last mentioned line to the line dividing ranges two and three west, of the second principal meridian, thence north with said range line to the Indian boundary, thence southeastwardly with said boundary to the line of Orange and Jackson counties, thence south with the same to the beginning, to be designated and known by the name and style of the county of Monroe." *Laws of Indiana,* 1817-18 (special), pp. 14-15.

Lawrence County was created out of Orange County by an act of January 7, 1818.

COUNTY SEAT: Commissioners appointed under the act forming the county reported on April 11, 1818, their selection of a county-seat site in sections 32 and 33, township 9 north, range 1 west. The county seat has never been removed from this first location at Bloomington. *Ibid.,* 15; *History of Lawrence and Monroe Counties,* 225-26; Blanchard (ed.), *Counties of Morgan, Monroe and Brown,* 374.

MONROE COUNTY I

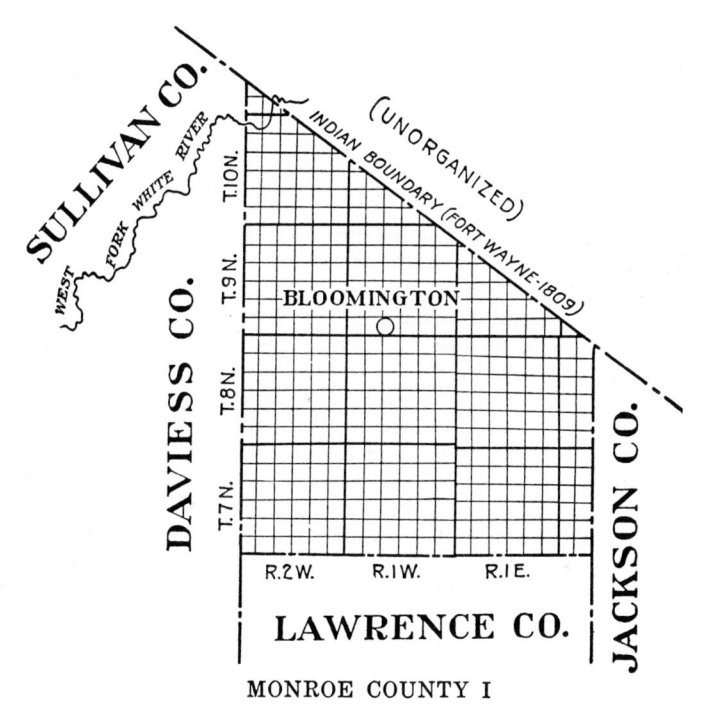

[Law: Jan. 14, 1818, effective Apr. 10, 1818]

MONROE COUNTY II

DECEMBER 31, 1821: Alteration by statute, effective on passage.

BOUNDARY CHANGE: The act provided that "All that part of Monroe county lying west of White river be . . . attached to Owen County," and that "so much of the new purchase as is contained in the following boundary to wit, Beginning on White river where the township line dividing ten and eleven north crosses the same thence east with said line to the corners of section four and five in township ten range two east of the second principal meridian thence south to Monroe county line . . . form and constitute a part of Monroe county." *Laws of Indiana*, 1821-22, p. 80.

The "new purchase" was the purchase made from the Indians at the Treaty of St. Mary's, October 2-6, 1818.

By an act of January 9, 1821, Monroe County had been given jurisdiction over Wabash County; the act was repealed January 2, 1822. *Ibid.*, 1820-21, p. 84; 1821-22, pp. 118-19.

MONROE COUNTY BOUNDARIES 603

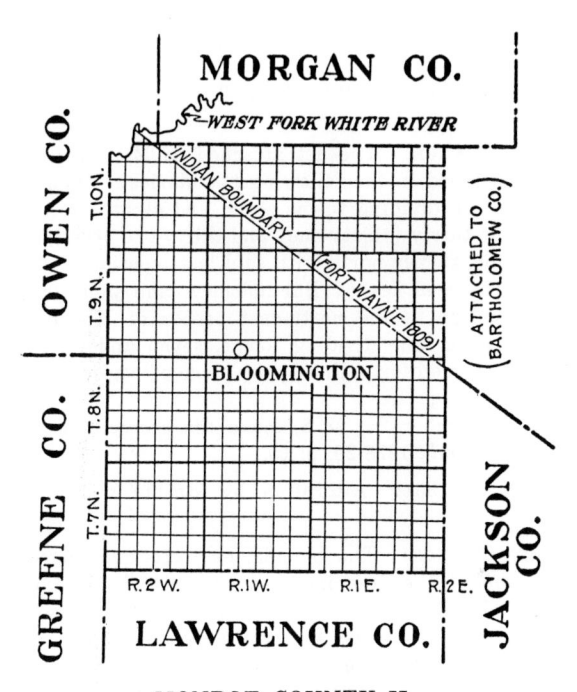

MONROE COUNTY II
[Law: Dec. 31, 1821, effective on passage]

MONROE COUNTY III

JANUARY 16, 1828: Alteration by statute attaching territory to Monroe County.

BOUNDARY CHANGE: The act attached to Monroe County all the territory included in the following boundaries: "Beginning at a point on the line dividing towns seven and eight where the line dividing sections thirty [thirty-one] and thirty-one [thirty-two] intersects the same, thence north with said last mentioned line to the line dividing the counties of Bartholomew and Johnson, thence west with said line to the north-east corner of Monroe county, thence south to the line dividing towns. seven and eight, thence east with the last mentioned line to the place of beginning." *Laws of Indiana*, 1827-28, p. 15.

A law of December 23, 1828, made the corrections shown in brackets above. *Ibid.*, 1828-29, p. 15.

FEBRUARY 10, 1831: Alteration by statute defining county boundaries.

BOUNDARY CHANGE: The boundaries were unchanged except for the addition of the area included by a line beginning on the township line dividing townships 10 and 11, at "the south east corner of section thirty-three, in town eleven north, of range two west; thence north with the last mentioned section line, until it strikes the west fork of White river; thence down said river" to the old Monroe boundary. *Revised Laws of Indiana*, 1830-31, pp. 115-16.

This area is marked (a) on the map.

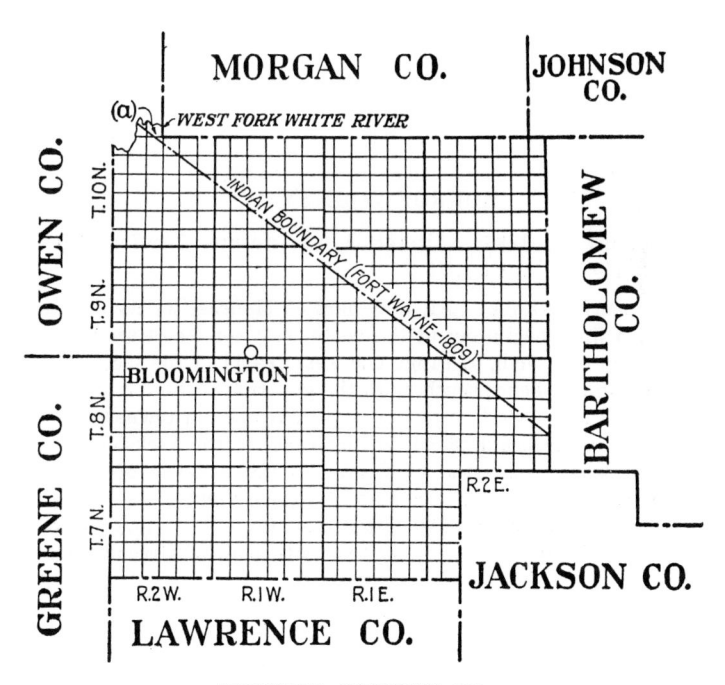

MONROE COUNTY III
[Laws: Jan. 16, 1828; Feb. 10, 1831]

MONROE COUNTY IV

FEBRUARY 4, 1836: Alteration by statute forming Brown County, effective April 1, 1836.

BOUNDARY CHANGE: All that part of Monroe County east and north of a line "beginning at the north west conner of section one, in township ten north, of range one west [east] of the second principal meredian; thence south, with the government land line twenty miles to the south west corner of section twelve, in township seven north, of the aforesaid range; thence east" to the Jackson County boundary was transferred to Brown County. *Laws of Indiana*, 1835-36 (general), p. 52. See map of Brown County.

For a note on a proposed later transfer of territory between Greene and Monroe counties, see text with map of Greene County.

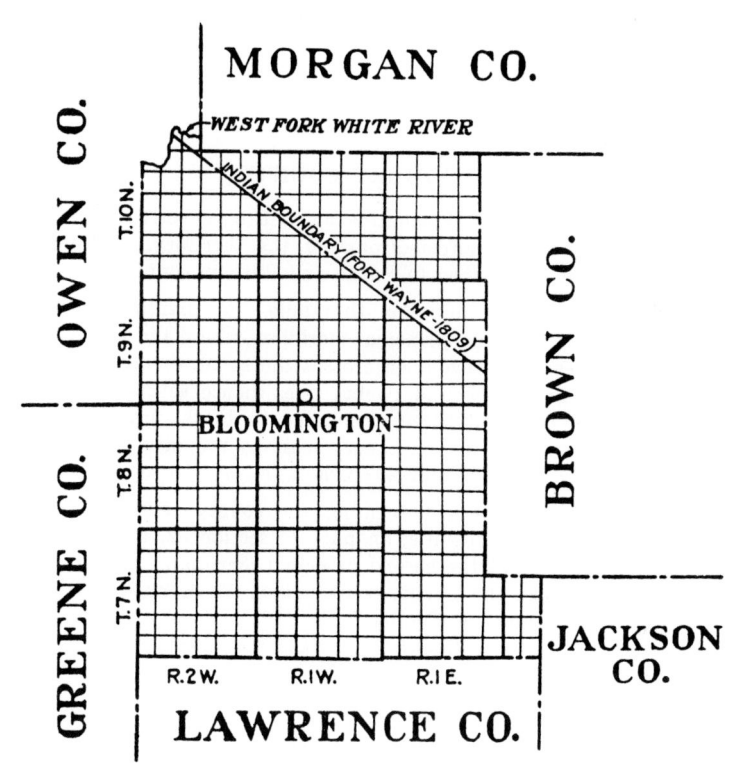

MONROE COUNTY IV
[Law: Feb. 4, 1836, effective Apr. 1, 1836]

MONTGOMERY COUNTY I

DECEMBER 21, 1822: Formation by statute, effective March 1, 1823. The formation affected part of the territory in Wabash County which was attached to Parke and Putnam counties.

BOUNDARIES: "Beginning on the range line dividing six and seven, west of the second principal meridian, where the line dividing towns sixteen and seventeen crosses the same, thence north to the line dividing twenty and twenty one, thence east to the line dividing range two and three, thence south to the line dividing towns sixteen and seventeen, thence west to the place of beginning." *Laws of Indiana*, 1822-23, p. 7.

COUNTY SEAT: The act forming the county established the county seat at Crawfordsville, on part of section 32, township 19 north, range 4 west of the second principal meridian. Crawfordsville has remained the county seat. *Ibid.*, 8; Kennedy, P. S., "History of Montgomery County," 15, 116, in Beckwith, H. W., *History of Montgomery County* . . . (Chicago, 1881).

MONTGOMERY COUNTY I

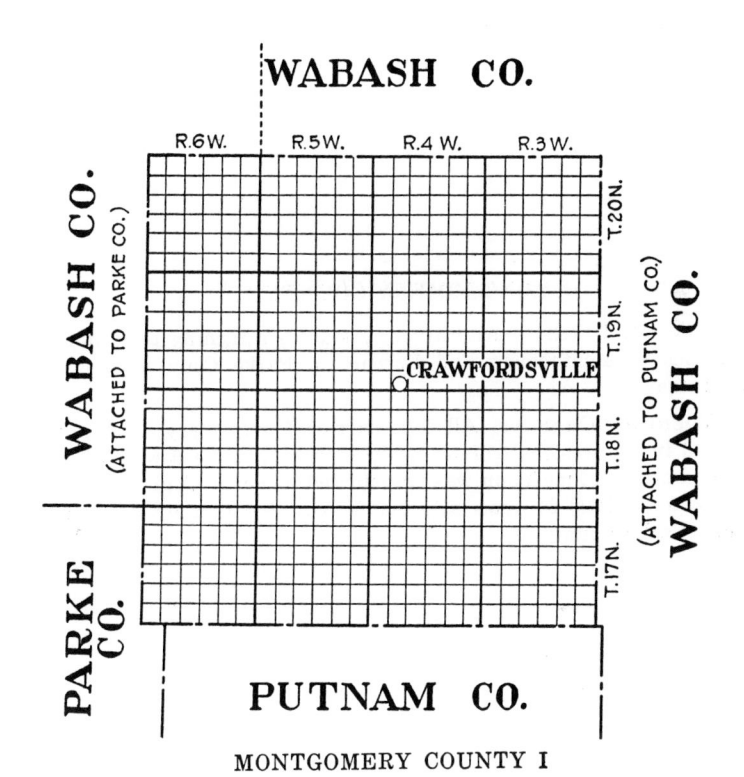

[Law: Dec. 21, 1822, effective Mar. 1, 1823]

MONTGOMERY COUNTY II

JANUARY 2, 1824: Alteration by statute attaching part of the counties of Montgomery and Putnam to Parke County, effective on passage.

BOUNDARY CHANGE: All that part of Montgomery County included in the west half of township 17 north, range 6 west of the second principal meridian was transferred to Parke County. *Laws of Indiana*, 1823-24 (special), pp. 53-54. See text of law, with map, Parke County II.

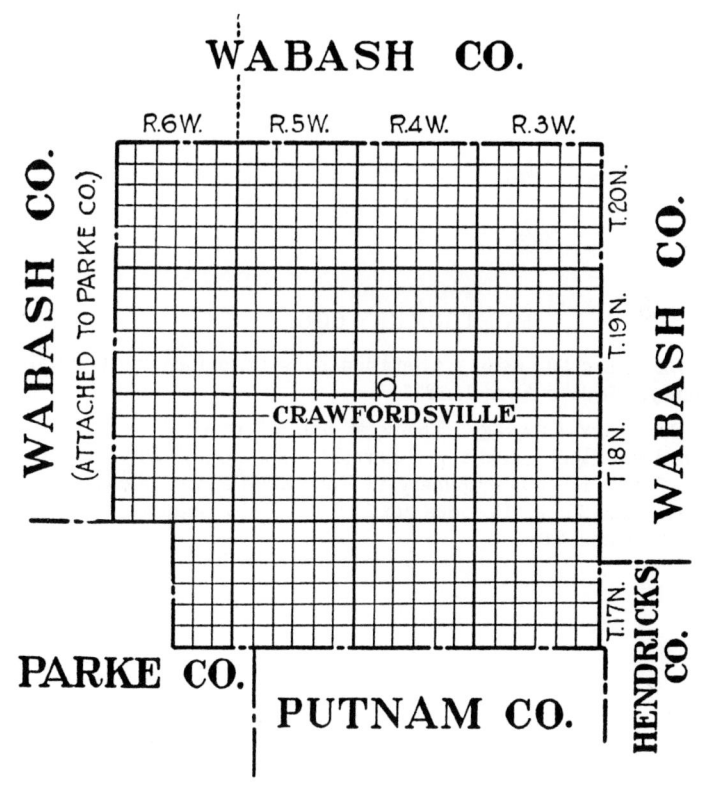

MONTGOMERY COUNTY II
[Law: Jan. 2, 1824, effective on passage]

MONTGOMERY COUNTY III

DECEMBER 30, 1825: Alteration by statute forming Fountain County, effective April 1, 1826.

BOUNDARY CHANGE: The west half of range 6, west of the second principal meridian, in townships 18, 19, and 20 north, was transferred from Montgomery to Fountain County. *Laws of Indiana*, 1825-26, p. 13. See text of law, with map of Fountain County, same date.

TIPPECANOE CO.

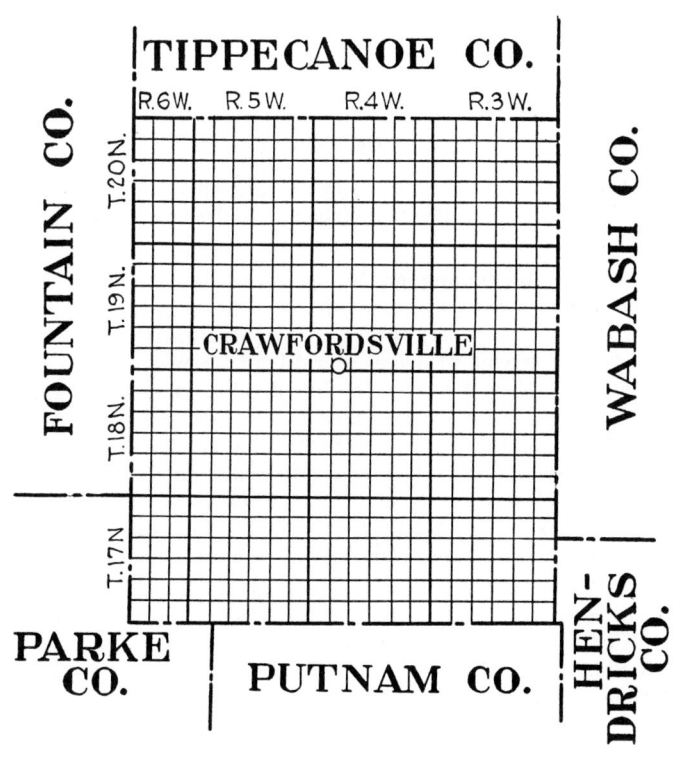

MONTGOMERY COUNTY III
[Law: Dec. 30, 1825, effective Apr. 1, 1826]

MORGAN COUNTY I

DECEMBER 31, 1821: Formation by statute, effective February 15, 1822. The formation affected Wabash and Delaware counties, New Purchase.

BOUNDARIES: "Beginning on the township line, dividing ten and eleven north, where the line dividing the ranges two and three east crosses the same; thence west to the centre of range two west of the second principal meridi[a]n, thence north nine miles, thence west three miles, to the line dividing ranges two and three west, thence north eleven miles to the corners of sections nineteen and thirty, thence east with said line twenty four miles to the line dividing ranges two and three east, thence south to the place of beginning." *Laws of Indiana*, 1821-22, pp. 35-36.

Marion County was formed by an act of December 31, 1821, effective April 1, 1822. *Ibid.*, 135-36.

COUNTY SEAT: Commissioners appointed by the act forming the county reported in June, 1822, their location of the county seat at Martinsville. The county seat has never been removed. *Ibid.*, 36; Blanchard (ed.), *Counties of Morgan, Monroe and Brown*, 15; Shockley, "County Seat Wars," *op. cit.*, 10:no.1:23.

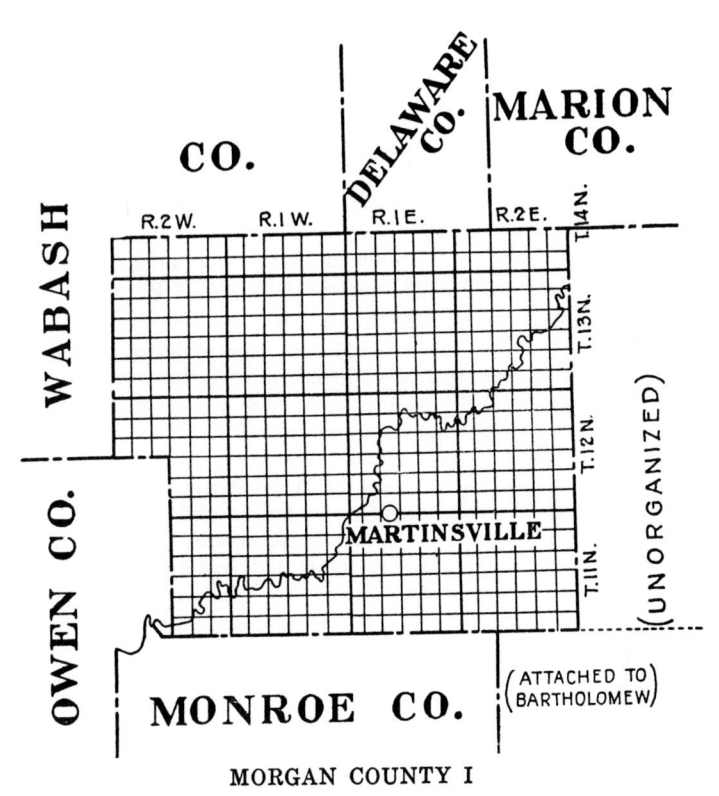

MORGAN COUNTY I
[Law: Dec. 31, 1821, effective Feb. 15, 1822]

MORGAN COUNTY II

MARCH 11, 1861: Alteration by statute changing the boundaries of Morgan and Putnam counties, effective on passage.

BOUNDARIES: "Beginning on the township line dividing townships ten and eleven north, where the line dividing ranges two and three east crosses the same; thence west to the center of range two west; thence north to the south-east corner of section sixteen, township twelve, north of range two west; thence west to the line dividing ranges two and three west; thence north to the point where Mill Creek crosses the line between ranges two and three west; thence following the meanders and channel of said Mill Creek to the point where the same crosses the line between sections twenty-one and twenty-eight, in township fourteen north of range two west; thence east to the line dividing range two and three east; thence south to the place of beginning." *Laws of Indiana*, 1861, p. 98.

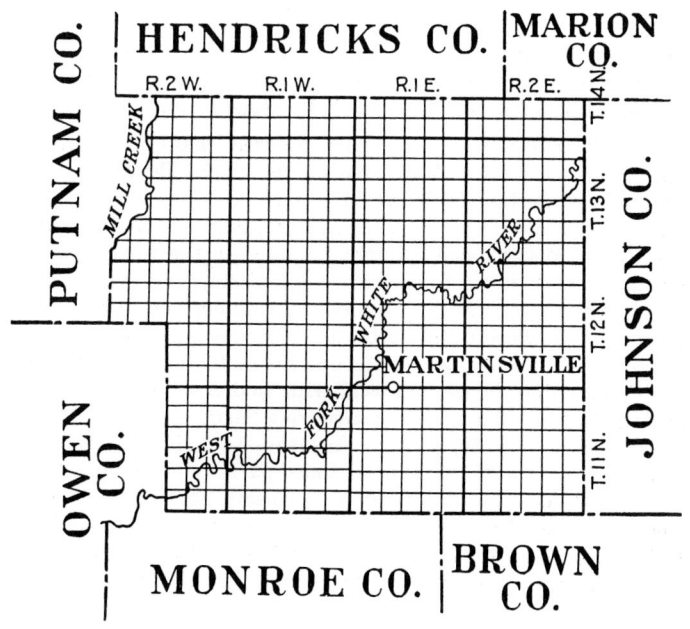

MORGAN COUNTY II

[Law: Mar. 11, 1861, effective on passage]

MORGAN COUNTY III

JUNE, 1868: Alteration by report of county commissioners, changing the boundaries of Morgan and Hendricks counties, presented March 3, 1868, and granted at the June term.

BOUNDARY CHANGE: The report ordered that the territory "commencing where the South line of Hendricks County crosses 'Mill Creek in Section 28 Township 14 N. R. 2 W and running South westerly along the meanderings of said 'Mill Creek' which is the line of Morgan and Putnam Counties to the Congressional Township line dividing Townships 13 and 14, and where said Township line crosses 'Mill Creek' thence running due east on said Congressional Township line to the principal meridian line, thence with said meridian line two miles due north to the present Hendricks County line thence due west with said line to the place of beginning: embracing in said boundaries Sections 25, 26, 27, 28, 29, 30, 31, 32, 33, 34, 35, & 36 in Township 14 N R 1 W and Sections 25, 26, 27, 34, 35, 36 and all those parts of Sections 28, 32, & 33 that lie east of 'Mill Creek' in Township 14 N R 2 W lying in the County of Morgan be detached from said County and attached to the County of Hendricks, all in the State of Indiana: And . . . further ordered that the boundaries of the County of Hendricks be changed so as to include in its area the territory described above." Commissioners' Record 10, Auditor's Office, Morgan County. See pages 122 and 123 for comment on the constitutionality of the change.

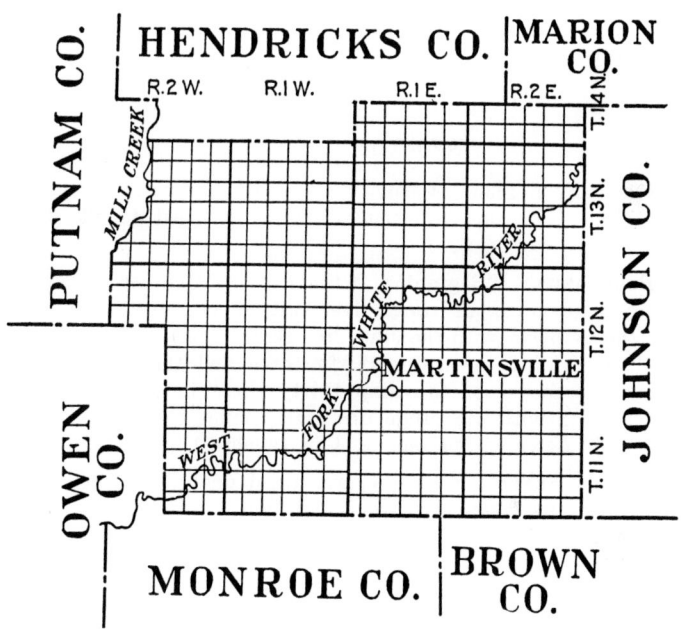

MORGAN COUNTY III

[Commissioners' Report: Mar. 3, 1868, granted June, 1868]

NEWTON COUNTY I

FEBRUARY 7, 1835: Formation by statute, effective on publication. The formation affected territory attached to St. Joseph County.

BOUNDARIES: "Beginning at the south east corner of township twenty nine north, of range five west, thence west to the state line, thence north with the state line thirty miles, thence east with the line dividing townships thirty three and thirty-four, to the north east corner of township thirty three in range five west, thence south with the range line thirty miles to the place of beginning." *Laws of Indiana*, 1834-35 (general), pp. 46-47.

COUNTY SEAT: The county remained unorganized for several years after its boundaries were first laid out. It had no county seat during this period.

NEWTON COUNTY I

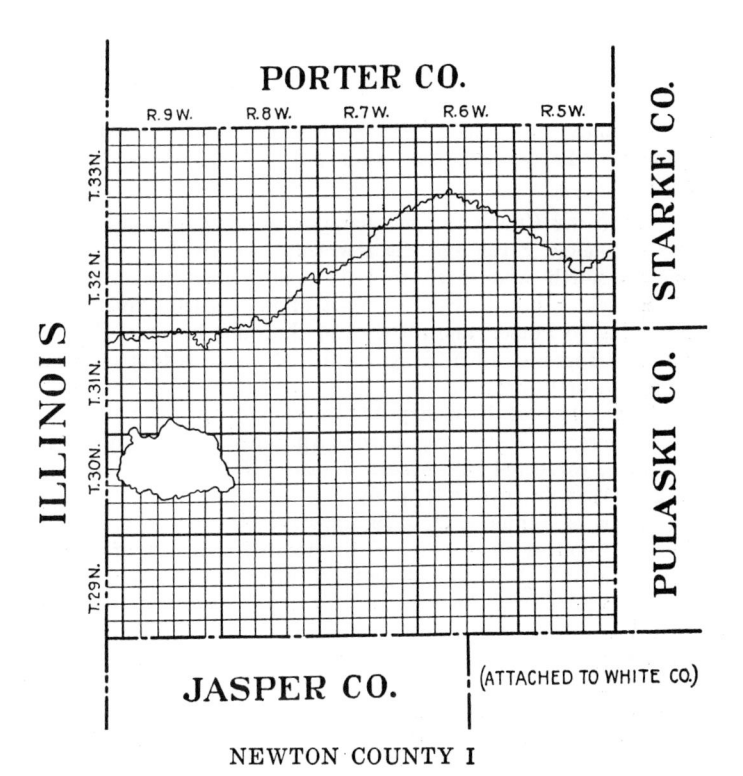

[Law: Feb. 7, 1835, effective on publication]

NEWTON COUNTY II

JANUARY 28, 1836: Alteration by statute organizing the county of Porter, and for other purposes, effective February 1, 1836.

BOUNDARY CHANGE: All that part of Newton County between the Kankakee River and the township line dividing townships 33 and 34 north was given to Lake and Porter counties, all east of the center line of range 7 west of the second principal meridian going to Porter, and all west of the same line to Lake County. *Laws of Indiana*, 1835-36 (general), p. 51. See text of law, with map, Porter County II.

In the law of February 17, 1838, defining county boundaries, these changes were overlooked. An amending act of February 11, 1839, corrected this error. *Laws of Indiana*, 1837-38 (local), p. 263; 1838-39 (general), p. 68.

A law of January 29, 1839, appointed commissioners "to examine the counties of Jasper and Newton, with a view of their being consolidated." It provided that "if, after examination, they shall be of opinion that the interest of the two counties would be promoted by the union of the same, from thenceforth the territory, known by the names of Jasper and Newton counties, shall be known as Jasper county." *Ibid.*, 83. The consolidation took place that year and lasted until 1859, when a new Newton County was formed. See following map, and maps, Jasper County II and III.

NEWTON COUNTY BOUNDARIES 623

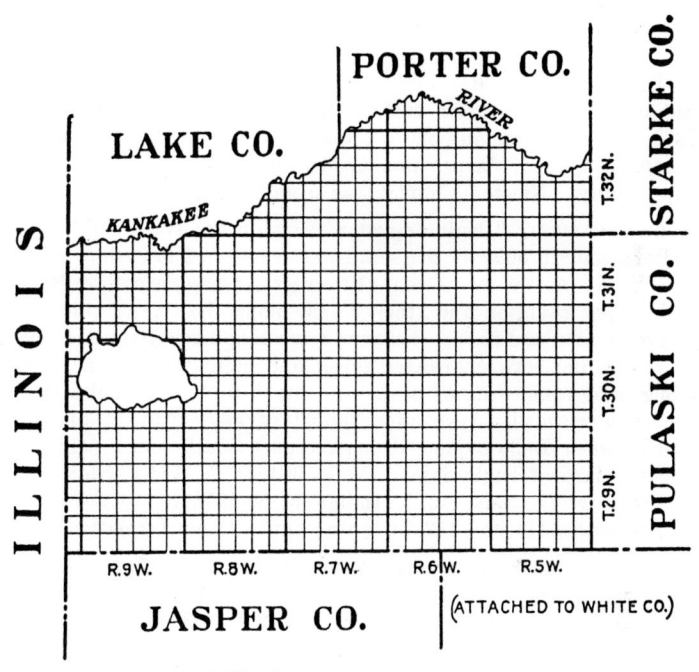

NEWTON COUNTY II
[Law: Jan. 28, 1836, effective Feb. 1, 1836]

NEWTON COUNTY III

DECEMBER 8, 1859: Formation, pursuant to a decision of the Indiana Supreme Court sustaining the report of February 27, 1858, made by commissioners appointed by the Board of County Commissioners of Jasper County, to lay out the boundaries of a new county. Newton County was organized in 1860.

BOUNDARIES: "Beginning at a point on the state line between Indiana and Illinois, at the south-west corner of township twenty-seven (27) north, range ten (10) west, at the corner of Benton and Jasper counties, Ind., thence east along the line of said counties of Benton and Jasper, between townships twenty-six and seven, to range line between ranges seven and eight west, thence north along said range line of seven and eight to the Kankakee river, thence westwardly down the channel of said river to the state line between Indiana and Illinois, thence south along said state line to place of beginning." Davis, Edwin A. (ed.), *Statutes of the State of Indiana*, 1:212 (Indianapolis, 1878).

See pages 111 and 112 for an account of this formation.

COUNTY SEAT: A site in section 22, township 27 north, range 9 west was chosen as the county seat for Newton County. The original name, Kent, was soon lengthened to Kentland. In this town the seat of justice has remained, although there have been attempts to remove it. Shockley, "County Seat Wars," *op. cit.*, 10:no.1:42-44; Hamilton and Darroch (eds.), *Standard History of Jasper and Newton Counties*, 1:189-96; Ade, *Newton County*, 129-33.

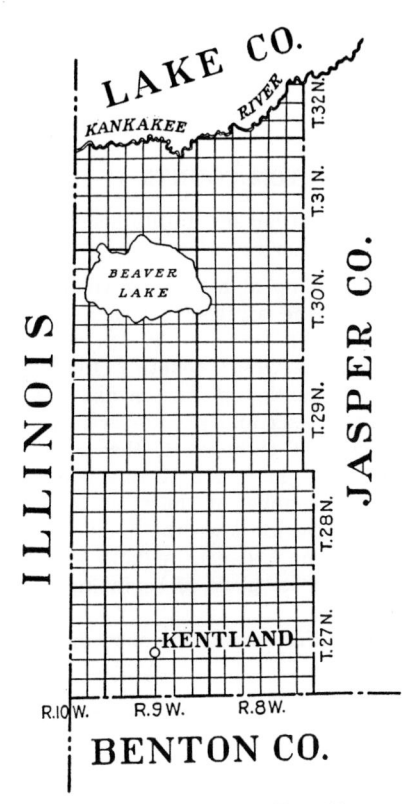

NEWTON COUNTY III

[Commissioners' Report: Feb. 27, 1858, recorded Dec. 8, 1859]

NEWTON COUNTY IV

MARCH 8, 1923: Alteration by statute defining the boundaries of Newton, Jasper, and other counties.

BOUNDARIES: "Beginning at a point on the state line between Indiana and Illinois, at the southwest corner of [section thirty-five] township twenty-seven north, range ten west, at the corner of Benton and Jasper [Newton] counties, Indiana, thence east along the line of said counties of Benton and Jasper [Newton], between townships twenty-six and twenty-seven, to the range line between ranges seven and eight west, thence north along said range line of seven and eight to the Marble Powers ditch, thence down the middle of the channel of the same to the beginning of the Williams ditch, and thence down the middle of the channel of the same to the state line between Indiana and Illinois, thence south along said state line to place of beginning." *Laws of Indiana*, 1923, pp. 464-65.

The corrections supplied in brackets above have not been made by law.

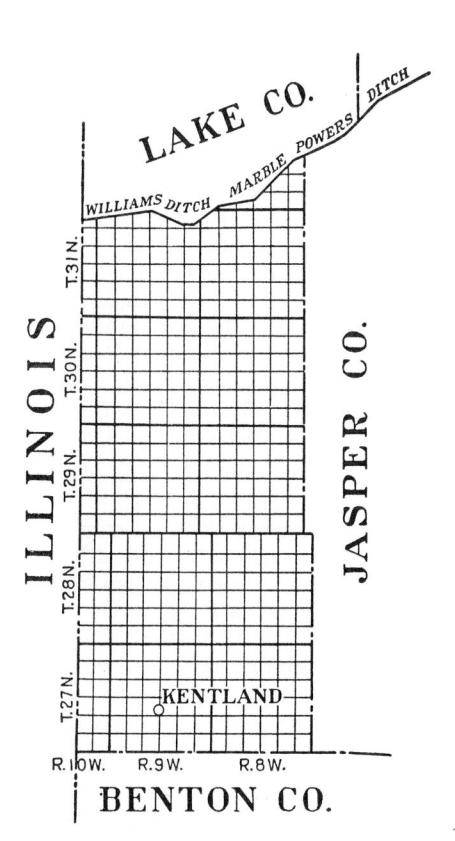

NEWTON COUNTY IV
[Law: Mar. 8, 1923]

NOBLE COUNTY I

FEBRUARY 7, 1835: Formation by statute, effective June 1, 1835. The formation affected territory attached to Elkhart, La Grange, and Allen counties. Noble was organized by an act of February 6, 1836, effective March 1, 1836.

BOUNDARIES: "Beginning at the north east corner of township thirty-five, range eleven east, thence west with the township line, dividing townships thirty-five and thirty-six, to the range line, dividing range eight and seven east, thence south with said range line to the south-west corner of township thirty-three range eight east, thence with said range [township] line dividing thirty-three and thirty-two, to the south east corner of township thirty-three, range eleven east, thence north with the range line, dividing ranges eleven and twelve, to the place of beginning." *Laws of Indiana,* 1834-35 (general), p. 43.

COUNTY SEAT: Commissioners appointed in the organization act, on May 3, 1836, reported their selection of a site in section 24, township 34 north, range 8 east, which was named Sparta but is now called Kimmel. Commissioners appointed under an act of February 4, 1837, to relocate the county seat, chose Augusta. After the destruction of the Augusta courthouse by fire, the legislature, in an act of January 13, 1844, appointed commissioners to again relocate the seat of government. In March, 1844, Port Mitchell became the county seat. The legislature, by an act of January 10, 1846, provided for a further change by a series of county elections. Center was the final choice in the election of August, 1846. This has remained the county seat, although the name has been changed to Albion. *Ibid.,* 1835-36 (general), pp. 54-55; 1836-37 (general), pp. 113-15; 1843-44 (local), pp. 155-56; 1845-46 (local), pp. 66-67; Kaler and Maring, *History of Whitley County,* 57-58; *Counties of La Grange and Noble,* pt.2:41-43.

NOBLE COUNTY BOUNDARIES 629

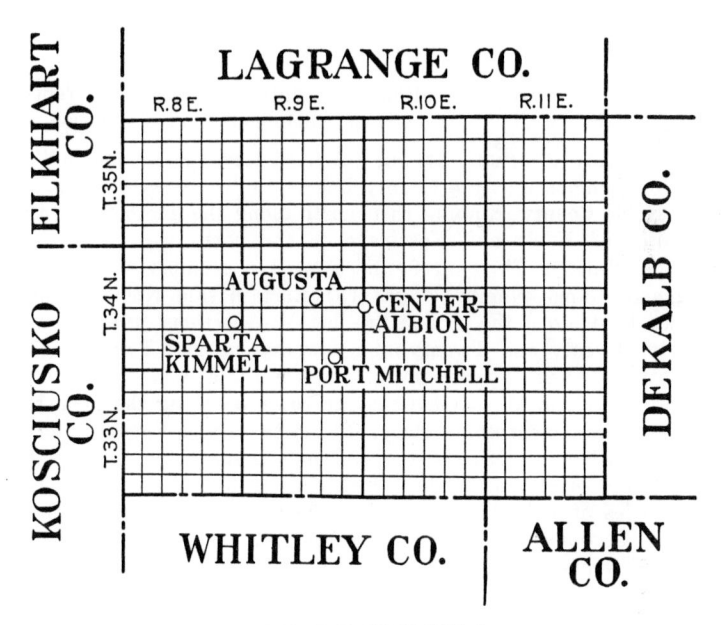

NOBLE COUNTY I
[Law: Feb. 7, 1835, effective June 1, 1835]

NOBLE COUNTY II

JUNE 11, 1859: Alteration by county commissioners' report changing the boundary line between Noble and Whitley counties.

BOUNDARY CHANGE: It was provided that the change in line should "commence at the County line at the south west corner of said Noble County, running then north along the line between the Counties of Noble and Kosciusko to the north west corner of Section Number Thirty (30) in Township Number Thirtythree North of Range Number Eight (8) East in said Noble County, thence East along the section line between Sections Nineteen and Thirty, Twenty and Twenty-nine, Twenty-one and Twenty-eight, Twenty-two and Twenty-seven, Twenty-three and Twenty-six, Twenty-four and Twenty-five, thence south on along the township line between Townships Number Thirty-three and Range Number Eight and Number Nine to the present boundary line between the said Counties of Noble and Whitley so as to include within the boundaries of said Whitley County the following named Sections, 'towit', Sections Twentyfive, Twentysix, Twenty-seven, Twenty-eight, Twentynine, Thirty, Thirtyone, Thirtytwo, Thirtythree, thirtyfour, Thirtyfive and Thirtysix, of Township Number Thirty-three (33) North of Range Number Eight (8) East." Whitley County Records.

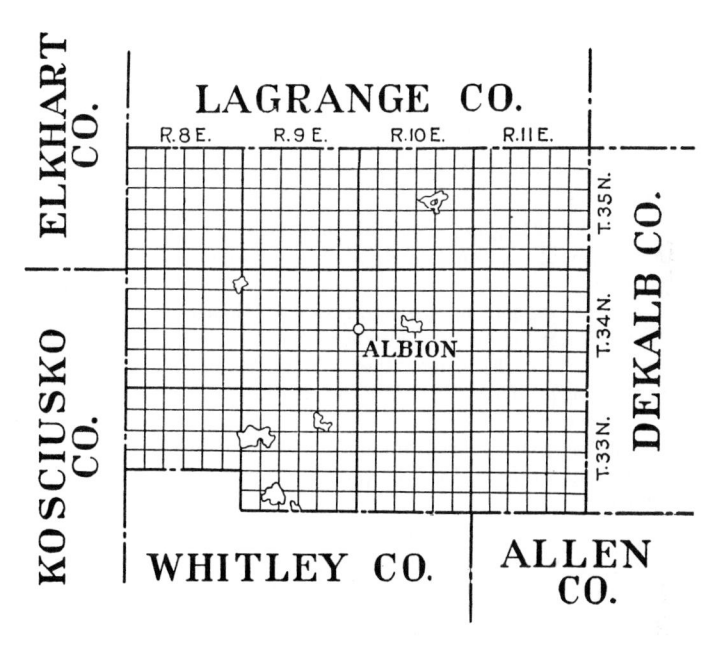

NOBLE COUNTY II
[Commissioners' Report: June 11, 1859]

OHIO COUNTY I

JANUARY 4, 1844: Formation by statute, effective March 1, 1844. The organization of the county was provided for in the same law, to be effective May 1, 1844. The formation affected Dearborn County.

BOUNDARIES: "Beginning on the Ohio river on the section line, between fractional sections number twenty-five and thirty-six, in town four, range one west, thence west with said line to the north west corner of section number thirty-two; thence south to the north west corner of section number five, in town three, range one; thence west to the range line between range one and range two; thence south to the line dividing Switzerland and Dearborn counties; thence with said line east to the Ohio river; thence up said river to the place of beginning, shall constitute the county of Ohio." *Laws of Indiana*, 1843-44 (general), p. 7.

See page 83.

COUNTY SEAT: Commissioners appointed in the act forming the county met on April 8, 1844, at Rising Sun, and selected a site within the town in fractional section 2 and section 3, township 3 north, range 1 west. This was in contravention of a section of the law which stipulated that the seat of justice be near the center of the county. It has, however, remained the county seat. *Laws of Indiana*, 1843-44 (general), p. 7; *History of Dearborn and Ohio Counties*, 116, 118, 356.

OHIO COUNTY BOUNDARIES 633

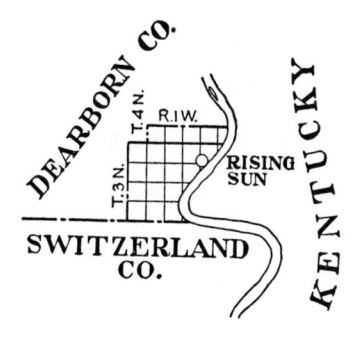

OHIO COUNTY I

[Law: Jan. 4, 1844, effective Mar. 1, 1844]

OHIO COUNTY II

JANUARY 7, 1845: Alteration by statute, attaching additional territory to the county of Ohio, effective on publication in the *Indiana Blade*, of Rising Sun.

BOUNDARY CHANGE: "All the territory which now belongs to Dearborn county, and which lies south of the main channel of Laughery Creek . . . is hereby attached to the county of Ohio, and shall form a part of said county of Ohio." The county boundaries are outlined in the same law as follows: "Beginning at the Ohio river in the centre of the mouth of Laughery Creek, and running up said Laughery Creek in the centre of the channel of the main creek with the meanders thereof, to where the same crosses the west boundary line of Dearborn county, commonly called the old Indian boundary line; thence southwardly on said old Indian boundary line to where the same intersects the line dividing the counties of Dearborn and Switzerland; thence east on the section line to the Ohio river; thence up said river with the meanders thereof to the place of beginning." *Laws of Indiana*, 1844-45 (local), p. 225.

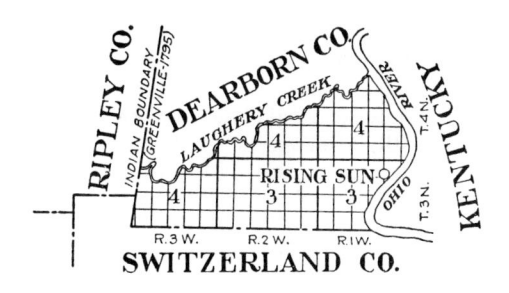

OHIO COUNTY II

[Law: Jan. 7, 1845, effective on publication in *Indiana Blade*]

ORANGE COUNTY I
[Indiana Territory]

DECEMBER 26, 1815: Formation by statute, effective February 1, 1816. The formation affected Knox, Gibson, and Washington counties.

BOUNDARIES: "Beginning on the Indian boundary line, where the range line dividing ranges two and three west of the second principal meridian intersects said boundary line; thence south with said range line until it intersects the line dividing the counties of Perry and Gibson; thence east with said line until it intersects the western boundary line of Harrison county; thence north with said line to the south-west corner of Washington county, and north-west corner of Harrison county; thence east with the line dividing Harrison and Washington counties, until it intersects the line dividing sections sixteen and seventeen in range two east, town one south; thence north with said line dividing sections sixteen and seventeen to the Indian boundary line; thence westwardly with said Indian boundary line to the place of beginning." *Acts of Indiana Territory*, 1815, pp. 57-58.

COUNTY SEAT: Commissioners appointed under the law forming the county, reported in February, 1816, their selection of a site which was named Paoli. *Ibid.*, 59; *History of Lawrence, Orange and Washington Counties*, 412.

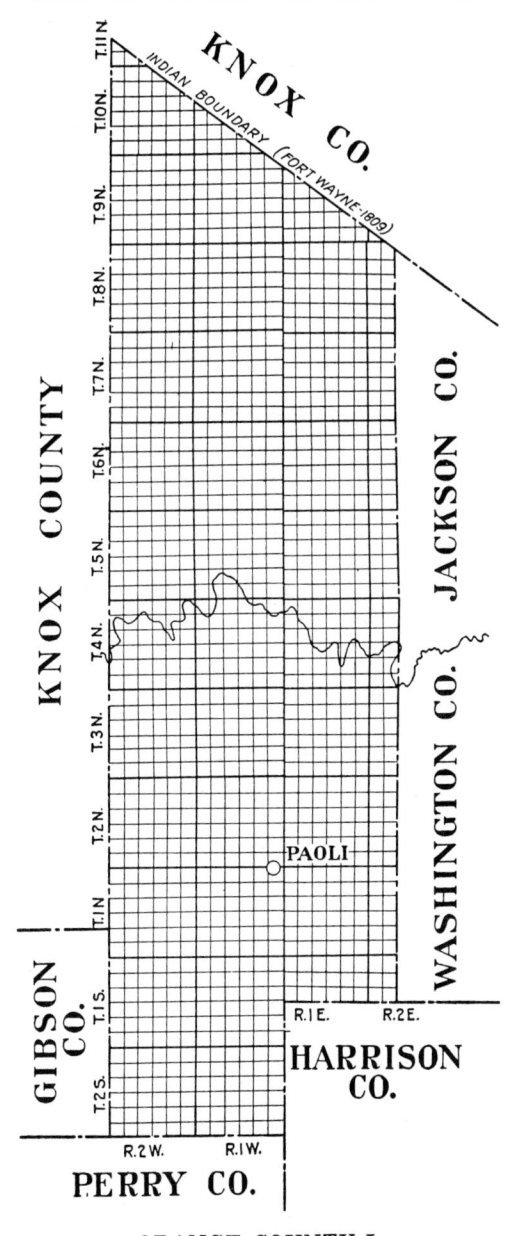

ORANGE COUNTY I

[Law: Dec. 26, 1815, effective Feb. 1, 1816]

ORANGE COUNTY II

JANUARY 29, 1818: Alteration by statute attaching a part of the county of Harrison to the county of Orange, effective February 15, 1818, and forming Crawford County, effective March 1, 1818.

BOUNDARY CHANGE: All that part of Harrison County included in the following boundaries was attached to Orange County: "Beginning on the second principal meridian line, where an east and west sectional line dividing sections thirty and thirty one, in township one south, and range one east strikes the same; thence east with said sectional line to the south-east corner of section number twenty nine, in township one south and range two east; thence north with a sectional line to the corner of Orange County; thence west with the line of Orange county to the aforesaid meridian line; thence south with the same to the place of beginning." *Laws of Indiana,* 1817-18 (special), pp. 25-26.

All that part of Orange County south of a section line beginning at the southeast corner of section 25, township 1 south, range 1 west of the second principal meridian, running thence west with the sectional line to the line dividing ranges 2 and 3 west, was transferred to Crawford County. *Laws of Indiana,* 1817-18 (special), p. 27. See text of law with map, Crawford County I.

ORANGE COUNTY BOUNDARIES 639

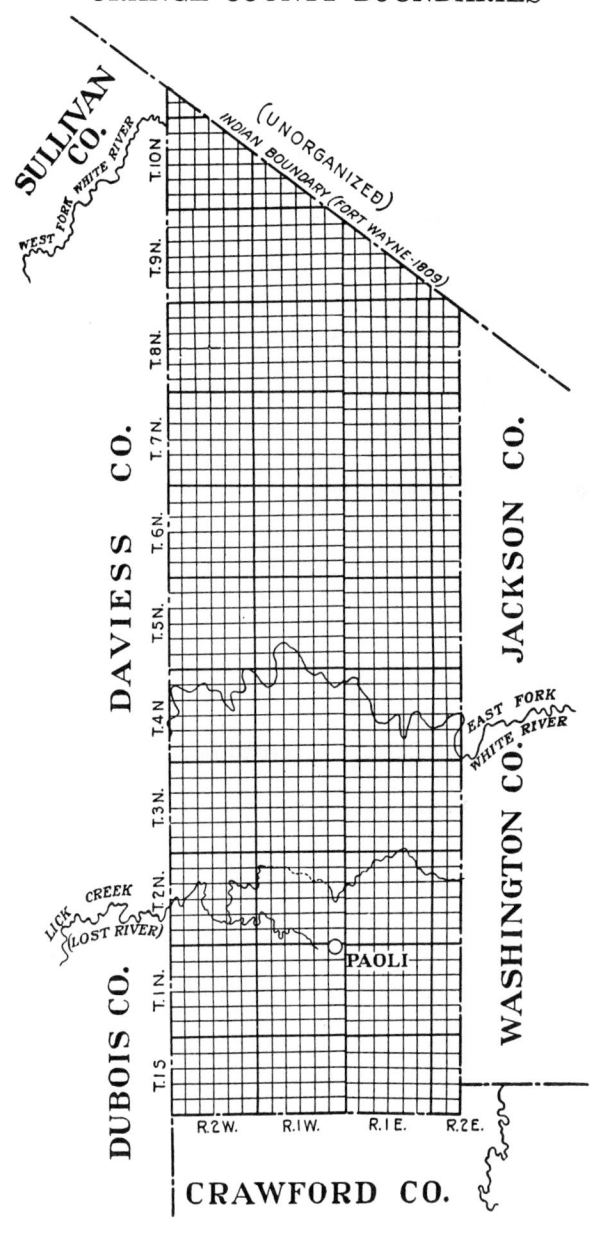

ORANGE COUNTY II

[Law: Jan. 29, 1818, effective Feb. 15 and Mar. 1, 1818]

ORANGE COUNTY III

JANUARY 7, 1818: Alteration by statute forming Lawrence County, effective March 16, 1818.

BOUNDARY CHANGE: All that part of Orange County included in the following boundaries was formed into Lawrence County: "Beginning at the range line dividing ranges two and three west, at the centre of town three north, and running thence east to the line dividing the counties of Washington, Orange and Jackson, thence north with said line to the line dividing townships six and seven north, thence west with said line [to the line] dividing ranges two and three west, thence south with said range line to the place of beginning." *Laws of Indiana*, 1817-18 (special), pp. 12-13.

JANUARY 14, 1818: Alteration by statute forming Monroe County, effective April 10, 1818.

BOUNDARY CHANGE: All that part of Orange County included in the following boundaries was formed into Monroe County: "Beginning on the line of Orange and Jackson counties, where the line dividing townships six and seven crosses the same, thence west with the last mentioned line to the line dividing ranges two and three west, of the second principal meridian, thence north with said range line to the Indian boundary, thence southeastwardly with said boundary to the line of Orange and Jackson counties, thence south with the same to the beginning." *Ibid.*, 14-15.

ORANGE COUNTY III

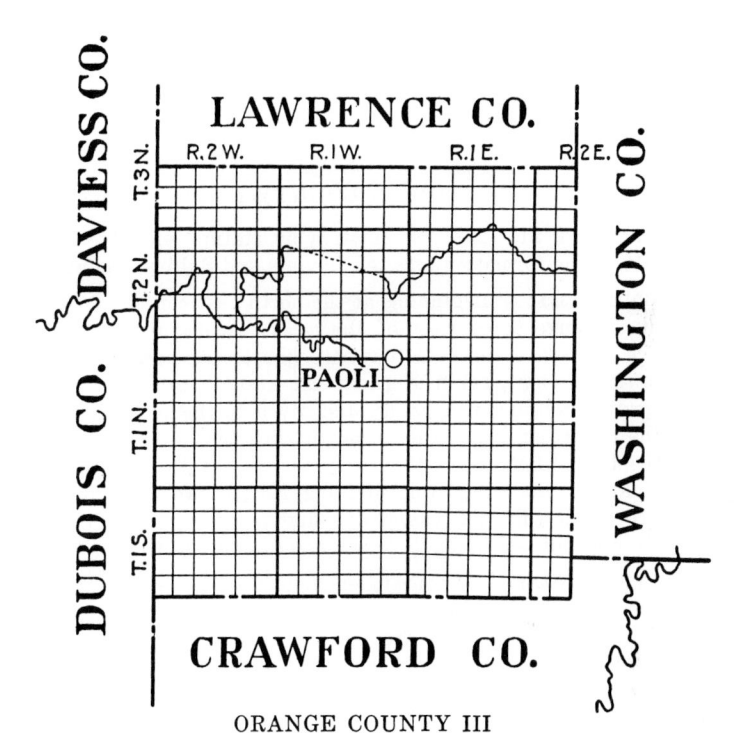

[Laws: Jan. 7, 1818, effective Mar. 16, 1818; Jan. 14, 1818, effective Apr. 10, 1818]

OWEN COUNTY I

DECEMBER 21, 1818: Formation by statute, effective January 1, 1819. The formation affected Daviess and Sullivan counties.

BOUNDARIES: "Beginning at the north east corner of township eight of range three west of the second principal meridian line, thence west with the said township line to the north west corner of township eight, north of range six west, thence north with the range line dividing ranges six and seven to the south east corner of the county of Vigo; thence north with the line of Vigo county to the Indian boundary; thence south eastwardly with the Indian boundary to the range line dividing ranges two and three west; thence south with the range line dividing ranges two and three to the place of beginning." *Laws of Indiana*, 1818-19, p. 96.

COUNTY SEAT: Commissioners appointed under the law forming the county reported in favor of the site of Lancaster, about half a mile up the river from the present Spencer. The county seat was later removed. *Ibid.*, 97; Blanchard (ed.), *Counties of Clay and Owen*, 561-62.

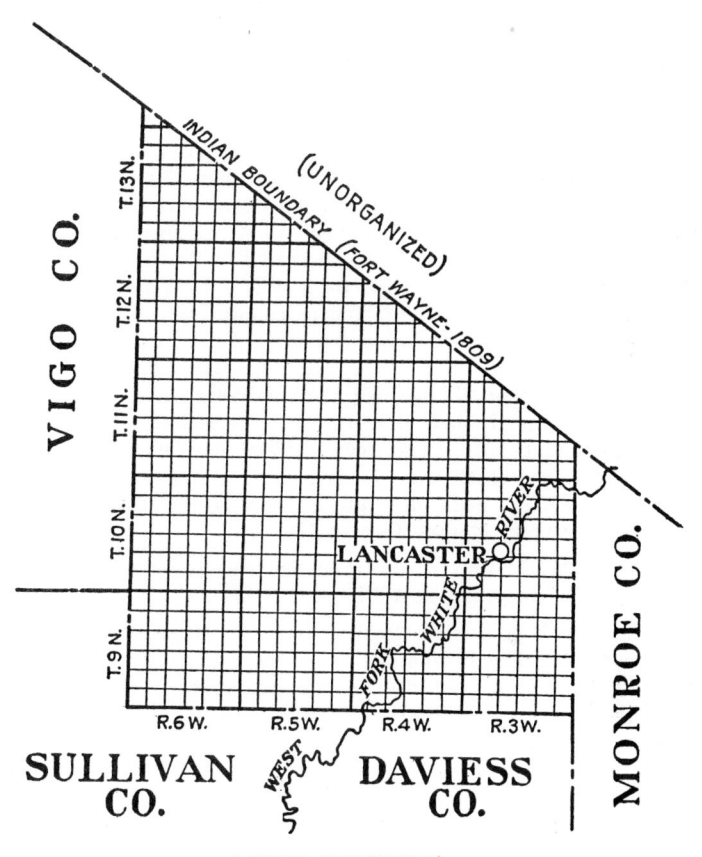

OWEN COUNTY I

[Law: Dec. 21, 1818, effective Jan. 1, 1819]

OWEN COUNTY II

DECEMBER 31, 1821: Alteration by statute attaching territory to Owen County, effective on passage.

BOUNDARY CHANGE: The act attached to Owen County "all that part of the county of Wabash contained in the following boundaries to wit, Beginning on the range line dividing ranges four and five west of the second principal meridian line at the centre of township twelve north thence east to the centre of range two west thence south to the west branch of White river thence down said river with the meanders of the same to Owen county where the line dividing ranges two and three west crosses said river.

"SEC. 2. All that part of Monroe county lying west of White river be . . . attached to Owen county." *Laws of Indiana*, 1821-22, pp. 79-80.

This attachment disregarded the small area above the center line of township 12 north, and between the Indian boundary and the east boundary of Putnam County, which had belonged to Owen. A tiny area west of Morgan County, north of Monroe County, and south of the West Fork of White River was not attached to any county. See map, Monroe County III.

DECEMBER 31, 1821: Alteration by statute forming Putnam County, effective April 1, 1822.

BOUNDARY CHANGE: All that part of Owen County north and west of a line beginning where the line between townships 10 and 11 north crosses the line dividing ranges 6 and 7 west, running thence east with the township line to the line dividing ranges 4 and 5 west, thence north with said range line to the Fort Wayne Treaty line of 1809, was transferred to Putnam County. *Laws of Indiana*, 1821-22, p. 65.

COUNTY SEAT: By an act of December 29, 1819, in response to a petition from citizens of Owen County, new commissioners were appointed to select a county seat. On February 12, 1820, they reported their selection of a site in sections 20, 21, 28, and 29. It was given the name of Spencer. *Ibid.*, 1819-20, pp. 11-12; Shockley, "County Seat Wars," *op. cit.*, 10:no.1:17; Tipton's Journal as commissioner to locate the seat of justice of Owen County, February 3-15, 1820, Tipton Papers, Indiana State Library.

OWEN COUNTY BOUNDARIES 645

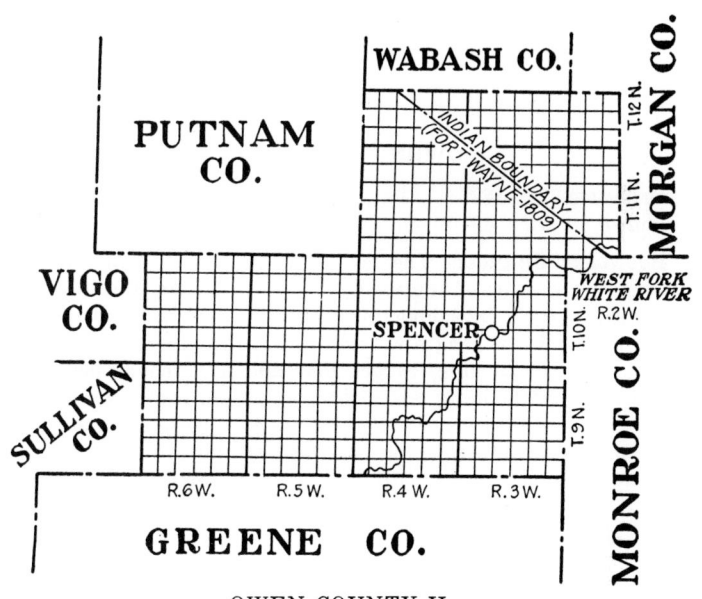

OWEN COUNTY II

[Laws: Dec. 31, 1821, effective on passage; Dec. 31, 1821, effective Apr. 1, 1822]

OWEN COUNTY III

DECEMBER 21, 1822: Alteration by statute amending act of December 31, 1821, effective on passage.

BOUNDARY CHANGE: The law provided that "all that part of the present county of Putnam, contained within the following boundary, to wit: beginning in the centre of town twelve north, on the line dividing ranges six and seven west, thence east twelve miles to the line dividing ranges four and five, thence south nine miles to the line dividing towns ten and eleven, thence west twelve miles with said line, to the line dividing ranges, six and seven, thence north nine miles, to the place of beginning . . . be attached to, constitute, and form a part of the county of Owen." *Laws of Indiana*, 1822-23, pp. 5-6.

OWEN COUNTY BOUNDARIES

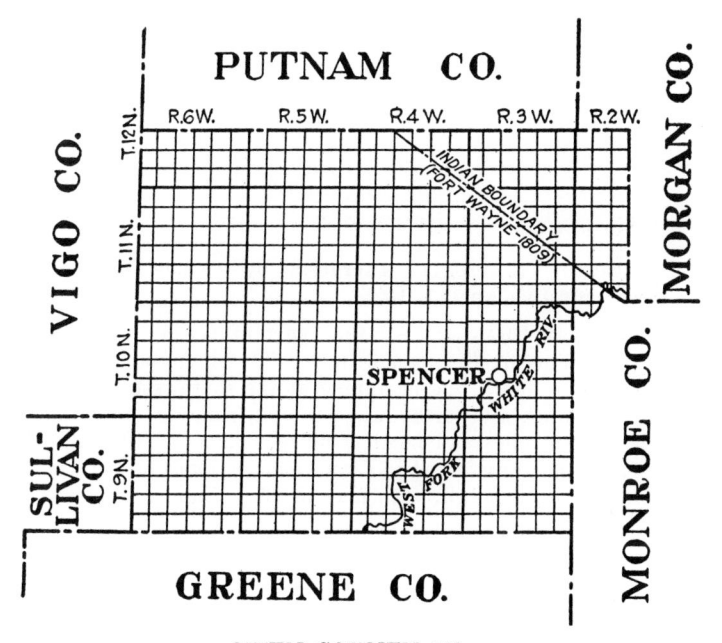

OWEN COUNTY III

[Law: Dec. 21, 1822, effective on passage]

OWEN COUNTY IV

FEBRUARY 12, 1825: Alteration by statute forming Clay County, effective April 1, 1825.

BOUNDARY CHANGE: All that part of Owen County between the range line dividing ranges 6 and 7 west of the second principal meridian and a line beginning at the southwest corner of section 35, township 9 north, range 6 west, running thence north 12 miles, east 6 miles and north 9 miles to the Owen-Putnam boundary line was transferred to Clay County. *Laws of Indiana*, 1825, p. 17. See text of law, with map of Clay County.

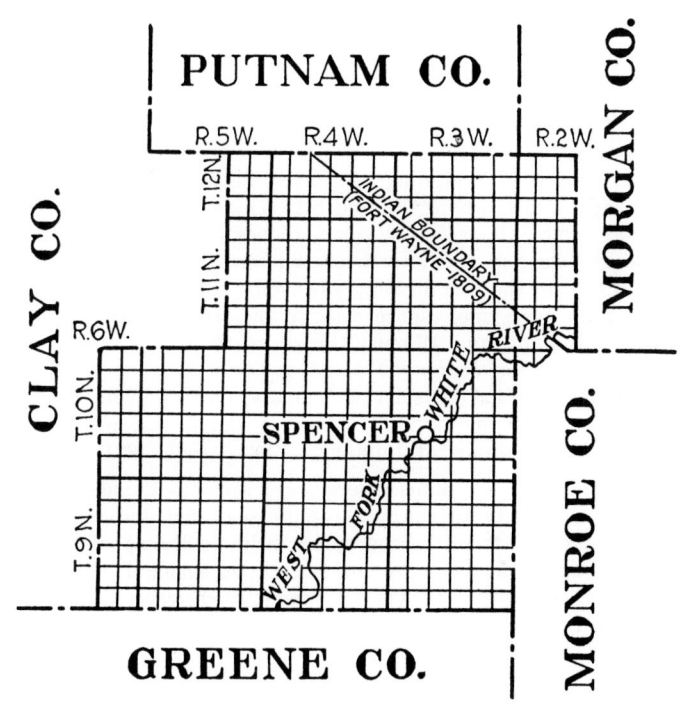

OWEN COUNTY IV
[Law: Feb. 12, 1825, effective Apr. 1, 1825]

PARKE COUNTY I

JANUARY 9, 1821: Formation by statute, effective April 2, 1821. The formation affected Vigo and Wabash counties.

BOUNDARIES: "Beginning at the line dividing the states of Indiana and Illinois, where the line between townships thirteen and fourteen north intersects the same, thence east to the line dividing ranges six and seven west, of the second principal meridian, thence north to the line dividing townships seventeen and eighteen north of the base line, thence west to the state line, dividing the states of Indiana and Illinois, thence south to the place of beginning." *Laws of Indiana*, 1820-21, p. 63.

Civil and criminal jurisdiction over that part of Wabash County lying west of the line dividing ranges 5 and 6 west was granted Parke County in an act of January 2, 1822. *Ibid.*, 1821-22, p. 119.

COUNTY SEAT: Commissioners were appointed under the act forming the county to select a county seat, but the removal of one commissioner from the county necessitated the appointment of another. This was done by an act of December 7, 1821. The selection of a county seat was not completed, however, before 1824 or 1825. In the meantime Roseville and Armiesburg served as temporary seats of government for the county. *Ibid.*, 1820-21, p. 64; 1821-22, p. 14; *History of Parke and Vermillion Counties*, 60-61; Shockley, "County Seat Wars," *op. cit.*, 10:no.1:22.

PARKE COUNTY BOUNDARIES 651

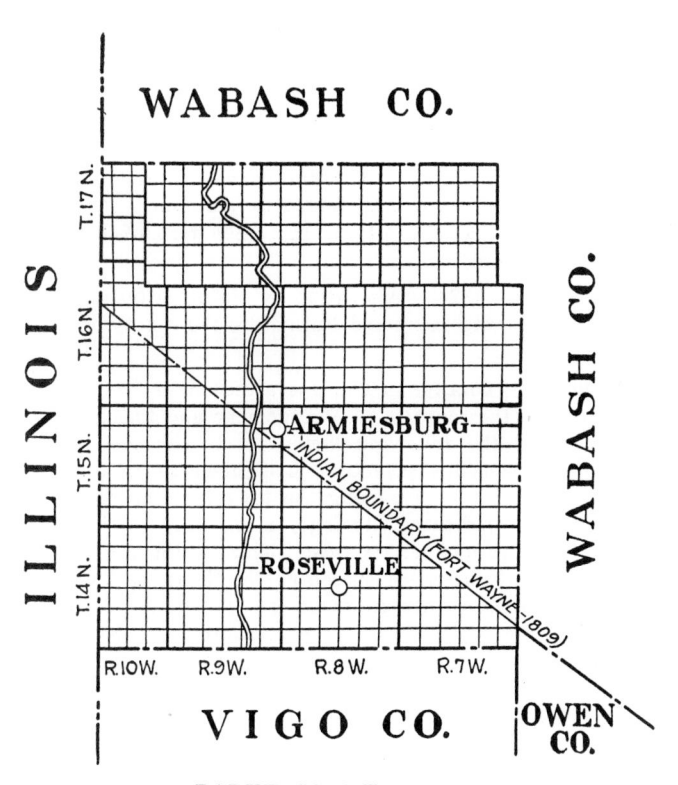

PARKE COUNTY I

[Law: Jan. 9, 1821, effective Apr. 2, 1821]

PARKE COUNTY II

JANUARY 2, 1824: Alteration by statute forming Vermillion County, effective February 1, 1824.

BOUNDARY CHANGE: All that part of Parke County west of the Wabash River was transferred to Vermillion County. *Revised Laws of Indiana*, 1823-24, p. 113. See text of law, with map, Vermillion County.

JANUARY 2, 1824: Alteration by statute attaching part of the counties of Montgomery and Putnam to the county of Parke, effective on passage.

BOUNDARY CHANGE: The act attached to Parke County "all that part of the counties of Montgomery and Putnam, lying south and west of the following boundary, to wit: Beginning at the corner of townships seventeen & eighteen north of range six & seven west; thence east along the township line, to the corner of sections numbered three and four, in township numbered seventeen north, of range number six west; thence south to the line dividing townships sixteen and seventeen north; thence east with the township line, to the corner of townships sixteen and seventeen north, of ranges five and six west; thence south with the range line, to the corner of townships thirteen and fourteen, and thence west to the present boundary of Parke county." *Laws of Indiana*, 1823-24 (special), pp. 53-54.

COUNTY SEAT: Rockville became the permanent seat of justice. See text with preceding map. Shockley, "County Seat Wars," *op. cit.*, 10:no.1:22.

PARKE COUNTY BOUNDARIES 653

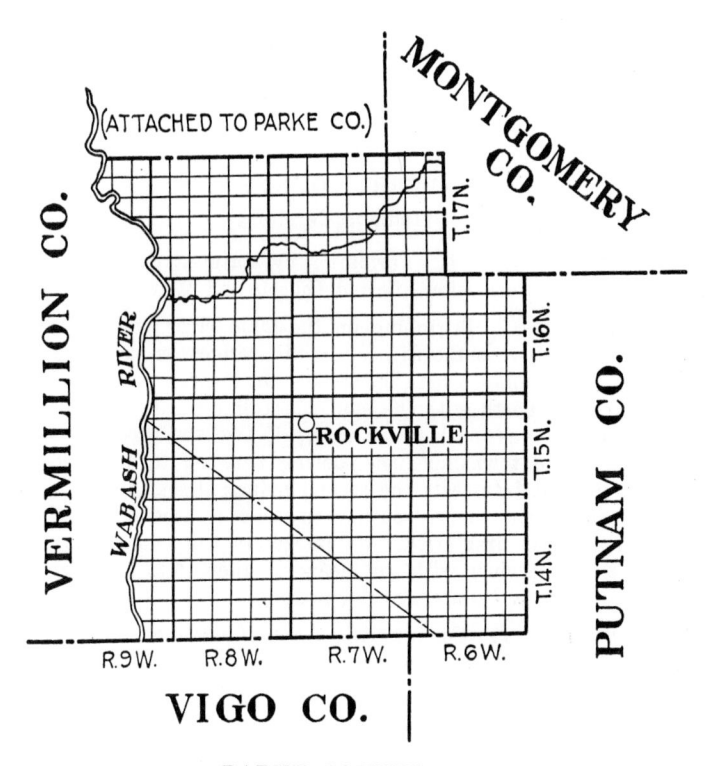

PARKE COUNTY II

[Laws: Jan. 2, 1824, effective Feb. 1, 1824; Jan. 2, 1824, effective on passage]

PERRY COUNTY I
[Indiana Territory]

SEPTEMBER 7, 1814: Formation by statute, effective November 1, 1814. The formation affected Gibson and Warrick counties.

BOUNDARIES: "Beginning on the Ohio river where the range line passes between the fifth and sixth ranges, west of the second principal meridian where it strikes or intersects the said Ohio river, thence north with the said range line until it intersects the township line passing between township two and three, thence east with the said township line, passing between township two and three, until it intersects the second principal meridian, or line of Harrison county, thence south with the said second principal meridian until it first strikes or intersects the Ohio river, thence down the Ohio river with the meanders thereof to the beginning." *Acts of Indiana Territory*, 1814, p. 19.

COUNTY SEAT: Commissioners appointed under the act forming the county, in November, 1814, chose a site on the Ohio and called it Troy. *Ibid.*, 21; Shockley, "County Seat Wars," *op. cit.*, 10:no.1:7.

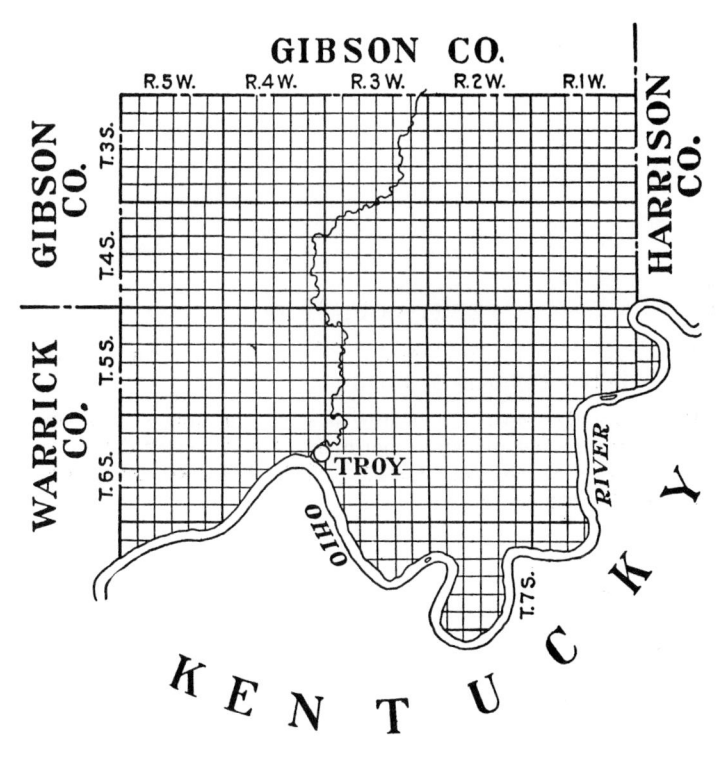

PERRY COUNTY I

[Law: Sep. 7, 1814, effective Nov. 1, 1814]

PERRY COUNTY II

DECEMBER 21, 1816: Alteration by statute forming Pike County, effective February 1, 1817.

BOUNDARY CHANGE: Townships 3 south, in ranges 3, 4, and 5 west of the second principal meridian were transferred to Pike County. *Laws of Indiana*, 1816-17, p. 208. See text of law with map, Pike County I.

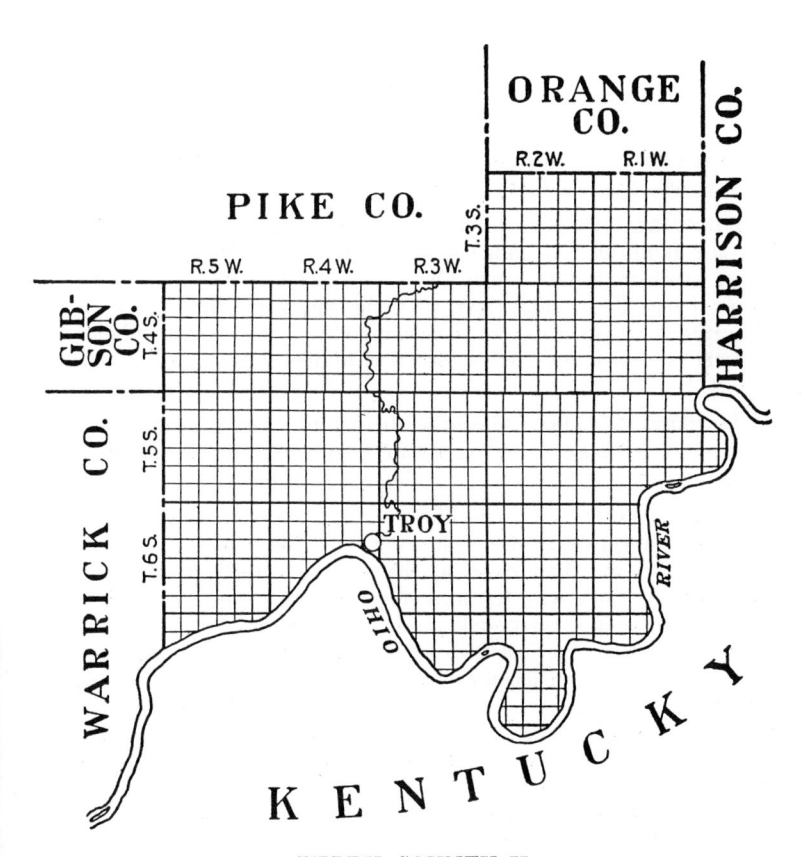

PERRY COUNTY II
[Law: Dec. 21, 1816, effective Feb. 1, 1817]

PERRY COUNTY III

JANUARY 10, 1818: Alteration by statute forming Spencer County, effective February 1, 1818.

BOUNDARY CHANGE: All that part of Perry County west of a line beginning at "the range line dividing ranges three and four, thence south with said range line until it first strikes Anderson's river, thence down said river with the meanders thereof to the Ohio river," was transferred to Spencer County. *Laws of Indiana,* 1817-18 (special), pp. 20-21. See text of law with map, Spencer County I.

JANUARY 10, 1818: Alteration by statute for attaching part of Harrison County to the county of Perry, effective February 1, 1818.

BOUNDARY CHANGE: The law provided that "all that part of Harrison county, which lies within the following boundary, to wit: Beginning on the Ohio river, at the mouth of Little Blue river; thence up the same with the meanders thereof to the line dividing sections thirty and thirty-one, in town 3, south and range one, east; thence with the last mentioned line to the second principal meridian, the western boundary of Harrison county; thence south with said meridian to the Ohio river; thence up the same to the place of beginning, be separated from the county of Harrison and attached to and form a part of the said county of Perry." *Laws of Indiana,* 1817-18 (special), p. 29.

This law also appointed commissioners to relocate the county seat of Perry County. See following map.

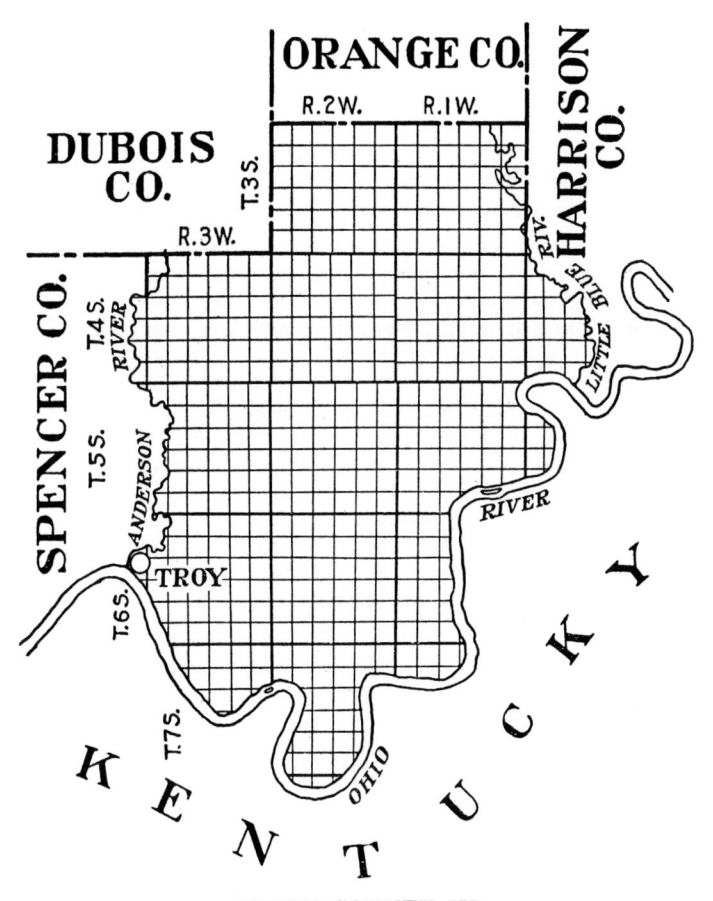

PERRY COUNTY III

[Laws: Jan. 10, 1818, effective Feb. 1, 1818; Jan. 10, 1818, effective Feb. 1, 1818]

PERRY COUNTY IV

JANUARY 29, 1818: Alteration by statute attaching a part of the county of Dubois to the county of Perry, effective February 15, 1818, and forming Crawford County, effective March 1, 1818.

BOUNDARY CHANGE: All that part of Dubois County included within boundaries "Beginning at the south east corner of township three south, and range three west; thence west with said township line to the line dividing ranges three and four west; thence north with the same three miles; thence east through the centre of said township to the line dividing ranges two and three west; thence south with the same to the place of beginning," was attached to Perry County. *Laws of Indiana*, 1817-18 (special), p. 26.

All that part of Perry County in ranges 1 and 2 west of the second principal meridian, between "an east and west line, four miles north of the line dividing townships three and four south," and the township line dividing townships 2 and 3 south, and that part of Perry County east of the meridian line in township 4 south, was transferred to Crawford County. *Ibid.*, 27.

COUNTY SEAT: On March 2, 1818, commissioners appointed by a law of January 10, 1818, met to relocate the county seat. The town plat of Washington was selected, but before the removal from Troy, the name of the new county seat had been changed to Franklin. The plat was reëntered under that name in the fall of 1818. By 1819 the name had been changed to Rome. *Ibid.*, 30; De la Hunt, *Perry County*, 38-39, 40-41; Shockley, "County Seat Wars," *op. cit.*, 10:no.1:7-8.

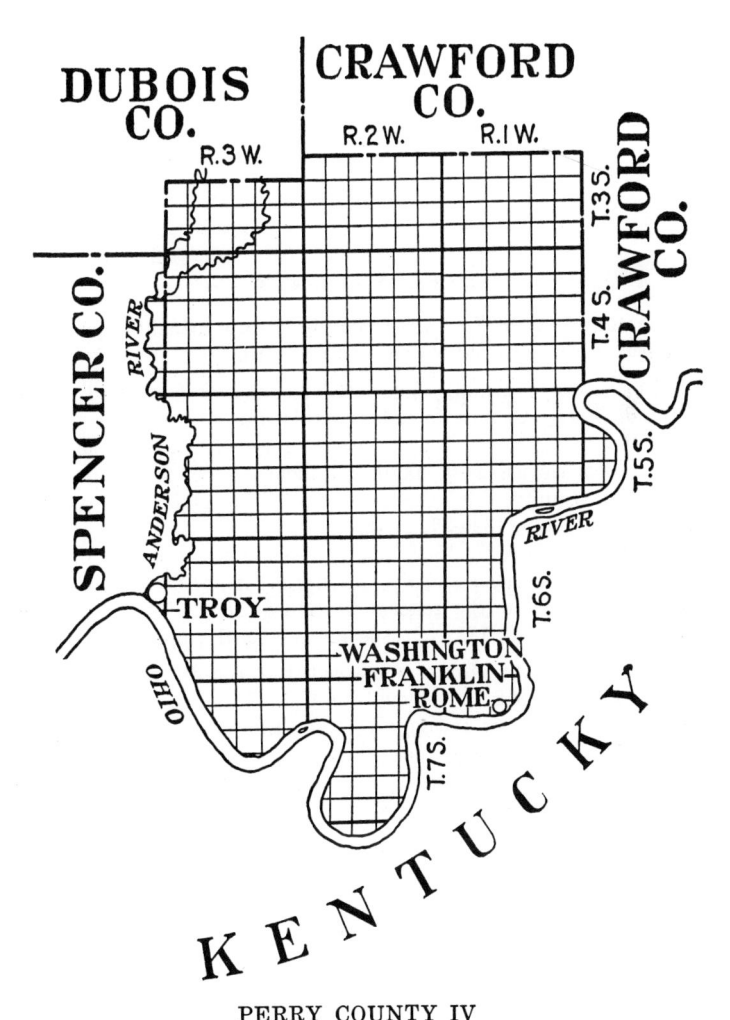

PERRY COUNTY IV

[Law: Jan. 29, 1818, effective Feb. 15 and Mar. 1, 1818]

PERRY COUNTY V

JANUARY 23, 1827: Alteration by statute attaching part of the county of Perry to the county of Crawford.

BOUNDARY CHANGE: The act attached to Crawford all that part of Perry County included within the following boundaries: "Beginning at the north east corner of Perry county, thence south four miles, thence west six miles, thence north four miles to the Crawford county line, thence east to the place of beginning." *Laws of Indiana*, 1826-27, p. 12.

A law of May 7, 1852, made possible the erection of a new county out of Spencer and Perry counties, if approved by the voters of those counties in the general election of 1852. The proposal was voted down. *Ibid.*, 1851-52 (special and local), pp. 132-34.

COUNTY SEAT: Rome remained the county seat until 1859 when, on March 8, a removal to Cannelton was ordered. This followed a four-year struggle between the two towns. The actual removal of the records took place December 7, 1859. Shockley, "County Seat Wars," *op. cit.*, 10:no.1:8; De la Hunt, *Perry County*, 156-64; *History of Warrick, Spencer and Perry Counties*, 604-5.

PERRY COUNTY V
[Law: Jan. 23, 1827]

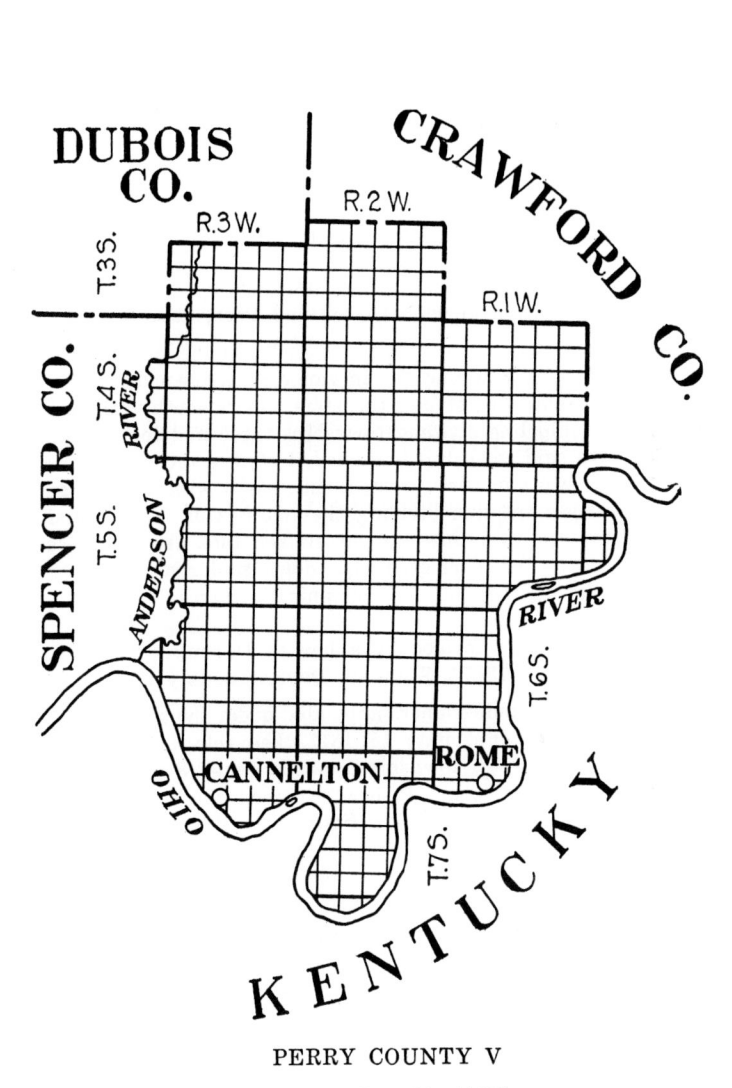

PIKE COUNTY I

DECEMBER 21, 1816: Formation by statute, effective February 1, 1817. The formation affected Gibson and Perry counties.

BOUNDARIES: "Beginning at a point on White river where the line dividing sections nine and ten in range nine, town one north of Buckingham's base line strikes the same, thence south with said line to the township line dividing townships three and four south, thence east with said township line until it strikes the range line dividing ranges two and three west, thence north with said range line until it strikes the line dividing the counties of Orange and Gibson, thence with said line until it strikes Lick creek, thence down said creek to White river, thence down said river with the meanders thereof to the place of beginning." *Laws of Indiana*, 1816-17, p. 208.

Daviess County was formed by a law of December 24, 1816, effective February 15, 1817. See map, Daviess County I.

COUNTY SEAT: Commissioners appointed under the act forming the county reported on February 15, 1817, their selection of a site in sections 22, 26, and 27, township 1 north, range 8 west. The town was called Petersburg. It has remained the county seat. *Laws of Indiana*, 1816-17, p. 209; *History of Pike and Dubois Counties*, 335-37.

PIKE COUNTY BOUNDARIES 665

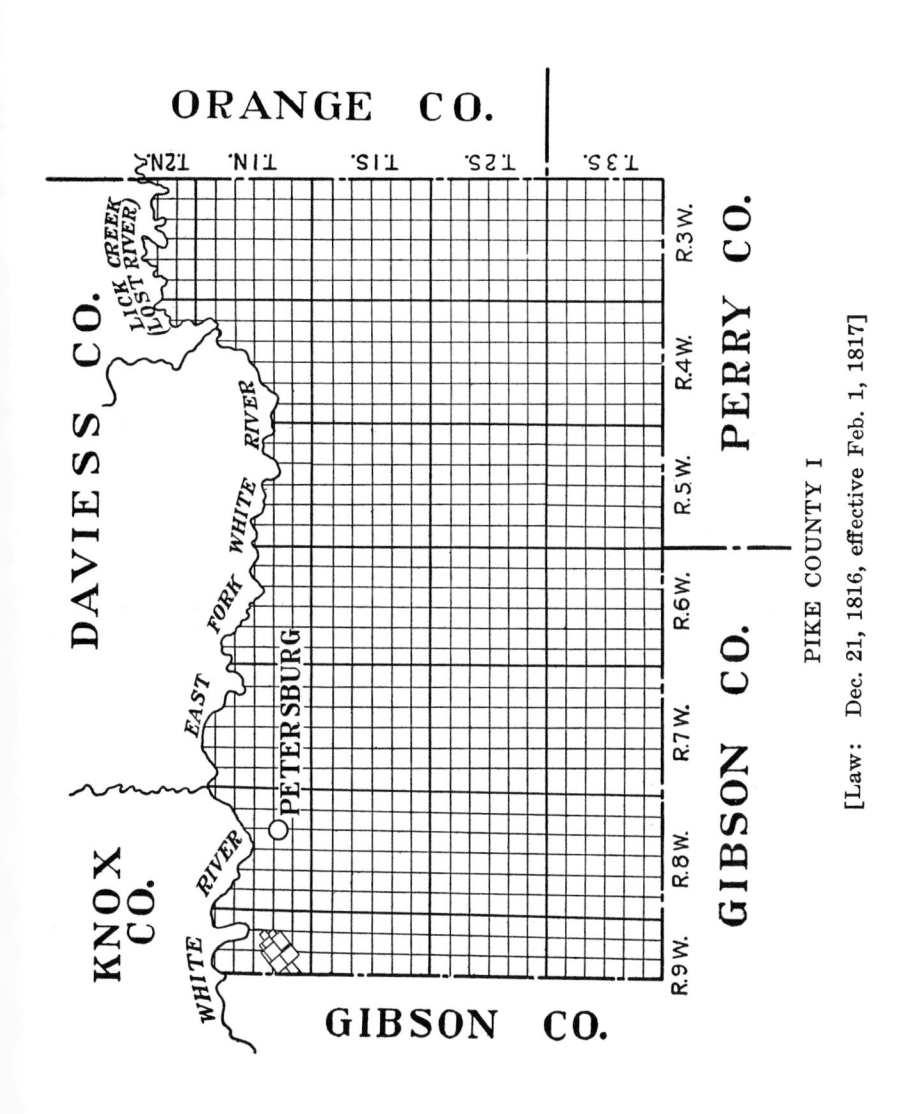

PIKE COUNTY I

[Law: Dec. 21, 1816, effective Feb. 1, 1817]

PIKE COUNTY II

DECEMBER 20, 1817: Alteration by statute forming Dubois County, effective February 1, 1818.

BOUNDARY CHANGE: All that part of Pike County east of a line "Beginning at a point on the bank of the east fork of White river, at which the centre line of range six shall intersect said fork of White river; thence running south with said centre line, until said centre line intersects the present line, dividing Warrick [Gibson] and Pike counties," was transferred to Dubois County. *Laws of Indiana*, 1817-18 (special), pp. 16-17.

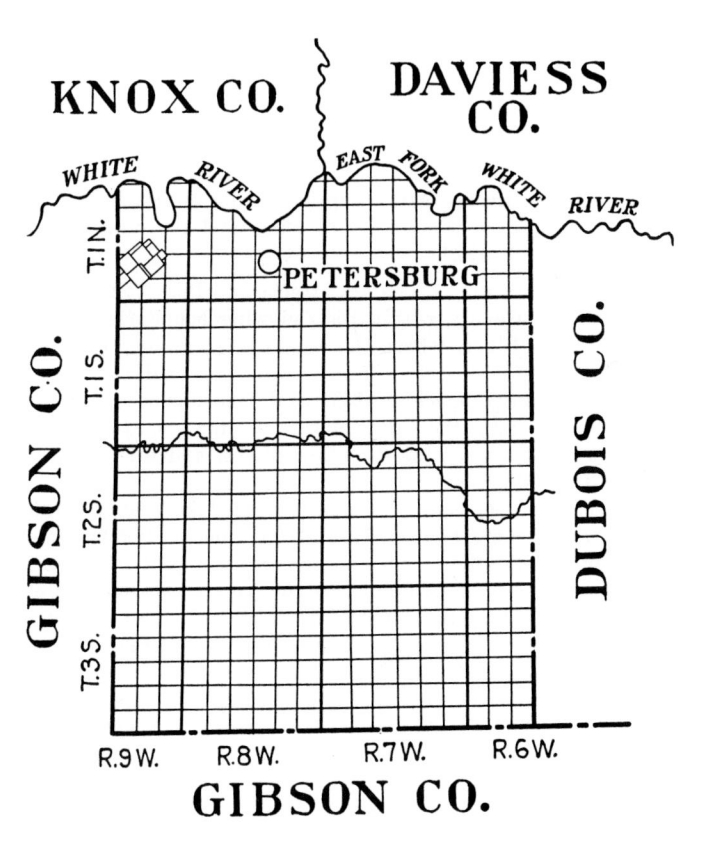

PIKE COUNTY II
[Law: Dec. 20, 1817, effective Feb. 1, 1818]

PIKE COUNTY III

JANUARY 26, 1824: Alteration by statute to attach part of the county of Gibson to the county of Pike, and for other purposes, effective March 1, 1824.

BOUNDARY CHANGE: The act attached to Pike County all that part of Gibson County within the following boundaries: "Beginning on White River, where the range line dividing ranges nine and ten strikes the same; thence south with said range line, to the river Patoka; thence up the said last named river, to the present line dividing the said counties of Pike and Gibson; thence north with said county line to White River, and thence down the same to the beginning."

It also provided that "all that part of Pike county contained within the following bounds, be and the same is hereby attached to, and shall hereafter form and constitute a part of the county of Gibson, to wit: Beginning on the river Patoka, where the present line dividing the counties of Pike and Gibson crosses the same; thence up said river, with the meanders thereof, to the line dividing sections four and five, in township one [two] south, of range eight west; thence south with said section line, to the line dividing the counties of Pike and Warrick; thence west to the present line of Gibson and Pike counties; and thence north to the place of beginning." *Revised Laws of Indiana*, 1823-24, pp. 115-16.

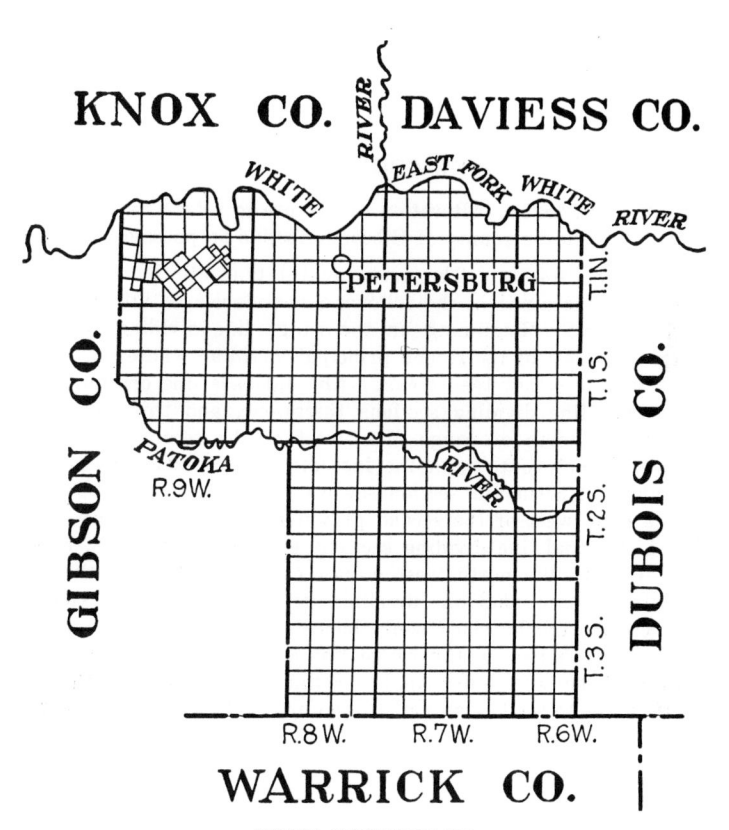

PIKE COUNTY III

[Law: Jan. 26, 1824, effective Mar. 1, 1824]

PIKE COUNTY IV

FEBRUARY 3, 1825: Alteration by statute to attach part of the county of Pike to the county of Gibson, effective on passage.

BOUNDARY CHANGE: The act provided that all that part of Pike County contained in the following boundaries be attached to Gibson County: "Beginning on the range line dividing ranges nine, and ten west of the second principal meridian where the base line crosses the same; thence east with said base line one mile to the sectional line dividing sections thirty-one, and thirty-two in township one north of range nine, west of the second principal meridian; thence south with the last mentioned sectional line to the north west corner of section seventeen in township one south of range nine, west of the second principal meridian; thence east with the sectional line dividing sections eight and seventeen, nine and sixteen, to the north west corner of section fifteen; thence south with the sectional line dividing sections fifteen and sixteen, until it crosses the Patoka River; thence down the said river with the meanders thereof to the range line dividing ranges nine and ten, west of the second principal meridian; thence north with the said range line to the beginning." *Laws of Indiana*, 1825, pp. 15-16.

KNOX CO. DAVIESS CO.

R.9W.   R.8W.   R.7W.   R.6W.

WHITE RIVER   EAST FORK WHITE RIVER

T.1N.

T.1S.

PETERSBURG

GIBSON CO.

PATOKA RIVER

T.2S.

DUBOIS CO.

T.3S.

WARRICK CO.

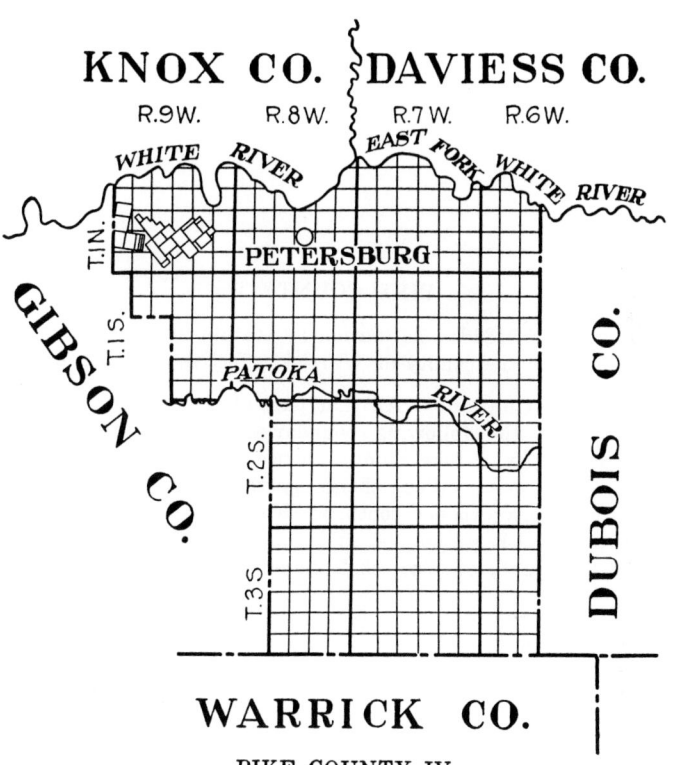

PIKE COUNTY IV

[Law: Feb. 3, 1825, effective on passage]

PIKE COUNTY V

JANUARY 20, 1826: Alteration by statute attaching a part of Pike County to the county of Warrick, effective on passage.

BOUNDARY CHANGE: "All that part of the county of Pike included within the following boundaries, viz: beginning at the south-east corner of Pike county; thence running north two miles; thence west, twelve miles; thence north, one mile; thence west, to Gibson county; thence south, to Warrick county; thence east, to the place of beginning, shall hereafter constitute and form a part of the county of Warrick." *Laws of Indiana*, 1825-26, p. 12.

PIKE COUNTY V

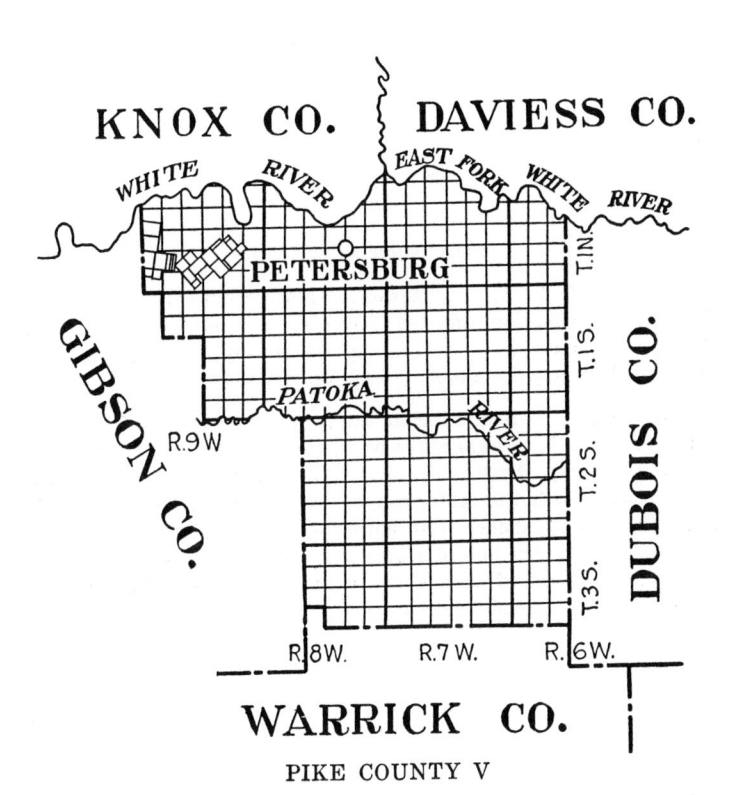

[Law: Jan. 20, 1826, effective on passage]

PORTER COUNTY I

FEBRUARY 7, 1835: Formation by statute, effective on publication. The formation affected territory attached to St. Joseph County. Porter was organized by an act of January 28, 1836, effective February 1, 1836.

BOUNDARIES: "Beginning at the south east corner of township thirty four north, of range five west, thence with the line dividing townships thirty three and thirty four north, to the state line, thence north with the state line, to the north west corner of the state of Indiana, thence east with the northern boundary of Indiana to the eastern line of range five west, thence south with the line dividing ranges four and five west to the place of beginning." *Laws of Indiana*, 1834-35 (general), p. 47.

PORTER COUNTY BOUNDARIES

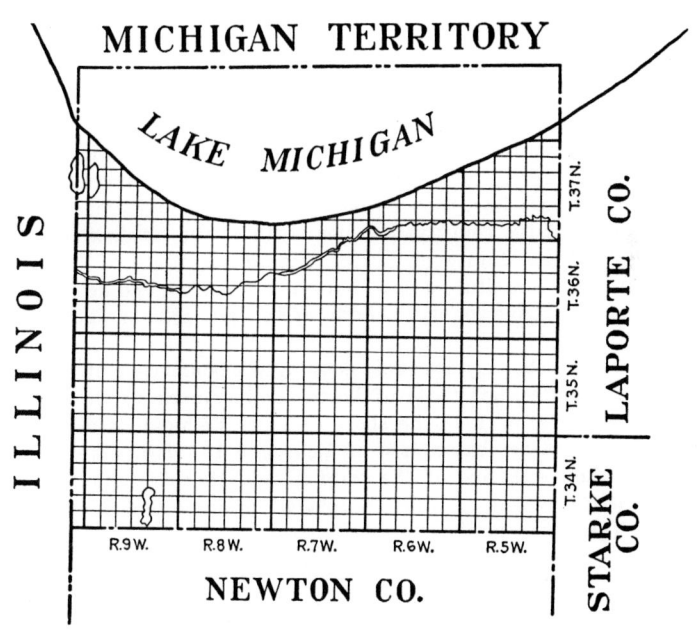

PORTER COUNTY I

[Law: Feb. 7, 1835, effective on publication]

PORTER COUNTY II

JANUARY 28, 1836: Alteration by statute to organize the county of Porter, and for other purposes, effective February 1, 1836.

BOUNDARIES: "Commencing at the north west corner of Laporte county, thence running south to the Kankakee river, thence west with the bed of said river, to the centre of range seven, thence north to the state line, thence east to the place of beginning. And all that part of the country that lies north of the Kankakee river, and west of the county of Porter, within the State of Indiana, shall form and constitute a new county, to be known and designated by the name of Lake county." *Laws of Indiana,* 1835-36 (general), p. 51.

An act of February 16, 1839, defining the boundaries of several northern counties, left those of Porter County unchanged. In the *Revised Statutes* of 1843 the shore of Lake Michigan is made the northern boundary, but a law of February 10, 1851, extended it again to the north line of the state. *Ibid.,* 1838-39 (general), p. 70; *Revised Statutes of Indiana,* 1842-43, p. 89; *Laws of Indiana,* 1850-51 (general), p. 58.

COUNTY SEAT: Commissioners appointed under the organizing act, on June 9, 1836, reported their selection of a site in section 24, township 35 north, range 6 west. The town was named Portersville. The location of the county seat has remained the same, although the name was changed to Valparaiso by an act of January 6, 1837. *Laws of Indiana,* 1835-36 (general), p. 51; 1836-37 (local), p. 382; Shockley, "County Seat Wars," *op. cit.,* 10:no.1:31; *History of Porter County,* 1:47-49.

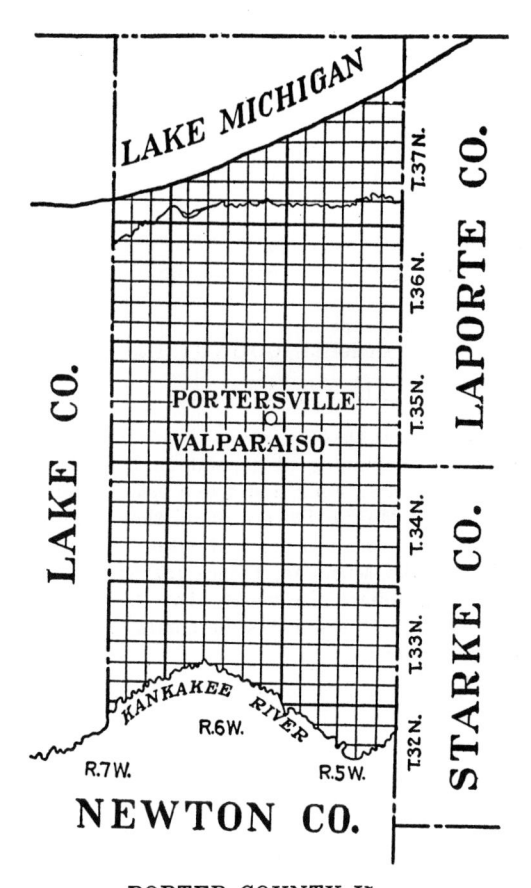

PORTER COUNTY II
[Law: Jan. 28, 1836, effective Feb. 1, 1836]

PORTER COUNTY III

MARCH 8, 1923: Alteration by statute defining the boundaries of Porter County.

BOUNDARIES: "Beginning at a point on Lake Michigan where the line dividing ranges four and five west intersects the same, thence south to the Marble Powers ditch, thence down the middle of the channel of the same to the center line of range seven west, thence north to Lake Michigan, thence eastwardly with the lake to the place of beginning: *Provided*, That the northern boundary of said county shall be the same as the northern state line." *Laws of Indiana*, 1923, p. 465.

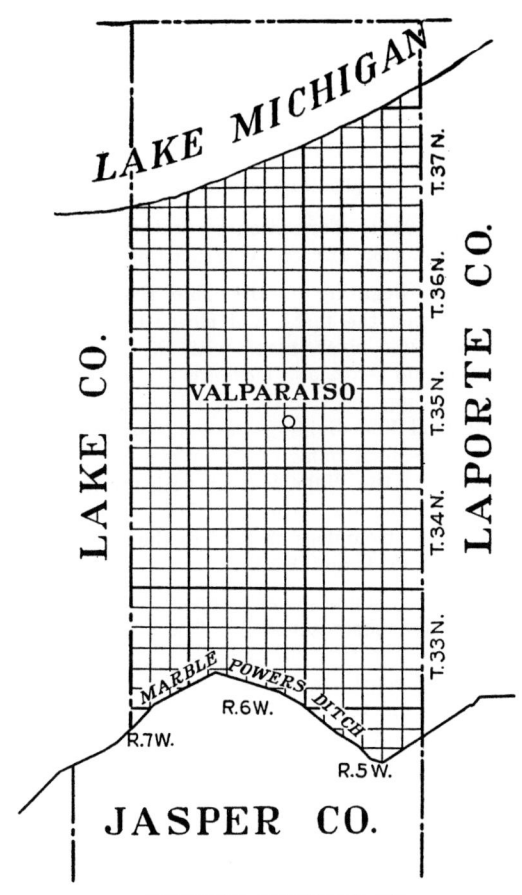

PORTER COUNTY III
[Law: Mar. 8, 1923]

POSEY COUNTY I
[Indiana Territory]

SEPTEMBER 7, 1814: Formation by statute, effective November 1, 1814. The formation affected Warrick County.

BOUNDARIES: "Begining on the Ohio river, where the range line passing between the tenth and eleventh range strikes or intersects the said Ohio river, north with the said range line passing between the said tenth and eleventh ranges, to its intersection with the line dividing the counties of Gibson and Warrick, thence west with the said line dividing the said counties of Gibson and Warrick to the western bank of the Wabash river, thence down the western bank of the Wabash river with the line of the Illinois Territory to its junction with the Ohio river, thence up the Ohio river with the meanders thereof to the beginning." *Acts of Indiana Territory*, 1814, pp. 18-19.

COUNTY SEAT: Commissioners appointed in the act forming the county reported their selection of a county-seat site in the northeast quarter of section 30, and the southeast quarter of section 19, township 6 south, range 12 west. The report came before the county officers on January 17, and on January 19 it was ordered that the seat of justice be called Blackford. *Ibid.*, 20-21; *History of Posey County*, 331-32.

POSEY COUNTY I
[Law: Sep. 7, 1814, effective Nov. 1, 1814]

POSEY COUNTY II
[Indiana Territory]

DECEMBER 18, 1815: Alteration by statute attaching part of Gibson County to Posey County, effective March 1, 1816.

BOUNDARY CHANGE: "Beginning on the township line dividing townships four and five, where the line dividing ranges thirteen and fourteen crosses said township line; thence with said range line north till it strikes the Wabash river; thence with the meanders of said river to a point, where the township line aforesaid, strikes said river; thence eastwardly with said township line to the place of beginning, shall be, and the same is hereby separated or taken from the . . . county of Gibson, and added or attached to . . . Posey county; and the said part of the present county of Gibson so separated and attached, shall in law and in fact, at all times thereafter, be to all intents and purposes, held, deemed and taken, as part of the said county of Posey." *Acts of Indiana Territory*, 1815, pp. 7-8.

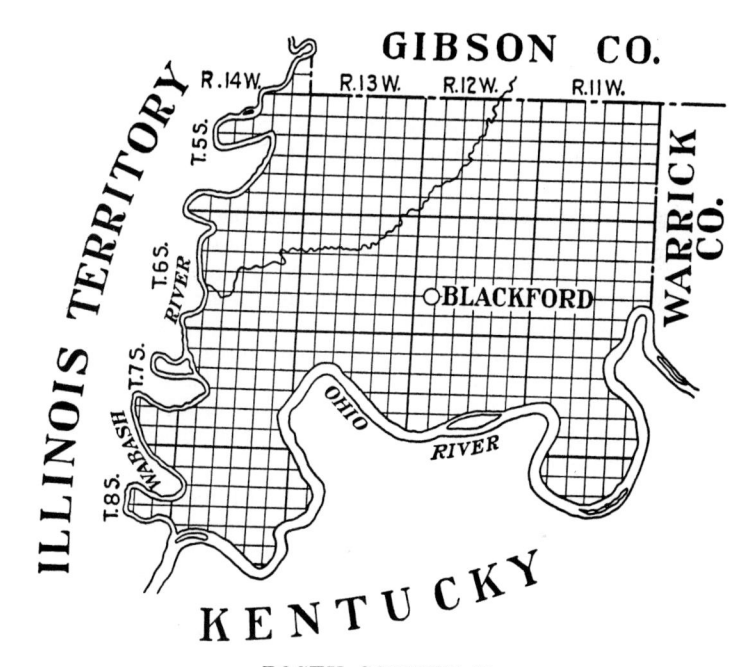

POSEY COUNTY II
[Law: Dec. 18, 1815, effective Mar. 1, 1816]

POSEY COUNTY III

JANUARY 1, 1817: Alteration by statute to attach part of the county of Gibson to the county of Posey, effective February 1, 1817.

BOUNDARY CHANGE: "From and after the first day of February next, all that part of the county of Gibson included within the following bounds be attached to and form a part of Posey county, to wit: beginning at the north east corner of Posey county, running thence north with the line dividing ranges ten and eleven, six miles to the line dividing townships, three and four south; thence west with said line dividing said townships to the Wabash river; thence down said river with the meanders thereof, to where the present line of Posey county strikes said river." *Laws of Indiana*, 1816-17, pp. 202-3.

COUNTY SEAT: Commissioners appointed under this law of January 1, 1817, to relocate the county seat, chose a site in section 33, township 5 south, range 13 west. Their report of February 22, 1817, was received on May 12, 1817. A few days later the town was named Springfield. *Ibid.*, 203; *History of Posey County*, 335-36; Shockley, "County Seat Wars," *op. cit.*, 10:no.1:7.

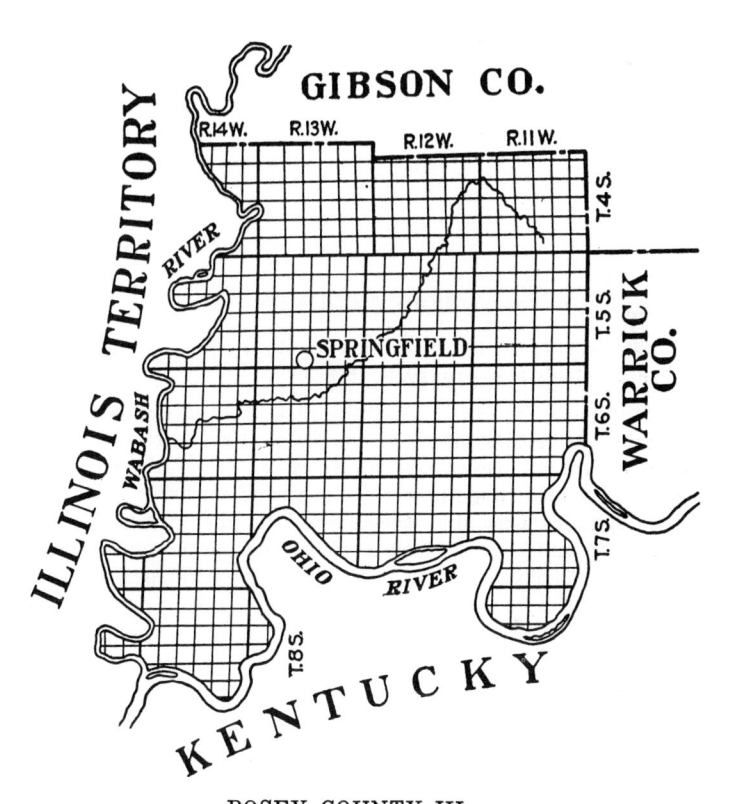

POSEY COUNTY III

[Law: Jan. 1, 1817, effective Feb. 1, 1817]

POSEY COUNTY IV

JANUARY 7, 1818: Alteration by statute forming Vanderburgh County, effective February 1, 1818.

BOUNDARY CHANGE: All that part of Posey County east and south of a line "Beginning on the Ohio river where the range line dividing ranges eleven and twelve west, strikes the same, thence north with said range line to the centre of township four, south of Buckingham's base line, thence east" to the range line dividing ranges 10 and 11 west of the second principal meridian was transferred to Vanderburgh County. *Laws of Indiana*, 1817-18 (special), p. 22.

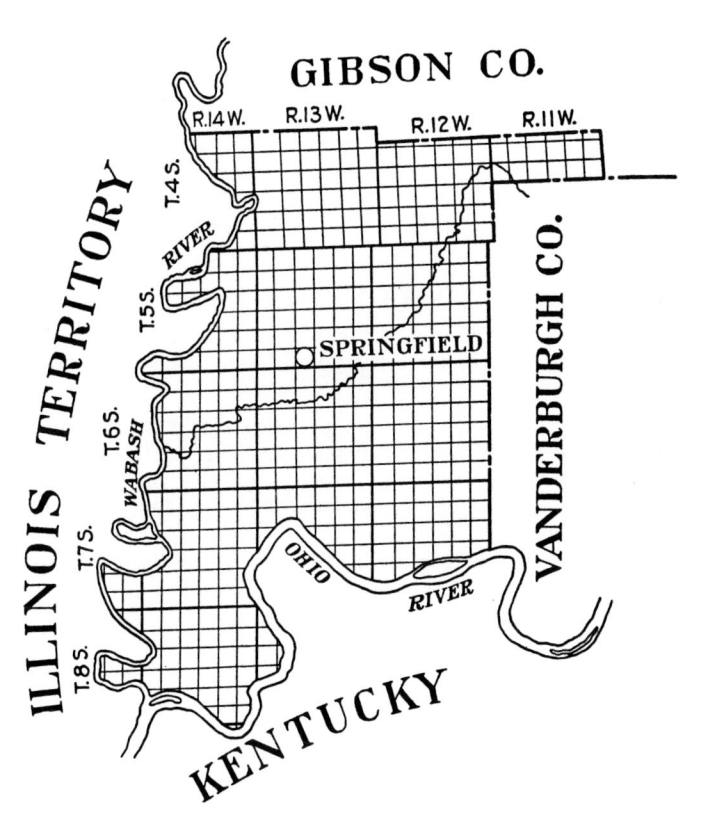

POSEY COUNTY IV
[Law: Jan. 7, 1818, effective Feb. 1, 1818]

POSEY COUNTY V

DECEMBER 31, 1821: Alteration by statute attaching part of the county of Posey to the county of Gibson, effective February 1, 1822.

BOUNDARY CHANGE: The act provided that "all that part of the county of Posey that lies in township four south of Buckingham's base line, in range eleven west be separated from said county of Posey and attached to the county of Gibson." *Laws of Indiana,* 1821-22, p. 120.

See note on Buckingham's base line with map, Gibson County VI.

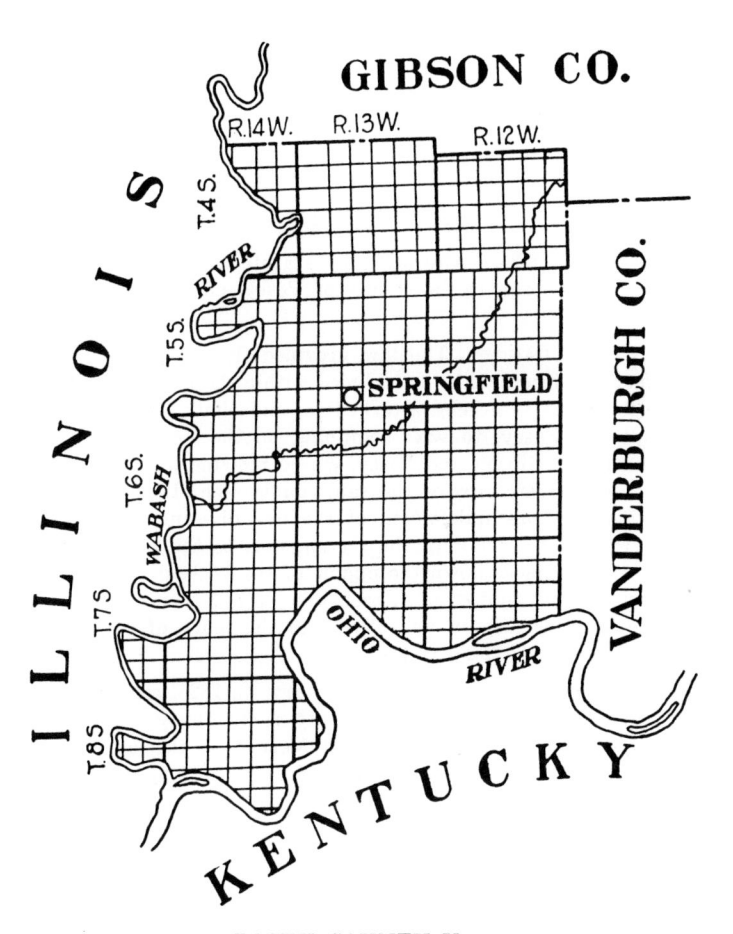

POSEY COUNTY V
[Law: Dec. 31, 1821, effective Feb. 1, 1822]

POSEY COUNTY VI

JANUARY 6, 1823: Alteration by statute to attach a part of the county of Gibson to the county of Posey, effective January 1, 1823.

BOUNDARY CHANGE: The law provided that "all that part of the county of Gibson, which is included within the following bounds, be and the same is hereby attached to, and shall form a part of the county of Posey, to wit: beginning on the line dividing the said counties of Gibson and Posey, where the line dividing ranges twelve and thirteen, crosses the said county line; thence north to the section line, one mile north of the line dividing the counties aforesaid; thence west with the section line, to the middle of the Wabash river; thence down the middle of the Wabash river, to the line dividing the counties of Gibson and Posey; thence east along said line dividing Gibson and Posey, to the place of beginning." *Laws of Indiana*, 1822-23, p. 116.

COUNTY SEAT: By an act of February 12, 1825, commissioners were appointed to relocate the county seat. They reported on May 10, 1825, their choice of Mount Vernon as the county seat. *Ibid.*, 1825, p. 90; Shockley, "County Seat Wars," *op. cit.*, 10:no. 1:7; *History of Posey County*, 340.

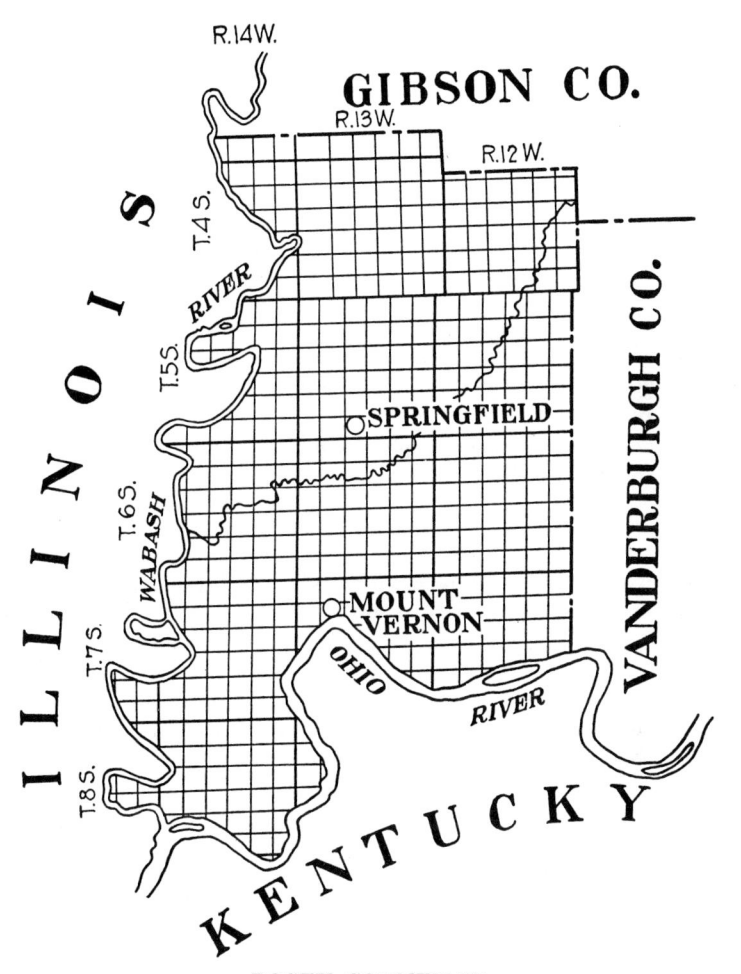

POSEY COUNTY VI
[Law: Jan. 6, 1823, effective Jan. 1, 1823]

PULASKI COUNTY

FEBRUARY 7, 1835: Formation by statute, effective on publication. The formation affected territory attached to Cass and St. Joseph counties. Pulaski was organized by an act of February 18, 1839, effective May 6, 1839.

BOUNDARIES: "Beginning at the north west corner of township thirty one north, of range four west, thence east twenty four miles, thence south with the meridian line eighteen miles, thence west with the line dividing townships twenty eight and twenty nine north, twenty four miles, thence north with the line of ranges four and five west, eighteen miles to the place of beginning." *Laws of Indiana*, 1834-35 (general), p. 46.

COUNTY SEAT: Commissioners appointed under the act organizing the county met May 6, 1839, at Winamac, and chose a site in that town as the county seat. Winamac has remained the seat of justice. *Ibid.*, 1838-39 (general), p. 34; *Counties of White and Pulaski*, 452.

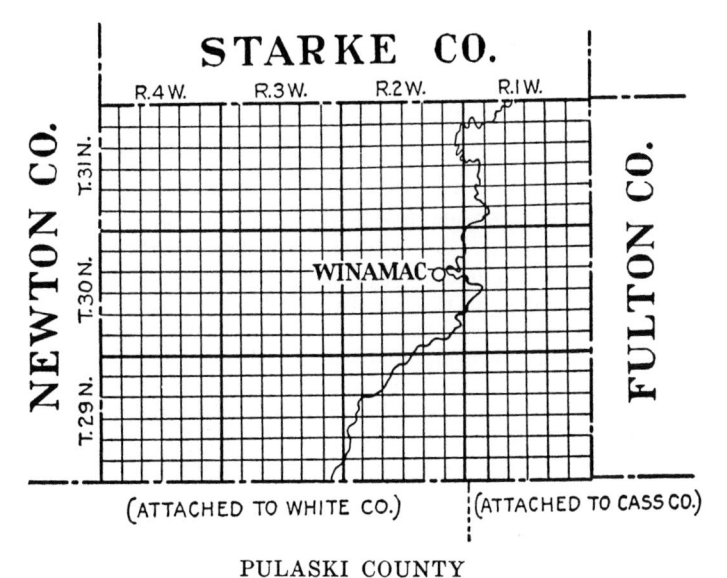

PULASKI COUNTY
[Law: Feb. 7, 1835, effective on publication]

PUTNAM COUNTY I

DECEMBER 31, 1821: Formation by statute, effective April 1, 1822. The formation affected Owen, Vigo, and Wabash counties.

BOUNDARIES: "Beginning in the centre of range seven west, on the line dividing townships ten and eleven north, thence east fifteen miles to the line dividing ranges four and five west, thence north twelve miles, to the line dividing townships twelve and thirteen north, thence east three miles, thence north twelve miles to the line dividing townships fourteen and fifteen, thence west fifteen miles to the line dividing ranges six and seven west, thence south six miles, thence west three miles, thence south eighteen miles to the beginning." *Laws of Indiana*, 1821-22, p. 65.

By a law of January 2, 1822, Putnam County was given civil and criminal jurisdiction over all that part of Wabash County lying east of the line dividing ranges 5 and 6 west as far as the second principal meridian. *Ibid.*, 119.

COUNTY SEAT: Commissioners were appointed by the act forming the county to select a county seat, but failed to act.

PUTNAM COUNTY BOUNDARIES 695

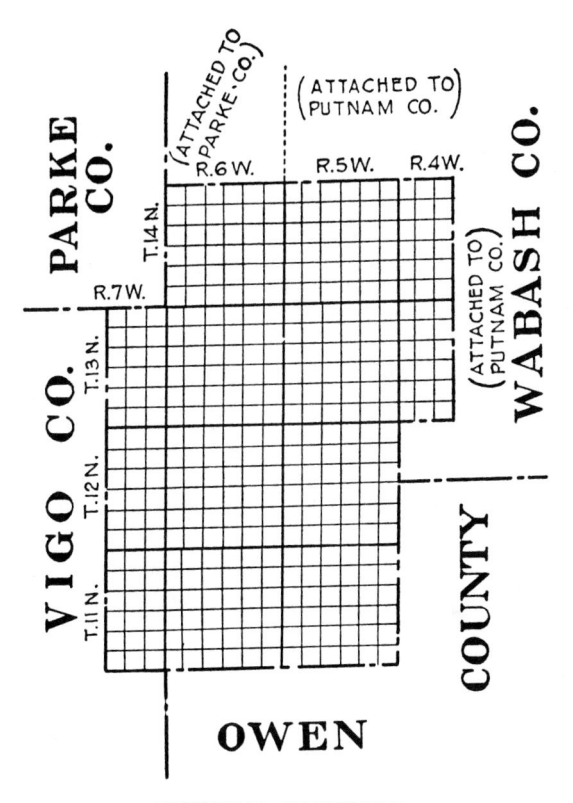

PUTNAM COUNTY I
[Law: Dec. 31, 1821, effective Apr. 1, 1822]

PUTNAM COUNTY II

DECEMBER 21, 1822: Alteration by statute amending act of December 31, 1821, effective on passage.

BOUNDARIES: The act provided "That the following boundaries, to wit: beginning in the centre of town twelve north, on the range line dividing ranges six and seven west, thence east twenty four miles, to the line dividing ranges two and three, thence north with said line, twenty seven miles to the line dividing townships sixteen and seventeen, thence west with said line twenty four miles, to the line dividing ranges six and seven, thence south twenty seven miles, to the place of beginning . . . constitute and form the boundaries of the county of Putnam." *Laws of Indiana,* 1822-23, pp. 5-6.

For descriptions of the territory transferred to Vigo and Owen counties, see maps, Vigo County V, and Owen County III.

COUNTY SEAT: Commissioners appointed under the formation law having failed to act, a second group was appointed by an act of January 7, 1823, with instructions to meet on the second Monday of April, 1823, to choose a county seat. After some delay a site in the southwest quarter of section 21, township 14 north, range 4 west was decided upon, and the town of Greencastle was laid out. This has remained the county seat. *Laws of Indiana,* 1822-23, pp. 125-26; *Biographical and Historical Record of Putnam County,* 212, 313.

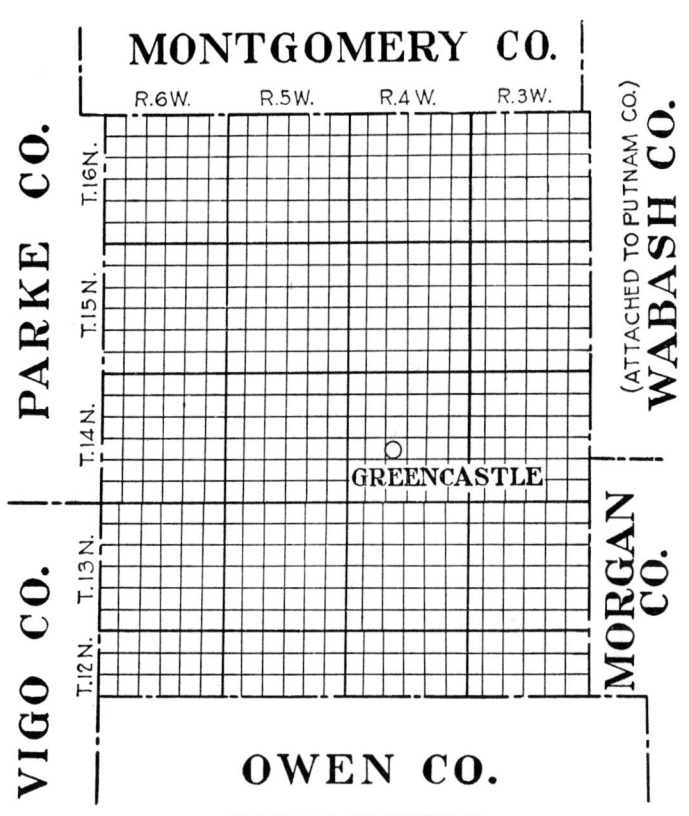

PUTNAM COUNTY II
[Law: Dec. 21, 1822, effective on passage]

PUTNAM COUNTY III

JANUARY 2, 1824: Alteration by statute attaching part of the counties of Montgomery and Putnam to the county of Parke, effective on passage.

BOUNDARY CHANGE: All that part of Putnam County in range 6 west of the second principal meridian, and townships 14, 15, and 16 north, was transferred to Parke County. *Laws of Indiana*, 1823-24 (special), pp. 53-54. See text of law with map, Parke County II.

Hendricks County was formed by an act of December 20, 1823, effective April 1, 1824.

PUTNAM COUNTY BOUNDARIES 699

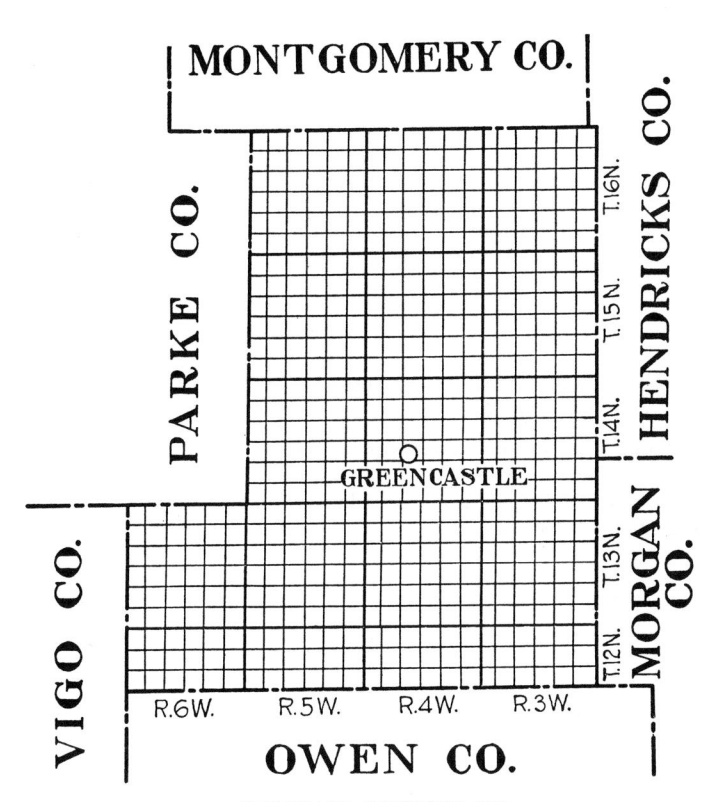

PUTNAM COUNTY III
[Law: Jan. 2, 1824, effective on passage]

PUTNAM COUNTY IV

FEBRUARY 12, 1825: Alteration by statute forming Clay County, effective April 1, 1825.

BOUNDARY CHANGE: Township 13 north, and the north half of township 12 north, range 6 west of the second principal meridian were transferred from Putnam to Clay County. *Laws of Indiana,* 1825, p. 17. See text of law with map of Clay County.

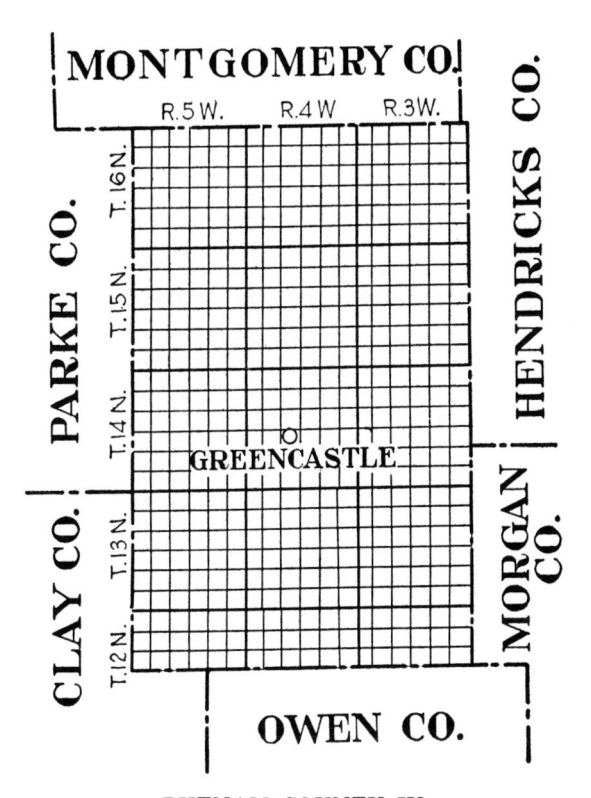

PUTNAM COUNTY IV
[Law: Feb. 12, 1825, effective Apr. 1, 1825]

PUTNAM COUNTY V

MARCH 11, 1861: Alteration by statute changing the boundaries of Morgan and Putnam counties, effective on passage.

BOUNDARIES: "Beginning at the south-east corner of section thirteen, in township twelve, north of range three west; thence north to the point where Mill Creek crosses the line between ranges two and three west; thence following the meanders and channel of said Mill Creek to the point where the same crosses the line between sections twenty-one and twenty-eight, in township fourteen, north of range two west; thence west to the line between range two and three west; thence north to the line dividing townships sixteen and seventeen north; thence west to line dividing ranges five and six west; thence south to the south-west corner of section eighteen, township twelve north, of range five west; thence east to the place of beginning." *Laws of Indiana*, 1861, p. 99.

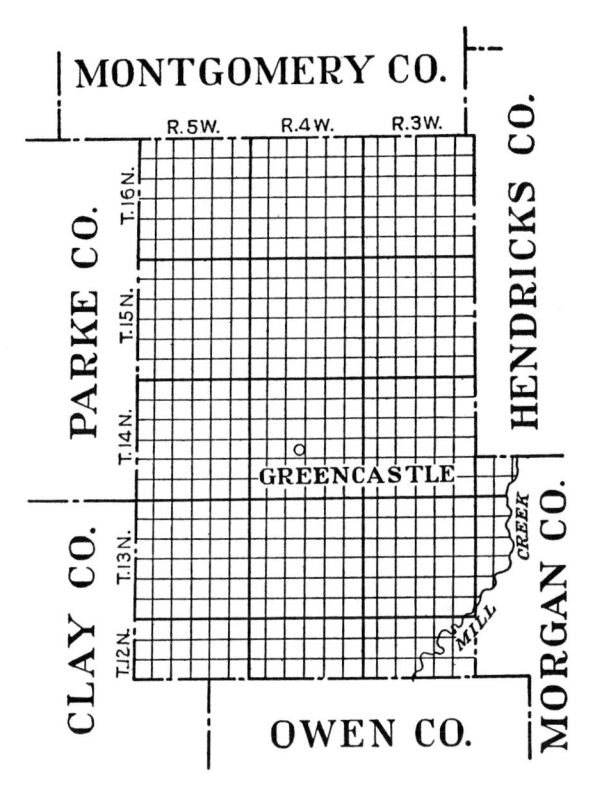

PUTNAM COUNTY V

[Law: Mar. 11, 1861, effective on passage]

RANDOLPH COUNTY I

JANUARY 10, 1818: Formation by statute, effective August 10, 1818. The formation affected Wayne County.

BOUNDARIES: "Beginning at the state of Ohio line, where the line that divides the fifteenth and sixteenth township strikes said Ohio line; thence west with said township line until it strikes the old boundary; thence westward with the centre line of the 18th township in the new purchase until it strikes the Indian boundary; thence northward with said boundary line until it strikes the state of [O]hio line; thence south with said line to the place of beginning." *Laws of Indiana*, 1817-18 (special), p. 18.

COUNTY SEAT: Commissioners appointed under the act forming the county met in September, 1818, and selected a site in sections 20 and 21, township 20 north, range 14 east of the second principal meridian. Winchester has remained the county seat. *Ibid.*, 19; Smith and Driver, *Past and Present of Randolph County*, 122.

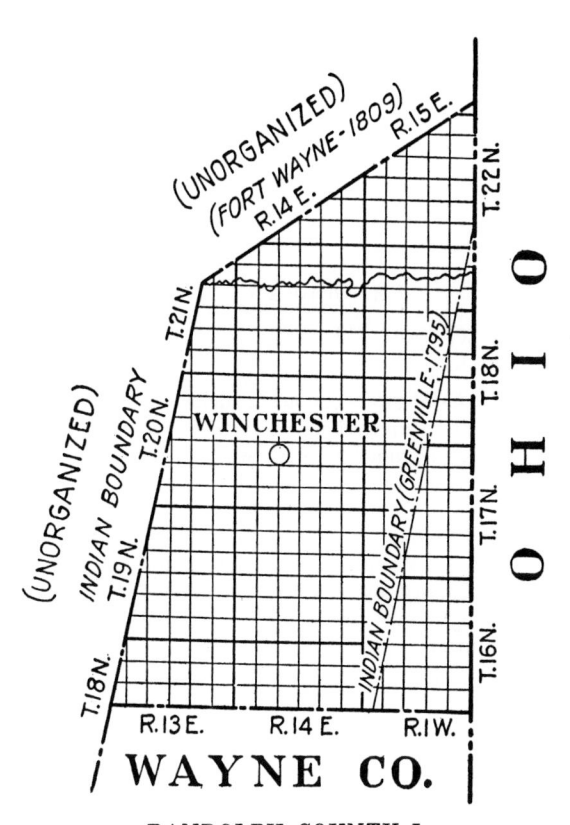

RANDOLPH COUNTY I
[Law: Jan. 10, 1818, effective Aug. 10, 1818]

RANDOLPH COUNTY II

JANUARY 20, 1820: Alteration by statute making provision for the New Purchase.

BOUNDARY CHANGE: The act attached to Randolph County "all that part of the aforesaid new purchase, which lies east of a due north line, drawn from the north west corner of Randolph county, and north of . . . Randolph county." *Laws of Indiana*, 1819-20, pp. 95-96.

The New Purchase was that territory ceded by the Indians at the Treaty of St. Mary's, October 2-6, 1818.

Randolph County, by this act, was given concurrent jurisdiction over Delaware County, with Wayne, Franklin, Ripley, and other bounding counties.

RANDOLPH COUNTY BOUNDARIES 707

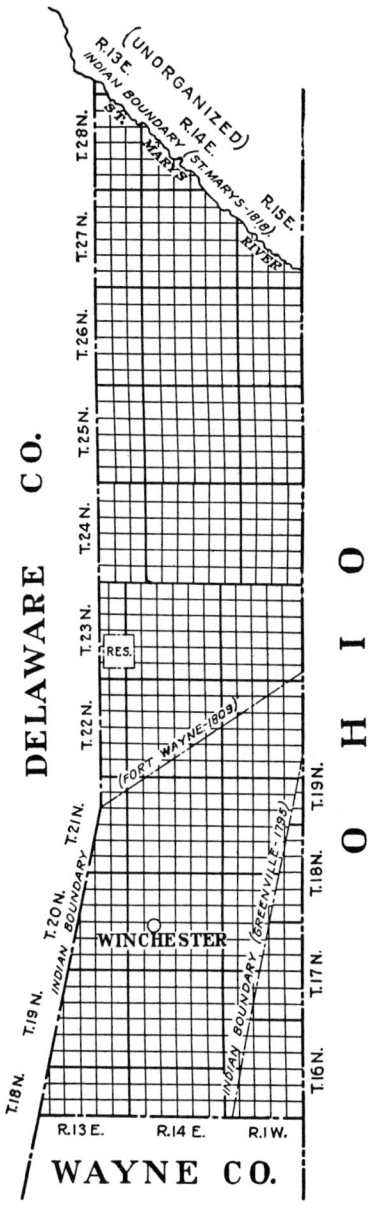

RANDOLPH COUNTY II

[Law: Jan. 20, 1820]

RANDOLPH COUNTY III

DECEMBER 23, 1820: Alteration by statute extending Randolph County, effective upon publication.

BOUNDARY CHANGE: The law provided that "all that part of the new purchase lately acquired from the Indians contained in the following boundaries, to wit: Beginning at the south west corner of Randolph county, thence west four miles, thence due north until it strikes the northern boundary of Indiana, shall from henceforth form and constitute a part of the county of Randolph in as full and complete a manner as though it had been attached to and formed a part of said county at the time of its formation." *Laws of Indiana*, 1820-21, pp. 117-18.

Note that this extension disregarded the Indian title to lands north of the St. Mary's River.

RANDOLPH COUNTY BOUNDARIES 709

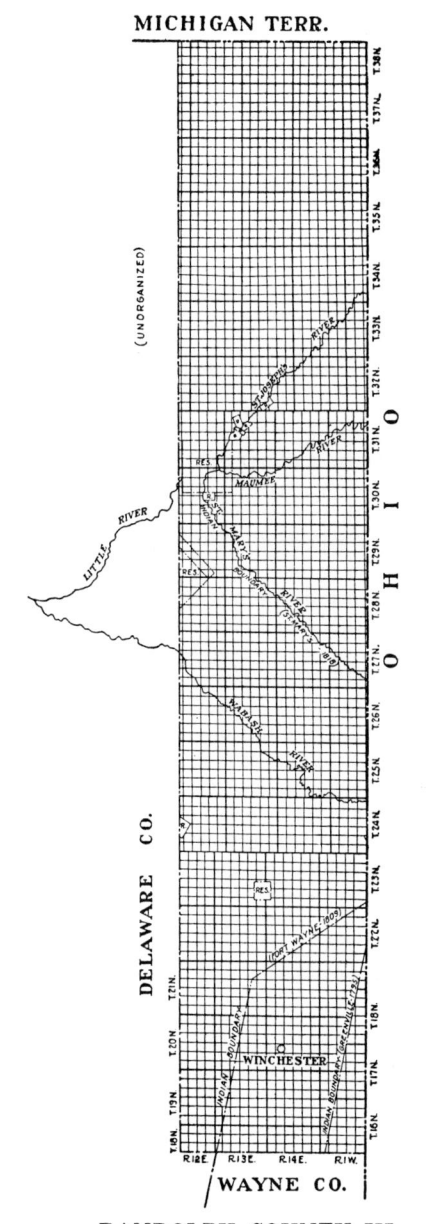

RANDOLPH COUNTY III

[Law: Dec. 23, 1820, effective on publication]

RANDOLPH COUNTY IV

JANUARY 31, 1824: Alteration by statute defining county boundaries.

BOUNDARIES: "Beginning at the Ohio state line, where the line dividing townships fifteen and sixteen strikes the same; thence west with said township line, until it strikes the old Indian boundary; thence to, and with the centre line of township eighteen, to the north-west corner of section twenty, in township eighteen, and range twelve east of the second principal meridian; thence north to the line dividing townships twenty-one and twenty-two; thence east to the Ohio state line, and thence with said state line to the place of beginning." *Revised Laws of Indiana*, 1823-24, p. 94.

A law of December 17, 1823, provided that Randolph County should have "civil and criminal jurisdiction over all that tract of country west of the said county of Randolph, to the . . . line dividing ranges seven and eight, and so far north as to where the township line dividing townships twenty-five and twenty-six, intersects the said range line." *Ibid.*, 111.

A law of February 10, 1831, attached "all the territory north of the counties of Randolph and Delaware, to the line dividing townships twenty-five and twenty-six . . . to said counties respectively." *Laws of Indiana*, 1830-31 (special), pp. 17-18.

RANDOLPH COUNTY IV
[Law: Jan. 31, 1824]

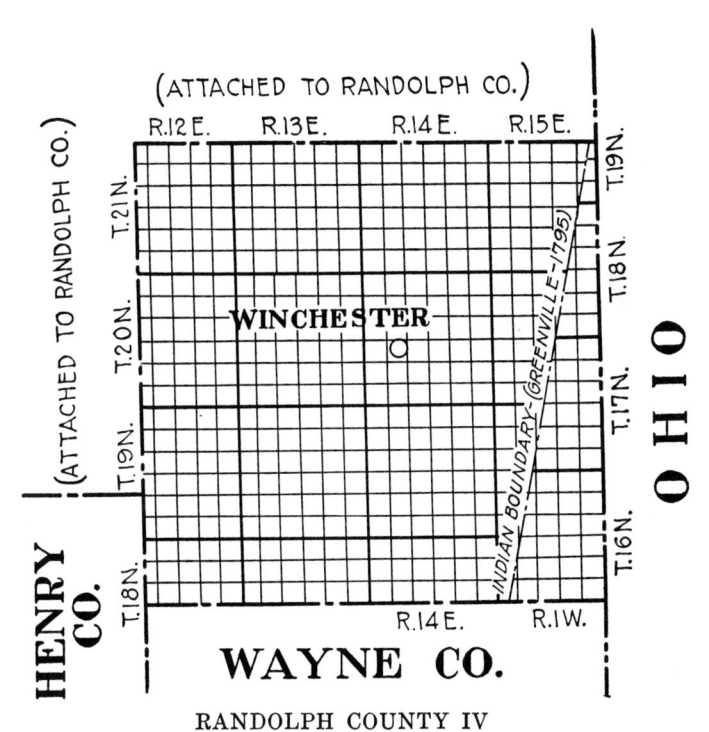

RIPLEY COUNTY I

DECEMBER 27, 1816: Formation by statute, affecting Dearborn and Jefferson counties. The county was organized by an act of January 14, 1818, effective April 10, 1818.

BOUNDARIES: "All that part of the county of Jefferson, lying north of the line dividing townships five and six north, and east" of a line beginning at "the south east corner of section thirty one in township six north, range ten east; thence north with the sectional line to the Indian boundary," also "all that part of Dearborn county west of the old boundary line." *Laws of Indiana*, 1816-17, pp. 197, 199.

The boundaries of Ripley County were thus laid out in the law forming Jennings County, with the provision that all that part of Ripley which was formerly Jefferson County be attached to Jennings County, and all that part of Ripley which was formerly Dearborn County remain attached to Dearborn until Ripley should be organized. The organization law of January 14, 1818, outlined the boundaries of Ripley County as follows: "Beginning at the south east corner of section number thirty-one, in township six, north of range number 10 east, being the south east corner of Jennings county, running thence north with the line of Jennings county to the Indian boundary, thence north-eastwardly with said Indian boundary, to the line of Franklin county, thence east with the said line to the old boundary line, thence south with said old boundary line to the corner of Switzerland county, thence west with the line of said county to the north-west corner thereof, thence south with another line of said county to the north east corner of Jefferson county; thence west with the line of Jefferson county to the place of beginning." *Ibid.*, 1817-18 (special), pp. 32-33.

COUNTY SEAT: Commissioners appointed under the act organizing the county reported on April 27, 1818, their selection of a site in part of section 12, township 7 north, range 11 east of the second principal meridian. Versailles is still the county seat. Courts were held the first year at Marion. *Ibid.*, 33; Shockley, "County Seat Wars," *op. cit.*, 10:no.1:16; *Historical Atlas of Indiana*, 322.

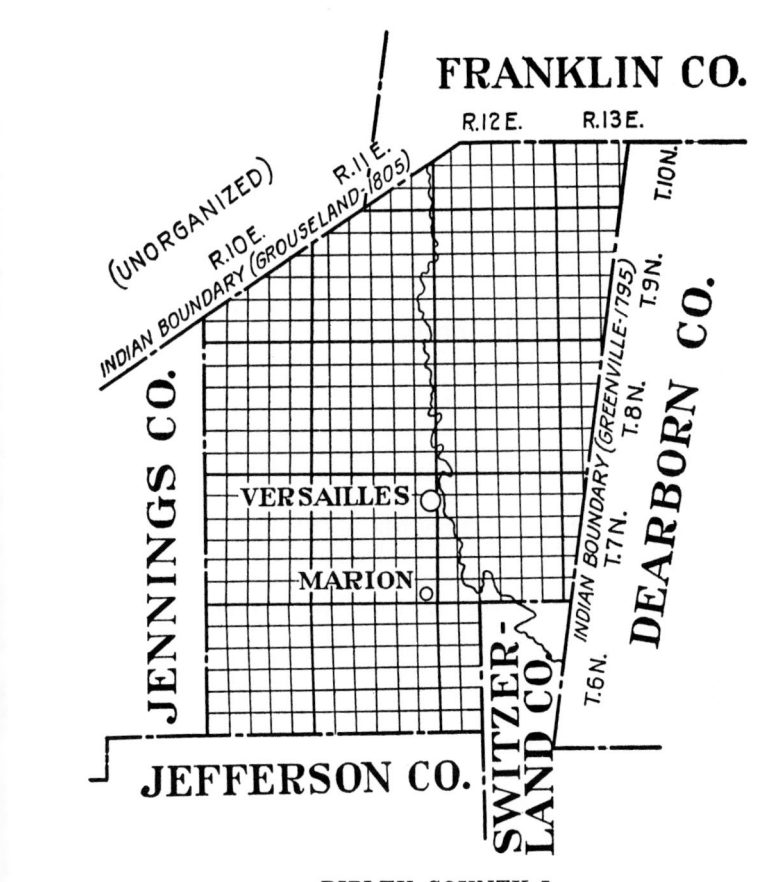

RIPLEY COUNTY I

[Law: Dec. 27, 1816; Jan. 14, 1818, effective Apr. 10, 1818]

RIPLEY COUNTY II

DECEMBER 31, 1821: Alteration by statute attaching part of Switzerland County to the county of Ripley, effective March 1, 1822.

BOUNDARY CHANGE: The act provided that "all that part of the connty [county] of Switzerland which lies north of the line running east from the north-west corner of section thirty three in town No. six north of range No. twelve east in the district of public lands sold at Jeffersonville, to the Dearborn county line, be, and the same is hereby attached to the county of Ripley." *Laws of Indiana*, 1821-22, p. 127.

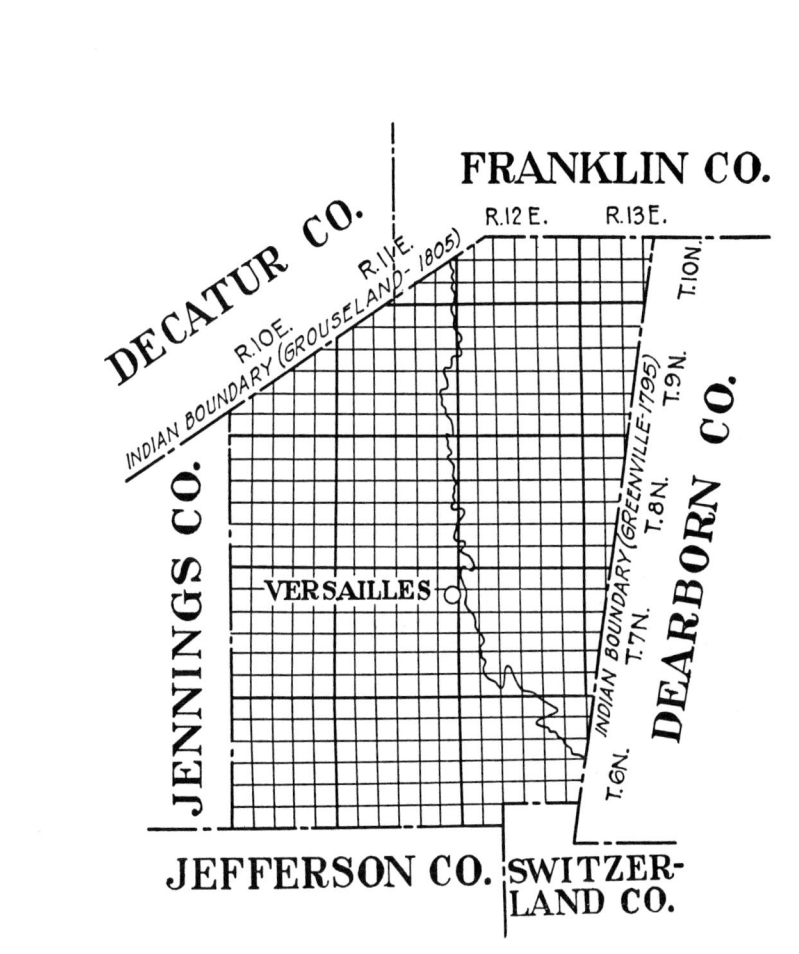

RIPLEY COUNTY II

[Law: Dec. 31, 1821, effective Mar. 1, 1822]

RUSH COUNTY

DECEMBER 31, 1821: Formation by statute, effective April 1, 1822. The formation affected Delaware County, New Purchase.

BOUNDARIES: "Beginning at the south-west corner of section twenty-seven in township twelve north of range eight east of the second principal meridian; thence east eighteen miles to the south-east corner of section twenty-eight in township twelve north of range eleven east, thence north to the line dividing townships fifteen and sixteen; thence west eighteen miles to the north-west corner of section three in township fifteen north of range eight east; thence south to the place of beginning." *Laws of Indiana,* 1821-22, pp. 61-62.

A law of February 12, 1839, restated the east boundary of Rush County as it is given in the formation law above and repeated in the law of February 17, 1838, with the addition of the words "pursuing said section line" after the word "north." The added provision that "all laws and parts of laws contravening the provisions of this act, be and the same are hereby repealed," suggests that there had been some ambiguity or controversy as to the original east boundary. What that was, does not appear from the wording of the laws. *Ibid.,* 1837-38 (local), p. 242; 1838-39 (general), pp. 85-86.

COUNTY SEAT: Commissioners appointed under the act forming the county, reported on June 17, 1822, their selection of a site for the county seat. It was named Rushville and has remained the county seat. *Ibid.,* 1821-22, p. 62; *History of Rush County,* 286; *Historical Atlas of Indiana,* 296.

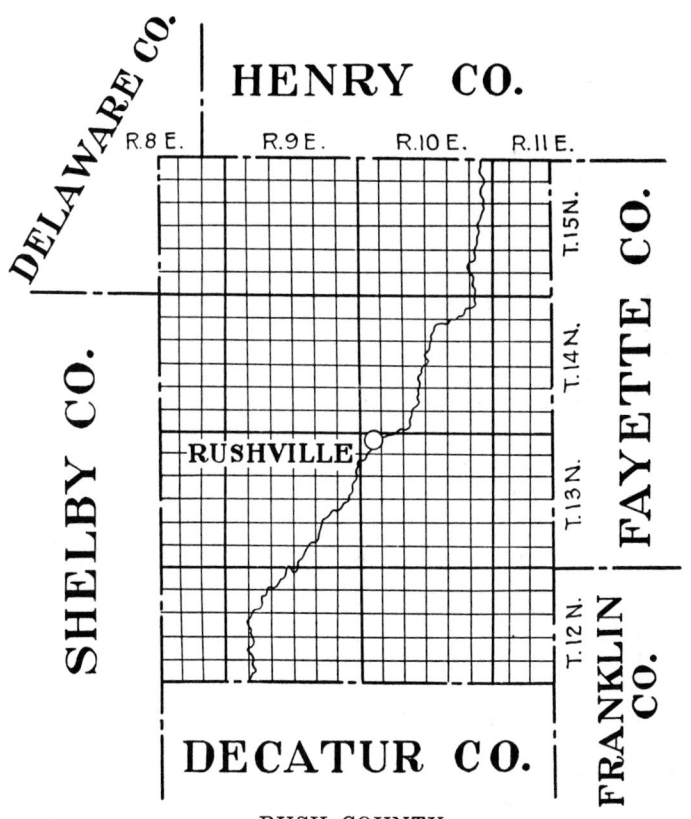

RUSH COUNTY BOUNDARIES 717

DELAWARE CO.
HENRY CO.
SHELBY CO.
RUSHVILLE
FAYETTE CO.
FRANKLIN CO.
DECATUR CO.

RUSH COUNTY
[Law: Dec. 31, 1821, effective Apr. 1, 1822]

ST. JOSEPH COUNTY I

JANUARY 29, 1830: Formation by statute, effective April 1, 1830. The formation affected territory attached to Cass County.

BOUNDARIES: "Beginning at range No. 2 west from the second principal meridian, of the state of Indiana, on the northern line of the state, thence running east, to where range No 3 east, intersects the state line; thence south with the range line, thirty miles; thence west to range two west; thence north to the place of beginning." *Laws of Indiana*, 1829-30, p. 28.

The same act attached to St. Joseph County for civil and criminal jurisdiction "all the territory lying west of said county, to the state line." *Ibid.*, 29. That part of St. Joseph County south of the Mississinewa Treaty line, and south and west of the Carey Mission Treaty line, was not ceded by the Indians until October, 1832.

COUNTY SEAT: Commissioners appointed under the act forming the county, on May 24, 1830, named a site at the portage between the St. Joseph and Kankakee rivers as the first county seat. It was called St. Joseph. Actually, county business was conducted at the home of Alexis Coquillard in South Bend. South Bend was formally made the county seat by commissioners appointed under a law of February 1, 1831. Their report of May 12, 1831, was made at the September meeting of the county board. *Ibid.*, 28-29; 1830-31 (special), pp. 21-22; Shockley, "County Seat Wars," *op. cit.*, 10:no.1:28-29; Howard, *History of St. Joseph County*, 173-75.

ST. JOSEPH COUNTY BOUNDARIES   719

MICHIGAN TERRITORY

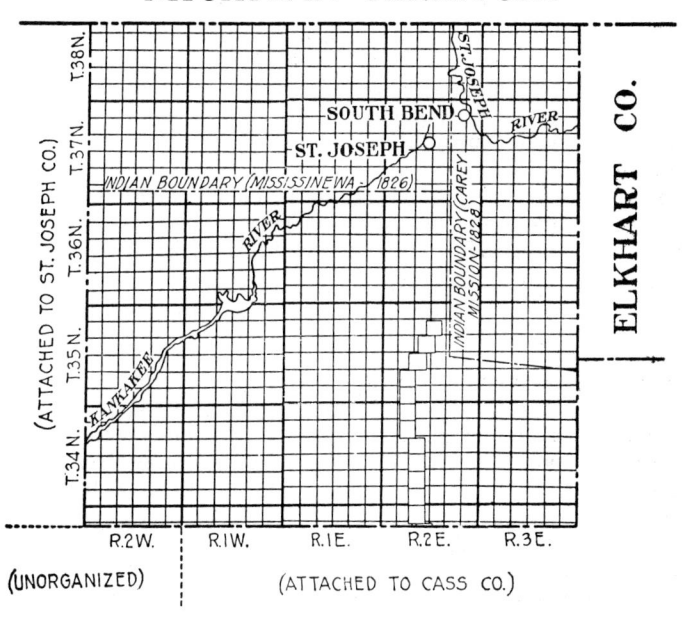

ST. JOSEPH COUNTY I

[Law: Jan. 29, 1830, effective Apr. 1, 1830]

ST. JOSEPH COUNTY II

JANUARY 9, 1832: Alteration by statute forming La Porte County, effective April 1, 1832.

BOUNDARY CHANGE: All that part of St. Joseph County west and north of a line beginning on the state line at the center line of range 1 west of the second principal meridian, running thence south twenty-two miles, thence west parallel with the state line to the range line dividing ranges 2 and 3 west, was transferred to La Porte County. *Laws of Indiana*, 1831-32, p. 9. See text of law with map, La Porte County I.

The south boundary of La Porte County was apparently run on the township line between townships 34 and 35 north. A definition of the boundary as made in a law of February 16, 1839, establishes it there. *Laws of Indiana*, 1838-39 (general), p. 70.

JANUARY 31, 1832: Alteration by statute changing the boundary line between St. Joseph and Elkhart counties, effective on passage.

BOUNDARY CHANGES: The law provided that "the boundary line between the counties of Elkhart and St. Joseph, be . . . a north and south line, three miles east, and parallel with range line, number three, east of the second principal meridian line. And all that portion of territory so stricken off of Elkhart county, be . . . attached to, and . . . constitute a part of St. Joseph county." *Laws of Indiana*, 1831-32, p. 114.

By a law of February 2, 1832, the south half of township 35 north, in ranges 4 to 7 east was attached to Elkhart County. See map, Elkhart County II.

By a law of February 10, 1831, all the territory west of the line dividing ranges 3 and 4 east, not otherwise attached, was attached to St. Joseph County for jurisdiction. *Ibid.*, 1830-31 (special), p. 18.

ST. JOSEPH COUNTY BOUNDARIES 721

MICHIGAN TERRITORY

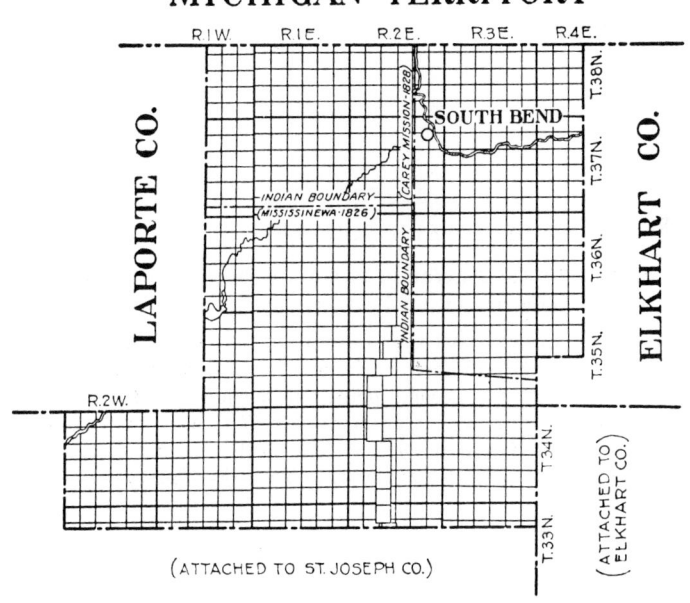

ST. JOSEPH COUNTY II

[Laws: Jan. 9, 1832, effective Apr. 1, 1832; Jan. 31, 1832, effective on passage]

ST. JOSEPH COUNTY III

FEBRUARY 7, 1835: Alteration by statute forming Marshall and Starke counties, effective on publication.

BOUNDARY CHANGE: All that part of St. Joseph County south of the township line dividing townships 34 and 35 north, in ranges 1, 2, and 3 east of the second principal meridian and 1 and 2 west of that meridian was transferred to Marshall and Starke counties. *Laws of Indiana*, 1834-35 (general), p. 46. See text of law with maps, Marshall County I, and Starke County I.

MICHIGAN TERRITORY

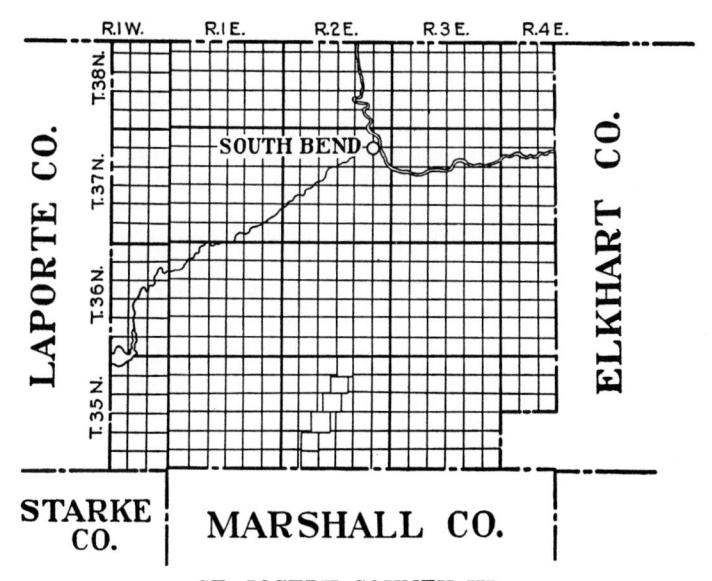

ST. JOSEPH COUNTY III

[Law: Feb. 7, 1835, effective on publication]

ST. JOSEPH COUNTY IV

FEBRUARY 4, 1836: Alteration by statute organizing the county of Marshall, effective April 1, 1836.

BOUNDARY CHANGE: All that part of St. Joseph County south and east of a line beginning at the southwest corner of township 35 north, range 1 east, running thence north with the range line to its intersection with the center line of township 35 north, thence east with the center section line of said township to the Elkhart boundary line, was transferred to Marshall County. See text of law with map, Marshall County II. *Laws of Indiana*, 1835-36 (general), p. 50.

The law of February 17, 1838, defining county boundaries incorrectly gave the south boundary of St. Joseph as the line between townships 34 and 35 north, and the west boundary of the county as the range line dividing ranges 1 and 2 west of the second principal meridian. A law of February 16, 1839, corrected these errors and defined the county boundaries as they appear on this map: "By a line commencing on the north boundary of this state at the intersection thereon of the section line running north and south through the centre of range four east, thence south to the centre of township thirty-five north, thence west to the second meridian line, being that line between ranges one east and one west, thence south to the township line between townships thirty-four and thirty-five north, thence west to the section line running north and south through the centre of range one west, thence north by said section line to the north boundary of this state, thence east to the place of beginning." *Ibid.*, 1837-38 (local), p. 257; 1838-39 (general), p. 70.

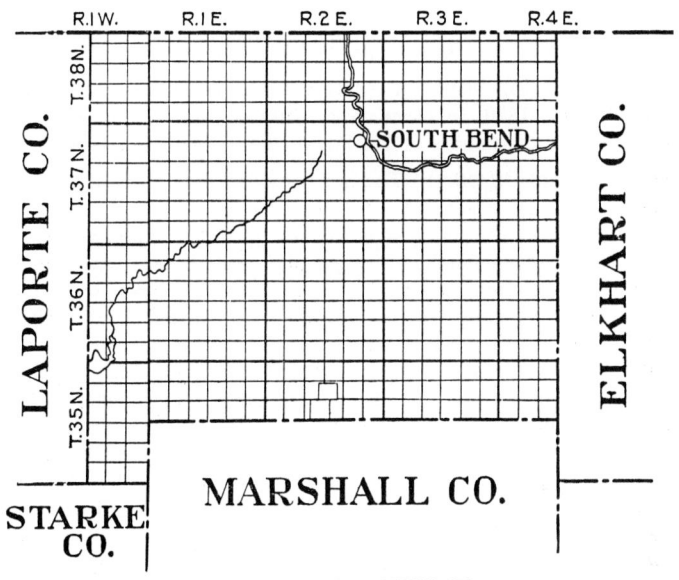

ST. JOSEPH COUNTY IV
[Law: Feb. 4, 1836, effective Apr. 1, 1836]

ST. JOSEPH COUNTY V

JANUARY 14, 1850: Alteration under provisions of statute of January 14, 1850, in force from July 4, 1850, made effective by order of commissioners of La Porte County, July 10, 1850.

BOUNDARY CHANGE: The act provided that all that part of St. Joseph County described as follows: "beginning at the present county line, at the north-west corner of section twenty-two, township thirty seven north, of range one west, thence with the north line of said section, and that of section twenty-three, to the northeast corner of said section twenty-three, thence south with the section line, until it shall strike the Great Kankakee river, thence with said river to the present county line, may be attached to the county of Laporte." The board doing county business in and for the county of La Porte was authorized "at their first or any subsequent meeting, after the taking effect of this act, to attach the said territory to any of the townships in the said county of Laporte." By an order of July 10, 1850, the Board of Commissioners of La Porte County divided the territory described between Wills and Pleasant townships, La Porte County. *Laws of Indiana,* 1849-50 (general), pp. 114-15; *History of La Porte County,* 442-43; Howard, *History of St. Joseph County,* 1:179.

ST. JOSEPH COUNTY BOUNDARIES 727

MICHIGAN

ST. JOSEPH COUNTY V

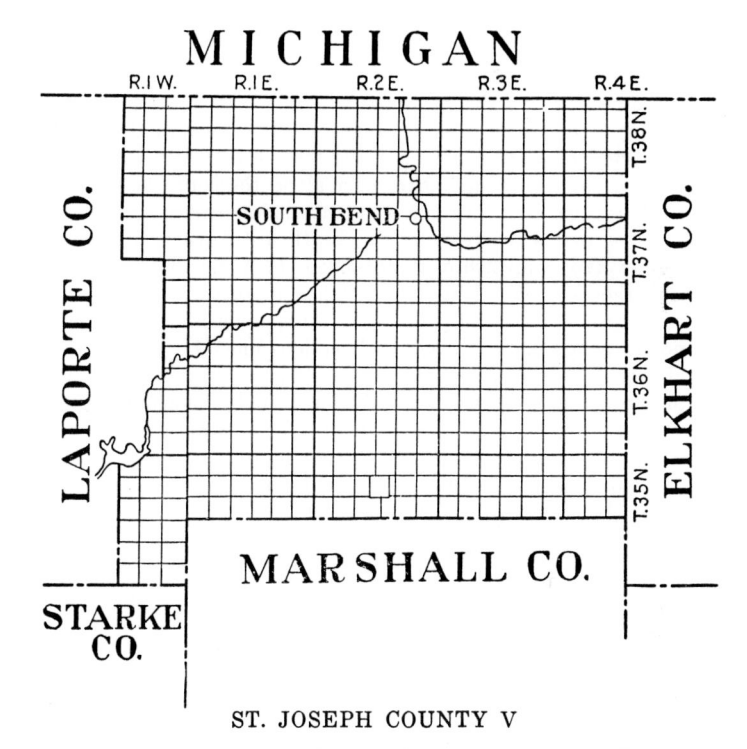

[Law: Jan. 14, 1850, in force July 4, 1850, made effective by County Commissioners' Report, July 10, 1850]

ST. JOSEPH COUNTY VI

MARCH 9, 1931: Alteration by statute defining the boundaries of St. Joseph and La Porte counties, effective on passage.

BOUNDARIES: "Beginning at the point where the center line of range one (1) west of the second principal meridian intersects the state line between the State of Michigan and Indiana, thence south along said center line of range one (1) west to the southwestern corner of section fifteen (15), township thirty-seven (37) north, range one (1) west, thence east along the south line of sections fifteen (15) and fourteen (14), township thirty-seven (37) north, range one (1) west to the northwest corner of section twenty-four (24), township thirty-seven (37) north, range one (1) west, thence south along the west line of sections twenty-four (24), twenty-five (25) and thirty-six (36), township thirty-seven (37) north, range one (1) west and sections one (1), twelve (12) and thirteen (13), township thirty-six (36) north, range one (1) west to the center of the Dixon W. Place ditch, thence down the center of said Dixon W. Place ditch to a point where a line protracted due north from the center of the channel of the beginning of the east branch of the Horace Miller ditch would intersect with said Dixon W. Place ditch, thence south along said line to said center of the channel of said Horace Miller ditch, thence down the center of said Horace Miller ditch to the intersection with the center line of Mud Lake Channel of the Dixon W. Place ditch, thence on the center line of said Mud Lake Channel of the Dixon W. Place ditch to the center line of range one (1) west, thence south along said center line of range one (1) west to the south line of township thirty-five (35) north, thence east to the meridian line, thence north along said meridian line to the center line of township thirty-five (35) north, thence east along said center line of township thirty-five (35) north to the center line of range four (4) east, thence north along said center line of range four (4) east to the state line between the states of Indiana and Michigan, thence west along said state line to the place of beginning." *Laws of Indiana*, 1931, pp. 451-52.

ST. JOSEPH COUNTY BOUNDARIES 729

ST. JOSEPH COUNTY VI

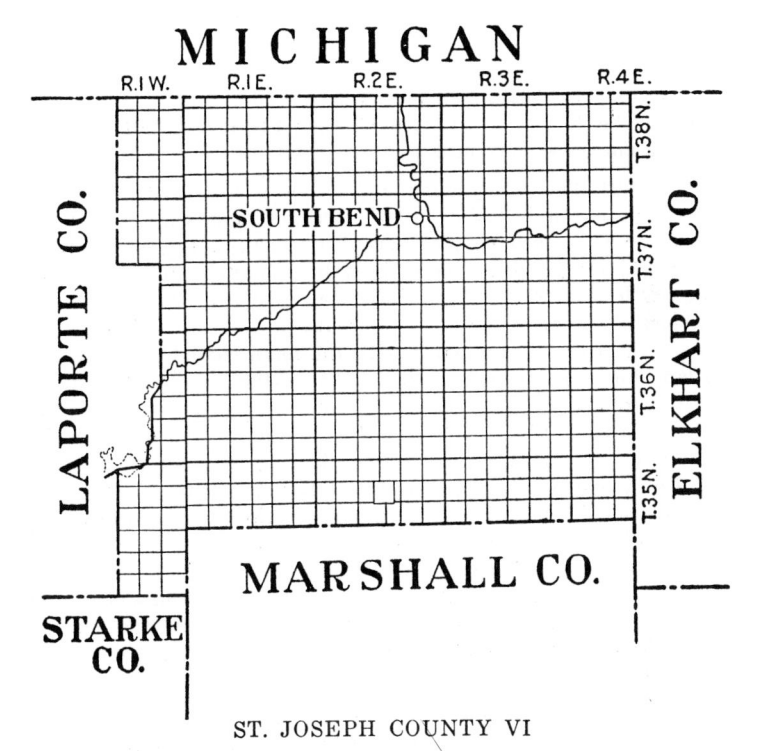

[Law: Mar. 9, 1931, effective on passage]

SCOTT COUNTY I

JANUARY 12, 1820: Formation by statute, effective February 1, 1820. The formation affected Clark, Jefferson, Jennings, Washington, and Jackson counties.

BOUNDARIES: "Beginning at the south east corner of section number thirteen, in township two north, of range eight east, thence north to the south east corner of township three, north of the aforesaid range, thence on a direct line through said township, to the north west corner thereof, thence north with the line dividing ranges seven and eight, to the south fork of the Muscackituck river, thence down the same with the main channel thereof, until a land line running due south, will touch the south west corner of section thirty-two, township two north, in range six east, thence directly east until it touches the line dividing Clark and Washington counties, thence with the line dividing the aforesaid counties of Clark and Washington, north eastwardly, until it touches the south west corner of section number eighteen, of township two north, of range seven east, thence east to the place of beginning." *Laws of Indiana*, 1819-20, pp. 51-52.

An act of January 22, 1820, appointed commissioners from Clark, Washington, and Scott counties to survey and mark so much of the boundary of Clark as was not defined by any survey. *Ibid.*, 121-22.

COUNTY SEAT: Commissioners appointed by the act forming the county, on March 6, 1820, reported their selection of Lexington as county seat. *Ibid.*, 52; Shockley, "County Seat Wars," *op. cit.*, 10:no.1:17; *Historical Atlas of Indiana*, 279.

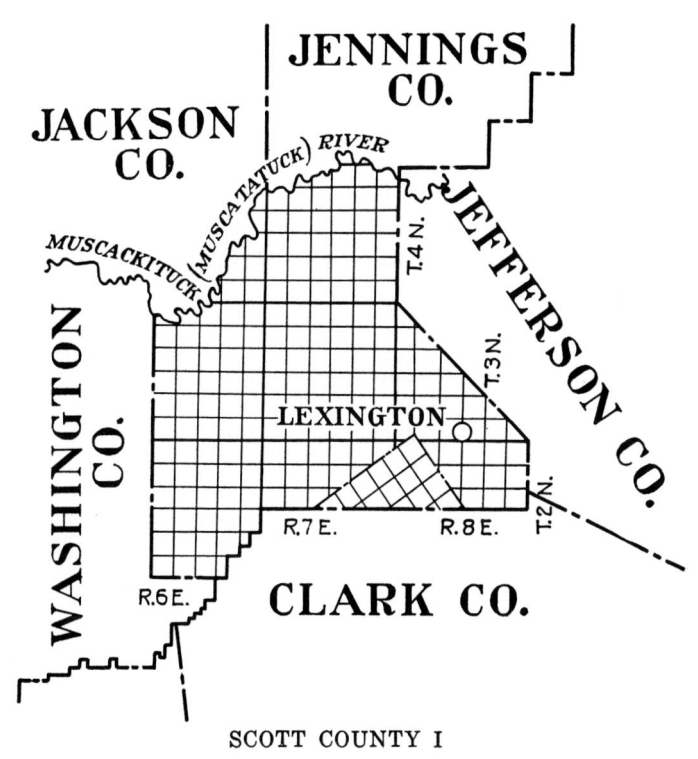

SCOTT COUNTY I
[Law: Jan. 12, 1820, effective Feb. 1, 1820]

SCOTT COUNTY II

DECEMBER 26, 1820: Alteration by statute arranging the boundary line between the counties of Washington and Scott, effective on passage.

BOUNDARY CHANGE: The act attached to Washington County "so much of the county of Scott as is south of a line commencing on the boundary line between the counties of Washington and Scott, at the southwest corner of section twenty in town two north of range six east; thence running east with the sectional line, until it intersects the Clark county line." *Laws of Indiana*, 1820-21, p. 58.

There is a discrepancy in the descriptions of the Clark-Washington boundary as given under the two counties in the 1824 Revision of the laws. See *Revised Laws of Indiana*, 1823-24, p. 97.

An act of January 12, 1829, appointed commissioners to mark the Scott-Clark boundary line. *Laws of Indiana*, 1828-29, p. 17.

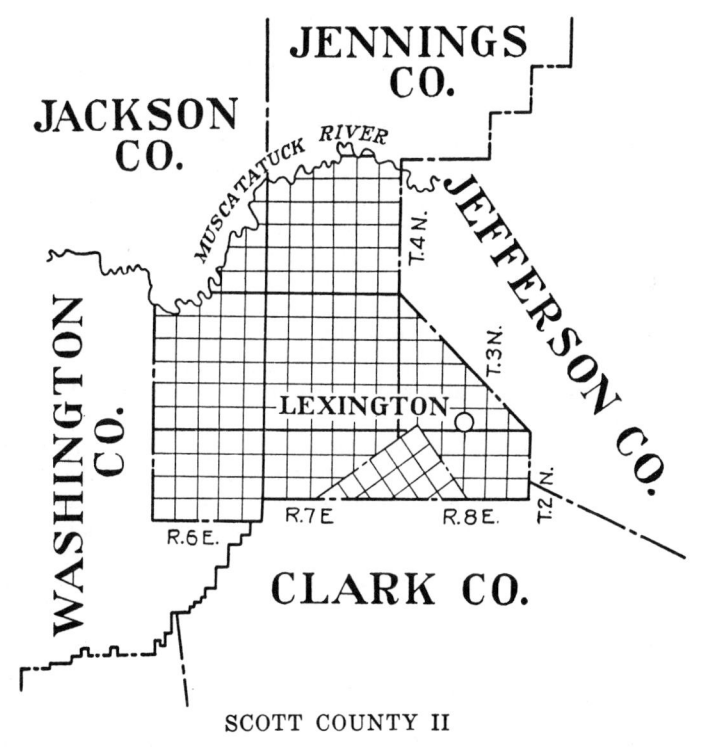

SCOTT COUNTY BOUNDARIES 733

SCOTT COUNTY II
[Law: Dec. 26, 1820, effective on passage]

SCOTT COUNTY III

JANUARY 22, 1830: Alteration by statute altering the line dividing the counties of Jefferson and Scott, effective on passage.

BOUNDARY CHANGE: The act provided that "the dividing line between the counties of Jefferson and Scott, where the same runs through township three, north of range eight east, in the Jeffersonville district . . . be as follows, viz: Beginning at the south east corner of said township; thence north two miles to the line dividing sections twenty-four and twenty-five; thence west two miles to the north east corner of section twenty-seven; thence north two miles to the north east corner of section fifteen; thence west two miles to the north east corner of section seventeen; thence north one mile to the north east corner of section eight; thence west one mile to the north east corner of section seven; thence north one mile, to the township line; thence west one mile to the north west corner of said township: And that all the territory south and west of said lines, and formerly belonging to the county of Jefferson, be . . . attached to the county of Scott." *Laws of Indiana*, 1829-30, p. 21.

The law defining county boundaries in the *Revised Laws* of 1831 contains a discrepancy between the descriptions of the Scott-Washington boundary as given under the two counties. The boundary as given under Scott County does not coincide with that shown on this map. It provided that beginning on the Muscatatuck River, at its intersection by the line dividing sections 5 and 6, township 3 north, range 6 east of the second principal meridian, the line should run due south to "the south-west corner of section twenty-nine, in town two north, of range six east; thence east two miles; thence south one mile, to the township line dividing one and two; thence east with said line, to the Clark county line; thence north-eastwardly, until it touches the south-west corner of section eighteen, of town two, range seven." The description of the Washington County boundaries in the same law, does not show this change, but coincides with the line as drawn on this map. *Revised Laws of Indiana*, 1830-31, pp. 127-28. See, however, Scott County map for February 16, 1839.

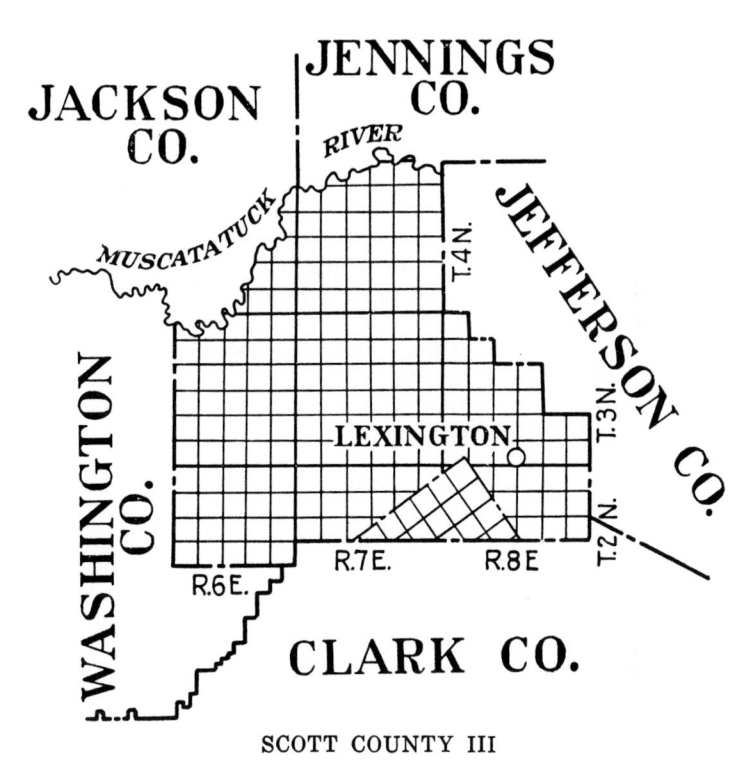

SCOTT COUNTY BOUNDARIES 735

SCOTT COUNTY III
[Law: Jan. 22, 1830, effective on passage]

SCOTT COUNTY IV

FEBRUARY 16, 1839: Alteration by statute more particularly defining the western and southern boundaries of the county of Scott, effective on passage.

BOUNDARY CHANGE: The line is described as "beginning in the main channel of the south fork of the Muscatitack river on the section line dividing sections five and six, in township three, north of range six east, and running thence southwardly upon the said section line to the south-west corner of section twenty-nine, in township two north of the same range, and running thence eastwardly upon said section line two miles to the south-west corner of section twenty-seven; and thence south upon the section line one mile to the township line dividing townships one and two, and running thence eastwardly upon said township line, two miles to the south-west corner of section thirty-six; thence north with said section line one mile to the south-west corner of section twenty-five; thence east with said section line one mile to the range line dividing ranges six and seven; thence north with said range line two miles to the south-west corner of section eighteen, township two, north of range seven east, intersecting at this point the line heretofore dividing the counties of Scott and Clark, running thence east with said county line as heretofore." *Laws of Indiana*, 1838-39 (local), pp. 323-24.

SCOTT COUNTY BOUNDARIES 737

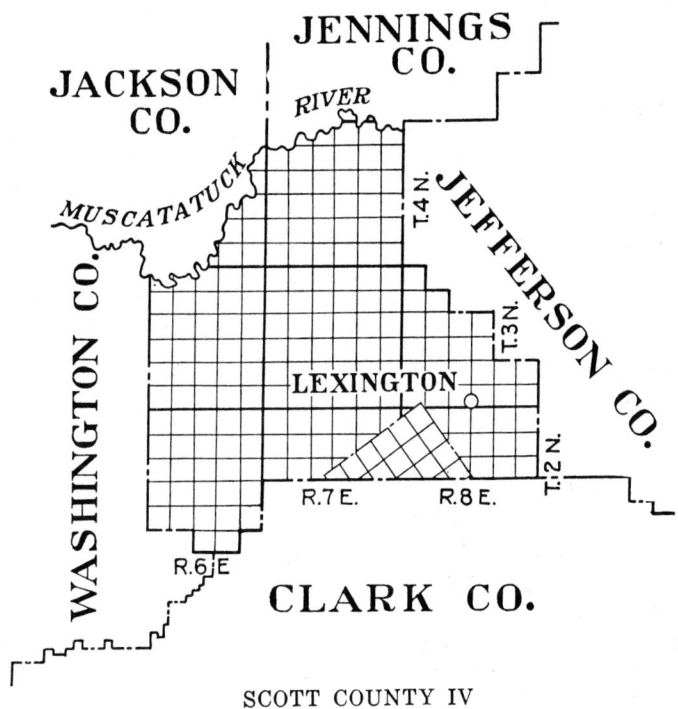

SCOTT COUNTY IV
[Law: Feb. 16, 1839, effective on passage]

SCOTT COUNTY V

1842-43: Alteration by statute defining county boundaries.

BOUNDARIES: "Beginning at the southeast corner of section thirteen, township two north, range eight east, thence north to the north-east corner of section twenty-five, township three north, range eight east, thence west two miles, to the northeast corner of section twenty-seven, thence north to the northeast corner of section fifteen, thence west to the northwest corner of section sixteen, thence north to the northeast corner of section eight, thence west to the northwest corner of same, thence north to the line dividing townships three and four north, thence west to the southeast corner of township four north, range seven east, thence north to the south fork of the Muscatituck river, thence down the same with the main channel thereof to the line dividing sections five and six, township three north, range six east, thence south to the southwest corner of section twenty-nine, township two north, range six east, thence east two miles, thence south one mile, to the line dividing townships one and two north, thence east one mile and a half, thence north one mile, thence east a half mile, thence north a half mile, thence east a half mile, thence north a half mile, thence east a half mile to the line dividing ranges six and seven east, thence north to the northwest corner of section nineteen, township two north, range seven east, thence east to the place of beginning." *Revised Statutes of Indiana*, 1842-43, p. 76.

FEBRUARY 13, 1851: Alteration by statute attaching territory to Scott County, effective on passage.

BOUNDARY CHANGE: The law provided that "the south half of section five, in township number three north, of range eight east, in the county of Jefferson, be . . . attached to the county of Scott." This area is marked (a) on the map. *Laws of Indiana*, 1850-51 (general), p. 58.

COUNTY SEAT: The question of removing the county seat from Lexington was under discussion in 1823, 1839, and 1840, but no change was made until 1871. On March 10 of that year, a petition was presented asking for removal of the county seat, and the new town of Scottsburg was laid out, although the removal of the county seat to that place did not occur until 1874. This has remained the county seat. *Ibid.*, 1822-23, pp. 45-47; 1838-39 (general), pp. 55-57; 1839-40 (general), pp. 37-38; Shockley, "County Seat Wars," *op. cit.*, 10:no.1:17-18.

SCOTT COUNTY V

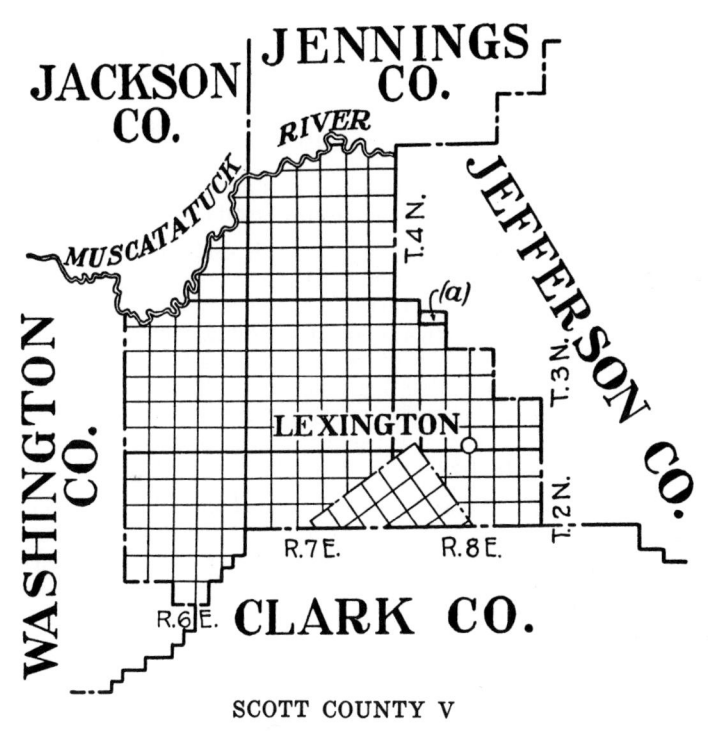

[Laws: 1842-43; Feb. 13, 1851, effective on passage]

SHELBY COUNTY

DECEMBER 31, 1821: Formation by statute, effective April 1, 1822. The formation affected Delaware County, New Purchase.

BOUNDARIES: "Beginning at the south east corner of section thirty-three in township eleven north of range eight east of the second principal meridian; thence north twenty-four miles, to the north-east corner of section four in township fourteen north of range eight east; thence west seventeen miles to the north west corner of section two in township fourteen north of range five east; thence south twenty-four miles to the north boundary of Bartholomew county; thence east seventeen miles to the place of beginning." *Laws of Indiana*, 1821-22, p. 52.

COUNTY SEAT: Commissioners appointed under the act forming the county selected part of sections 5 and 31, townships 12 and 13 north, range 7 east of the second principal meridian. Their report was accepted July 5, 1822. Shelbyville remains the county seat. *Ibid.*, 53; *History of Shelby County.* 275.

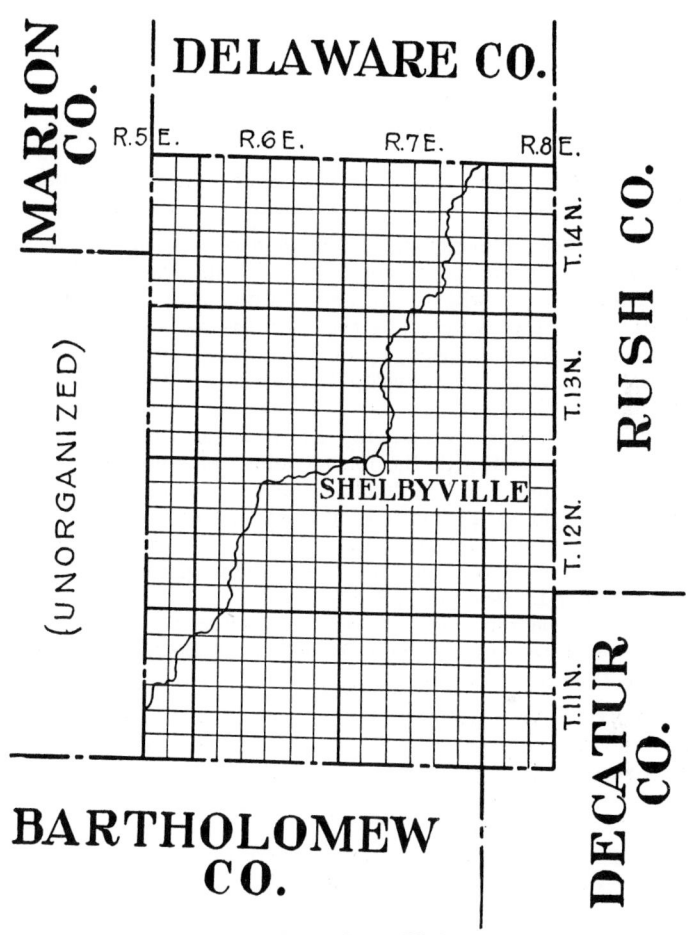

SHELBY COUNTY BOUNDARIES 741

SHELBY COUNTY
[Law: Dec. 31, 1821, effective Apr. 1, 1822]

SPENCER COUNTY I

JANUARY 10, 1818: Formation by statute, effective February 1, 1818. The formation affected Perry and Warrick counties.

BOUNDARIES: "Beginning on the Ohio river where the section line passes through the centre of the seventh range strikes the same; thence north with the said section line until it strikes Little Pigeon creek; thence up said creek, with the meanders thereof, to the Polk Patch Fork; thence up the Polk Patch Fork, with the meanders thereof, to the township line passing between townships four aad [and] five; thence east with said . . . line to the range line dividing ranges five and six; thence north to the line of Pike county, thence east with the line dividing the counties of Perry and Pike to the range line dividing ranges three and four, thence south with said range line until it first strikes Anderson's river, thence down said river with the meanders thereof to the Ohio river, thence down the same to the place of beginning." *Laws of Indiana*, 1817-18 (special), pp. 20-21.

By the time this law had become effective, "the line of Pike county" had become the south boundary of the new county of Dubois. See map, Dubois County I.

COUNTY SEAT: Commissioners appointed under the act forming the county, in a report of March 11, 1818, announced their selection of a site for the county seat in sections 23 and 26, township 7 south, range 6 west. The town was given the name Rockport. *Laws of Indiana*, 1817-18 (special), p. 21; *History of Warrick, Spencer and Perry Counties*, 278-79, 326-28; Shockley, "County Seat Wars," *op. cit.*, 10:no.1:10.

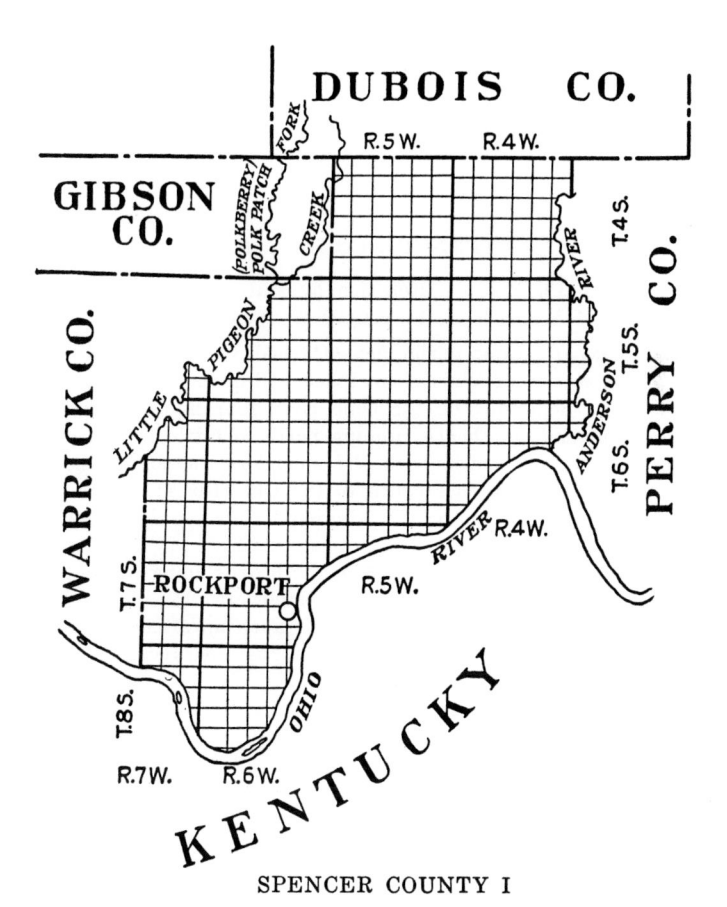

SPENCER COUNTY I
[Law: Jan. 10, 1818, effective Feb. 1, 1818]

SPENCER COUNTY II

FEBRUARY 10, 1825: Alteration by statute attaching part of the county of Warrick to the county of Spencer.

BOUNDARY CHANGE: The act attached to Spencer "all that part of the county of Warrick included within the following boundaries, viz: Beginning on the Ohio river four miles west of the Spencer county line; thence running north to Little Pigeon creek; thence up the said creek, with the meanders thereof to the line of Spencer county; thence south to the Ohio River; thence down the Ohio River to the place of beginning." *Laws of Indiana*, 1825, p. 16.

By an act of February 18, 1839, the boards doing business for Warrick and Spencer counties were empowered to confer on the common boundary line. If they agreed upon an alteration it was to become law. *Ibid.*, 1838-39 (local), p. 254. No record has been found of action on the matter.

SPENCER COUNTY BOUNDARIES 745

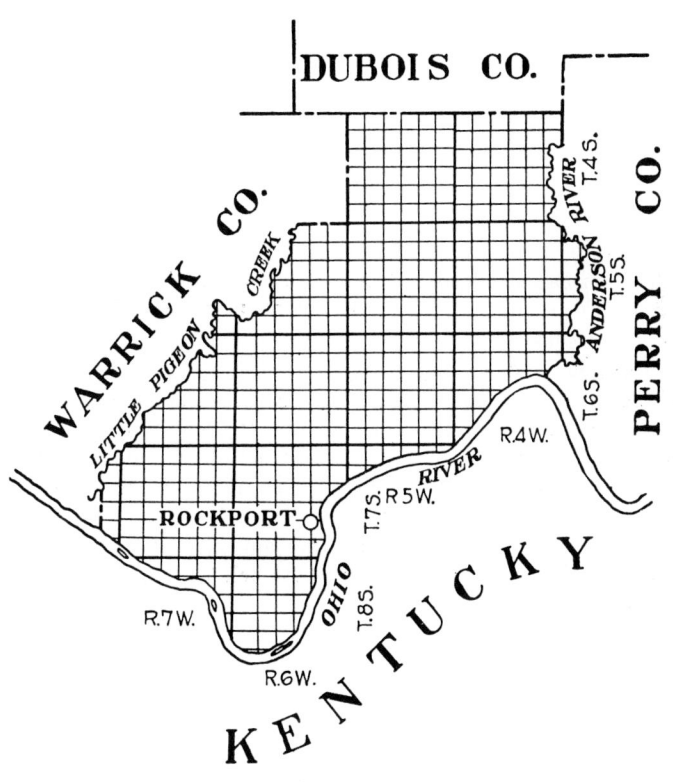

SPENCER COUNTY II
[Law: Feb. 10, 1825]

STARKE COUNTY I

FEBRUARY 7, 1835: Formation by statute, effective on publication. The formation affected St. Joseph County and attached territory. Starke was organized by an act of January 15, 1850, effective on passage.

BOUNDARIES: "Beginning at the north west corner of township thirty four north, of range four west, thence east twenty four miles, thence south with the meridian line eighteen miles, thence west twenty four miles, thence north with the line dividing ranges four and five west, eighteen miles to the place of beginning." *Laws of Indiana*, 1834-35 (general), p. 46.

COUNTY SEAT: No county seat was laid out until after the act of organization in 1850. See text with following map.

STARKE COUNTY I

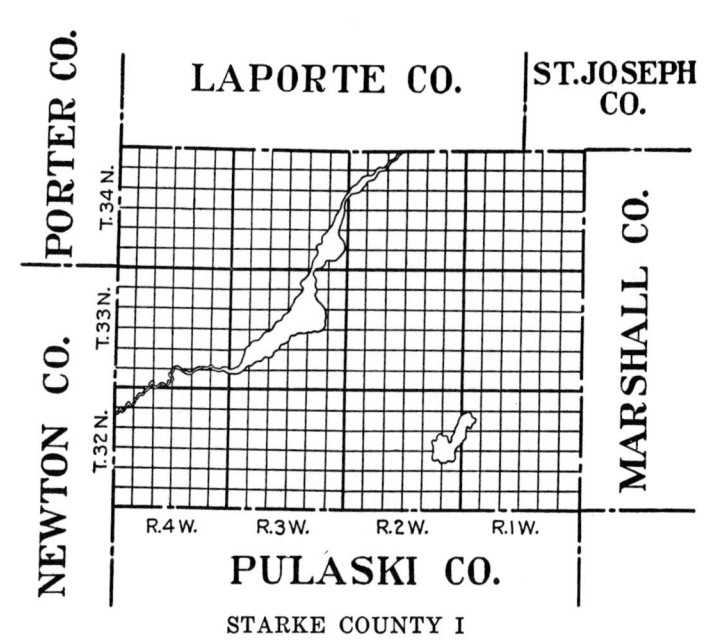

[Law: Feb. 7, 1835, effective on publication]

STARKE COUNTY II

JANUARY 29, 1842: Alteration by a statute for the attachment of a part of Starke County to the county of La Porte, effective on passage.

BOUNDARY CHANGE: The law provided that "all that part of Stark county which lies north of the Kankakee river be, and the same is hereby attached permanently to the county of Laporte." *Laws of Indiana*, 1841-42 (general), p. 152.

COUNTY SEAT: Commissioners appointed in the act of January 18, 1850, organizing the county, selected a site in section 22, township 33 north, range 2 west, on April 1, 1850. The town of Knox, which was laid out on this site, has continued to be the county seat. *Ibid.*, 1849-50 (general), p. 213; Shockley, "County Seat Wars," *op cit.*, 10:no.1:41; *Historical Atlas of Indiana*, 276; McCormick, Joseph N., *A Standard History of Starke County, Indiana* . . ., 154 (Chicago and New York, 1915).

STARKE COUNTY II

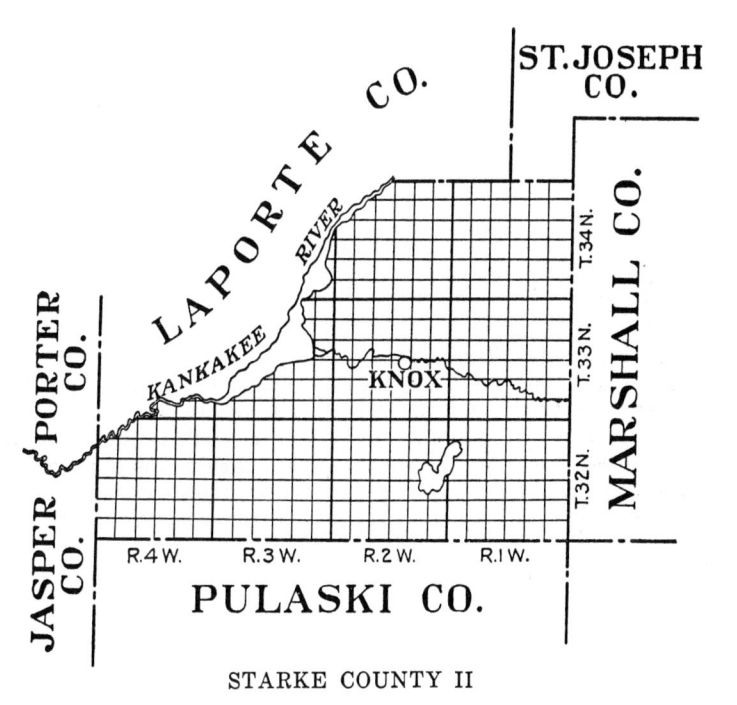

[Law: Jan. 29, 1842, effective on passage]

STARKE COUNTY III

MARCH 2, 1925: Alteration by statute defining the boundaries of Starke County.

BOUNDARIES: "Beginning at the northeast corner of township thirty-four, range one west, thence south to the south-east corner of township thirty-two, range one west, thence west to the line dividing ranges four and five west, thence north to the Dixon W. Place ditch, thence up the middle of said ditch to the line dividing townships thirty-four and thirty-five north, thence east along said line to the place of beginning." *Laws of Indiana*, 1925, p. 123.

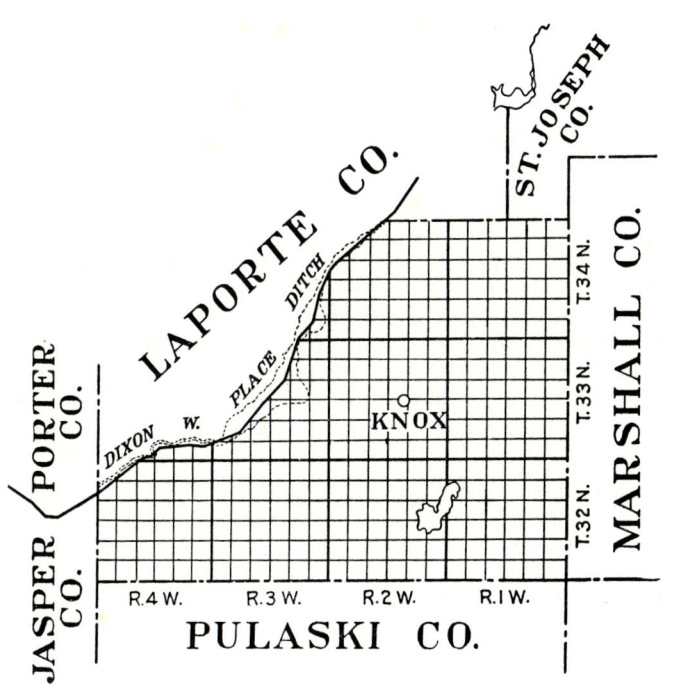

STARKE COUNTY III

[Law: Mar. 2, 1925]

STEUBEN COUNTY

FEBRUARY 7, 1835: Formation by statute, effective on publication. The formation affected territory attached to La Grange County. Steuben was organized by an act of January 18, 1837, effective May 1, 1837.

BOUNDARIES: "Beginning at the south west corner of township 36 north, of range twelve east, thence east with the line dividing townships thirty five and thirty six north to the line, of the state of Ohio, thence north with the state line to the line of Michigan territory, thence west with the territorial line to the eastern boundary line of Lagrange county, thence south with said county line to the place of beginning." *Laws of Indiana*, 1834-35 (general), p. 45.

COUNTY SEAT: Commissioners appointed under the act organizing the county selected Angola as the county seat, and the town was surveyed in April, 1838. No change of county seat has been made. *Ibid.*, 1836-37 (general), pp. 56-57; *History of Steuben County*, 273-74, 659; Shockley, "County Seat Wars," *op. cit.*, 10:no.1:35-36.

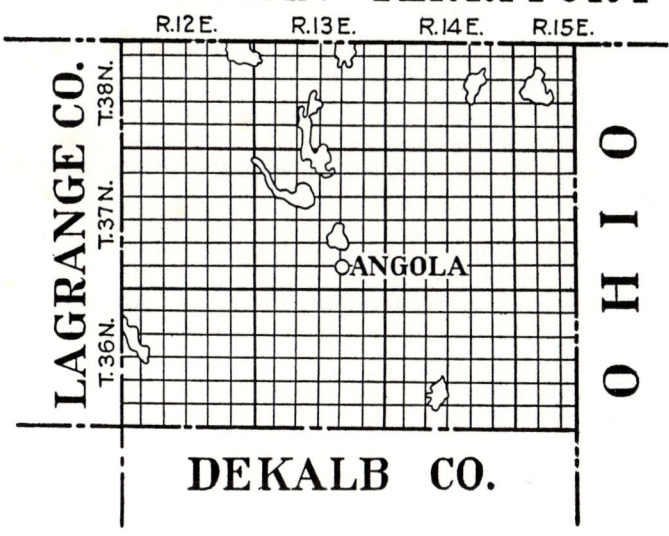

STEUBEN COUNTY
[Law: Feb. 7, 1835, effective on publication]

SULLIVAN COUNTY I

DECEMBER 30, 1816: Formation by statute, effective January 15, 1817. The formation affected Knox County.

BOUNDARIES: "Beginning on the Wabash river, where the line dividing township five, and six, crosses the same; running thence east, with said line, until it strikes the west fork of White river; thence up the said west fork of said river, to the Orange county line; thence with said line, to the Indian boundary line; thence with said boundary line, crossing the Wabash river, to the line dividing the state of Indiana, and the Illinois territory; thence with said line south, to the Wabash river; thence down the said river, with the meanders thereof to the place of beginning." *Laws of Indiana*, 1816-17, p. 205.

Daviess County was formed by an act of December 24, 1816, effective February 15, 1817. See map, Daviess County I.

COUNTY SEAT: A temporary seat of justice was established in Carlisle by the act forming the county. Commissioners to select a permanent county seat were appointed in the same act. *Laws of Indiana*, 1816-17, pp. 205-6; Shockley, "County Seat Wars," *op cit.*, 10:no.1:9; Wolfe (ed.), *History of Sullivan County*, 1:30.

SULLIVAN COUNTY BOUNDARIES 755

SULLIVAN COUNTY I

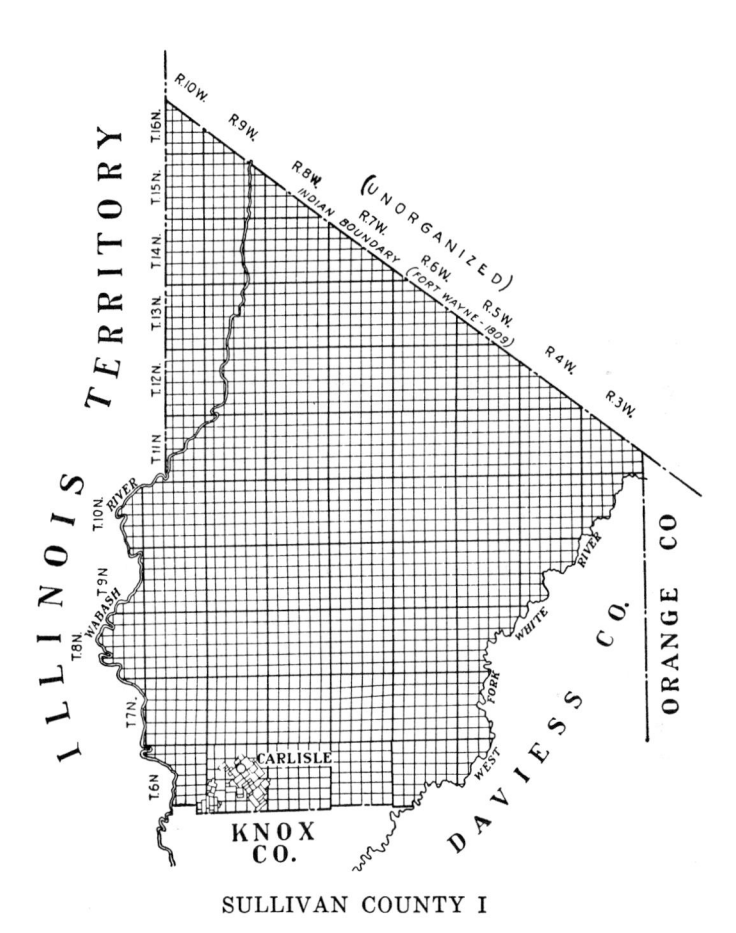

[Law: Dec. 30, 1816, effective Jan. 15, 1817]

SULLIVAN COUNTY II

JANUARY 21, 1818: Alteration by statute forming Vigo County, effective February 15, 1818.

BOUNDARY CHANGE: "All that part of the county of Sullivan included in the following bounds, shall form and constitute a new county, that is to say: Beginning at a point on the Wabash river, where the section line between fractions fourteen and twenty-three, in range eleven west, township ten north strikes the same; thence east with said line, to where it intersects the range line dividing ranges six and seven west, township ten north; thence north with said range line, to the Indian boundary; thence with said boundary to the division line between the state of Indiana and the Illinois Territory; thence south with said line to where it strikes the Wabash river; thence down said river to the place of beginning." *Laws of Indiana*, 1817-18 (special), p. 34.

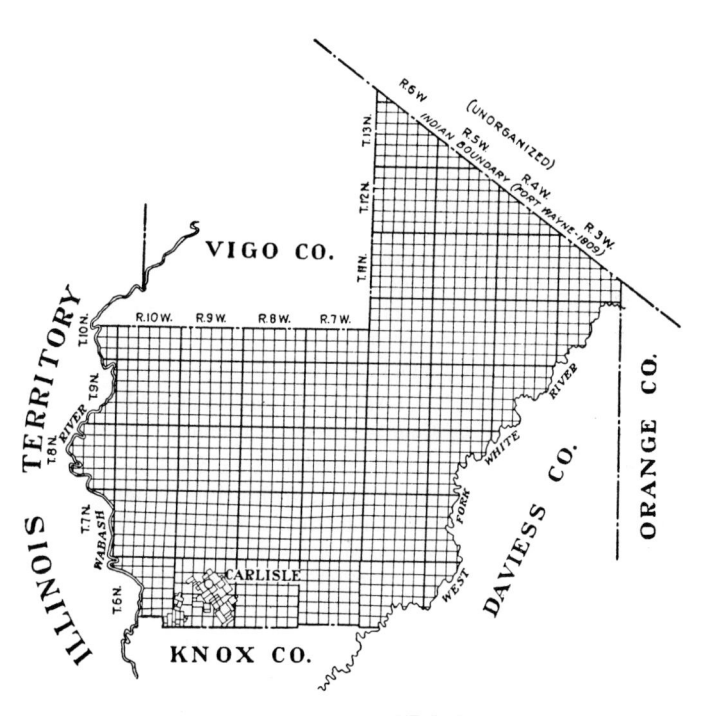

SULLIVAN COUNTY II
[Law: Jan. 21, 1818, effective Feb. 15, 1818]

SULLIVAN COUNTY III

DECEMBER 21, 1818: Alteration by statute forming Owen County, effective January 1, 1819.

BOUNDARY CHANGE: All that part of Sullivan County north and east of a line beginning on the West Fork of White River at its intersection by the line dividing townships 8 and 9 north, in range 4 west of the second principal meridian, running "thence west with the said township line to the north west corner of township eight, north of range six west, thence north with the range line dividing ranges six and seven" to the Fort Wayne Treaty line of 1809, was transferred to Owen County. *Laws of Indiana,* 1818-19, p. 96. See map, Owen County I.

JANUARY 1, 1819: Alteration by statute attaching part of Sullivan County to Vigo County, effective January 10, 1819.

BOUNDARY CHANGE: All that part of Sullivan County north of a line beginning "where the township line dividing towns nine and ten intersects the Wabash, thence east with the said line to the range line dividing ranges six and seven" west of the second principal meridian, was transferred to Vigo County. *Laws of Indiana,* 1818-19, p. 107. See map, Vigo County II.

COUNTY SEAT: Merom was made the seat of justice by commissioners appointed in the act forming the county. Although a sale of lots in Merom probably took place as early as June, 1817, county business does not appear to have begun there before 1818 or 1819. *Laws of Indiana,* 1816-17, pp. 205-6; Wolfe (ed.), *History of Sullivan County,* 31-32, 193-94.

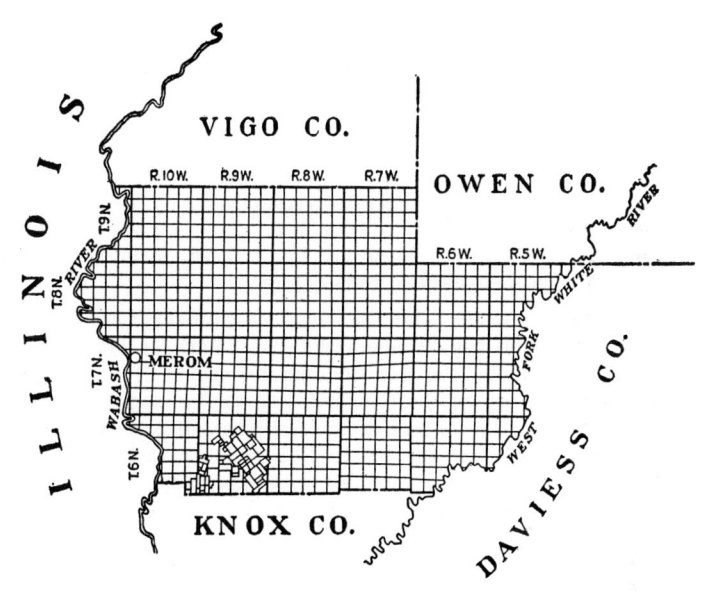

SULLIVAN COUNTY III

[Laws: Dec. 21, 1818, effective Jan. 1, 1819; Jan. 1, 1819, effective Jan. 10, 1819]

SULLIVAN COUNTY IV

JANUARY 5, 1821: Alteration by statute forming Greene County, effective February 5, 1821.

BOUNDARY CHANGE: All that part of Sullivan County south and east of a line beginning on the West Fork of White River at its intersection by the line dividing townships 8 and 9 north, running thence west on the township line to the northeast corner of township 8 north, range 8 west of the second principal meridian, thence south with the range line dividing ranges 7 and 8 west to the north boundary of Knox County, was transferred to Greene County. *Laws of Indiana*, 1820-21, p. 114. See text of law with map of Greene County.

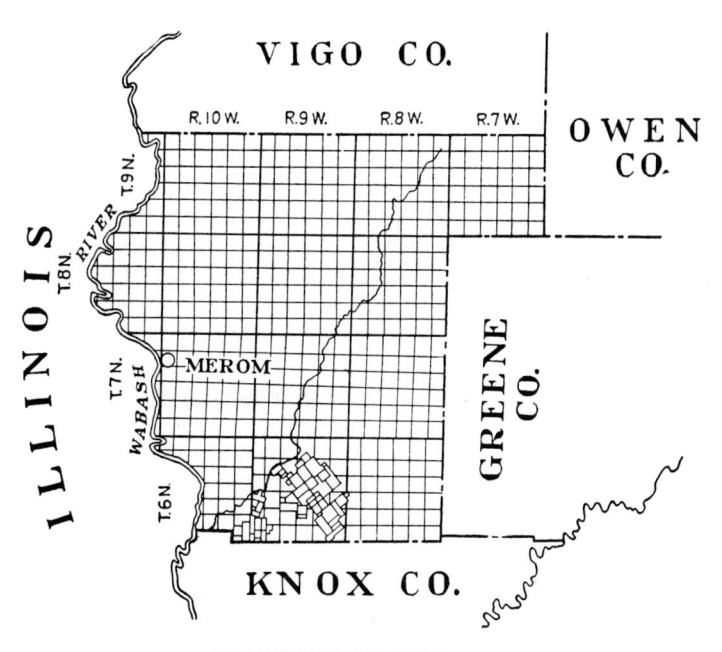

SULLIVAN COUNTY IV

[Law: Jan. 5, 1821, effective Feb. 5, 1821]

SULLIVAN COUNTY V

FEBRUARY 12, 1825: Alteration by statute forming Clay County, effective April 1, 1825.

BOUNDARY CHANGE: Township 9 north, range 7 west of the second principal meridian was transferred from Sullivan to Clay County. *Laws of Indiana*, 1825, p. 17. See text of law with map of Clay County.

COUNTY SEAT: In spite of an act of January 29, 1830, providing for a relocation, Merom remained the county seat of Sullivan County until an act of February 15, 1841, ordered the relocation of the seat of government in the geographical center of the county, if an election should prove favorable to the change. The move to Sullivan was made about 1842. *Laws of Indiana*, 1829-30, pp. 35-37; 1840-41 (local), p. 198; Shockley, "County Seat Wars," *op. cit.*, 10:no.1:10; Wolfe (ed.), *History of Sullivan County*, 163-65; *History of Greene and Sullivan Counties*, 481-84.

SULLIVAN COUNTY BOUNDARIES   763

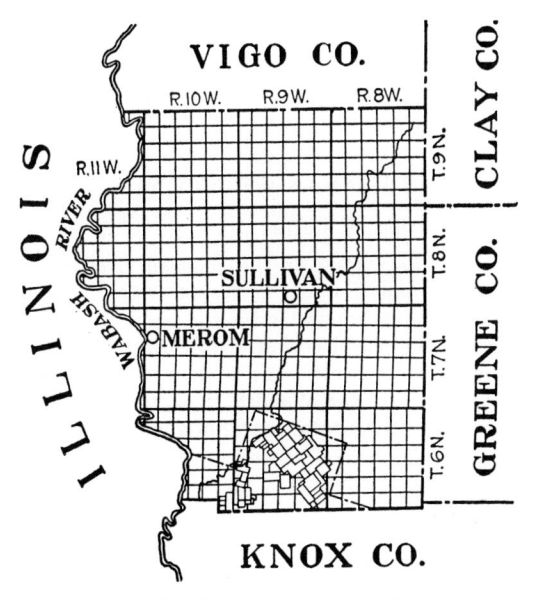

SULLIVAN COUNTY V

[Law: Feb. 12, 1825, effective Apr. 1, 1825]

SULLIVAN COUNTY VI

1842-43: Alteration by statute defining county boundaries.

BOUNDARIES: "Beginning on the Wabash river where the line dividing townships nine and ten north intersects the same, thence east to the line dividing ranges seven and eight west, thence south to the southwest [southeast] corner of township six north, of range eight west, thence west to the line dividing ranges nine and ten west, thence due west to the Wabash river, thence up the river to the beginning." *Revised Statutes of Indiana,* 1842-43, p. 81.

SULLIVAN COUNTY BOUNDARIES 765

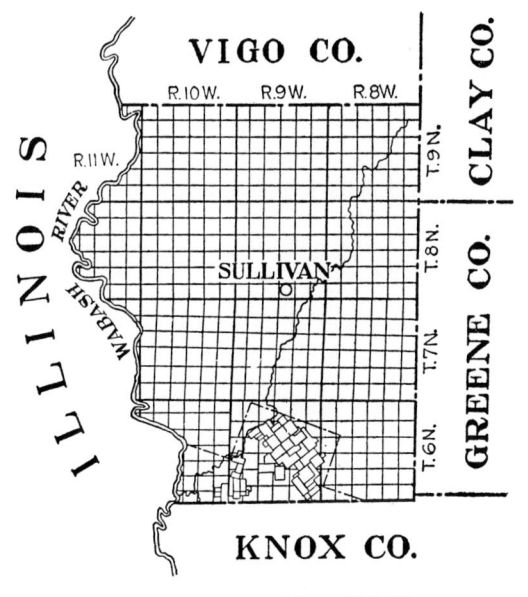

SULLIVAN COUNTY VI
[Law: 1842-43]

SWITZERLAND COUNTY I
[Indiana Territory]

SEPTEMBER 7, 1814: Formation by statute, effective October 1, 1814. The formation affected Dearborn and Jefferson counties.

BOUNDARIES: "Beginning at a point between fractional sections number twenty two and twenty seven, on the Ohio river, in town three range one, west, thence due west with said sectional line to the old Indian boundary, thence nearly north running with said boundary to the north east corner of section thirteen, town six, range twelve in the new purchase, thence due north with said section line to the north east corner of town six, range twelve, thence west with the line dividing town six, range twelve, and town seven, and range twelve to the sectional line, dividing sections five and four, in town six, range twelve, in the new purchase, thence south with said sectional line, to the Ohio river, at a point between fractional sections number twenty and twenty one, about one mile below the old Indian boundary, in town three range twelve in the new purchase, thence with the meanders of the Ohio river and up the same to the place of begining." *Acts of Indiana Territory*, 1814, pp. 30-31.

COUNTY SEAT: Vevay was chosen county seat on October 28, 1814, by commissioners appointed under the law forming the county. The site included part of sections 23 and 24, township 2 north, range 3 west. *Ibid.*, 32; Dufour, *Swiss Settlement of Switzerland County*, 41-44.

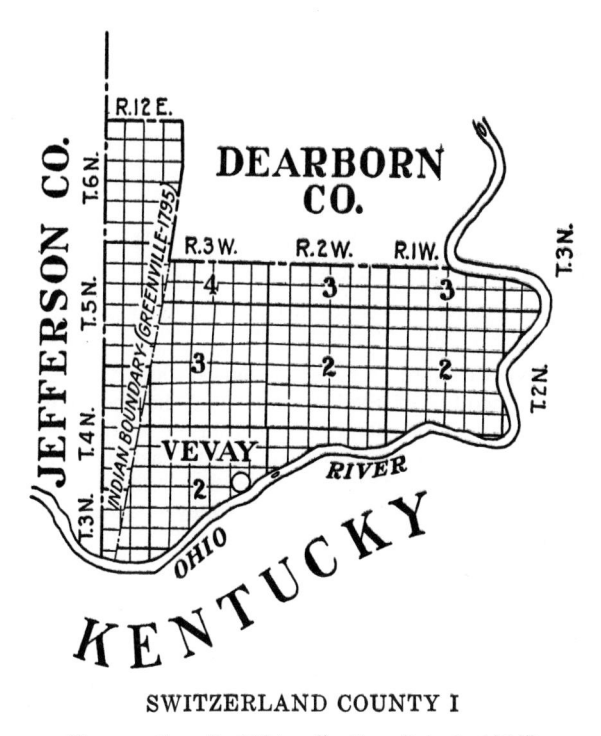

SWITZERLAND COUNTY I
[Law: Sep. 7, 1814, effective Oct. 1, 1814]

SWITZERLAND COUNTY II

DECEMBER 31, 1821: Alteration by statute attaching part of Switzerland County to the county of Ripley, effective March 1, 1822.

BOUNDARY CHANGE: The act provided that "all that part of the connty [county] of Switzerland which lies north of the line running east from the north-west corner of section thirty three in town No. six north of range No. twelve east in the district of public lands sold at Jeffersonville, to the Dearborn county line, be . . . attached to the county of Ripley." *Laws of Indiana*, 1821-22, p. 127.

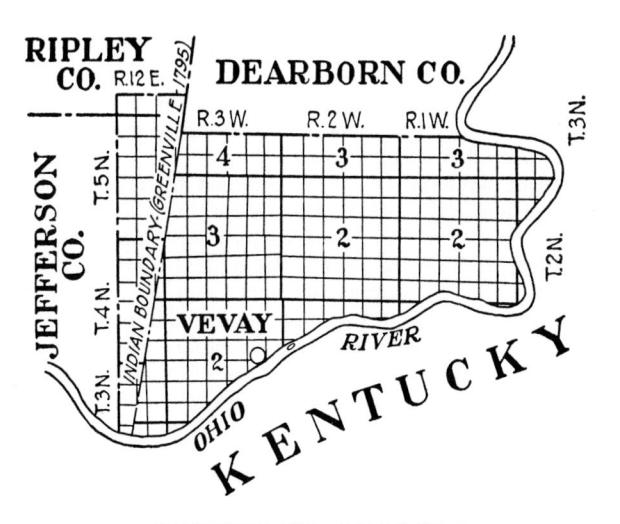

SWITZERLAND COUNTY II
[Law: Dec. 31, 1821, effective Mar. 1, 1822]

TIPPECANOE COUNTY

JANUARY 20, 1826: Formation by statute, effective March 1, 1826. The formation affected Wabash County, including that part attached to Parke.

BOUNDARIES: "Beginning at the north east corner of the county of Montgomery, on the township line dividing ranges two, and three west of the second principal meridian; thence north twenty-four miles; thence west, twenty-one miles; thence south twenty-four miles; thence east twenty-one miles, with the north line of Montgomery county, to the place of beginning." *Laws of Indiana*, 1825-26, p. 14.

The small area of territory bounded by the north boundary of the county and the Tippecanoe and Wabash rivers, was not ceded by the Indians until October, 1826.

An act of January 24, 1828, attached to Tippecanoe County for criminal and civil jurisdiction the territory within the following bounds: "Beginning on the eastern boundary line of Tippecanoe county, at the point where the central section line of town. twenty-three, north, intersects the same; thence east with said line . . . twenty-four miles, to the range line dividing ranges two and three, east of the second principal meridian; thence south, with said line, eighteen miles to the centre of town. twenty; thence west with the sectional line to the range line dividing ranges two and three west; thence north, with said line, to the place of beginning."

The same law provided that "all the country north of the counties of Tippecanoe and Carroll, and west of the second principal meridian, to the northern boundary of the state, and not otherwise attached . . . be attached to the counties of Tippecanoe and Carroll, with concurrent civil and criminal jurisdiction." *Ibid.*, 1827-28 (local), pp. 13-14.

The boundaries of the county as given in the law of February 17, 1838, defining county boundaries, contained an error in the wording which was corrected by a law of February 11, 1839. *Ibid.*, 1837-38 (local), p. 255; 1838-39 (general), p. 79.

Fountain County was formed by an act of December 30, 1825, effective April 1, 1826.

COUNTY SEAT: Commissioners appointed in the act organizing the county, selected Lafayette as the county seat. *Ibid.*, 1826-27, pp. 14-15; De Hart (ed.), *Past and Present of Tippecanoe County*, 1:150-51.

TIPPECANOE COUNTY BOUNDARIES 771

TIPPECANOE COUNTY

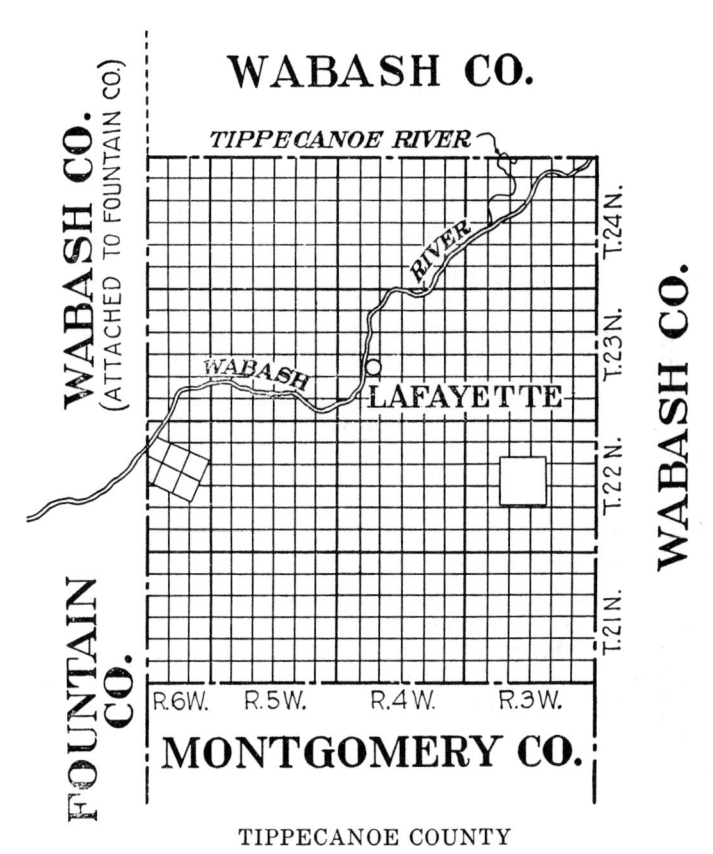

[Law: Jan. 20, 1826, effective Mar. 1, 1826]

TIPTON COUNTY

JANUARY 15, 1844: Formation by statute, effective on passage. The organization of Tipton County was provided for by this law, to be effective May 1, 1844. Tipton was formed from territory attached to Hamilton, Cass, and Miami counties.

BOUNDARIES: "Beginning at the north east corner of section thirty-six, in township twenty-three north, range two east; thence east to the north west corner of section thirty-three, in township twenty-three north, range six east; thence south to the line dividing townships twenty and twenty-one; thence west to the line dividing ranges two and three; thence north to the place of beginning." *Laws of Indiana*, 1843-44 (general), p. 10.

COUNTY SEAT: The act forming the county appointed commissioners to locate the county seat. On October 14, 1844, a site in section 11, township 21 north, range 4 east was made the seat of government. It was first called Canton, but in 1848 was renamed Tipton. *Ibid.*, 10-11; Pershing, *History of Tipton County*, 63-65.

RICHARDVILLE CO.
(HOWARD)

TIPTON COUNTY

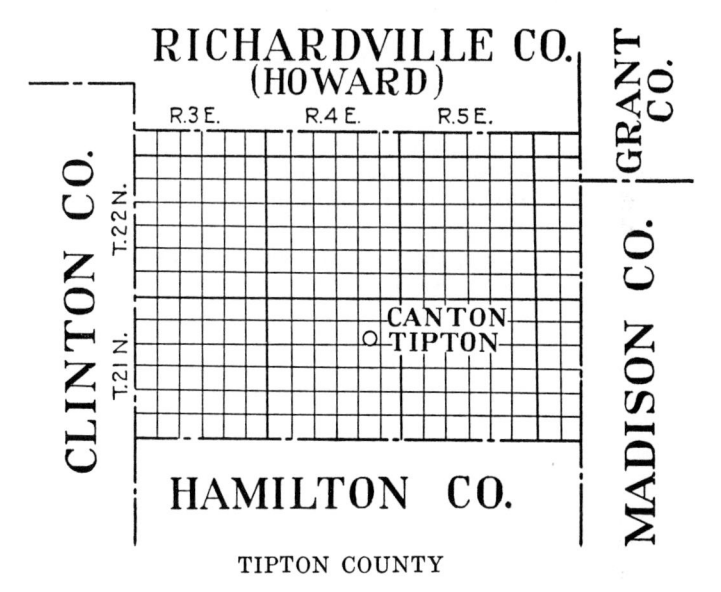

[Law: Jan. 15, 1844, effective on passage]

UNION COUNTY I

JANUARY 5, 1821: Formation by statute, effective February 1, 1821. This formation affected Fayette, Franklin, and Wayne counties.

BOUNDARIES: "Beginning at the south west corner of section twenty-four in township thirteen range thirteen east second principal meridian, thence east to the south east corner of section one town ten range one west of the first principal meridian, it being the line dividing the state of Ohio from this state; thence north twelve miles to the north east corner of section twelve in town twelve range one west of the first principal meridian; thence west twelve miles to the north west corner of section twenty-five in town fifteen range thirteen east second principal meridian; thence south twelve miles to the place of beginning." *Laws of Indiana*, 1820-21, pp. 126-27.

COUNTY SEAT: Commissioners appointed in the act forming the county failed to select a county seat. Others, appointed by an act of December 31, 1821, reported on February 14, 1822, their selection of Brownsville. An act of December 21, 1822, appointed commissioners to select a new county seat. Their choice of Liberty was made in 1823. It has remained the county seat. *Ibid.*, 127-28; 1821-22, pp. 103-4; 1822-23, pp. 10-11; Shockley, "County Seat Wars," *op cit.*, 10:no.1:21.

UNION COUNTY BOUNDARIES 775

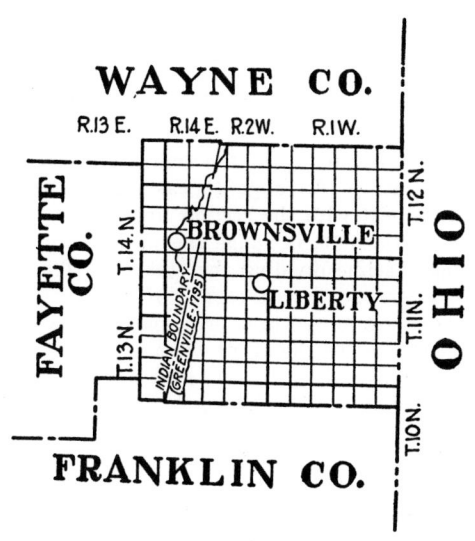

UNION COUNTY I
[Law: Jan. 5, 1821, effective Feb. 1, 1821]

UNION COUNTY II

JANUARY 16, 1826: Alteration by statute attaching territory to Union County.

BOUNDARIES: "Beginning at the south west corner of section thirty-six, in township 13, range 13 east of the second principal meridian; thence east with the section line, to the south east corner of section 13, town 10, in range one west, of the first principal meridian, being the line dividing the states of Ohio and Indiana; thence north, to the north-east corner of section 12, in township 12, of range one west of the first principal meridian; thence west, with the section line, to the north-west corner of section 25, in township 15, in range 13 east of the 2d principal meridian; and thence south to the place of beginning." *Laws of Indiana*, 1825-26, p. 11.

This attached to Union County all that territory south of a line beginning on the Ohio boundary at the southeast corner of section 1, township 10 north, range 1 west of the first principal meridian and running thence due west to the southwest corner of section 24, township 13 north, range 13 east of the second principal meridian.

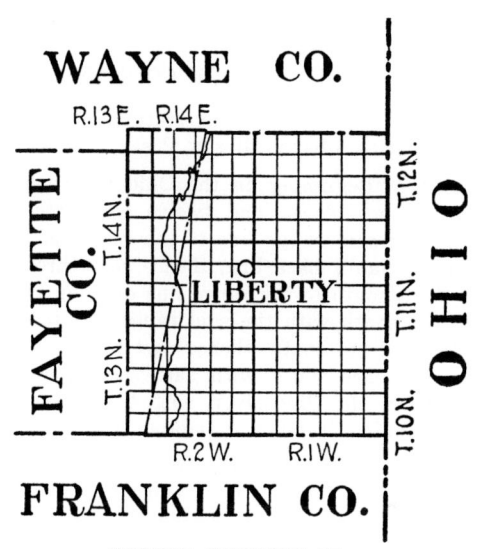

UNION COUNTY II
[Law: Jan. 16, 1826]

VANDERBURGH COUNTY

JANUARY 7, 1818: Formation by statute, effective February 1, 1818. The formation affected Gibson, Posey, and Warrick counties.

BOUNDARIES: "Beginning on the Ohio river where the range line dividing ranges eleven and twelve west, strikes the same, thence north with said range line to the centre of township four, south of Buckingham's base line, thence east through the centre of township four, south to the range line dividing ranges nine and ten west, thence south with the said range line to a line dividing townships five and six south, thence east to the first section line in range nine, thence south with said section line to the Ohio river, thence down the Ohio river, with the meanders thereof, to the place of beginning." *Laws of Indiana*, 1817-18 (special), p. 22.

COUNTY SEAT: Five commissioners, two of whom had been appointed under the act forming the county, submitted their report, selecting a county-seat site in Evansville, on March 11, 1818. Evansville has remained the county seat. *Ibid.*, 23; *History of Vanderburgh County*, 47-48, 104; Shockley, "County Seat Wars," *op. cit.*, 10:no.1:10.

VANDERBURGH COUNTY
[Law: Jan. 7, 1818, effective Feb. 1, 1818]

VERMILLION COUNTY

JANUARY 2, 1824: Formation by statute, effective February 1, 1824. The formation affected Parke County and territory attached to Parke.

BOUNDARIES: "Beginning on the west bank of the Wabash river, where the township line dividing townships numbered thirteen and fourteen north of the base line, of range number nine west of the second principal meridian crosses the same; thence west to the state line; thence north to the line dividing townships numbered nineteen and twenty north; thence east to the Wabash river; and thence south, with the meanders of the said river, to the place of beginning." *Revised Laws of Indiana*, 1823-24, p. 113.

The north boundary of the county has been drawn with the township line, rather than on a due east and west line. The line was defined, as drawn here, by a law of January 15, 1833. *Laws of Indiana*, 1832-33, p. 13. See *ante*, 59-61.

The law forming the county attached for civil and criminal jurisdiction "all the country north of said county, which is or may be included in ranges nine and ten west, to the northern boundary of the state." *Revised Laws of Indiana*, 1823-24, p. 115.

COUNTY SEAT: The site of Newport was selected by commissioners appointed in the act forming the county, in March, 1824. It was not named until May. Newport has remained the county seat. *Ibid.*, 114; *Historical Atlas of Indiana*, 308; *History of Parke and Vermillion Counties*, 251-52, 254-55.

VERMILLION COUNTY

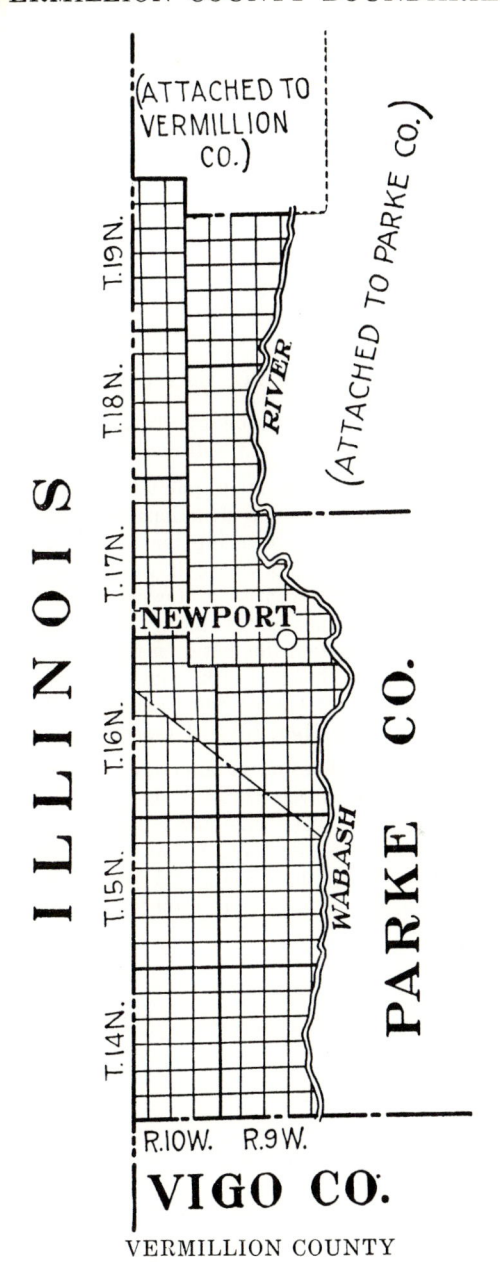

[Law: Jan. 2, 1824, effective Feb. 1, 1824]

VIGO COUNTY I

JANUARY 21, 1818: Formation by statute, effective February 15, 1818. The formation affected Sullivan County.

BOUNDARIES: "Beginning at a point on the Wabash river, where the section line between fractions fourteen and twenty-three, in range eleven west, township ten north strikes the same; thence east with said line, to where it intersects the range line dividing ranges six and seven west, township ten north; thence north with said range line, to the Indian boundary; thence with said boundary to the division line between the state of Indiana and the Illinois Territory; thence south with said line to where it strikes the Wabash river; thence down said river to the place of beginning." *Laws of Indiana*, 1817-18 (special), p. 34.

COUNTY SEAT: Commissioners appointed under the act forming the county, met on March 21, 1818, and selected a county-seat site in Terre Haute. There has never been a removal of the county seat. *Ibid.*, 34-35; Gookins, Judge S. B., "History of Vigo County," 10, 32, in Beckwith, *History of Vigo and Parke Counties;* Andreas, A. T., *Atlas Map of Vigo County, Indiana,* 9 (Chicago, 1874).

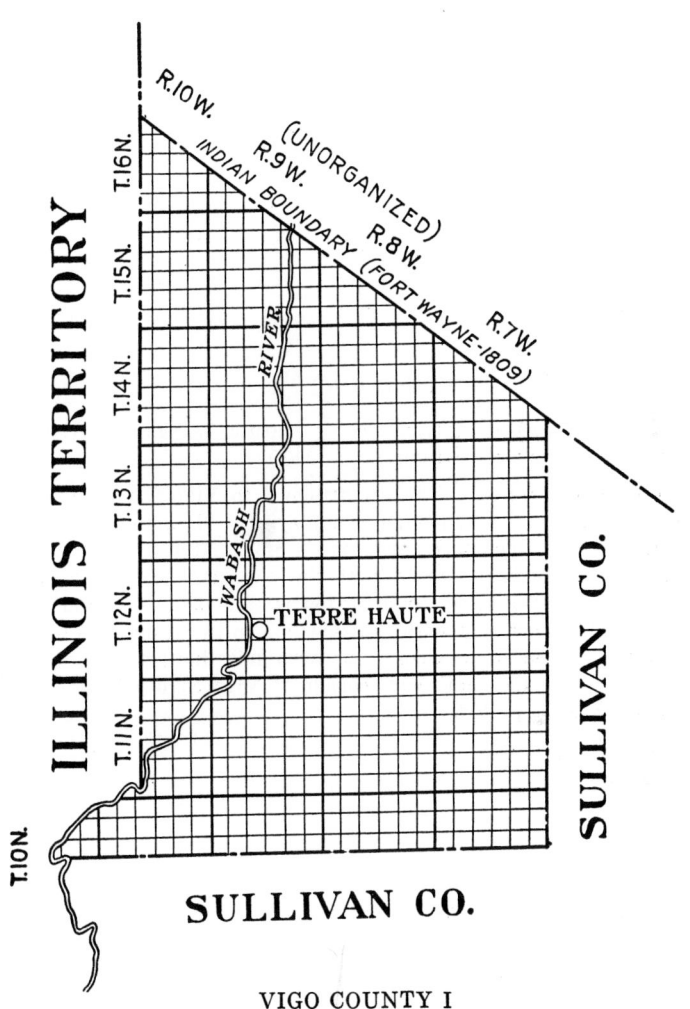

VIGO COUNTY I
[Law: Jan. 21, 1818, effective Feb. 15, 1818]

VIGO COUNTY II

JANUARY 1, 1819: Alteration by statute, attaching territory to Vigo County, effective January 10, 1819.

BOUNDARY CHANGE: The act attached to Vigo County all the territory within the following boundaries: "Beginning on the Wabash river at the south west corner of said county of Vigo on the said river Wabash, thence with the meanders of the same, to where the township line dividing towns nine and ten intersects the Wabash, thence east with the said line to the range line dividing ranges six and seven then north with said line between ranges six and seven to the south east corner of Vigo county." *Laws of Indiana*, 1818-19, p. 107.

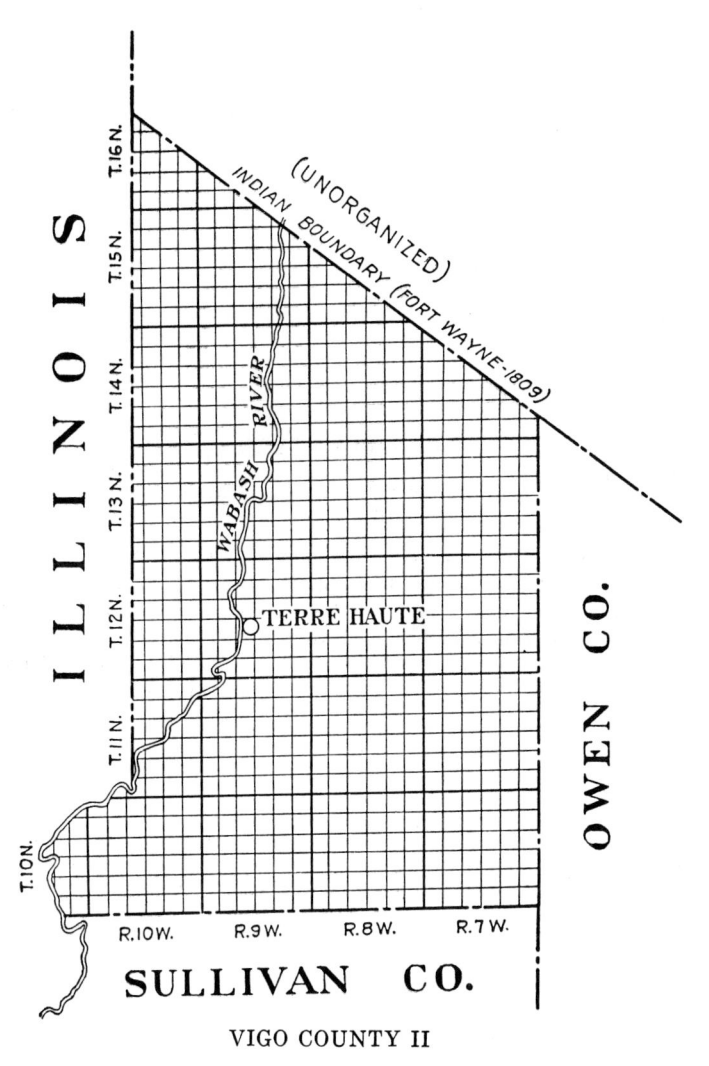

VIGO COUNTY II
[Law: Jan. 1, 1819, effective Jan. 10, 1819]

VIGO COUNTY III

JANUARY 9, 1821: Alteration by statute forming Parke County, effective April 2, 1821.

BOUNDARY CHANGE: All that part of Vigo County north of a line "beginning at the line dividing the states of Indiana and Illinois, where the line between townships thirteen and fourteen north intersects the same, thence east to the line dividing ranges six and seven west, of the second principal meridian," was transferred to Parke County." *Laws of Indiana*, 1820-21, p. 63.

VIGO COUNTY III
[Law: Jan. 9, 1821, effective Apr. 2, 1821]

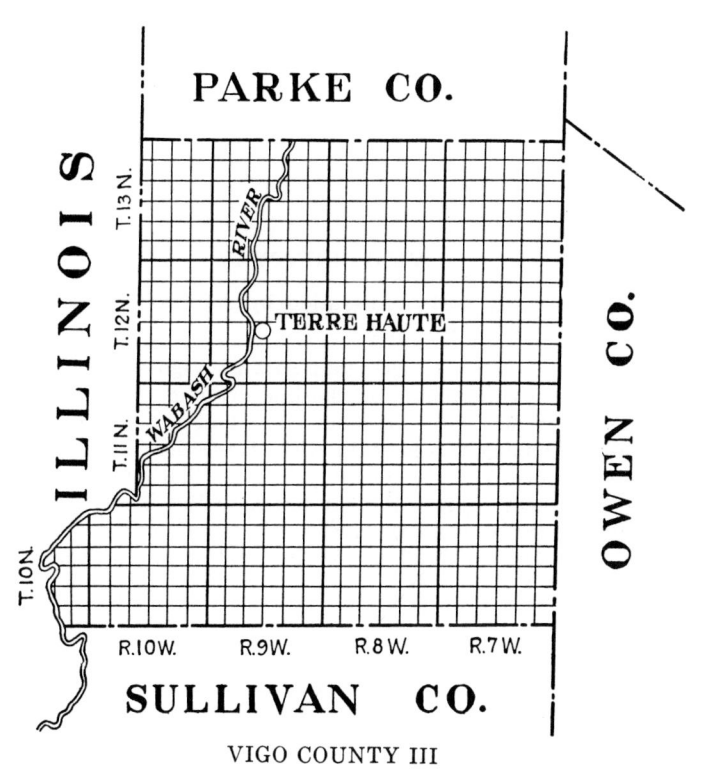

VIGO COUNTY IV

DECEMBER 31, 1821: Alteration by statute forming Putnam County, effective April 1, 1822.

BOUNDARY CHANGE: All that part of Vigo County east and north of a line beginning on the line dividing townships 13 and 14 north, at the center of range 7 west of the second principal meridian, running thence south with the section line through the center of range 7 to the township line dividing townships 10 and 11 north, thence east with that township line to the range line dividing ranges 6 and 7 west, was transferred to Putnam County. *Laws of Indiana*, 1821-22, p. 65. See text of law with map, Putnam County I.

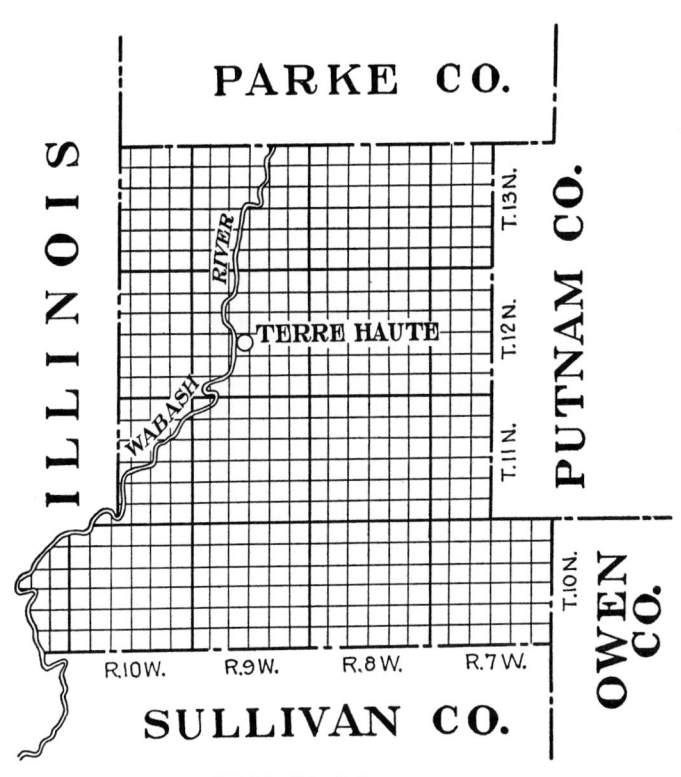

VIGO COUNTY IV
[Law: Dec. 31, 1821, effective Apr. 1, 1822]

VIGO COUNTY V

DECEMBER 21, 1822: Alteration by statute amending act of December 31, 1821, effective on passage.

BOUNDARY CHANGE: The territory taken from Vigo by Putnam County, on the latter's formation by law of December 31, 1821, that is, all that territory between the range line separating ranges 6 and 7 west of the second principal meridian, and a line drawn through the center of range 7 in townships 11, 12, and 13 north, was restored by the act of December 21, 1822, to Vigo County. *Laws of Indiana*, 1822-23, pp. 5-6. See text of law, with map, Putnam County II.

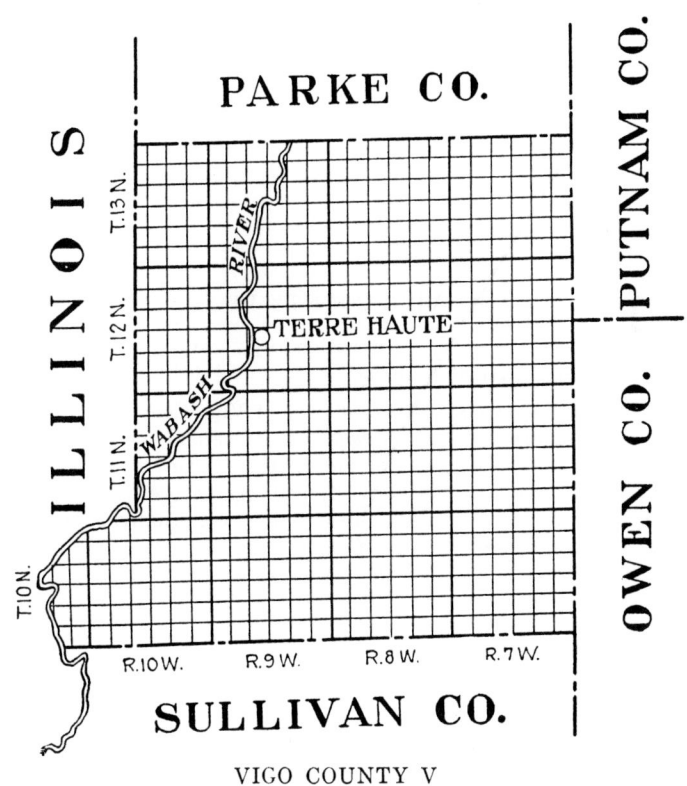

VIGO COUNTY V
[Law: Dec. 21, 1822, effective on passage]

VIGO COUNTY VI

FEBRUARY 12, 1825: Alteration by statute, forming Clay County, effective April 1, 1825.

BOUNDARY CHANGE: All that part of Vigo County between the line dividing ranges 6 and 7 west of the second principal meridian, and a line beginning at the northeast corner of section 5, township 13 north, range 7 west, running thence south 6 miles, west 2 miles, and south 18 miles to the Vigo-Sullivan boundary line, was transferred to Clay County. *Laws of Indiana*, 1825, p. 17. See text of law with map of Clay County.

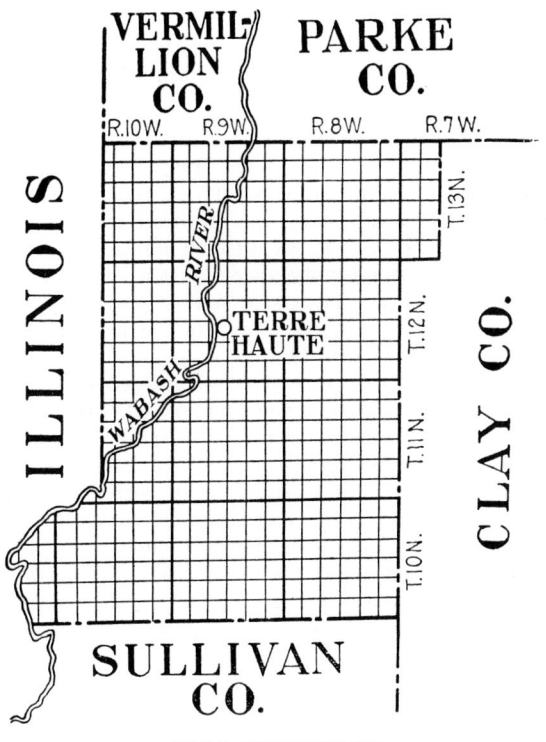

VIGO COUNTY VI

[Law: Feb. 12, 1825, effective Apr. 1, 1825]

WABASH COUNTY I

FEBRUARY 2, 1832: Formation by statute, effective on passage, corrected by statute of January 30, 1833, effective on publication. The formation affected territory attached to Cass and Grant counties. The county was organized by a law of January 22, 1835, effective March 1, 1835.

BOUNDARIES: In the original act of formation the county boundaries were outlined as follows: "Beginning at the south east corner of section five, in town twenty-six north, in range eight east, on the northern boundary line of Grant county; thence west sixteen miles, thence north twenty-four miles with the western boundary of Huntington county, thence east with the township line, to the north east corner of section five, in township twenty-nine north, thence south twenty-four miles to the place of beginning." *Laws of Indiana*, 1831-32, p. 113.

This ambiguous description was superseded by the following one, outlined in a corrective act of January 30, 1833: "Beginning at the north east corner of section five, in township twenty-five north, in range eight east, on the northern boundary line of the county of Grant, being the south west corner of Huntington county, running thence west sixteen miles, thence north twenty-four miles, thence east with the township line between townships twenty-nine and thirty north, sixteen miles to the north west corner of Huntington county, thence south twenty-four miles with the western boundary of said county to the place of beginning." *Ibid.*, 1832-33, p. 39.

Part of the Indian lands not yet ceded were included within these boundaries.

COUNTY SEAT: The report of commissioners appointed under the act organizing the county, made in May, 1835, was accepted June 15, 1835. They chose the site of Wabash as the county seat, and it has remained so to the present time. *Ibid.*, 1834-35 (general), p. 42; Weesner (ed.), *History of Wabash County*, 1:155-57; Shockley, "County Seat Wars," *op. cit.*, 10:no.1:31.

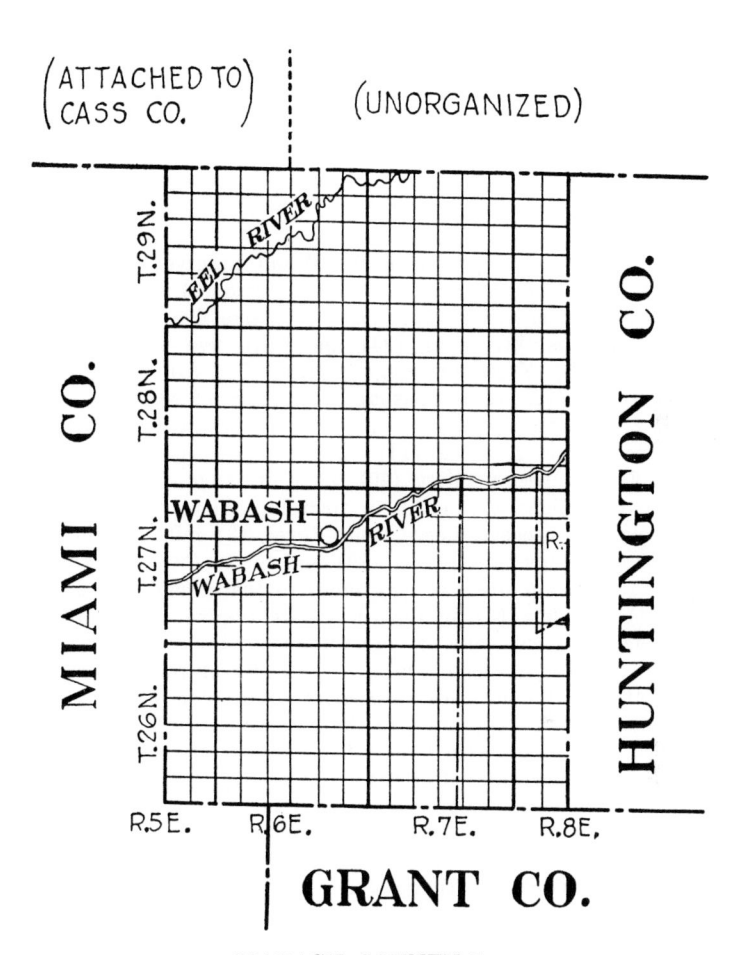

WABASH COUNTY I

[Law: Feb. 2, 1832, effective on passage, corrected by statute of Jan. 30, 1833, effective on publication]

WABASH COUNTY II

FEBRUARY 17, 1838: Alteration by statute defining county boundaries.

BOUNDARIES: "Beginning in the Miami Reserve, where when surveyed it will be the corners of sections two (2) and three (3) in townships twenty-five (25) north of range five (5) east and corners, sections thirty-four (34) and thirty-five (35) township twenty-six (26) North of range number five (5) east; thence north twenty-seven (27) miles to the corners of sections 14, 15, 22 and 23 in township number thirty (30) north of range five (5) east; thence east fourteen (14) miles to the corners of sections 13 and 24 in township thirty (30) north of range seven east, and corners of sections 18 and 19 in township thirty (30) north of range eight (8) east; thence south three (3) miles to the line dividing townships twenty-nine (29) and thirty (30); thence east with the township line two (2) miles to the corners of sections four (4) and five (5) in townships twenty-nine (29) north of range eight (8) east, and corners of sections thirty-two (32) and thirty-three (33) township thirty (30) north of range eight (8) east, that being the north-west corner of Huntington county; thence south twenty-four (24) miles to the corners of sections four (4) and five (5) in township twenty-five (25) north of range eight (8) east, and corners of sections thirty two (32) and thirty-three (33) in townships twenty-six (26) north of range eight (8) east, the same being the south-west corner of Huntington county; thence west sixteen (16) miles to the place of beginning." *Laws of Indiana*, 1837-38 (local), pp. 263-64.

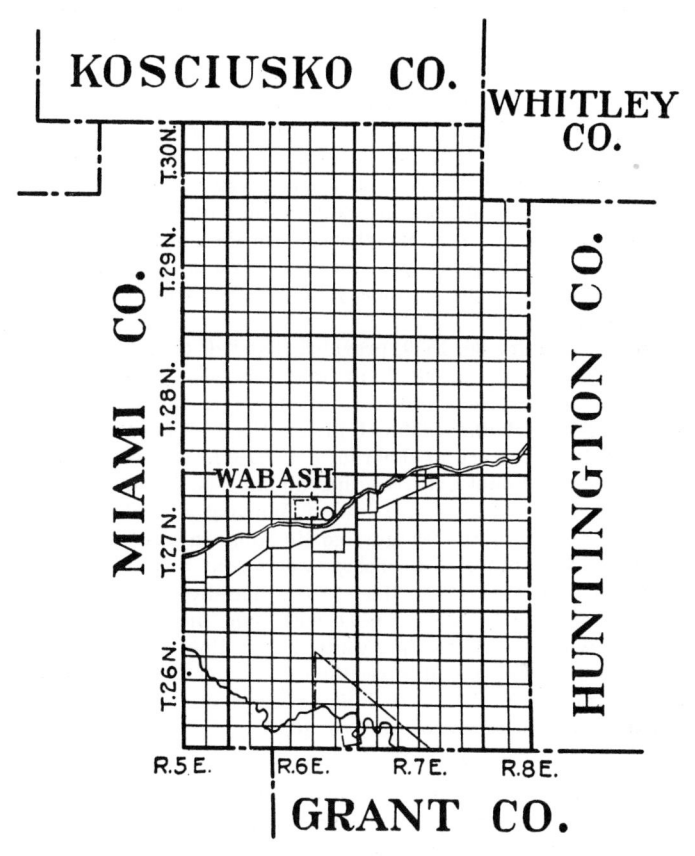

WABASH COUNTY II
[Law: Feb. 17, 1838]

WARREN COUNTY

JANUARY 19, 1827: Formation by statute, effective March 1, 1827. The formation affected that part of Wabash County attached to Fountain.

BOUNDARIES: "Beginning at the north east corner of Vermillion county, on the Wabash river, thence west to the state line, thence north to the line dividing townships twenty-three and twenty-four, thence east with said line to the western line of Tippecanoe county, thence south on the said western line of Tippecanoe county to the Wabash river, and thence with the meanders of said river to the place of beginning." *Laws of Indiana*, 1826-27, p. 14.

See note on the south boundary of Warren with map, Vermillion County.

An act of January 30, 1830, provided that "all that part of the county of Wabash, lying north of the said county of Warren, and west of Tippecanoe . . . be . . . attached to the said county of Warren, for civil and criminal jurisdiction." The attachment was extended by an act of February 10, 1831, to the territory north of Warren County, to the line dividing townships 30 and 31 north. It was redrawn in a law of January 31, 1835, as follows: "beginning on the range line dividing ranges seven and eight west, at the corner of township twenty-four and twenty-five, thence north with said range line, to the line dividing townships twenty-nine and thirty, thence west with said line, to the State line, thence with the State line, south to the line dividing townships twenty-four and twenty-five, thence east on said line to the place of beginning." *Laws of Indiana*, 1829-30, p. 26; 1830-31 (special), p. 18; 1834-35 (general), p. 86.

COUNTY SEAT: Commissioners appointed under the act forming the county, in March, 1828, reported their choice of a site in section 31, township 22 north, range 7 west. The county seat was called Warrenton. Under an act of January 22, 1829, commissioners were appointed to relocate the county seat. In June, 1829, the seat of justice was established at Williamsport, where it still remains. *Ibid.*, 1826-27, p. 14; 1828-29, pp. 129-31; Shockley, "County Seat Wars," *op. cit.*, 10:no.1:24; *Counties of Warren, Benton, Jasper and Newton*, 54, 56.

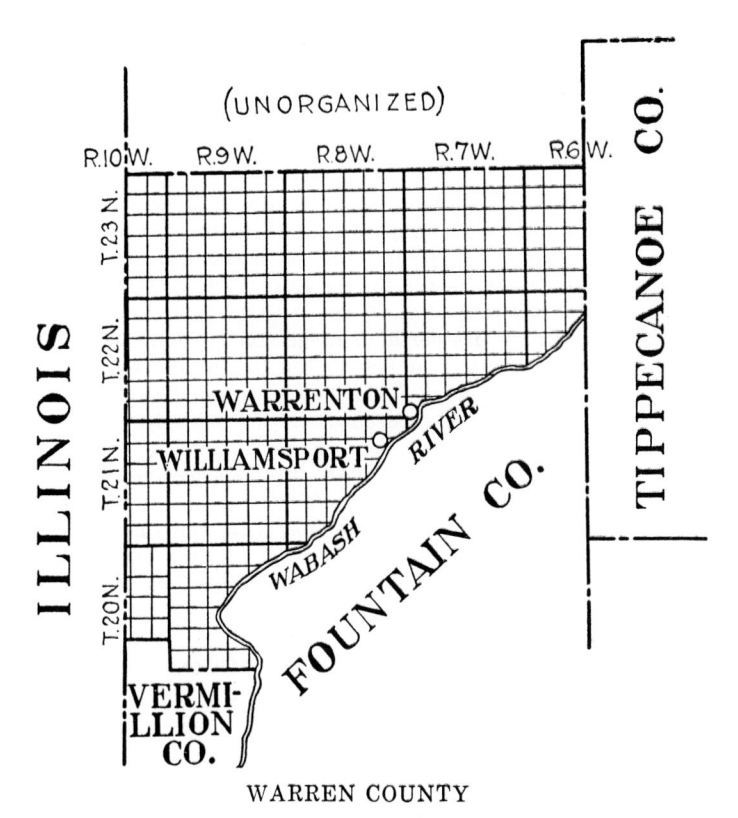

WARREN COUNTY
[Law: Jan. 19, 1827, effective Mar. 1, 1827]

WARRICK COUNTY I
[Indiana Territory]

MARCH 9, 1813: Formation by statute, effective April 1, 1813. The formation affected Knox County.

BOUNDARIES: "Beginning at the mouth of the Wabash, thence up the same with the meanders thereof to the mouth of White river, thence up White river with the meanders thereof to the forks of White river, thence up the East Fork of White river to where the line between sections number twenty and twenty nine, in township number one, north, of range number four, west, strikes the same, thence with said line to the line of Harrison county, thence with the said line dividing the counties of Knox and Harrison to the Ohio river, thence down to the Ohio river to the beginning.

". . . the same is hereby divided into two separate and distinct counties by a line beginning on the Wabash river and known . . . by the name of Rector's base line, and with said line East until it intersects the line of Harrison county . . . the tract of country falling within the southern division thereof shall be known . . . by the name . . . of the county of Warrick." *Acts of Indiana Territory*, 1813, pp. 67-68.

See note on Rector's base line with map, Gibson County I.

COUNTY SEAT: Commissioners appointed by an act of December 14, 1813, with several substitutions for original members, reported on June 13, 1814, their selection of Evansville. *Acts of Indiana Territory*, 1813-14, p. 74; *History of Warrick, Spencer and Perry Counties*, 36-37.

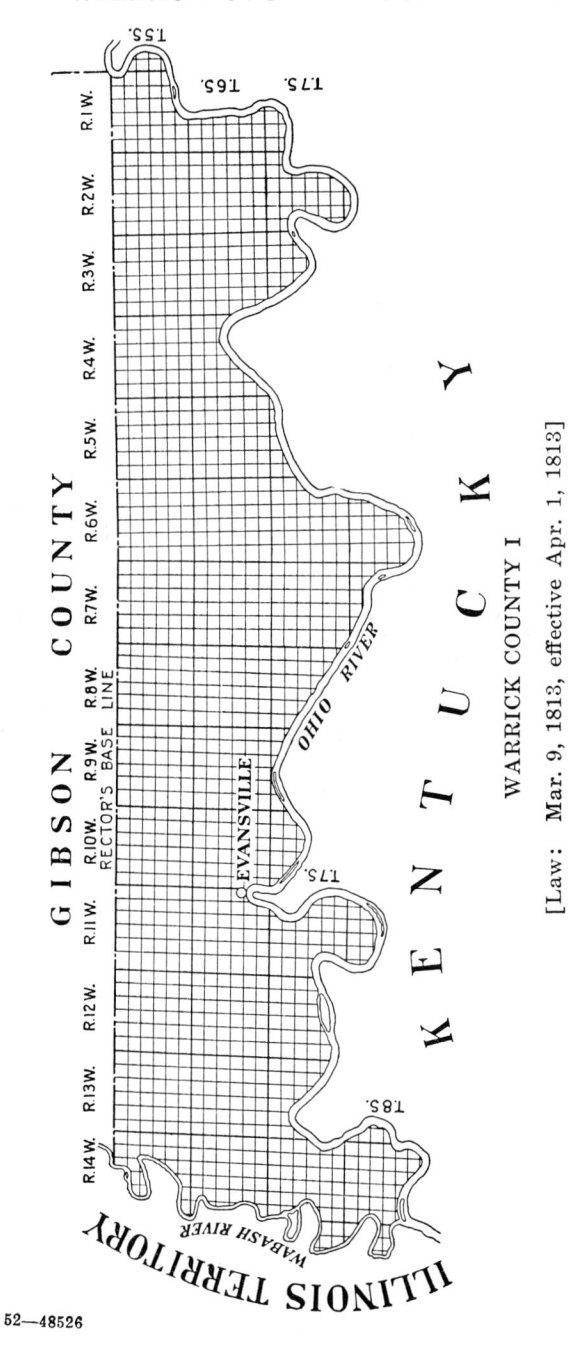

WARRICK COUNTY BOUNDARIES

WARRICK COUNTY I

[Law: Mar. 9, 1813, effective Apr. 1, 1813]

WARRICK COUNTY II
[Indiana Territory]

SEPTEMBER 7, 1814: Alteration by statute forming Perry and Posey counties, effective November 1, 1814.

BOUNDARY CHANGES: All of Warrick County east of the line dividing ranges 5 and 6 west of the second principal meridian was given to Perry County.

All of Warrick County west of the line dividing ranges 10 and 11 west, was transferred to Posey County. *Acts of Indiana Territory*, 1814, pp. 18-19. See text with maps, Perry County I and Posey County I.

COUNTY SEAT: By an act of September 1, 1814, fractional section 7, township 7 south, range 8 west was made the site of the county seat. It was called Darlington. *Acts of Indiana Territory*, 1814, p. 16; *History of Warrick, Spencer and Perry Counties*, 37-38.

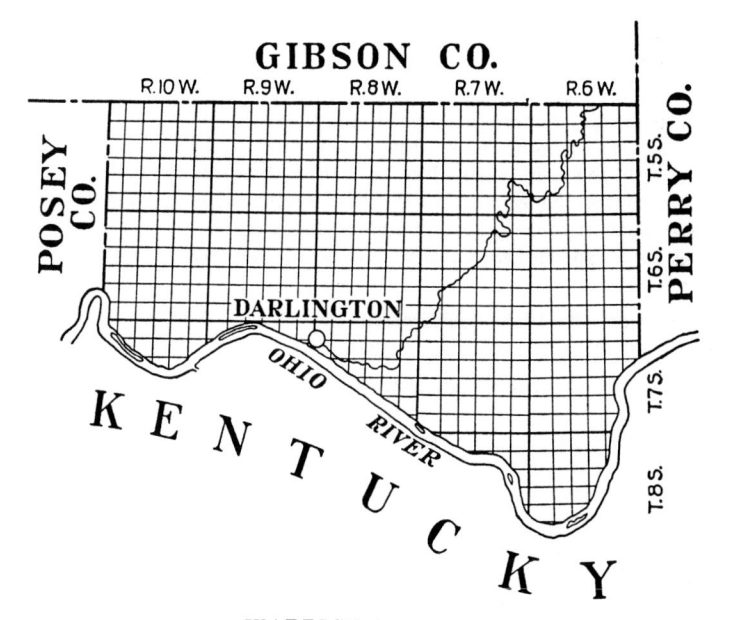

WARRICK COUNTY II
[Law: Sep. 7, 1814, effective Nov. 1, 1814]

WARRICK COUNTY III

JANUARY 7, 1818: Alteration by statute forming Vanderburgh County, effective February 1, 1818.

BOUNDARY CHANGE: All that part of Warrick County west of a line beginning where the line dividing townships 4 and 5 south intersects "the range line dividing ranges nine and ten west, thence south with the said range line to a line dividing townships five and six south, thence east to the first section line in range nine, thence south with said section line to the Ohio river," was transferred to Vanderburgh County. *Laws of Indiana*, 1817-18 (special), p. 22.

JANUARY 10, 1818: Alteration by statute forming Spencer County, effective February 1, 1818.

BOUNDARY CHANGE: All that part of Warrick County east of a line "beginning on the Ohio river where the section line passes through the centre of the seventh range strikes the same; thence north with the said section line until it strikes Little Pigeon creek; thence up said creek, with the meanders thereof, to the Polk Patch Fork; thence up the Polk Patch Fork, with the meanders thereof, to the township line passing between townships four aad [and] five," was transferred to Spencer County. *Ibid.*, 20.

COUNTY SEAT: Commissioners appointed under the act of January 7, 1818, to relocate the county seat, reported March 19, 1818. They selected a site in sections 26 and 25, township 5 south, range 8 west of the second principal meridian. The new county seat was called Boonville. *Ibid.*, 24; *History of Warrick, Spencer and Perry Counties*, 41; Shockley, "County Seat Wars," *op. cit.*, 10:no.1:5.

WARRICK COUNTY III

[Laws: Jan. 7, 1818, effective Feb. 1, 1818; Jan. 10, 1818, effective Feb. 1, 1818]

WARRICK COUNTY IV

JANUARY 31, 1824: Alteration by statute defining county boundaries.

BOUNDARIES: "Beginning on the Ohio river, where the section line passes through the centre of range seven strikes the same; thence north with said line to Little Pigeon creek; thence up said creek with the meanders thereof to the Polk Patch fork; thence up the last named stream, with the meanders thereof, to the line dividing townships four and five south, thence east with said township line, to the line dividing ranges five and six; thence north to the line of Dubois county; thence west with the same to the Gibson county line; thence with the line of Gibson county, to the eastern line of Vanderburgh county; thence south with the same to the Ohio river; and thence with the said river to the place of beginning." *Revised Laws of Indiana*, 1823-24, p. 103. See text with map, Gibson County VIII.

WARRICK COUNTY IV
[Law: Jan. 31, 1824]

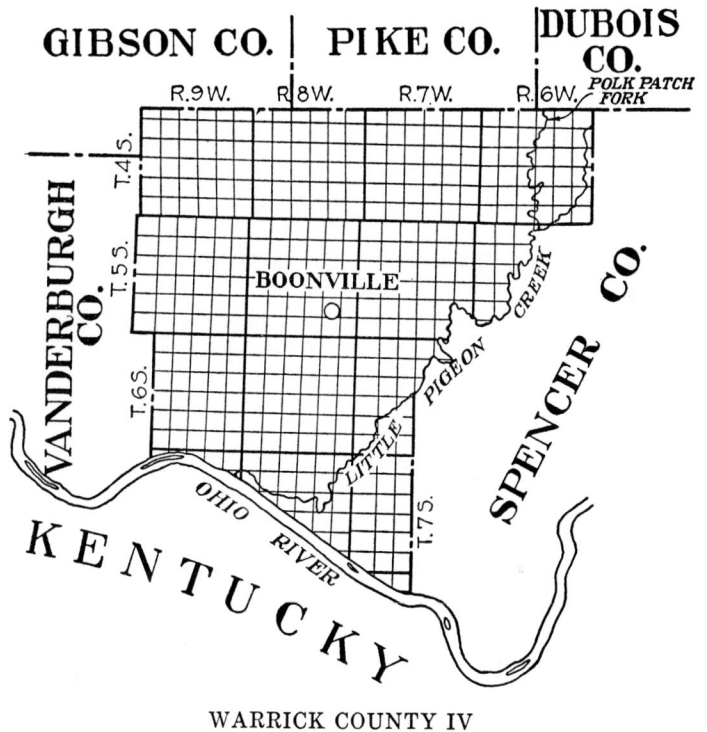

WARRICK COUNTY V

FEBRUARY 10, 1825: Alteration by statute attaching part of the county of Warrick to the county of Spencer.

BOUNDARY CHANGE: The act attached to Spencer County all that part of Warrick within the following boundaries: "Beginning on the Ohio River four miles west of the Spencer county line; thence running north to Little Pigeon creek; thence up the said creek, with the meanders thereof to the line of Spencer county; thence south to the Ohio River; thence down the Ohio River to the place of beginning." *Laws of Indiana*, 1825, p. 16.

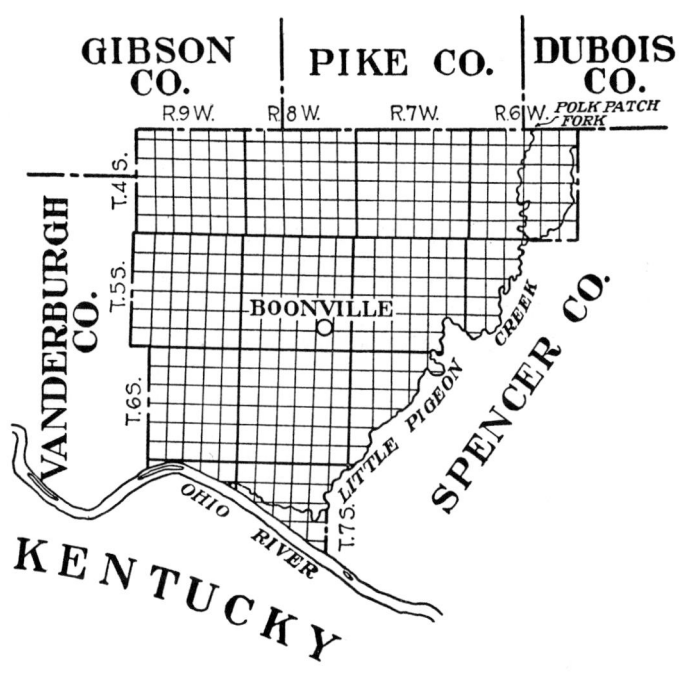

WARRICK COUNTY V

[Law: Feb. 10, 1825]

WARRICK COUNTY VI

JANUARY 20, 1826: Alteration by statute, attaching a part of Pike County to the county of Warrick, effective on passage.

BOUNDARY CHANGE: "All that part of the county of Pike included within the following boundaries, viz: beginning at the south-east corner of Pike county; thence running north two miles; thence west, twelve miles; thence north, one mile; thence west, to Gibson county; thence south, to Warrick county; thence east, to the place of beginning," was attached to Warrick County. *Laws of Indiana*, 1825-26, p. 12.

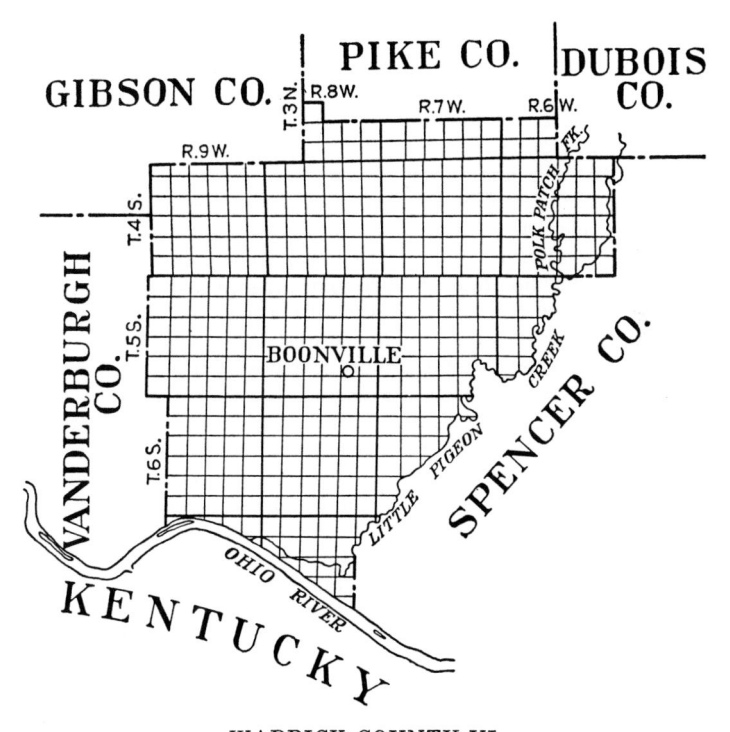

WARRICK COUNTY VI

[Law: Jan. 20, 1826, effective on passage]

WARRICK COUNTY VII

1842-43: Alteration by statute defining county boundaries.

BOUNDARIES: "Beginning on the Ohio river where the sectional line running north and south one mile west of the line dividing ranges six and seven [seven and eight] west strikes the same, thence north to Little Pigeon creek, thence up said creek, with the meanders thereof, to the Poke Patch Fork, thence up the last mentioned stream, with the meanders thereof, to the line dividing townships four and five south, thence east to the line dividing ranges five and six west, thence north to the northeast corner of township four south, range six west, thence west to the southwest corner of section thirty-four, in township three south, of range six west, thence north to the northeast corner of section twenty-eight, township three south, range six west, thence west to the southeast corner of section twenty-one, in township three south, of range eight west, thence north to the northeast corner of the same section, thence west to the northwest corner of the same, thence south to the southwest corner of section sixteen, in township four south, of range eight, thence west to the northwest corner of section nineteen, township four south, range nine west,· thence south to the line dividing townships five and six south, thence east to the northeast corner of section six, township six south, of range nine west, thence south to the Ohio river, thence up the same to the place of beginning." *Revised Statutes of Indiana*, 1842-43, p. 79.

The error corrected in brackets above was rectified by statute in 1853.

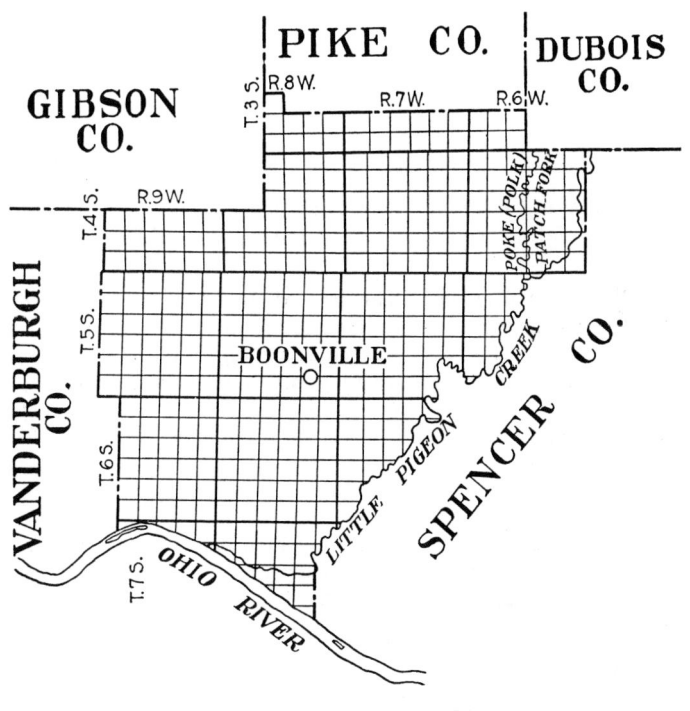

WARRICK COUNTY VII
[Law: 1842-43]

WARRICK COUNTY VIII

JANUARY 13, 1844: Alteration by statute, effective on passage, regulating the boundaries of the counties of Warrick and Gibson.

BOUNDARY CHANGE: The law of January 13, 1844, provided that "the boundary lines between the counties of Warrick and Gibson be . . . fixed and established according to the provisions of the act entitled 'An act relative to county boundaries,' approved February 10, 1831, and all acts passed subsequent to said mentioned act, altering or changing said act in any manner whatever, be . . . repealed, so far as the same relates to the said boundary between the counties of Warrick and Gibson." *Laws of Indiana*, 1843-44 (general), p. 87.

The law of February 10, 1831, which defined the boundaries of each county, repeats the Gibson-Warrick County boundary as given in the *Revised Laws* of 1823-24. See map, Warrick County IV; *Revised Laws of Indiana*, 1830-31, p. 116.

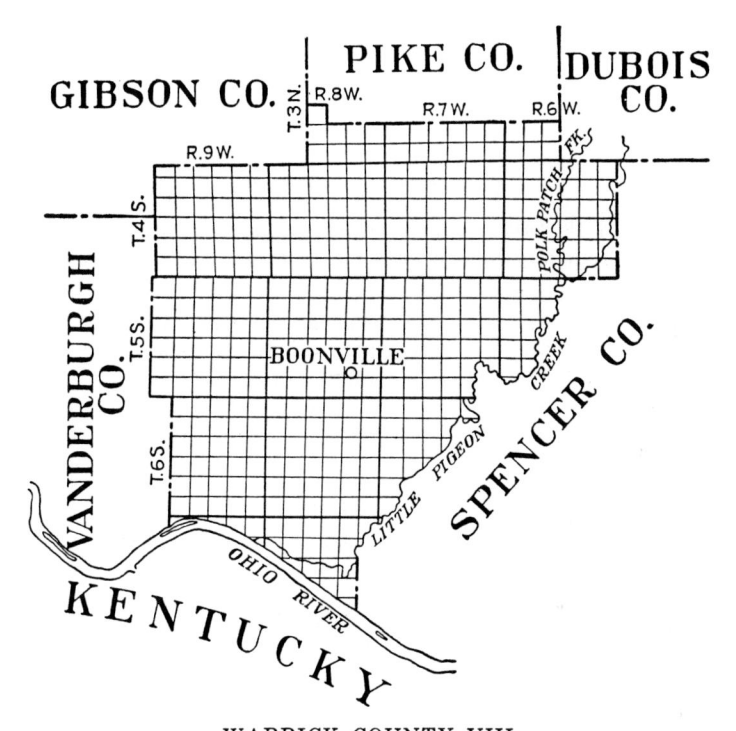

WARRICK COUNTY VIII
[Law: Jan. 13, 1844, effective on passage]

WARRICK COUNTY IX

JANUARY 18, 1847: Alteration by statute more particularly defining the boundary line between the counties of Gibson and Warrick.

BOUNDARY CHANGE: "The following described line shall form and be the boundary line between the counties of Gibson and Warrick, so far as said counties lie contiguous to each other, to wit: Beginning at the north-east corner of Vanderburgh county; thence running east to the south-east corner of section fifteen, in township four south, of range nine west; thence north to the northeast corner of section three, in township four south, of range nine west; thence east with the township line dividing townships three and four south, to the south east corner of section thirty-two, in township three south, of range eight west; thence north to the north-west corner of section twenty-one, in township three south, of range eight west." *Laws of Indiana*, 1846-47 (local), p. 272.

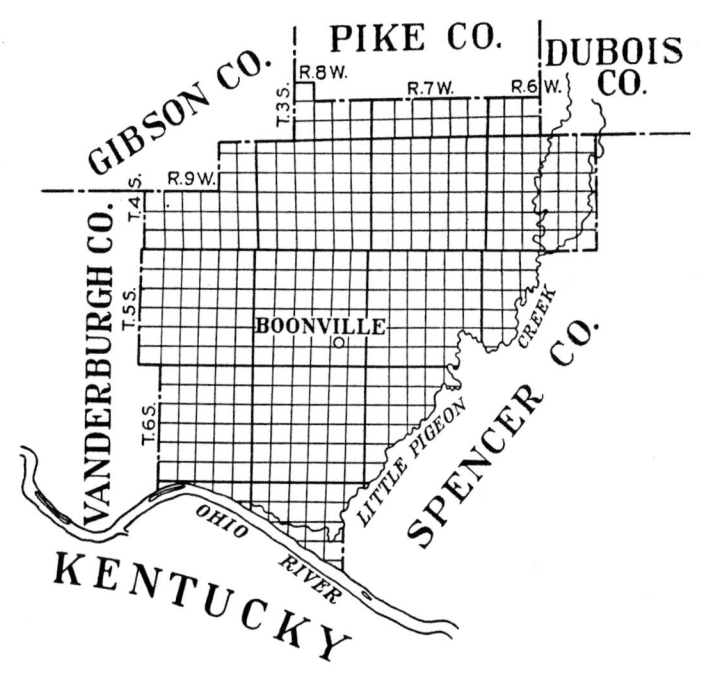

WARRICK COUNTY IX
[Law: Jan. 18, 1847]

WARRICK COUNTY X

JUNE 7, 1852: Alteration by statute defining county boundaries.

BOUNDARIES: "Beginning on the Ohio river where the sectional line running north and south one mile west of the line dividing ranges six [seven] and seven [eight] west strikes the same, thence north to Little Pigeon creek, thence up said creek, with the meanders thereof, to the Poke Patch fork, thence up the last mentioned stream, with the meanders thereof, to the line dividing townships four and five south, thence east to the line dividing ranges five and six west, thence north to the north-east corner of township four south, range six west, thence west to the south-west corner of section thirty-four, in township three south, of range six west, thence north to the north-east corner of section twenty-eight, township three south, range six west, thence west to the south-east corner of section twenty-one, in township three south, of range eight west, thence north to the north-east corner of the same section, thence west to the north-west corner of the same, thence south to the line dividing townships three and four south, thence west to the line dividing ranges nine and ten west, thence south to the line dividing townships five and six south, thence east to the northeast corner of section six, of township six south, and range nine west, thence south to the Ohio river, and thence up the same to the place of beginning." *Revised Statutes of Indiana,* 1851-52, vol.1:194-95.

The errors corrected in brackets above were rectified by an act of March 1, 1853, defining the boundary between Warrick and Spencer counties. The Spencer County boundaries were correctly given in the law of 1852. *Laws of Indiana,* 1852-53, p. 15.

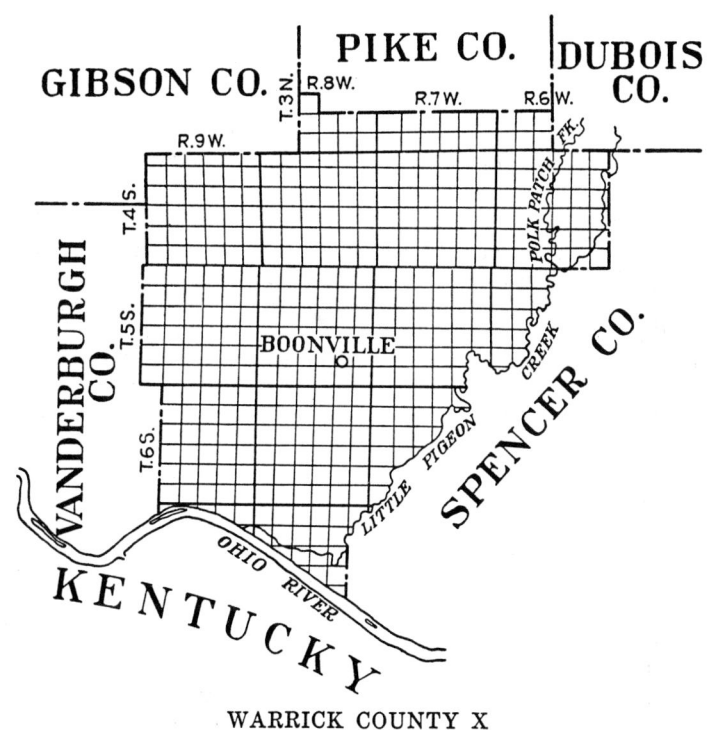

WARRICK COUNTY X
[Law: June 7, 1852]

WASHINGTON COUNTY I
[Indiana Territory]

DECEMBER 21, 1813: Formation by statute, effective January 17, 1814. The formation affected Clark, Harrison, and Jefferson counties.

BOUNDARIES: "Beginning at Freemans' corner, on the meridian line, thence southwardly with said line to the intersection of an east and west line running through the centre of township one south; thence with the same eastwardly to the summit of the Silver creek knobs; thence north-eastwardly with the extreme heighth of the same between the waters of Silver creek and Blue river, to the line dividing ranges six and seven east; thence with said range line northwardly to the Indian boundary; thence with said boundary to the place of beginning, shall compose one new county, called and known by the name of Washington." *Acts of Indiana Territory*, 1813-14, p. 91.

Freeman's Corner was the northeast corner of the purchase made at Fort Wayne in 1803, and Thomas Freeman was the surveyor of the land ceded. The line along the height of the Knobs was the subject of much controversy and later legislation.

COUNTY SEAT: Commissioners appointed under the act forming the county met in February, 1814, and a site in sections 17 and 20, township 2 north, range 4 east, was chosen for the county seat. This is now Salem. *History of Lawrence, Orange and Washington Counties*, 707.

WASHINGTON COUNTY BOUNDARIES 821

WASHINGTON COUNTY I

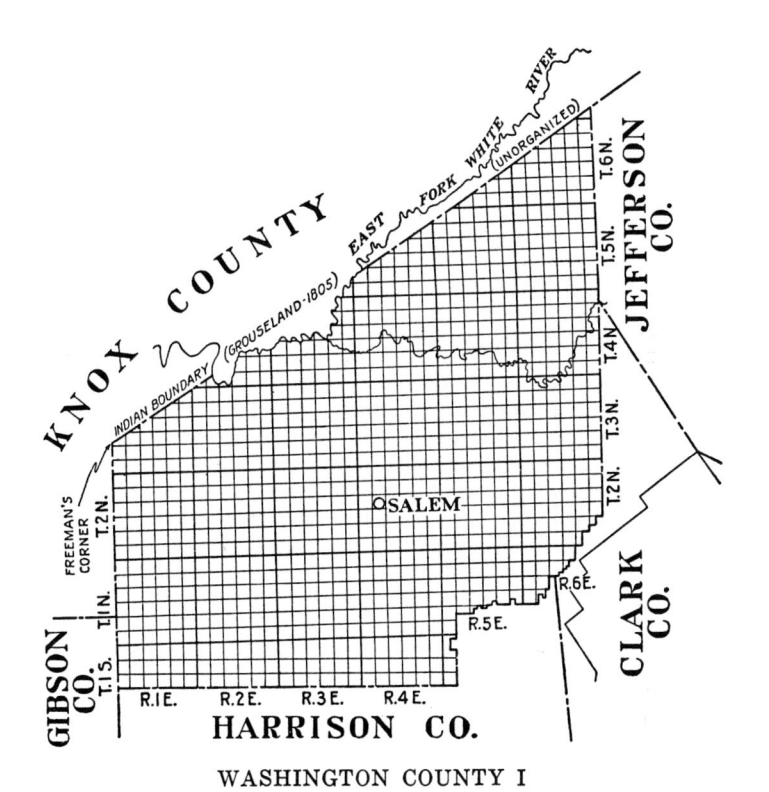

[Law: Dec. 21, 1813, effective Jan. 17, 1814]

WASHINGTON COUNTY II
[Indiana Territory]

SEPTEMBER 1, 1814: Alteration by statute extending the bounds of Washington County.

BOUNDARY CHANGE: All that tract of country within a boundary "begining at Freeman's corner on the meridian line, thence north to the present Indian boundary line, thence with said Indian boundary to the line established by the treaty of Grousland, thence with said line to the place of beginning," was attached to Washington County. *Acts of Indiana Territory*, 1814, p. 15.

The "present Indian boundary" was the line established by the Treaty of Fort Wayne, September 30, 1809. For a statement about Freeman's Corner, see text with preceding map.

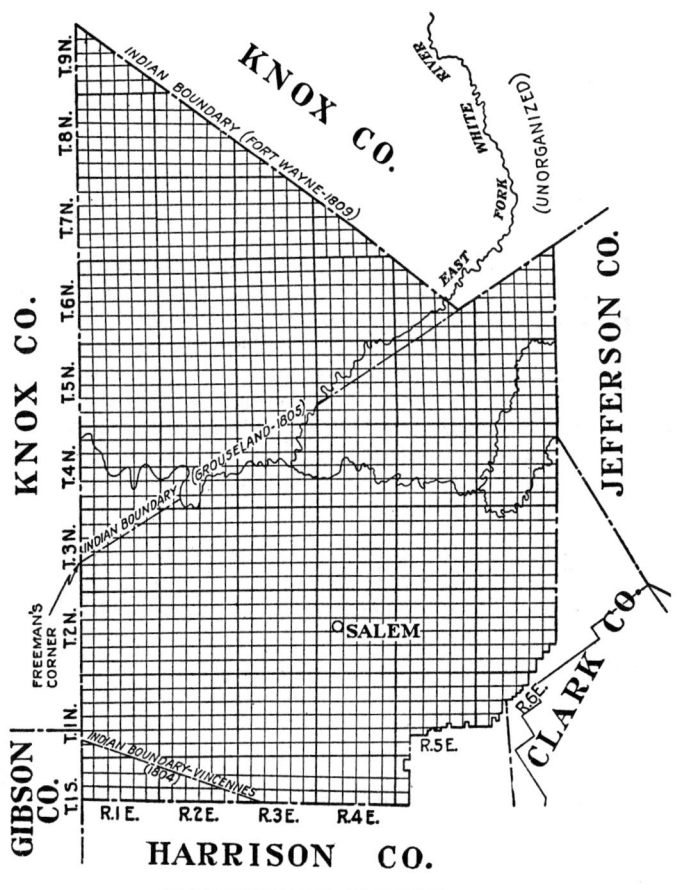

WASHINGTON COUNTY II
[Law: Sep. 1, 1814]

WASHINGTON COUNTY III
[Indiana Territory]

DECEMBER 18, 1815: Alteration by statute forming Jackson County, effective January 1, 1816.

BOUNDARY CHANGE: That part of Washington County north of a line beginning at the northeast corner of township 3 north, range 6 east, running thence with the township line "west, to the east fork of the Muscacketuck river; thence down the said river, with the meanders thereof, to the junction of Drift fork of White river; thence down the same with the meanders" to the "point on the east fork of White River where the line dividing sections four and five, in range two east, town three north crosses the same," was transferred to Jackson County. *Acts of Indiana Territory*, 1815, pp. 3-4.

DECEMBER 26, 1815: Alteration by statute forming Orange County, effective February 1, 1816.

BOUNDARY CHANGE: That part of Washington County west of a line beginning where the line between Harrison and Washington counties "intersects the line dividing sections sixteen and seventeen in range two east, town one south; thence north with said line . . . to the Indian boundary line" was transferred to Orange County. *Ibid.*, 57-58.

The Indian boundary line mentioned was the Fort Wayne Treaty line of September 30, 1809.

WASHINGTON COUNTY BOUNDARIES 825

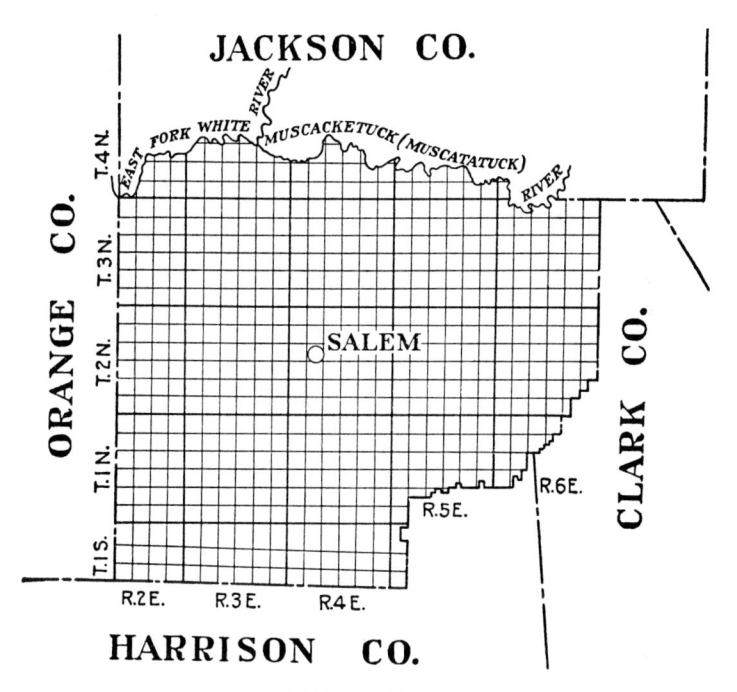

WASHINGTON COUNTY III

[Laws: Dec. 18, 1815, effective Jan. 1, 1816; Dec. 26, 1815, effective Feb. 1, 1816]

WASHINGTON COUNTY IV

JANUARY 12, 1820: Alteration by statute forming Scott County, effective February 1, 1820.

BOUNDARY CHANGE: All that part of Washington County east and north of a line beginning on the Muscatatuck River where "a land line running due south, will touch the south west corner of section thirty-two, township two north, in range six east, thence directly east until it touches the line dividing Clark and Washington counties," was transferred to Scott County. *Laws of Indiana,* 1819-20, pp. 51-52. See map, Scott County I.

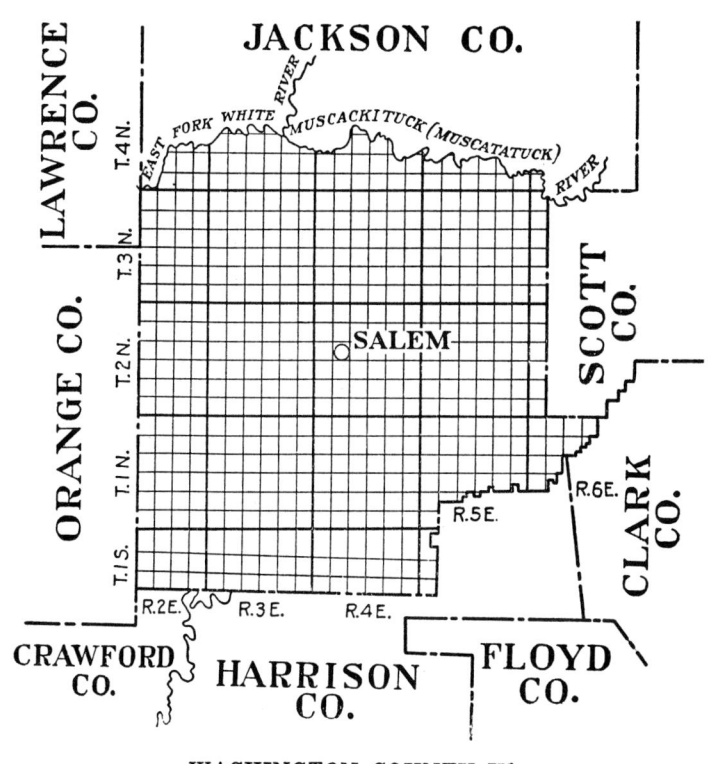

WASHINGTON COUNTY IV

[Law: Jan. 12, 1820, effective Feb. 1, 1820]

WASHINGTON COUNTY V

DECEMBER 26, 1820: Alteration by statute arranging the boundary line between the counties of Washington and Scott, effective on passage.

BOUNDARY CHANGE: The law provided that "so much of the county of Scott as is south of a line commencing on the boundary line between the counties of Washington and Scott, at the southwest corner of section twenty in town two north of range six east; thence running east with the sectional line, until it intersects the Clark county line be . . . attached to . . . Washington." *Laws of Indiana*, 1820-21, p. 58.

In the descriptions of county boundaries in the 1824 Revision of the laws, there is a discrepancy between the descriptions of the Scott-Washington boundary given under the two counties. See *Revised Laws of Indiana*, 1823-24, p. 97.

By a law of December 19, 1828, commissioners were appointed to survey the Clark-Washington line. *Laws of Indiana*, 1828-29, p. 16.

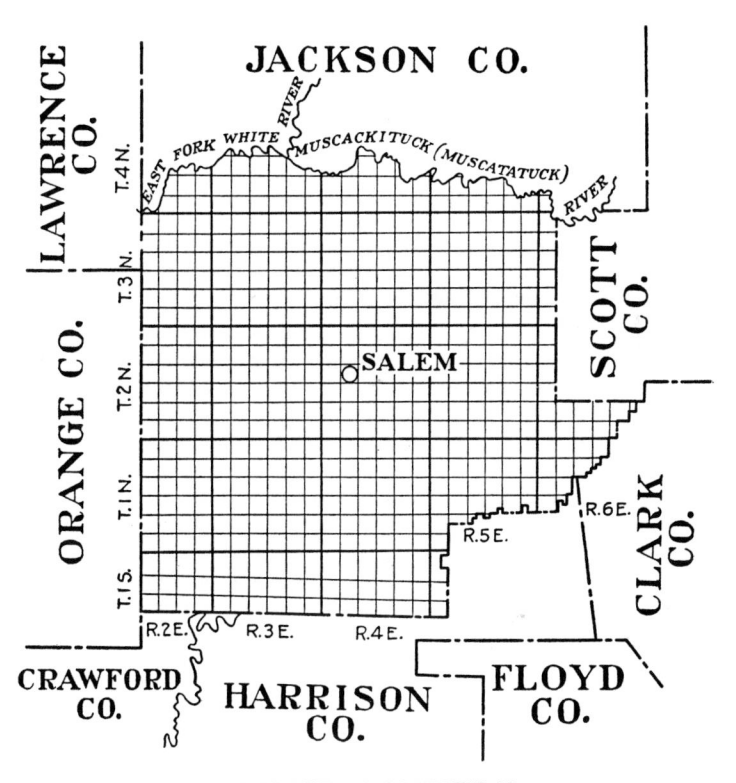

WASHINGTON COUNTY V
[Law: Dec. 26, 1820, effective on passage]

WASHINGTON COUNTY VI

FEBRUARY 16, 1839: Alteration by statute more particularly defining the western and southern boundaries of the county of Scott, effective on passage.

BOUNDARY CHANGE: The line between Scott and Washington counties is described as "beginning in the main channel of the south fork of the Muscatitack river on the section line dividing sections five and six, in township three, north of range six east, and running thence southwardly upon the said section line to the south-west corner of section twenty-nine, in township two north of the same range, and running thence eastwardly upon said section line two miles to the south-west corner of section twenty-seven; and thence south upon the section line one mile to the township line dividing townships one and two, and running thence eastwardly upon said township line" until it intersects the line between Clark and Washington counties. *Laws of Indiana*, 1838-39 (local), pp. 323-24.

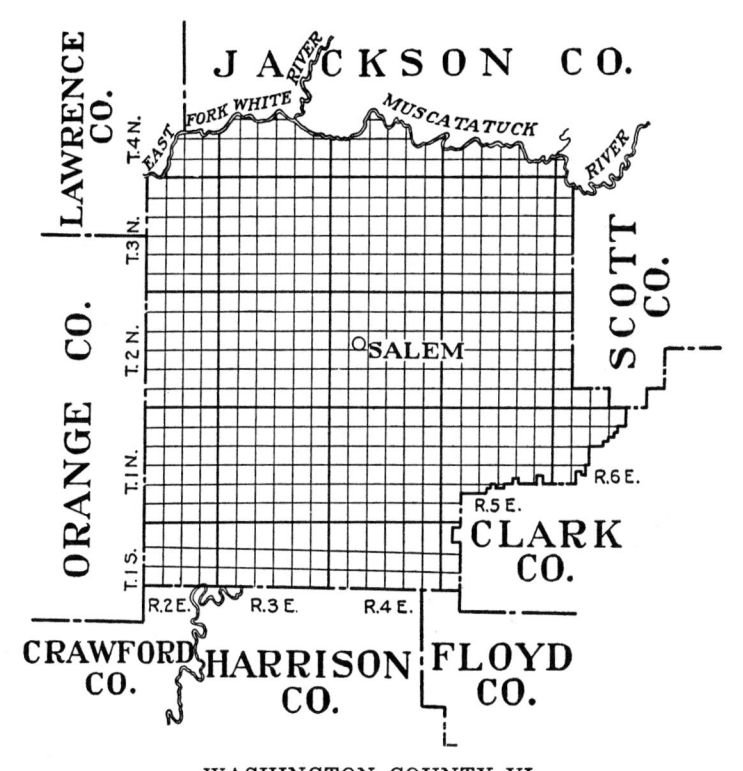

WASHINGTON COUNTY VI
[Law: Feb. 16, 1839, effective on passage]

WASHINGTON COUNTY VII

1842-43: Alteration by statute defining county boundaries.

BOUNDARIES: "Beginning at the southwest corner of section sixteen, in township one south, of range two east, thence due east to the southeast corner of section eighteen, township one south, range five, thence north two miles, thence east one half mile, thence north to the north line of section thirty-two, township one, range five east, thence east one half mile, thence north one half mile, thence east one mile and a half, thence north one half mile, thence east one mile, thence north one half mile, thence east to the centre of section nineteen, township one north, range six east, thence north one half mile, thence east one half mile, thence north one half mile, thence east one mile, thence north one half mile, thence east one half mile, thence north one half mile, thence east one half mile, thence north to the line dividing townships one and two north, thence west one mile, thence north one mile, thence west to the southwest corner of section twenty-nine, in township two north, of range six east, thence north to the Muscatituck river, thence down the same and White river to where a sectional line running north from the beginning crosses said White river, thence south with said sectional line to the place of beginning." *Revised Statutes of Indiana*, 1842-43, p. 75.

The description of Washington County's boundaries in the *Revised Statutes* of 1852 incorrectly substitutes the words "section twenty" for "section twenty-nine." *Ibid.*, 1851-52, vol. 1:195.

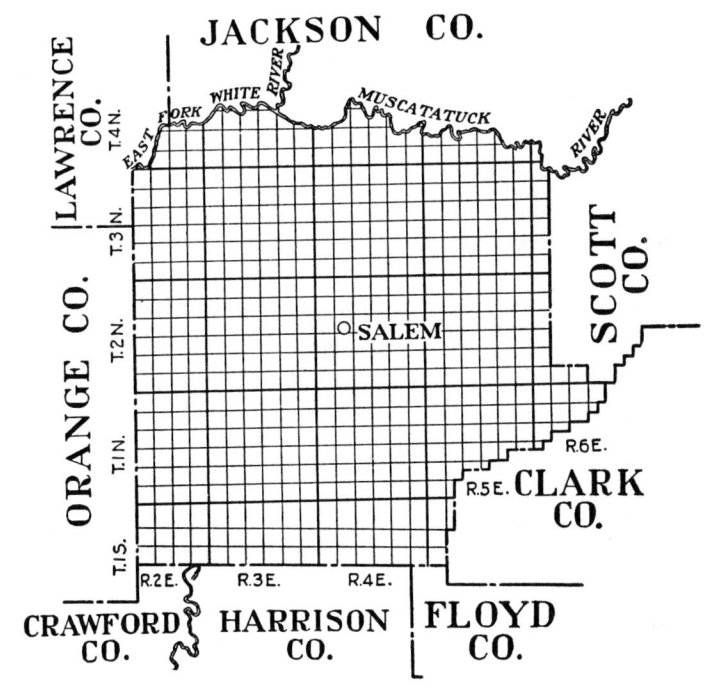

WASHINGTON COUNTY VII

[Law: 1842-43]

WASHINGTON COUNTY VIII

JANUARY 14, 1846: Alteration by statute defining the boundaries between the counties of Clark and Washington, effective on publication.

BOUNDARY CHANGE: The Washington-Clark boundary line, established in the *Revised Statutes* of 1842-43, was altered by the provision that "so much of the revised statutes of 1831 as defines the boundary line between said counties . . . is hereby revived and declared to be in full force." *Laws of Indiana*, 1845-46 (general), pp. 111-12.

The law of 1831 here mentioned defined the boundary between Washington and Clark counties as it was laid out at the formation of Washington County, December 21, 1813, along the height of the Silver Creek Knobs. The line had not yet been surveyed.

WASHINGTON COUNTY BOUNDARIES 835

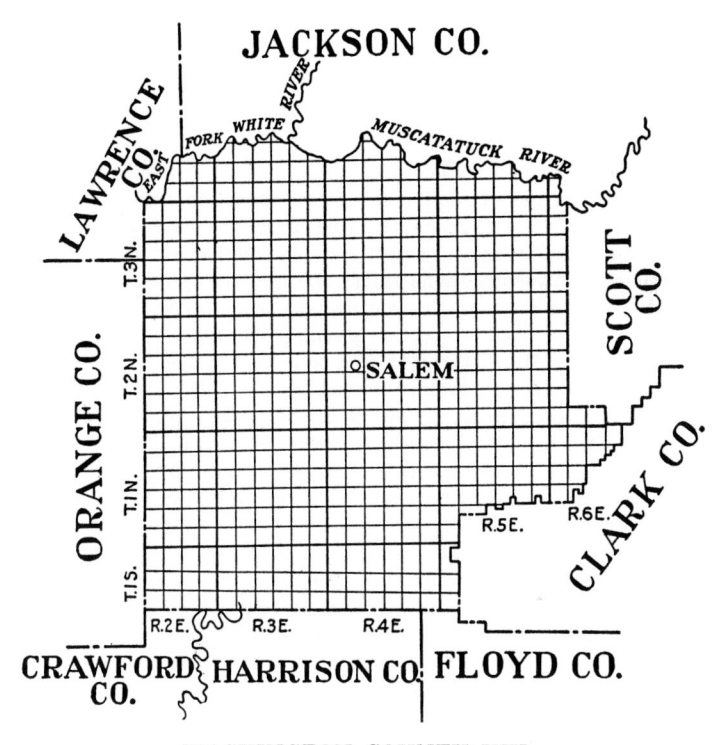

WASHINGTON COUNTY VIII

[Law: Jan. 14, 1846, effective on publication]

WASHINGTON COUNTY IX

MARCH 7, 1873: Alteration by statute changing the Washington-Clark boundary line, effective on passage.

BOUNDARY CHANGE: The line is defined as "Commencing at the southwest corner of section seventeen, town one, south of range five, east, thence north along the line dividing sections seventeen and eighteen, and seven and eight, and five and six, to the base line; thence north between sections thirty-one and thirty-two, town one, north, range five east, to the southwest corner of section twenty-nine; thence east between section twenty-nine and thirty two, and twenty-eight and thirty-three of said town and range, to the southwest corner of section twenty-seven; thence north to the northwest corner of section twenty-seven, in said town one, north, range five, east; thence between sections twenty-two and twenty-seven, and twenty-three and twenty-six, and twenty-four and twenty-five in said town one, north, range six [five], east; thence east between sections nineteen and thirty, of town one, north, range six, east, to southwest corner of section twenty; thence north between nineteen and twenty, to southwest corner of section seventeen in said town one, north of range six, east; thence east to southwest corner of sixteen; thence north between sections sixteen and seventeen, and eight and nine, to the northwest corner of nine, of said town and range; thence east between four and nine, to southwest corner of section three; thence north between three and four in said town one, north, range six, east, to Scott county line." *Laws of Indiana*, 1873, pp. 105-6.

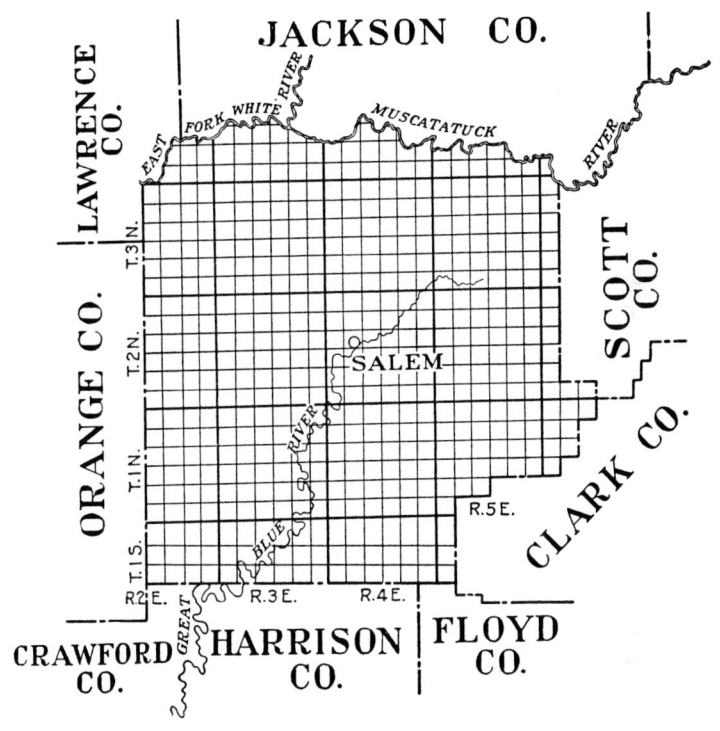

WASHINGTON COUNTY IX

[Law: Mar. 7, 1873, effective on passage]

WAYNE COUNTY I
[Indiana Territory]

NOVEMBER 27, 1810: Formation by statute, effective January 1, 1811. The formation affected Clark and Dearborn counties.

BOUNDARIES: "Beginning at the corner of townships number 7 and 8, on the line of the state of Ohio, thence north, until the same arrives at fort Recovery, thence, from fort Recovery southwardly, with the line of the western boundary of the purchase made at fort Wayne, in the year one thousand eight hundred and nine, until the same intersects the line of the northern boundary of the purchase made at Grouseland, thence northwardly, with the line of the last mentioned purchase until the same arrives at a point from which a due east and west line will strike the corner of town seven and eight on the aforesaid state of Ohio line.

". . . The same is hereby divided into two separate and distinct counties by a line beginning at the corner of townships number eleven and twelve, on the line of the state of Ohio, and from thence due west until the same intersects the line of the western boundary of the before mentioned purchase of fort Wayne . . . the northern division thereof shall be known and designated by the name and style of the county of Wayne." *Acts of Indiana Territory*, 1810, pp. 19-20, 114.

The state line did not pass through Fort Recovery, though the boundary between Indiana Territory and the Northwest Territory had intersected that point. The Fort Wayne treaty line of 1809 also ran to Fort Recovery.

COUNTY SEAT: Commissioners appointed under the act forming the county, located the county seat at Salisbury. Their choice was ratified by the Territorial Assembly in an act of December 5, 1811. *Acts of Indiana Territory*, 1810, pp. 21-22; 1811, p. 14.

WAYNE COUNTY BOUNDARIES 839

SALISBURY

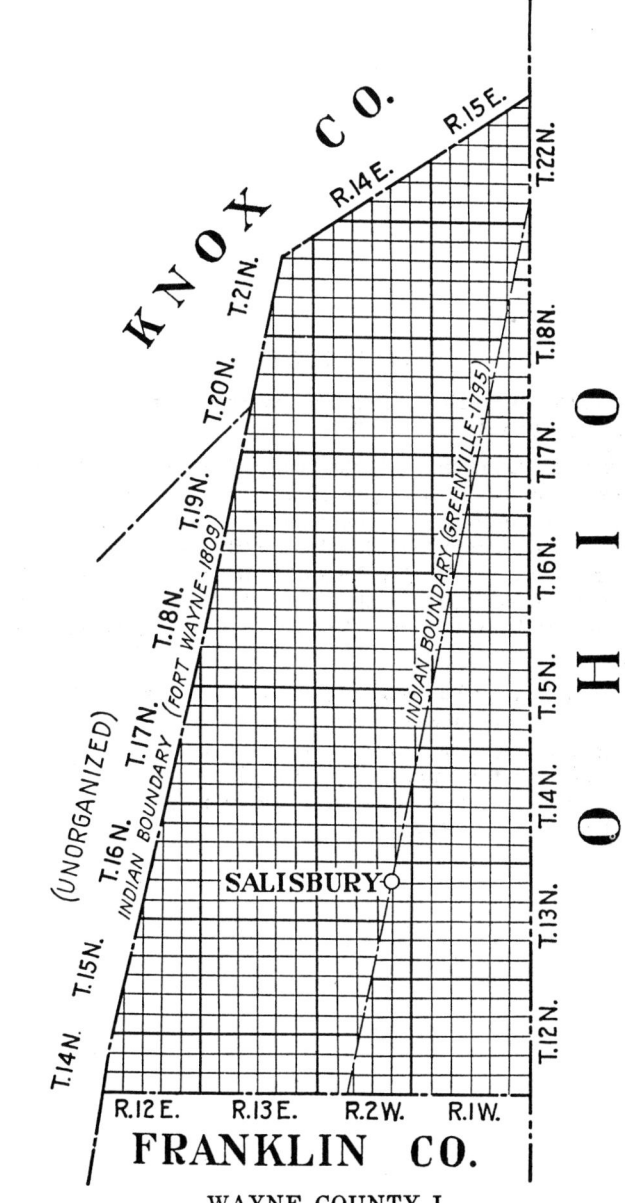

R.12E. R.13E. R.2W. R.1W.

FRANKLIN CO.

WAYNE COUNTY I

[Law: Nov. 27, 1810, effective Jan. 1, 1811]

WAYNE COUNTY II

JANUARY 10, 1818: Alteration by statute forming Randolph County, effective August 10, 1818.

BOUNDARY CHANGE: All that part of Wayne County north of a line "Beginning at the state of Ohio line, where the line that divides the fifteenth and sixteenth townships strikes said Ohio line; thence west with said township line until it strikes the old boundary; thence westward with the centre line of the 18th township in the new purchase until it strikes the Indian boundary," was transferred to Randolph County. *Laws of Indiana*, 1817-18 (special), p. 18.

COUNTY SEAT: The county seat had been removed from Salisbury to Centerville under an act of December 21, 1816. The last meeting of county commissioners was held at Salisbury in August, 1817. *Ibid.*, 1816-17, pp. 216-18; Shockley, "County Seat Wars," *op. cit.*, 10:no.1:3; Fox (ed.), *Memoirs of Wayne County and the City of Richmond*, 1:37-38.

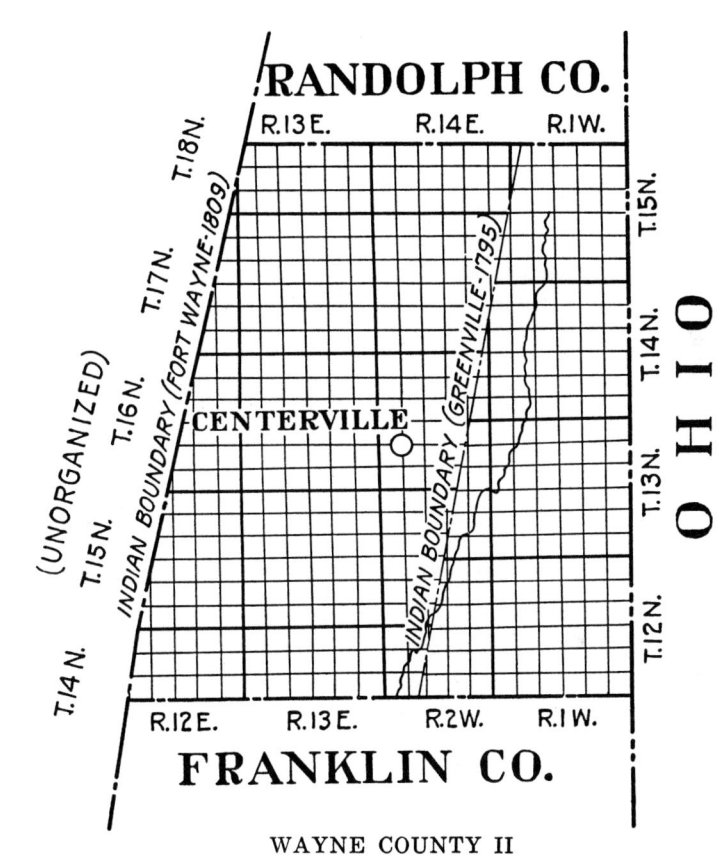

WAYNE COUNTY II
[Law: Jan. 10, 1818, effective Aug. 10, 1818]

WAYNE COUNTY III

DECEMBER 28, 1818: Alteration by statute forming Fayette County and attaching territory to Wayne County, effective January 1, 1819.

BOUNDARY CHANGE: All that part of Wayne County south and west of a line beginning where the Greenville Treaty line of 1795 crosses the line between townships 11 and 12 north, range 2 west of the first principal meridian, running thence with the Indian boundary northwardly "to fractions twenty-eight and thirty-three in the fifteenth township, range fourteen east of the second principal meridian, thence west on said line, to a line dividing sections twenty-seven and twenty eight in the fifteenth township range twelve east of the second principal meridian, thence north on said line to a line dividing townships fifteen and sixteen," thence west to the Fort Wayne Treaty line of 1809, was transferred to Fayette County. *Laws of Indiana*, 1818-19, pp. 103-4. See map, Fayette County I.

The same law provided that "all that tract of land lying east of a line drawn due north from the south east corner of section thirty-four in township sixteen and range twelve east of the second principal meridian, until it extends as far north as the north end of Wayne county" be made a part of Wayne County. *Laws of Indiana*, 1818-19, pp. 106-7.

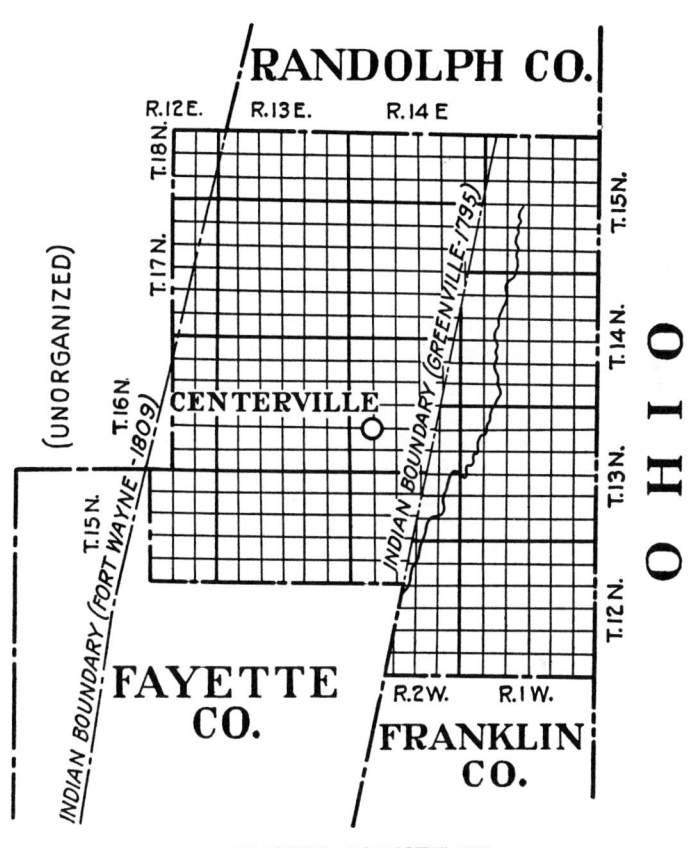

WAYNE COUNTY III
[Law: Dec. 28, 1818, effective Jan. 1, 1819]

WAYNE COUNTY IV

JANUARY 5, 1821: Alteration by statute annexing territory to Wayne County, effective upon publication in the *Indiana Gazette*, and forming Union County, effective February 1, 1821.

BOUNDARY CHANGES: The act annexed to Wayne County "all that part of the new purchase lying east of a due north line commencing on the north line of Fayette county, one mile west of the north west corner of fractional section 4 town 15 range 12 east of the second principal meridian and running north until it intersects the line dividing Randolph and Wayne counties." *Laws of Indiana*, 1820-21, pp. 129-30.

Wayne lost to Union County all her territory south of a section line running west from the southeast corner of section 1, township 12 north, range 1 west of the first principal meridian, to the southwest corner of section 24, township 15 north, range 13 east of the second principal meridian. *Ibid.*, 126-27.

WAYNE COUNTY BOUNDARIES 845

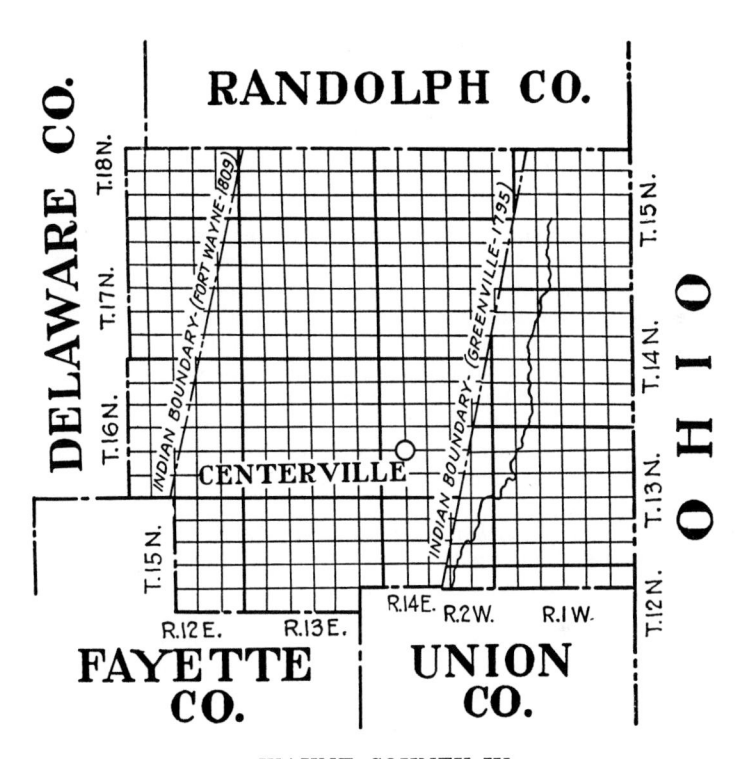

WAYNE COUNTY IV

[Law: Jan. 5, 1821, effective Feb. 1, 1821, and on publication in *Indiana Gazette*]

WAYNE COUNTY V

JANUARY 11, 1823: Alteration by statute changing the western boundary line of Wayne County.

BOUNDARY CHANGE: It was provided by the act "That the said line, dividing Wayne and Henry counties, as fixed by the General Assembly of this state, in the year A. D. 1819, be and the same is hereby altered; the said boundary line, dividing the said counties of Wayne and Henry, to commence at the south west corner of section thirty four, in township sixteen, range twelve, east of the second principal meridian; thence north on said section line, to the [point where the] line dividing towns sixteen and seventeen, crosses the said line; thence east to the section line dividing sections thirty three and thirty four; thence due north, to the north boundary line of Wayne county.

"SEC. 2. *Be it further enacted*, That hereafter all that part of Henry county, falling by this line, within the said county of Wayne, be and the same is hereby attached to, and made a part of the county of Wayne. And all that part of the county of Wayne, which may fall by the said line, in the boundary of the county of Henry, be and the same is hereby attached to, and made a part of the county of Henry." *Laws of Indiana*, 1822-23, pp. 138-39.

See notes on the text, with map, Henry County II.

WAYNE COUNTY BOUNDARIES 847

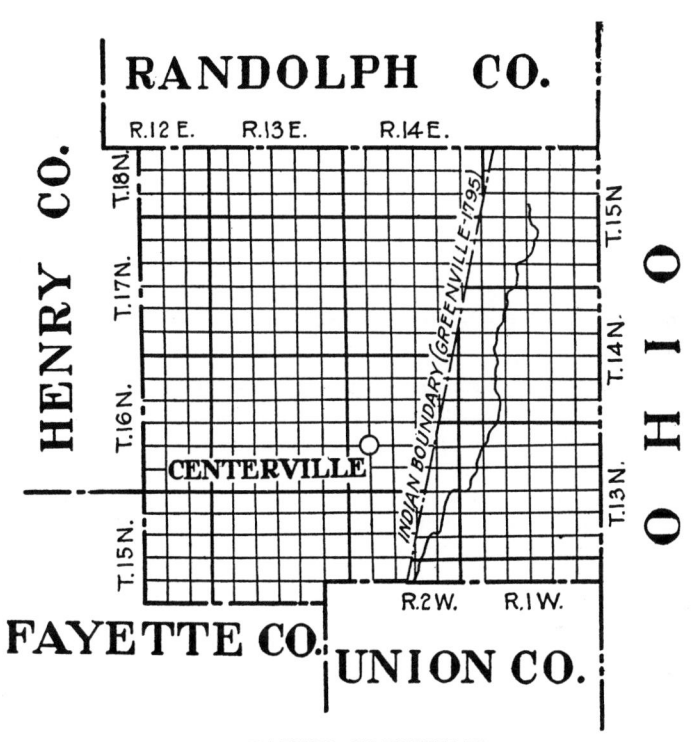

WAYNE COUNTY V
[Law: Jan. 11, 1823]

WAYNE COUNTY VI

JANUARY 22, 1824: Alteration by statute repealing act of January 11, 1823, and redefining the boundary line between Henry and Wayne counties, effective on passage.

BOUNDARY CHANGE: The act provided that "the western boundary line of Wayne county be known and designated as follows, to wit: Beginning at the south west corner of section thirty two, on the line dividing townships fifteen and sixteen in range twelve east of the second principal meridian, thence north on the said line, to the township line dividing townships sixteen and seventeen, thence with said line to where the section line dividing sections thirty one and thirty two, in township seventeen in range twelve, intersects the same, thence north with the last mentioned line to the section line dividing the counties of Wayne and Randolph." *Laws of Indiana*, 1823-24 (special), p. 52.

WAYNE COUNTY BOUNDARIES 849

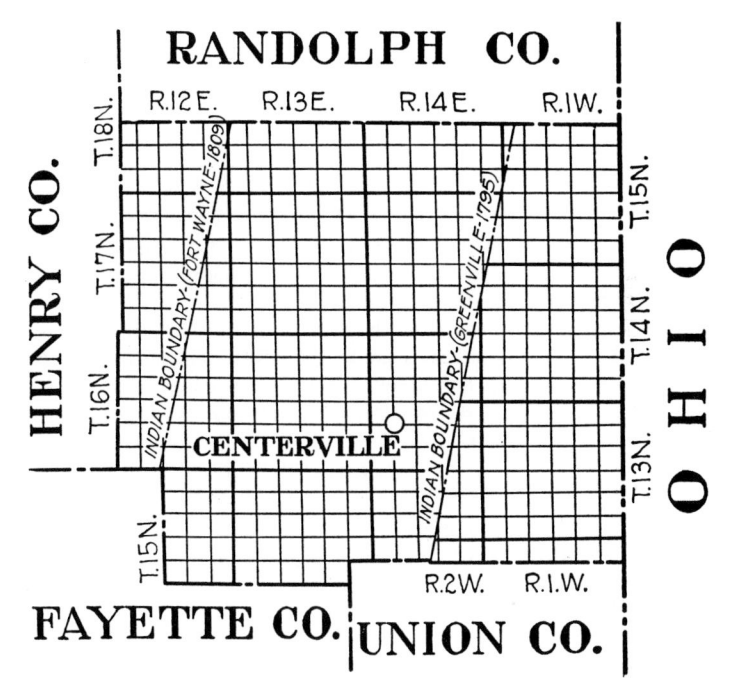

RANDOLPH CO.

HENRY CO.

FAYETTE CO. UNION CO.

OHIO

CENTERVILLE

WAYNE COUNTY VI

[Law: Jan. 22, 1824, effective on passage]

WAYNE COUNTY VII

JANUARY 26, 1827: Alteration by statute to establish the eastern boundary of Henry County, effective on passage.

BOUNDARY CHANGE: The act described the boundary between Wayne and Henry counties as follows: "Beginning at the south west corner of section thirty-two, town sixteen, north of range twelve east, thence north to the township line dividing towns sixteen and seventeen, thence east to the south east corner of section thirty-two, township seventeen, range twelve, thence north to the north east corner of section twenty, town eighteen, range twelve, thence west to the range line dividing eleven and twelve, thence north to the northern boundary of Henry county." *Laws of Indiana*, 1826-27, pp. 11-12.

COUNTY SEAT: Centerville remained the county seat until August 15, 1873, when the seat of government was removed to Richmond. This was the final step in a long struggle between the two towns. Shockley, "County Seat Wars," *op. cit.*, 10:no.1:3-4; *Historical Atlas of Indiana*, 295; *History of Wayne County*, 1:425.

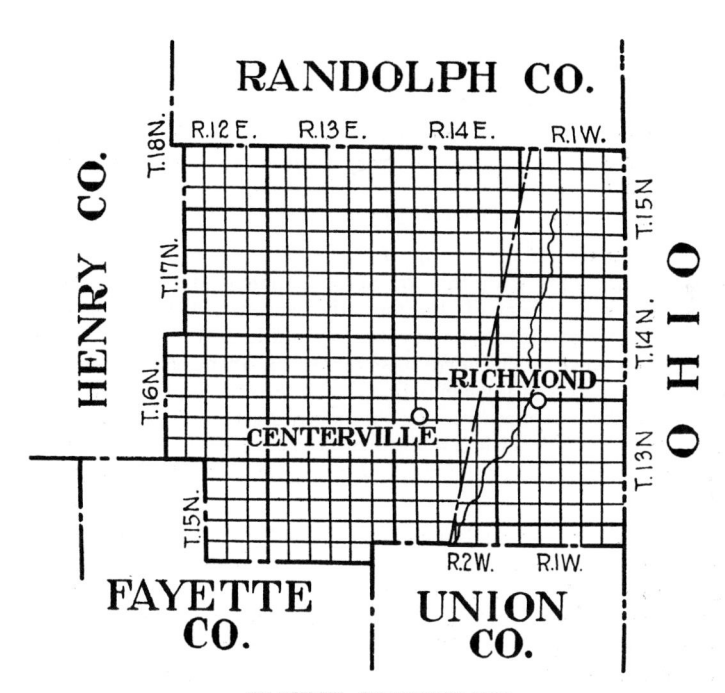

WAYNE COUNTY VII

[Law: Jan. 26, 1827, effective on passage]

WELLS COUNTY

FEBRUARY 7, 1835: Formation by statute, effective on publication. The formation affected territory attached to Allen, Delaware, and Randolph counties. Wells was organized by an act of February 2, 1837, effective May 1, 1837.

BOUNDARIES: "Commencing at the north west corner of Adams county, thence west with the southern boundary of Allen county, to the south west corner of the same, thence south with the eastern boundary of Huntington county to the south east corner of the same, thence west to the north east corner of Grant county, thence south six miles to the township line deviding township twenty four and twenty five, thence east to the south west corner of Adams county, thence north with the western boundary of Wells [Adams] county to the place of beginning." *Laws of Indiana*, 1834-35 (general), p. 44.

COUNTY SEAT: Commissioners appointed under the law to organize the county, failed to act. New commissioners appointed under an act of January 20, 1838, on March 9, 1838, reported their selection of a site in section 4, township 26 north, range 12 east. The original county seat, Bluffton, has remained to the present time. *Ibid.*, 1836-37 (general), p. 59; 1837-38 (local), p. 430; Tyndall and Lesh (eds.), *Standard History of Adams and Wells Counties*, 304-6; Shockley, "County Seat Wars," *op. cit.*, 10:no.1:36.

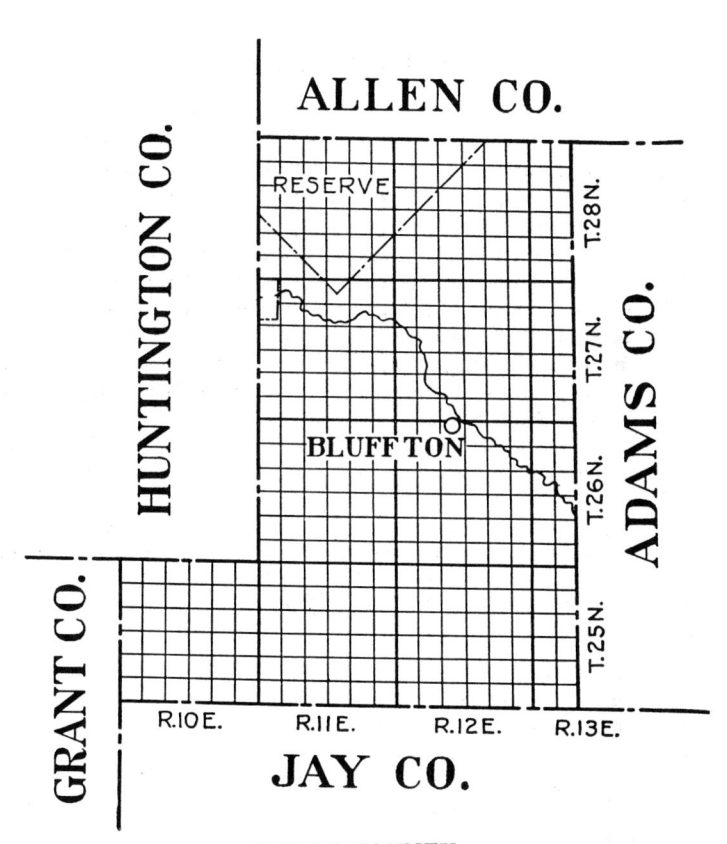

WELLS COUNTY
[Law: Feb. 7, 1835, effective on publication]

WHITE COUNTY I

FEBRUARY 1, 1834: Formation by statute, effective April 1, 1834. The formation affected territory attached to Carroll County.

BOUNDARIES: "Beginning at the north west corner of Tippecanoe county, thence running east with the north line of Tippecanoe county to the south western corner of Carroll county, thence north with the west line of Carroll county, to the north west corner of the same, thence east with the north line of Carroll county to the west line of Cass county, thence north with the west line of Cass county to the north west corner of the same, thence west to the centre section line of range six west, thence south to the north west corner of Tippecanoe county to the place of beginning." *Laws of Indiana*, 1833-34, p. 67.

The same law attached to White County for jurisdiction "all the territory lying west of the county . . . to the state line." *Ibid.*, 68.

An act of December 24, 1834, attached to White County "all the territory lying north of the county of White, and of the territory attached thereto," to "the line dividing townships thirty two and thirty three north" for judicial and representative purposes. *Ibid.*, 1834-35 (general), p. 77.

COUNTY SEAT: Commissioners appointed under the act forming the county reported on September 5, 1834, their selection of a site in section 33, township 27 north, range 3 west for the county seat. The town, which was named Monticello, has remained the seat of county government. *Ibid.*, 1833-34, p. 67; Hamelle (ed.), *Standard History of White County*, 1:65-66; Shockley, "County Seat Wars," *op. cit.*, 10:no.1:30.

WHITE COUNTY BOUNDARIES 855

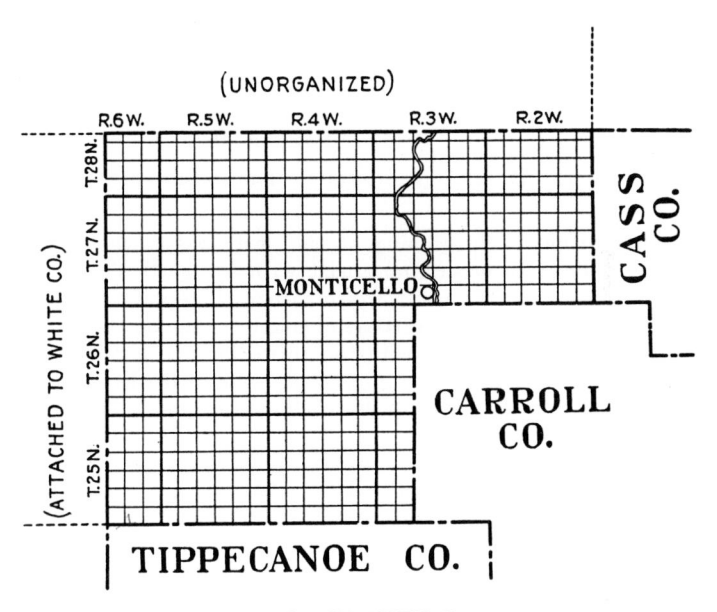

WHITE COUNTY I
[Law: Feb. 1, 1834, effective Apr. 1, 1834]

WHITE COUNTY II

FEBRUARY 17, 1838: Alteration by statute defining county boundaries.

BOUNDARIES: "Beginning at the north-west corner of Tippecanoe county; thence running east with the north line of Tippecanoe county, to the north-western corner of Carroll county; thence north with the west line of Carroll county to the north-west corner of the same, thence east with the north line of Carroll county, to the west line of Cass county; thence north with the west line of Cass county to the north-west corner of the same, thence west to the centre section line of range six west, thence south to the north west corner of Tippecanoe county to the place of beginning." *Laws of Indiana*, 1837-38 (local), p. 264.

Although there is no apparent distinction between this description and that of the formation of the county, an actual change occurred due to the northward extension of Cass County by the same law. See map, Cass County IV.

WHITE COUNTY BOUNDARIES 857

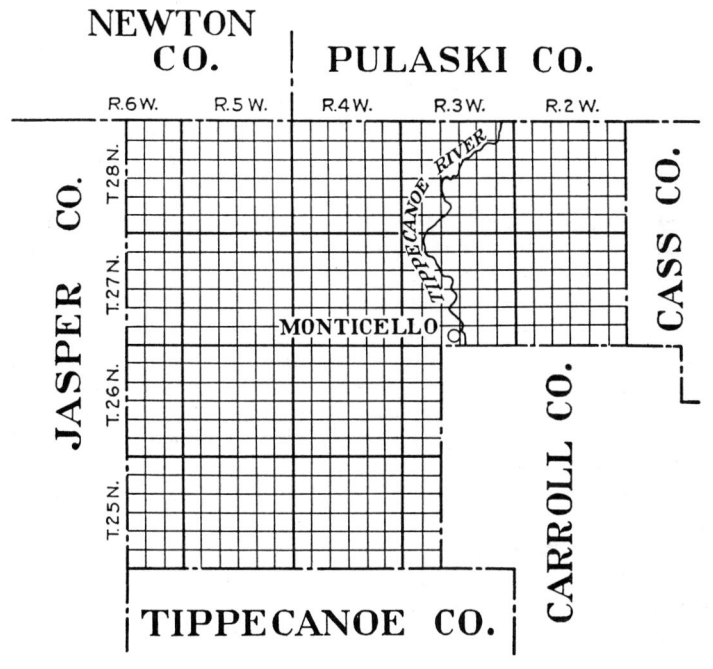

WHITE COUNTY II
[Law: Feb. 17, 1838]

WHITE COUNTY III

FEBRUARY 14, 1839: Alteration by statute to change the boundary line of the counties of Carroll and White, effective on passage.

BOUNDARY CHANGE: "Hereafter the Tippecanoe river shall be the western boundary of Carroll county, from where the north line of said county strikes the river, until said river strikes the section line dividing thirty-three and twenty-eight, in township twenty-six, and all the territory west of said river and north of said line in township twenty-six, and range three west, is hereby attached to the county of White, as intended by the act, entitled, "an act to alter the boundary line between Carroll and White," approved, February 4, 1837." *Laws of Indiana*, 1838-39 (general), p. 93.

The law of February 4, 1837, incorrectly mentioned township six north, instead of twenty-six north. *Ibid.*, 1836-37 (local), p. 379.

The consolidation of Jasper and Newton counties was not actually effected until June, 1839, although carried out under provisions of a law of January 29, 1839.

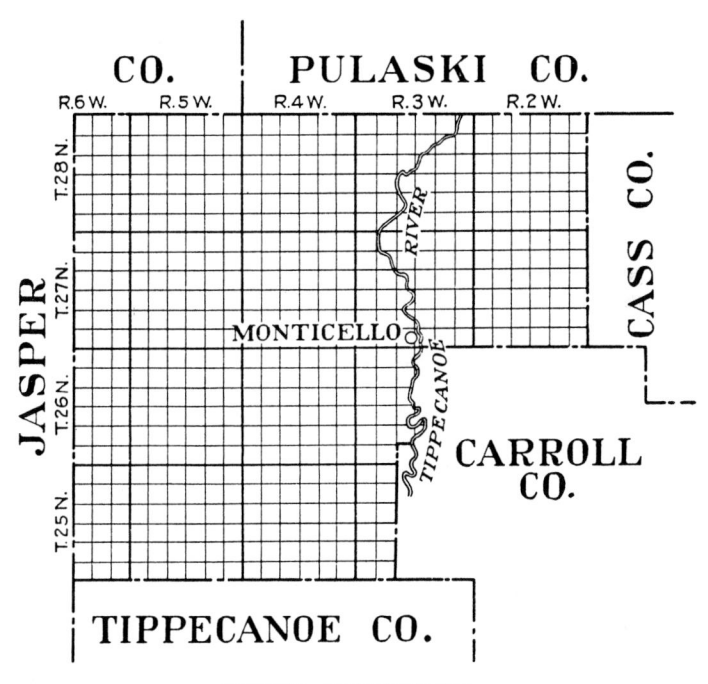

WHITE COUNTY III

[Law: Feb. 14, 1839, effective on passage]

WHITE COUNTY IV

FEBRUARY 10, 1841: Alteration by statute to attach certain territory to Jasper County, effective on passage.

BOUNDARY CHANGE: All that part of White County within the following boundaries was attached to Jasper: "Commencing at the northwest corner of White county; thence east six miles; thence south five miles; thence west six miles to the county line dividing the counties of White and Jasper; thence north with said line to the place of beginning." *Laws of Indiana*, 1840-41 (general), p. 135.

WHITE COUNTY BOUNDARIES 861

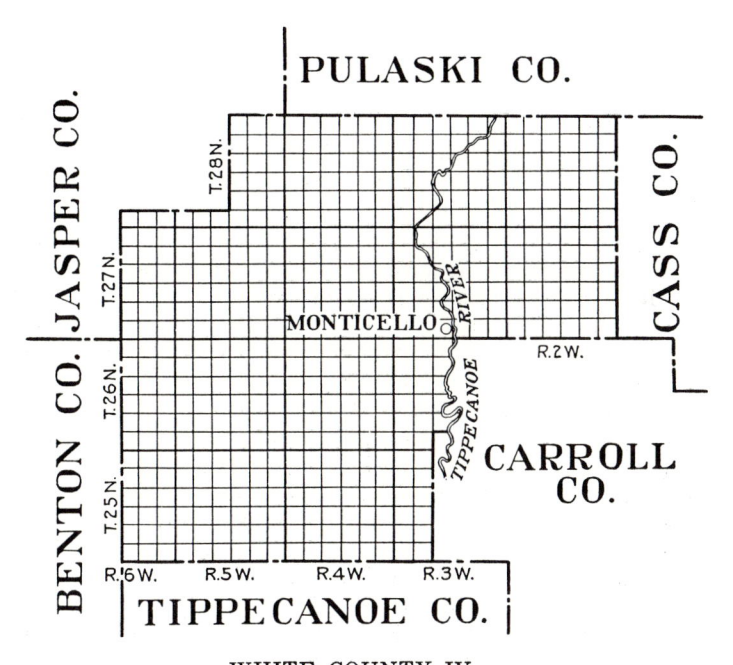

WHITE COUNTY IV

[Law: Feb. 10, 1841, effective on passage]

WHITLEY COUNTY I

FEBRUARY 7, 1835: Formation by statute, effective on publication. The formation affected territory attached to Elkhart and Allen counties. Whitley was organized by an act of February 17, 1838, effective April 1, 1838.

BOUNDARIES: "Beginning at the north-east corner of township thirty two north, of range seven east, thence east with the township line eighteen miles, thence south with the line dividing ranges ten and eleven east eighteen miles, thence west with the township line eighteen miles, thence north with the line of ranges seven and eight east, eighteen miles to the place of beginning." *Laws of Indiana*, 1834-35 (general), p. 45.

COUNTY SEAT: Commissioners appointed under the act organizing the county, in June, 1838, reported their selection of a site in section 19, township 31 north, range 9 east, on land owned by L. S. Bayless. By an act of February 18, 1839, commissioners were appointed to relocate the county seat. At their meeting in October they chose the site of Columbia on fractional section 11, township 31 north, range 9 east. *Ibid.*, 1837-38 (local), p. 408; 1838-39 (local), pp. 317-18; Kaler and Maring, *History of Whitley County*, 53-55; Goodspeed and Blanchard (eds.), *County of Whitley*, 57-58; Shockley, "County Seat Wars," *op. cit.*, 10:no.1:38.

WHITLEY COUNTY BOUNDARIES 863

NOBLE CO.

KOSCIUSKO CO.

ALLEN CO.

COLUMBIA CITY

RES.

R.

R.8E. R.9E. R.10E.

T.32N.
T.31N.
T.30N.

(UNORGAN-IZED)

WABASH CO. HUNTINGTON CO.

WHITLEY COUNTY I

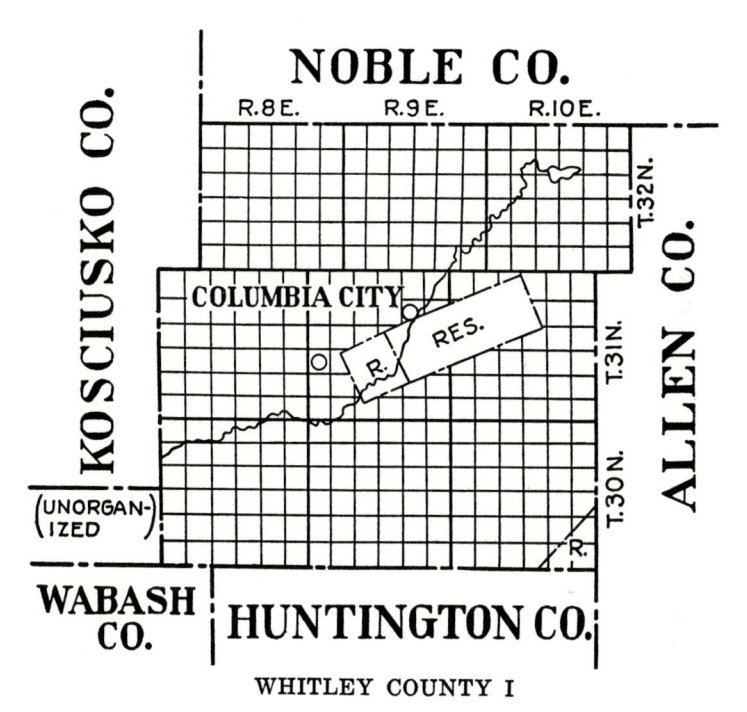

[Law: Feb. 7, 1835, effective on publication]

WHITLEY COUNTY II

JUNE 11, 1859: Alteration by county commissioners' report changing the boundary line between Whitley and Noble counties.

BOUNDARY CHANGE: It was provided that the change in line should "commence at the County line at the south west corner of said Noble County, running then north along the line between the Counties of Noble and Kosciusko to the north west corner of Section Number Thirty (30) in Township Number Thirtythree North of Range Number Eight (8) East in said Noble County, thence East along the section line between Sections Nineteen and Thirty, Twenty and Twenty-nine, Twenty-one and Twenty-eight, Twenty-two and Twenty-seven, Twenty-three and Twenty-six, Twenty-four and Twenty-five, thence south on along the township line between Townships Number Thirty-three and Range Number Eight and Number Nine to the present boundary line between the said Counties of Noble and Whitley so as to include within the boundaries of said Whitley County the following named Sections, 'towit', Sections Twentyfive, Twentysix, Twentyseven, Twentyeight, Twentynine, Thirty, Thirtyone, Thirtytwo, Thirtythree, thirtyfour, Thirtyfive and Thirtysix, of Township Number Thirtythree (33) North of Range Number Eight (8) East." Whitley County Records.

COUNTY SEAT: The name of the county seat was changed from Columbia to Columbia City when the town was incorporated in 1853. Goodspeed and Blanchard (eds.), *County of Whitley*, 101, 113.

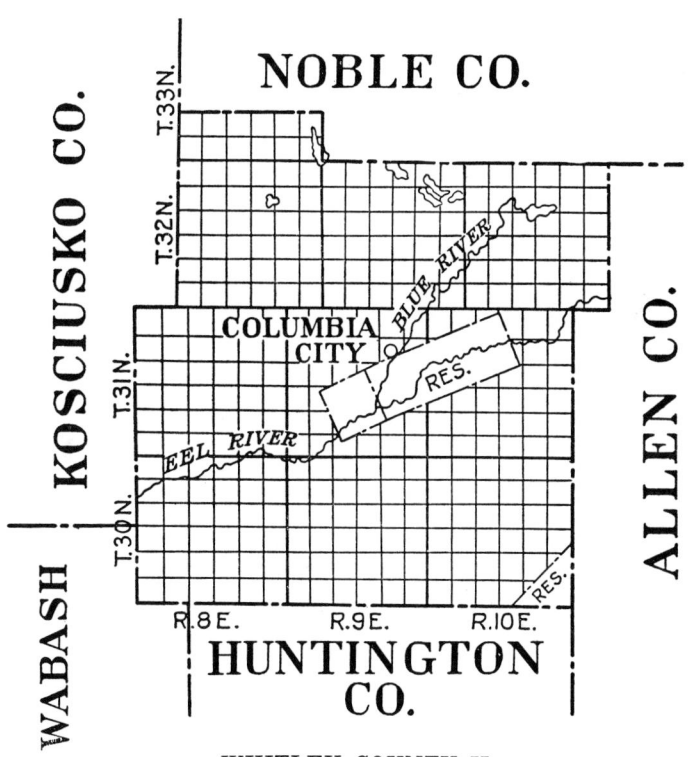

WHITLEY COUNTY II

[Commissioners' Report: June 11, 1859]

INDEX

INDEX

Adams County, formation, 65-66; organization, 67; description and map, 224-25; mention, 92.
Ade, John, 112n.
Albion, 628.
Allen County, formation, 41; jurisdiction, 41, 49, 50, 52, 57, 226; proposed change, 118; description and map, 226-27.
Alton, 376.
Alves, Gaston M., commissioner, Kentucky boundary dispute, 18-19.
Anderson, 578.
Andersontown, 570, 574, 578.
Angola, 752.
Armiesburg (Parke Co.), 650.
Attachments, for civil and criminal jurisdiction, 28-29. *See also* jurisdiction, under names of counties.
Auburn, 322.
Augusta (Noble Co.), courthouse fire, 628.

Bartholomew County, formation, 36-37; addition, 49; reduction, 67, 71; proposed change, 118; jurisdiction, 36-37, 38, 222, 228; county seat, 228; descriptions and maps, 228-35; mention, 45; *and others*, petition for formation of new county, 71, 77, 90.
Bayless, L. S., 862.
Bedford (Lawrence Co.), 568.
Bedford (Madison Co.), 574.

Benton County, formation, 75; proposed disorganization, 79-80; proposed change, 96; description and map, 236-37.
Blackford (Posey Co.), 680.
Blackford County, formation, 71; organization, 73; proposed changes, 77-78, 87, 93, 95, 96-97, 98-99, 101, 120-21, 126, 127; discussed in Constitutional Convention (1850-51), 104; description and map, 238-39; mention, 90.
Bloomfield (Greene Co.), 406.
Bloomington, 600.
Bluffton, 852.
Boon, Ratliff, 32n.
Boone County, formation, 51-52; description and map, 240-41.
Boonville, 32n, 804.
Bourbon, proposed name for county, 118.
Bowling Green, 288.
Brazil, 288.
Brookville, 354.
Brown, proposed name for county, 58.
Brown County, move for formation, 66; formation, 67; description and map, 242-43.
Brownstown, 452.
Brownsville, 774.
Buckingham's base line, 386.
Burlington (Greene Co.), 406.
Butler, McDonald and, 18.

Cahokia (St. Clair Co.), 208, 210.
California, state of, establishment of counties in, 28n.

57—48526 (869)

870   INDIANA HISTORICAL COLLECTIONS

Cannelton, 116, 120, 662.
Canton (Tipton Co.), name changed, 772.
Carey Mission Treaty (1828), 51, 334.
Carlisle, 754.
Carroll County, movement for formation, 46; formation, 48; jurisdiction, 50, 52, 63, 73, 244, 246; proposed changes, 51, 66, 68-69, 75-76, 79, 81, 95, 96; loss to White, 72; county seat, 244; descriptions and maps, 244-47;
and others, petition for formation of new county, 71, 76-77, 78, 85.
Carrollton, name changed, 244.
Cass County, formation, 50; jurisdiction, 50, 52, 66, 73, 248, 250, 252, 254; loss to Miami, 63; extended north, 70; proposed changes, 66, 76, 77, 79, 96; county seat, 248; descriptions and maps, 248-55;
and others, petition for new county, 94-95.
Cave Spring, location, 202, 204, 206.
Center (Noble Co.), name changed, 628.
Centerville, 840, 850.
Centre, proposed name for county, 38n.
Charlestown, 264.
Chester, proposed name for county, 74.
Chicago (Ill.), treaty of (1821), 51.
Cicero, proposed name for county, 84.
Cincinnati (Ohio), interest in division of Northwest Territory, 3n; legislative sessions at, 136.

Clark, J. W., 123n.
Clark County, formation, 22; additions, 22, 42, 68; loss to Dearborn, 22; to Floyd, 34, 87; to Harrison, 23; to Harrison, Jefferson, and Washington, 24; to Jackson, 26; to Jefferson, 68; boundary defined, 80; change with Washington, 91-92; ambiguous act concerning, 37; proposed changes, 23, 38-39, 40-41, 50, 53, 55, 64, 76, 93; boundary surveys, 31, 35, 44, 48, 49, 50, 59, 72, 78, 82, 124, 268, 274, 278, 488, 496, 730, 732, 828; county seat, 256, 258, 264, 286; descriptions and maps, 256-87; mention, 62, 69, 100.
Clarksville, 256.
Clay County, movement for formation, 43; formation, 43; proposed changes, 50, 51, 59, 72, 74, 76, 79, 100; description and map, 288-89;
and others, petition for new county, 79.
Clinton, proposed name for county, 40.
Clinton County, formation, 51-52; proposed change, 90; loss to Howard, 114-15; protests against act of 1857, p. 116n; county seat, 290; descriptions and maps, 290-93;
and others, propose formation of new county, 71, 76-77, 78, 85, 94-95.
Colorado, state of, establishment of counties in, 28n.
Columbia City (Columbia), 862, 864.
Columbus, 228.
Connersville, 27n, 338.
Constitutional conventions, provisions regarding counties

INDEX

(1816), 29-30; (1850-51), 103-4.
Coquillard, Alexis, 718.
Corydon, 412.
Counties, cycle of development, 129; factors determining establishment, 21; Indian titles to be recognized in formation of, 20n, 22, 32n;
method of forming: Northwest and Indiana Territory, 20, 22-23; in new state, 28-30; under the second constitution, 103-4; act of 1857, pp. 109-11n; acts of 1858 and 1859, pp. 112-15; act of 1861, pp. 116-17;
method of changing boundaries (1840-41), 78, 80; (1844-45), 90-91; (1850-51), 103-4; (1853), 108; (1857), 109-11n; (1858, 1859), 112-15; (1861), 116-19; (1875), 124-25; (1883), 126; (1887, 1889), 128; (1932), 131;
size of: under first constitution, 29-30; under second constitution, 103; under act of 1857, p. 110; under act of 1859, p. 114; under act of 1861, p. 117; proposed change (1895), 128;
problem of unorganized territory, 31, 48-49, 64-65; number of (1816), 27; (1823-24), 43; (1830-31), 55; (1843-44), 83; solidarity of development lost, 57; interpretation of boundary descriptions (1842-43), 81; effect of changes on taxation, 99, 107; consolidation considered (1931-33), 130-31.

County seats, importance of rivalries, 32n, 69-70, 83, 116, 117-18; mention, 78n.
Covington, 352.
Crawford County, formation, 32; addition, 47; proposed changes, 40, 42, 44, 66, 68, 90, 92; county seat, 294, 296; descriptions and maps, 294-97;
and others, petition for new county, 94.
Crawfordsville, 608.
Crown Point, 550.
Cynthiana, proposed name for county, 100.
Cynthiana (Posey Co.), 100n.

Danville, 428.
Darlington (Warrick Co.), 32n, 802.
Daviess County, movement for formation, 27; formation, 30; division suggested, 33; loss to Owen, 33; to Greene, 36; to Martin, 49; jurisdiction, 35; proposed changes, 41, 42, 44, 46, 48, 69, 77, 105; protests against act of 1857, p. 116n; controversy with Martin, 118; county seat, 298; descriptions and maps, 298-307;
and others, propose new county, 81, 92.
Dearborn County, formation, 22; move for division, 23; addition, 25; loss to Ripley, 30; to Ohio, 83, 88; objects to formation of Ohio County, 69-70, 96; jurisdiction, 31, 712; proposed changes, 94, 97, 99-100; discussed in Constitutional Convention (1850-51), 104; county seat, 308, 316; descriptions and maps, 308-19.
Decatur, 224.

Decatur County, formation, 37-38; proposed changes, 44, 51, 59, 62, 67, 74, 80, 96, 109, 122; description and map, 320-21; *and others*, propose new county, 71, 90.

De Kalb, proposed name for new county, 57n.

De Kalb County, formation, 65-66; organization, 69; description and map, 322-23.

Delaware, proposed name for county, 39n.

Delaware County, formation, 46; jurisdiction, 49, 54, 324, 710; proposed changes, 69, 92, 96-97, 98-99, 101; discussed in Constitutional Convention (1850-51), 104; description and map, 324-25; *and others*, propose new county, 106.

Delaware County (New Purchase), formation, 34-35; organization in, 55; description and map, 222-23.

Delaware Indians, 34.

Delphi, 244.

Detroit, courts held at, 216, 218.

Dover Hill, 590.

Drayton, proposed name for county, 62.

Dubois County, formation of foreseen, 30; formation, 31; loss to Martin, 35; proposed changes, 41, 42, 46, 96, 105, 119; protests against act of 1857, p. 116n; county seat, 326, 330; descriptions and maps, 326-31.

Dunlap, 332.

Elkhart County, formation, 52; loss to St. Joseph and addition, 57; loss to Marshall, 67-68; proposed changes, 55, 118; jurisdiction, 332, 334; county seat, 332; descriptions and maps, 332-37; mention, 87.

English, 296.

Evansville, 15, 32n, 778, 800.

Fairfield, suggested name for county, 44n.

Fayette County, movement for formation, 31, 33; formation, 34; loss to Union, 36; addition, 45; proposed changes, 35-36, 47, 49, 55, 59, 72; jurisdiction, 222; county seat, 338; descriptions and maps, 338-43; mention, 72n.

Floyd County, movement for formation, 26, 31, 33; formation, 34; ambiguous act concerning, 37; additions, 40, 49, 87, 106; proposed changes, 39, 50, 53, 55, 59, 62, 64, 68, 69, 76; boundary surveys, 72, 78, 82, 350; county seat, 344; descriptions and maps, 344-51.

Fort Recovery (Ohio), 3, 4, 22, 522, 838.

Fort Wayne, 226.

Fort Wayne Treaty line (1809), 23, 24, 25, 26, 30, 32, 33, 35, 36.

Fountain County, movement for formation, 44; formation, 44-45; jurisdiction, 45, 46, 352; proposed changes, 47, 53, 122, 123-24; description and map, 352-53;
and others, propose formation of new county, 71, 75, 95.

Fowler, 236.

Frankfort, 290.

Franklin (Johnson Co.), 512.

Franklin (Perry Co.), name changed, 660.

Franklin County, formation, 24; addition, 34; loss to Fayette,

INDEX

34; to Union, 36; to Fayette and Union, 45; proposed changes, 47, 55, 62, 74; jurisdiction, 358; county seat, 354; descriptions and maps, 354-63; mention, 26.

Fredonia, 294, 296.

Freeman's Corner, 530, 820, 822.

Fulton, proposed name for county, 54n.

Fulton County, formation, 65-66; organization, 67; jurisdiction, 70; additions, 75, 85, 91; loss to Kosciusko, 80; proposed changes, 67, 76, 77, 89, 109, 119; county seat, 364; descriptions and maps, 364-75.

Gallatin, proposed name for county, 89.

Gibson County, formation, 24; loss to Perry, 25; to Orange and Posey, 26, 27; to Pike and Posey, 30; to Posey, 40; to Warrick, 106; additions, 38, 43; proposed changes, 36, 76, 105; dispute with Warrick, 41-42, 72, 74, 80, 85-86, 93, 106-7, 108-9, 109; county seat, 376; descriptions and maps, 376-401; mention, 90n.

Gore, the, 4, 5n, 22, 258, 260.

Goshen, 332.

Grant County, formation, 54; loss to Madison, 70; proposed changes, 77-78, 87, 90n, 93n, 95, 127; discussed in Constitutional Convention (1850-51), 104; jurisdiction, 402, 404; county seat, 402; descriptions and maps, 402-5; mention, 69;
and others, petition for new county, 106.

Grass, Daniel, 32n.

Gray, Isaac P., 17.

Great Cave, location of, 204.

Great Miami Reserve, organization of considered, 73, 79, 81, 83-84; mention, 41, 43, 46, 48, 49, 54, 55, 64-65, 76, 78, 85, 244, 246, 248, 290, 402, 404, 408, 576, 596.

Green River Island (Ky.), boundary controversy concerning, 15-19.

Greencastle, 696.

Greene County, movement for formation, 33, 35, 36; formation, 36; proposed changes, 42, 43n, 44, 47, 49, 50, 51, 69, 71, 406; description and map, 406-7;
and others, petition for new county, 81, 92, 94.

Greenfield, 410.

Greensburg, 320.

Greenville Treaty line, 3, 4, 5, 22, 258, 260, 488.

Grouseland Treaty line, 22, 25, 33, 35, 262, 264, 412, 414, 488, 524.

Hamilton County, formation, 39; jurisdiction, 45, 73, 408; description and map, 408-9.

Hamilton County (Ohio), 518.

Hancock County, formation, 46; organization, 48; proposed changes, 50, 63; description and map, 410-11; mention, 61.

Harris, William, surveys Ohio-Indiana line, 5.

Harrison, William Henry, 2, 22.

Harrison County, formation, 23; addition, 24; loss to Washington, 24; to Crawford, 32; to Floyd, 34, 40, 106; to Clark, 42; proposed changes, 39, 59, 62, 64, 66, 68, 92; county seat, 412; descriptions and maps, 412-27; mention, 37, 109;

874   INDIANA HISTORICAL COLLECTIONS

and others, petition for new county, 94.
Harrisonville (Martin Co.), 590.
Hart, proposed name for county, 90.
Hartford City, 238.
Hendricks, Thomas A., 16.
Hendricks, proposed name for county, 32n.
Hendricks County, formation, 41; jurisdiction, 49, 428; proposed changes, 44, 45, 62, 90, 93; loss to Marion, 54; addition, 122-23; county seat, 428; descriptions and maps, 428-33.
Henrie, Arthur, surveyor, 14n.
Henry County, formation, 37-38; alterations, 40, 42, 47; proposed changes, 45-46, 50, 53, 59; county seat, 434; descriptions and maps, 434-41; mention, 61.
Highland, proposed name for county, 52-53.
Hillsborough (Martin Co.), name changed, 590.
Hindostan (Martin Co.), 588.
Howard County (Richardville), formation of, as Richardville County, 83-84; additions, 88, 114; proposed changes, 90, 95; name changed, 95n, 444; county seat, 442; descriptions and maps, 442-47;
and others, petition for new county, 94-95. *See also* Richardville.
Huntington, 448.
Huntington County, move for formation, 54; formation, 58; description and map, 448-49.

Illinois, state of, eastern boundary, 12-14.
Illinois County, 1, 135, 514.

Illinois Grant, the, 22.
Illinois Territory, formation, 8-9, 144-45; eastern boundary, 9, 9n-10n, 12; St. Clair and Randolph counties become part of, 21.
Indian titles, 20n, 22-23, 43, 47, 51, 55, 61-62, 454, 554, 592, 708, 770, 794.
Indiana, state of, boundaries foreshadowed, 1; formation, 10-12; Illinois boundary, 12-14; Michigan boundary, 14-15; Kentucky boundary, 15-19; descriptions and maps, 146-201. *See also* Counties.
Indiana Territory, formation of, 2-4; division of: Ohio, 4-7; Michigan Territory, 7; Illinois Territory, 8-10n; descriptions and maps, 138-45. *See also* Counties.
Indianapolis, 580.

Jackson County, formation, 26; loss to Jennings, 30; to Bartholomew, 36; to Lawrence, 40, 115; of northern territory, 42; additions, 49, 71, 80; proposed changes, 36, 38, 59, 66-67, 68, 80, 92, 96, 97, 100, 102; jurisdiction, 222, 456; county seat, 450, 452; descriptions and maps, 450-71; mention, 35n, 121;
and others, propose new county, 52-53.
Jacksonburg (Brown Co.), name changed, 242.
Jamestown, 240.
Jasper, 330.
Jasper County, formation, 65-66; organization, 71; consolidation with Newton, 73, 622; loss to Benton, 75; proposed change, 69; addition, 77; divi-

INDEX

sion, 111-12; Kankakee boundary, 115, 128-29; county seat, 472, 474, 476; courthouse fire, 474; descriptions and maps, 472-83;
and others, petition for new county, 108.

Jay County, formation, 65-66; organization, 67; proposed changes, 69, 77-78, 97; loss to Blackford, 71; boundaries defined, 75; descriptions and maps, 484-87; county seat, 484.

Jefferson, Thomas, 1.

Jefferson County, formation, 24; loss to Washington, 24; to Switzerland and Dearborn, 25; to Jackson, 26; to Jennings, 30, 53, 66; to Scott, 53, 101; to Clark, 68; boundary surveys, 31, 268, 488, 496; proposed changes, 36, 40-41, 42-43, 44, 49-50, 50, 59, 62, 124, 126; addition, 68; county seat, 488; descriptions and maps, 488-505;
and Clark, propose new county, 35.

Jeffersonville, 258, 286.

Jennings, Jonathan, 10n, 11.

Jennings County, formation, 30; jurisdiction, 31, 222, 496, 506, 508, 712; additions, 34, 53, 66; proposed changes, 42-43, 44, 49-50, 59, 67, 80, 124, 126; county seat, 506; descriptions and maps, 506-11; mention, 35n.

Johnson County, formation, 39; proposed changes, 44, 45, 48, 49; description and map, 512-13; mention, 59;
and others, propose new county, 77.

Jurisdiction, civil and criminal, in unorganized territory, 28, 54, 65-66. *See also* under names of counties.

Justus, Basil, 236.

Kaskaskia (Randolph Co., Northwest and Indiana territories), 202, 208.

Kendricks, E. P., surveyor, 14.

Kent (Newton Co.), name changed, 624.

Kentland, 624.

Kentucky, state of, boundary controversy with Indiana, 15-19.

Kimmel, 628.

Knox (Starke Co.), 748.

Knox County, formation, 21; loss to Harrison, 23; to Gibson and others, 24; to Washington, 25-26; to Orange, 26; to Sullivan and Daviess, 30; to Sullivan, 80; protests loss to Sullivan, 86; proposed changes, 27, 105, 107-8; descriptions and maps, 514-39;
and others, petition for new county, 81, 92, 94.

Kokomo, 442.

Kosciusko, formation, 65-66; organization, 67; proposed changes, 67, 89, 119; addition, 80; loss to Fulton, 75, 91; county seat, 540; descriptions and maps, 540-47;
and others, propose new county, 74, 74-75, 76, 78.

Lafayette, 770.

La Grange, county seat, 548.

La Grange County, formation, 57; proposed changes, 66, 126; consolidation with Noble proposed, 76, 102; jurisdiction, 548; description and map, 548-49;

and *Noble*, propose new county, 75.
Lake County, formation, 67; organization, 69; northern boundary, 101, 129, 550, 552; protests against act of 1857, p. 116n; descriptions and maps, 550-53; mention, 72n.
Lake Court House, name changed, 550.
Lancaster (Owen Co.), 642.
La Porte, county seat, 554.
La Porte County, formation, 57; jurisdiction, 63; additions, 80, 101; proposed changes, 87, 97-98, 108; proposed transfer to Starke, 124; northern boundary, 101, 556, 560; Kankakee River boundary, 129; county seat, 554; descriptions and maps, 554-63; mention, 69, 72n;
and *others*, propose new county, 108, 117-18.
Lawrence County, formation, 32; proposed changes, 38, 44, 45, 48, 59, 66-67, 68, 92, 96, 97, 100, 102; additions, 40, 115; protests against act of 1857, p. 116n; county seat, 564, 568; descriptions and maps, 564-69; mention, 121;
and *others*, propose new county, 52-53.
Lawrenceburg, boundary marker at, 6-7; asks transfer to Kentucky, 68; county-seat rivalries, 69, 83, 308, 316; mention, 96.
Leavenworth, 296.
Lebanon, 240.
Leesburg, courts held at, 540.
Lexington, 730, 738.
Liberty, 774.
Lima, 548.

Lincoln Township (La Porte Co.), 558.
Liverpool (Daviess Co.), name changed, 298.
Liverpool (Lake Co.), 550.
Logan, proposed name for county, 54n.
Logansport, 248.
Loogootee, 590.
Louisiana Territory, 7, 8.
Ludlow, Israel, surveyor, 6.

McClintoc, Samuel, surveys Indiana-Illinois line, 13.
McDonald, John, surveyor, 13.
McDonald and Butler, attornies in Kentucky boundary dispute, 18.
McGary, Hugh, 32n.
Macomb, proposed name for county, 77.
Madison, 488.
Madison County, formation, 39; alterations, 42, 46; proposed changes, 45, 53, 63, 69, 92; loss to Grant, 54; addition, 70; eastern boundary, 82; county seat, 570, 574, 578; jurisdiction, 576; descriptions and maps, 570-79; mention, 61;
and *others*, propose new county, 106.
Marietta (Ohio), 136.
Marion, proposed name for county, 38n.
Marion (Grant Co.), county seat, 402.
Marion (Ripley Co.), courts held at, 712.
Marion County, formation, 37-38; jurisdiction, 38, 43-44, 580; proposed changes, 44, 45, 90, 93; addition, 54; county seat, 580; descriptions and maps, 580-83.

INDEX 877

Marshall County, formation, 65-66; organization, 67; addition, 67-68; proposed change, 77; county seat, 586; descriptions and maps, 584-87; mention, 69, 72n.
Martin County, formation, 35; proposed changes, 41, 42, 69, 77, 96; addition, 49; controversy with Daviess, 118; county seat, 588, 590; descriptions and maps, 588-91.
Martinsville, 614.
Memphis (Martin Co.), 590.
Menzies, Gustave V., commissioner, Kentucky boundary controversy, 18-19.
Mercer, proposed name for county, 52.
Merom, 758, 762.
Miami County, move for formation, 54-55; formation, 58, 61; addition, 63; jurisdiction, 70, 73, 596; proposed changes, 74-75, 79; loss to Fulton, 84-85, 89; county seat, 594; descriptions and maps, 592-99.
Miami Indians, 34n.
Miami Reserve, *see* Great Miami Reserve.
Miamisport (Miami Co.), 594.
Michigan, state of, boundaries foreshadowed, 1, 2, 4n.
Michigan City, 117.
Michigan Territory, formation, 7, 142-43; boundary survey, 7, 14-15; reduced on admission of Indiana to Union, 12; Wayne County becomes part of, 21-22.
Milroy (Benton Co.), name changed, 236.
Mississinewa Treaty line, 49, 51, 554.
Mississippi Territory, 7.

Mongoquinong (La Grange Co.), name changed, 548.
Monroe County, formation, 32; proposed changes, 37, 50, 69, 71, 100; additions, 38, 49, 54; loss to Brown, 67; jurisdiction, 220, 602; county seat, 600; descriptions and maps, 600-7;
and others, propose new county, 52-53.
Montgomery County, formation, 40; loss to Fountain, 44-45; protests against act of 1857, p. 116n; county seat, 608; descriptions and maps, 608-13;
and others, propose new county, 47-48, 50, 52, 54, 58, 68, 75, 89-90, 92, 100, 118.
Monticello, 854.
Morgan County, formation, 37-38; proposed changes, 40, 44, 48, 49, 62, 100; loss to Putnam, 119; to Hendricks, 122-23; county seat, 614; descriptions and maps, 614-19.
Mount Pleasant (Martin Co.), 590.
Mount Sterling, 294.
Mount Vernon, 690.
Muncie (Munseytown, Muncietown), 324.

Nashville, 242.
New Albany, 344.
New Carlisle, 118.
New Castle, 434.
New Design, 202, 206.
New Harmony, 26-27, 376.
New Purchase, the, division into counties, 28, 34-35, 37, 40; descriptions and maps, 220-23.
Newport, 780.
Newton (Jasper Co.), 474, 476.
Newton County, formation, 65-66; loss to Lake and Porter,

878 INDIANA HISTORICAL COLLECTIONS

67; jurisdiction, 71; consolidation with Jasper, 73, 622; reorganization of, 111-12; reorganization ratified, 118; Kankakee boundary, 115, 129; county seat, 624; descriptions and maps, 620-27.

Noble County, move for formation, 63; formation, 64; organization, 67; consolidation with La Grange proposed, 76, 102; loss to Whitley, 115; proposed change, 126; county seat, 628; descriptions and maps, 628-31;

and La Grange, new county proposed, 75.

Noblesville, 408.

Northwest Territory, organization under Ordinance of 1787, pp. 1-2; division, 2-4; counties in, 20, 21-22; description and map, 136-37.

Ohio, state of, formation of, 4-7, 140-41; boundary survey, 5-7.

Ohio County, movement for formation, 31, 33, 58, 68, 69-70; formation, 83; extended, 87-88; proposed changes, 92, 93-94, 96, 97, 99-100; discussed in Constitutional Convention (1850-51), 104; county seat, 632; descriptions and maps, 632-35.

Ohio River, boundary controversy over course of, 15-19; jurisdiction on, 19.

Orange County, formation, 26; loss to Lawrence and Monroe, 32; proposed changes, 45, 119; protests against act of 1857, p. 116n; county seat, 636; descriptions and maps, 636-41.

Ordinance of 1787, pp. 1, 4, 12, 20, 22.

Orth, Senator Godlove S., 89-90.

Ouiatanon (Ouiatenon), 135.

Owen County, formation, 33; loss to Putnam, 38; to Clay, 43; additions, 38, 39; proposed changes, 50, 62, 74, 76, 100; jurisdiction, 220, 644; county seat, 642, 644; descriptions and maps, 642-49;

and others, propose new county, 35.

Oxford, 236.

Palestine (Lawrence Co.), 564.

Paoli, 636.

Paris, on Jefferson-Jennings boundary, 49-50, 53, 66, 500, 510.

Parish Grove (Jasper Co.), 472.

Parke County, formation, 36; jurisdiction, 38, 40, 45, 220, 650; proposed changes, 44, 47; protests against act of 1857, p. 116n; county seat, 650, 652; descriptions and maps, 650-53;

and others, propose new county, 47-48, 50, 52, 54, 58, 68, 75, 79, 89-90, 92, 100, 118.

Pendleton, 570, 574.

Perry County, formation, 25; loss to Pike, 30; to Crawford, 32, 47; proposed changes, 36, 40, 42, 44, 90, 92; county seat, 654, 658, 660, 662; descriptions and maps, 654-63;

and Spencer, new county proposed, 50, 78, 104, 105-6n, 116.

Peru, 594.

Petersburg, 107, 664.

Pfafflin, August, commissioner, Kentucky boundary controversy, 16.

INDEX

Pike County, formation, 30; loss to Dubois, 31; to Gibson, 43; to Warrick, 45; exchange with Warrick, 41-42; proposed changes, 90, 105, 107-8, 109; county seat, 664; descriptions and maps, 664-73.

Pleasant Township (La Porte Co.), 558.

Plymouth, 586.

Polk, proposed name for county, 90.

Port Mitchell (Noble Co.), 628.

Porter County, formation, 65-66; organization, 67; alteration, 67; northern boundary, 101, 676; Kankakee River boundary, 129; protests against act of 1857, p. 116n; county seat, 676; descriptions and maps, 674-79; mention, 72n;

and La Porte, propose new county, 117-18.

Portersville (Dubois Co.), 326, 330.

Portersville (Porter Co.), name changed, 676, 678.

Portland, 484.

Posey County, formation, 25; additions, 26-27, 30, 40; proposed changes, 36; loss to Gibson, 38; petition for new county, 90, 100; part of, west of Wabash River, 14; county seat, 680, 684, 690; descriptions and maps, 680-91.

Post Vincent's, see Vincennes.

Potawatomi Indians, 34n.

Prairie du Rocher, courts held at, 208.

Princeton, 376.

Pulaski County, formation, 65-66; organization, 73; protests against act of 1857, p. 116n; description and map, 692-93; and others, propose new county, 108.

Putnam County, formation, 37-38; jurisdiction, 38, 40, 220, 694; boundaries reformed, 39; loss to 'Clay, 43; proposed changes, 59, 62; addition, 119; descriptions and maps, 694-703;

and others, propose new county, 47-48, 50, 52, 54, 58, 68, 75, 79, 89-90, 92, 100, 118.

Randolph County (State of Indiana), formation, 33; extended, 34, 37; loss to Allen, 41; jurisdiction, 41, 222, 358, 706, 710; Delaware boundary in question, 69; county seat, 704; descriptions and maps, 704-11.

Randolph County (Northwest and Indiana territories), formation, 21; county seat, 202; descriptions and maps, 202-7; petitions for territorial division, 8.

Ray, proposed name for county, 52, 57n.

Ray, James Brown, 14.

Rector's base line, 376.

Rensselaer, 476. See also Newton.

Richardville County, movement for formation of, 73, 79. See also Howard (Richardville).

Richmond, 850.

Ripley County, formation, 30, 31; jurisdiction in, 31, 712; jurisdiction in New Purchase, 222; addition, 38; proposed changes, 44, 53; protests against act of 1857, p. 116n; county seat, 712; descriptions and maps, 712-15.

Rising Sun, 58, 69-70, 83, 632.

880 INDIANA HISTORICAL COLLECTIONS

Robinson, Milo, courts held at home of, 550.
Rochester, 364.
Rockport, 32n, 742.
Rockville, 652.
Rome, 116, 660, 662.
Roseville (Parke Co.), 650.
Ross, proposed name for county, 52.
Rush County, formation of, 37-38; proposed changes, 45, 50, 62; eastern boundary, 87; description and map, 716-17; mention, 72n;
and others, propose formation of new county, 71.
Rushville, 716.

St. Clair, Arthur, governor of Northwest Territory, 3, 21.
St. Clair County (Northwest and Indiana territories), formation, 21; petitions for territorial division, 8; descriptions and maps, 208-15.
St. Joseph (St. Joseph Co.), 718.
St. Joseph County, formation, 52; addition, 57; loss to La Porte, 57, 101; to Marshall, 67-68; proposed changes, 87, 96, 97-98; protests against act of 1857, p. 116n; Kankakee River boundary, 129; county seat, 718; jurisdiction, 718, 720; descriptions and maps, 718-29; mention, 69, 72n;
and La Porte, propose new county, 118.
St. Mary's, Treaty of (1818), 34, 220, 222, 454.
St. Omer, proposed name for county, 71.
St. Paul, on Shelby-Decatur line, 122.
Salem, 127, 820.
Salisbury (Wayne Co.), 838, 840.

Scott County, movement for formation, 31; formation, 35; boundary changes, 37, 53, 72, 80, 101; proposed changes, 40-41, 44, 66, 125-26, 127; boundary surveys, 50, 274, 730, 732; county seat, 730, 738, 740; descriptions and maps, 730-39; mention, 69.
Scottsburg, 127, 738.
Secession, of Ohio River counties, proposed, 120.
Shelby County, formation, 37-38; proposed changes, 51, 59, 62, 96, 109, 122; description and map, 740-41;
and others, propose new county, 71, 77.
Shelbyville, 740.
Shoals, 590.
Silver Creek Knobs, 24-25, 29, 42, 78, 80, 92, 127, 266, 274, 278, 284, 416, 418, 820, 834.
Sink Hole Spring, location, 204, 206.
Smith, proposed name for county, 90.
South Bend, 718.
Sparta (Noble Co.), name changed, 628.
Spencer, county seat, 642, 644.
Spencer County, formation, 31-32; proposed changes, 36, 40, 42, 43, 87; Warrick boundary survey, 72; county seat, 742; descriptions and maps, 742-45;
and Perry, new county proposed, 50, 78, 104, 105-6n, 116.
Spitler's Cabin (Jasper Co.), 472.
Springfield, 684.
Springville (Clark Co.), courts held at, 256.
Squibb, Nathaniel L., surveyor, 6.

INDEX 881

Standing Stone Forks (Ohio), location, 514.
Starke County, formation, 65-66; loss to La Porte, 80; organization, 101; proposed changes, 108, 111-12, 118, 124; protests against act of 1857, p. 116n; Kankakee River boundary, 129; county seat, 748; descriptions and maps, 746-51; mention, 69, 72n;
and others, propose new county, 108.
Steuben County, formation, 65-66; organization, 69; description and map, 752-53.
Stickney, Colonel Amos, commissioner, Kentucky boundary dispute, 18-19.
Sullivan, 762.
Sullivan County, formation, 30; loss to Vigo, 32, 33; to Owen, 33; to Greene, 36; to Clay, 43; division suggested, 33; proposed changes, 42, 43n, 44, 47, 49, 51, 87; addition, 80; retains added territory, 86; protests against act of 1857, p. 116n; county seat, 754, 758, 762; descriptions and maps, 754-65; course of Wabash near, 14n; corrective act, 115-16;
and others, propose new county, 81, 94.
Surveys, territorial and state boundaries: Ohio, 5-7; Michigan, 7, 14-15; Illinois, 9, 10n, 12-14; Kentucky, 15-19; irregularity of, 20-21, 29.
Switzerland County, formation of, 25; loss to Ripley, 38; proposed changes, 36, 42, 92, 93-94, 104; county seat, 766; descriptions and maps, 766-69.

Taxation, affected by boundary changes, 99, 107, 125.
Tecumseh, proposed name for county, 46n, 57n, 63.
Ten o'Clock Line, *see* Fort Wayne Treaty line.
Terre Haute, 782.
Thomas, Jesse B., territorial delegate, 8-9.
Tiffin, Edward, surveyor-general, 14.
Tippecanoe County, formation, 45; jurisdiction, 49, 52, 770; proposed changes, 51, 63, 75-76, 77, 78, 81, 96; description and map, 770-71;
and others, propose new county, 71.
Tipton, John, 10n, 13, 36n, 448.
Tipton, proposed name for county, 75n, 79, 81.
Tipton, county seat, 772.
Tipton County, move for formation, 81; formation, 83-84; description and map, 772-73; mention, 101-2.
Tiptona, name suggested for county seat, 228.
Troy, 116, 654.
Twelve Mile Purchase, 23, 24, 34.

Union County, formation, 36; addition, 45; proposed changes, 47, 59, 92-93; county seat, 774; descriptions and maps, 774-77.
United States Coast and Geodetic Survey, examine Ohio-Indiana line, 6.

Vallonia (Velonia), 450, 452.
Valparaiso, 676.
Van Buren, proposed name for county, 74, 75n.

Vanderburgh County, formation, 31-32; description and map, 778-79.
Vermillion County, movement for formation, 40; formation, 41; jurisdiction, 41, 780; proposed changes, 44, 47; northern boundary controversy, 59-61; description and map, 780-81.
Vernon, 506.
Versailles, 712.
Vevay, 766.
Vigo County, formation, 32; additions, 33, 39; loss to Parke, 36; to Putnam, 38; to Clay, 43; proposed changes, 79, 87; jurisdiction in New Purchase, 220; county seat, 782; descriptions and maps, 782-93; *and others,* propose new county, 79.
Vincennes (Post Vincent's), 2, 9, 9n-10n, 11, 12, 13, 107, 136, 138, 514.
Vincennes, Treaty of (1804), 22, 412, 414.
Vincennes Tract, the, 22.
Virginia, plans for northwestern country, 1, 2.

Wabash, 794.
Wabash and Erie Canal, 57-58, 64.
Wabash County, movement for formation, 54; formation, 58, 61; organization, 66; jurisdiction, 70; proposed changes, 74-75, 89, 91; county seat, 794; descriptions and maps, 794-97; mention, 69; *and Kosciusko,* propose new county, 76, 78.
Wabash County (New Purchase), 34-35, 55, 220-21.

Wabash River, transfer of land by alteration of course, 14.
Walden, D. N., commissioner, Indiana-Kentucky boundary controversy, 16.
Warren County, formation, 46; proposed changes, 51, 53, 63, 68, 69, 100, 122, 123-24; jurisdiction, 52, 66, 798; southern boundary dispute, 59-61; protests against act of 1857, p. 116n; description and map, 798-99; *and others,* propose new county, 71.
Warrenton (Warren Co.), 798.
Warrick County, formation, 24; loss to Posey and Perry, 25; to Spencer and Vanderburgh, 31-32; to Spencer, 43; boundary dispute with Gibson, 41-42, 72, 74, 80, 85-86, 93, 106-7, 108-9, 109; addition, 45; Spencer boundary survey, 72; proposed changes, 76, 109; county seat, 800, 802, 804; descriptions and maps, 800-19; mention, 87.
Warsaw, proposed name for county, 57n.
Warsaw, 540.
Washington, George, plan for division of western territory, 4n.
Washington (Daviess Co.), 298.
Washington (Perry Co.), name changed, 660.
Washington County, formation, 24; extension northward, 25; loss to Jackson, 26; proposed changes, 27, 38-39, 93, 125-26, 127; alterations, 37, 80, 91-92; boundary surveys, 44, 48, 49, 50, 59, 72, 124, 274, 730, 838; county seat, 820; descriptions

INDEX 883

and maps, 820-37; mention, 35n, 69, 100; *and others*, propose new county, 94.
Watson, John A., 5-6.
Watts, proposed name for county, 65n.
Wayne County (State of Indiana), formation, 25; loss to Randolph, 33; to Fayette, 34; to Union, 36; Henry County boundary, 40, 42, 47; proposed changes, 47, 49, 50, 53, 59, 72, 93; jurisdiction, 222, 358; county seat, 838, 840, 850; descriptions and maps, 838-51.
Wayne County (Northwest and Indiana territories), formation, 21; descriptions and maps, 216-19.
Wea Indians, 34n.
Wells County, formation, 65-66; organization, 69; proposed changes, 77, 92, 96-97; description and map, 852-53.
West Shoals (Martin Co.), 590.

Whitcomb, proposed name for county, 84.
White County, move for formation, 58, 62; formation, 63; jurisdiction, 63, 66, 71; proposed changes, 66, 68-69, 77; additions, 70, 72; loss to Jasper, 77; county seat, 854; descriptions and maps, 854-61; *and others*, propose new county, 71.
Whitley County, formation, 65-66; organization, 71; addition, 115; proposed change, 118; county seat, 862, 864; descriptions and maps, 862-65.
Williams, Micajah T., 5-6, 14.
Williamsport, 798.
Wills Township (La Porte Co.), 558.
Wilmington, 69, 316.
Winamac, 692.
Winchester, 704.
Windsor, proposed name for county, 71n.
Wolcottville, on La Grange boundary, 126.